THE STUDENT NEWSPAPER SURVIVAL GUIDE

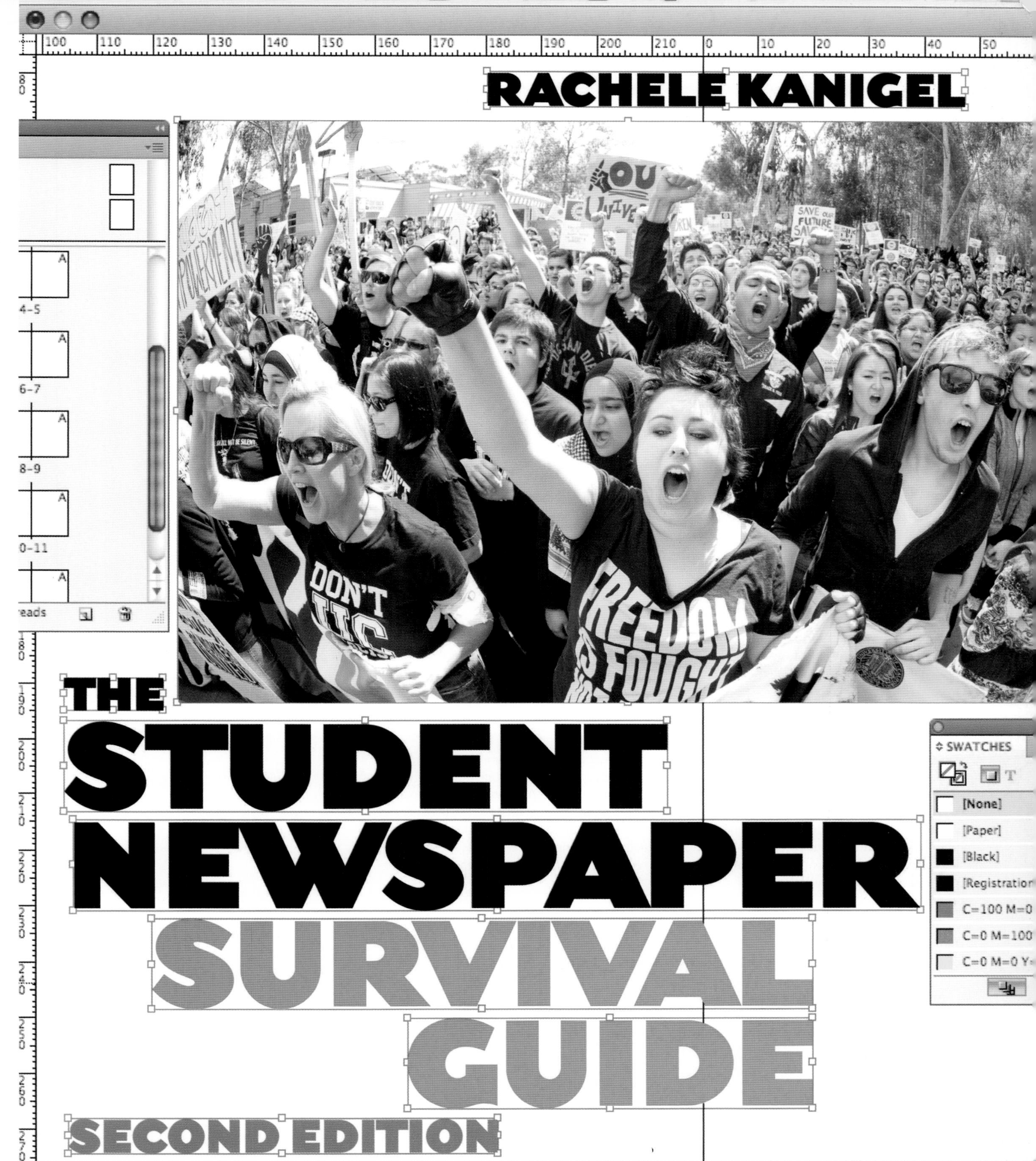

WILEY-BLACKWELL
A John Wiley & Sons, Ltd., Publication

This second edition first published 2012

Edition history: Blackwell Publishing Professional (1e, 2006)

Blackwell Publishing was acquired by John Wiley & Sons in February 2007. Blackwell's publishing program has been merged with Wiley's global Scientific, Technical, and Medical business to form Wiley-Blackwell.

Registered Office
John Wiley & Sons Ltd, The Atrium, Southern Gate, Chichester, West Sussex, PO19 8SQ, United Kingdom

Editorial Offices
350 Main Street, Malden, MA 02148-5020, USA
9600 Garsington Road, Oxford, OX4 2DQ, UK
The Atrium, Southern Gate, Chichester, West Sussex, PO19 8SQ, UK

For details of our global editorial offices, for customer services, and for information about how to apply for permission to reuse the copyright material in this book please see our website at www.wiley.com/wiley-blackwell.

Library of Congress Cataloging-in-Publication Data

Kanigel, Rachele.
The student newspaper survival guide / Rachele Kanigel. – 2nd ed.
p. cm.
Includes bibliographical references and index.
ISBN 978-1-4443-3238-4 (pbk.)
1. College student newspapers and periodicals. I. Title.
LB3621.65.K36 2011
378.1′9897–dc22

2011017891

A catalogue record for this book is available from the British Library.

This book is published in the following electronic formats: ePDFs [9781444344486]; ePub [9781444344493]; Kindle [9781444344509]

Set in 9.5/11pt Century book by SPi Publisher Services, Pondicherry, India
Printed and bound in Malaysia by Vivar Printing Sdn Bhd

2 2012

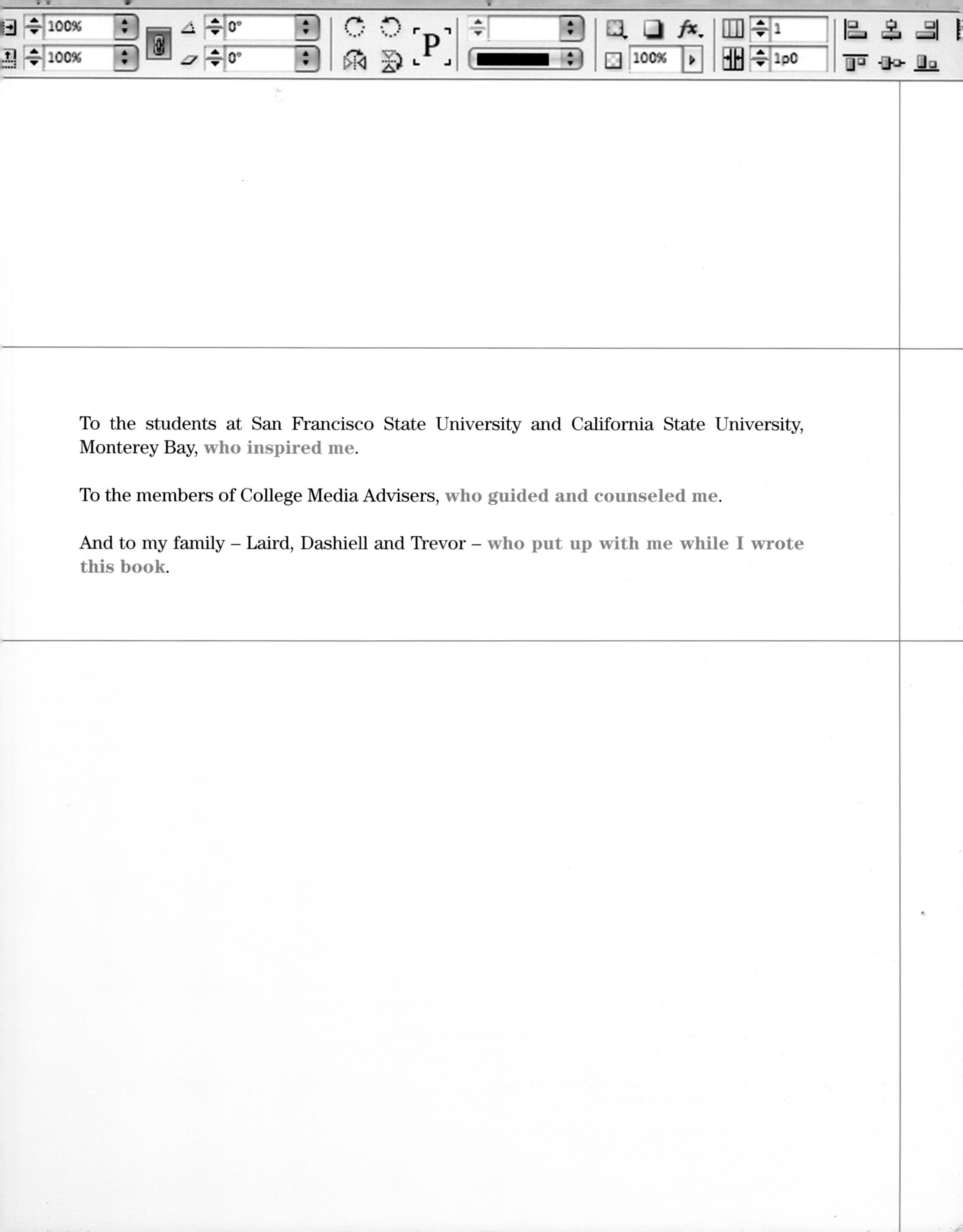

To the students at San Francisco State University and California State University, Monterey Bay, **who inspired me**.

To the members of College Media Advisers, **who guided and counseled me**.

And to my family – Laird, Dashiell and Trevor – **who put up with me while I wrote this book**.

CONTENTS

PREFACE

In 2005, when I wrote ***The Student Newspaper Survival Guide***, less than 40 percent of North Americans had broadband Internet service at home, Facebook was still called thefacebook.com, YouTube had just launched and Twitter was something little birds did. Most student newspapers at the time published stories in print before posting them online, and few had taken more than a tentative step into the world of multimedia storytelling.

It's hard to believe how much things have changed in just a few years. Today, people are accustomed to watching video not just on their computers (more than 68 percent have high-speed Internet at home), but also on iPods, cell phones and tablet PCs. Many college students spend more time on social media than they do sleeping. Mobile media and multimedia have radically transformed student newspapers into 24-hour news organizations that publish on multiple platforms.

This new edition of *The Student Newspaper Survival Guide* is designed to help you make sense of these changes and figure out how to make your news organization more effective, more efficient and more creative.

In it you'll find:

- A new chapter on multimedia that explains the basic concepts of digital storytelling and offers tips on recording audio, shooting and editing video, producing slideshows and creating interactive graphics, maps and databases
- A new chapter on social media that will help you use Facebook, Twitter, CoveritLive, Storify and other tools to find news, report it and distribute it widely
- An expanded chapter on covering a campus that offers tips on localizing international and national stories, reporting on higher education and writing about science and medicine
- A new section on computer-assisted reporting
- A revised chapter on websites that explores in greater detail how to use online and mobile technology to report breaking news
- An expanded chapter on newswriting that includes more examples from award-winning student stories
- Tips from a veteran sportswriter on how to produce a great college sports section
- 10 ethical dilemmas you can discuss with co-workers at a training session or editors meeting
- An expanded chapter on advertising that now includes sections on marketing and distribution
- More examples of page design from some of the top student designers in the country
- An expanded chapter on editing that includes sections on planning special projects and working with a student media board
- A revised chapter on reporting that includes advice on how to cover breaking news and traumatic events.

To research *The Student Newspaper Survival Guide* I studied campus newspapers from around North America – struggling publications with small staffs as well as impressive, professional-quality newspapers that routinely sweep awards contests. I interviewed professional journalists, journalism educators, student newspaper advisers and business managers.

I also talked to students – hundreds of reporters, editors, photographers, columnists, ad sales people and webmasters – asking each of them what challenges they faced and what advice they had for the next generation of student newspaper staffers. This volume is a compendium of their suggestions.

If you've picked up this book, you're probably part of a student newspaper staff, or soon will be. You may be an editor or reporter, a photographer or designer, an ad salesperson or a business manager. Or perhaps you're a student newspaper adviser looking for new ways to train, motivate and inspire your staff.

Whatever your role, welcome. Whether you're doing this for a class, checking out a potential profession, or just want to have fun, working for a student newspaper is one of the most eye-opening and empowering experiences you can have in college.

It also can be one of the most challenging. Over the months or years you work on a newspaper, you will encounter many obstacles. People you need to interview won't want to talk with you, subjects will decline to be photographed, businesses will refuse to buy ads. People you depend on will let you down. Heated debates will break out in the newsroom over photos and stories and headlines and ads. You'll face ethical and legal issues you don't know how to deal with.

This book is designed to help you cope with these challenges and to give you the resources you need to make reasoned decisions.

The first chapters of the book focus on editorial issues – everything from recruiting and training a staff, to photographing sports and campus events, to steering clear of legal minefields. Here's where advisers, editors, reporters and photographers can look for guidance and ideas on the issues they deal with on a day-to-day basis.

Later chapters address design and production – how to put out a readable and attractive paper that invites readers to pick it up and a website readers will turn to.

The last chapter deals with advertising and marketing, including training and motivating your sales staff, promoting your publication and keeping your revenue flowing.

Each section includes tipsheets, checklists, Q&As and essays from professionals, some of them well-respected leaders in their fields, others who are just barely out of college themselves. At the end of each chapter is a list of projects, readings and websites you can explore to deepen your understanding of your craft and make your news organization run more smoothly.

My inspiration for this book comes from my students at *The Otter Realm* at California State University, Monterey Bay, where I taught for a year and a half, and those at *Golden Gate [X]press* at San Francisco State University, where I teach now. On both staffs, students were always hungry for ideas to make their papers better. I hope they and other students will see this book as a valuable resource. I thank them for their help, advice and support in preparing these pages.

One thing to remember: Student newspapers are training grounds for journalists, yes, but they are also boot camps for life. Your campus newsroom may end up the most valuable classroom you have during your college years. Take full advantage of your rights. But be mindful, too, of your responsibilities. As a journalist you have the power to help and to harm, to expose wrongs and ruin careers. If you understand this power and use it wisely, you can change your corner of the world.

RACHELE KANIGEL

ACKNOWLEDGMENTS

When I set out to write this book, I knew I'd need help. I wanted this to be a compendium of advice from student journalists, college newspaper advisers, advertising and business managers, media lawyers, professional journalists and others dedicated to sustaining and nurturing the student press.

But I had no idea how much help I would receive. Now, as I think back over the two years I worked on this book – and the year I spent revising it – I'm overwhelmed by the generosity of my colleagues in journalism and journalism education. What touched me most was how much people were willing to share. Often I'd post a query to the College Media Advisers' Listserv on some esoteric topic (Who owns the copyright to material your student newspaper publishes? Does your paper have a mission statement? Can anyone recommend a good student sex columnist?) and within an hour I would have half a dozen helpful responses, many from people I'd never met in person. Thanks to all the advisers who contributed tidbits of information. I promise not to bombard the list with questions for a while – at least not until I start working on the next edition!

It's hard to imagine this book would exist without the help of my mentor, friend and colleague, Kenneth Kobré, whose wise insights, demanding criticism and rousing pep talks kept me going when I felt overwhelmed. Thanks, too, to his wife, designer Betsy Brill, who helped me envision how the book should look and who brought her design expertise to the first edition.

My tireless research assistant Eugenia Chien was a tremendous help in many different ways – from her technical expertise and her youthful perspective to her sharp eye for math mistakes. Daniel Jimenez proved to be an adept copy editor. Thanks to San Francisco State University, the College of Humanities and Dean Paul Sherwin for the Affirmative Action Faculty Development Grant that made their contributions possible and for the sabbatical that gave me time to write the second edition.

Several people read chapters and provided much-needed feedback: Amy Emmert, Nils Rosdahl, Cynthia Mitchell, Dave Waddell, Sylvia Fox, Joe Gisondi, Mike Spohn, Morgane Byloos. Thanks for your encouraging words and helpful criticism. In addition, Mark Goodman's legal advice – for my readers, my students and for me as an author – was invaluable.

My colleagues at San Francisco State University, many of whom have co-advised student publications with me, have all taught me useful lessons about teaching and advising: Cristina Azocar, Staci Baird, Justin Beck, John Burks, Eva Charles, Harriet Chiang, Kevin Cox, Yvonne Daley, Andrew DeVigal, Roland DeWolk, Jon Funabiki, David Greene, Lesley Guth, Tom Johnson, Dottie Katzeff, Barbara Landis, Edna Lee, Austin Long-Scott, Don Menn, Jim Merithew, Raul Ramirez, Beth Renneisen, Erna Smith, Jim Toland, Scot Tucker, Venise Wagner, James Wagstaffe and Yumi Wilson.

Sylvia Fox and the founding board of the California College Media Association – Paul Bittick, Amy Emmert, Rich Cameron, Michelle Carter, Melinda Dudley, Tom Clanin, Tim Hendrick, Tom Nelson, Jennifer Poole, Dave Waddell, Jenifer Woodring – helped me understand the needs of college newspapers. Their passion for student publications was a constant source of inspiration.

And when I was stuck on what to do for graphics, Bradley Wilson saved the day.

I am thankful to Mark Barrett, Dede Pedersen, Judi Brown and the others at Blackwell Publishing who believed in this book and helped bring the first edition to publication. Tracy Petersen not only proved to be a crackerjack copyeditor, but an astute and sensible adviser on the text. Thanks to Elizabeth Swayze, Matthew Baskin, Allison Kostka and Amanda Banner at John Wiley & Sons, Inc. for shepherding through the second edition. A special note of appreciation to Louise Ennis, who worked tirelessly to make sure all the i's were dotted and the t's were crossed. Her patience with last-minute changes and her attention to detail were admirable.

Thanks to my brother, Robert Kanigel, who always asked how the book was going, and to my mother, Beatrice Kanigel, who reminded me not to work too hard.

To Dashiell and Trevor, I pledge to be a better, more attentive mother, now that this book is done. I am enduringly grateful to my husband, Laird Harrison, who provides me with time, writing and editing advice, a ready ear and love. I can't imagine a more perfect life partner.

Finally, thanks to my students, who each day remind me why I love journalism.

The following journalists and journalism educators contributed material or information to this book. (Affiliations are current as of when I was last in touch with them.)

Robert Adams, *College Heights Herald*, Western Kentucky University
The late David L. Adams, *Indiana Daily Student*, Indiana University, Bloomington
Jordin Thomas Althaus, photographer
Brad Arendt, *The Arbiter*, Boise State University
Kaylene D. Armstrong
Michael Arrieta-Walden, *The Oregonian*
Harry Austin, *Chattanooga Times Free Press*
Jennifer Bass, The Kinsey Institute
Nate Beeler, *The Washington Examiner*
Paul Bittick, *Mustang Daily*, California Polytechnic State University, San Luis Obispo
Robert Bohler, *The Daily Skiff*, Texas Christian University
Ed Bonza, *The Sentinel*, Kennesaw State University
Timothy Michael Bowles, *Orbis*, Vanderbilt University
Karla Bowsher, *University Press*, Florida Atlantic University
Ralph Braseth, Loyola College Chicago
Elinor J. Brecher, *The Miami Herald*
Daniel Burnett, *The Red and Black*, University of Georgia
Marcy Burstiner, *The Lumberjack*, Humboldt State University
Jerry Bush, *The Daily Egyptian*, Southern Illinois University, Carbondale
Steve Buttry, TBD
Dan Carino, cartoonist
Emery Carrington, *The Daily Mississippian*, University of Mississippi
Chris Carroll, *The Vanderbilt Hustler*, Vanderbilt University
Brian Cassella, *The Daily Tar Heel*, University of North Carolina at Chapel Hill
Steven E. Chappell, *The Simpsonian*, Simpson College
Nathaniel Christopher, *Toast*, Trent University
Betty Clapp, Cleveland State University
Mac Clemmens, *The Otter Realm*, California State University, Monterey Bay
Aly Colón, The Poynter Institute
Paul Conley, media consultant
Michael Conti, *The Harvard Crimson*, Harvard University
Autumn Cruz, *Sacramento Bee*
David Cuillier, University of Arizona
Tonya Danos, *The Nicholls Worth*, Nicholls State University
Juanita Darling, San Francisco State University
Christopher Dinn, Canadian University Press
Mike Donoghue, *The Burlington* (Vt.) *Free Press*
David Downham, *The Ball State Daily News*, Ball State University
Andrew Dunn, *Wilmington StarNews*
Roger Ebert, *Chicago Sun-Times*
Charlie Eisenhood, *NYU Local*, New York University
Joel Elliott, *The Toccoa Record*
Amy Emmert, *Daily Bruin*, University of California, Los Angeles
Taylor Etchison, *The Rebel Yell*, University of Nevada-Las Vegas
Mark Fainaru-Wada, *ESPN*
Robert Faturechi, *Los Angeles Times*
Vincent Filak, University of Wisconsin Oshkosh
Jenny Fischer, Colorado State University
Annette Forbes, *Iowa State Daily*, Iowa State University
John Frank, *The News and Observer*
Julie Freeman, *The Baylor Lariat*, Baylor University
Jessica Fryman, *The Nevada Sagebrush*, University of Nevada, Reno
Dante Gallan, *The Daily Californian*, University of California, Berkeley
Sean Gallagher, photographer
Jessie Gardner, Primo Advertising
Matt Garton, *Cleveland Plain Dealer*
Susan Goldberg, Bloomberg News
Lloyd Goodman, *The Shorthorn*, University of Texas at Arlington
Mark Goodman, Student Press Law Center
Jeremy Gragert, *The Flip Side*, University of Wisconsin-Eau Claire
Gideon Grudo, *University Press*, Florida Atlantic University
Andy Guess, *The Cornell Sun*, Cornell University
Shannon Guthrie, *State Journal-Register*
Gerry Lynn Hamilton, *The Daily Collegian*, Pennsylvania State University
Kami Hammerschmith, *The Daily Barometer*, Oregon State University
Terrence G. Harper, Society of Professional Journalists
Christy Harrison, *The Exponent*, Purdue University
Tim Harrower, design consultant
Patricia Hartranft, *The Daily Collegian*, Penn State University
Elaine Helm, *The Daily Northwestern*, Northwestern University
Sarah Hemus, *Golden Gate [X]press*, San Francisco State University
Jennifer Herbenick, Indiana University
Megan Hermida, *DoG Street Journal*, College of William and Mary
Robert Hernandez, University of Southern California
Brant Houston, Investigative Reporters and Editors, Inc.
Megan Irwin, *The State Press Magazine*, Arizona State University
Eric Jacobs, *The Daily Pennsylvanian*, University of Pennsylvania
Tracy Jan, *The Boston Globe*
Joe Jaszewski, *Idaho Statesman*
Lee Jenkins, *The New York Times*
Erik Jepsen, *The Guardian*, University of California San Diego
Danielle Jurski, *The Campus*, Ottawa University
Tyler Kepner, *The New York Times*
Jim Killam, *Northern Star*, Northern Illinois University
Harry Kloman, *The Pitt News*, University of Pittsburgh
Kenneth Kobré, *Golden Gate [X]press*, San Francisco State University
Amy Koeckes, *The Nevada Sagebrush*, University of Nevada, Reno
Michael Koretzky, *University Press*, Florida Atlantic University
Brian Krans, *The Dispatch/Rock Island Argus/The Leader* newspaper group
Tyler Krome, *University Press*, Florida Atlantic University
Jill "J.R." Labbe, *Fort Worth Star-Telegram*
Melissa Lalum, *Daily Sundial*, California State University, Northridge
Jack Lancaster, *Daily O'Collegian*, Oklahoma State University
Al Lanier, *Chicago Tribune*
Kathy Lawrence, *The Daily Texan*, University of Texas at Austin
Ira David Levy, Wilbur Wright College
Scott Lindenberg, *The Gamecock*, University of South Carolina

Charles Little, *el Don*, Santa Ana College
Mark Ludwig, Sacramento State University
Chris Lusk, *The Oklahoma Daily*, University of Oklahoma
Robert Mays III, *The Missourian*, University of Missouri
Sherrie Mazingo, University of Minnesota School of Journalism
Mindy McAdams, University of Florida
Sean McCourt, freelance writer
Michael G. McLaughlin, *The Daily Evergreen*, Washington State University
Melvin Mencher, *News Reporting and Writing*
Jim Merithew, *San Francisco Chronicle*
Kristin Millis, *The Daily*, University of Washington
Cynthia MItchell, *The Observer*, Central Washington University
Derek Montgomery, *The Badger Herald*, University of Wisconsin, Madison
Miguel M. Morales, *The Campus Ledger*, Johnson County Community College
Nick Mrozowski, *The State News*, Michigan State University
Colin Mulvaney, Spokane *Spokesman-Review*
Erika B. Neldner, *The Sentinel*, Kennesaw State University
Ashley Nelson, *The Orion*, California State University, Chico
Michael Newsom, *The Daily Mississippian*, University of Mississippi
Jeremy Norman, washingtonpost.com
Jared Novack, *The Daily Orange*, Syracuse University
Christopher Null, Filmcritic.com
Andrew O'Dell, *Student Life*, Washington University, St. Louis
Jake Ortman, Utterlyboring.com
Rob Owen, *Pittsburgh Post-Gazette*
Pat Parish, *The Daily Reveille*, Louisiana State University
Perry Parks
Erica Perel, *The Daily Tar Heel*, University of North Carolina, Chapel Hill
Jason Perlmutter, *The Cornell Sun*, Cornell University
Mandy Phillips, Missouri State University
Chris Poore, *Kentucky Kernel*, University of Kentucky
John Puterbaugh, *Kane County Chronicle*
Lilah Raptopoulos, *The Minaret*, University of Tampa
Daniel Reimold, *The Minaret*, University of Tampa
Cera Renault, *Golden Gate [X]press*, San Francisco State University
Alison Roberts, *The State*, Columbia, S.C.
Josie Roberts, *Pittsburgh Tribune-Review*
Michael Roberts, NewsTrain
Tom Rolnicki, Associated Collegiate Press
Amy Rolph, *The Daily*, University of Washington, Seattle
Ed Ronco, KCAW Raven Radio
Nils Rosdahl, *The Sentinel*, North Idaho College
Mike Rosenberg, *Detroit Free Press*
Laurel Rosenhall, *The Sacramento Bee*
Misha Rosiak, *Golden Gate [X]press*, San Francisco State University
Adam Rubin, *New York Daily News*
Kenneth Rystrom, *The Why, Who and How of the Editorial Page*
Leigh Sabey, *Northern Colorado Business Report*
Peter S. Scholtes, *City Pages*
Lauren Schuker, *The Harvard Crimson*, Harvard University
Kevin Schwartz, *The Daily Tar Heel*, University of North Carolina at Chapel Hill
Davis Shaver, *Onward State*, Penn State University
Becky Sher, Knight Ridder/Tribune
Cheri Shipman, *The Battalion*, Texas A&M University
Brian Singler, *The Missourian*
Melissa Silverberg, *The Daily Illini*, University of Illinois at Urbana-Champaign
Emmet Smith, *The Plain Dealer*
Chris Snider, Drake University
Lance Speere
Ron Spielberger, College Media Advisers
Mike Spohn, *The State Press*, Arizona State University
Sree Sreenivasan, Columbia University
George Srour, *DoG Street Journal*, College of William and Mary
Brian Steffen, *The Simpsonian*, Simpson College
Emily Stephenson, *The Daily Tar Heel*, University of North Carolina
Robert F. Stevenson, *The Forum*, Lander University
Brian Stewart, *The Daily Iowan*, University of Iowa
John Strauss, *The Ball State Daily News*, Ball State University
Scott Strazzante, *Chicago Tribune*
Sean Patrick Sullivan, Canadian University Press
Patricia Tisak, *The Philadelphia Inquirer*
Brian Vander Kamp, *The Flip Side*, University of Wisconsin-Eau Claire
Peter Velz, *Collegiate Times*
Dave Waddell, *The Orion*, California State University, Chico
Brian Wagner, *The Daily Herald*
James M. Wagstaffe, Kerr & Wagstaffe, LLP
Matt Waite, *St. Petersburg Times*
Arvli Ward, Student Media UCLA
Tom Warhover, *The Columbia Missourian*, University of Missouri-Columbia
Megan Watzin, *The Diamondback*, University of Maryland
Tom Whisenand, photographer
Kyle Whitfield, *The Daily Reveille*, Louisiana State University
Denny Wilkins, St. Bonaventure University
David Williams, Oregon State University
Bradley Wilson, *Technician*, North Carolina State University
John K. Wilson, Collegefreedom.org
Carie Windham, *Technician*, North Carolina State University
Mark Witherspoon, *Iowa State Daily*, Iowa State University
Kelly Wolff, Educational Media Company at Virginia Tech, Inc.
Stacy Wynn, *The Daily Tar Heel*, University of North Carolina at Chapel Hill
Suzanne Yada, *The Spartan Daily*, San Jose State University
Christine Yee, *Contra Costa Times*
John Zeratsky, *The Badger Herald*, University of Wisconsin-Madison

THE STUDENT NEWSPAPER SURVIVAL GUIDE

Howard Stone

William Townsend

Jordan Williams

INSIDE...

MONDAY
AUGUST 30, 2004
Vol. 96, No.006

THE DAILY MISSISSIPPIAN

The University of Mississippi — *Serving Ole Miss and Oxford since 1911.* — www.thedmonline.com

Bound as brothers

J.D. Johnson The Daily Mississippian

An **Alpha Tau Omega member** comforts friends outside his fraternity house Friday morning. The ATOs spent most of the early hours in the Beta Theta Pi house.

Fire scene investigation concludes, memorial service set for Thursday

MICHAEL NEWSOM
DM CAMPUS NEWS EDITOR

Fire scene investigations at the Alpha Tau Omega house ended over the weekend as the community prepares to say goodbye to three of its members.

Federal, State and local agencies have wrapped up their on site look into the cause of the fraternity house fire that killed three Ole Miss students early Friday morning. All the while, memorials were being planned.

The investigation into the fire that killed William Townsend, Jordan Williams and Howard Stone has been turned over to the University Police Department.

The investigators said that they found no evidence of foul play and no evidence the fire was intentionally set.

The starting point of the fire has been isolated to one of the basement bedrooms along the south side of the structure on the east wall.

Investigators found several possible points of origin for the fire, therefore samples must be sent to the Alcohol, Tobacco, Firearms and Explosives (ATF) laboratory in Maryland to be analyzed to help determine the cause of the fire.

Joey Hall, an ATF special agent assigned to the Oxford bureau, commented on the samples.

"It will be a priority for them to turn it around, get some answers," Hall said.

Hall said that about 25 agents trained to investigate the cause of fire were summoned to campus.

He said that it is common for his office to deal with on-the-scene fire investigations.

"It is kind of what we do every day. With the amount of loss, along with the fatalities, once we got the calls, we jumped in with open arms," Hall said.

He also said the samples would be analyzed today, and more will be known about the cause of the fire after the results are returned.

Hall worked with ATF agents, the Mississippi Bureau of Investigations, University Police, Lafayette County Sheriff's and Oxford Police Departments.

Investigators took pictures, collected physical evidence at the scene and interviewed witnesses throughout the community.

The fire investigation has been turned over to UPD, so that engineers can be brought in to determine if the structure of the ATO house is sound enough for students to go in and collect any of their belongings that are salvageable.

Stone was the last casualty of the fire to be identified. Authori-

See THURSDAY → page 5

FIGURE 1.1 A fraternity house fire at the University of Mississippi in August 2004 highlighted the many roles a student newspaper serves. *The Daily Mississippian*, University of Mississippi.

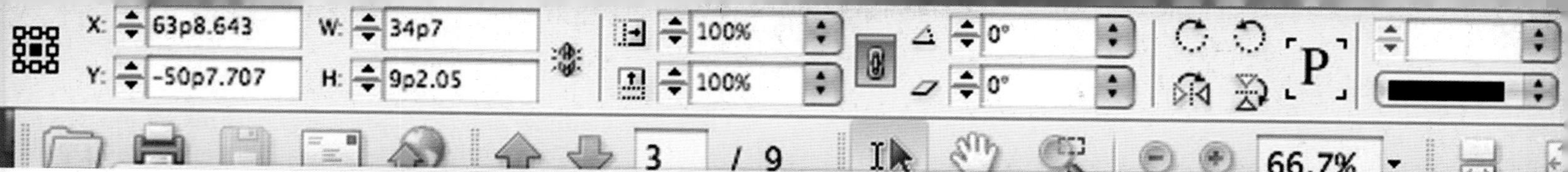

CHAPTER 1
THE ROLE OF THE STUDENT PRESS

It was about 6:15 on a Friday morning when Michael Newsom, the campus news editor for *The Daily Mississippian* (thedmonline.com) at the University of Mississippi, got a wake-up call from Elizabeth Ogden, the paper's former photo editor.

"Michael, I heard that the ATO (Alpha Tau Omega) house is on fire. It's probably nothing, but you should check it out," she said.

Newsom rolled over and went back to sleep. But five minutes later the phone rang again. It was Ogden.

"Michael, it's bad. Get down here," she said.

Newsom dressed quickly and drove toward Fraternity Row at the Oxford, Miss. campus. As he neared the neighborhood of Greek residences, he saw smoke billowing around the Alpha Tau Omega house, a once stately, brick building with white columns in front.

As firefighters battled the blaze, dazed fraternity members milled about, looking for information about their missing brothers.

Newsom set to work interviewing students, fraternity members, the fraternity's adviser – anyone who would talk, anyone who could help him piece together the facts of the story.

The Student Newspaper Survival Guide, Second Edition. Rachele Kanigel.

CHAPTER CONTENTS

Later that morning, *The Daily Mississippian* reported the grim news on its website: Three students had died in the fire.

Over the next several hours and through the weekend, the staff posted updates, stories and photos, as well as radio and video reports from the newspaper's sister student broadcast stations, about the fire on the newspaper's website (Figure 1.2). On Monday, the print edition of the paper was filled with in-depth coverage of the tragedy, including profiles of the victims, a timeline of events and information about how to help the surviving fraternity brothers.

The fire on August 27, 2004 challenged *The Daily Mississippian* staff in many ways. Official sources were tight-lipped, making it difficult to get information. Photographers were shooed away from the scene. Reporters and editors, just settling into their new roles on the fourth day of classes, grappled with unfamiliar equipment and difficult decisions.

But the fire reminded the University of Mississippi of how essential the paper, along with its affiliated radio and television stations, were to the campus and larger community.

"The nation wanted to know exactly what was going on in Oxford, Miss., and we told them," says Emery Carrington, the newspaper's editor-in-chief that year. "Ole Miss. parents,

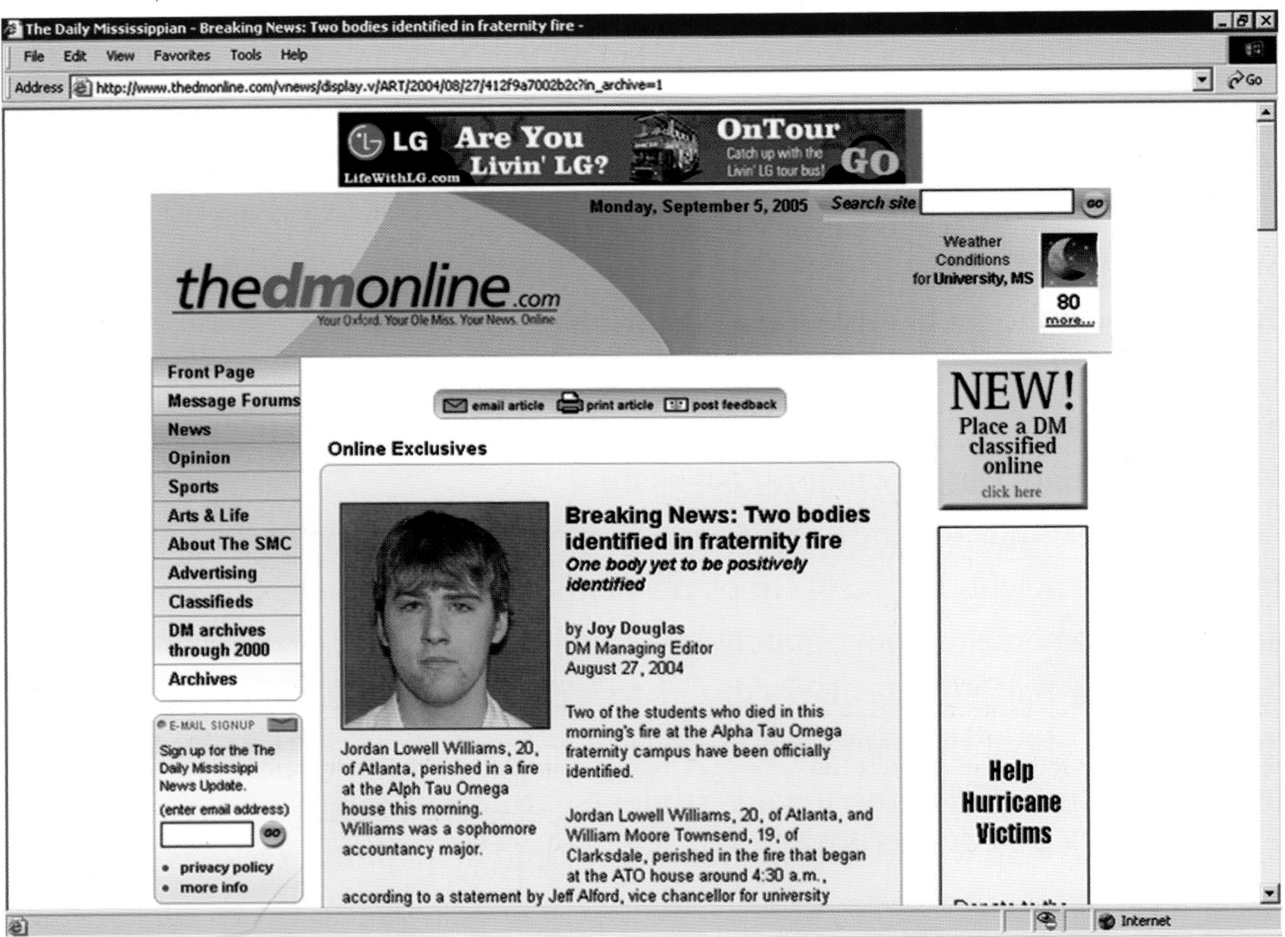

FIGURE 1.2 Though news of the fire broke after the Friday edition of *The Daily Mississippian* was printed, the staff was able to post updates throughout the weekend on the newspaper's website. *The Daily Mississippian*, University of Mississippi.

TIPS FROM A PRO Susan Goldberg

The college newspapers where you now work don't need to look like the city newspaper in the nearest town. In fact, they shouldn't. They should be laboratories for cutting-edge journalism.

In addition to the late nights and pizza and camaraderie, make the most of every assignment. Do things that help make your college paper indispensable to readers. Don't be afraid to try new, unconventional approaches. What kind of approaches? Here are a few you might consider:

1 **Make sure to reflect your community.** Is your front page attuned to what college students are talking about – music, sex, stress, the job market? Do those boring and often inconsequential student government stories really belong out there?

2 **Make use of the latest technology.** Can you podcast your news so students can download it and listen to it when they want to?

3 **Make other people do your work.** Provide a platform for a series of different Web logs – a dorm blog, a Greek blog, a rate-the-prof blog.

4 **Make a local mark.** Leave national and international stories to someone else. It's not your area of expertise and folks can get that information off any number of national websites. Instead, focus on news that is local and useful for your campus readers.

5 **Make the stories you write accessible.** Use everything in your toolbox of tricks – lists, charts, highlights, summaries, tips – to help quickly usher people into your content.

6 **Make watchdog stories your hallmark.** Your on-campus location puts you in the catbird seat to see what the university is up to. Exploit that advantage. How is the administration spending money? Who gets a free car? Whose lover just got a high-paying job? Nothing you do will be more compelling to your readers than revelatory and exclusive local content.

7 **Make change; be a crusader.** Editorial pages too often are boring. Set out to make your pages provocative. Take up a cause. Work in concert with the news side. Get some action!

8 **Make some hard choices.** Newspapers are drowning in dull, turn-of-the-screw 12- to 20-inch stories. Figure out the handful of stories you are going to tell really well on a given day – stories where you can really add value. Brief everything else.

9 **Make hearing your readers a priority.** Ask your readers what they'd like to see you cover. I'm sure you think you know – but do you really? Invite them to tell you, and actually listen to their answers. Maybe you'll learn something that will surprise you and suggest a groundbreaking avenue of presentation or coverage.

10 **Learn your craft.** Newspapers are the public trust. Be proud of that responsibility, and take it seriously. But don't shy away from being bold about it.

SUSAN GOLDBERG is executive editor of Bloomberg News. She got her start at *The State News* (statenews.com) at Michigan State University, where she was a general assignment reporter, county reporter and assistant editor.

These tips are adapted from a speech she gave at the National College Newspaper Convention in San Francisco in 2005.

alumni, fellow fraternity members, the media and the general public created an unprecedented amount of traffic on our website – over 1 million hits within the first 24 hours of the fire, 2 million by the end of the weekend."

THE ROLE OF THE STUDENT PRESS

The tragedy at the University of Mississippi highlights the vital role a student newspaper plays on a college campus. Whether it's a stapled sheaf of photocopied pages distributed every couple of weeks or a professional-looking daily broadsheet, a college newspaper serves many functions.

- It's a chronicle of campus life that informs the campus about everything from scientific research and protest demonstrations to championship basketball games and out-of-control fraternity parties.
- It's a community forum where students, faculty, administrators and staff can debate issues of common concern.
- It's a watchdog that barks when a cafeteria is cited for health code violations or hale athletes drive around with handicapped parking placards.
- It's a training ground for the next generation of journalists.

Let's look at these roles and the responsibilities and challenges that come along with them.

THE CHRONICLE OF CAMPUS LIFE

Every campus has its events, issues and personalities, and a student newspaper is often the only unbiased publication for reporting on the life of a college community. While the primary audience for college papers is students, a good paper covers the whole campus.

"One of the responsibilities of a newspaper is to reflect the nature of the community it serves," says Melvin Mencher, a longtime journalism educator and author of *News Reporting and Writing* (Mc-Graw Hill, 2008), a leading journalism textbook. "A student newspaper should be able to understand and display all dimensions of a campus community, not just student life but the concerns of the university employees, faculty, administrators and staff."

THE COMMUNITY FORUM

A college campus can be a fragmented place. Freshmen and transfer students may feel lost and alienated. Seniors and commuters may be so wrapped up in their majors and schoolwork that they're unaware of what's happening on the rest of the campus. And students can feel overwhelmed at times by a monolithic entity that can raise their tuition, their rents and their health care costs with little warning.

"The student paper can be a unifying force," says Mencher. "It should represent students from around the campus. And it should establish some kind of leadership, demanding the highest quality education for students, so students have an outlet for their frustrations, their excitements, their passions."

In the days and weeks after the University of Mississippi fire, for example, the opinion section and the website comment boxes overflowed with letters and email messages expressing prayers, sadness and outrage (Figure 1.3).

ATO fire leaves three students dead

Post your feedback on this topic here

Date	Subject	Posted by:
08/27/2004	God bless and be with you, men of...	Candy
08/27/2004	All the Taus in Western Michigan wish...	Kurt Pease
08/27/2004	God be with the families of these...	Missy
08/27/2004	I am so saddened about this and my...	Julie
08/27/2004	First I want to let the ATO...	Mike
08/27/2004	I heard about this tragedy on the...	Lindsay
08/27/2004	I feel terrible for all of those...	Josh Loper
08/27/2004	Were the 3 dead before the fire?	M
08/27/2004	Thoughts and support are with you...	Brother Leighton Mohl
08/27/2004	As the father of an Ole Miss Student,...	Charley Cook
08/27/2004	Pray for these kids and their...	prayers
08/27/2004	As a Beta alum, my prayers go out to...	Tom Rice
08/27/2004	The loss of our interfraternal...	Stephen Rupprecht
08/27/2004	My heart goes out to the families of...	Sympathy

FIGURE 1.3 As news of the fire spread students, faculty, alumni, parents of students and members of the community shared prayers and messages of mourning on *The Daily Mississippian*'s website. *The Daily Mississippian*, University of Mississippi.

Journalism and the movies **Eugenia Chien**

Movies about journalism are great for inspiration, motivation and illumination. Stick a video in the newsroom's DVD player, throw some popcorn in the microwave and gather the staff for an evening of fun flicks and discussion.

The Front Page (1931) What are you willing to do to cover a big story? In this classic comedy, an editor convinces a top reporter to put off his marriage long enough to cover the hottest story in town. The original film stars Pat O'Brien, Adolphe Menjou and Mary Brian. B&W, 99 minutes. (A 1974 remake features Jack Lemmon, Walter Matthau and Susan Sarandon. Color, 105 minutes.)

Foreign Correspondent (1940) A crime reporter turned foreign correspondent is caught up in the espionage and danger of World War I. Alfred Hitchcock's famous scene of an assassin escaping into a sea of rippling umbrellas is just one of the unforgettable images from this movie. Joel McCrea and Laraine Day star. B&W, 120 minutes.

His Girl Friday (1940) In a clever remake of *The Front Page*, the tables are turned when an editor (Cary Grant) tries to stop his female star reporter (Rosalind Russell), who happens to be his ex-wife, from leaving the newspaper business. Howard Hawks directs. B&W, 92 minutes.

Citizen Kane (1941) If you don't know what "Rosebud" refers to, you've got to check out this thinly disguised biopic about newspaper publisher William Randolph Hearst. Orson Welles writes, directs and stars. B&W, 119 minutes.

Teacher's Pet (1958) Clark Gable plays a tough city editor who doesn't believe in college-taught journalism. He goes head to head with a journalism professor, played by Doris Day, when he pretends to be a student in her class. B&W, 120 minutes.

All The President's Men (1976) This riveting movie tells the story of how two journalists brought down President Richard Nixon in the Watergate scandal. Dustin Hoffman and Robert Redford play Carl Bernstein and Bob Woodward of *The Washington Post*. Color, 139 minutes.

Absence of Malice (1981) A Miami reporter, played by Sally Field, unknowingly ties an innocent man (Paul Newman) to the murder of a union leader. Color, 116 minutes.

The Year of Living Dangerously (1982) A group of journalists grapples with the political upheaval of the Indonesian government in 1960s Jakarta. Linda Hunt becomes the only actress ever to win an Academy Award playing a man – with no cross-dressing or gender confusion involved. Mel Gibson stars. Color, 117 minutes.

Under Fire (1983) A photojournalist finds himself on a mission to photograph a rebel leader in war-torn Nicaragua. Along the way, it becomes difficult for the journalists to stay neutral. Nick Nolte, Ed Harris star. Color, 128 minutes.

The Killing Fields (1984) Based on a true story, this movie explores the relationship between *New York Times* journalist Sidney Schanberg and his Cambodian assistant Dith Pran when Schanberg is unable to help Pran escape the Khmer Rouge. Sam Waterston, Haing S. Ngor star. Color, 142 minutes.

Salvador (1986) A freelance journalist leaves his out-of-control life in San Francisco to cover the bloody civil war in El Salvador. James Woods and James Belushi star. Oliver Stone writes and directs. Color, 122 minutes.

The Paper (1994) This movie captures 24 hours in a hectic New York newsroom, after two young black men are arrested for the murder of two white businessmen. Ron Howard directs. Michael Keaton, Glenn Close and Robert Duvall star. Color, 112 minutes.

Welcome to Sarajevo (1997) American and British journalists find an orphanage in Sarajevo and walk past the line of ethics when they decide to rescue the children. Stephen Dillane, Woody Harrelson star. Color, 102 minutes.

Fear and Loathing in Las Vegas (1998) Legendary gonzo journalist Hunter S. Thompson (Johnny Depp) takes a dizzying, hallucinogenic road trip to Las Vegas with his sidekick, Dr. Gonzo (Benicio Del Toro). Color, 128 minutes.

The Insider (1999) Russell Crowe plays a scientist who violates his contract with a tobacco company when he exposes addictive ingredients in cigarettes. Ethical quandaries arise when broadcast veteran Mike Wallace (Christopher Plummer) and producer Lowell Bergman (Al Pacino) report the story. Color, 157 minutes.

Live from Baghdad (2002) CNN made television news history when it became the only news network remaining in Baghdad on the eve of the first Gulf

War. Michael Keaton and Helena Bonham Carter star. Mick Jackson directs. Color, 108 minutes.

Shattered Glass (2003) Stephen Glass, a young journalist at *The New Republic*, had everything: talent, a coveted job and adoring friends. This movie explores how Glass betrayed everyone by fabricating stories. Hayden Christensen, Chloe Sevigny and Peter Sarsgaard star. Color, 94 minutes.

The Pentagon Papers (2003) James Spader plays Daniel Ellsberg, a military analyst who risks treason charges when he seeks to publish a series of classified government documents detailing the true nature of America's involvement in the Vietnam War. Color, 92 minutes.

Capote (2005) Philip Seymour Hoffman plays the young Truman Capote as he reports on the murder that inspired his true-crime classic *In Cold Blood*. Color, 114 minutes.

State of Play (2009) A grizzled investigative reporter and a young blogger investigate the murder of a congressman's mistress. Color, 127 minutes.

The wounded community needed to vent, and *The Daily Mississippian* provided a place to do that.

THE WATCHDOG

Colleges and universities may be institutions of learning, but they can also be hotbeds of corruption and scandal. Some undertake questionable research, some misuse state funds, some employ sexual predators.

And on many campuses, the student newspaper is the only institution able to investigate and report such matters.

The Daily Mississippian took its watchdog role seriously after the fraternity house fire. When fire investigators seemed to be holding back information about the cause of the blaze, a *Daily Mississippian* editorial demanded answers. Reporters filed several Freedom of Information Act requests to find out what investigators knew. When government officials finally turned over the investigation report more than six months after the fire, Carrington, the editor-in-chief, posted the entire document on the newspaper's website.

"People really wanted to know what happened," she says. "We felt the community could use it to gain some closure on this tragedy."

THE TRAINING GROUND

Countless professional journalists got their start at college newspapers. Broadcast journalists Bill Moyers and Walter Cronkite worked at *The Daily Texan* (dailytexanonline.com), the student newspaper of the University of Texas at Austin. Michael Isikoff, who broke the Monica Lewinsky story for *Newsweek*, reported for *Student Life* (studlife.com) at Washington University in St. Louis. James Fallows, David Halberstam, Michael Kinsley and Susan Faludi all served as editors of *The Harvard Crimson* (thecrimson.com). Columnist Molly Ivins began to hone her razor-sharp pen in the pages of *The Sophian* (smithsophian.com) at Smith College, and Garry Trudeau created the prototype for Doonesbury for the *Yale Daily News* (yaledailynews.com).

Many believe student newspapers, more even than journalism degree programs, are the best way to launch a career in the field. The clips and experience you get at your college paper can pave the way to internships and jobs.

This training role is even more important today as the field of journalism undergoes cataclysmic changes. The industry is looking to the next generation of journalists – that's you! – for leadership and innovation. Experiments tried at college news organizations – new ways of reporting the news, new ways of communicating with readers, new ways of delivering content, new ways of telling stories – could well pave the way for what journalism becomes in the future.

THE ENHANCED ROLE OF ONLINE PUBLICATIONS

Now that virtually all student newspapers are online – and in fact a few are online-only – they have the potential to play an even more important role than ever. For one thing, the audience is vastly bigger; student publications are not just seen by students, faculty and staff and a few campus neighbors but by alumni, prospective students, parents of students, media professionals and Google searchers from around the world. The immediacy of the Web allows student journalists to report vital information in seconds – often before campus or police officials or the professional press. Student journalists are often the ones to break a campus story of national or international significance, such as a shooting, a bomb threat or a protest that turns into a riot.

In addition, the Web presents opportunities for student journalists to do much more than simply report the news. With social networking tools and mobile technology you can mobilize a community in a matter of minutes.

These new opportunities bring with them new responsibilities. In the old days, if a college newspaper reported a scandal or made a mistake, it would cause a stir on campus. Period. Now a big story – or a major error – can make its way around the world. Professional news organizations often pick up on stories first reported on a college news website, sometimes replicating facts in student news reports without checking them (unfortunate but true). If you paint someone in a negative light or get a vital fact

REFLECTIONS OF A COLLEGE NEWSPAPER EDITOR **Ed Ronco**

Shortly before I graduated from Michigan State University, I had a conversation with my mom about what I had learned. You know, the "how was it?" discussion. College was great, and my professors and classes taught me innumerable things about academic subjects and life in general.

But I had to admit that my most valuable lessons came from working on the student newspaper, *The State News*. Filling the pages of that paper as a reporter, a news editor and finally editor-in-chief my last year gave me insight into every aspect of journalism, and, also, every aspect of humanity.

I had the chance to write about people who were grieving and celebrating, frustrated and elated. I talked to countless readers on the phone, some who said nice things and others who told me I was a buffoon. (That's fine; maybe I was.)

I got to cover – or lead the coverage of – hundreds of stories, from the formation of a graduate student labor union, to the departure of the university president, to the war in Iraq.

When some students on our campus rioted in March 2003, our offices were half-newsroom, half-triage unit. As reporters and photographers ran out the door to gather more news, others came back with red and swollen eyes, seeking relief from the tear gas.

When the United States invaded Iraq, we had stories written 30 minutes after President Bush announced the invasion. After watching Bush's statement, our reporters conducted reaction interviews, calling university administrators, local politicians and others, and then returned to the newsroom to assemble it into something coherent, all with lightning speed.

And then there was election night 2004. I'll never forget the scene of that full newsroom in the early hours of the morning, with more than 80 people throwing papers and yelling election totals across the room.

Those were the big successes. The big stories. But it's the smaller things that I hope you get to experience.

I hope you see the lights burning late in your newsroom and hear the crackle of the police scanner that's always on.

I hope you see people going in and out at all hours of the day, forgoing social lives, and sometimes academic lives, for the sake of an informed campus.

I hope you get to see the presses roll – blurs of gray and black and red and blue that shoot by at astronomical speeds. Our presses were in a warehouse 60 miles away. I'll never forget the smell of the ink.

I hope you see your staff step up to the plate for some of the biggest stories of their lives. And when they do, I hope they hit it out of the park.

I hope you feel the thrill of getting on Page One for the first time, or if you're an editor, I hope you see the look on the face of a rookie reporter when you help her get there.

I hope you hear the sadness in your co-worker's voice after he's interviewed friends and family members of someone who just died.

I hope you talk to each other at 4 a.m., when one of you can't sleep because you're worried about a story in the next day's paper.

I hope you see a really talented photographer hard at work. I still remember driving one of ours down a two-lane highway in rural Michigan as she snapped photos of a runner from the back of my pickup truck.

I hope you watch your copy desk kick into action – these people actually argue about commas – and see your page designers turn raw text and photos into works of art.

I hope you take time to get to know the people who prepare your paper for press and troubleshoot your technical problems. Ours were the finest and smartest bunch of people I have ever met, and modest, too – they never once stood up and took a bow or even asked for the opportunity.

And I hope you get to know the people who get up before the sun, the ones who complete the miracle. We had a group of 12 carriers who rose at 5:30 every morning to distribute 28,500 copies of our newspaper around the campus and city by 8 a.m.

When the time comes for you to walk away from it all, I hope you leave secure in the knowledge that people will continue to sweat and toil over keyboards and continue to produce good journalism night after night so your campus can read it morning after morning.

And when you get out into the professional world, I hope you can say to an editor, "Oh yeah, I've done that before."

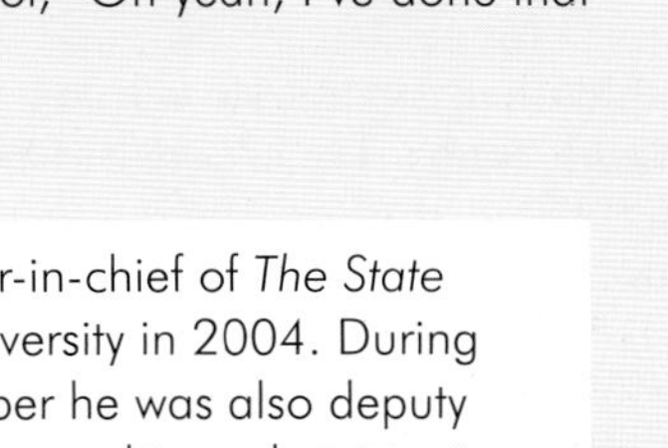

ED RONCO served as editor-in-chief of *The State News* at Michigan State University in 2004. During his previous years at the paper he was also deputy managing editor, campus news editor, administration reporter and graduate issues reporter. He graduated in 2004 with a bachelor's degree in journalism and went on to do internships with the *St. Louis Post-Dispatch* and *The Grand Rapids* (Mich.) *Press*. He is a reporter and host for KCAW Raven Radio in Anchorage, Alaska.

wrong, you can do irreparable damage. An offensive column or cartoon on a student news website can stir outrage not just locally but globally.

Now, more than ever, student journalists must act professionally and responsibly.

CHALLENGES OF STUDENT NEWSPAPERS

Putting out a student paper can be one of the most exciting parts of your college career, but it can also be filled with frustrations. Student journalists often don't feel the power and confidence that professionals do. Among the common problems:

Lack of respect. "As a student journalist, it can be tough to get readers and sources to take you seriously," says Becky Sher, former editor-in-chief of the *GW Hatchet* (gwhatchet.com) at George Washington University in Washington, D.C. who went on to work for McClatchy-Tribune in Washington, D.C. and now teaches at her alma mater. "Off-campus sources can present a particular problem." Administrators and faculty also sometimes fail to give students due consideration.

Conflicts of interest. Even more than professional journalists, student journalists face the challenge of covering the community in which they live. That sometimes means writing about the health violations at the dining hall, the melee after your friend's dorm party or the tenure battle of your favorite English professor. "There are times you can recuse yourself from a story you're too close to, but there are other times that you can't," says Sher. "After all, the latest tuition hike affects you, too."

Inexperience. The most seasoned college newspaper staffer may have three or four years under his belt, but many start writing stories, shooting photographs, selling ads, or designing pages with little or no training. That lack of experience can lead to serious mistakes that are on display for the whole campus – or, in the case of an error picked up by the mass media, the whole world.

Interference. While some student newspapers exist in a climate of complete respect for their First Amendment rights, many don't. Every year, administrators at colleges across the country challenge student newspapers that stir up trouble or embarrass the campus.

GETTING HELP

Fortunately, there are resources to help. Most college newspapers have an adviser to guide students through the sometimes-choppy waters of newspaper publishing. If yours doesn't, find a professor or professional journalist you trust to become a mentor or unofficial adviser. Take advantage of local press clubs, Society of Professional Journalists chapters and other media groups in your area that can offer advice.

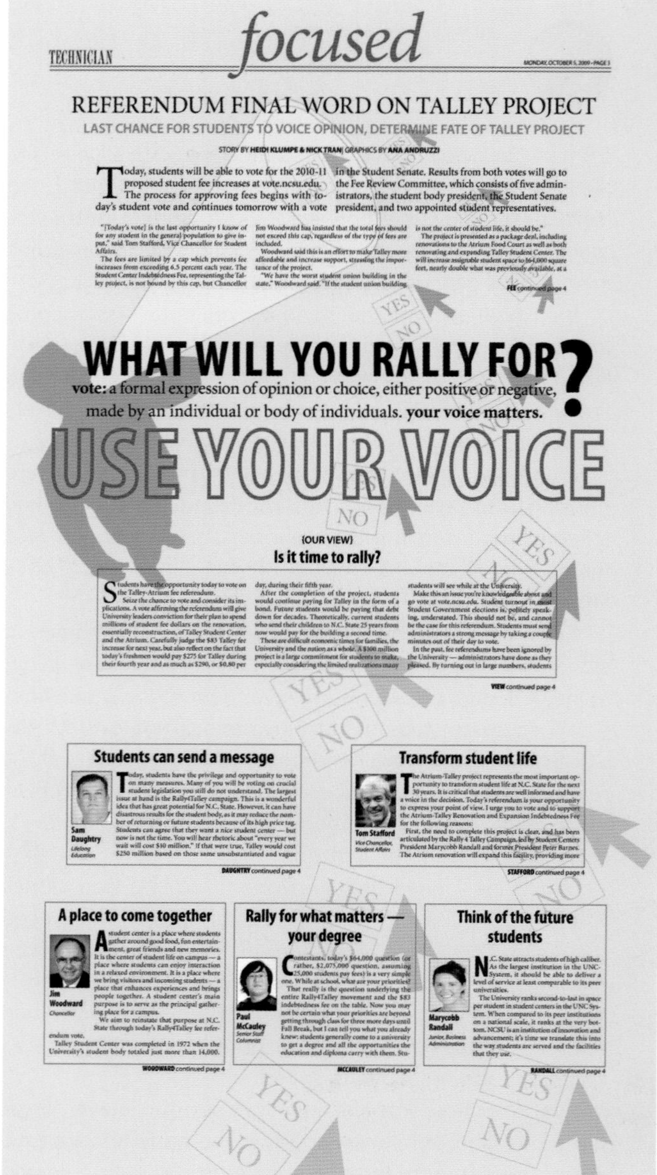
TECHNICIAN *focused* MONDAY, OCTOBER 5, 2009 • PAGE 3

REFERENDUM FINAL WORD ON TALLEY PROJECT

LAST CHANCE FOR STUDENTS TO VOICE OPINION, DETERMINE FATE OF TALLEY PROJECT

STORY BY **HEIDI KLUMPE & NICK TRAN** | GRAPHICS BY **ANA ANDRUZZI**

Today, students will be able to vote for the 2010-11 proposed student fee increases at vote.ncsu.edu. The process for approving fees begins with today's student vote and continues tomorrow with a vote in the Student Senate. Results from both votes will go to the Fee Review Committee, which consists of five administrators, the student body president, the Student Senate president, and two appointed student representatives.

"[Today's vote] is the last opportunity I know of for any student in the general population to give input," said Tom Stafford, Vice Chancellor for Student Affairs.

The fees are limited by a cap which prevents fee increases from exceeding 6.5 percent each year. The Student Center Indebtedness Fee, representing the Talley project, is not bound by this cap, but Chancellor Jim Woodward has insisted that the total fees should not exceed this cap, regardless of the type of fees are included.

Woodward said this is an effort to make Talley more affordable and increase support, stressing the importance of the project.

"We have the worst student union building in the state," Woodward said. "If the student union building is not the center of student life, it should be."

The project is presented as a package deal, including renovations to the Atrium Food Court as well as both renovating and expanding Talley Student Center. The will increase assignable student space to 164,000 square feet, nearly double what was previously available, at a

FEE continued page 4

WHAT WILL YOU RALLY FOR?

vote: a formal expression of opinion or choice, either positive or negative, made by an individual or body of individuals. **your voice matters.**

USE YOUR VOICE

{OUR VIEW}

Is it time to rally?

Students have the opportunity today to vote on the Talley-Atrium fee referendum.

Seize the chance to vote and consider its implications. A vote affirming the referendum will give University leaders conviction for their plan to spend millions of student fee dollars on the renovation, essentially reconstruction, of Talley Student Center and the Atrium. Carefully judge the $83 Talley fee increase for next year, but also reflect on the fact that today's freshmen would pay $275 for Talley during their fourth year and as much as $290, or $0.80 per day, during their fifth year.

After the completion of the project, students would continue paying for Talley in the form of a bond. Future students would be paying that debt down for decades. Theoretically, current students who send their children to N.C. State 25 years from now would pay for the building a second time.

These are difficult economic times for families, the University and the nation as a whole. A $100 million project is a large commitment for students to make, especially considering the limited realizations many students will see while at the University.

Make this an issue you're knowledgeable about and go vote at vote.ncsu.edu. Student turnout in most Student Government elections is, politely speaking, understated. This should not be, and cannot be the case for this referendum. Students must send administrators a strong message by taking a couple minutes out of their day to vote.

In the past, fee referendums have been ignored by the University — administrators have done as they pleased. By turning out in large numbers, students

VIEW continued page 4

Students can send a message

Sam Daughtry, *Lifelong Education*

Today, students have the privilege and opportunity to vote on many measures. Many of you will be voting on crucial student legislation you still do not understand. The largest issue at hand is the Rally4Talley campaign. This is a wonderful idea that has great potential for N.C. State. However, it can have disastrous results for the student body, as it may reduce the number of returning or future students because of its high price tag. Students can agree that they want a nice student center — but now is not the time. You will hear rhetoric about "every year we wait will cost $10 million." If that were true, Talley would cost $250 million based on those same unsubstantiated and vague

DAUGHTRY continued page 4

Transform student life

Tom Stafford, *Vice Chancellor, Student Affairs*

The Atrium-Talley project represents the most important opportunity to transform student life at N.C. State for the next 30 years. It is critical that students are well informed and have a voice in the decision. Today's referendum is your opportunity to express your point of view. I urge you to vote and to support the Atrium-Talley Renovation and Expansion Indebtedness Fee for the following reasons:

First, the need to complete this project is clear, and has been articulated by the Rally 4 Talley Campaign, led by Student Centers President Marycobb Randall and former President Peter Barnes. The Atrium renovation will expand this facility, providing more

STAFFORD continued page 4

A place to come together

Jim Woodward, *Chancellor*

A student center is a place where students gather around good food, fun entertainment, great friends and new memories. It is the center of student life on campus — a place where students can enjoy interaction in a relaxed environment. It is a place where we bring visitors and incoming students — a place that enhances experiences and brings people together. A student center's main purpose is to serve as the principal gathering place for a campus.

We aim to reinstate that purpose at N.C. State through today's Rally4Talley fee referendum vote.

Talley Student Center was completed in 1972 when the University's student body totaled just more than 14,000.

WOODWARD continued page 4

Rally for what matters — your degree

Paul McCauley, *Senior Staff Columnist*

Contestants, today's $64,000 question (or rather, $2,075,000 question, assuming 25,000 students pay fees) is a very simple one. While at school, what are your priorities?

That really is the question underlying the entire Rally4Talley movement and the $83 indebtedness fee on the table. Now you may not be certain what your priorities are beyond getting through class for three more days until Fall Break, but I can tell you what you already knew: students generally come to a university to get a degree and all the opportunities the education and diploma carry with them. Stu-

MCCAULEY continued page 4

Think of the future students

Marycobb Randall, *Junior, Business Administration*

N.C. State attracts students of high caliber. As the largest institution in the UNC-System, it should be able to deliver a level of service at least comparable to its peer universities.

The University ranks second-to-last in space per student in student centers in the UNC System. When compared to its peer institutions on a national scale, it ranks at the very bottom. NCSU is an institution of innovation and advancement; it's time we translate this into the way students are served and the facilities that they use.

RANDALL continued page 4

FIGURE 1.4 A student newspaper should be a community forum where students, faculty and staff can discuss issues and share ideas. *Technician*, North Carolina State University.

Several national organizations exist solely to support the student press. The Student Press Law Center in Arlington, Va., a tireless advocate for student-press rights, offers free legal advice to student newspapers. Associated Collegiate Press, a nonprofit educational membership association in Minneapolis, Minn., and College Media Advisers, a professional association of advisers, sponsor contests, conventions and advocacy services for member newspapers. And many states have statewide student press associations to support student media.

As a journalist, it's up to you to seek out the resources you need and to use them to your advantage.

TO DO

1 Many people on college campuses – especially administrators – don't understand the role of the student press or the basic tenets of press freedom. Early in the school year, plan a meeting with key campus officials to discuss the various roles your paper plays and the importance of press freedom.

2 Plan an open house to acquaint the campus community with your paper. Create displays of major stories and photos. Explain how the paper works, how students can join the staff or contribute material on a freelance basis, how people can send in press releases and letters to the editor.

3 Invite a marketing class on campus to organize a focus group of students to critique your paper. (If you can't get a class to do it, organize a focus group yourself.) Ask participants what they see as the role of your student paper and how well you serve that role. Find out what they like and don't like. Then analyze the responses and see how you can better fulfill their expectations.

4 Conduct a reader survey to find out what readers like about your paper and what they don't like. Develop an action plan to address their concerns.

TO READ

Kovach, Bill and Tom Rosenstiel. *The Elements of Journalism*. New York, N.Y.: Crown Publishers, 2001.

TO CLICK

Associated Collegiate Press

Associated Collegiate Press is the largest and oldest national membership organization for college student media in the United States. A branch of the National Scholastic Press Association, the organization sponsors conventions, training workshops and contests for student journalists.

http://www.studentpress.org/acp

Canadian University Press

Canadian University Press is a national, nonprofit co-operative, owned and operated by more than 80 student newspapers in Canada.

www.cup.ca

Center for Innovation in College Media

Now a part of College Media Advisers, this nonprofit think tank was created to help college student media adapt and flourish in the new media environment. The blog is a must-read for student journalists.

http://www.collegemediainnovation.org/blog

College Media Advisers

College Media Advisers is a membership organization that helps student media professionals improve their media operations. The organization sponsors national conventions and training workshops and advocates for members. Its website is packed with tips and information about college media.

http://collegemedia.org

College Media Matters

This blog, written by college journalism scholar Dan Reimold of the University of Tampa, covers news and issues related to college media.

http://collegemediamatters.com

Columbia Scholastic Press Association

The Columbia Scholastic Press Association unites student editors and faculty advisers working with them to produce student newspapers, magazines, yearbooks and online media. The association is owned by Columbia University and operated as a program affiliated with its Graduate School of Journalism.

http://www.columbia.edu/cu/cspa

Society of Professional Journalists

The Society of Professional Journalists is the nation's most broad-based journalism organization, dedicated to encouraging the free practice of journalism.

www.spj.org

Student Media Sourcebook

The National Scholastic Press Association and Associated Collegiate Press have compiled this directory of links and contact information for resources and organizations of interest to student journalists.

http://www.studentpress.org/sourcebook

Student Press Law Center

The Student Press Law Center is an advocate for student free press rights and provides free legal help and information to students and the educators who work with them.

www.splc.org

FIGURE 2.1 *Technician* at North Carolina State University in Raleigh, N.C., hosts an open house every fall to recruit staff. *Technician*, North Carolina State University.

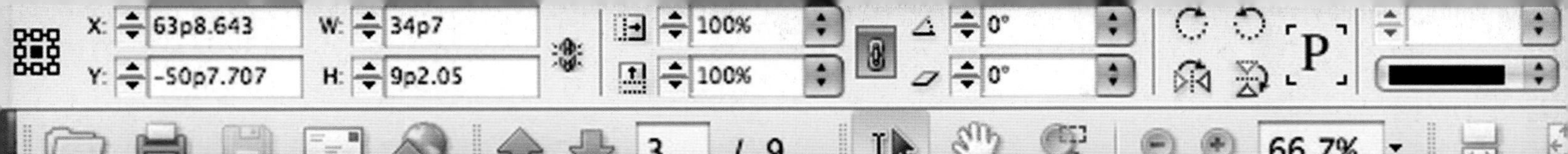

CHAPTER 2
RECRUITING AND TRAINING YOUR STAFF

Professional newspaper editors are always grumbling about the difficulties of recruiting, retaining and training a staff. But compared to student editors, they've got it easy. Most managing editors have a stack of résumés on their desks from young journalists eager to work for them. A phone call to the local college journalism program or a listing on a journalism jobs website will yield even more qualified applicants. Most have a seasoned reporter or two willing to show the newbies the ropes. And while pay for journalists is relatively low, professional newspapers can offer enough compensation to keep people coming to work every day.

Now think of the typical student newspaper editor trying to put together a staff. Where is she going to find a group of talented people willing to work for little or no pay? How will she train them if her most experienced staffers have only a couple of years – or sometimes only a couple of months – on the job? And how will she keep them motivated when they can make more money washing dishes in the cafeteria?

The key is to make working for your newspaper the best experience it can be.

The Student Newspaper Survival Guide, Second Edition. Rachele Kanigel.

CHAPTER CONTENTS

RECRUITING A STAFF

Well-established newspapers at large universities usually have systems and traditions for recruiting staff. At UCLA, for example, the *Daily Bruin* (dailybruin.com) recruits with an open house every quarter and information tables during orientation week. Application forms are posted on the newspaper's website, along with information about how the newspaper works. "We have about 200 students apply for positions every fall," says media adviser Amy Emmert. "We accept about half of those."

At smaller schools, however, recruiting enough students to put out even 12 or 16 pages every week or two can be a formidable task. Commuter schools, where most students live off campus and many students work, may find recruitment especially difficult.

Nils Rosdahl, former adviser to the award-winning *Sentinel* (nicsentinel.com) at North Idaho College, a community college in Coeur D'Alene with about 4,000 students, would start recruiting at the high school level. Each October, he organized a high school media day that attracted about 300 young journalists from 15 high schools in three states. Journalists from the two professional newspapers in town led most of the sessions but Rosdahl would take a few minutes at the beginning of the day to introduce his journalism program and the biweekly student newspaper. He also scheduled annual visits to many of the high school newspapers in Idaho and neighboring Montana and Washington. "I would give a constructive critique of their paper and then let them know what we offer," says Rosdahl, who worked as a sports writer and editor for newspapers in Chicago and Seattle before he started advising in 1986.

In the first week of school Rosdahl would visit photography, journalism, graphic design and marketing classes on campus to recruit potential staffers. "I let them know this is really good for developing their portfolio. Working for *The Sentinel*, they can get their work published and get their name in print. It's also a good opportunity for getting scholarships and internships."

FIGURE 2.2 *The Daily Nebraskan* recruits new staff in the early spring, shortly after the new editor-in-chief is selected. *The Daily Nebraskan*, University of Nebraska.

Rosdahl believes the best recruiting tool is developing the reputation of the paper as a fun and rewarding place to work. Over his 25 years as an adviser, Rosdahl created an inviting newsroom that many students came to think of as a second home. "We have lockers where they can keep their bookbags, a microwave oven, dishes, a refrigerator, a couch, comfortable chairs – everything to make them comfortable. It's really a homeroom atmosphere. They hang out there, their friends hang out there and then we recruit their friends."

TRAINING YOUR STAFF

Once you've assembled a staff it's important to orient the new players and make your expectations clear. Most newspapers schedule staff trainings in the late summer before the new term starts or at the beginning of each semester, trimester or quarter. Some newspapers organize distinct sessions for reporters, photographers, editors and designers as well as orientation events for the entire staff.

The *Daily Bruin* at UCLA has one of the most sophisticated and well-organized training programs around. All new editorial staffers are required to attend a series of four four-hour Saturday training sessions in one of nine departments – news reporting and writing, sports writing, copyediting, design, photojournalism, electronic media, column writing, arts reporting and writing, graphics and illustration, and cartooning. The sessions are led by professional journalists from the *Los Angeles Times*, *Orange County Register* and other Southern California news organizations.

Editors are required to attend summer training sessions – four weeks of sessions in leadership, management and editing skills. Throughout the term the paper offers optional training workshops in specific skills, such as accessing public documents, headline writing, feature writing and creating complex graphics.

Most student newspapers don't have such extensive resources, but every paper should have some kind of orientation for new staffers and leadership training for editors. If yours doesn't, talk to your adviser or editor. (For more on training see the Tipsheet for training your staff).

Patricia Tisak organized a leadership seminar for her editors when she was editor-in-chief of *The Daily Collegian* (collegian.psu.edu) at Pennsylvania State University in 2000. "We played the requisite cheesy bonding games, but we also discussed story ideas, major goals for the various departments, newspaper policy, and motivation techniques for our staff," says Tisak, who went on to become a copy editor for *The Philadelphia Inquirer*. "Because the dynamic of a college newspaper changes so quickly with the graduation of each class, it's important for editors to get together and have a discussion on the newspaper's standards. It's important to set the tone early so that the staff is on the same page."

And training should continue through the term. If someone on the staff has done exemplary work, invite him to speak about how he got that story or photo. Organize periodic brown-bag luncheons and invite professional journalists, journalism professors or others to speak. A time management expert on campus might be tapped for a workshop on handling deadlines; ask a meditation or yoga teacher to offer some tips on stress management.

Students can also take advantage of regional, statewide and national training programs and conventions offered by College Media Advisers, Associated Collegiate Press, the Cox Institute for Newspaper Management Studies, Investigative Reporters and Editors and other groups listed at the end of this chapter.

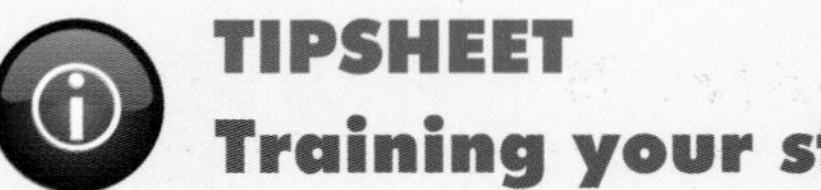

TIPSHEET
Training your staff

Student newspapers should schedule training sessions each time the staff turns over. If you have a large staff, you may want to organize special sections for reporters, editors, photographers and designers. If your staff is small, you'll probably want to have one training for editors and another for the staff as a whole. Here are some tips for making training sessions effective.

1. **Survey the staff.** Ask both returning and incoming staffers what skills they'd most like to learn.
2. **Get organized.** Assign a person or a committee to organize the training. Typically, advisers and top editors or teams of editors create training programs.
3. **Find time.** Decide how much time to devote to training. Some newspapers sponsor multi-day or even multi-week seminars. Others can only spare a day or two.
4. **Arrange the date early.** That way students can plan vacations and work schedules around it. A week or two before the term starts is usually best, although some papers find they get better attendance if they schedule training a day or two before classes start.
5. **Set a budget.** If your newspaper has the money, you may want to arrange for meals or a special venue for the training, such as a hotel, restaurant or conference center. If your budget is tight, you can hold the training in your newsroom or in classrooms and have students handle lunch on their own. If meals are too pricey, provide drinks and snacks to keep people's energy up.
6. **Recruit local journalists.** Invite pros to lead workshops. Alumni of your newspaper who are now working in the field can be especially effective and inspiring.
7. **Learn the law.** Invite your newspaper's attorney, a law professor or other media law expert to offer a session on legal issues, such as libel, copyright and open meetings and records laws.
8. **Break the ice.** If the staffers don't all know each other, open the training with introductions or ice breakers so people can get to know each other.
9. **Mix it up.** Make sure some of the activities are interactive; intersperse large-group sessions with small-group discussions or exercises.
10. **End on a high note.** Conclude the training with an informal social gathering, such as a pizza party. Encourage veteran staffers to mingle with new people.

CHECKLIST
Planning a training workshop

Topics for an editors' training workshop

- Coaching reporters and photographers
- Multimedia storytelling techniques
- Legal issues for editors – libel, copyright, invasion of privacy
- Ethical issues for editors – taste, profanity, conflicts of interest
- Design basics
- News judgment
- Managing a staff
- Editing copy
- Photo editing
- Leadership
- Disaster planning
- Critiquing the work of others
- Workflow, deadlines and story budgeting.

Topics for a staff training workshop

- Understanding your campus community – demographics, ongoing issues, sources
- Generating story ideas
- Covering breaking news
- Covering a beat, developing sources
- Freedom of information
- Review of policies and procedures of your news organization
- Computer-assisted reporting
- Multimedia skills – recording and editing audio and video, creating interactive maps
- Social media skills and policies.

CREATING A STAFF MANUAL

One of the most important tools for orientating your staff is a staff manual that includes all the rules and procedures your newspaper operates by.

If your paper is still using the same old staff manual that's been hanging around for years, it's probably time to update it. And if you don't have one at all, start work on one right away.

A good staff manual can:

Give the paper a foundation and sense of continuity, even in the face of high turnover

Serve as a newsroom reference book

Orient new staffers and help them understand what's expected of them

Help staffers resolve conflicts.

"I view the handbook as a bible – the highest ranking document in the newsroom," says Ira David Levy, former adviser to *Diversity*, the monthly college newspaper at Wright College in Chicago. "A handbook serves as a point of reference for continual newsroom policies. It also teaches new staff members how things work and what to expect."

The staff manual can also be used to educate your readers about how your newspaper works. Some student newspapers, including *The Sentinel* (ksusentinel.com) at Kennesaw State University in Georgia, prominently post their staff manuals on the newspaper's website for all to see.

Most staff manuals have several of the following sections:

1. A list of staff positions and job descriptions
2. An ethics policy
3. Policies about letters to the editor, anonymous sources, deadlines, freelance contributions, advertising, and other issues relevant to the working of the publication
4. A stylebook (which may be a separate document or included in the staff manual) Some staff manuals also include tips on reporting, writing, photojournalism, conflict resolution and avoiding libel and in recent years some have added a social media policy (for an example, see Chapter 19).

MENTORING

Mentor relationships are vital in journalism – both for learning the ropes and snagging jobs and internships – and the best student newspapers have systems in place to cultivate such relationships. A mentor is a person at a higher level in the field who can nurture, teach and counsel a young journalist. It can be a fellow reporter on the student paper who has been around a little longer, an editor, an adviser or a professional journalist.

Some student newspapers have a buddy system that links incoming reporters to more experienced staffers; others assign a senior staffer to act as a writing coach. Miguel M. Morales became a writing coach for the *Campus Ledger* (campusledger.org) when he was a student at Johnson County Community College in Overland Park, Kansas after serving as a staff reporter, features editor, managing editor and editor-in-chief for the biweekly paper. "I try to work with reporters in all stages of the process," Morales says. "I provide tips and introduce new skills for the stories they may have to write. I don't force my coaching on staff members, though sometimes their editors make them meet with me."

The *Daily Bruin* lines up professional journalists to serve as writing coaches. The Center for Integration and Improvement of Journalism at San Francisco State University has paired interested students with writing and photo coaches, most of whom work for local news organizations. Students are encouraged to meet with their coaches every week or two to talk about stories and review copy.

Ralph Braseth, manager of student media at Loyola University Chicago, urges student editors to contact their counterparts at a local professional newspaper to seek advice and counsel. Obviously, the top editor at a big city newspaper may not have time to meet with the college paper's editor-in-chief, but many editors are more than happy to mentor up-and-coming journalists. Students should also look for mentors in advisers, journalism faculty members or other writing teachers.

DIVERSITY TRAINING

Is it appropriate for a female reporter to shake hands with an Orthodox Jew? Will a person who uses a wheelchair be offended if you stand during an interview?

Should you refer to a transgender person as he or she – or is there a preferable term?[1]

Covering a diverse community can enrich you as a journalist and a human being. But it can also raise uncomfortable challenges. In recent years professional newspapers have begun to train staffers in cultural competency and student newspapers are beginning to follow suit.

When she was editor-in-chief of *The Daily Collegian*, Patricia Tisak organized a mandatory diversity training program for all new staff members. "During this training, I led discussions on race and ethnicity issues and went over *Collegian* guidelines and policies," Tisak says. "For example, I inevitably encountered at least one new staffer who didn't understand why the term 'Oriental' might be offensive to some when applied to a person of Asian heritage."

To organize a diversity training program, invite professors in ethnic and religious studies departments or student leaders of ethnic and religious groups to meet with your staff. Have someone from your campus disability resource center and the gay, lesbian, transgender groups on campus discuss issues pertinent to those groups. Professional journalists from mainstream newspapers and the ethnic or gay and lesbian press can also offer insights about covering various groups.

Be sure to incorporate what you learn into your newspaper's stylebook and staff manual.

For more ideas about diversity training, check out the website of the Poynter Institute, listed in the resources section at the end of this chapter.

MOTIVATING YOUR STAFF

It's the middle of the semester. Everyone's studying for mid-terms and frantically trying to catch up in the classes they've been ignoring while they devote themselves to the newspaper. The newsroom is virtually empty – except for that guy fast asleep on the couch. How are you going to put out a newspaper this week?

Motivation is a chronic problem at all newspapers – but student newspapers suffer most of all. With little or no pay and competing interests (classes, jobs, spring break, the Big Game, love, graduation, the bar down the street), work for the school paper often gets pushed down the priority list a month or two into the term. How can you keep your staff motivated?

Stroke them every way you can. That means rewards and awards, free food and drinks, pats on the back and shoulder massages. Everyone wants to feel appreciated.

Though *The Sentinel* at North Idaho College doesn't pay writers and photographers, the newspaper provides lots of incentives to keep staffers committed. The seven editors get full-ride scholarships "just as if they were on the basketball team," Rosdahl says. "Not only are they doing the school a service but they're actually going to use the skills they learn when they get out of school whereas a basketball player probably isn't." *The Sentinel's* journalism club raises about $4,000 each year through a book swap the first week of each semester. That pays for trips to national conventions as well as food and other perks. The paper also arranges a lot of ads in trade "so instead of money we get free food, free bowling, free car washes," Rosdahl says. "Students who do a good job win these prizes."

As a student you probably can't arrange for such enticing perks as full scholarships. But you can make working for the newspaper fun. When you see morale flagging, organize a party or invite the staff out for drinks.

Awards work, too. Advisers and editors shouldn't wait for the end of the semester to honor exemplary work. Best-of-the week awards lift staff morale. Dave Waddell, adviser to *The Orion* (theorion.com) at California State University, Chico, gives out mugs emblazoned with the paper's name each week to reward good work. Don't have money for promotional mugs? Even a paper citation and a round of applause will keep staff members coming back for more.

[1]Orthodox Jewish men generally don't shake hands with women who are not their wives. A person in a wheelchair probably will not be offended if you stand for an interview, but it's better to sit if you can. Transgender people generally prefer the pronoun that relates to how they are living their lives, regardless of surgical status. A female-to-male transsexual, for example, should be referred to as "he." Some use the pronoun "ze" for he/she and "hir" for his/her.

Q&A Miguel M. Morales

After serving as a reporter, features editor, managing editor and editor-in-chief of *The Campus Ledger* at Johnson County Community College in Overland Park, Kansas, Miguel Morales became the newspaper's writing coach. At a student paper, Morales says, a writing coach can facilitate student journalists' transition from the classroom to the newsroom.

What do you do as a writing coach?

My job is to act as a back-up editor-in-chief, a back-up managing editor and a front-end adviser. I catch things that fall through the cracks when reporters, section editors, the copy desk, the managing editor and the editor-in-chief don't. I anticipate problems and their solutions. I provide skills training and counseling. I am the personal and professional conscience of the newsroom.

I advocate for the staff. I give them what they need to do their jobs successfully. Sometimes it's a pep talk, a shoulder to cry on or researching the problem to find a handout or website that can help. Other times it means talking with the editor-in-chief and the managing editor about issue planning, motivating the staff or disciplinary action.

My job changes with the needs of the newsroom. Some days I am the peacekeeper, other days I light the fire, other days I bring down the hammer.

How did you prepare to become a writing coach?

I approached it the way I approach a story, through research. I found the best sources and interviewed them. They made time to help me, so I make time to help others.

Since writing coach is a new position, one I haven't seen another college paper institute, I take my lead from professional coaches like Steve Buttry, Don Fry (co-author of *Coaching Writers: Editors and Reporters Working Together Across Media Platforms, 2nd ed.*, Bedford/St Martins, 2003), and other members of Newscoach (a discussion list for newsroom trainers sponsored by The Poynter Institute).

How do you coach reporters?

Whenever I am in the office and a reporter or photographer has come back from an interview or shoot, I stop whatever I'm doing. I ask them how it went and what it covered. Reporters and photographers need to debrief. They need to talk about how the subject was a jerk or about something funny that happened. I also ask questions: What did he (or she) mean by that? Does that answer make sense based on the other interviews you've done? What did their office look like?

This helps them crystallize aspects of the interview they need for the story and helps them identify follow-up questions. I usually don't grill a photographer as hard as the reporter. I just ask them to tell me something interesting that happened while taking the photo and that usually helps them write the cutline.

Do you also coach editors?

Yes. Students find it difficult to go from being a reporter, where he or she is strictly responsible for his or her story, to a section editor responsible for five or more stories they didn't write.

I have three goals when coaching editors:

1. Help them learn the reporter's voice.
2. Help them edit in the reporter's voice.
3. When possible have the editor and the reporter edit together. If that's not possible, the editor needs to inform the reporter of needed changes and give the reporter the opportunity to make the changes before publication.

What resources have you found that may be useful to other college newspapers?

Every college paper has "trades." The trades are papers we receive from other schools in exchange for ours. I use these as coaching tools. I go through them for story ideas to see what other campus papers cover and how well (or badly) they do it. I tear out examples of good photography, graphics, layouts, headlines, ledes and even ads. I post these at the desk of the appropriate staff member. The staff members then use these as ways to help the paper.

Of the papers I haven't chopped up, I take and distribute these at a staff meeting (usually once a semester) and have the staff pick three things the paper does better than our paper and three things we do better than them. We gain insights on our paper. We also identify holes we've been overlooking all semester. I can't believe we used to throw them away. Now they are teaching tools. That's what I call recycling newspapers!

I constantly search for online resources for my staff. Obitpage.com offers examples of how to write an obituary. American Copy Editors Society (copydesk.org) offers AP and style quizzes, while Glossarist.com offers a searchable directory of glossaries and topical dictionaries. I also use Edward Miller's Reflections on Leadership website (reflections.edwardmillercoaching.com). I constantly rely on their insight in coaching my newsroom. Professional organizations like the Society of Professional Journalists, American Society of Newspaper Editors, National Association of Hispanic Journalists, National Association of Black Journalists, Asian American Journalists Association and National American Journalists Association offer scholarships, student membership and/or programs targeting student journalists. These organizations introduced me to coaching and professionalism in the newsroom.

TO DO

1 Take a look at your current recruiting practices. If your staff isn't as large or as committed as you'd like, try some new recruitment techniques such as those suggested in this chapter. Schedule an open house at the beginning of the term with tours of your newsroom (and don't forget munchies – there's nothing that brings in the crowds like free food.)

2 Review your staff training program. Is it sufficient or could you be doing more? Discuss options for more extensive training with your editor or adviser.

3 Invite local journalists to lead workshops on various topics such as photojournalism, headline writing, investigative reporting and page design.

4 Plan a field trip for your editors or your entire staff to a local newspaper. Ask to sit in on an editors' meeting. As an alternative, arrange for individuals or small groups of students to shadow a person or department, such as the copy desk, sports department, graphics team or editorial board, for a few hours.

5 If you don't already have one, set up a coaching program. Enlist reporters, editors, photographers, designers and graphic artists from local media organizations to meet on a regular basis with students. You may set up one-on-one relationships or ask a professional to hold regular office hours once or twice a month.

6 Find out about local, regional and national conventions and training programs (for information see websites below). If your newspaper cannot afford to pay the expenses, see about getting funding from a local news organization, student government, your journalism or communication program or other source. Or organize a fund-raising event to send staffers to training events.

TO READ

Clark, Roy Peter and Don Fry. *Coaching Writers: Editors and Reporters Working Together Across Media Platforms, 2nd ed.* New York, NY: Bedford/St. Martin's, 2003.

Coffey, Shelby III. *Best Practices: The Art of Leadership in News Organizations.*

(Available to download at http://www.freedomforum.org/templates/document.asp?documentID=16166).

TO CLICK

American Press Institute
API is one of the leading training centers for professional journalists. Its website offers descriptions of training programs and links to many journalism organizations.
www.americanpressinstitute.org

Associated Collegiate Press
This nonprofit educational membership association, a division of the National Scholastic Press Association, hosts three conventions a year. The National College Media Convention, co-sponsored with College Broadcasters Inc. and College Media Advisers, is held in the fall. The organization sponsors annual midwinter conventions in the West and Midwest. ACP also offers summer workshops for advisers and student journalists.
http://www.studentpress.org/acp/conventions.html

College Media Advisers
This national organization of media advisers hosts two conventions each year, featuring more than 200 training sessions, workshops, media tours and critique sessions for student journalists as well as advisers. The fall meeting, held in partnership with Associated Collegiate Press and College Broadcasters Inc, takes place in a different city each year. The spring convention is held in New York City in mid-March. CMA also offers summer workshops for advisers.
www.collegemedia.org

Cox Institute for Newspaper Management Studies
Every summer this institute at The University of Georgia sponsors a weeklong Management Seminar for College News Editors on the Athens campus. This intensive seminar enables editors-in-chief to acquire and sharpen skills in managing people, resources and time while meeting and working with their peers from across the country.
www.grady.uga.edu/CoxInstitute

Poynter Institute
The Poynter Institute offers training seminars for student journalists and journalism educators, as well as professional journalists. The website, which includes a useful search engine, also has articles and columns on nearly every aspect of journalism and links to other journalism websites. The site also allows you to join Newscoach-L, a Listserv for people interested in newsroom training.
http://about.poynter.org/training

Society for Collegiate Journalists
The nation's oldest organization designed solely to serve college journalists holds a convention every two years. The organization also sponsors contests.
www.scj.us

State College Press Associations
Many states have press associations or student media associations that offer training opportunities for student journalists. Among them are:

Arkansas Collegiate Press Association

California College Media Association
http://calcollegemedia.org

Florida College Press Association
http://floridacollegepress.com

Georgia College Press Association
http://www.gapress.org/gcpa.html

Illinois College Press Association
www.illinoiscollegepress.wordpress.com

Indiana Collegiate Press Association
www.indianacollegiatepress.org

Iowa College Media Association
http://iowacollegemedia.com

Kansas Associated Collegiate Press
www.kacponline.org

Kentucky Intercollegiate Press Association
www.kycollegepress.org

Michigan Collegiate Press Association
http://www.michiganpress.org

Missouri College Media Association
www.mcmachronicle.com

Nebraska Collegiate Media Association
www.nebraskacollegemedia.blogspot.com

New Jersey Collegiate Press Association
www.njpa.org/collegepress

North Carolina College Media Association
www.jomc.unc.edu/nccma

Oklahoma Collegiate Media Association
http://ocma.okstate.edu

Texas Intercollegiate Press Association
www.texasipa.org

Western Association of University Publications Managers
This organization of publication managers offers an annual retreat for student newspaper editors and an annual conference for media directors and general managers from its 29 member schools.
www.waupm.org

APPENDIX 2.A TRAINING EXERCISES

1 Story idea hunt

This exercise helps foster teamwork, allows people to get acquainted and encourages staffers to start generating story ideas.

Break participants into groups of three or four. Make sure each group has people in a variety of positions – editor, reporter, photographer, designer etc.

Send the groups out on campus for 30 to 45 minutes and instruct them to come back with at least five story ideas. You may assign each team to go to a certain building or part of campus or allow them to go wherever they choose. You could also be specific about the types of story ideas they should look for:

1 A news story
2 A trend story
3 A multimedia story
4 A personality profile
5 An newsworthy event.

When the groups return, have them pitch their story ideas to the whole staff. Make a list of the story ideas on a board and then discuss which would make good stories for the paper.

2 Project Planning

This exercise gets staffers to think about projects and helps develop planning skills. It also raises awareness about group dynamics.

Arrange participants in two concentric circles: In the smaller, inner circle place the editor-in-chief, opinion editor, photo editor or chief photographer, news editor, art director or lead designer, graphics editor, online editor. The rest of the group should sit in a circle around them.

Then propose a news scenario – a fire in a dormitory, a visit to campus by the president of the United States, a fraternity prank that ends in a student's death.

Have the inner group spend 15 minutes planning how the paper will cover the story. Then have the outer group critique the planning process by addressing these questions:

1 Did anyone dominate the conversation?
2 Did everyone get a chance to speak?
3 Did the group discuss photos as well as text?
4 Did the group come up with good ideas for graphics?
5 Did the group come up with innovative ideas for presenting the story on the Web?

6 Did the group miss any important angles on the story?

7 What was productive about the discussion? What wasn't productive?

Then break the rest of the staff into small groups to discuss real upcoming stories and how they can work together to enhance those stories with graphics, photos and special online features, such as discussion boards, links, polls, slide shows and multimedia reports.

3 Interviewing

This exercise helps develop interviewing skills and raises awareness of interpersonal communication issues.

Break participants into groups of three. In each, one person plays the role of a reporter and one the role of a source. The third person is an observer who will take notes on the interaction.

Have the reporter interview the source for five minutes for a short biographical profile.

Next, have members of the group rotate. The observer becomes the reporter, the reporter becomes the source, the source becomes the observer. Have the new reporter interview the source for five minutes.

Then switch one more time. By now, each person has played every role.

Finally, have the groups discuss the interactions.

1 What did the observers notice? Did the reporters establish rapport with the sources? How were the reporters at drawing out their sources? Did they follow up on interesting things the sources said?

2 How did the sources feel about the interaction? Did the reporters make them feel comfortable? Did they feel heard?

3 How did the reporters feel about the interaction? What do they think they did well? How do they think they could have improved?

If time permits, you could expand this exercise by giving each reporter time to write a brief profile of the source and then discuss the stories.

4 Scavenger hunt

This exercise is designed to help staffers get to know each other and see the campus in a new way.

During a training workshop for editors or for the whole staff, divide participants into groups of four or five. Try to group people with others they don't know well or with whom they don't normally work.

Hand each group a campus map, then tell the groups to come back in a set amount of time (an hour for a small to mid-sized campus, an hour and a half for a large campus) with as many of these items as they can collect (or come up with your own list):

A bus schedule for a line that goes to campus

Three fliers for different campus events

A brochure (or a condom?) from the student health center

A menu from a campus restaurant

A brochure from an academic department

A game schedule for an athletic team

A library map (or some other handout readily available at the library).

Reward the winning team with a gift certificate or coupons to a campus eatery and encourage them to celebrate their victory with a meal together.

5 Management scenarios

This exercise is designed to help editors develop management and leadership skills.

Break editors into groups of three or four. Have each group discuss one of the following scenarios for 15 minutes. Then have them share their responses with the larger group.

1 A reporter turns in excellent stories but consistently misses deadlines. The last story came in so late that the paper missed its production deadline. You're the reporter's direct supervisor; how would you approach the situation? What tools or penalties would you use to motivate the reporter to meet deadlines?

2 A reporter and an editor who had been dating for a few months have a big argument in the newsroom. The next day they're back together and are cuddling on the couch in the office. You believe they're acting in a less-than-professional way. How would you handle the situation?

3 A professor calls to say a reporter misquoted her in a story and demands a front-page correction. The reporter swears that the professor said the quote but he doesn't have an audio recording or notes to back him up. This is the second complaint from a source about the accuracy of the reporter's work. What would you tell the reporter? What would you say to the source?

4 It's the fifth week of school and only half your staff has attended the mandatory staff meeting. Reporters and photographers have been missing deadlines and turning in shoddy work. Morale is low. What would you do to motivate the staff?

5 A student complains that a staff photographer shot a photo of him drinking a beer in his dorm room without his permission. The photo was published in the newspaper and now the campus police are charging him with underage drinking. He demands that the photographer be fired. How would you handle the situation?

Look good
STYLE YOURSELF
in buzz

Issues remain for Chicago's 2016 Olympic bid
SPORTS, 1B

Thursday
September 24, 2009

The Daily Illini

High: 77° Low: 62°

The independent student newspaper at the University of Illinois since 1871 | **www.DailyIllini.com** | Vol. 139 Issue 25 | **FREE**

WHITE STEPS DOWN

The University of Illinois' Sixteenth President, B. Joseph White, waits to enter the Krannert Center for the Performing Arts on Tuesday afternoon.

THE DAILY ILLINI FILE PHOTO

Editor's note: The articles on President B. Joseph White's resignation and the campus' reaction were compiled by The Daily Illini staff.

President to vacate position on Dec. 31, replacement has yet to be named

B. Joseph White will resign as the 16th president of the University, effective Dec. 31.

In a press release from the University, Board of Trustees Chairman Christopher Kennedy accepted White's official resignation. Kennedy said the board will address the appointment of an interim president at a special meeting "within weeks."

He explained that a search committee of trustees, faculty, students and alumni will be named soon to recruit the next president. According to the release, the board intends to have a new president by the 2010-11 academic year.

"I take this action to enable you as a newly constituted board to select University leadership going forward," White said in his letter addressed to Kennedy.

In the release, White said he will remain active at the University by teaching and raising funds. His contract as president would have expired in June 2011, but now his last day will be Dec. 31.

White also said he will forgo a $475,000 retention bonus he would have soon earned.

"I'm sensitive to the University's difficult financial situation and the sacrifices being made by faculty and staff," White said in his letter.

Kennedy said the University needs to review other personnel at an ad-hoc committee meeting Thursday at the University system's Chicago campus at 9 a.m He said the meeting will be an organizational time to put together a plan for reviewing top administrators, including Chancellor Richard Herman.

Kennedy said he does not think it will hurt the board's ability to find quality leadership in the future.

"The scandal won't hurt us. There is a lot of passion about the University," Kennedy said. "We want the University to be the best in every class."

Kennedy said the remainder of the board is supportive of White and is looking to the future

See **RESIGNATION,** Page 4A

BOARD OF TRUSTEES

TREVOR GREENE THE DAILY ILLINI

Christopher G. Kennedy, chairman of the Board of Trustees, left, speaks to President B. Joseph White, right, during the Board of Trustees meeting at the Illini Union on Sept. 10.

Trustee reactions mixed about events

Past and current Board of Trustees members had mixed reactions to President White's resignation Wednesday.

Trustee Tim Koritz, who was appointed by Gov. Pat Quinn on Sept. 4, said White informed him about his decision Tuesday.

"President White called me yesterday and told me his intentions," Koritz said. "He's putting the interests of the University ahead of his own interests."

Koritz, however, said he was optimistic about the University's future leadership and admired and respected White for stepping down.

Lawrence Eppley, a former trustee, said White is a capable leader whom he respects.

"He's a very talented man and has a great track record in education, and I hope he is able to continue this," Eppley said.

He added that he thought White's departure will be detrimental to the University.

"If that is his decision, I support it," Eppley said. "But I think it's a big loss for the University."

See **TRUSTEES,** Page 5A

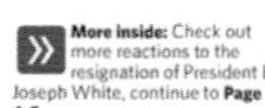

More inside: Check out more reactions to the resignation of President B. Joseph White, continue to **Page 4-5**

More online: For continuing coverage throughout the day, log on to **www.DailyIllini.com**

More on-air: For more information and further reactions, tune in at 5 p.m. to **WPGU 107.1-FM**

CAMPUS REACTION

Students, faculty respond to President White's resignation

"I guess I wasn't really that surprised. It seems pretty evident that he was involved in that."
ANGUS LANKER,
senior in LAS

"There was no reason for him to stay in his position. He should've resigned quicker."
KIANI LOVE,
sophomore in ACES

"He doesn't go with the glory and the grand exit that you would like to see when you retire, when you leave someplace. I think he tried very hard to be the protector of the faculty- to keep us shielded from things."
PETER SAUER,
professor of electrical engineering

"I had no idea he resigned today. I think it's a good thing. Anything to help our school's image."
ELLIE BRZEZENSKI,
freshman in LAS

See **CAMPUS,** Page 5A

FIGURE 3.1 When a major event, like the resignation of the university president, strikes your campus, your news organization is responsible for covering all the angles. *The Daily Illini*, University of Illinois, Champaign-Urbana.

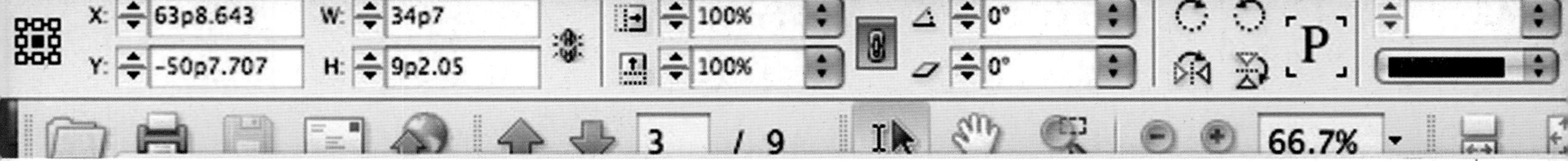

CHAPTER 3
COVERING A CAMPUS

A college campus, even a small one, is like a miniature city. It has its own political establishment (the administration), policy makers (faculty senate, student government), merchants (campus bookstore, food vendors, and other on- and off-campus businesses that serve the college community), residents (students, as well as the faculty and staff who spend their days there). It has its local celebrities (the president, university police chief, noted professors) and its disenfranchised (janitors, restaurant workers, and, some might argue, teaching assistants.) Most schools have some kind of health care system and police force.

The typical college campus also has the legal battles, crime, capital improvement projects, union disputes and political entanglements that every small city has, but on top of that it has fervent intellectual discussion and groundbreaking research that may reach far beyond the borders of the campus. Add to all that a dynamic cast of characters – with new faculty, new staff and new students joining the community every year – and you've got the makings of a darn good news town.

Any student journalist who says, "This campus is so dull. There's no news here," simply isn't looking.

But knowing where to look and how to look isn't second nature.

The Student Newspaper Survival Guide, Second Edition. Rachele Kanigel.

CHAPTER CONTENTS

As we discussed in Chapter 1, your paper may be the only consistent and unbiased vehicle for campus news. Even if local media organizations report on your college, they probably don't have the time, space and contacts to cover your school community as thoroughly as you can. With a staff of reporters dedicated to covering your campus, you should be able to snoop out stories even the most experienced professional reporter would have a hard time finding.

DEVELOPING A BEAT SYSTEM

The most efficient way to cover a campus is to develop a coordinated beat system. "The whole idea of reporting on a community is to place people at what I call 'surveillance points,'" says Melvin Mencher, a longtime journalism educator and author of the classic journalism textbook *News Reporting and Writing* (McGraw Hill Higher Education, 2010). "That way they're apt to find out what's happening."

Virtually all professional news organizations and many college newspapers assign reporters to cover a particular subject area, or beat. Beats may be organized by:

Subject matter (e.g. crime, politics, health)

Institution (campus police department, student government, student health center)

Academic unit (the law school, the political science department, the school of medicine)

or they may be organized by some combination of these three. The crime reporter, for example, may cover the campus police department as well as the academic department of criminology; the politics reporter may cover student government, the faculty senate and the political science department. (For examples of beat structures see College Newspaper Beats. Also see the beat report in Appendix 3.A at the end of this chapter.)

No single beat system will work for all campuses. Yours should be based on the size of your staff, the type of campus you cover and the issues that are most relevant to your community. A small paper might have one student covering science, health and technology, while a large paper on a big, research-oriented campus may have a team of six reporters assigned to life sciences, medicine, agriculture, nursing, technology and astronomy. A major campus issue, such as a fiscal crisis or the search for a new university president, may warrant its own beat. Some student papers that cover racially diverse campuses assign reporters to a diversity or race-relations beat.

If drinking is a major part of life on your campus you could even assign a reporter to the alcohol beat. Stories that could come out of such a beat: news reports on changes in enforcement of drinking laws or drinking-related injuries; profiles of local bartenders; features on the oldest bar or most popular bar in town or on special events like trivia or karaoke nights. One year *Golden Gate [X]press* (goldengatexpress.org), the student paper at San Francisco State University, created a sex, drugs and rock "n" roll beat that gave rise to a front-page story on students hooking up in the academic building bathrooms. To be sure, it was one of the best-read stories of the year.

Other papers have created special beats for senior reporters. *The State News*, the daily student paper at Michigan State University, has a "news enterprise" beat. "This has allowed one of our most experienced reporters to pursue more in-depth news and news-feature stories without the pressure of daily deadlines," says former Editorial Adviser Perry Parks. During the war in Iraq the reporter wrote about a former Iraqi nuclear scientist who attended Michigan State and a local company that produces the anthrax vaccine. He also produced an in-depth feature about a center on campus that researches and investigates identity theft.

Reporters aren't the only ones who can benefit from having a beat. Some newspapers assign photographers to beats, as well. At San Francisco State University's *Golden Gate [X]press*, photographers have been assigned to cover particular buildings or physical areas on campus. A photographer responsible for the Creative Arts Building, for example, may poke around rehearsal rooms and theaters, finding feature photos as well as potential stories.

One year a photographer covering the campus athletic fields discovered the university had spent a staggering $19 million on a new baseball field – this at a school that

College newspaper beats

How beats are divvied up depends on the size of your staff and the type of campus you cover.

Beats for a small newspaper staff

Here's a beat structure that might work for a staff of 10 or fewer reporters:

Crime and safety–campus and city police, crime, safety-oriented organizations

City/community–city politics, neighborhood issues around your campus

Academics (1 or 2 reporters)–all academic departments

Administration–school policies and administration officials

Campus politics–student government, faculty senate, political organizations on campus

Sports (1 or 2 reporters)–intramural and collegiate sports, recreation

Arts and entertainment–music, dance, theater, film, art, etc.

Lifestyle–including clubs, activities, recreation and housing

Science and health–personal health, scientific research.

Beats for a medium or large newspaper staff

Here's a sample beat structure that might work for a medium to large staff. Note that beats can be divided for a larger staff or combined for a smaller staff.

News beats

Administration–administration, budget, top campus administrators, admissions

Crime and safety–campus and city police departments (may include an academic criminal justice or criminology department if you have one)

City/community–city politics and community issues (you may assign several reporters to this beat if your newspaper covers the city as well as the campus)

Faculty/staff–academic senate, staff and faculty unions

Student government–student government elections, meetings, politics

Higher education–community college or state university system (at public schools), higher education trends

Race and ethnicity–demographics, racial and ethnic groups on campus such as Muslim Students' Association or Black Student Union

Religion–campus religious groups such as Newman Center, Hillel, Christian Campus Fellowship, Muslim Student Association, etc. (as well as religious studies departments or seminaries if you have them)

Politics–city politics, elections, political science department

Social sciences–including psychology, sociology, anthropology and other academic departments

International–this beat may include international students and study-abroad programs as well as academic departments in international relations, foreign languages and related fields.

Lifestyle beats

Housing–on-campus dorms and apartments, off-campus housing and related issues

Careers and jobs–campus career center, employment trends

Money–financial aid, grants and loans, credit issues, student jobs

Parking and transportation–campus parking facilities, campus shuttles and public transportation

Campus clubs/activities–depending on your campus and the size of your staff, you may have several reporters assigned to related beats, such as Greek life, service groups, ethnic groups, etc.

Fashion–fashion trends (as well as fashion, interior design departments if you have them)

Drugs and alcohol–drinking, the bar scene, trends, drug and alcohol law enforcement

Personal technology/social networking–how students are using social networking, new technology products.

Sports and fitness

- **Intercollegiate sports**–depending on the size of your staff and the importance of sports on your campus you may have a reporter assigned to each sport or reporters covering several sports at once
- **Extreme sports**–surfing, skateboarding, snowboarding, mountain climbing, etc.
- **Recreation**–recreational and intramural sports, gym and athletic facilities.

Arts and entertainment beats

Media–coverage of film, television and video games; campus broadcast stations (as well as journalism, film, multimedia studies and communication departments if you have them)

Theater and dance–coverage of performances (as well as theater and dance departments if you have them)

Visual arts–coverage of visual art (as well as art, graphic design departments if you have them)

Music–coverage of music (as well as the music department if you have one.)

Business and technology

Business–business school, employment issues

Technology–technology issues as well as coverage of information technology and computer science departments

Engineering–could be combined with technology or stand on its own if you have a large engineering school.

Health and science beats

Health–student health services, health issues (this beat may include academic departments in nursing, dentistry, and allied health fields if you have them)

School of medicine (if you have one)

Sex–sex and sexuality research (including academic department in human sexuality studies if you have one), sexually transmitted diseases

Environment–environmental issues as well as related academic departments such as geosciences, meteorology, environmental studies, etc.

Sciences–physics, astronomy, chemistry, biology, mathematics, etc.

was cutting classes in response to a budget crisis. The photographer brought the story to a reporter and the two produced an impressive investigative piece, complete with a photo essay on the construction of the field.

ON THE BEAT

Once you've been assigned a beat, your first job is to start developing sources – people who can clue you in to the issues and people you'll be covering. You want to meet the major players – the department chairs, administrators, coaches, club leaders – and other official sources. But you also want to get to know the other players, such as student employees and teaching assistants, janitors and secretaries, any of whom may tip you off to good stories.

Try to build relationships with your sources by developing rapport and letting them know you want to hear what they have to say. "Beat coverage involves a lot of talking that isn't formal interviewing," says Parks, author of the book *Making Important News Interesting: Reporting Public Affairs in the 21st Century* (Marion Street Press, 2006). "Part of your work is not just reporting specific stories but looking for your next story, or your next scoop."

With each potential source you meet, ask lots of questions. What are you working on now? What new programs or projects are you developing? What problems do you face? What would you like to change in your department or at your school? Most important, ask for ideas about what your paper *should* be covering. Keep in mind, journalism is a two-way street. You want story ideas; many of your sources want the publicity only you can offer.

After you've met a source, take note of the person's name and vital information, including title, phone numbers (when possible, get home and cell phone numbers as well as office numbers), email addresses and campus addresses. You may also jot down story ideas and other information the person provided. Develop a system for keeping track of your sources. Some reporters plug such information into a computer database; others use a cell phone or PDA. Some prefer an old-fashioned Rolodex or a card file. Whatever the system, make sure you're consistent about updating it and refer back to it regularly.

In addition to developing sources, beat reporters are expected to keep on top of significant events on their beats. A reporter assigned to cover the faculty senate or student government, for example, should cover all of that body's meetings. Even if a meeting seems to have a dull agenda, interesting stories may come out it. Sometimes a seemingly boring or bureaucratic issue will spark a heated debate. And interesting topics may come up during discussions or in before- and after-meeting informal chats.

Police or crime reporters should stop in at the campus police or public safety office on a regular basis – daily, if possible – to check the police log and see what people are up to. Even if your campus is relatively crime-free, these logs can be a gold mine of information, not just for crime stories but for trend pieces or features. Was there a drug bust in a dorm? Were police called three times last weekend to break up a rowdy party?

Student editors should think about ways to pass vital source information from one reporter to another. High staff turnover is a constant problem at college papers – even more so than in the professional world – and your paper shouldn't have to lose good sources each time a reporter graduates or leaves the staff. Some student papers have reporters post source lists on their content management system or stow them in files in the newsroom. Others require each reporter to write a beat report when they leave the publication.

At Keene State College in Keene, N.H., for example, editors at the weekly *Equinox* (keeneequinox.com) have reporters create "beat books." These three-ring binders contain background information about each beat, including contact information for sources and a list of stories that have been written. The books are handed off to the new staff at the end of each year.

Another way to get information on your beat is to network with professional reporters covering your beat or similar beats. Although it may be a little uncomfortable reaching out to your direct competitor, professionals at non-competing papers may be happy to share information about how to cover your beat. Join specialty groups of reporters. The website list at the end of this chapter includes contact information for organizations of journalists who cover education, medicine, environment, crime and other beats. These groups often have reduced-price memberships for students, and some sponsor conferences, workshops, Listservs and other events or services that could help you. Getting involved in such organizations can also provide good contacts for lining up internships and jobs down the line.

CHECKLIST
Covering a beat

As you begin to cover a new beat ask yourself these questions:

1 What does this beat encompass?
2 What do I know about this beat?
3 What do I want to learn about it?
4 Who are the official sources on this beat and how can I find them?
5 What sort of unofficial sources may be helpful?
6 What has the paper written about this beat in the past?
7 Who on the newspaper staff knows something about this beat?
8 What professional journalists or journalism organizations can I tap for guidance about covering this beat?
9 What books and websites might be useful?
10 Who would make for interesting profiles?
11 What trends are happening on this beat?
12 What meetings or events can I attend?
13 What are four stories I can write in the next month or two?
14 What are some of the larger issues I'd like to explore?
15 What long-term project can I produce on this beat?

DEALING WITH YOUR PUBLIC INFORMATION OFFICE

The most obvious source of information on your campus is the school's public information office. Depending on who's in charge and the relationship you have with the staff there, this office can be a news treasure chest – or your greatest obstacle to getting information. Good public information officers are always on the lookout for stories, and many are willing to share them even before a news release is written or a report is issued. They can tell you about upcoming events, important visitors, demographic trends and researchers who are about to publish significant studies.

If your university's PIOs are amenable, arrange a meeting between them and key newspaper staffers – or even the whole staff – early in the year. Ask about what stories are coming down the pike and what challenges the university may be facing. Do they anticipate budget cutbacks, accreditation reviews, administrative changes, fee increases or other notable developments in the coming months? Which professors are doing groundbreaking research? What new programs are being developed? What trends are they seeing in admissions or hiring? Ask how they want to be contacted – by phone, email, cell phone or pager – on breaking stories and who in the office should be contacted for different types of stories.

While you want to have a friendly relationship with university PIOs, never forget that they're unlikely to be your best source for bad news on campus. They won't write a press release when a popular professor doesn't get tenure or when there's a rat infestation in the student apartments or when the dining hall is cited for health violations. For those stories, you need to have a strong network of other sources.

COVERING THE ADMINISTRATION

Do you know where your college president is? As the newspaper of record for your school you should. Your campus news organization should cover top campus officials the way White House reporters cover the president of the United States. What boards or committees is your president on? Where is your president traveling? Does your president regularly attend sports events at your school?

The Red and Black (redandblack.com) at the University of Georgia has run a daily "Where's Mikey" feature on its front page and website, reporting on the comings and goings of President Michael F. Adams. Readers can learn, for example, when the university president is on vacation, when he's attending an administration retreat and when he has a 1 p.m. tee-time scheduled. The information comes from the president's calendar, a public record *The Red and Black* obtained with a Freedom of Information Act request, says Daniel Burnett, who was editor-in-chief when the paper launched the feature. "People are interested in just hearing where he is and what he's up to," says Burnett. He noted that once the paper got access to the calendar, it only took a few minutes each day to browse through it, choose an event and write it up.

If possible, you should set up regular meetings between your school's top administrators – president, chancellor, provost, dean of students, president or chair of the faculty senate, etc. – and the top brass at your news organization. You might invite others staffers to sit in from time to time. This keeps the lines of communication open and ensures you get a heads-up on new policies and other possible story ideas.

When covering the administration, remember to show the human side of the people governing your campus. *The State Press* (statepress.com) wrote an in-depth profile of Arizona State University President Michael Crow, following him through an entire day from the time he arrived on campus at 6:48 a.m. till he signed off his email just past midnight the following morning (Figure 3.2). The story included details about what Crow read on his computer, whom he met with and how he interacted with students.

STATEPRESS.COM | MONDAY, FEBRUARY 1, 2010 | VOL. 96 ISSUE 82

The State Press

A day in Crow's Nest

TESSA MUGGERIDGE
| THE STATE PRESS |

The Tempe campus is still surrounded by the eerie quiet of night as President Michael Crow walks toward the already-lit Fulton Center, an inky black sky behind him.

Crow moves steadily, his pace neither rushed nor lagging, appearing to mentally prepare himself for the day with each step.

He unlocks the building's main door with his Sun Card in one swift motion. The time is 6:48 a.m. on Wednesday, Jan. 27.

Setting the tone

Crow moves into his office, pausing to remove his suit jacket before settling into his desk.

The office is kempt, with neat stacks of papers and pens lining his desk among piles of class readers and textbooks. An analog clock labeled with time zones of major world cities ticks forward, a framed picture of the globe on the wall behind it.

Joyce Smitheran, Crow's personal assistant, steps in from her connected office to announce the arrival of Crow's 7 a.m. meeting, and he quickly moves to slide open the door to the adjoining conference room.

Within seconds he is greeting Johnnie Ray, president of the ASU Foundation and Ann Toca, the foundation's vice president of communications and marketing, at the door.

The trio spreads sheets of paper across the

See CROW page 9

SEE PHOTOS OF A DAY IN THE LIFE OF MICHAEL CROW ON PAGE 8

ILLUSTRATION BY TAESEOK YOON | THE STATE PRESS

A lifetime of learning

Low-cost ASU courses allow Arizonans over 50 to continue education

DANA SHEAFF
| THE STATE PRESS |

Starting next week, Valley residents 50 and older will have the chance to take classes and seminars from a number of prominent ASU professors and well-known scholars from across the country.

The courses, being offered at various locations statewide, are run by the ASU Osher Institute's Lifelong Learning program.

The classes, many of which start on Feb. 8, are held in six locations throughout the state, including at ASU's Polytechnic and West campuses, as well as the Tempe Public Library.

The Bernard Osher Foundation, a San Francisco-based group that grants endowments to educational programs, funds the classes.

"This is a program that attracts older adults, and some of them are snowbirds and are just here during the nice months in Arizona," said Patricia Feldman, director of the ASU Osher Institute.

The program serves an important function in its participants' lives, Feldman said.

"The program is geared for that 50-plus age group. Typically they are maybe not working full time," she said. "Most of them are retired, they like taking daytime classes — a lot of times for the social aspect of it — but also to keep their minds sharp and keep learning."

See LIFELONG page 3

88-70

Men's Basketball

Abbott, Sun Devils rebound against Stanford

Women's Basketball

Last-second shot gives ASU 63-61 victory over Cal

See Sports, page 11

WEATHER 65° | 49° | ONLINE To see a slideshow of *The State Press'* day with President Michael Crow, visit statepress.com. | An independent daily serving Arizona State University since 1890

FIGURE 3.2 When covering the administration, remember to show the human side of the people governing your campus. *The State Press* wrote an in-depth profile of Arizona State University President Michael Crow, following him through an entire day from the time he arrived on campus at 6:48 a.m. till he signed off his email just past midnight the following morning. *The State Press*, Arizona State University.

FINDING STORY IDEAS

As noted earlier in this chapter, college campuses are breeding grounds for news. There's always something going on that's worth writing about. Your job is to find those stories. The best news tips will come from your sources, be they professors, students, coaches or public information officers. But other good stories will come from your own observations. Was your financial aid check late? Does your psychology professor make sexually inappropriate remarks in class? Are campus police cracking down on late-night parties? Are the weight machines in your university fitness center continually marked "out of order"?

Let your own basic curiosity drive you. If something gives you pause or makes you say, "Hmmm, that's strange," keep snooping around. Ask some questions. You never know what you may find.

For more ideas on finding story ideas see Tipsheet: How to find story ideas.

TIPSHEET
How to find story ideas

1 **Look around.** Study bulletin boards – including electronic bulletin boards – and other places where public notices are posted. Is there a new club on campus? An unusual class? A protest rally coming up? Jot down the contact info and check it out.

2 **Explore your archives.** Read back issues of your own newspaper, keeping a particular eye out for stories worth a follow-up. What's happened since an affirmative action admissions program was discontinued? How has a rape prevention policy instituted five years ago affected sexual crimes on campus? Talk to your predecessors, people who previously covered your beat, and ask about stories that warrant a second look or ones the reporter never got a chance to write.

3 **Ask questions.** Set up an informal focus group of your friends or roommates. What would they like to read in the paper? What are they concerned about, excited about, frustrated about? What do they want to know?

4 **Eavesdrop.** Listen in on conversations in the cafeteria, the bookstore, the student union and other places students gather. What are people talking about on campus?

5 **Pay attention.** Take note of announcements made in class. Your professors – or other students – may be passing on news tips.

6 **Develop sources.** See everyone you talk to – roommates, friends, professors, service workers – as

a potential news source. Listen for trends, campus political developments, policy changes.

7 **Read everything.** Newspapers, magazines, newsletters, fliers, journals are all good sources of stories. Among the publications to pay particular attention to: *The Chronicle of Higher Education* and *The New York Times'* quarterly "Education Life" section. They can be great for tips on trend stories that you could localize to your campus. Local newspapers are also news story bonanzas, as are other campus newspapers. As long as you don't plagiarize and you do your own reporting, there's nothing wrong with stealing story ideas. (See Newslink's links to online campus newspapers at http://newslink.org/statcamp.html)

8 **Bring research home.** Look for studies about college students that you can localize to your campus. A Google search on "study," "college students" and the current year will reveal a host of recent studies on such things as drinking habits and video game use that you could use as a launch pad for a trend story.

9 **Mine your PIO.** Read campus publications, such as employee and faculty union newsletters and alumni magazines, as well as press releases issued by your university's public information office. Some PIOs also keep track of university staff and faculty in the news. A quote by a professor in a local or national newspaper or magazine may give you an idea for a deeper story on that person or her research.

10 **Open your eyes.** Look for changes – buildings being torn down, long lines, new businesses in neighborhoods near your campus. Anything fresh or different could be the beginning of a story.

11 **Peruse ads.** Read display and classified ads in your paper and in community publications. Are apartment rental prices on the rise? Are those too-good-to-be-true airfares for real? Check out unusual job opportunities – for exotic dancers, models, escort services.

12 **Do a records search.** Periodically check public records on your campus and its key players. Stop by the county courthouse and see if your school or the university president has been sued.

THE TICKLER FILE

Most professional news organizations and some college papers use a tickler file to remind the staff of upcoming events, anniversaries of major campus or community incidents and other important dates. If your newsroom doesn't have one, set one up. Tickler files can be electronic or physical; an easy-to-access file drawer works well.

To start, create 43 folders, one for each day of the month and one for each month of the year. Drop in press releases, event announcements, meeting agendas and other documents relating to upcoming events. If you don't have a document, write up a note with the significant details. If, for example, you're waiting for a coroner's report on a suspicious death or an announcement about curriculum changes, write something up and pop it in the tickler file when you expect some new development. Someone, usually an assigning editor or general assignment reporter, should be charged with checking the tickler file every single day to make sure important developments and events aren't forgotten.

LOCALIZING NATIONAL AND INTERNATIONAL STORIES

An earthquake strikes Chile, killing hundreds of people. The federal government passes new health care legislation that will extend coverage to millions. Israeli and Palestinian leaders gather at an Egyptian resort in an attempt to forge a peace plan. A gunman takes 15 hostages at a college campus halfway across the country.

Every minute, important news stories break around the nation and around the world. Is it the job of your student news organization to cover them?

It depends. Certainly, your primary responsibility is to cover your campus and immediate community. But there are times when you should localize national and international news, putting it into context for your readers. There's no clear answer on when your news organization should step in, but here are some guidelines and some examples of how student news outlets have covered national and international news.

What kinds of national and international stories should you localize?

- **Stories that have an impact on your readers.** How will the new health care legislation affect your readers? How do students feel about a proposed increase in the federal minimum wage? What do your readers need to know about a national recall of eggs?
- **Stories that break on another college campus.** When a student at California State University, Chico died in a hazing incident, student newspapers around the country took a hard look at fraternity pranks on their own campuses. Suicides, campus shootings, and drinking deaths are other news events that may be worth localizing because such stories are likely to resonate with your readers.
- **Stories that people are talking about.** When Michael Jackson died or Osama bin Laden was killed by U.S. forces in Pakistan, college campuses were abuzz with the news. If a lot of people are talking about an issue, you probably should cover it.
- **Stories with a local angle.** If a current or former student or faculty member makes news, that's grounds

'I, BARACK HUSSEIN OBAMA, DO SOLEMNLY SWEAR...'

THE 44TH PRESIDENT ★ SPECIAL INAUGURATION ISSUE

The Daily Northw

WWW.DAILYNORTHWESTERN.COM SERVING THE UNIVERSITY AND EVANSTON SINCE 1881 WEDNESDAY, JANUARY 21, 2009

"What is required of us now is a new era of responsibility – a recognition, on the part of every American, that we have duties to ourselves, our nation, and the world, duties that we do not grudgingly accept but rather seize gladly, firm in the knowledge that there is nothing so satisfying to the spirit, so defining of our character, than giving our all to a difficult task. This is the price and the promise of citizenship."

PRESIDENT OBAMA

When the 44th president of the United States was sworn in Tuesday, it was the culmination of a two-year campaign. In Hyde Park, it represented the elevation of a local as the first African-American president. In Washington, D.C., millions packed onto the Mall to watch President Barack Obama take the oath of office. And in Evanston as well as at Northwestern, both of which supported Obama by large margins, residents and students gathered to watch the ceremony and reflect on its meaning.

CHICAGO 5 In bars and barbershops, Obama's South Side home cheered the president.

WASHINGTON, D.C. 6 NU students joined with millions to watch Obama be sworn in as president.

NORTHWESTERN 7 In venues across campus, crowds gathered around TVs to watch the ceremony.

EVANSTON 8 Evanston mayor Lorraine Morton hosted a gathering, as did the library.

FORUM | THE VIEW FROM D.C., PAGE 4 ONLINE | MORE PHOTOS AND AUDIO, DAILYNORTHWESTERN.COM

FIGURE 3.3 When Barack Obama, a former Illinois senator, was sworn in as president, it wasn't difficult for *The Daily Northwestern* to localize the story. *The Daily Northwestern*, Northwestern University.

for coverage, even if the story breaks thousands of miles away. When a big story breaks check to see if members of your campus community are planning service or political activities in response.

- **Stories that affect a particular political, ethnic group or special-interest group on your campus.** If you've got a sizable LGBT community, there's likely to be heightened interest in gay rights issues. Does your campus have a large number of immigrants from Mexico, China or another country? Keep a special eye out for news from home that might interest them.
- **Stories similar to major events that have happened on your campus.** When there's a campus shooting anywhere in the United States, the *Collegiate Times* (collegiatetimes.com) at Virginia Tech and the *Northern Star* (northernstar.info) at Northern Illinois University pay special attention because such events may spur memories of the shootings at those campuses.

What can your news organization add to the coverage? When deciding whether to localize a story think about what your news organization can contribute to the discussion. Will experts on your campus be able to provide analysis or context for what has happened? Will you offer an opportunity for community members to vent on an issue they feel passionate about? Can you report the news in a way that will make it more meaningful to your readers?

How do you find local sources for a national or international story? Social media tools are a good way to start. When a major earthquake struck Haiti in January 2010, Emily Stephenson, then community manager for *The Daily Tar Heel* (dailytarheel.com), posted a Facebook message asking if anyone from the University of North Carolina, Chapel Hill community had been affected. She didn't expect much response. "As it turned out, the School of Public Health had a student there who was trying to get home, and another student had just returned from a mission trip," she says. "The second student wound up in the lede of the story."

Suzanne Yada of *The Spartan Daily* (spartandaily.com) also struck pay dirt with social media tools after learning that John Patrick Bedell, who had been shot to death after firing at two guards in front of the Pentagon, may have attended San Jose State University. Yada, then the online editor for the paper, scoured social media sites. "Bedell was quite tech-savvy and had accounts on LinkedIn, Wikipedia and Amazon that mentioned SJSU and revealed more pieces of his character," she says.

Another strategy for finding sources is to search for campus experts. If a coup breaks out in a distant land, look for professors who have done research on that country and its politics. If a major earthquake strikes, ask your geology department for someone who can explain the science behind seismic activity. Many university public information offices list professors with expertise in particular issues who can speak to the media.

Campus ethnic, religious and service groups may also be good sources for commentary and reaction to national or global news. Leaders of Jewish, Palestinian and Muslim student organization groups will often have comments on new developments in Middle East politics, for example. Think, too, about whether any individuals or groups on your campus may help in rescue efforts or take political action in response to a news event. College service groups often plan fundraisers or service trips to help survivors of natural disasters. Campus political groups may stage political activities in response to an important court ruling, crime or other news event.

If a major newsmaker has a connection to your campus – an alum is appointed to a high-level position or a former student engages in a high-profile crime – try to find professors, students and alumni who knew the person. When Elena Kagan was nominated to the Supreme Court, *The Daily Princetonian* (dailyprincetonian.com) provided extensive coverage of the Princeton alum, providing insights about her political activities and beliefs as an undergraduate. Reporters didn't have to look too far to find evidence; Kagan had been a news writer and editorial chairman for the

"Prince" and had penned a number of unsigned editorials, "many of which took decidedly liberal stances on national and campus issues," *The Daily Princetonian* wrote.

COVERING HIGHER EDUCATION

Whether it's a single beat or a collection of beats – administration, faculty affairs, the academic senate and financial aid – covered by different reporters, higher education is a critical area of coverage at any college newspaper. Part of your mission is to not only to cover how your institution works, but to put it into the context of other schools in your region, state or nation.

Higher education reporters at professional newspapers generally cover a range of issues from admissions to financial aid to housing to budget cuts. You should, too. And you ought to handily beat community and regional newspapers on any story that happens on your campus. You're there. You've got the sources. And you've got the resources. While a professional newspaper may have one or two reporters covering your school and others in the region, you have a whole staff.

So when your school's president resigns or massive budget cuts threaten the quality of education at your school, your newspaper should own the story.

Tracy Jan, a higher education reporter for *The Boston Globe*, advises students to take an aggressive approach to covering their schools. "Don't be afraid to take on your administration," says Jan, who covers Harvard University and other schools in the Boston area. "You shouldn't be beholden to the administration. Be sure to be fair and balanced but don't be intimidated to question authority."

Jan, who was a reporter, features editor and opinion editor for the *The Stanford Daily* (daily.stanford.edu) when she was in college, says students actually have a leg up on professional higher education reporters when it come to covering their campuses. "Just being a student and living on campus makes it easy to find features ideas and news ideas. My best stories come from hanging out and talking to people."

She recommends cultivating sources among students, staff and faculty. "There are always those key professors on campus who know everything and have opinions about everything."

Laurel Rosenhall, a higher education reporter for *The Sacramento Bee*, says some of her best sources are professors in leadership positions with academic senates or the faculty unions. "They are very dialed in and opinionated and are consistently a huge help in connecting me with instructors and students on many, many stories," says Rosenhall, who worked on the *Cooper Point Journal* (cooperpointjournal.com) when she was a student at Evergreen State College in Olympia, Wash.

Most higher education reporters read two publications religiously – the weekly *Chronicle of Higher Education* and the online InsiderHigherEd.com. Read these publications and you'll know what is going on at other schools. You're bound to find story ideas you can localize to your own campus or region.

Other campus newspapers are also good sources for keeping up on issues in higher education If you don't already subscribe to other college papers in your state, arrange for a regular exchange or follow coverage on their websites.

Rosenhall often gets news, tips and story ideas by following other education reporters, including some student reporters, on Twitter. She also tracks professors, education organizations, student groups and education bloggers.

"Twitter allows you to create your own community of people who are knowledgeable about the issues you're covering," says Rosenhall. "It's a good way to keep up to date."

Jan, who reads a lot of college papers as part of her research, says student newspapers are sometimes overly provincial in their coverage, looking at stories from the narrow perspective of a single school. She encourages students to take a broader view on issues and trends. "If you cover a state university or community college that's part of a bigger system, find out what's happening at other schools in that system. It helps to get the bigger picture to see where your school fits into the state or national context."

Jan has one last bit of advice for students: "Have fun. A lot of my fellow college newspaper staffers didn't have a life outside of the college newspaper. You need to have a life to be a good college newspaper reporter. Be involved in your dorm community and in other extracurricular activities. That way you not only have fun and meet new people; you get good story ideas."

COVERING HEALTH AND SCIENCE

Writing about science and medicine for a college newspaper can be daunting. How do you make scientific advances and medical concepts interesting to college students? How do you write about things you barely understand yourself? And how do you get people with all those initials after their names to speak English?

But don't let those things intimidate you. It's important to cover the scientific community and the intellectual life on your campus. Many students who report on science come to appreciate – and even to love – the intellectual and practical challenges that come along with it. With science writing, you're always learning something new. You get to understand cool stuff, like how the human body fights off invading organisms or what black holes really are.

And experience on a science beat can pay off down the career road. Some solid clips and a line on your resume that says "science writer" or "medical writer" can lead to lucrative and satisfying careers in medical journalism, public relations, government and private agency work, as well as health and science fields. For those thinking about graduate programs in science or science writing, experience covering science will help set you apart from the pack of applicants.

So how do you cover science and medicine? Here are some tips to get you started:

Cultivate sources. As with any beat, you're only as good as your sources. You can find them in the laboratories around campus, in student associations of medical or nursing students, in environmental groups, in the student health center, in academic departments. Don't feel that you have to only use top officials and professors. Graduate

Higher education story ideas

Here are some classic story ideas that would work at virtually any school.

- **Graduation rates:** How long does it take the average undergraduate to graduate from your school? How many students graduate within four, five or six years? How do those rates vary by race, gender or major? See how the rates compare to other nearby colleges and to the national average.
- **Super seniors:** How many students at your school have more than enough credits to graduate but stick around to take more courses? Interview some and find out what's keeping them. Is your school doing anything to move them along?
- **Hot majors:** What are the most popular majors at your school? How do they compare with the most popular majors of a decade ago? How do they mesh with the current job market?
- **Research funding:** Which college or department or professor brings in the most research dollars? Where does the money come from? How is it being used?
- **A day in the life of your college president (or chancellor):** Follow the leader of your school around for a day and give readers a sense of what the job entails. Or follow your student government president around for a day.
- **Financial aid:** How many students at your school receive financial aid? How does that compare with previous years? How much debt will the average student at your school graduate with?
- **Transfer rates:** If you're at a community college, what percentage of students transfer to a four-year college and eventually earn a bachelor's degree? Four year-colleges: How many students transfer in from community colleges, and do they graduate at the same rate as other students?
- **Rising costs:** How much have tuition and fees risen at your college over the past five or 10 years? Then look at how much financial aid students receive – has aid kept up with the rising cost? Again, compare to other colleges and the nation.
- **Out-of-state and international students:** If you're at a public school, look at recruitment of students from other states and countries. Find out how many students come from other states, and see how that's changed over the years. Do they pay higher tuition? Are they more academically qualified than in-state students? Has it gotten harder for in-state students to get in? Is your school doing things to lure more out-of-state or international students?
- **Admission rates:** How have the number of applicants and admission rates changed at your school over the past five or 10 years? Has it become easier or more difficult to get in? What percentage of students who are accepted actually enroll? How does your school handle its waiting list?
- **SAT scores:** What are the average SAT score and GPA for students admitted to your school? How do they compare with past years and with other schools? Is it getting harder or easier to get in?
- **Undocumented immigrants:** How does your university handle admission of undocumented immigrants? What's it like for students who aren't in this country legally to study at your school?
- **Unusual/popular courses:** What's the most popular course at your school? What new, unusual courses are being offered this semester?
- **Tenure:** Which professors weren't approved for tenure this year? What happened to them?
- **Disability access:** How does your university accommodate students with disabilities? Is it well set up for students with physical limitations? Borrow a wheelchair or blindfold a reporter and find out what it's like to navigate your campus.

students who work in a lab and receptionists who work in the health center can also be helpful sources of information.

Ask the right questions. In talking to sources, always ask: What's new? The answer may be a scientific advance, a troubling trend, the outbreak of an illness or the launch of a new treatment or product. You should also ask what's not going well. Are scientists frustrated because their funding is running out? Is there a shortage of equipment? Are cadavers being misused?

Do your homework. Read some of the major scientific journals like *Science*, the *New England Journal of Medicine*, and the *Journal of the American Medical Association*, as well as whatever other specialty publications you can find about the field you're covering.

Milk your public affairs office. Try to get a line not just on upcoming press releases but on ongoing research on your campus. Who are the major players? Who's getting the biggest grants? What kinds of research is your campus best known for?

Use online science information services. Regularly check Newswise and EurekAlert!, which distribute press releases from research institutions around the world.

Explore the science behind the news. Many news stories have a scientific angle – the injury that sidelined your team's starting quarterback, the earthquake that struck a nearby community, weird weather patterns. Find scientists and physicians who can put these stories into context for your readers.

Learn the lingo. Writing about science means translating foreign or complex concepts into simple language. Learn what the scientific terms mean and then figure out how to explain them to a lay audience. If you can find the right metaphor, you can explain nearly anything. But don't just make these up. Science writing is really a partnership between the experts and the journalists – make sure whatever you write is technically accurate.

Translate the information. A big part of science writing is translating unfamiliar terms and concepts for the lay reader. Ask scientists how they would explain their research to a seventh-grader. Quote that explanation rather than the more esoteric language they use with their colleagues.

Find the human application. Bring the research home to your readers. How will this advance in medicine affect patients or future generations of people with this condition? What are the long-term environmental implications for this finding?

Read good science writers. To find story ideas and to see how science writing is done, you should regularly read *The New York Times*, particularly "Science Times," the weekly science section that comes out on Tuesday, as well as science coverage in other newspapers and magazines. Take note of how the writers explain technical concepts to lay readers.

COVERING A DIVERSE COMMUNITY

Colleges are among the most diverse gathering places in our society. If your campus is like most, you have people from all over your state or province – and possibly from different parts of the country and the world – coming together to live and learn. In this community you most likely have people of different races and religions, different classes and different political persuasions, many of whom are venturing out of their home cultures for the first time.

Diversity is part of what makes college so interesting. But it can also make covering a college campus challenging.

The best way to start familiarizing yourself with diversity issues is to get to know your campus. Your college public information office should be able to give you a detailed demographic profile of your student body and the faculty and staff who serve them.

Some questions to ask yourself: Does the racial and ethnic makeup of the faculty reflect that of the students? Is one group substantially less diverse? If there is a gap, what is your school doing to bridge it? These are questions that may lead to stories.

Aly Colon, diversity program director for The Poynter Institute, suggests editors asks themselves these five W's of journalism from a diverse perspective:

Who–Who's missing from the story?

What–What's the context for the story?

Where–Where can we go for more information?

When–When do we use racial or ethnic identification?

Why–Why are we including or excluding certain information?

In addition to asking these questions, it can be useful to periodically evaluate your coverage. Betty Clapp, adviser to *The Cleveland Stater* (clevelandstater.com) at Cleveland State University, says, "Avoiding stereotyping really is based on awareness of stereotypes, so perhaps a useful exercise is to look at a story for its treatment and description of any specific groups. Does it perpetuate stereotyping? Is the description pertinent to the story? Why? Answering those questions and related ones that may develop tend to help people become more aware of stereotypes in general, and particularly in their own writing."

Covering a campus requires organization, enterprise and persistence. At times it may seem like a daunting task, particularly if your staff is small. But even just a handful of energetic, dedicated reporters, editors and photographers can be enough to take your newspaper to the next level and create an interesting, informative, even thought-provoking publication that truly covers your campus community.

TO DO

1. If your newspaper doesn't have a beat system, consider assigning reporters to particular coverage areas. If you already assign reporters to beats, think about alternate ways of covering your campus, such as combining academic departments with subject areas (creating a money beat, for example, that includes personal finance, financial aid and the business school) or devising brand new beats, such as sex and relationships, drinking or other topical issues that newspapers sometimes neglect.
2. At the beginning of your next editorial staff meeting, send the entire staff – reporters, photographers, editors and designers – out to hunt for stories. Have everyone come back in half an hour with three story ideas. Discuss the ideas as a group and decide which ones are worth pursuing.

Getting in touch with your readers **Robert F. Stevenson**

All week your staff works hard to create a paper for the vast campus just outside your newspaper office. You check your facts, you proofread your stories, you look for just the right photograph – and then you hope people will pick it up and read it.

But are you doing a good job? Do your stories interest your readers? Do your photographs capture their attention? Are your stories balanced and fair? Are you getting not just the facts, but the essence of your stories right?

It's often hard to tell. Some student newspapers don't get many letters to the editor and even when they do get a letter it can be difficult to know if the criticism is valid or just one wacky reader's opinion. Awards from state and national organizations are a great boost, but they don't tell you if you're truly serving your campus community.

Here are some ways to assess your newspaper and to reach out to readers:

Get to know your readers. Invite the campus to an open house to meet your staff and to see how the newspaper works. Sponsor a forum on a major issue in your community. Be sure to participate in school-sponsored student organization fairs. Maintain a portable information booth (a table with handouts, preferably manned by an editor and other staffers), and set it up around campus at various times.

Do some research. Surveying your readership is a great way to find out how you're doing and what your readers want more (and less) of. Telephone surveys are quick and inexpensive, but caller IDs and answering machines have taken a serious bite out of their effectiveness. Web surveys are useful for online readers. Questionnaires included in your newspaper are inexpensive and easy; keep in mind, though, that response rates are usually low. Suggestion boxes strategically placed outside your office or in the student union give readers a way to talk back to the paper. (See Appendix 3.B for an example of a newspaper readership survey.)

Hire an ombudsman. Have one staffer serve as a liaison between the staff and the campus – a sort of middleman. This ombudsman should spot check accuracy and reader satisfaction with the paper. After the paper is distributed, the ombudsman can call sources mentioned in the current issue to confirm the articles' accuracy. In addition, this liaison can call students at random to determine their level of satisfaction with that issue of the newspaper. The ombudsman should report results to the editor, who can use them to plan future coverage.

Advertise your newspaper. Keep telling your readers why they should read your paper. Put the ad in your school's weekly bulletin or similar publication. Always have notices in the paper inviting reader's comments and questions. *The Forum* (landerforum.com) student newspaper staff at Lander University regularly posts teasers around campus – something like: "Check out who's coming to campus next week – page three next *Forum*." This has proven to be an effective method to get non-readers to check the paper out.

Engage in gorilla warfare. Some newspaper staffs get downright inspired in their battle to overcome poster blindness – the condition many students develop to ignore the flood of fliers on campus. Some student newspaper staffs rent costumes, such as a gorilla or the school mascot, to hand deliver the paper. At least one college wrote the newspaper's name on hundreds of ping pong balls and dropped them in strategic places, such as a busy cafeteria. Other newspapers take the town-crier approach: a student wearing a placard advertising the newspaper rings a bell, hands out the newspaper and shouts current headlines followed by, "Read All About It!"

The goals are simple: get to know your readers and find out how satisfied they are with your newspaper. The best method to realize your goals is probably as varied as student newspaper mission statements across the country. A combination of approaches like those just described is a good place to start. Be persistent and proactive. If your strategies work well, keep them up; if not, it's probably time to stir up the mix. The results for all this hard work, simply put, will be a better newspaper for you and your campus.

ROBERT F. STEVENSON is chair of the department of mass communication and theatre and an associate professor of journalism at Lander University. He received his Ph.D. in Higher Education Administration from the University of South Carolina. Dr. Stevenson is a columnist for two South Carolina newspapers, the *Greenville News* and the *Greenwood Index Journal*.

TIPSHEET
Covering meetings

Many beats – including student government, faculty senate and city government – involve covering meetings. David Cuillier, a veteran journalist who teaches at the University of Arizona School of Journalism, offers these tips on what to cover.

Before (preparation)

1. **Know the meeting schedule:** Find out when regular meetings are held for the organization you are covering. Mark them down on the calendar.
2. **Get the agenda:** Get a copy of the agenda, including supplementary documents that are referenced in the agenda. Read through it and identify the topics that are most likely to be of interest to readers.
3. **Write meeting advance:** Let readers have a chance of going too. Write a brief a few days before the meeting explaining the main subjects on the agenda that readers would care about and the time, date, place of the meeting.
4. **Write issue story:** For the advance, focus on the most newsworthy issue. Talk to the players on all sides and get a photo. Make it a good issue piece and then mention in a box the fact the matter will be discussed at the upcoming meeting. It gets people interested in a topic and then provides them a way to act.

During (coverage)

1. **Mingle:** Use the time before the meeting, during breaks and afterwards to talk with sources and anyone else there. Introduce yourself and initiate a conversation. Sometimes they will tell you why they are there and will fill you in on what's really behind the story.
2. **Take good notes:** Get lots of quotes. Be thinking through the meeting what you are going to focus your story on.
3. **Look for different stories:** Listen to what is being said and make note of potential stories. Half a dozen things will be mentioned but not embellished. Check up on those later and follow up with stories.
4. **Zero in on your turn-around story:** Your editor is going to want you to write at least one story out of the meeting. Figure out what that will be and make sure you have all the information you need. Most likely it will be what you advanced. You want to tell readers what happened regarding the issue you raised in your advance story. Then, you will have a lot of information already. Rarely are all the facts needed to write a complete story presented in a meeting.
5. **Snag people:** After the meeting snag people and ask them questions to complete the information needed to write a solid story. If someone speaks at a public hearing and you didn't get their name, track them down in the crowd.

After (writing)

1. **Write fast:** If your deadline is the day or night of the meeting, write fast. As you are in the meeting and heading back to the office, already have a lede in mind.
2. **Don't be a stenographer:** Write the story focused on a single news angle just like any other news story, mentioning that the matter was discussed at the meeting. Do not simply list a chronology of what happened at the meeting. The news isn't the fact a meeting happened.
3. **Follow up:** Make sure to follow up on the other stories that came out of the meeting.

3. If your photographers don't have beats, try giving them buildings to cover. Suggest that photographers cruise their assigned buildings every few days in search of news and feature story ideas and stand-alone photos.
4. Have reporters write a beat report (see Appendix 3.A at the end of this chapter) that they can use to guide their reporting. Before they leave a beat, ask reporters to update and file the beat report so it can be passed down to the next reporter who will cover that topic.

TO READ

Blum, Deborah and Mary Knudson, eds. *Field Guide for Science Writers*. New York, N.Y.: Oxford University Press, 1997.

Hancock, Elise. *Ideas into Words: Mastering the Craft of Science Writing*. Baltimore: Johns Hopkins University Press, 2003.

Schulte, Henry H. and Marcel P. Dufresne. *Getting the Story: An Advanced Reporting Guide to Beats, Records*

TIPS FROM A PRO Mike Donoghue

The police beat at most professional newspapers is normally considered the most stressful assignment. It probably is no different at a college or university. You are dealing with people – police, college officials, classmates, victims, etc. – who are under stress.

You, too, are under stress to produce a story, often with a short deadline.

School officials love to talk about a major grant won by the college or a winning season for a university team. Student leaders will tell you how hard they are working for students. When it comes to bad news, however, everybody runs for cover. It is often your job to overcome the stone wall that is erected.

People have a right to know about crime and how safe a campus is for students, faculty, staff and visitors. Informed people make informed decisions about their personal safety habits. Knowledge is the basis for making those informed decisions. The presence of the media at a crime scene or major incident plays an important and necessary role in meeting its responsibility to educate the public.

It is also the responsibility of the media to tell the public about the performance of authorities and how they reacted to a situation.

The following are a few basic tips for dealing with law enforcement and campus officials:

1. **Explain deadlines to campus law enforcement personnel.** They need to know why you need the information now, in two hours or two days. Deadlines are different for daily and weekly campus newspapers and for the college radio or television station.

2. **All comments made to you as a reporter should be considered "on the record."** If somebody tries to use "off the record," "between you and me," or "for deep background," make sure you are in agreement as to what these phrases mean. People have different definitions.

   For example, if a security guard tells you, "Off the record, there was a major theft of computers from the lab," it might mean: "Don't use this until I tell you officially." It might also mean, "Chase this story – it's true, but I'm not authorized to tell you." Alternatively, the tipster might let you use it but not want you to make any reference to an anonymous campus police officer as being the source. Some police/security departments are so small that leaks can easily be traced.

3. **If you are at a public institution, know your state's (or province's) Freedom of Information laws backwards and forwards.** Some groups, like the Society of Professional Journalists and state press associations, have wallet-sized copies of the law. If you are at a private institution, appeal to their instincts to do the right thing by voluntarily disclosing campus crime information.

4. **Always be polite in seeking information.** Use a written request under a state open records law only as a last resort. If you are too formal, the custodian of the record might make you jump through every hoop required by the law.

5. **Make copies of any documents that might be available, especially in sensitive cases.** You might not think something is important when you read it, but when you write your story it might become a key point.

6. **Check the numbers.** Some colleges and universities provide the full police log. Many private institutions, however, provide only a breakdown of what they think is important. Some major incidents are deleted because college administrators believe they put the school in a negative light. If you get a police log, try to check the case numbers assigned to each complaint. Complaints or cases are normally assigned numbers in numerical order. If one is missing from the log or list you are given, don't be afraid to ask about it. Don't easily accept an excuse that the record is not available or is locked up. Records can usually be "found" when necessary.

7. **Get out of the newspaper office or radio/TV station and go down to the campus police station.** Don't expect campus police to make news judgments for you. Some campus police telephone lines are audio-recorded. Somebody who might want to give you a tip is less likely to if the line is recorded. You will often learn the most simply by hanging around the police office. (And don't be afraid to bring an extra soda or coffee to share when you stop by!)

8. **Ask the right questions.** If you contact the campus police office every day and ask, "Is anything happening?" it is too easy for them to simply say,

"No." Instead, ask an open-ended question like: "What's the most important thing (or three most important) things the department has done in the last 24 hours?"

9 **Quote people by name**. Don't attribute everything to "Police said." Names make news. You like to see your byline, don't you? Well, some cops like to see their names in print, also.

10 **In a tragedy, never ask a victim's family, "How do you feel?"** Learn something positive about the victim before you approach family or friends. The family will respect you more if you are able to say up front that you knew the victim was "a history major and a real leader for the field hockey team."

11 **Look to other sources, including public records**. One private college president once said that two on-campus rapes were confidential and could not be discussed. Yet, down the street at the courthouse the case was spelled out in public court records, including the names of the victims and witnesses.

12 **Try to develop a relationship with the local police before you have to do it in the heat of battle.** That way you are likely to get information the college is not inclined to release. The local police department will usually either be handling the case, assisting the college police, or at least have the information, composite photograph or other material that will be helpful to you. Neighboring departments might also have the information. Don't be afraid to play to their sense of justice. "The paper wants to make sure the person responsible is caught. We'll run the composite or any information." Unfortunately, some colleges and universities have a "circle the wagon" mentality. They don't realize that when they try to hide things, journalists by nature tend to dig deeper, wondering what else is hidden.

13 **Don't be afraid to turn to the local media to help you dig out the story.** If you are stonewalled by the college or university, the school may be less likely to offer a "no comment" to the local daily newspaper when one of their reporters calls about a rape, major theft or serious assault on campus. The local reporter might also be able to help you with possible sources to check. In return, you can be a valuable campus resource for the local newspaper or electronic media outlet. It's a two-way street.

14 **If you are denied access to records, don't be afraid to write about it.** You can also share the story of the denial with the local news media, which may also have an interest in the story. It might be interesting to see if local reporters are denied the same information.

15 **Don't compromise your position as an ethical, independent observer.** Even if the police lie to you, don't think it is acceptable to lie to them.

16 **Join up.** Consider having your media outlet support one or more of the following: Student Press Law Center, Society of Professional Journalists or the Reporters Committee for Freedom of the Press. They can provide needed resources and help if you run into roadblocks.

MIKE DONOGHUE is an award-winning journalist with *The Burlington (Vt.) Free Press*. He has worked as a reporter for more than 30 years, much of it as a police/court reporter. He is also an adjunct professor in the journalism department at St. Michael's College and has been a co-adviser to its award-winning student newspaper, *The Defender* (journalism.smcvt.edu/defender).

This piece, under the title, "Tips from the Front Line: A Veteran Police Reporter Shares Some Tricks of the Trade," is reprinted with permission from *Covering Campus Crime: A Handbook for Journalists,* a publication of the Student Press Law Center, Arlington, Va.

and Sources. Needham Heights, Mass.: Macmillan Publishing, 1994.

TO CLICK

The Chronicle of Higher Education

This weekly newspaper for the academic community is a great source for story ideas. If your newspaper or journalism department doesn't already subscribe, you can probably find copies of the print edition in your school library. Ask about gaining access to the publication's vast website.
http://chronicle.com

EurekAlert!

EurekAlert! is an online, global news service operated by the American Association for the Advancement of Science. It provides a central place through which universities, medical centers, journals, government agencies, corporations and other organizations engaged in research

bring their news to the media and it's a great resource for story ideas.
www.eurekalert.org

Inside Higher Ed
This online publication covers news and trends in higher education; a must-read for college newspaper reporters.
http://insidehighered.com

National Center for Education Statistics
The center is the primary federal entity for collecting and analyzing data related to education. The center's website has scads of data that allows you to compare your school to others, as well as studies and reports on many issues.
http://nces.ed.gov

Newswise
Newswise is a newswire service for journalists, and a press release distribution service for public relations professionals. You'll find lots research news from around the world that you can localize to your campus and community.
www.newswise.com

The Poynter Institute
The Poynter website offers numerous useful articles on beat reporting, including:
"Beat Reporting: What Does it Take To Be The Best?" by Chip Scanlan.
"Anatomy of a Beat Memo" by Richard Kipling.
"The Heart of the Beat" by Chip Scanlan.
"Tracking News by Beat" by Jonathan Dube.
www.poynter.org

Professional Organizations for Beat Writers:

American Medical Writers Association
www.amwa.org

Association of Food Journalists
www.afjonline.com

Association of Health Care Journalists
www.healthjournalism.org

Council for the Advancement of Science Writing
www.casw.org

Criminal Justice Journalists
www.crimjj.wordpress.com

Education Writers Association
www.ewa.org

Military Reporters and Editors
http://militaryreporters.org

National Association of Science Writers
www.nasw.org

North American Travel Journalist Association
http://natja.org

Religion Newswriters Foundation
www.religionwriters.com

Society of American Business Writers and Editors
www.sabew.org

Society of Environmental Journalists
www.sej.org

Beat Report

Name ______________________________

Beat ______________________________

Sources:

Name	Title	Phone Numbers	Office	Email Address	Notes

Upcoming Events (meetings, conferences, performances, exhibits, etc.):

____

____

____

Documents (reports, public records, publications, etc. that will help you cover your beat):

____

____

____

List six story ideas:

1

2

3

4

5

6

APPENDIX 3.B NEWSPAPER READERSHIP SURVEY

How often do you read (NAME OF NEWSPAPER)?

___ Every issue

___ Most issues

___ Occasionally

___ Never

Is the paper distributed at convenient locations?

___ Yes, I can find it if I want to

___No, I never see it

___ I'd like to see it at _____(specify location)

Which best describes how thoroughly you read (NAME OF NEWSPAPER)?

___ Front page only

___ Skim entire paper and headlines

___ Read one or two sections

___ Read it cover to cover

___ Don't read it

How often do you read each section of (NAME OF NEWSPAPER)?

News

___ Every issue

___ Most issues

___ Occasionally

___ Never

Sports

___ Every issue

___ Most issues

___ Occasionally

___ Never

Lifestyle

___ Every issue

___ Most issues

___ Occasionally

___ Never

Arts and entertainment

___ Every issue

___ Most issues

___ Occasionally

___ Never

Opinion

___ Every issue

___ Most issues

___ Occasionally

___ Never

How would you rate the overall quality of the newspaper?

___ Excellent

___ Good

___ Fair

___ Poor

What are you interested in reading about (check all that apply)?

___ On-campus events

___ Administration

___ Student government

___ Entertainment and culture

___ Campus clubs and organizations

___ Crime

___ Sports

___ Faculty

What would you like to see more of in (NAME OF NEWSPAPER)? (Check all that apply)

___ Information about student activities

___ Student government news

___ Entertainment coverage

___ Academic news

___ Photos

___ Sports coverage

___ Opinion columns

___ Comics and cartoons

___ Features and profiles

___ Crossword puzzles

How often do you visit the (NAME OF NEWSPAPER) website?

___ Several times a week

___ Weekly

___ Monthly

___ Never

What is your affiliation with the university?

___ Freshman

___ Sophomore

___ Junior

___ Senior

___ Graduate student

___ Faculty

___ Staff

___ Other (please describe) ________

Are you:

___ Male

___ Female

Where do you live?

___ Residence hall

___ On-campus apartment

___ Off-campus rental

___ Own home

___ With family

Please list any suggestions you have for improving the (NAME OF NEWSPAPER).

____

____

____

Thank you for sharing your thoughts about (NAME OF NEWSPAPER).

Adapted from surveys created by the *Washington Square News*, New York University; *The Spectator*, University of Wisconsin–Eau Claire; *The Broadside*, Central Oregon Community College.

CAMPUS SHOOTING | 5 killed, 16 more injured

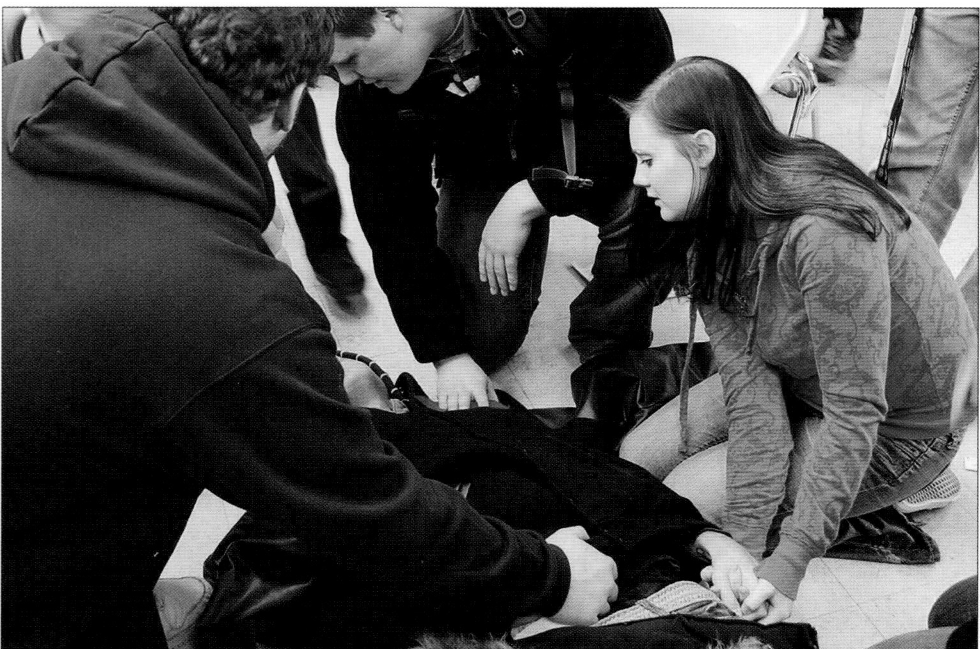

Stacey Huffstutler | Northern Star

Student Emily Fuller helps calm a shooting victim in DuSable Hall while they wait for paramedics to arrive. The victim was shot in the leg while in Cole Hall and then helped away from the scene by student Tim Mayerbock.

TRAGEDY

Stacey Huffstutler | Northern Star

A friend of the shooting victim pictured above reacts to the situation. Students gathered in the lobby of DuSable Hall for almost 30 minutes after the attack before officials were on hand to secure the building.

"I'm going to begin the process of talking to students, and I'll do what I can personally to help them through this; and they'll help me."

- John Peters,
NIU President

SPECIAL ISSUE COVERING THURSDAY'S COLE HALL SHOOTING

FIGURE 4.1 Student reporters have to be ready to cover breaking news at a moment's notice. When a former student at Northern Illinois University shot 23 people and then killed himself, the staff of the *Northern Star* sprang into action to report the story. *Northern Star*, Northern Illinois University.

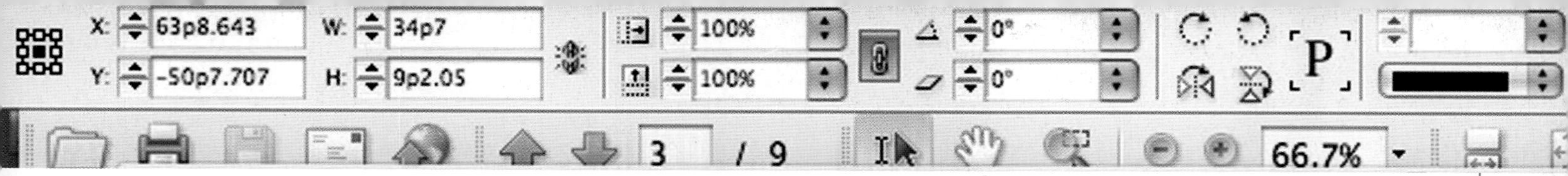

CHAPTER 4 REPORTING

John Puterbaugh, editor-in-chief of the *Northern Star* (northernstar.com) at Northern Illinois University, was meeting with a professor on Valentine's Day 2008 when he heard people running past the office. As the sound of the commotion rose, his professor's office mate rushed into the office and locked the door, saying she'd heard there had been a shooting on campus.

Puterbaugh, the two professors and a couple of other students stayed in the office for a few minutes, texting friends and trying to figure out what was happening. Puterbaugh's professor called 911; the dispatcher confirmed there had been multiple reports of a shooting on campus.

"At first I didn't think it could be the real thing," Puterbaugh says. "Once I realized it was for real, I just knew I had to get out there and start finding out anything and everything I could."

As he walked into the cold February air, Puterbaugh could see people fleeing Cole Hall, where the shooting had reportedly occurred. Some students were gathered in small groups, talking about what had happened. Puterbaugh listened and asked people what they knew, what they had seen. "Some girl got hit in the eye," he wrote in his notebook. "A guy got hit in the leg … 10 shots … Shotgun, maybe."

The Student Newspaper Survival Guide, Second Edition. Rachele Kanigel.

CHAPTER CONTENTS

As he dashed down notes, faster than he'd ever written before, he could see rescue personnel tending to bleeding students. After 10 to 15 minutes of interviewing, he ran back to the *Northern Star* office and posted a few hurried paragraphs to the newspaper's website.

But even then, Puterbaugh didn't know the extent of the tragedy.

Puterbaugh and another *Northern Star* editor were the first journalists on the scene of what would end up the fourth deadliest campus shooting in United States history. On Feb. 14, 2008, Steve Kasmierczak, a graduate student at the University of Illinois who had graduated from NIU, shot 23 people before turning the gun on himself. Six people, including the gunman, died.

Within minutes of the shooting the campus was in a state of shock. Everyone was looking for answers. Who was shot? Had anyone died? Who was the gunman? What happened to him? Where should students go? Was there still a danger?

The *Northern Star's* website became the destination for students, faculty, alumni, parents and others looking for information. In the months before the tragedy, the website typically had 15,000 page views a day, Puterbaugh says. In the 24 hours after the shootings, it had about 600,000.

The experience of covering the shooting "reinforced my desire to become a journalist," says Puterbaugh, who went on to become a reporter and editor for the *Kane County Chronicle*. "I enjoyed being able to serve the community. I felt like I accomplished something I didn't even know I was supposed to do."

NEWS JUDGMENT

While few students cover anything as emotionally wrenching as the 2008 shooting at Northern Illinois

Shootings at Northern Illinois University: A timeline of coverage

The following is a minute-by-minute timeline of how the *Northern Star* – Northern Illinois University's student-run, daily newspaper – covered the February 14, 2008 campus shooting.

THURSDAY, FEB. 14, 2008

ABOUT 3:10 p.m. Newsroom scanner picks up DeKalb Fire Department personnel being directed to "shooting in Cole Center." As chatter continues, news staffers realize the shooting is in Cole Hall, about 400 yards from the Campus Life Building where the *Northern Star* is located.

3:15 p.m. About a dozen *Northern Star* journalists arrive outside Cole Hall. Most come from the newsroom; others from nearby classes. They are the first journalists on the scene, arriving just after rescue personnel. Yellow crime-scene tape is being stretched around Cole Hall and surrounding sidewalks. Rescue workers are tending to wounded students on sidewalks near Cole Hall. A class period has just ended, so hundreds of students are milling about, adding to the general chaos. The student journalists huddle briefly, then fan out to nearby buildings to gather information. Some encounter wounded students and help apply First Aid.

3:45 p.m. Several *Star* staffers return to the newsroom. Someone has pulled the fire alarm in the Campus Life building. There's no one immediately available to turn it off, so the deafening, screeching noise continues for about 45 minutes. Every newsroom phone is ringing, with national and Chicago media wanting information.

3:55 p.m. The *Star's* first story is posted to *www.northernstar.info*. Numerous updates follow closely behind. The *Star* is the first to report that the gunman is dead.

5 p.m. *Northern Star* photos have been sent to The Associated Press and already are appearing all over the world on network television and news websites. Every phone continues to ring, with interview requests for national and Chicago evening newscasts.

6 p.m. Students and advisers decide to produce an eight-page paper for the following morning, and to remove all advertising.

7 p.m. The *Northern Star* learns that one of its student employees, advertising sales representative Dan Parmenter, was among those killed.

EVENING. The staff assembles Friday's edition, finishing well after midnight. Media calls from all over the world continue throughout the night.

FRIDAY, FEB. 15

6–8 a.m. Papers are delivered around campus and the cities of DeKalb and Sycamore.

8 a.m. A half-dozen *Star* reporters and editors attend the NIU press conference, where the shooter's identity will be announced. A few minutes earlier, acting on credible tips from several law-enforcement officers, the *Star* has posted an online update naming the gunman.

Online updates continue all day and all weekend.

SUNDAY, FEB. 17

3 a.m. News staffers and advisers gather to decide whether to publish a print edition for Monday. Classes are canceled and most faculty and staff will be gone. After lengthy discussion, the staff decides to publish online-only for Monday and throughout the week when students are gone.

SUNDAY, FEB. 24

Staffers cover NIU's memorial service and prepare a 24-page special edition for Monday. This time, advertising is included; many ads contain messages of support and condolence.

MONDAY, FEB. 25 The *Star* resumes its daily print edition and NIU classes resume.

More at: northernstar.info/tragedy.

Reprinted with permission from the *Northern Star* and the Dart Center for Journalism and Trauma, which first published this piece.

University, every staff member should be trained to collect information for a news story. The process of gathering those facts – interviewing sources, collecting statistics, finding experts, seeking documents, reviewing reports – is called reporting.

Good reporting begins with good news judgment, knowing how to recognize information that is timely, interesting and important to your readers. For a college newspaper, that means identifying stories that will have impact and meaning for students, specifically, and for the college community (staff, faculty, alumni, parents of students, neighbors) as a whole. Journalists must be able to sift out the most important details from the many bits of information they collect.

To have good news judgment, you need to be able to identify what's news.

All news stories have at least one of these basic elements:

Timeliness. It's happening now. With a daily paper, that may mean covering a fire or a speech or a football game today for tomorrow's paper or the website that day; with a monthly, it means covering the events of this month and putting them into context for people who will read the paper next month.

Proximity. It has impact or meaning for people living in your geographic area, or, in the case of a college newspaper, people involved with your school.

Novelty. Out-of-the-ordinary events get people talking. Readers enjoy stories about the 77-year-old pursuing a bachelor's degree or the engineering student who invents a mechanical leech.

Impact. These are stories that have consequences, such as a fee hike or the adoption of a new smoking policy on campus. News reports help readers understand the impact news events have.

Drama. Reporters look for stories that have mystery, suspense, emotion. A story about a promising athlete recovering from a serious injury or an adopted woman who finds her birth mother has emotional appeal.

TIPSHEET
Student journalists share advice on covering a campus shooting

JOHN PUTERBAUGH, BEN BURR, BEN GROSS, HERMINIA IRIZARRY, MARIEL MENTINK, AND JESSICA SABBAH

Staff of the *Northern Star*, the Northern Illinois University student newspaper, share wisdom from their coverage of the 2008 school shooting. For more information about covering campus shootings go to http://dartcenter.org/content/school-shooting-package.

Immediate coverage

Write down everything you hear. A full half-hour probably passed between when I heard that there was a shooting in the building next door and when I realized how serious and grave the situation really was. In that time, I was scratching notes all over the pages of my notebook, piecing things together based on what was coming from the lips of the students who were in the room and building. This process of piecing things together based only on what I was hearing from fellow students allowed my mind and personal thoughts to stay out of the way of the work at hand.

Let autopilot kick in. Despite the enormity of the situation and story at hand, the fundamentals of covering the story still applied. By keeping the journalist hats on and personal feelings and thoughts aside, student journalists for the *Star* were able to focus on doing interviews and other work the same way they would for a more routine story.

Call, text, or email loved ones to tell them you are OK. After the events of Feb. 14 it took me about six hours to tell my family I was OK. They were hysterical during this period of time, wondering if I was all right.

Always be prepared. Pen, paper, press pass, voice recorder. Cell phone camera or something better.

Work hard to develop good working relationships with police and rescue workers BEFORE anything like this happens. This will pay off immediately by the access you get and by preferential treatment granted to local journalists whom the sources already know.

Accuracy above all. The world is not only watching, it's stealing stories from your website. They'd better be accurate. This is make-or-break time for your paper's credibility.

Doing the work

Remember whom you work for: the people in the community. As students fled town and parents all over the state searched for answers and found northernstar.info in the process, the *Northern Star* took on a powerful responsibility. People wanted and deserved accurate answers and information as soon as possible. The *Northern Star* provided the message board for the community, giving all sorts of organizations the avenue to get their message out to students and community members. People from within and beyond the NIU community expressed their feelings and messages of solidarity in the pages of the *Northern Star*.

Remember what you are covering. Never let the adrenaline of covering a big story become a thrill. In our case, one of our own student-newspaper colleagues was among the students killed, and two others had escaped that classroom. That immediately made the story personal.

Support your co-workers. The weight of the work of covering a shooting was enormous and required incredible teamwork from everyone involved. Specific job titles and descriptions were almost totally arbitrary; everyone did anything they could to help one another. Everyone was helping each other, doing whatever they could to distribute the weight of the responsibility as evenly as possible.

At some point you have to pull yourself away from what is going on and get some sleep. I stayed in the newsroom or was covering events after the tragedy for 13 hours. I finally drew myself away from the office and found how exhausted I was. I got about four hours of sleep, and it was very much needed, because the next day there was just as much work to do as the day before. There's no way I could have pulled an all-nighter.

Work as a team. You can't do everything by yourself. Take time, sit down and make a game plan in which you delegate responsibilities. Make sure to include everyone who wants to be included. Those who are sitting around in the newsroom want to be doing something; otherwise they wouldn't be there. So give everyone a job.

Be sensitive. Watch how the national media acts, and don't act that way. Don't be vultures. Don't do or ask anything that makes you uncomfortable, and keep your voice down.

Think of the victims and their families. Be careful not to glorify the killer or the bad in your coverage.

Remember you are a student, too. This gives you an advantage in coverage by having connections with the campus and community that outside media does not.

Outside media

Be careful when speaking to the press. In a high-profile event, before you even know fully what's happening, the world is watching you and hanging on your every word. You are everyone's story of the day. In interviews: Say what you know and what you saw. Don't speculate. Don't generalize.

Designate one or two editors to answer media requests. Otherwise, the whole newsroom can be consumed with it and you can't get your own work done.

After the story

Take time to socialize. A couple days after the shootings and after putting what seemed like a million hours into the work of covering this story, a dozen or so *Northern Star* staffers and editors went out to eat and share a few drinks. The release and uplift this provided us was so helpful and really gave us renewed energy and purpose in doing a good job.

Be sad. After the immediate work was done, it was important to realize that what happened was a tragedy and was horribly sad. No one should have to feel like their job as a journalist is to not be affected by tragedy they may have to cover. While it is a journalist's job to cover the tragedy, the journalist is also a person who must reconcile the two separate approaches to the situation. Emotion is important to recognize, and to allow for the sake of moving on as a person.

Talk about your experience. By reporting what is going on, sometimes you aren't dealing with what has been happening. While everyone else in the world has been experiencing the event, you haven't. So once things go back to normal, it's almost like you realized what just happened.

Take care of yourself. Don't get so lost in your work that you completely distance yourself from what has happened. You have to distance yourself to an extent to cover the event for your readers, but you are also experiencing it too. If you completely escape from it into your work, then recovering will become extremely hard. It's OK to escape for a bit, but not forever.

Keep an eye on your co-workers. Everyone copes differently. Some may be dealing with the incident by hiding their feelings. If you notice something, ask if everything is OK. Sometimes just talking to someone who is going through what you are can help a great deal.

Don't ever take for granted the camaraderie that can be found in the newsroom.

Be sensitive with images. Graphic photos of the carnage may be legit for a day or two. After that, your community does not want to see them.

 For more information about covering campus shootings go to http://dartcenter.org/content/school-shooting-package.

Prominence. In every community, certain people are minor celebrities because of their position or achievement. This is equally true on a college campus, where readers want to know if the president resigns or the star quarterback is arrested on drug charges.

Conflict. Readers love a good conflict, whether it's rival teams meeting on the basketball court or political factions trying to capture the leadership of student government.

Human interest. People like stories about people. It's interesting to read about the blind student who makes her way around campus with a seeing-eye dog or the English major who strips for a living.

Usefulness. Readers want to know where to buy low-cost textbooks, when to file graduation applications, how to make it through an all-night study session.

Once you understand what makes news, you can begin to make decisions about how to report it.

THE REPORTING PROCESS

The reporting process is about going from ignorance to knowledge. As a reporter you may know little about a topic when a story is assigned; by the time it's published, you will be a minor expert. Whether they're covering a shooting like the one at Northern Illinois University or a commencement speech or the demolition of an unsafe building, reporters follow a basic process. To see how the reporting process works, let's trace a reporter's steps from the moment a story is assigned.

You walk into the newsroom at 10:45 a.m. and your editor hands you a flier. "Students for the Ethical Treatment of Animals is organizing a rally in front of the student union today at noon," she says. "Bring me back a story. We've already assigned a photographer; Jennifer will meet you over there."

> What do you do next?
>
> Start reporting!

As you begin the reporting process it's a good idea to ask yourself some basic questions:

What is the story?
In this case, People are gathering on campus to protest animal research.

What makes the story news?
By definition, a protest involves conflict and may involve drama. The rally is also timely and geographically relevant.

What do I need to know?
What is Students for the Ethical Treatment of Animals? Why are people protesting? How many people will participate? What do organizers hope to achieve?

Where can I find information?
The best way to get information about the rally itself is to go to it. But even before it starts you should do some background research.

Developing a reporting plan

For every story, be it a breaking news story you report and write in two hours, or a long feature you work on for weeks, you should develop a reporting plan. Such a plan will act as a roadmap for your reporting, guiding you and helping you keep your focus.

Draft your reporting plan as you begin work on a story. It may change as you find out more information.

Step One. Write a focus statement for your story.

Step Two. Write a list of questions.

Step Three. Look over your questions and figure out where you can get each piece of information.

Step Four. Make a list of individuals you want to interview and documents you want to find. Look up phone numbers and email addresses for your sources.

BACKGROUND RESEARCH

A Web search is a good place to start. You go on Google and search for "Students for the Ethical Treatment of Animals" and the name of your school. Then you do another search for "lab animals" and your school. You find out:

- Two years ago there was a big animal rights demonstration on your campus. Five students were arrested.
- A philosophy professor on campus is a leader in the local animal rights movement.
- A number of professors have published medical research based on lab experiments with animals.
- Your university is accredited by the Association for Assessment and Accreditation of Laboratory Animal Care, a private, nonprofit organization that promotes the humane treatment of animals in science.

You jot down some names and facts and then go to your student newspaper archive and find the article about the students who were arrested for protesting animal research.

You take note of the people quoted in the article. You also check the university directory and get phone numbers, email addresses and office numbers for the professors on either side of the animal research issue.

Before going out to the rally, you go back to your original list of questions and add a few more:

- What kind of animal research is conducted on this campus?
- Why is the rally happening now?
- Is Students for the Ethical Treatment of Animals related to People for the Ethical Treatment of Animals?
- How much animal research is being done on campus?
- Are animals being mistreated? If so, how and by whom?

By now it's 11:45 a.m., time to head over to the student union. You don't know much yet, but you've got a start – you have contact information for a list of potential sources, you have a little background on the issues and you've got some ideas about what else you need to know.

REPORTING RESOURCES

A good reporter learns how to quickly gather information from various sources. These may include:

Directories. Phone books and online directories are vital tools for reporters. They help not only with phone numbers and email addresses but also with names and titles. (Be aware, though, that directories can be out-of-date or contain errors; always double-check name spellings and titles with human sources.)

TIPSHEET
Evaluating information on the Web

The Web is a fabulous resource for finding information. It's also a frighteningly effective vehicle for spreading misinformation, propaganda and disinformation. When considering information presented on a website, think critically, asking yourself the following questions:

1. Is the person or organization responsible for the contents of the page clearly identified?
2. What is the URL domain (.org, .gov, .edu, etc.)? If the domain is .gov, you know this is an official governmental organization, whereas anyone can get a .net or .com domain.
3. Does the site clearly describe its goals?
4. Can you verify the legitimacy of the organization? Is there a phone number or postal address to contact for more information? (An email address is not enough.)
5. Can you tell if the page has the official approval of the organization?
6. Are the sources for any factual information clearly listed so they can be verified?
7. Does the site have many grammatical, spelling and typographical errors? (These kinds of errors don't just indicate a lack of quality; they can lead to factual errors.)
8. Is the factual information consistent with other sources?
9. Does the organization have a political or ideological bias? If so, is this bias clearly stated?
10. If the page has advertising, is it clearly differentiated from the informational content?
11. Does the organization or individual behind the site have a commercial stake in the information presented?
12. Is the topic covered in a comprehensive and balanced way? Be wary of one-sided views with critical information missing.
13. Are there dates on the page to indicate when the page was written, when it was put on the Web and when it was last revised?
14. Is there any outdated information on the site?
15. Are there many dead links? This suggests the page has not been updated recently.

Documents. Reports, lawsuits, police records and other documents provide a paper trail in reporting. Reporters can use documents to verify facts, confirm hunches or track down new information.

Newspaper archives. Past news stories in your paper and others can provide invaluable background information.

Websites. The Internet has revolutionized reporting. Information that used to take hours or days or weeks to find is now accessible in seconds with the click of a mouse. Social networking sites like Facebook and Twitter are particularly useful for finding students at your university. Be aware, however, that much of the information on the Web is biased, inaccurate or incomplete. (For more information about using the Internet as a research tool see Tipsheet: Evaluating information on the Web.)

Listservs and newsgroups. Email discussion groups and Web-based bulletin boards can be a great way to find story ideas and sources. Just be sure to check people out before quoting them. People who present themselves anonymously may not feel bound by truth.

Human sources. Interviewing people remains a reporter's stock-in-trade. People provide the anecdotes, quotes, eyewitness accounts, opinions and perspectives that make a news story come alive.

THE POWER OF OBSERVATION

On your walk to the student union, you hear drumming and chanting. "Liberate the animals! Liberate the animals!" the crowd shouts. You pull out your notebook and start to take notes. When you get to the front of the student union, you see a large crowd of people, some of them carrying signs. A young man with a bullhorn is standing on the steps addressing the crowd.

You feel a bit overwhelmed. What should you take notes on?

Let your senses guide you. What do you hear? What do you see? What captures your attention?

Note the slogans on the signs. Listen to what the speaker is saying. When he utters something catchy or important, jot it down, but don't feel you have to write down every single word. Observe the crowd's reaction. Do people look bored or fired up? Do they seem angry? Try to estimate the size of the group by counting a section of the crowd and then extrapolating. (You can also get crowd estimates from police and organizers; typically organizers overestimate and police come in with a lower count.)

INTERVIEWING

During and after the rally, you'll want to interview people. Choose a variety of sources – organizers (who may not be available until after the event is over), participants, onlookers, university officials, scientists who conduct research with animals, science students who work in labs with animals.

When doing interviews you're looking for a number of things.

- **Factual information** (such as when the organization was formed, why this rally is happening today, what its objective is).
- **Reactions and opinions** from a variety of perspectives (how people feel about what they've seen and heard).
- **Statistics** that will quantify the story (how many labs on campus do animal research? How many people attended the rally?)
- **Anecdotes**, or vignettes, that will help tell the story (someone drove 200 miles to come to this rally, a woman with diabetes supports animal research because it's helped pave the way for treatments).

RECORDING INTERVIEWS

There are two kinds of reporters in the world: those who prefer to record interviews and those who prefer not to.

Nearly all reporters use an audio recorder at some time in their careers – for a Q&A, for example, or a meeting with a potentially litigious source, or any interview where the source whips out his own recorder. Political reporters typically record interviews with politicians in case someone wants to challenge their quotes. In addition, audio recorders have become indispensable for the multimedia journalist who produces stories for the Web (and sometimes radio and television), as well as print.

Audio recorders are useful for:

Getting verbatim quotes

Picking up tone or accent

Collecting sound and voice recordings for audio reports

Interviewing fast talkers.

However, many reporters believe audio recorders interfere with the interviewing process. For one thing, they sometimes intimidate sources. For another, reporters who rely on them often don't take good notes. And many newspaper reporters feel they don't have the time to listen to and transcribe recordings after the interview.

The most important thing to keep in mind when recording an interview is that recorders can fail. Batteries run out, machines break, a plane roars overhead at a key moment and your interview is lost. The solution, of course, is to take good notes whether or not you're taping. Don't rely on your recorder. In terms of notetaking you should pretend it's not there. Some other tips for using an audio recorder:

1. **Come prepared.** Always bring extra batteries and storage devices.
2. **Test the recorder first.** Do a trial run before meeting your source and then again in the place where you'll be doing the interview. Make sure not only that your equipment works but that background noises don't interfere.
3. **Use the counter.** Turn the counter to zero when you start and then write down numbers in your notes every now and then so you can find key passages easily.
4. **Know the law before recording phone interviews.** State laws on recording phone conversations vary. Some states require consent from all parties before a phone conversation can be recorded. (For information on laws that apply to you, check out "Can We Tape? A Practical Guide to Taping Phone Calls and In-Person Conversations in the 50 States and D.C." by the Reporters Committee for Freedom of the Press, listed at the end of this chapter.)

NOTETAKING

Probably the best way to develop your notetaking skills is to study old-fashioned stenography. A course or book on shorthand is an excellent investment, particularly at this point in your career.

If you don't learn a formal shorthand system, you should develop your own method of speedwriting. Look for ways to shorten words – drop vowels, use symbols, abbreviate commonly used words – bc for because, w/ for with, etc. The key is to find a system that works for you.

You also have to find a system that you can read. There's no point in taking notes quickly if you can't read your jottings a few days later when you sit down to write your story.

When taking notes on an interview, don't feel you have to write down every single word the person says. Listen for key information or catchy quotes. When the subject says something you may want to quote, get it all down, even if it means a pause in your questions. Some reporters even ask throwaway questions to buy them time to finish writing a good quote.

TIPSHEET Interviewing

Before the interview

1 **Do as much background research as possible.** Read articles and websites about the topic you're covering as well as the person you are interviewing. The more you know, the more intelligent the questions you'll be able to ask.

2 **Make a list of questions.** Begin with the who, what, where, when, why and how, and go from there. Think about what this source may be able to provide.

3 **Organize the questions.** Put them in a format that's easy to access and an order that makes sense. Start with easy, factual questions and build to more complex or pointed ones.

4 **Make an appointment.** Unless you're on a tight deadline, it's best not to just drop in on people. Try to find an hour when both of you will have time to devote to the interview.

5 **Dress appropriately.** Generally you want to dress as much like your source as possible. If you're interviewing the college president, wear business attire; if you're interviewing students or construction workers you should dress more informally.

6 **Be prepared.** Make sure you have a notebook, pens, an audio recorder if you use one (plus extra storage devices and batteries), documents you'll be discussing and anything else you may need.

During the interview

7 **Introduce yourself.** Always identify yourself as a reporter working on a story for publication.

8 **Build rapport.** It's good to start with a little small talk to make the source feel comfortable. Talk about the weather or current events or mutual acquaintances or remark on a picture or something in the room.

9 **Describe your story.** Explain the purpose and scope of the piece you plan to write.

10 **Write it down.** Even if you're using an audio recorder, always take notes. Don't assume you'll remember details.

11 **Ask open-ended questions.** Avoid questions that can be answered with yes, no or other one-word answers. Questions that begin with how, why or "tell me about" tend to elicit fuller answers.

12 **Show you're listening.** Nod your head or utter agreeing sounds to demonstrate you understand and are interested in what the person is saying.

13 **Make eye contact.** Even if you're frantically scribbling notes, take time to look at your source every now and then. Eye contact helps you stay focused and maintain rapport.

14 **Listen for quotable quotes.** When you hear a likely quote, take careful notes. It's OK to ask people to repeat themselves or slow down; demonstrate your commitment to quote them accurately.

15 **Follow up.** Don't feel you have to slavishly stick to the prepared questions. If your source says something unexpected or interesting, pursue a new line of questioning.

16 **Take charge.** Remember that *you* are conducting the interview. If the source strays from the topic or doesn't answer the question, it's your job to keep the person on track.

17 **Save tough questions for the end.** Build up to challenging, hard-to-ask questions. Be sure to pace the interview so that you don't run out of time before you ask the difficult questions.

18 **Wrap it up.** End each interview by asking for other things the source would like to tell you and recommendations for other good sources of information.

19 **Be appreciative.** Thank the source for taking the time to talk with you and ask permission to check back, if need be, if more questions arise. Make sure you have the source's phone numbers and email address for follow-up.

After the interview

20 **Review your notes.** Fill in missing words and spell out troublesome abbreviations while they are still fresh in your mind.

21 **Mark your notes.** Highlight key facts or quotes you may want to use in your story with a highlighter or by underlining or marking key passages with stars.

22 **Transcribe key sections.** Most reporters don't transcribe full interviews but it's good to type up significant quotes, scenes, anecdotes or details you're likely to use. This will help later when you sit down to actually write the story.

EMAIL INTERVIEWS

Email has given reporters a powerful new tool for reporting. Now you can reach people thousands of miles away in different time zones with the click of a few keys. Busy professionals often answer email before they'll pick up a phone. It's fast. It's efficient. And it's also potentially dangerous.

Some of the pitfalls of email interviews:

You're never really sure who is answering your message. Is it the university president – or her secretary? The student you wrote to – or her boyfriend? Or is it the next person who got on the lab computer when your intended source forgot to log off?

You can't ask spontaneous questions. With email, it's impossible to have a real conversation with back and forth chat and follow-up questions.

Responses can be stilted or carefully crafted. That's OK in certain circumstances, but most of the time you want quotes that are natural and unscripted.

It's hard to read nuances. It's often difficult to tell from an email if the writer is being funny or serious, sarcastic or sincere. You don't have tone of voice, facial expressions and gestures to help you interpret the words.

Your email messages can be forwarded. You may not want one source to pass on all your comments and questions to another person.

Despite these drawbacks, email does have its place in the reporter's toolbox. Here are some guidelines to follow:

1 Use email for making contact with people and setting up interviews.

2 Try to conduct interviews by phone or in person. Do primary interviews by email only as a last resort.

3 Use email to ask quick follow-up questions or to check information.

4 Make sure you know the email source's name. Don't use interviews from an anonymous source.

Be professional in your messages. Keep in mind that anything you write may be forwarded to other people.

When using email, try to verify that the information comes from the intended source. If any information provided via email sounds fishy, check it out.

MATH FOR JOURNALISTS

Statistics, percentages and other numbers add specificity and context to stories. But many journalists – professionals as well as students – get uncomfortable when they have to explain concepts in numbers instead of words. Here's a primer on some of the basic math journalists have to deal with.

Percentages

Percentages are useful for comparing two or more numbers without regard to their differing size. For example, you can look at the raw numbers of African-American, white and Asian students at your university but it's more telling to compare the percentages of each racial group.

To understand how percents work, it helps to look at the root of the word. "Per" means "out of" and "cent" means "one hundred." So percent after a number means that many out of 100.

To calculate X *as a percentage of* Y: Divide X by Y and multiply the result by 100.

Example: Of the 25,000 students who attend your university, 5,000 live on campus. The percentage of students who live on campus is:

(5,000 divided by 25,000) × 100
= 0.2 × 100
= 20 percent

If X is larger than Y, the result is a percentage greater than 100.

To calculate *the percentage change* from X to Y: Calculate the difference and divide it by X. Then multiply by 100.

Example: Your university's budget was $12 million last year and $15 million this year. The percentage change is:

[(15 – 12) divided by 12] × 100
= [3 divided by 12] × 100
= .25 × 100
= 25 percent

Therefore, the budget is 25 percent higher this year.

To change a decimal to a percent: Move the decimal point two places to the right.

Example: .75 = 75 percent

To change a percent to a decimal: Move the decimal point two places to the left.

Example: 75 percent = .75

Keep in mind that a 100 percent increase is a doubling, a 200 percent increase is a tripling, and so forth.

Example: Your university police department charged 15 students with drug violations last year and 45 students with drug violations this year. You can express this increase two ways, A. Drug violations tripled in the past year or B. Drug violations increased 200 percent from last year to this year.

Ratios and rates

A ***ratio*** describes the number of times larger one number is than another.

To calculate the ratio of X to Y: Divide X by Y.

Example: Your university has 12,000 students and 600 faculty. The student-faculty ratio is:

12,000 divided by 600
= 20 to 1

A ***rate*** describes a number in terms of how it fits into a larger population, usually expressed per hundred, per thousand, per hundred thousand, etc.

To calculate the rate of X cases in a population of Y: Divide X by Y and multiply by a basis number (such as 1,000).

Example: Your campus has a population of 25,000 and there were three sexual assaults last year. The sexual assault rate was:

3 per 25,000
= 3 divided by 25,000
= 0.000012

Then multiply by the number to express it in various ways:

$0.000012 \times 1{,}000 = 0.012$ per 1,000
$0.000012 \times 10{,}000 = 0.12$ per 10,000
$0.000012 \times 100{,}000 = 1.2$ per 100,000

Averages

An average is a way to summarize a set of numbers with a single number. This is useful for stories that deal with professor's salaries, grade-point averages, the costs of a college education at different schools, etc.

There are three types of averages: the **mean**, the **median** and the **mode**.

- The **mean** is the sum of all numbers divided by the number of numbers in the set.
- The **median** is the one in the middle.
- The **mode** is the most common answer.

The most common way of calculating an average is to find the mean, or arithmetic average.

To calculate the mean of X numbers: Add up the numbers and divide by X.

Example: Full professors in one department at your university are paid $76,000, $68,000, $83,000, $152, 000 and $65,000 a year. What is their average salary?

(76,000 + 68,000 + 83,000 + 152,000 + 65,000) divided by 5
= an average salary of $88,800.

The problem with the mean is that it can be misleading. In the example above, one high-paid professor skews the whole equation. All but one of the professors are making $83,000 or less but the mean average is $88,000.

A **median** is often used to average dollar amounts to avoid distortion caused by a few extreme values. The median is the middle number in a series.

To calculate the median of several numbers: Arrange them from smallest to largest and choose the middle number.

Example: Using the example of professors' salaries above, the median is $76,000.

If you have to find the median of an even number of numbers, it's the mean of the two middle numbers. In the example above, if you had another professor making $72,000 you would find the mean of $72,000 and $76,000 by adding the numbers and dividing by 2.

(72,000 + 76,000) divided by 2 = 74,000.

The median would be $74,000.

The third kind of average is a **mode**, the number that appears most often. This is rarely used. But let's say you're trying to figure out the most common price students are paying for a particular textbook. You interview a dozen students and you find:

Jan paid $49.99.
Alex, Grace, Mark, Stephen and Rodrigo paid $59.99.
Esperanza paid $51.
Joyce and Trevor paid $61.
Tom, Carla and Yasmin paid $55.99.

The most common price paid for the book was $59.99.

ACCURACY

Being a reporter is an enormous responsibility. When people read an article in the newspaper, they expect it to be true. If you get the facts wrong you won't just embarrass yourself, you'll let down your whole paper–and you may even leave yourself open to a lawsuit (more about that in Chapter 13). So the No. 1 rule of journalism is Get it Right.

Factual accuracy means checking and rechecking every statement, fact and detail and also making sure the overall account – the way the details are assembled – is true. Professional reporters work painstakingly to achieve accuracy and you should, too. The fact that you work for a college newspaper, that you're still learning, doesn't excuse sloppy reporting.

This is easy to say but hard to do. Virtually every reporter, student and professional, can remember (with a

CHECKLIST
Reporting for accuracy

The process to achieve accuracy ends with editing and proofreading, but it starts with reporting. To report for accuracy, ask yourself:

1 **Did you use primary sources?** You should base most of your reporting on primary sources – official documents; reports; and interviews with eyewitnesses, leaders and spokespersons for groups, or people who have direct knowledge of a situation or event. Secondary sources, such as other news articles and people who don't have direct knowledge of the topic, should be used for background research.

2 **Did you double-check all names?** Ask people you interview to spell their name, even if it's a common one. John can be Jon and Jane can be Jayne.

3 **Did you double-check phone numbers, addresses and Web addresses?** Don't just review the number, dial it. Same goes for website addresses; look up the URL.

4 **Did you double-check dates and times?** Make sure all dates and times, especially for upcoming events, are correct. You don't want to tell people the lecture starts at noon when it really begins at 11 a.m.

5 **Did you use credible sources?** Check out the people you talk to. If a source gives you suspect information, confirm it with another source.

6 **Did you double-check math and numbers?** Every number in a story – whether you got it from a source or calculated it yourself – should be verified.

7 **Do you have varying versions of events?** If one person says something and another source contradicts it, go back to the first source. If both sources stand by their statements, look for additional sources. Or include both accounts with proper attribution and note the discrepancy.

8 **Did you check the documents?** If the university president says your school passed its accreditation review, ask to see the accreditation documents. If an alleged crime victim says she reported a crime to the police, look for the police report. Whenever a document is available, seek it out.

Northern Star

MONDAY, FEBRUARY 25, 2008 NORTHERNSTAR.INFO

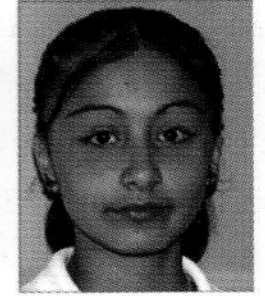

Ryanne Mace
"Ryanne put a smile on everyone's face; I never saw her in a bad mood."
- Matt LeCompte
coworker

Daniel Parmenter
"He always cared about others first and making someone else's life better."
- Tim Smerz
fraternity brother and coworker

Catalina Garcia
"She kept me positive; she kept my head on straight."
- Anthony Hayes
friend

Julianna Gehant
"If you saw her smiling, you'd never forget it."
- John Galan
NIU Veterans Club member

Gayle Dubowski
"She was so kind and nice and just ... genuine."
- Stephanie Franz
friend

TOGETHER FORWARD

Alan Cesar | Northern Star

Lights shine in the Convocation Center at the end of the memorial service Sunday night. The Convo was filled beyond capacity for the service, with satellite locations drawing large crowds at the Campus Recreation Center, the Barsema Alumni and Visitors Center and the Holmes Student Center.

SPECIAL ISSUE

Memorial coverage	3, 5	Letter from John Peters	2
Virginia Tech support	4	Perspective	6-7
Letters to the editor	8-12	Online comments	10, 13
Cole Hall info	14	Student support	15
Flavor	17	Community support	18
Classifieds	19	Sudoku	19
Sports	21-23	Memorial Back Cover	24

For more coverage, archived stories and video from Sunday night's memorial, go to northernstar.info.

"AN ACT OF VIOLENCE DOES NOT DEFINE US."

- PRESIDENT JOHN PETERS IN A LETTER TO STUDENTS

FIGURE 4.2 Ten days after a former student shot 23 people at Northern Illinois University, the *Northern Star* prepared a special 24-page issue memorializing the slain students and reflecting on the impact the tragedy had had on the campus. *Northern Star*, Northern Illinois University

grimace) a time they got a fact wrong. Maybe it was a quote they misheard or a number they miscopied or a name they misspelled.

Remember that most errors are preventable. It's just a question of taking the time to check your facts.

TO DO

1 Make a reporting plan for the next story you're assigned. Write the focus statement and questions. Then think about who or what could answer those questions and make a list of sources.

2 Create a reporting sourcebook or database for your newspaper. Have students share lists of useful sources, including reports, documents and helpful

people. Put it in a form and place – a binder in a corner of the newsroom, an electronic database accessible from the Web – that will be available to your entire staff.

3 Organize a staff discussion about interviewing. Discuss challenges and solutions. Encourage green reporters to share their fears about interviewing and have others share what they've learned. Invite skilled reporters – professionals or veterans on your staff – to share how they get reluctant sources to talk.

4 Develop a disaster plan for your newsroom. Consider possible scenarios and think about how your staff would deal with challenges like a power outage, a campus evacuation, flooding, etc. Once you have a plan in place review it with your staff.

TO READ

Adams, Sally. *Interviewing for Journalists.* New York, N.Y.: Routledge, 2001.
Blum, Walter and C. Theo Yerian. *Personal Shorthand for the Journalist.* Portland, Ore: ERA Learning, 1980.
Brady, John Joseph. *The Craft of Interviewing.* New York, N.Y.: Vintage Books, 1977.
Schwartz, Jerry. *The Associated Press Reporting Handbook.* New York, N.Y.: McGraw-Hill, 2001.

TO CLICK

The Art of the Interview
Neal Conan, Poynter Online
http://poynter.org/content/content_view.asp?id=9572

The Art of Interviewing
Gregory Favre, Poynter Online
http://poynter.org/content/content_view.asp?id=5165

The Bare Facts of Interviewing
Jim Alexander, Poynter Online
http://www.poynter.org/content/content_view.asp?id=60317

Can We Tape?
"A Practical Guide to Recording Phone Calls and In-Person Conversations in the 50 States and D.C."
Reporters Committee for Freedom of the Press
www.rcfp.org/taping

Facebook.com
Facebook is an invaluable reporting resource because you can look up students who come from a particular place or who are in a particular major.
http://facebook.com

Guidelines for Interviewing Confidential Sources: Who, When, and Why?
Al Tompkins, Poynter Online
http://www.poynter.org/content/content_view.asp?id=4361

Guidelines for Interviewing Juveniles
Al Tompkins, Poynter Online
http://poynter.org/content/content_view.asp?id=4571

To Tape or Not to Tape
Chip Scanlan, Poynter Online
(This article contains a link to a fascinating feedback board on the pros and cons of recording interviews)
http://www.poynter.org/column.asp?id=52&aid=15200

Monday, March 28, 2005

The Exponent

Vol. 119 · No. 50 www.purdueexponent.org Purdue's Independent Daily Student Newspaper

TWO DIE IN ON-CAMPUS PLANE CRASH

Officials look over the wreckage from an early morning plane crash Saturday near the Ackerman Hills Golf Course at Purdue. Both of the plane's occupants were killed. Jason Tang/Senior Photographer

Weather may have led to Saturday crash

By Brent Forgues
Campus Editor

On Sunday, the Tippecanoe County coroner's office identified the man and woman that died in a plane crash Saturday morning on Purdue's campus.

Dustin L. Walters, 22 of Lafayette, piloted the 1975 Piper Arrow four-seat aircraft and Tiesa L. Knoth, 34 of West Lafayette, rode as passenger when it crashed at about 5:40 a.m. into McCormick Woods. Neither were affiliated with Purdue.

Although a federal investigation is underway to determine the cause of the crash, the weather at the time of the aircraft's flight is suspected as being the greatest factor.

Walters rented the airplane from Lafayette Aviation and took it out from the Purdue airport between 5 and 5:30 a.m. A plane crash was reported at 5:42 a.m.

Police found the crash site at 7 a.m. near Purdue's Ackerman Hills Golf Course.

Jeff Pittard, president of Lafayette Aviation, said Walters was an employee who was terminated in 2001. Walters received his piloting license with Lafayette Aviation during his employment with the company, he said.

Pittard said he heard that Walter was practicing take-offs and landings.

Ed Malinowski, air safety investigator with the National Transportation Safety Board, said, "The three main things we look at are the weather at the time, the pilot's background and the aircraft."

A timeline of the day's events

Between 5 and 5:30 a.m.

Dustin L. Walters, 22 of Lafayette, and Tiesa L. Knoth, 34 of West Lafayette, take off from Purdue University Airport in a 1975 single-engine Piper Arrow four-seat airplane.

5:40 a.m.

The plane crashes into McCormick Woods near Ackerman Hills Golf Course at the intersection of Cherry Lane and McCormick Road.

5:42 a.m.

A nearby resident calls 911 and informs police that he heard the sound of a sputtering airplane followed by a boom.

7:00 a.m.

Purdue University police locate the crash site.

Between 1 and 1:30 p.m.

Physical facilities constructs a makeshift road to the crash site from gravel and large rocks to allow bulldozers and other large machinery access to the wreckage since rain the night before softened the ground.

4:05 p.m.

The coroner removes the bodies of Walters and Knoth from the crash site and moves them to the county morgue for identification. The bodies cannot be identified until the following afternoon.

4:30 p.m.

Emergency management moves the wreckage of the plane on to a flat-bed pulled by a pick-up truck.

5:45 p.m.

The remains of the airplane are transported from the crash site to a hangar at the Purdue University Airport for the National Transportation Safety Board to begin its investigation and the woods are reopened to the public.

526
Birck Boilermaker Golf Complex
Cherry Lane
126
McCormick Road
Site of plane crash
N
Stadium Avenue

INSIDE

For expanded coverage and more information on the investigation, **see Page 4**.

About the aircraft

Piper Arrow

- It's typically used by students who are learning how to fly.
- This model typically costs around $65,000.
- It has 200 horse power.
- Wing span of 35.4 feet.
- 24.7 feet long.
- 7.9 feet high.
- A maximum take-off weight of 2,750 pounds.

A history of recent local crashes

April 23, 2002

A Purdue student experienced what appeared to be an engine malfunction in her single-engineer Piper Warrior 3 aircraft, crash-landing the plane on the 14th fairway of the Lafayette Municipal Golf Course. The pilot and plane received minor injuries.

July 26, 2000

A Purdue student died when his self-made aircraft crashed east of Lafayette. It was the first flight of the plane, which had been checked by the Federal Aviation Authority.

Sept. 12, 1997

A crash shortly after takeoff from the Purdue airport killed three. The incident was the first crash involving aviation students and staff at the airport since the flight education program began 41 years earlier.

March 15, 1989

Two crew members died instantly when a Mid-Pacific Air cargo plane crashed 200 yards short of a Purdue runway. Rescue workers found the wreckage in three pieces east of the airport.

April 13, 1981

Two students were killed shortly after takeoff from Aretz Airport when their private plane crashed into a nearby yard.

[INSIDE]

PSG ELECTION COVERAGE

For expanded information about PSG senate candidates, **see Page 5.**

DEBATE

At 7 p.m. today in Rawls Hall Room 1086, there will be an open forum discussion for presidential and vice presidential candidates.

Senator candidates will be available afterward to answer questions.

VOTING

Elections for Purdue Student Government begin at 12:01 a.m. on March 29 and end at 11:59 p..m. on March 31. To vote, point your Web browser to http://ssinfo.purdue.edu.

[WEATHER]

>> Sunny
Tonight: Clear
62/38 Tue: 67/50 | Wed: 65/45

[INDEX]

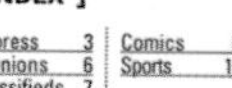

[CONTACT]

460 Northwestern Ave.
PO Box 2506
West Lafayette, IN 47996-0506
Hours: 8:30 a.m. to 5 p.m.
Monday through Friday
Phone: (765) 743 - 1111
Fax: (765) 743 - 6087
http://www.purdueexponent.org

FIGURE 5.1 When a major news story breaks on or near your campus, your reporters should be ready to write concise, informative news stories on a tight deadline as *The Exponent* staff did when a small plane crashed on the Purdue University campus. *The Exponent*, Purdue University.

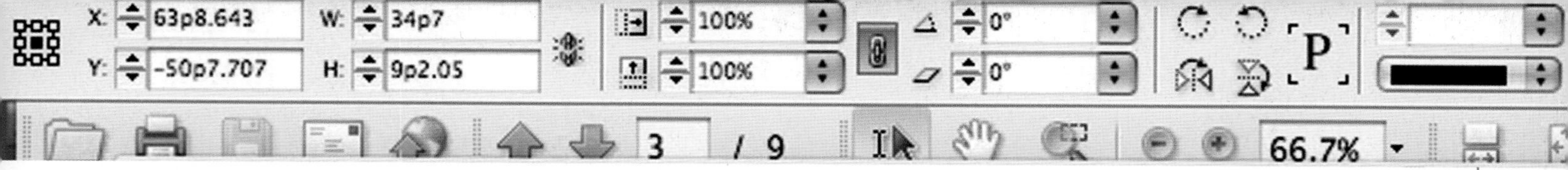

CHAPTER 5 NEWSWRITING

"Student dies after five-story fall."

Who died? Where did it happen? When did it happen? Why did the student fall?

These are some of the questions that would go through a typical reader's mind after reading the headline that appeared in the *Washington Square News* (nyunews.com), New York University's daily student newspaper one fall day.

A reporter's job is to answer these questions clearly and quickly. Here's how Kate Meyer, the reporter, wrote the story:

> Police are investigating the death of an NYU student who fell from a University Place apartment building Saturday night.
>
> Michelle Gluckman, a 19-year-old in the General Studies Program, fell at about 10 p.m. from a sixth-story window to the enclosed courtyard on the second floor of a non-NYU apartment building at 1 University Place, police said. She was taken to St. Vincent's Hospital where she lay in critical condition until she died seven hours later.

The Student Newspaper Survival Guide, Second Edition. Rachele Kanigel.

CHAPTER CONTENTS

> The details surrounding the death remain unclear, but the police said Gluckman likely jumped and was not pushed. "There's no criminality involved," said Sgt. John Grimpel, a police spokesman.
>
> Gluckman's death is the second at NYU in nine days and the third this semester. A College of Arts and Science freshman jumped to his death from the tenth floor of Bobst Library on Oct. 10, and a CAS junior leapt from the same floor of the library Sept. 12.

Notice how in four paragraphs – just a little over 150 words – the writer has answered the basic questions and even put the story into the context of the previous suicides. Interested readers can continue reading for more details; others can move on in the paper, having gotten the gist of the story.

Clear, succinct, informative prose – that's what newswriting is all about.

THE BASIC NEWS STORY

The goal of newswriting is to convey a lot of information efficiently. Journalists do this by using a spare, clean, direct writing style and organizing stories so that readers can get the main points quickly.

Though there are many ways to write a news article, the basic news story often follows a simple formula, known as the inverted pyramid. In this technique the writer presents information in descending order of importance. The most important facts are presented first in the lede – the opening paragraph (the base of the upside-down pyramid). Succeeding paragraphs provide added details (Figure 5.2).

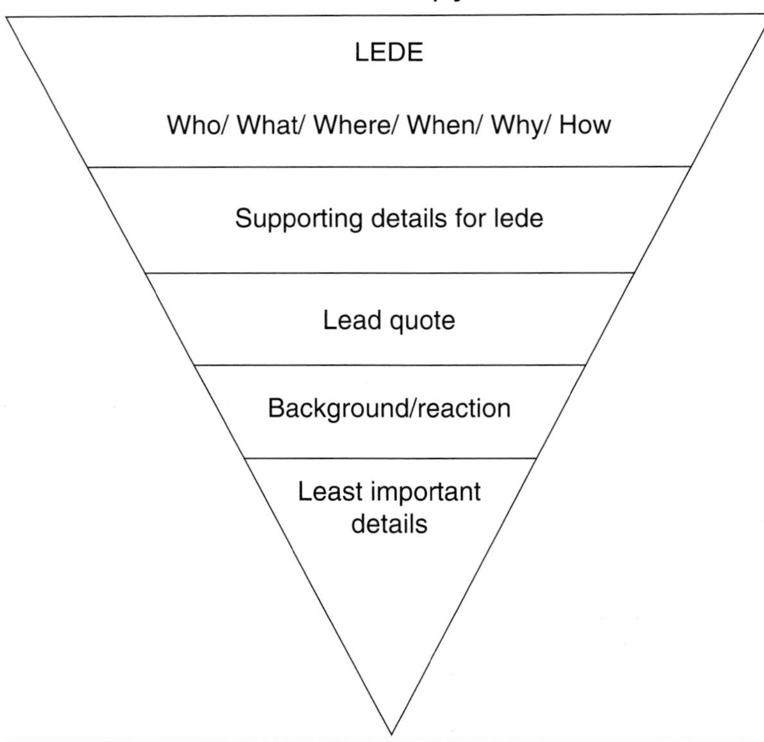

FIGURE 5.2 The inverted pyramid is the traditional form for a news story, with a lede that summarizes the news, followed by less important details in descending order of importance.

The *who, what, where, when, why* and *how* – known as the "five W's and an H" of journalism – are generally answered in the first two or three paragraphs.

An inverted pyramid story usually starts like this:

1 A lede that hooks the reader and captures the essence of the story.

2 A second paragraph that amplifies, or backs up, the lede. This paragraph often explains the impact of the story and answers the "who, what, where, when, why and how" questions not addressed in the lede.

3 A lead quote that augments the lede. It's often the strongest quote of the story and adds a human dimension.

4 A nut graph, a paragraph or two that provides context and tells readers why they should care.

The rest of the story typically includes reaction and background, more quotes and other information in descending order of importance.

Some people call the inverted pyramid old-fashioned, but it actually works well in the age of the Web because online readers often just scan the headline and the first couple of paragraphs of the story. Even if they don't read the article all the way through they will get the gist of a story written in the inverted-pyramid format.

LEDES

The lede of a story is crucial. "Three seconds and the reader decides to read or turn to the next story," Donald M. Murray writes in his book *Writing for Your Readers: Notes on the Writer's Craft from the Boston Globe* (out of print). "That's all the time you have to catch a reader's glance and hold it; all the time you have to entice and inform."

The goals of the lede are to:

Report the essential details of the story

Lure the reader into the story

Make the reader want to read more.

Ledes are generally divided into two categories: hard-news ledes and feature ledes. (Lead is sometimes spelled lede, harkening back to the days when editors wanted to distinguish the beginning of the story from the lead type used in printing.)

Hard-news ledes

A hard-news lede, also known as a summary lede or direct lede, delivers the news immediately:

> The Student Center was evacuated for about an hour Wednesday as a result of a phoned-in bomb threat. It was the second threat made on the building in less than a month.
>
> *THE TEMPLE NEWS* (TEMPLE-NEWS.COM), TEMPLE UNIVERSITY

> Former Northwestern linebacker Braden Jones, who left the university in March after being charged with assaulting and trying to rob a taxi driver, will return to NU as a student and football player this week, he said Monday.
>
> *THE DAILY NORTHWESTERN* (DAILYNORTHWESTERN.COM), NORTHWESTERN UNIVERSITY

> A CSU sorority was quietly ousted from the university in the spring as a result of a campus police investigation that found numerous alleged incidents of hazing, harassment and cruelty that one whistle-blower victim called "torture."
>
> *THE ROCKY MOUNTAIN COLLEGIAN* (COLLEGIAN.COM) COLORADO STATE UNIVERSITY

Feature ledes

A feature lede, also known as a soft lede or delayed lede, takes more of a storytelling approach. It may start with an anecdote or a scene that draws a picture for the reader like these:

> When friends of 2003 College alumnus Arshad Hasan notified him that he was pictured on the cover of this year's commencement brochure, he was initially flattered. But upon closer examination, Hasan and his friends realized that one detail from his costume was missing – the rainbow tassel that had hung beside the standard black tassel from his cap.
>
> Hasan distinctly remembered having the rainbow tassel – distributed by the Lesbian Gay Bisexual Transgender Center to be worn during graduation ceremonies – as part of his academic regalia. He also knew that it was distinct enough that it could not simply be covered up due to the angle of the photograph.
>
> But while University officials in charge of commencement materials have admitted since then that the photograph was edited, they have also said that slight alteration to published images is standard procedure.
>
> *THE DAILY PENNSYLVANIAN* (DAILYPENNSYLVANIAN.COM), UNIVERSITY OF PENNSYLVANIA

> Kevin Costello should have spent last Friday doing what every college freshman does during his or her first couple of weeks at their new campus and home – settling into dorm life, getting to know his classmates and looking forward to the semester ahead.
>
> Instead, Costello's family and friends remembered the 17-year-old in a private memorial along the coast of Monterey Bay, after he died Aug. 31 from serious injuries sustained in an accidental fall in the Marin Headlands.
>
> *GOLDEN GATE [X]PRESS* (GOLDENGATEXPRESS.ORG), SAN FRANCISCO STATE UNIVERSITY

> When John Soloski first arrived at the University in 2001, he couldn't wait to get to his office at the Grady College of Journalism and Mass Communication.
>
> Now he can't wait to leave it.
>
> Every day as the former journalism dean walks alone from his 2002 Toyota 4Runner to Grady College, he

retraces the steps he's taken while fighting the University to clear his name of sexual harassment charges.

THE RED AND BLACK (REDANDBLACK.COM), UNIVERSITY OF GEORGIA

Feature ledes may be several paragraphs long. Because readers don't always know from the start where the story is heading, writers need to provide a nut graph to guide them. A nut graph, or focus graph, explains the point of the story and why readers should care. It should come early in the story, usually in the third to fifth paragraph.

Here's an example of a soft lede and a nut graph from *The Arkansas Traveler* (uatrav.com) at the University of Arkansas:

> When Charles Martin left the UA (University of Arkansas) in 1941 to fly C-87s across the infamous Himalayan passage to China called "The Hump," he was a senior and "president of everything," he said, chuckling as he looked through his UA Razorback yearbook.
>
> Now, while working through UA correspondence courses, he suffers occasional "senior moments" of another type.
>
> "It's so much more difficult now," he said. "I don't know if you know what a senior moment is, but sometimes I have senior moments and it makes taking examinations a lot harder."
>
> Martin, his hair grayed and his 6-foot-2-inch frame bent by arthritis, will walk with the class of 2005 and earn a Bachelor of Arts in Journalism, the degree he started in 1937.

The fourth paragraph, the nut graph, explains why Charles Martin is newsworthy.

Another type of soft lede, sometimes known as a "scene setter," evokes a vivid image.

> It is mid-July, and piles of papers are scattered across the floor and tables of assistant dean of freshman Lesley Nye Barth's Hurlbut Hall apartment. As she sorts through the collection of papers, her cat wanders into the room, stepping on and destroying a few carefully ordered stacks – groups of four roommates that she had spent hours assembling as she culled 550 or so housing applications for the perfect match. The cat's romp sends her back to step one, and she gathers the papers to rematch the students.
>
> Such is the life of the three assistant deans of freshman (ADFs), Lesley Nye Barth, James N. Mancall, and Sue Brown, who spend nearly two-and-a-half months hand-picking rooming groups and then assigning these groups to create entryways.
>
> It's a process that takes hundreds of hours and turns the summer – when most administrators take a relaxing break from the frenetic pace of the school year – into some of the busiest months for the Freshman Deans Office (FDO).

THE HARVARD CRIMSON (THECRIMSON.COM), HARVARD UNIVERSITY

Another popular technique is to use an anecdotal lede, one that employs an anecdote or vignette to illustrate the main point of the story.

Anecdotal ledes work particularly well for trend and issue stories because they bring broad topics or problems down to a personal level. Such ledes must be followed by a nut graph that puts the anecdote into context.

TIPSHEET
Writing ledes

1 **Hard-news ledes are generally short – one sentence or two at the most – and include the most important details.** Writers typically try to limit hard-news ledes to 30 words or fewer so they'll be easy to read.

Example:

Weak lede: The Kansas Board of Regents met yesterday in regular session. The board discussed several issues related to financial aid for students in the state university system and approved a plan that would create a need-based financial aid program for students who do not qualify for Pell grants and whose family income is below the state's median level.

Better lede: The Kansas Board of Regents approved a plan that would create a need-based financial aid program for students who do not qualify for Pell grants and whose family income is below the state's median level.

2 **Don't overdramatize.** Let the facts speak for themselves.

Example:

Weak lede: A construction site turned into a scene of tragedy Monday when a steel beam collapsed at Johnson University, claiming the life of one young

worker and sending five more to the hospital with serious injuries.
Better lede: A steel beam collapsed at a Johnson University construction site, killing one worker and injuring five others.

3 **Ledes generally contain only the most relevant details and should be free of clutter – unimportant details, addresses, ages, times.**
Example:
Weak lede: Northern University faculty members, who have been working without a contract for 52 days and who have held an informational picket every Monday since the semester started, voted overwhelmingly to approve a two-year contract that would increase salaries, backing a deal today by a vote of 265 to 18.
Better lede: Northern University faculty members, who have been working without a contract for 52 days, approved a two-year contract by a vote of 265 to 18.

4 **Leave names out of a news lede unless the person is familiar to your readers.**
Example:
Weak lede: Derek Smith, a freshman engineering major, died in a car accident after a Delta Chi fraternity party late Saturday night.
Better lede: A freshman engineering major died in a car accident after a Delta Chi fraternity party late Saturday night.

5 **Generally put attribution at the end of a lede:**
Example:
Weak lede: A spokesman for Jackson University said the school will establish a liberal arts college in the United Arab Emirates that will be financed entirely by the government there.
Better lede: Jackson University will establish a liberal arts college in the United Arab Emirates that will be financed entirely by the government there, according to a university spokesman.

Steps to writing a story

1 **Review your notes.** Mark key passages you plan to use – statistics, facts, quotes.
2 **Talk through the story.** If possible, discuss the story with an editor, fellow reporter or friend. Talking will often help you understand what's most important or most interesting about the story.
3 **Decide what's most important.** Think about what's most current, what's most interesting, what has the greatest impact.
4 **Write a focus statement.** Ask yourself: What is the story about? How will it affect readers?
5 **Write an outline.** It needn't be formal, but sketch out a roadmap for the story, including facts, quotes, anecdotes and observations you want to include.
6 **Write a draft.** Write it quickly, without worrying too much about style. You can revise and polish later.
7 **Craft the lede.** Make sure the opening is short and punchy, that it captures the essence of the story and makes readers want to read more.
8 **Revise.** Read the story aloud to see how it flows. Then go back and rewrite.
9 **Check your facts.** That includes names and titles, all numbers, addresses, phone numbers, etc.
10 **Turn it in.** Let the editor know you'll be available to do additional reporting and revising.

Indiana Daily Student (idsnews.com) reporter Gavin Lesnick used this approach in 2005 for a story on how Indiana University was taking in student refugees after Hurricane Katrina closed several Gulf Coast universities:

> John Spotts strolled down Bourbon Street last Friday night, about to begin his freshman year at the University of New Orleans. The next morning, Spotts awakened to a city evacuating ahead of Hurricane Katrina and a college education put on hold.
>
> "It actually happened really quickly," said Spotts, a Brownsburg, Ind., native. "Friday night I was walking around the city and Saturday I woke up and evacuated. I drove to Houston and I realized I wasn't going to be back in New Orleans for awhile."

TIPSHEET
Newswriting

1 **Write tight.** Use short sentences, short paragraphs. A good rule on sentences: If you can't say it in one breath, break it into two sentences.

2 **Leave unnecessary details out of the lede.** Street addresses, times, even unfamiliar names, should go lower in the story.

3 **Avoid passive verbs.** Use active verb construction, where the subject is doing something rather than having something done to him, her or it.
Example:
Poor: Last week's allegation of rape on campus was retracted Monday, said a university police spokesman.
Better: A woman who claimed last week she had been raped retracted the story Monday, said a university police spokesman.

4 **Translate jargon.** Interpret bureaucratic, legal, scientific or technical language for readers.

5 **Steer clear of clichés.** Avoid tired, overused phrases. Strive for original language.

6 **Omit unnecessary words.** After writing a story, read through it and see how many words you can take out.

7 **Vary sentence lengths.** Stories become dull when all the sentences are the same length.

8 **Back up your lede and nut graph.** Make sure you provide adequate evidence – quotes, facts, statistics – to prove what you say in the beginning of your story.

9 **Read your lede out loud.** Ask yourself: Does it make you want to read more?

10 **Read your story out loud.** Listen for word repetition, overly long sentences, awkward phrasing.

> Spotts is one of a growing number of students who are transferring to IU from universities forced to close in Katrina's wake. Colleges in Louisiana, Mississippi and Alabama have been shut down for an undetermined time. IU has received calls from at least 25 to 30 families and 10 to 15 students have already begun enrolling, said Registrar Roland Coté.

The third paragraph in this story is a classic nut graph. It explains how John Spotts is part of a trend and why the story is timely and important.

OTHER ELEMENTS OF A NEWS STORY

Once you've crafted a lede, you need to think about what else goes into your story. Most news stories should include some, if not all, of the following elements.

- **Numbers.** Statistics, dimensions, percentages and population figures quantify and give context to a story. How many people does this affect? How big is this new building?
- **History/background.** Historical details put a story into context. What happened in the past? How long has this been going on? What do readers need to know about the past to understand what's happening now?
- **Financial figures**. How much will this cost? What are the financial implications of this policy or program?
- **Reaction**. How are different types of people reacting to this news? Be sure to include a variety of perspectives – students, faculty, staff; opponents and proponents; winners and losers. In many stories, it's also important to tap people of different races, ethnicities, religions, genders and socioeconomic groups.
- **Chronology**. In a story with several developments, it may help to lay out a sequence of events. What happened first? Then what happened? What is expected to happen next?
- **Description**. What do the places, people and things you're writing about look like? Use your senses – sight, taste, touch, smell, hearing – to help you describe what you're reporting on.
- **Impact**. What effect will this news have on people?

In deciding how to order these elements, ask yourself which are the most interesting or most important for the reader to know. Put those elements up high. Then place the less important, less interesting (but still relevant) details lower in the story.

TELLING DETAILS

When writing a news story, you want to look for telling details – facts that add meaning to the story. This story by Mark Dent from *The University Daily Kansan* (kansan.com) at the University of Kansas offers some good examples of telling details:

> The lights go out at 11 p.m., no exceptions, not even for the resident of Unit 7A, cell number 264.
>
> Maybe he could've gotten a break on team curfew in 1996, when he left Kansas as the No. 1 rushing leader in school history. Not anymore. June Henley's turned his lights off at 11 for the last 892 days, the time he's spent at a county jail and at Ross Correctional Institution, a prison located an hour south of

> Columbus, Ohio, where he's two and a half years into a four-year sentence.
>
> They put him here, in the gray slate building behind the 20-foot-tall razor-wire covered fences, for aggravated robbery and burglary. He wears a light blue T-shirt and denim button-up over his softened but still imposing 5-foot-11 240-pound frame, counts a Bible, radio and tiny TV among his few possessions and spends a good portion of his days sitting in his closet-sized cell, staring at the white walls wondering how he got here and what life holds for him when he gets released.

Note how the time of lights out, the unit and cell number of Henley's cell, the exact number of days Henley has been at the prison and the description of his cell together give readers a sense of the confined life he leads. These details were carefully selected by the writer.

This story by Hayley Peterson of *The Red and Black* at the University of Georgia is also packed with meaningful details, in this case dollar amounts:

> On a Tuesday evening in May, University President Michael Adams had a dinner date in Macon with donors.
>
> Adams piled into the University's twin-engine Super King Air 200 turboprop plane with his assistant Mary McDonald, Provost Arnett Mace, Senior Vice President of External Affairs, Tom Landrum and his wife, and external affairs director Greg Daniels, for a 15-minute flight to a city 90 miles from Athens.
>
> At $1,000 an hour, Adams' flight to dinner and back cost $700. But it costs $45 an hour for the pilot and co-pilot's time in the air, and $35 an hour for the plane to sit on the tarmac while the party enjoyed its four-and-a-half-hour dinner.
>
> The grand total for dinner in Macon that Tuesday night in May came to $1,363.64, according to documents obtained by *The Red and Black*.
>
> In one month – from April, 20, 2009 to May 30, 2009 – Adams spent $20,667 on flights. His itinerary included a trip to Destin, Fla., with his wife "to attend SEC meetings and related events," a trip to Valdosta to play in the South Georgia Golf Classic – and to meet with donors – with Mace, Executive Director of Legal Affairs Stephen Shewmaker and Executive Director of the Office of Development Keith Oelke, and a trip to Memphis for the funeral of a family member.

When deciding which details to include and which to leave out, choose bits of information that will help your reader see, hear, feel, taste or smell the scene. Also take note of the surprising or the unusual. If your college president wears a blue suit, it's probably not worth noting, but if he's wearing socks with orange pumpkins on them or a Grateful Dead necktie, put that in your story.

FAIRNESS AND ACCURACY

Every news story should have several sources representing multiple points of view. If you simply interviewed your college president or public information officer about a new master plan for your campus, they'd probably offer a pretty rosy picture of the school's plans for growth. If you also interviewed someone who lives across the street from the campus, you might get a different perspective. If you interviewed three students and four professors and half a dozen neighbors, you'd get a much richer, more complex view of the master plan.

When writing your story, try to get as many points of view as you can and then present a fair and balanced account of what you've found out. If you quote one student who hates the design of the new psychology building, try to find others who like it. If a financial aid officer says the office has streamlined its process of filing applications, talk to several students to see how the new system works.

The more sources you have, the more complete your account will be.

ATTRIBUTION

In academic writing, scholars generally use footnotes to show where they got their information. In newswriting, journalists use attribution.

All quotations, opinions and statements of fact (unless they are commonly known) should be attributed. Here are some examples:

Factual attribution: The crash occurred at 5:29 p.m., according to the National Transportation Safety Board.

Direct quote: "This is an important time for our campus," said Darlene Smith, vice president for student affairs.

Indirect quote/paraphrase: Assistant Coach Jason Peters said the quarterback will not be allowed to play for the team until the case is resolved.

Attribution tells your readers where information is coming from so they can better interpret the news. Any time information in your story comes from a source, and not from your own firsthand observation, it should be attributed.

QUOTES

Quotations from sources add human voices to a newspaper story. Quotes capture emotion, offer varying perspectives and add authority to your stories.

But not just any quote will do. Just as strong quotes can enliven a story, dull quotes can bog it down.

So, what's a good quote? It's vivid, colorful or personal. It expresses a strong opinion (the source's, not necessarily yours). It conveys drama.

When deciding what to quote, listen to the words. Look for quotes that are colorful or original, funny or poignant. The best rule on quoting: If the source says it better than you can, use the quote. If you can say it better – more clearly, more powerfully, more succinctly – paraphrase.

The first quotation in a story is sometimes called the lead quote. The lead quote is usually the strongest quote you have and often sums up the theme or main points of the story or adds a note of emotion, humor or irony.

This story by Elizabeth Cook for *The Minnesota Daily* (mndaily.com) at the University of Minnesota demonstrates the power of a strong lead quote:

> A man convicted of killing a University student in 1997 was executed Thursday.
>
> David Martinez was executed in Huntsville, Texas, for the July 1997 murder of University student Kiersa Paul.
>
> "Only the sky and the green grass goes on forever, and today is a good day to die," Martinez said as his last statement before the lethal injection began.

Some guidelines for using quotes:

Punctuate quotes properly. Start the quote with open quotation marks and close with close quotation marks. Commas and periods always go inside the quotation marks. A question mark goes within the quotation marks if it's part of the quoted material. Otherwise, it goes outside the quotation marks.

Example: She said, "Do you really think that's funny?"

Attribute. Identify the speaker, not just by name but by title or the role the person plays in the story. Put attribution high in the quote, usually after the first sentence.

Example: "We want this team to be the strongest it can be," said Roger Johnson, coach of the women's basketball team. "We're not going to let a few losses get us down."

Make a transition between speakers. Each time you quote a new source you should start a new paragraph. A good way to transition between speakers is by introducing the speaker first and then running the quote like this:

> Junior Sarah Anderson said the college atmosphere helps students hook up without worrying about consequences.
>
> "College students don't feel a societal pressure to commit, which makes a hooking-up lifestyle easier," Anderson said. "It's a fun age to just be able to go out and have fun."
>
> *THE DAILY NORTHWESTERN,*
> NORTHWESTERN UNIVERSITY

Only use quotes you've heard. Don't lift quotes from other news reports; do your own reporting. If you must use a quote from another newspaper, say where you got it.

Example: "Torture is never acceptable, nor do we hand over people to countries that do torture," President Bush said in an interview with *The New York Times*.

Clean up quotes – a little. Journalists frequently disagree about how much to correct quotes. Most agree writers should eliminate "ums" and "ers" and many believe poor grammar should be corrected. If you do make a slight change, use an ellipsis (...) to represent deleted material and put any additional words in brackets [ ]. And make absolutely sure you don't change the sense of a quote. If a quote needs too much correcting, it's best not to use it at all.

Use "said." Don't feel you have to come up with synonyms for "said" in attributing quotes. Verbs like stated, remarked, opined, avowed and declared usually sound stilted or overly formal. Readers generally don't notice repeated use of said.

Keep quotes tight. Don't feel you have to quote long passages from an interview. Look for short, snappy quotes that express the point succinctly.

Save a catchy quote for the ending. A quote often makes a nice kicker, an ending that finishes a story with a climax, surprise, or punch line.

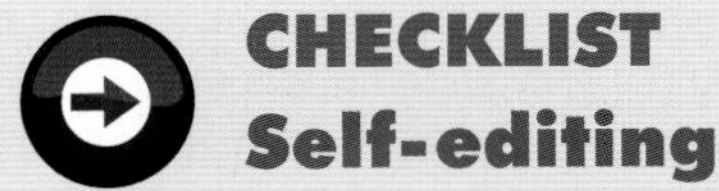

CHECKLIST Self-editing

When writing a news story, ask yourself these questions:

1. Does the lede capture the essence of the story?
2. Is it 30 words or less? If not, can you tighten it?
3. Does the lede entice readers to read more?
4. Is the main idea of the story explained clearly in the lede or the nut graph?
5. Is the story concise? Can you remove any unnecessary words?
6. Do the first few paragraphs of the story answer the who, what, where, when, why and how questions?
7. Are the paragraphs short?
8. Is the writing objective, free of editorializing?
9. Does the story have quotes? Are they properly attributed?
10. Are all the facts right? Are they properly attributed?
11. Are the tenses consistent?
12. Is the story free of spelling, punctuation, grammar problems?
13. Does the story follow the newspaper's style?
14. Are all names in the story spelled right?
15. Are all phone numbers correct? (Check by dialing.)
16. Are all dates and addresses correct?
17. Are all website addresses correct? (Check by going to the website.)

TO DO

1. Look over the ledes in your paper. Are they brief and concise? Do they entice readers into the story? Do they make readers want to learn more? Do the ledes tend to be similar or do they take a variety of approaches?
2. Plan a lede-writing workshop to help your reporters write better ledes. Invite a professional journalist, journalism instructor or one of your staff's best writers to conduct it or just have a group discussion about the ledes in your paper.
3. Set up a buddy system for reporters. Have two reporters talk through stories and read each other's work before turning copy in to their editors.
4. If other media (college newspapers or professional papers, including the *The Chronicle of Higher Education*) cover events and issues you cover, compare the stories. Look at the ledes – which were better and why? What details did each story stress? Are the stories equally fair and balanced?
5. Draft a focus statement for every story you write. This will help you organize your stories and write ledes and nut graphs.

TO READ

Baker, Bob. *Newsthinking: The Secret of Making Your Facts Fall Into Place.* Boston, Mass.: Allyn & Bacon, 2001.

Cappon, Rene J. *The Associated Press Guide to News Writing.* Forest City, Calif.: IDG Books Worldwide, 2000.

Fink, Conrad C. *Writing to Inform and Engage: The Essential Guide to Beginning News and Magazine Writing.* Boulder, Colo.: Westview Press, 2003.

Fox, Walter. *Writing the News: A Guide for Print Journalists, 3rd ed.* Ames: Iowa State University Press, 2001.

Franklin, Jon. *Writing for Story: Craft Secrets of Dramatic Nonfiction.* New York, N.Y.: Plume, 1994.

Goldstein, Norm, ed. *The Associated Press Stylebook and Briefing on Media Law.* Cambridge, Mass.: Perseus Publishing, published annually.

Jackson, Dennis and John Sweeney, eds. *The Journalist's Craft: A Guide to Writing Better Stories.* New York, N.Y.: Allworth Press, 2002.

Kessler, Lauren and Duncan McDonald. *When Words Collide: A Media Writer's Guide to Grammar and Style, 8th ed.* Belmont, Calif.: Wadsworth Publishing, 2011.

Knight, Robert M. *A Journalistic Approach to Good Writing: The Craft of Clarity.* Ames, Iowa: Iowa State University Press, 2003.

LaRocque, Paula. *The Book on Writing: The Ultimate Guide to Writing Well.* Oak Park, Ill.: Marion Street Press, 2003.

Murray, Donald M. *The Essential Don Murray: Lessons from America's Greatest Writing Teacher.* Boynton/Cook Publishers, 2009.

Woods, Keith, Christopher Scanlan, Karen Brown, Don Fry and Roy Peter Clark, eds. *Best Newspaper Writing.* St. Petersburg, Fla.: Poynter Institute and Chicago: Bonus Books. Published annually 1979–2005, published every other year since.

Zinsser, William. *On Writing Well, 30th Anniversary Edition: The Classic Guide to Writing Nonfiction.* New York, N.Y.: Harper Resource, 2006.

TO CLICK

The Power of Words: Weekly lessons on the craft of newspaper writing.

The Power of Words has published writing tips by the staff of *The Providence Journal* almost every week from 1997 to 2004. Though they are no longer updated, there are still a lot of valuable lessons here.

http://www.projo.com/words/past.htm

Poynter Online

The Poynter Institute's website has many resources on writing. Click on the Reporting and Writing tab on the home page.

www.poynter.org

POOL BALL: 'U' water polo club to host conference tournament. **page 8B**

MS&U

The State News

Section

WEDNESDAY
April 7, 2004

¡Salsa!

Sounds and styles from Latin America carry over into Lansing's Metro Bowl where Salsa sways a diverse crowd

By Megan Frye
The State News

It's a well-known fact that the Caribbean clock is not in sync with our tickers in the United States.

Things happen when they happen in this free-spirited lifestyle. The stress-free Caribbean clock carries over to Lansing on Saturday nights.

Saturday night is, and has been for the past two years, salsa night at the Metro Bowl Entertainment & Sports Complex, 5141 S. Martin Luther King Jr. Blvd. in Lansing.

The building houses a bowling alley and multiple bars. Salsa nights are held in a relaxing lounge area with a bar and a dance floor and ample seating.

By 11 p.m., about 50 people are congregated in the lounge, catching up with old friends and making new ones. The music is on, the lights are low and there's a multicolored strobe light hanging from the ceiling. Scents of women's perfume and burning tobacco fill the room, adding a haze to the atmosphere.

Saturday night at the Metro Bowl is the ideal time to witness amazing salsa dancers in action. Many of them have been dancing their entire lives and the ages in the lounge range from 18 to late 60s and early 70s.

Couples hit the dance floor for an intense and exciting dancefest to songs often lasting between six and 10 minutes. On a good night, an average of 50 men and women of all ages, ethnicities and dancing abilities show up to the warm lounge to have the time of their lives.

please see **SALSA**, page 2B

▲ Rosa Quinones dances with Marino Martec on Saturday night at the Metro Bowl Entertainment and Sports Complex. The pair came from Grand Rapids for the Latin dancing hosted at the Lansing club.

◄ Dancers fill the floor Saturday night at the Metro Bowl Entertainment and Sports Complex, 5141 S Martin Luther King Jr. Blvd in Lansing.

Photos by Megan Spelman
THE STATE NEWS

1 • 2 • 3 • salsa

Salsa is danced in eight beats, with stress on the even beats. On the even beats, dancers shift their weight, and on the odd beats, they break (split their feet apart). The leader usually starts with the right foot and, after four beats, repeats the steps with the left. Here are the basic salsa steps (advanced salsa dancers can embellish them):

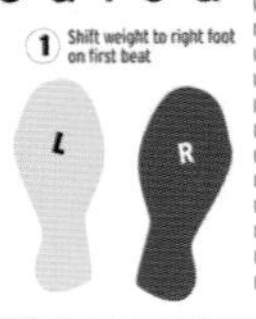

1 Shift weight to right foot on first beat

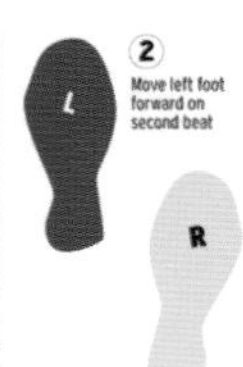

2 Move left foot forward on second beat

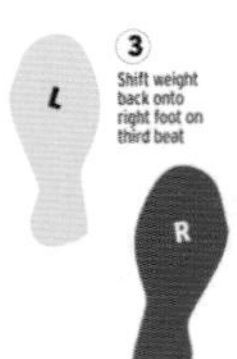

3 Shift weight back onto right foot on third beat

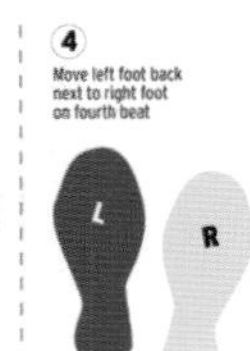

4 Move left foot back next to right foot on fourth beat

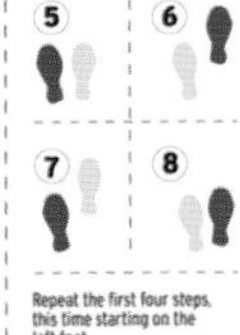

Repeat the first four steps, this time starting on the left foot

Source: http://www.geocities.com/Broadway/Orchestra/3202/salsa_patterns.htm

Nick Mrozowski/The State News

A.P. KRYZA

Classes create another stakes game when dealer holds Scantrons in deck

I am a compulsive gambler, perhaps even a gambling junkie. But I don't know how to shoot craps. I can't tell you the difference between Caribbean Stud and Texas Hold 'Em. I don't get comped drinks, nor do I wager money.

I gamble on standardized testing, my definition of which is any test that relies on Scantrons and multiple choices. Any test that has no personality, where the outcome could very well hinge on the professor's word choice, good or bad, time of day and luck of the draw.

The incentives for gambling on standardized testing are so sweet.

Have you ever had a class where you take five tests and get to drop the lowest score? Or one where you take three tests, and if you're happy with your grade, you don't have to take a final? It gets me feeling lucky every time.

The train of thought that goes down is frighteningly irresponsible; it's a cross between apathy, laziness and optimism. "Okay. Test one is in a month, so I'll hold off on buying the book and take the test based on the notes. That way, instead of buying $100 worth of books I'll forget within three hours of reading and selling them back for $15 worth of beer money, I can invest it ALL toward beer. Plus, if I do good, it means I can do good without the extra reading."

Three weeks later …

"Okay, test is in a week, need to get the notes. Naw, let's just wing it on what I learned in class. That way, I can see just what I can get away with."

Test one comes and goes, and I find I've done pretty well. I knew when to hold 'em, knew when to fold 'em and when to flip a coin. Now I'm on top.

Test two, same deal, worse grade. Test two is the dropped grade and the signal to cash in your chips and take a better approach — maybe earn the grade by reading and analyzing. "Flash cards, gotta get some flash cards. Maybe I'll study with the girl in front of me, she seems smart."

But the dealer, the guy in front of the class with the lesson plan, wants you to keep playing the game and he throws you a marker by curving the exam. Suddenly, test two's score is better than test one, and it's back to throwing caution to the wind.

Each gambler has his own style, but mine works well to

please see **KRYZA**, page 2B

Elysia A. Smith MS&U editor • **phone** (517) 355-8252 • **fax** (517) 353-2599 • **e-mail** MSandU@statenews.com

FIGURE 6.1 Lifestyle pages should capture the passions of your readers and bring graphics, photos and text together into an enticing package. *The State News*, Michigan State University.

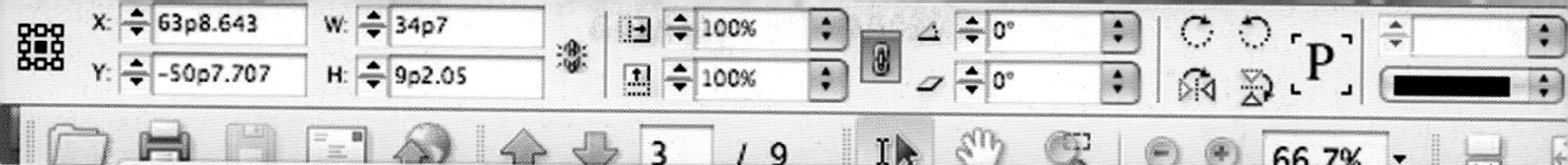

CHAPTER 6 THE LIFESTYLE PAGES

"What to do with the roommate from hell."
"The price of partying."
"Queer eye for the Greek guy."

Perhaps more than any other section, the lifestyle pages in a student newspaper should be relevant, edgy and fresh.

Don't simply look to the big daily newspaper in town for ideas; you don't want stories about home decorating or how to plan for retirement.

Your lifestyle coverage should capture the obsessions, frustrations, gripes and passions of your student population. For possible models, look to your favorite magazines or alternative weeklies. Better yet, look and listen around you. You should be writing about the things people talk about in dorm rooms and cafeterias, at parties and in the laundry room.

The Student Newspaper Survival Guide, Second Edition. Rachele Kanigel.

CHAPTER CONTENTS

YOUNG BLOOD: Spartans hockey team signs 5 new recruits for next season. **page 6B**

Prof reflects on past ties to eco-underworld

Check out next week's Faces & Places for more on MSU's encounters with environmental terrorism.

TOPSY-TURVEY: *Much-debated skatepark might face more changes*

FIGURE 6.2 The weekly "Faces and Places" section in *The State News* offers in-depth coverage of the people and places that make Michigan State University unique. *The State News*, Michigan State University.

LIFESTYLE COVERAGE

Lifestyle, or feature, stories may be light, frothy pieces about fads and fashions or serious and insightful ones about such weighty issues as date rape, binge drinking or suicide. The best newspapers make room for both.

The State News (statenews.com) at Michigan State University, for example, produces a daily "MS&U" page with a mix of lifestyle and entertainment coverage. On Tuesdays the paper runs "Faces & Places," a weekly section devoted to in-depth feature stories and photos Figure 6.2). "The section tries to capture the character of MSU and its community," says Perry Parks, former editorial adviser to the newspaper. "The students try to do stories that branch out, ones that don't quite fit into the other features sections."

The Daily Illini (dailyillini.com) at the University of Illinois has themed feature pages. Tuesday is "Business and Technology," Wednesday is "Health and Living," and Thursday is "Greeks and Campus." "Our school is known for our engineering and science departments, it's a Big Ten university and it has one of the largest Greek systems in the country," says Melissa Silverberg, who was editor-in-chief when the paper started the themed pages. "These topics seemed to really draw in a readership – and an ad base we had been missing before."

Lifestyle pages shouldn't limit themselves to straight text stories. "A relevant, hip college features section must include alternative storytelling: lists, Q&As, first-person squibs, '5 minutes with' shorts, the list goes on," says Alicia Roberts, who became features editor for *The State* in Columbia, S.C., after working on *The Flyer News* (flyernews.com) at the University of Dayton. "Think of your favorite magazine; it usually has a handful of meaty stories and a raft of short, easily digestible items. Features sections should be planned the same way."

TYPES OF LIFESTYLE STORIES

Whether they run in a designated lifestyle section or on the front page, feature stories usually fall into one of several categories.

- **Profiles**–feature stories about a particular person.
- **Trend features**–stories that capture a trend, such as an increase in foreign students, or a fad, like sexting or clothes swapping.

- **Service features**–how-to where-to-go or what-to-do stories that provide a service to your readers.
- **First-person accounts**–stories in which the writer shares his or her own experiences.

Features linked to a news event are called news features. Other timely pieces may hang on a holiday, season or cultural happening. Stories without a time peg are known as evergreens because they can run any time. A good features editor always has a few evergreen stories on tap in case another story falls through.

Profiles

Profiles are a great way to humanize your coverage and bring people to your pages. Some newspapers have a regular spot for profiles. *The Otter Realm* (otterrealm.net) at California State University, Monterey Bay, for example, has used its back page for "Artist Spotlight," a full-page profile of a student in the arts. One semester, the page focused on visual artists and included photographs of their art pieces; the scope was later expanded to include student musicians, dancers, actors and other artists.

Other newspapers regularly profile interesting professors or staff members.

Profiles needn't be told in straight prose. Q&As and list formats also work well. *The Auburn Plainsman* (theplainsman.com) at Auburn University has run a regular feature called "Joe/Jane Random," a Q&A with a random student on campus. Questions include: What's your favorite place in the world? What's the best advice you've ever received? What was your most embarrassing moment? What's the easiest class you've taken?

The Simpsonian (thesimpsonian.com) at Simpson College in Indianola, Iowa, has run a weekly feature called "The FlipSide," a "Dewar's Profile"-style piece on a student, faculty or staff member that lists the subject's favorite movie, food, drink, motto, etc. "These stories are very well-received by our readers," says Brian Steffen, former faculty adviser to the newspaper.

CHECKLIST Profile writing

A profile is a portrait of a person drawn in words. When writing a profile, ask yourself these questions:

1. Does the lede entice readers into the story? Does it capture the essence of the story?
2. Does the profile include a graphic physical description of the person?
3. Are the quotes vivid and telling?
4. Does the story include anecdotes – little vignettes or stories – about the person?
5. If there is a news peg for the feature (the subject recently won an award or is the person at the center of a current controversy), is it clearly and prominently stated?
6. Does the profile include observations of the subject in different environments (at home, at work, at play, at school)?
7. Does it include observations and comments about the subject from other people (family members, friends, co-workers, etc.)?
8. Does the profile include age and relevant background material about the subject's life (where the person grew up and currently lives, schools, jobs, past accomplishments)?
9. Does the story include information that will be new or surprising to readers?
10. Does the profile offer a well-rounded view of the person, including personality flaws and failures, as well as successes?

Trend stories

Are toga parties back in vogue? Are more students studying Arabic than ever before? Are ballet slippers or flip-flops or belly button rings or charm bracelets all the rage? Trend stories capture fads, fashions and, well, trends.

The best way to spot a trend is to look and listen around you. What are people wearing, doing, talking about? What's hip? What's new? What's different?

When a hookah bar opened in the college town of Chico, California, Ashley Nelson, staff writer for *The Orion* (theorion.com) at the California State University campus there, wrote a story on the Middle Eastern water pipes for the features section. It began:

> When you hear students talking about a load of shisha, they're not talking dirty, they're talking hookah.
>
> Taking a hit of the 'hubbly-bubbly' has become one of the latest crazes around college campuses, and Chico is no exception.
>
> With the smokin' opening of Café Nile at 243 W. Ninth St., students can sit down, relax and buy a load off the latest hookah lounge in town.

Nelson did her research. The story went on to include the history of hookahs, comments from one of the café's owners and even health information about the risks of hookah smoking. Colorful illustrations and interesting graphic packaging made the story appealing (see Figure 6.3).

When writing a trend story, try to track down statistics that capture the phenomenon. If, for example, you're writing a story about the bhangra dance craze, it would be impossible to find out how many people on your campus do bhangra dancing. However, you can ask local Indian dance teachers if they've had more interest in their classes and find out if ethnic music clubs are doing more bhangra events.

And with the Internet it's easy to find publications, associations and trade groups associated with virtually any hobby, business or health condition you can think of. Such groups can often provide just the statistics you seek.

FEATURESONLINE
www.orion-online.net

INSIDE
Bella's Sports Pub D2
Earth Haven Institute D3
Powers of being profs D5

» CRUISING ACROSS CAMPUS D2

» GREAT GARDENS D5

FEATURES

D
Wednesday
April 27, 2005

Kelly Parker
Features Editor

ET CETERA

Under the weather

Being sick sucks.

I usually only get really sick about once a semester, but I've been lucky enough to get struck by the dreaded Cold of Death twice this semester. And the illness always seems to hit at the worst possible times.

No, it would be too convenient to get sick during the part of the semester when there's a nice lull in all the tests and papers and projects due.

Clearly, my body just hates me and wants me to flunk out of my last semester with only four weeks left.

I can't afford to miss any more class, and I can't call in sick to my jobs because I would just feel too damn guilty. Not to mention that here at The Orion, I'm not even sure calling in sick is an option. Looks like my co-workers will just have to breath in my germy goodness for a while.

Surely I can suffer through in a cold-medicine haze.

Maybe I'll be too doped up on drugs to really understand what my teacher is talking about, but I can at least pretend like I'm functional.

I'm just kicking myself now for all the times I used up one of my freebie absences for no good reason.

I just can't win when I'm sick. I can go about my normal business because I don't want to get too far behind and risk making everyone around me sick as well, or I can shut myself up in my room for days and emerge feeling better, but more stressed out than ever.

You know, the worst part about being sick when you're an adult is that there's no mommy and daddy to take care of you anymore.

I'm forced to take my own temperature, make my own soup and fetch myself more Kleenex.

Plus, I hate going to the doctor. It takes 10 years to get seen by an actual doctor, and in the time I've been sitting in the waiting room, Lord knows how many other germs I've breathed in from the other sickies in there, only prolonging my illness, I'm sure.

And at my age, I don't even get a lollipop anymore for being brave. Guess what, doc? Going to the doctor at any age is scary.

So I did it. I wrote a whole column while high on DayQuil.

And I've managed to create a pretty impressive mountain of used Kleenex.

Kelly can be reached at
featureseditor@orion-online.net

RANDOM LAWS

- In Nevada, it is illegal to drive a camel on the highway.
- In New Mexico, state officials ordered 400 words of "sexually explicit material" to be cut from Romeo and Juliet.

SMOKE ON THE NILE

ASHLEY NELSON
Staff Writer

When you hear students talking about a load of shisha, they're not talking dirty, they're talking hookah.

Taking a hit of the "hubbly-bubbly" has become one of the latest crazes around college campuses, and Chico is no exception.

With the smokin' opening of Café Nile at 243 W. Ninth St., students can sit down, relax and buy a load off the latest hookah lounge in town.

In addition to an impressive array of coffees and teas, Café Nile also provides 15 fruity flavors of hookah tobacco. Each type allows customers to experience everything from pineapple to mint to apricot or cherry, all the while sitting outside and breathing in the sweet smell of the shisha tobacco.

For $7, a four-person load will last about 45 minutes. And for couples that really have time to burn, a load for two can last up to an hour.

For those who don't know what the heck hookah is and what the hoopla is all about, it's a water pipe of Middle Eastern and African origin dating back hundreds of years. A long tube passes through an urn of water, and cools the smoke as it's drawn. The pipes, which are large and usually made of decorated glass, are used to smoke fruit-flavored tobacco or smokable dried fruit. (And if there's still any confusion, one can always turn to an old tape of "Alice in Wonderland" and watch for the contraption that the caterpillar smokes from.)

While people on the other side of the world have used it for centuries, hookah is just starting to get hot in Western culture.

"It's really a huge hype right now," said Amie Lucas, one of Café Nile's four owners. "Just in the last three or four years it's started to get as popular as coffee shops, especially around colleges."

But this cozy Internet café has much more to

please see HOOKAH | D3

Illustration by Shawna Kirby

Interns gain experience, fun from jobs

MARIA DAVALOS
Staff Writer

Internships that require power suits and remembering if your boss takes cream with his coffee are a thing of the past.

As the season of summer internship applications heats up, the Chico State Internship Center is helping students obtain jobs with organizations like the Sacramento Kings, PepsiCo Inc. and Lucas Films.

More than 1,000 companies are entered into the center's job-placement database. Chico State juniors, seniors and graduate students who have a GPA of 2.5 or better are eligible to apply for part- or full-time positions.

Though only about 65 percent are paid internships, Internship Center Director William Lerch said he encourages students to apply.

Students can learn so much with the hands-on experience, Lerch said.

"Even though sometimes you don't get paid, the experience will help in the future," he said.

About 600 of the internships available are offered in California. Others are in Boston, New York, Chicago and overseas. Currently, there are three Chico State students preparing to take internships out of the country–two marketing majors are traveling to Australia and a public

please see INTERN | D5

The Orion • BRIAN KENNEDY

Kelly Campbell, an intern at the Barry R. Kirshner Wildlife Foundation, cleans up some old meat while Chaffy, a white bengal tiger, keeps an eye on things Thursday. Campbell gets 13 units for her internship.

WORD OF MOUTH:

Have you ever smoked out of a hookah?

"Yeah. It was as much fun as smoking out of any other smoking device."
—Matt Martin
Senior
Music

"No, I don't like smoking at all."
—Vanessa Garcia
First year
Business management

"Yeah. I don't know, I like it, socialize with people."
—Nolan Pevone
Senior
Recreation

"I'm a kinesiology student. I definitely wouldn't recommend that."
—Ryan Locklin
Graduate student
Kinesiology

FIGURE 6.3 When a hookah bar opened in the college town of Chico, California, Ashley Nelson, staff writer for *The Orion* at California State University, Chico wrote a story on the Middle Eastern water pipes for the features section. Colorful illustrations and interesting graphic packaging made the story appealing. *The Orion*, California State University, Chico. Illustration by Shawna Kirby.

Service features

Where can you take a date for dinner for under twenty bucks? How should you prepare for a semester abroad? How do you get into the most elite sororities and fraternities? What are some ways to reduce stress around final exams?

Service features offer expert advice and useful tips on meeting the challenges of life.

To come up with service feature ideas think about the challenges you face as a student. If you're trying to think of something novel to do with your sweetie on Valentine's Day, write a story about offbeat ways to celebrate the holiday. If you've discovered some ways to divide household chores among your roommates, share them with your readers.

As with trend stories, the key to a good service feature is research. If you're doing a story about reducing stress, don't just ask five random students how they cope with tension. Talk to experts. Interview a psychology professor who has written a book on stress. Look for research studies on stress reduction. Sit in on a meditation or yoga class on campus, and follow up by interviewing the teacher and some of the students. The more thorough your research, the more useful your story will be.

First-person accounts

Unlike news stories, features occasionally use first person. When should you use this more personal writing style? When you've got a unique perspective on the story.

Take Thor Nystrom, a former student at the University of Kansas. He rarely told people about his struggle with Attention Deficit Hyperactivity Disorder and mental illness but in his last year of school, after emerging from a period of anxiety, depression, extreme weight gain, suicidal thoughts and other side effects of medications, he decided to write about his experiences for *The University Daily Kansan*. Using his own medical records, police records, his diaries, interviews with family and his own recollections, he pieced together a poignant first-person account of his descent into what he called the "depths of hell."

The piece, which in 2008 won first place in the feature-writing category for *Rolling Stone* magazine's annual College Journalism Competition, was graphic and illuminating, shining a light into the world of mental illness and psychiatric medications. After the story was published Nystrom received more than 100 emails from readers. "Oh my God, it was amazing," Nystrom said in an interview with *The University Daily Kansan* after winning the *Rolling Stone* contest. "I didn't get one negative comment. It was validation that I had written it the way I needed to."

That's the kind of story that warrants first-person writing.

Often, though, first-person writing is simply a crutch. Think about whether you have something extra to offer the reader. If you don't, stick to third person.

FINDING AN ANGLE

College newspapers often write about the plagues of young adulthood – drug addiction, credit card debt, eating disorders, abortion. These are interesting and important topics for college students and absolutely appropriate fodder for a college newspaper.

However, these stories can often sound like generic term papers on social problems. The trick is to find a fresh angle.

Recent statistics or research studies will often provide such an angle. News events are even better. When a 21-year-old student at California State University, Chico died in a fraternity hazing incident, student newspapers (as well as professional papers) around the country wrote about hazing in their communities. A rash of suicides at New York University prompted student papers to explore the issue of student suicide.

If there's no news to peg a feature to, prowl the Web looking for organizations, news stories and published research that may help you find a fresh angle. Look for experts on your campus by asking the public affairs office, checking your school's online database of experts or talking to professors in related departments. With each potential source, look for something new. Is there a new treatment for this condition? Is a professor doing research on this topic? Are police seeing an increase or decrease in reports of this type of crime?

REPORTING THE FEATURE STORY

Whether it's a light story about the newest craze in body piercing or a serious piece on date rape, lifestyle stories must be thoroughly reported. You should talk to as many sources as possible and gather multiple points of view. If you're writing about a new online service for matching roommates, don't just talk to one set of roommates. Interview as many as you can find. It's best if you can come up with examples showing the plusses and minuses of such services. If there are multiple roommate matching services that serve your school, mention several of them, exploring their advantages and weaknesses.

In lifestyle stories, sensory detail is vital. You want your reader to be able to hear the whir of the tattoo wand, smell the coffee the professor is drinking, feel the spinning clay on the potter's wheel in the ceramics studio. In-person interviews where you can observe your sources and collect sensory information are best. Go beyond simply interviewing and observing. Spend a few minutes – or better yet a few hours – watching, listening, smelling, tasting. Take careful notes.

STRUCTURING THE FEATURE STORY

Many established writers use a writing technique developed by former *Wall Street Journal* reporter William E. Blundell, who immortalized it in *The Art and Craft of Feature Writing* (Penguin, 1988), still a classic decades after it was published.

Blundell divides the feature story into four main parts:

1. **The lede (or introduction)** for the article is usually about one to three paragraphs long and often starts with an anecdote. In writing this kind of opening it's vital that the anecdote captures not just a random scene or story but illustrates the main point you are trying to make.
2. **The nut graph**, sometimes called the "so-what" graph, explains in a nutshell what your entire article is about. Blundell calls it "the main theme statement, the single most important bit of writing I do on any story."
3. **The main body** of the article consists of several blocks, each representing a different aspect of the main story. Drive home each point you are trying to make with examples, anecdotes, quotes and statistics. Make sure paragraphs flow smoothly from one to another.
4. **The conclusion** is something that ends your story with a punch. A catchy quote or an ending scene can either sum up your story or reinforce its central message.

SEX AND RELATIONSHIPS COLUMNS

It's hard to say if Carrie Bradshaw, the fictional columnist of *Sex and the City*, spawned them, but sex columns have become a staple of 21st century college newspapers. Daniel Reimold, author of the book *Sex and the University: Celebrity, Controversy and a Student Journalism Revolution* (Rutgers University Press, 2010), estimates about 20 to 25 percent of college newspapers run sex columns at any given time. "Literally, as recently as 15 years ago they didn't exist and now they're a mainstay of many larger and some smaller college publications," says Reimold, who teaches at the University of Tampa, where he advises *The Minaret* (theminaretonline.com).

Reimold believes sex and relationships columns serve an important role in college publications. "These columns are tackling worthwhile issues," he says. "They're dealing with an area of news that has largely been ignored by the professional press."

From "The Bed Post" in *The Towerlight* (thetowerlight.com) at Towson University to "Sex on Tuesday" in the University of California, Berkeley's *Daily Californian* (dailycal.org), these columns have raised eyebrows around the country.

In a number of cases, they've also raised the hackles of campus officials.

In 2005, the editor of *The Campus Communicator* (cravenccnews.com) at Craven Community College in North Carolina, cancelled the paper's sex column, "Between the Sheets," after getting complaints from readers and administrators. In 2009, the editor of *The Towerlight* resigned under pressure after the university's president publicly condemned the paper for publishing an anonymous column about masturbation.

But sex columns don't always lead to calamity. Lena Chen parleyed her *Sex and the Ivy* blog about her sexcapades at Harvard into a successful freelance writing career. She continues to write about sexuality for *The Boston Globe Magazine* and SexReally.com, a project of the National Campaign To Prevent Teen and Unplanned Pregnancy.

One defense for writing a sex and relationships column is to keep it educational. That means doing real research – scouting for studies, reading books on sexuality, interviewing experts (scientific researchers and therapists, not just the Casanova down the hall). A number of universities have sexuality research centers on campus. (see resources list at the end of this chapter.)

Reimold offers these tips for sex and relationship columnists:

1. **Be yourself and stick with what you know.** "A lot of criticism that's coming down on students – I think unfairly – is that they're supposed to be sexperts," Reimold says. "There's this expectation that the students have some sort of formal qualification or expertise to talk about sex. The best columnists I've seen are the opposite. They're ordinary students stuck

TIPS FROM THE PROS Debby Herbenick and Jennifer Bass

Want to write a sex column but don't know where to start? Running out of ideas for topics? Wondering where to get quality information? The Kinsey Institute, which publishes the syndicated sex Q&A column, *Kinsey Confidential*, offers these tips on writing sex and relationships columns.

1 **DO be clear about your goal for the column.** Is it to provide information? Advice? Entertainment? Or some combination of these?

2 **DO search for accurate, research-based information.** Thanks to the Internet, it's possible to search online in a range of professional, scholarly journals. You can find these through your campus library, Ovid, EBSCOhost or http://scholar.google.com.

3 **DO use clear language and specify behaviors.** For example, "having sex" may not mean the same thing to all of your readers.

4 **DON'T assume the gender or sexual orientation of readers.** For example, if a woman writes in asking how to perform oral sex on her partner, don't presume that her partner is a man.

5 **DO ask professionals with expertise in public health, medicine or psychology to review your column.** Sexual health is an important area of life that many students struggle with, and accurate information can be tough to come by.

6 **DON'T sacrifice accurate information for a laugh.** Respect the fact that your newspaper's column may be some students' only source of sex education.

7 **DON'T use the column for the sake of self-exposure.** Yours is a forum for ideas and information, not exhibitionism.

8 **DO refer to resources for additional information.** A website with reference links is a good addition to any column. For suggested references, see the list at the end of this column.

9 **DO strive for a balance between accurate information and interesting writing.** Accurate information is only useful if students actually *read* the column.

10 **DO have fun with the column!** Sexuality is often portrayed exclusively through a lens of disease and difficulty. Let's not forget how pleasurable sexuality can be.

To learn more about the *Kinsey Confidential* column and how to syndicate it to your student newspaper, email Kinsey@indiana.edu.

As a sexual health educator at The Kinsey Institute, Debby Herbenick, Ph.D, M.P.H., writes the *Kinsey Confidential* column and hosts the affiiliated podcasts. She is also a research scientist at Indiana University and author of *Because It Feels Good: A Woman's Guide to Sexual Pleasure and Satisfaction* (Rodale Books, 2009).

Jennifer Bass, M.P.H., is communications director at The Kinsey Institute.

Q&A Josie Roberts

JOSIE ROBERTS started making newspapers in second grade, when she created the *Peters Creek Press* on primitive fax paper and tucked it behind all her neighbors' mailbox flags. She's never stopped reporting. At the University of Virginia, she served as life editor (2000–01) and assistant managing editor (2002) of *The Cavalier Daily* (cavalierdaily.com). After an internship with National Public Radio in Washington, D.C., she landed her first paid job in Niagara Falls, New York with the Greater Niagara Newspaper chain and later worked for the *Pittsburgh Tribune-Review*.

What did you get out of your college newspaper experience?

Working on my college paper helped me develop a voice and work quickly on deadline. By editing other people's stories, I learned to see the holes in my own. Writers often get wrapped up in the details and forget to give the reader a straightforward, one-sentence summary of what the story is about (often called the "nut graph," or it could be considered your thesis statement). I make sure I always put these three or four paragraphs into my story so the reader is comfortable and isn't still asking "What's this story about?" on the jump page.

What do you know now that you wish you had known when you were on your college newspaper?
That paid circulation is much harder to achieve than a free newspaper passed out to students! Also, that if you want a job in this industry, you need to hammer the cops and breaking news stories to be taken seriously by employers. Features can be a great outlet, but no rookie college grad is going to land a general-assignment lifestyle or entertainment position. You have to pay your dues.

What can student newspapers do to make their features and lifestyle stories more relevant and interesting to readers?
Pull them to the front page. If you think features should only be confined to the features page, you're only writing fluff. Feature writing gives stories room to breathe. They're the crucial articles that uncover trends that don't happen overnight, that won't be in a breaking news article, but tell us something important about the world we live in. Think of features like enterprise articles, or news articles written in a narrative style. Don't pigeonhole them as fashion articles, celebrity news and quirky profiles.

A strong feature would be about students using Ritalin to stay up late and study for exams – why is this happening, where do they get the prescription, what are the dangers, how prevalent is it? Just because there's a news angle, doesn't mean it can't be approached as a feature. This would be one to plant as the centerpiece on the front page.

What kinds of stories would you want to see in a student newspaper lifestyle/features section?
I think the features should mine the pulse of the campus. In 10 years, if someone picks up an old issue of the newspaper, it will be less important who won the student council election and more important that you catalogued the trends on campus, the attitudes of the students, the political swayings, the unique quirks that made that year so distinct. It's like a cultural study. I always say that you should look at the lifestyle pages as entries to a time capsule.

What advice do you have about finding and writing personality profiles?
Talk to your friends – you're surrounded by interesting people on campus. *The Washington Post* once did a story where the reporter hammered six nails into a phone book and profiled the people where the nails stopped. It was fascinating and proved that everyone has a story.

Don't overquote. Use details. Make the person's character come out.

Any tips for finding trend stories?
Look around you. When you have an idea, write it down right then. Otherwise, you will forget it. And trust your instinct. If you think something is interesting, pitch it to the editor. If it caught your eye, it probably will catch others' too.

We once did a "reporters' challenge" where four teams (two reporters and a photographer each) met at 9 a.m. at a central location, ventured north, south, east and west, and had to have a story and photos in by 9 p.m. We were forced to find stories in everyday situations and found some of our strongest features by just talking to a bakery owner out in the countryside and interviewing people passing through our town at a rest stop.

Any other advice for college newspaper reporters or editors?
Get an internship at a *daily* paper.

Get a second internship in another medium like radio, television or the Internet. Media is becoming mass media and the next generation of journalists will have to do it all.

Finally, read, read, read. Read *The New York Times*. Read *The Washington Post*. Read *Smithsonian* magazine. Read *People*. Read everything.

in the college quagmire of love and lust. A lot of the great columnists ask questions and readers respond because they see the person is like them."

2 **Be prepared for criticism.** When you're writing about a touchy subject like sex, there's bound to be controversy. Reimold suggests columnists think carefully about the possible ramifications of what they write. "You should have a surefire explanation ready of why you're doing what you're doing," he says.

3 **Consider writing anonymously or under a pseudonym.** This may go against your newspaper's policies but it's something columnists and editors should discuss. In interviewing dozens of sex columnists from student newspapers, Reimold found that many later regretted writing under their own name. "They're not ashamed of their work but they found the Google prints can be nasty. If you write a popular sex column, your name will pop up pretty high on a Google search. That may not be the first thing you want people to know about you when you're

Confessions of a sex columnist **Jessie Gardner**

I've been stopped in the street, pointed at, whispered about, hit on and hollered at. In the small, middle-of-nowhere town of Chico, Calif., with just over 70,000 people and a university where everyone knows your name and 15,000 students binge with pride, even the average student can find it hard to go unnoticed.

I volunteered to write a weekly sex column for the school's award-winning newspaper, *The Orion*. I crossed my fingers hoping the community would enjoy reading about all the times I uncrossed my legs.

Every Wednesday, I taught 20-somethings how it was, how it could be, how it is, and of course, how it should be. Every day, as I strolled through campus, almost everyone passing by knew my sexual resumé. I revealed things I hadn't even told my best friends about. Oscar-worthy fake orgasms, threesomes, dentist chairs, home videos, vibrators, oral sex and back doors – nothing was too hot for me to handle.

Gaining celebrity status in such a small town was quite an adventure. Within the first 10 weeks I managed to make a name for myself as "the sex girl." And once I realized that my audience reached far beyond the town of Chico, that's when it really climaxed. Imagine your parents knowing all your sexual experiences – in print. Weird.

It's funny how it happened. I wasn't a writer and I didn't study journalism; I was a graphic design major.

I was the art director of *The Orion* and just happened to be around when the editorial staff were throwing around the idea of adding a sex column. With the recent prevalence of sex columns in college newspapers throughout the nation, it sounded like a great idea.

So one night in September 2003, I fell asleep an average college student and woke up a "sexpert."

Some moments were a little creepy, like going to a party and finding my picture cut out of the newspaper and hung on the refrigerator. Or when the person next to me in class would be reading my column and look up at me, then back down at the picture and up again, realizing that there I was, in the flesh, while reading about my anal sex preferences.

But it was the emails that shocked me the most. One person blamed me for AIDS and cultural decay, while others actually thought I would call and have sex with a complete stranger because they sent me their number. Just because I wrote a sex column didn't mean I was easy.

A few of my ex-boyfriends got mad after they read the column and found out I didn't mean it when I said "I love you, too." And some got back in touch with me after they learned how I felt about sex with an ex.

I wasn't sure how being the sex columnist would affect my sex life, but it made it better. I didn't even know it could get any better. My text messages got steamier and I found new ways to make sex fun outside of the bedroom.

Even though my parents were mortified, other women were resentful and ex-boyfriends sent me hate mail, it felt so good to be naked – stripped of society's baggage and free to own my sexuality and share it with anyone who wanted to read about it.

In college, there's a lot to deal with. School, stress, work, roommates, relationships and, yes, sex. There was a lot of it going on where I went to school, and not many sexually active college students are willing to be open about it, so why not write a sex column, address the issue and encourage a healthy sexual lifestyle?

JESSIE GARDNER was the sex columnist for *The Orion*, the weekly newspaper at California State University, Chico, from September 2003 to May 2004. During her four years with *The Orion* she also served as designer and art director. She graduated in 2004 with a degree in communication design. She now lives in Reno, Nevada where she works as a designer for Primo Advertising.

applying for a job or grad school or going out on a first date."

4 **Branch out to related topics.** A sex column does not have to be solely about the act itself. Dating, relationships, friendships, socializing and sexual health should all have a place in this kind of column.

5 **Don't glorify sex.** "The stereotype is that every student sex columnist is Samantha Jones," Reimold says, referring to the sex-crazed character on *Sex and the City*. "The truth is the best columnists are more like Carrie Bradshaw. They're a bit more cautious. You don't need to promote sex; you can offer a cautionary tale every now and then."

TO DO

1. Organize a features brainstorming session for your lifestyle staff (if you work for a small paper without a dedicated features staff, put together a group of reporters, editors and designers or even invite the whole staff). Start with a particular question like: "What's hard about being a student?" or "What are the best things about this school?" or "What's frustrating about going to school here?"
2. Come up with a theme for a standing feature or column for your lifestyle section. It could be student-artist-of-the-week or professor-of-the-week profile or some kind of tips list (such as a weekly 10 best – the 10 best places to kiss on campus, the 10 best classes, the 10 best places for a first date, etc.)
3. Designate at least one designer to focus on your lifestyle section. Make sure that person comes to meetings, including lifestyle staff brainstorming sessions and editorial budget meetings.
4. Look for service feature ideas and try to assign one for each lifestyle page.

TO READ

Blundell, William E. *The Art and Craft of Feature Writing.* New York, N.Y.: Penguin, 1988.

Franklin, Jon. *Writing for Story, Craft Secrets of Dramatic Non-Fiction by a Two-Time Pulitzer Prize Winner.* New York, N.Y.: Penguin, 1986.

Friedlander, Edward Jay and John Lee. *Feature Writing for Newspapers and Magazines: The Pursuit of Excellence, 6th ed.* New York, N.Y.: Longman, 2008.

Johnson, Carla. *21st Century Feature Writing.* Boston, Mass.: Pearson Education, Inc., 2005.

Reimold, Daniel. *Sex and the University: Celebrity, Controversy and a Student Journalism Revolution.* New Brunswick, NJ: Rutgers University Press, 2010.

TO CLICK

American Association of Sunday and Features Editors
This organization of editors from the United States and Canada supports its membership with an annual conference, a writing contest, an annual magazine and a website.
www.aasfe.org

Association of Food Journalists
The association's website includes information about contests and events, recipes and resources for food journalists.
www.afjonline.com

Sex information sites

Alan Guttmacher Institute
www.guttmacher.org

American Association of Sexuality Educators, Counselors and Therapists
www.aasect.org

The Center for Sex and Gender Research at California State University Northridge
http://www.csun.edu/~sr2022

Center for Sexual Health Promotion
www.sexualhealth.indiana.edu

Kinsey Confidential
http://kinseyconfidential.org

The Kinsey Institute for Research in Sex, Gender, and Reproduction
www.kinseyinstitute.org

National Sexuality Resource Center
www.nsrc.sfsu.edu

Planned Parenthood Federation of America
www.plannedparenthood.org

Sexuality Information and Education Council of the United States
www.siecus.org

Society for Human Sexuality
www.sexuality.org

Society for the Scientific Study of Sexuality
www.sexscience.org

Sports editor: **Mark F. Barnett** | tel. 882-5729 | e-mail barnettm@missouri.edu

PLAY

The sporting life, both in the stands and in the air.

NEWSUNDAY MISSOURIAN · September 19, 2004

With a 7-0 win against Arizona, the Cardinals clinch a playoff spot. **MAJOR LEAGUE BASEBALL, PAGE 4B**

A friendship between two Missouri volleyball players from China has spanned six years and many miles. **PLAYERS, PAGE 5B**

Skydiving isn't just for the deranged. B.J. Wolters shares tips for beginners. **GEARHEADS, PAGE 16B**

MISSOURI 48, BALL STATE 0

BACK ON THEIR FEET

Tigers' crushing win sets stage for Big 12 play

Gary Pinkel knew his team needed to improve after a disappointing game at Troy.

"I think there's an expectation level out there, and there should be," Pinkel said. "I told our football team after the game a week ago is that we let a lot of people down, and there's an expectation level out there. Missouri fans expect us to have a very good football team."

On Saturday at Memorial Stadium, the Tigers treated the 57,279 fans in attendance to a 48-0 win against Ball State, the biggest shutout since they defeated Kansas in 1986.

"I thought it was more of a complete game," Pinkel said. "Obviously, it feels a little bit better, get some of that bad taste out of our mouth from a week ago. Offensively, defensively, kicking-wise, it was probably our best team performance."

Pinkel and the Tigers have a little time to enjoy this one. They have a bye before beginning the crucial section of their schedule, Big 12 Conference play.

"Now it's Big 12 time, and we've got to become a better football team," Pinkel said. "That's the message I've sent to my team. I think we're a lot better than what we have shown, but we have got to become a better team."

The Tigers open Big 12 play Oct. 2 when they host Colorado, which has won five straight games against Missouri.

Now the expectations get heavier.

— **S. Scott Rosenberg**

MORE INSIDE

Missouri's defense keeps getting stronger, holding Ball State to 142 total yards of offense. **Page 10B**

Highs and lows: Thomson Omboga cranked up the speed, but false starts hurt Missouri in the fourth quarter. **Page 10B**

The Tigers prevented Ball State from gaining ground in the second quarter. **Page 10B**

Players of the game. **Page 8B**

Reserve running back Tyrone Roberson runs Ball State's Chris Allen over Saturday. Due to the large margin of victory, most of MU's back-ups played in the fourth quarter.
SHAUNA BITTLE/MISSOURIAN

5 KEYS ANSWERED

1 **STARTING QUICKLY:** The Tigers came out slowly, going three plays and out on their first possession but soon had their offense working methodically. They outgained the Cardinals 111-56 in the first quarter but scored three points. They scored on the first play of the second quarter, though.

2 **SUSTAINING THE QUICK START:** The Tigers played their best second quarter of the season, scoring 28 points and turning the game into a rout. Quarterback Brad Smith ran for 50 yards and passed for 98 in the quarter. The Tigers scored 14 points in 17 seconds late in the quarter.

3 **STRENGTHENING THE DEFENSE:** Excluding the effort of Adell Givens, the Cardinals struggled to produce. The Tigers became the third team this season to hold the Cardinals to less than 220 yards, allowing 142. The Tigers had three sacks.

4 **TURNING AROUND TURNOVERS:** The Tigers finished with a plus-two turnover ratio, but more important, they did not commit a turnover, the first time this year that has happened.

5 **ELIMINATING MISTAKES:** Although they did well for most the day, the Tigers committed some offsides penalties, six for 44 yards. The penalties didn't stop any drives, though. Still, the Tigers committed several penalties on punt returns, which negated long returns from wide receiver Thomson Omboga.

— **Missourian staff**

FIGURE 7.1 Large photos and information boxes in the sports section sometimes tell the story better than long text articles can. *The Missourian*, University of Missouri.

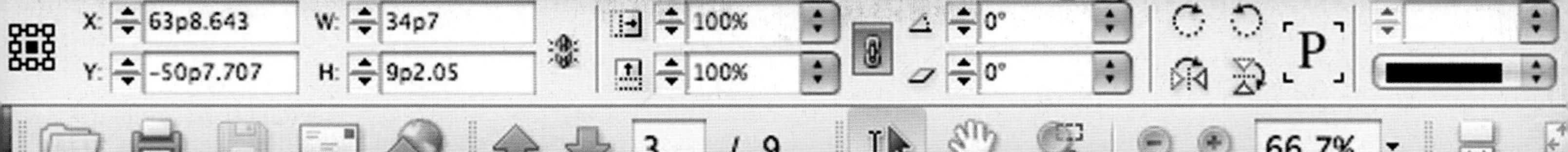

CHAPTER 7
SPORTSWRITING

Whether it's fall football games that bring thousands of shivering, beer-swilling fans to the stands every weekend or boisterous pick-up soccer games on the quad, sports is a vital element of college life and the sports pages are an integral part of any college paper.

Good sports stories not only inform and entertain, they help build a sense of community on campus. Here's where your readers can follow the ups and downs of your school's teams, learn about the people inside the uniforms and get an understanding of the role athletics play on your campus.

In the professional world, sports sections are among the best read – and often among the best written – pages of the newspaper. Readership studies show that 50 to 70 percent of newspaper readers turn to the sports sections. This can be equally true – or even more so – at the college level where team loyalty can get downright obsessive.

If you're passionate about sports, being a sportswriter can be one of the most fun and most creative jobs on the newspaper. "It allows you a lot of latitude," says Tyler Kepner, a former sports writer, sports editor and editor-in-chief for *The Vanderbilt Hustler* (vanderbilthustler.com) who went on to cover the Yankees for *The New York Times*.

CHAPTER CONTENTS

"You can express yourself a lot more than you can in other sections of the paper while still abiding by the rules of journalism."

But the sports section needn't be the "toy department," as some have called it. College sports is big business and there are myriad opportunities for hard-hitting investigative stories. Why is your school spending millions on a new stadium when classes are being cut? What's the graduation rate for your basketball players? How does your football coach's salary compare to that of your most popular English professor? To what lengths are your college's recruiters going to lure star athletes?

In this chapter we'll look at the ins and outs of sports coverage, from reporting on tonight's basketball game to interviewing the next stars of the NFL.

THE ROLE OF THE SPORTSWRITER

In the *Associated Press Sports Writing Handbook* (McGraw-Hill, 2001), Steve Wilstein, a national AP sports writer and columnist, writes, "The sports writer's challenge is to describe events with elegance and passion and wit, to make readers share their laughter or tears or rage, to entertain and inform, to break the news that no one else knows or describe a game that everyone has seen, to impart a feeling for what it was like to be there in the stands or on the field or in the locker room, to give the event meaning and put it in perspective."

Sports writing is about sports, yes, but it's also about good reporting and good writing, about observing and describing, about seeing what's really going on and transmitting that information to the reader.

One of the best ways to understand how sportswriters work is to watch the pros sitting next to you in the press box, advises Mike Rosenberg, a sports writer and columnist for the *Detroit Free Press*. "Figure out which ones do the best job, figure out what makes them the best and if possible, ask them what you could do better." Such informal friendships with professional sportswriters can also lead to internships and jobs later on.

After you've written your story, see how the professional reporters covered the same event. Did they lead with a similar anecdote? How did they describe that key play? What structural devices did they use? Which statistics did they include? Take note of their use of quotes and description.

Most sports stories fall into one of these categories: advances, game stories, profiles, sports news stories and sports columns. Let's take a look at each type of story.

ADVANCES

A sports advance, or *precede*, is a preview story that gives readers insights and information about an upcoming game. Such stories typically include background on the rivalry between the teams and quotes from coaches and key players about what they expect.

In an advance story, it's vital to find a fresh angle. You don't want to simply report that your team is playing the Tigers on Saturday. If your coach or one of your players used to be associated with the competing team, that's your angle. Or focus on the long-simmering rivalry between the two schools, including the last-minute upset the last time they played. Or get players to discuss their concerns about facing the best team in the division.

And don't just stick to your usual sources. Try interviewing coaches and players from opposing schools who can offer a different perspective.

GAME STORIES

Game stories – accounts of a particular game or a series of games – are the bread and butter of most sports sections. Written on a tight deadline, particularly for a daily newspaper or website, they're essentially breaking news stories.

"You should treat a game like a news story with the same who-what-where-when-why questions," advises Rosenberg, who worked at the University of Michigan *Daily* (michigandaily.com) as a sportswriter, sports editor, editor-in-chief and humor columnist in the mid-1990s. "Why was it important? Why did the team you cover win or lose? If the team lost because of rebounding, feel free to write the whole story about that."

While you want to incorporate details from important moments in the game, Rosenberg adds, "Don't write too much play-by-play. Nobody wants to read about who scored to tie the game in the first half, unless it was a spectacular play. Three or four specific plays are often enough."

For each game story, think about what your readers want to know:

What made the team (or, in individual events, the athlete) win?

How did the star athletes perform?

How did an individual athlete's efforts affect the outcome?

Were any of the players injured and if so, how did those injuries affect the game?

Did weather or other environmental factors, such as the condition of the facilities, affect the game?

How does this game affect the teams' standings and future prospects?

How did the fans respond?

A game story should include a summary of the game, significant details, key statistics and quotes from players and coaches that offer analysis about what happened. Game stories are often written in inverted pyramid structure, like news stories (as described in Chapter 5), although reporters may use a feature lede rather than a summary news lede.

For daily reports you generally want to open the story with the element that made the difference: Why did the victorious team win? How did a key player save the game? "A game almost always turns on something," says Mark Fainaru-Wada, an investigative sports reporter for ESPN who worked for *The Daily Northwestern* (dailynorthwestern.com) when he was a student at Northwestern University. "You want to be looking for a single play or a period in time or something that dramatically shifts the game."

Here are some examples:

> For Travis Mayle, game-winning kicks are becoming just as routine as putting on his uniform every Saturday.
>
> Mayle's third field goal of the game – a 33-yard field goal with 13 seconds to play – gave Kent State (2–1, 1–0 Mid-American Conference) the 16–13 win over Youngstown State (2–1) Saturday at Dix Stadium.
>
> ROB MEYER, *THE DAILY PENNSYLVANIAN* (DAILYPENNSYLVANIAN.COM), UNIVERSITY OF PENNSYLVANIA

> It could have been Jason Dourisseau's final game as a Nebraska Cornhusker.
>
> That's why the senior guard did everything in his power to make sure that didn't happen.
>
> With a game-high 20 points on 8 of 13 shooting and six rebounds, Dourisseau helped the Huskers pull off a 71–64 win over Missouri on Thursday night in the first found of the Big 12 Conference Tournament in Dallas.
>
> ROBIN WASHUT, *DAILY NEBRASKAN* (DAILYNEBRASKAN.COM), UNIVERSITY OF NEBRASKA

It's been traditional for game stories to run in the print edition following the event, but more and more, college sports editors understand that game stories can – and should – be posted online as soon as the game is over. Some college sportswriters are even using live blogging tools like CoveritLive and Twitter to report on games as they are unfolding.

Joe Gisondi, author of the *Field Guide to Covering Sports* (CQ Press, 2010) and adviser to the *Daily Eastern News* (dennews.com) at Eastern Illinois University, says student newspapers should post games stories online, whether the print newspaper is a daily, a weekly or monthly. "At the very least, write a quick overview of a football, basketball or softball game online that offers results, key plays and a few quotes," he writes on his blog, *Sports Field Guide* (sportsfieldguide.com/sports). "In print you can then offer

CHECKLIST
The game story

When writing or editing a game story ask yourself these questions:

1 Does the story say early on who won and what the score was?
2 Does it include the full names of all teams involved?
3 Does it clearly describe the turning point of the game and explain what made the difference?
4 Does the story quote players and coaches explaining the outcome of the game and what it means?
5 Does the story graphically describe key plays?
6 Does it include information about streaks or records by the teams or players?
7 Does it state where the event occurred (school, stadium or field)?
8 Does it include the day and time of the event?
9 Does it describe the significance of the event (division title, etc.) and effect on standings, rankings and individual records?
10 Are weather conditions relevant? If so, is this explained in the story?
11 Does the story include background about rivalry between the schools or the players?
12 Does it include key player statistics?
13 Was the size and/or behavior of the crowd notable?
14 Did any players sustain significant injuries?
15 Was the length of the game remarkable?

a game story with far more context, depth and sources. This is the way of the sports journalism world."

Gisondi recommends reworking the story for the print edition. "If you work for a daily, you may only have an hour or so. Those writing for weeklies may have several days," he says. "Either way, find a storyline – a running back who played well despite a major injury, a softball team that executed the basics to win a game, a soccer team that struggled offensively – for this revised story. Make sure you mix in comments from players and coaches on both teams, insert analysis, address key plays or stats, and offer some context for this story."

SCORING AND NOTETAKING

To help keep track of each play, Fainaru-Wada recommends sportswriters come up with an effective notetaking and scoring system. "It's useful to keep a running log of what's going on," he says. "You want to come up with some sort of formula that works for you and that's easily readable."

When he covers a baseball game, for example, Fainaru-Wada uses a scorecard but he also keeps a log in his notebook as each player comes to bat. He marks every pitch and notes details about the expression on the player's face or movements made by the coach. At the back of his notebook he writes random notes, ideas for the angle he may take with his story or impressions he wants to include.

"It's kind of a juggling act," Fainaru-Wada admits, commenting that he frequently makes notations in his laptop computer as well as his notebook and scorecard when covering a game. "Most of the stuff I won't use but it helps keep me really focused on the game."

PROFILES

A profile is a portrait of a particular player, coach, trainer or athletics official. Alumni are also good subjects, particularly if they are still working in the sports field. One of Tyler Kepner's most memorable profiles for *The Vanderbilt Hustler* focused on Joey Cora, a Vanderbilt alum who was then playing for the Chicago White Sox. "It was all about his college days. He talked about his coach and how he was great in math," Kepner says. "He hadn't really talked about those times for years."

Players and coaches who have overcome obstacles are also good profile subjects, as are those from sporting families and athletes who play multiple sports. Jonathan Jones landed a centerpiece story on the front page of *The Daily Tar Heel* (dailytarheel.com) when he wrote a profile of University of North Carolina freshman football quarterback Bryn Renner, who played baseball for the UNC Tar Heels in the spring. The story traced Renner's career from his days as a ball boy for his dad's football team through his grueling days on the practice field at UNC.

When writing a profile, look for key moments, like when one of your players faces his brother on the basketball court or when a player returns to the game after weeks or months of being out with an injury. The Renner profile opens with a telling scene of the Tar Heel at bat, while teammates from both teams look on:

> As designated hitter Bryn Renner approached the batter's box in his first collegiate at-bat, the crowd at Boshamer Stadium rose to their feet.
>
> Most cheered for North Carolina to finally get on the board in the seventh inning of the Saturday afternoon game with the freshman's bat. UNC quarterback T.J. Yates and offensive coordinator John Shoop rose to encourage their teammate.
>
> Renner has been moonlighting this spring, splitting his time between baseball and football, where he redshirted last season at quarterback and is vying to start next season. Recruited to play football by Butch Davis, Renner has essentially been on loan to Mike Fox's baseball team this season.
>
> He finds himself jumping from Boshamer to Kenan Stadium daily, trying to balance the act of playing two varsity sports in college. And at the end of each day, he's exhausted. "It's pretty tough," Renner said. "It's a lot of walking back and forth, but luckily it's so close. It definitely gets tiring.

Bruce Tran of the *Daily Bruin* (dailybruin.com) at UCLA won a national award from the Society of Professional Journalists in 2004 for his profile of a football player who was injured in a motorcycle accident. Here's how it began:

> For several seconds, Keith Carter could not have cared less about the National Football League.
>
> Instead of dreams about the NFL draft and lucrative contracts, Carter's thoughts turned to his family, his friends and his life. Despite side-splitting pain, the UCLA tight end couldn't help but wonder about his coaches and teammates.
>
> Even as he was being lifted into the ambulance, even after he had come so close to losing his life, and even as his mangled motorcycle lay on the ground just yards away, he muttered to the paramedics, "You guys have no idea how bad my coaches are going to kill me for this."
>
> And in that instant, everything about Keith Carter changed. His thoughts no longer centered on professional football.
>
> They focused on simply making it back to the Rose Bowl in a UCLA uniform.

When you're reporting for a profile, try to interview the source off the field or the court. The best profile interviews are conducted in people's homes, where you can see how they live and gain insights about their personal lives.

Robert Mays III of the *Columbia Missourian* opened his four-part series profiling University of Missouri Tigers wide receiver Jeremy Maclin with a scene from the player's home shortly before the NFL draft. Note the telling details Mays uses to draw a picture not just of the room but of Maclin:

> Three helmets, stacked on a set of shelves in a small alcove, are almost lost in the clutter of sports memorabilia that decorate the Chesterfield basement. They don't stand out as prominently as the All-American certificate or the *Sports Illustrated* clippings. But each is important in understanding how Jeremy Maclin got here, and where exactly here is.

The replica helmet on the bottom of the stack is the most familiar and the most recent – black with a gold "M." It symbolizes Maclin's arrival in the consciousness of football fans throughout the country and the surest sign of what is to come.

The helmet on top is the red of Kirkwood High School, and just like the one that Maclin wore when football became more than fun. That's when football became a future. Football could make you a legend.

The helmet in the middle is the oldest and the only authentic one. White with a red "1" on the side, multicolored streaks of paint record the collisions that were the thrill of a game still in its infancy.

Another set of helmets sits in a case across the basement, a collection of miniature replicas from each of the NFL teams. Thirty-two teams and 32 possible destinations, each helmet the potential next symbol of a football journey more than a decade in the making.

Of the thousands of college football players who harbor what-if dreams of going pro, Maclin is a given to be one of the 250 who will be picked in next weekend's NFL Draft. The 6-foot, 200-pound wide receiver is expected to be tapped in the first round and offered a contract worth up to $20 million.

When interviewing sports profile subjects ask about their goals, their motivations, their strengths and insecurities. Find out when they started playing and what obstacles they faced. Ask about the person's childhood and how it influenced their commitment to the game. And don't forget to watch your subject in action – at practices, at games, even in the classroom.

Good profiles have multiple sources. Coaches, fellow players, roommates, family members, lovers and friends can all offer insights into what makes the person tick. Try to gather anecdotes from each source that shine a light on one facet of the subject's personality. What did the coach do to bolster morale when the team was behind? How did the player celebrate when he learned he had been picked to play on the team? The best profiles are a collection of little detail-packed vignettes that together draw a vivid picture of a person.

Gameday

B8 • SEPTEMBER 29, 2009

ROCK THE VOTE

➤ Will the Wolf Pack beat the Rebels?

➤ Should football head coach Ault be fired if the Wolf Pack goes 0-4?

➤ Vote on these polls and more online at:

NEVADASAGEBRUSH.COM

www.nevadasagebrush.com

SEPT. 5	SEPT. 19	SEPT. 25	Saturday	OCT. 9	OCT. 17	OCT. 24	OCT. 31	NOV. 8	NOV. 14	NOV. 21	NOV. 27
at Notre Dame	at Colorado St.	Missouri	UNLV	La. Tech	at Utah St.	Idaho	Hawaii	at San Jose St.	Fresno St.	at New Mexico St.	at Boise St.
L 35-0	L 35-20	L 31-21	TIME: 1:05 p.m.	TIME: 6:05 p.m.	TIME: 12 p.m.	TIME: 1:05 p.m.	TIME: 1:05 p.m.	TIME: 5:30 p.m.	TIME: 1:05 p.m.	TIME: 5 p.m.	TIME: TBA

AP TOP 25

1. Florida (55)	4-0
2. Texas (1)	4-0
3. Alabama (4)	4-0
4. LSU	4-0
5. Boise State	4-0
6. Virginia Tech	3-1
7. USC	3-1
8. Oklahoma	2-1
9. Ohio State	3-1
10. Cincinnati	4-0
11. TCU	3-0
12. Houston	3-0
13. Iowa	4-0
14. Oklahoma State	3-1
15. Penn State	3-1
16. Oregon	3-1
17. Miami (FL)	2-1
18. Kansas	4-0
18. Georgia	3-1
20. BYU	3-1
21. Mississippi	2-1
22. Michigan	4-0
23. Nebraska	3-1
24. California	3-1
25. Georgia Tech	3-1

OTHERS RECEIVING VOTES
Missouri 175, Auburn 171, South Carolina 154, South Florida 145, UCLA 41, Utah 35, Wisconsin 20, Notre Dame 7, Arizona State 4, Stanford 2, North Carolina 2

USA TODAY TOP 25

1. Florida (58)	4-0
2. Texas (1)	4-0
3. Alabama	4-0
4. LSU	4-0
5. Boise State	4-0
6. Virginia Tech	3-1
7. USC	3-1
8. Oklahoma	2-1
9. Ohio State	3-1
10. TCU	3-0
11. Cincinnati	4-0
12. Oklahoma State	3-1
13. Penn State	3-1
14. Georgia	3-1
15. Houston	3-0
16. Kansas	4-0
17. Iowa	4-0
18. Mississippi	2-1
19. California	3-1
20. Michigan	4-0
21. Miami (FL)	2-1
21. BYU	3-1
23. Missouri	4-0
24. Nebraska	3-1
25. Oregon	3-1

OTHERS RECEIVING VOTES
Georgia Tech 186, South Florida 112, Auburn 103, South Carolina 92, Wisconsin 53, Utah 40, UCLA 27, Notre Dame 23, Stanford 20, North Carolina State 8, North Carolina 7, Florida State 4, Minnesota 2, Arizona 2, Rutgers 1, Texas A&M 1

THIS WEEK'S GAME

UNLV at Nevada

When: 1:05 p.m. Saturday

Where: Mackay Stadium (29,993; Field Turf)

Radio: ESPN Radio 630

Meet the coaches: Head coach Mike Sanford is 13-38 in his fifth year at UNLV. Nevada coach Chris Ault is in his 25th season as Nevada's coach and has a 198-94-1 record.

Records don't matter: Rivalry week is here

When Pack and Rebels play, it's more than a game

By Juan López

Nevada could lose all of its games this season, but beating the University of Nevada, Las Vegas would make it a good year. The Wolf Pack could get smashed by 50 points every game, but beating the Rebels by one point would make it a good season. Nevada could — you see where I'm going with this.

Saturday's matchup between Nevada and UNLV is for all of the state's marbles. As soon as the final horn sounded in the Wolf Pack's 31-21 loss last week to No. 21 Missouri, Nevada's focus shifted to UNLV.

The Wolf Pack's players are very adamant about not losing the Fremont Cannon, but willpower will be just one of the factors in this hatred-filled civil war.

ROLE REVERSAL

Prior to the college football season, Nevada was picked to finish second in the Western Athletic Conference. The team was often seen on ESPN and proclaimed to be a possible Bowl Championship Series buster.

Fast-forward four weeks and the Wolf Pack is 0-3 with no talks of a bowl game, much less a BCS game.

As for the Rebels, they were picked to finish fifth in the Mountain West Conference. Expectations were low for the team, which had gone 11-36 in its previous four years under head coach Mike Sanford.

Well, through four games, UNLV is 2-2 and could very easily have been undefeated (its two losses have come by a combined five points).

The quality of football has done a complete 180 and the higher quality now resides in Sin City. So much for preseason predictions.

START OF A NEW STREAK?

When the cannon leaves, it doesn't come back for a long time.

In the UNR-UNLV series, which goes back 34 games, only five times has a team won the game to start a streak and then lost the next meeting.

During the past two decades, the elongated winning streaks have been the trademark of this series. From 1989-93 and from 1995-99, the Wolf Pack kept the cannon. From 2000-04, the cannon was red. And since 2005, the cannon has been blue.

Needless to say, there is a very good chance the Rebels will come into Mackay Stadium and walk out with a victory. If UNLV wins this game, history shows that we won't see our darling cannon for a long time.

MORE THAN JUST A GAME

The Wolf Pack played Notre Dame earlier this season. The Irish are one of the most storied college football programs in the nation. UNLV took on a Pac-10 foe, Oregon State, earlier in the year.

Yet, no matter who else each team plays throughout the year, this game is always the biggest of the season.

There's much more that makes this rivalry one of the top in the country. For one, the schools are the only two universities in the seventh-largest state in the U.S.

Secondly, a lot of the students who attend each school have friends at the other school, making the football game personal. There's year-long bragging rights at stake here.

Finally, there is a genuine hatred between the schools. Not a hatred which would result in major crimes (hopefully), but a hatred which pulls for the other team's quarterback to roll his ankle during pregame warm-ups.

When it comes to rivalries, little compares to wishing injury on your opponents, but that's what makes Nevada vs. UNLV so special.

Juan López can be reached at jlopez@nevadasagebrush.com.

BRIAN BOLTON/NEVADA SAGEBRUSH
Wolf Pack running back Mike Ball

TALE OF THE TAPE

*National ranking in parentheses

Nevada	Category	UNLV
	OFFENSE	
180.00 (43)	Rushing	136.00 (65)
183.67 (85)	Passing	269.50 (23)
106.25 (100)	Pass Efficiency	140.27 (44)
363.67 (66)	Total	405.50 (43)
13.67 (116)	Scoring	30.00 (47)
	DEFENSE	
145.00 (71)	Rushing	112.50 (40)
312.00 (118)	Passing	255.50 (101)
203.21 (120)	Pass Efficiency	144.71 (101)
457.00 (112)	Total	368.00 (75)
33.67 (109)	Scoring	22.24 (50)
	SPECIAL TEAMS/MISC.	
35.14 (80)	Net Punting	39.55 (17)
8.75 (63)	Punt Returns	8.00 (66)
26.56 (24)	Kickoff Returns	25.12 (31)
-9.00 (119)	Turnover Margin	-6.00 (108)

LEADERS

UNLV

Player	Category	Avg./Game
Channing Trotter	Rushing	73.8
Ryan Wolfe	Receiving	96.0
S. Fuimaono	Tackles	9.25
J. Beauchamp	Tackles for loss	1.38

Nevada

Player	Category	Avg./Game
Vai Taua	Rushing	69.7
B. Wimberly	Receiving	72.0
Mike Bethea	Tackles	7.33
Dontay Moch	Tackles for loss	2.16

WAC STANDINGS

Standings	Conference	Overall
Boise State	1-0	4-0
Idaho	1-0	3-1
Hawaii	0-0	2-1
Louisiana Tech	0-0	1-2
Utah State	0-0	1-2
San Jose State	0-0	1-3
Nevada	**0-0**	**0-3**
Fresno State	0-1	1-3
New Mexico State	0-1	1-3

REBELS' SCHEDULE

Date	Opponent	Time/Result
Sept. 5	Sacramento State	W 38-3
Sept. 12	Oregon State	L 23-21
Sept. 19	Hawaii	W 34-33
Sept. 25	at Wyoming	L 30-27
Saturday	**at Nevada**	**1:05 p.m.**
Oct. 10	BYU	7 p.m.
Oct. 17	Utah	7 p.m.
Oct. 24	at New Mexico	5 p.m.
Oct. 31	at TCU	1 p.m.
Nov. 7	Colorado State	7 p.m.
Nov. 14	at Air Force	3 p.m.
Nov. 28	San Diego State	6 p.m.

MAKING THE CALL

STAFF PICKS

OPTIMIST SAYS: This is Nevada's biggest game. Colin Kaepernick will have a repeat of last season's performance and single-handedly dismantle the Rebels. The defense continues to play better and the offense cuts down on turnovers. The Rebels may be better than they were, but the Wolf Pack is still the superior team and wins running away.

CANNON STAYS BLUE: Nevada wins 42-27

PESSIMIST SAYS: UNLV is a lot better than the two-win and five-win teams Nevada has beaten in the past. The Wolf Pack continue to be plagued by turnovers and the Rebels take advantage by building an early lead. UNLV's defense, which gives up 22 points per game, shuts down Nevada's running game. Kaepernick keeps it close, but UNLV is too much.

CANNON TURNS RED: UNLV wins 34-24

DIFFERENCE MAKER | *CHANNING TROTTER*

Since being held to 39 yards against Oregon State, running back Channing Trotter has found his groove. After rushing for 68 yards during the Rebels' victory over Hawaii, he rushed for 90 yards and a touchdown against Wyoming. Nevada is giving up 145 rushing yards per game, but will likely see a much heavier dose of the running game than previous opponents. This appears to be UNLV's best chance to beat Nevada in the last four years and the outcome of the game could depend on whether the Wolf Pack can stop Trotter. While many teams pass against Nevada, the Rebels will depend on Trotter to control the clock and keep the Wolf Pack's offense off the field.

UNLV MEDIA RELATIONS
UNLV running back Channing Trotter

FIGURE 7.2 A well designed sports section packages game schedules, conference standings, game results and other tidbits of information for sports fans. *The Nevada Sagebrush*, University of Nevada, Reno.

SPORTS FEATURES

Feature stories capture a trend or a slice of life about a sport or a team. When writing feature stories about a team, look for winning or losing streaks, how a team works together, tensions that lead to divisiveness. You can also do features on recruiting, tryouts, training regimens, coaching philosophies or how a particular news event such as the resignation of a coach or a series of player injuries – affects the team.

Unusual sports like kickboxing and roller derby can also make good features like the one Krystal Peak wrote for *Golden Gate [X]press* (goldengatexpress.org) at San Francisco State University when the local television station televised the San Francisco Bay Bombers for the first time in 21 years:

A group of women skate around a banked track. As the whistle blows, they pick up speed.

Two women break ahead of the pack, and as suddenly as one lifts her arm to strike the other, they are both hurtling over the outside rail with helmets and fists flying.

The crowd roars in support of the rumble.

The non-stop antics of full contact Roller Derby bring all the showmanship of entertainment wrestling to the roller circuit.

This is the sport where body slams, throws to the ground, hair pulling and general clobbering by folding-chairs are all commonplace sportsmanship.

Action, drama, vivid description – that's sportswriting at its best.

The pressures, demands and health challenges college athletes face can also make for good sports feature stories. Robert Samuels wrote an insightful piece for *The Daily Northwestern* in 2003 about African-American athletes on the mostly white campus and the stereotyping they face. Joe Watson blew the lid off college football recruiting in a piece for *The State Press* (statepress.com) at Arizona State University. And David Agrell of *Golden Gate [X]press* won first-place honors from the California College Media Association for this feature on the dangers of head injuries among college athletes:

> In the week following an on-field collision that set her slamming head-first into the ground, Gator soccer player Sarah Ordaz was in a cognitive fog.
>
> She couldn't concentrate in class because of debilitating headaches and blurry vision, and her short-term memory became glitchy.
>
> "I would tell my friends something, and then, like five minutes later, I would tell them the same thing," she said. "They'd be like, 'Yeah, you told us that already.'
>
> Ordaz, 19 is one of an estimated 3,750 college athletes who suffer a concussion in the United States every year. The injury is now one of the fastest growing in college sports, according to reports recently published in the Journal of Athletic Training.

Note how Agrell smoothly transitions from anecdotal lede to nut graph. By bringing together a riveting personal story with scientific research he was able to craft a compelling trend story.

SPORTS NEWS STORIES

When a coach resigns, is hired or fired, that's news. When a melee breaks out after a basketball game, that's news. When an athlete is charged with sexually assaulting another student, that's news.

Many of the stories on sports pages around the country are news stories. They follow the structure of standard news stories and should respect the same rules of balance, objectivity and fairness. And sports news needn't be relegated to the sports section; an important story can start on the front page and jump inside to the sports section.

One of the biggest college sports news stories of the past decade began to unfold in 2006 when three members of the Duke University lacrosse team were charged with raping an exotic dancer who had been invited to perform at a team party. All charges were eventually dropped but *The Chronicle* (dukechronicle.com) at Duke followed the story for years as the head lacrosse coach resigned, civil suits were filed against the university and the prosecutor was brought up on ethics charges and disbarred. The story raised questions about race, culture and the relationship between the elite private university and the hard-scrabble town of Durham where it is based. "It's hard to imagine an event that shaped the decade at Duke more forcefully than the lacrosse case," David Graham, who was a reporter and later editor of *The Chronicle* as the saga unfolded, wrote in a column for the paper after he graduated.

When reporting sports news, it's important to take the same investigative approach you'd take with other news stories. Don't accept "no comment" for an answer; try to dig behind the sketchy press releases sent out by the public information office. If you're at a public university, public records may come in handy.

When Louisiana State University women's basketball coach Pokey Chatman abruptly resigned in 2007 with the briefest of explanations, *The Daily Reveille* (dailyreveille.com) investigated. The day after the resignation, Amy Brittain, the newspaper's chief sportswriter, filed a public records request asking for correspondence between members of the Athletic Department. The following week she received emails between department officials suggesting that Chatman left because of allegations of "inappropriate conduct" with a former player. (After the story was published the LSU Athletic Department warned staff members to be careful what they write in emails, noting that they may be subject to state public records laws.)

Brittain didn't let the story drop. Five months after Chatman left LSU, the reporter caught up with her at a summer camp where she was teaching pre-teens the basics of basketball. During an interview on the bleachers there, Brittain got Chatman to open up. Here's how her story began:

> Hurt. Shocked. Angry. Disappointed. Bewildered. Bombarded. Scared. Sad. Lost. Unknown. No Answer.
>
> It's a list of emotions Pokey Chatman stoically conveys when asked to describe her feelings about March 7, the day she announced her resignation as LSU women's basketball coach amid allegations of inappropriate conduct with one or more former players.

Though Chatman declined to offer details of the events leading up to her resignation, Brittain was able to write a moving portrait of a sports figure under siege.

INVESTIGATING COLLEGE SPORTS

College athletics is also prime territory for investigative stories. Athletes' grades and graduation rates, recruitments strategies, how game tickets are distributed and how teams are funded are all topics that can lead to enlightening investigative reports.

Reporters Andrew Mannix and Briana Bierschback won several awards for *The Minnesota Daily* (mndaily.com) with their investigation of University of Minnesota wrestlers and coaches who had bought up large chunks of housing around the campus. Their story revealed that Coach J. Robinson owned more than $3 million in real estate and that people with ties to the team owned more than 55 housing units near the University of Minnesota campus. Though no improprieties were found, the newspaper's report led university and NCAA officials to scrutinize the financial relationships between the head wrestling coach and his players and staff.

Using public records, *The Daily Tar Heel* at the University of North Carolina, Chapel Hill was able to find out that the university had distributed thousands of dollars worth of free football and basketball tickets to elected officials. The newspaper even put a searchable database with the information on its website so readers could find out just which officials had gotten tickets for which games.

SPORTS COLUMNS

Columns can personalize your sports pages, and really good ones can build a loyal fan base. But that doesn't mean you should hand out regular columns to every aspiring columnist who steps into your newsroom.

Column writing is hard work. And it demands three qualities that most people don't have: an inspired understanding of the sport being covered, an engaging writing style and the creativity to come up with a new angle for each column.

Many wannabe columnists have great ideas for two or three columns and then they run dry. Before assigning someone a regular column ask for a few sample columns and a detailed description of how they plan to approach the column. Make sure the person knows the sport. And ask what they plan to offer readers. Columns can't just report on games or team changes; they must give readers added value.

The best college sports columns focus on local teams, not the pros. It gets back to the old adage: Write what you know. A college sportswriter probably doesn't have great access to Tiger Woods or Derek Jeter or know the inside scoop on Alex Rodriguez's $275 million, 10-year contract with the New York Yankees. But with thorough reporting he can offer insights into his college teams, players and coaches.

Like all opinion pieces, successful sports columns must go beyond top-of-the-head musings. They should be laced with facts, figures, even quotes. The best sports columns are as thoroughly researched as any news story. "Columnists are reporters with an opinion," Joe Gisondi writes in his blog, *OnSports*, (onsportz.blogspot.com). "The best columnists are also keen observers, precise writers, and excellent storytellers."

Sports columns must have a point. Too many columnists ramble on, never really saying anything. "A columnist's role is also to get people to react to an issue so some change of mind or policy or action will take place," Gisondi writes. Make sure that any column you write or edit has an opinion and that it makes a forceful, well-reasoned case for that point of view.

COVERING SPORTS FOR A NON-DAILY

Game stories are fine if you're working for a daily paper. But what if your newspaper comes out weekly or even biweekly? A report on a game a week or two after the event can be about as enticing as the turkey sandwich you left in your backpack last week. Don't despair. Here are two approaches you can take:

One is you can post game stories between editions on your newspaper's website. Brief reports on games with photos or photo galleries will give fans the information they need and keep your website fresh. *The State News* (statenews.com), Michigan State's 5-day-a-week newspaper, for example, posts "Web updates" on games throughout the weekend.

If your paper doesn't post games on your site between editions – or if your online game coverage is brief – take the *Sports Illustrated* approach: Use great writing and analysis to keep game stories fresh. "If you're writing for a non-daily paper, you're not writing game stories, you're using the game to tell a broader story about the team or

FIGURE 7.3 Sports preview sections help whet fans' appetites for a new season or a big game. *The Ball State Daily News*, Ball State University.

1B | Sports

Wednesday
March 17, 2010
The Daily Illini
www.DailyIllini.com

TOP 20 ILLINI ATHLETES OF THE DECADE

THE TOP 20 ILLINI ATHLETES OF THE DECADE

NO. 2 JUSTIN SPRING Men's gymnastics 2002-2006

NO. 3 PERDITA FELICIEN Women's track 2000-2003

NO. 4 ANGELA BIZZARRI Women's track 2006-present

NO. 5 DERON WILLIAMS Men's basketball 2002-2005

NO. 6 AMER DELIC Men's tennis 2000-2003

NO. 7 MATT LACKEY Wrestling 1998-2003

NO. 8 PAUL RUGGERI Men's gymnastics 2007-present

NO. 9 ADAM TIRAPELLE Wrestling 1997-2001

NO. 10 KEVIN ANDERSON & RYAN ROWE, Men's tennis 2004-2007

NO. 11 LAURA DEBRULER Volleyball, 2007-present

NO. 12 ELLA MASAR Soccer 2004-2007

NO. 13 EMILY ZURRER Soccer 2004-2007

NO. 14 JOHN LOCKHART Wrestling 1998-2002

NO. 15 YVONNE MENSAH Women's track 2004-2007

NO. 16 J LEMAN Football 2003-2007

NO. 17 RYLER DEHEART Men's tennis 2003-2006

NO. 18 WES HAAGENSEN Men's gymnastics 2005-2006

NO. 19 JENNA SMITH Women's Basketball 2006-present

NO. 20 GAKOLOGELWANG MASHETO Men's track 2006-2009

ILLINI OF THE DECADE

NO. 1

MEMBER OF 2005 NATIONAL RUNNER-UP TEAM

2005 SPORTING NEWS PLAYER OF THE YEAR

TWO-TIME ALL-AMERICAN

Men's Basketball
DEE BROWN
Guard | 2002-2006

"He was the face of not only Illinois basketball, but the face of college basketball."

JERRANCE HOWARD, former teammate and current Illinois assistant coach

BY RICH MAYOR
SPORTS COLUMNIST

What makes Dee Brown so special?

We could revisit why Dee was such a sought-after recruit at Proviso East High School in Maywood, Ill.: Illinois Mr. Basketball, Illinois' Gatorade Player of the Year, McDonald's All-American, First-Team All-State by the IBCA, Chicago Tribune, Chicago Sun-Times and News-Gazette; ranked by RivalsHoops.com as the No. 2 point guard and No. 11 overall player in his class.

We could revisit his 3.7 grade-point average and 16-of-382 students class ranking at Proviso East, the stats that makes his mother, Cathy, proudest.

"He started playing basketball when he was seven or eight years old, so I kind of knew he was gonna have a skill anyway, he was going to have that talent of playing ball," Cathy said. "But I wanted him to understand that education was important and that getting good grades and being able to manage your money is better than just having money without the education."

We could revisit the process of Dee's college choice, one that resulted in "so much mail... I mean unbelievable mail, boxes of mail, boxes and boxes," according to Cathy. The search might have led him away from the Orange and Blue, if not for his mother. Initially, Dee approached her with his desire to attend Arizona. That didn't go over too well.

"Arizona?" Cathy said, with her displeasure still shining through, nine years later. "When am I gonna be able to see you play? I can't afford to fly out to Arizona!"

This conversation led Dee toward the Midwest, and the search narrowed to Illinois and Michigan State. Cathy remembers a time at the Moody Bible Institute in Chicago, when then-Illinois head coach Bill Self and then-assistant coach Billy Gillespie took her in a room and asked if Dee was going to commit. Cathy didn't know — Dee hadn't told her anything, and she demanded that Dee tell her first, so she didn't find out from someone else.

We could revisit the drive Cathy and Dee took soon after, the drive during which Dee told his mother he was going to commit to Self and the Illini.

"I was ecstatic," Cathy remembers. "I could not even tell you, I was so thrilled. I was like, 'Oh, he's going somewhere that I can drive to. Even if I didn't have anybody to ride with me, I could ride by myself.'"

Underclassman

We could revisit his relationship with

See **BROWN,** Page 6B

More online: For a photo gallery of past Illini of the Decade recipients, visit **DailyIllini.com**

Editor's note: It was a long journey, but today finally wraps up one of The Daily Illini sports staff's biggest and most ambitious projects ever — an opinionated look at the Top 20 Illini Athletes of the Decade, from 2000-2009. Preparation and planning for this series began more than a year ago, and countless hours were put in by many to get to this point. But it was worth every minute of it from our end.

For a breakdown of how the voting worked and who was eligible for the list, visit the following link:

DailyIllini.com/special/athletes-of-the-decade

The site will remain live at the conclusion of this series, so if you missed any of the previous stories or want to take a look back, go ahead and visit any time.

This series might not have been a book, but there's still countless people to acknowledge. A special thanks goes out to all those in the UI sports information department who were so kind in providing us contact information for the many athletes and sources we used in this series.

Another thanks to all those who graciously gave their time to be interviewed, helping bring these stories to life with their countless tales and memories.

And to everyone in the newsroom, thank you. From the Web site crew that stays so late to post these stories to the copy desk that helped make these stories error-free, from the photographers who went through countless old photos to the design team that made everything look terrific, you all did a great job. And of course, a thanks to all the writers who so vividly described why these athletes were so great.

But the biggest thanks goes out to all you readers. You're the reason we wrote these stories, and we hope you had fun reading them. We know we had a blast writing them.

FIGURE 7.4 A project or special section highlighting accomplishments of top student athletes may be popular with fans. *The Daily Illini*, University of Illinois at Urbana-Champaign.

a certain player," says Fainaru-Wada of ESPN. "If a guy is emerging as a star on the team or having troubles, you're going to use that game to tell part of your story." Details from games can also help with trend stories or mood pieces on the team.

Nils Rosdahl, a former sports editor who advised *The Sentinel* (nicsentinel.com) at North Idaho College in Coeur d'Alene, recommends students working on non-dailies open game stories with a look-ahead lede. "Write about what's coming up, what do you expect of your team's next opponent, what's the team doing to prepare? Then you can do a roundup of games since the last issue and talk about what worked and what didn't."

BEYOND TEAM SPORTS

What if you don't have a championship football or basketball team on campus? What if only 25 fans – most of them parents, girlfriends and roommates of the players – show up for a typical game? What if the biggest sport on campus is ultimate frisbee? Then you write about ultimate frisbee. Fill your sports pages with news about the sports that people are talking about – the new women's rugby club on campus, how the gym just got three new elliptical trainers, the cool sailing class that has a waiting list each spring.

At North Idaho College's *The Sentinel*, some of the most popular sports stories are features about non-team pursuits, many of which occur off campus. The paper frequently writes features and columns on hunting and fishing, whitewater rafting and frisbee golf. "We find these stories lend themselves to some of the best photos in the paper," former adviser Rosdahl says. "We always have full color on the back and we often reserve the back page for these kinds of stories."

SPECIAL SECTIONS

One of the best ways to whet your readers' interest in a new sports season is to produce a special preview section (Figure 7.3). Such special sections help to build reader loyalty; your paper gets to be seen as the authority on your team.

Components of a typical preview section include:

- A game schedule
- A team roster
- Player profiles
- Team and player statistics
- Bios on coaches
- History timelines.

Make sure your preview section includes plenty of art. If you don't have photos of key players from last season, have a photographer go out to practices and shoot the players on the field. You may use some portraits or headshots, but try to include as many action photos as possible.

You can also create special sections for championship events or "the big game" with your school's archrival or mark noted accomplishments by athletes. In 2010, *The Daily Illini* (dailyillini.com) at the University of Illinois at Urbana-Champaign, for example, produced a 20-part series about the top athletes of the decade (Figure 7.4). "Our sports department ... worked on the project for nearly a year, going through old stats and compiling a list of athlete achievements both during and after college," Melissa Silverberg, who was managing editor at the time of the series and later editor-in-chief of the paper, wrote in an email interview. "The sports desk voted on who deserved the honors. We ran the series several times a week from January until March, counting down the top athletes from the past 10 years - culminating in #1 Dee Brown, a basketball player who took the Illini to the final four in 2005 and had a spirit that brought Illini fans together."

The long, in-depth profiles, she said, were a big hit with the athletic department, students and alumni.

WEB COVERAGE

The potential content for sports coverage is virtually limitless. Most college sports editors find they have more information than they can possibly put in two or three pages of a newspaper. So more and more, savvy sports editors are looking to the Web to enhance their sports coverage.

Game stories should not be covered the same way in both editions, Gisondi advises. "For example, online you can create live game-blogs that offer a mix of play-by-play, analysis and fan interaction. After the game concludes, you can post a short game story online that includes basic information, such as the score, team names, location, key plays or stats, and the game's significance, like a team clinching a postseason berth.

"Afterward, rush to the locker rooms or press conference to interview coaches and players. Then, insert a few quotes, a few updated details, and additional perspective into the original story."

Associated Press Sports Editors' ethics guidelines

Does your news organization's ethics policy consider the particular ethical challenges of covering sports? You may want to consider the APSE's ethics guidelines as a model.

1 The newspaper pays its staffer's way for travel, accommodations, food and drink. A If a staffer travels on a chartered team plane, the newspaper should insist on being billed. If the team cannot issue a bill, the amount can be calculated by estimating the cost of a similar flight on a commercial airline. B When services are provided to a newspaper by a pro or college team, those teams should be reimbursed by the newspaper. This includes providing telephone, typewriter or fax service.

2 Editors and reporters should avoid taking part in outside activities or employment that might create conflict of interest or even appearance of a conflict.
A They should not serve as an official scorer at baseball games. B They should not write for team or league media guides or other team or league publications. This has the potential of compromising a reporter's disinterested observations. C Staffers who appear on radio or television should understand that their first loyalty is to the paper.

3 Writers and writers' groups should adhere to Associated Press Managing Editors and APSE standards: No deals, discounts or gifts except those of insignificant value or those available to the public.
A If a gift is impossible or impractical to return, donate a gift to charity. B Do not accept free memberships or reduced fees for memberships. Do not accept gratis use of facilities, such as golf courses or tennis courts, unless it is used as part of doing a story for the newspaper. C Sports editors should be aware of standards of conduct of groups and professional associations to which their writers belong and the ethical standards to which those groups adhere, including areas such as corporate sponsorship from news sources it covers.

4 A newspaper should not accept free tickets, although press credentials needed for coverage and coordination are acceptable.

5 A newspaper should carefully consider the implications of voting for all awards and all-star teams and decide if such voting creates a conflict of interest.

6 A newspaper's own ethical guidelines should be followed, and editors and reporters should be aware of standards acceptable for use of unnamed sources and verification of information obtained other than from primary news sources.

A Sharing and pooling of notes and quotes should be discouraged. If a reporter uses quotes gained secondhand, that should be made known to the readers. A quote could be attributed to a newspaper or to another reporter.

7 Assignments should be made on merit, without regard for race or gender.

Guidelines can't cover everything. Use common sense and good judgment in applying these guidelines in adopting local codes.

A number of student newspapers, including the *Daily Bruin* and *The Daily Pennsylvanian* have a Web page for each sport – from golf to football to women's soccer. Each sport-specific page includes recent photos and links to the last dozen or so stories posted and then sends readers to the archive for more coverage.

Many newspapers have dedicated sports Twitter feeds to report games and other sports news. And some are using CoveritLive, a live blogging program, to report play-by-play coverage of games.

The Daily Reveille uses databases to enhance its sports coverage. The paper has put together a database showing which LSU athletes have signed with professional teams. The database goes all the way back to 1910 when Roland Howell left LSU to pitch for the St. Louis Cardinals. Another database compares graduation rates of LSU athletes in 21 sports with other teams in the Southeastern Conference.

Non-daily papers can take advantage of the Web's immediacy by using blogs to report games scores and sports updates between editions. Slideshows and galleries of game photos are also popular features on many student newspaper websites.

AVOIDING BIAS

If you're covering sports, you're probably a sports fan and if you're writing for your college newspaper, you're probably rooting for your school's team. **Don't let it show**.

"The trickiest part of sportswriting is not showing that you're rooting for the team you're covering," says Lee Jenkins, a former *Vanderbilt Hustler* sportswriter and editor who went on to become a sportswriter for *The New York Times*. "You have to learn not to cheer in the press box, even if you want to. Your stories should cover the team through the eyes of someone interested in the team but not rooting for that team. You have to take the bias out."

That means not wearing a college sweatshirt or hat to games, not raising your fist when your team scores a touchdown, not using "we" when writing about the team. "Every sports writer was a fan at one time," Jenkins says. "You have to learn to restrain that part of you."

Q&A Adam Rubin

ADAM RUBIN started covering sports for *The Daily Pennsylvanian* in 1991, in his freshman year at the University of Pennsylvania. He served as sports editor in 1994. After graduating from Penn in 1995, he did a one-year internship with *The Birmingham* (Ala.) *News*, where he covered the U.S. men's Olympic soccer team and then worked in the news department for about six months. He worked as a sportswriter at the *Shreveport* (La.) *Times* before returning to a full-time position in the sports department in Birmingham. In 2000, the *New York Daily News* hired him as a general-assignment sports writer; he took over the Mets beat in 2003.

What do you think college papers should do with their sports sections? What can college papers do to compete with professional papers on sports coverage?

Don't believe that just because you're a college paper, you should accept the professional paper in your city breaking the significant news. You're the one on campus. You're the one in class with the student-athletes. And as a journalist, you should want to break news. There are disadvantages here: Coaches and administrators often purposely leak information to the professional paper's beat writer because they're perceived to have more power. But that can be overcome to some extent with diligence.

Also, a college paper typically will have more space to devote to that university's athletics, except in extreme cases like, say, Alabama football or Kentucky basketball, so use that to your advantage.

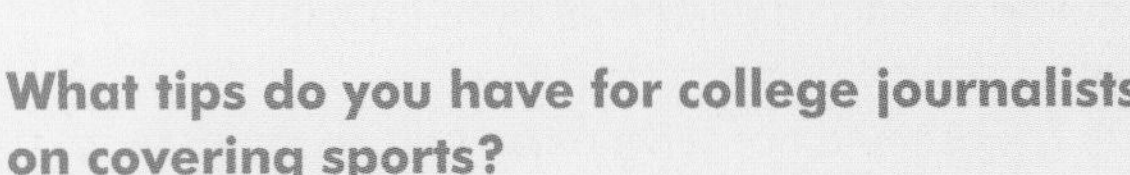

What tips do you have for college journalists on covering sports?

Remember to tell a story. At major colleges, everyone is already going to know how each important point was scored by the time they read the article recapping the event. And at smaller colleges, which don't receive the same scrutiny, or possibly the same interest level from fans, no one wants to read a recitation of how every point was scored.

Also, don't discount the importance of being a reporter, even if you're on the sports staff. In nearly every story, there ought to be a nut graph summarizing what happened and why it's important. And there are plenty of issues in sports. Good sports reporters ought to be able to produce issue pieces – known as enterprise stories – and features to complement game coverage.

Do you have any specific suggestions for covering games?

Use the advantages you have over professional sports writers – including time. Even during games that begin in the afternoon, I'm frequently on deadline. While I try to spend as much time interviewing after the game, I often must return to my laptop sooner than I would like to begin writing so that I make deadline. College journalists, just like those working for *Sports Illustrated* and magazines that cover sporting events, can spend extra time speaking with the athletes and coaches, getting stories and details about what transpired. Also, don't squander that extra time by heading to the newspaper office to write up the story late on the night it's due. Start early.

How about going beyond game coverage?

Again, use the built-in advantages you have. Sometimes it's difficult for a professional journalist – perhaps a guy in his 40s or 50s – to get an athlete to feel comfortable speaking with him, because he comes from a different background and has different interests and an age gap to overcome. You and the athlete you're covering have so much in common, being fellow students, taking similar classes, living in the same dorms, etc. The best interviews come when you're having a conversation with the person you're interviewing, not from a dry Q&A session.

Any thoughts on finding feature ideas?

You glean feature ideas by simply having conversations with the people you cover, being visible and maximizing the amount of time you spend with them.

Features don't only cover the on-field exploits of the best athlete on the team. It's finding out about their personalities and interesting things that have occurred in their lives. You get that by spending time with them and making them feel comfortable, with a pad or tape recorder away.

What advice do you have for sports writers and editors at schools with not-very-competitive or no sports teams?

Whether you're at a university where the athletics teams draw little interest, or covering what's perceived as a minor beat at a major Division I college (I initially covered men's tennis and women's fencing), you do yourself a tremendous disservice by worrying about the actual interest. You need to treat your beat like it's important. The athletes and coaches will notice the interest you're taking and reward you by opening up. Plus, sometimes off-the-radar teams are the best to cover. It's very hard on a major professional beat to write a feature about an athlete that hasn't already been told. You're telling stories for the first time. And often these people will have fascinating backgrounds if you dig deep enough to uncover it. Also, you're probably underestimating the actual readership, especially with most newspapers now on the Internet. Parents and other relatives read the stories, as do fraternity brothers, sorority sisters and other friends of the athletes, plus opposing coaches.

What were your most memorable moments as a college journalist?

From a journalism perspective, the most exciting moment was the night before Penn was to name its new athletics director, Steve Bilsky. As sports editor, I found out Bilsky would be arriving on an Amtrak train from Washington the night before the news conference. We dispatched a reporter and photographer to meet him at the 30th Street Station. As he's riding the escalator up from the tracks, we're shooting pictures of him arriving in Philly. He also consented to a brief interview. His first words were, "Boy, you guys are good."

From a sports perspective, it was a thrill to cover Penn's trip to the NCAA basketball tournament and clinching the Ivy League football title at rival Princeton. While you're supposed to be dispassionate as a journalist, you're still a student at the university and (quietly) revel in the success.

How can college papers make better use of their websites in covering sports?

College papers, whether they publish Monday–Friday or weekly, may want to post a short recap quickly after weekend sporting events – like after a Saturday football game – on their websites to address the competition from professional papers if it exists, or merely to increase hits on the site.

Consider creating pages on your website for each team, with links to the most recent stories, roster, schedule, statistics, etc. With technology these days, you can also put up audio or video of interviews, etc.

How did your experience on the college paper prepare you for your professional career? What do you wish you had known about sports writing then that you know now?

I would not be a sports writer today without *The Daily Pennsylvanian*. I was enrolled in Wharton, the business school at Penn. But I enjoyed so much working for the DP – first because of my affinity for sports, then because of my affinity for journalism – that I decided to seek internships with newspapers rather than in business. By the time I graduated, it was a natural choice to enter journalism.

There are so many things you learn about sports writing after college that it's difficult to cite just one. One warning, though, would be that journalism in competitive markets can be all-consuming. As a baseball beat writer, I'm typically on the road 170 days a year.

TIPS FROM A PRO
How to build a great sports section
Joe Gisondi

To create a top-notch sports section, you need to plan like a coach and generate a game plan. That means you'll need to develop daily, weekly and monthly news budgets, hold regular meetings with staffers, and work closely with the photo and design desks to ensure you have top-quality pictures that lead to equally impressive pages.

To budget, ask each staff member to pitch stories for the week that include gamers, precedes, features, notes packages and multimedia projects. Propose photos and art with every story, along with a prescribed length and specific deadline. If you are a daily, plan next week's five days during a Friday afternoon meeting. If you know the number of pages you'll have, also assign stories to pages, leaving room to re-adjust and change assignments based upon the news of that day.

Before you plan, you'll need to assign reporters to specific sports beats. Sometimes, staffs will rotate reporters so everybody has a chance to cover the so-called prestigious beats like football or basketball, but that is a disservice to reporters who won't properly develop sources, to players and coaches who won't know their main contact person, and to readers who won't receive sufficient insights. Beat sports reporters are like embedded journalists who receive, in many situations, almost unfettered access to coaches, players, locker rooms, executives and private conversations. Beat reporters should become part of the daily landscape, spending as much time with the athletes as team managers, personnel directors and team physicians. As a result, team members will feel comfortable speaking around and to this writer, which will yield breaking news and insights worth reading.

Once reporters get their beats, they should introduce themselves to the sports information director, who, in turn, will introduce them to the assistants in charge of other beats. Dress and act professionally for these meetings, if you expect to be treated like a pro.

Then, reporters should meet informally with coaches, asking them to offer information about their teams and their sports off the record. But make sure you review the team's roster and read stories about the team before you meet.

And don't try to impress anybody with your knowledge of the game. Frankly, you won't know nearly as much as the coaches and, frequently, not as much as players. Be honest. Let the coaches know you know this. As a result, maybe a coach will help educate you about a sport along the way.

Here are a few other print features you may consider.

- If you don't already have one, start a weekly athlete profile that focuses on an impressive athletic performance or that reveals an interesting student-athlete. Find players from all teams, not just the football and basketball teams. You can offer this as a traditional feature or in Q&A format.
- Write precedes for as many games, or beats, as possible. Frequently, these stories focus more on the opposing teams, offering trends or interesting stories found from researching and interviewing coaches and players. Set up these interviews either by speaking with your sports information director or by directly contacting the other school's SID.
- Publish conference standings alongside game precedes and game stories, along with the most recent results and schedule (Figure 7.2). That means publishing the current Saturday game results and next weekend's schedule for football games, for example. These give readers an additional perspective on the local team's progress.
- Make sure your staff develops in-depth stories, which can lift your section up to the next level. Write a sports budget story every year, focusing on financial adjustments during the past year – and noting, when relevant, changes or trends over the past five to 10 years. Pull every coach's contract for review. Investigate trends (the dominance of pitchers in your conference), find dramatic human stories (focus on individuals outside the lines as well), and explain esoteric or medical terms.

Ultimately, your sports section will be judged by its content in print and online. The best sections are comprehensive, timely, professional – as well as innovative, creative and fun.

So what else can a staff do to create '*the*' place where fans turn for sports news on your campus?

College newspapers have to deliver more content on many more multimedia platforms much more frequently, if they are to remain relevant. And many colleges are already doing such things.

Nearly all sports sections now offer information daily on a blog that includes notes from practices, honors for players and general updates. Ask reporters to post an item, even if it is a few paragraphs, from each day's practice.

Make sure you also use social media like Twitter and Facebook to promote coverage. It's as simple as creating a site with your newspaper's name, such as *Daily Eastern News sports*. Set it up so all Facebook feeds are also tweeted.

In addition, post photo galleries from games, practices or feature packages. Don't let all those terrific photos go to waste, using just one or two for the print edition. Besides, fans love viewing and downloading pictures of their teams.

Ask reporters to use digital recorders for all interviews so short audio clips can be inserted with stories online. Try to keep these clips to about 90 seconds. Better to post several shorter clips than to post a lengthy one that few people will listen to all the way through.

Don't get overwhelmed. Start with one new item at a time. In time, your newspaper and website will grow stronger and your reporting will drill deeper.

JOE GISONDI, a sports reporter and editor for more than 20 years, is the author of the *Field Guide To Covering Sports* (CQ Press, 2010). He is also an associate journalism professor at Eastern Illinois University. You can find more tips and suggestions about sports journalism at his website, SportsFieldGuide.com.

TO DO

1 Invite a sportswriter or sports editor from your local professional paper to speak to your sports staff.

2 Think about ways to enhance your sports coverage on your website. Consider posting slide shows and Web updates or creating team pages fans can use to get complete, up-to-the-minute coverage.

3 If you don't already have one, consider creating a preview section for the biggest sport or sports on campus. Include profiles of athletes, Q&As with a coach, game schedules, history timelines and other elements that will be useful and interesting to readers.

4 Try to go beyond day-to-day sports coverage by planning a special project or feature. Study National Collegiate Athletic Association statistics and reports or look for interesting trends worth exploring.

5 If you haven't already used CoveritLive, Twitter or another live blogging program to report on a game, give it a try. Experiment with getting readers involved by asking questions. After the game see what kind of responses you got.

6 If your news website doesn't already publish sports-related databases, produce one. You can look at athletes' graduation rates, game attendance, athletic department salaries. See if you can compare your school to others.

TO READ

Fensch, Thomas. *The Sports Writing Handbook, 2nd ed.* Hillsdale, N.J.: Lawrence Erlbaum & Associates, 1995.

Fink, Conrad C. *Sportwriting: The Lively Game*. Ames, Iowa: Iowa State Press, 2001.

Gisondi, Joe. *Field Guide to Covering Sports*. Washington, D.C.: CQ Press, 2010.

Swan, Jennifer. *Sports Style Guide and Reference Manual: The Complete Reference for Sports Editors, Writers, and Broadcasters*. Worcester, Mass.: Triumph Books, 1996.

Wilstein, Steve. *Associated Press Sports Writing Handbook*. New York, N.Y.: McGraw-Hill, 2001.

TO CLICK

Association for Women in Sports Media

AWSM is a nonprofit support network and advocacy group for women who work in sports writing, editing, broadcast, production, and media relations. The group has a reduced membership rate for students as well as an internship/scholarship program.

http://awsmonline.org/

College football history

Learn everything you ever needed to know about college football history.

www.collegefootballhistory.com

National Collegiate Athletic Association

The NCAA website offers news, statistics, press releases and other information about collegiate sports.

www.ncaa.org/

Sports Field Guide

The companion blog to the *Field Guide to Covering Sports* by Joe Gisondi offers tips on every aspect of covering college sports. Earlier posts can be found at onsportz.blogspot.com.

http://sportsfieldguide.com

The Sports Institute

The Sports Institute at Boston University's College of Communication offers an intensive four-week summer study program on the sports industry.

http://www.bu.edu/com/sports_institute

on the web:
www.statenews.com/lowdown

the lowdown

MS&U entertainment • The State News

Section **B**
THURSDAY
March 4, 2004

grand ole
LANSING

Why does such a large and unique mix of country exist in a Midwest, capital city?

2B

Animal science senior Curtis Shoup sits and plays the banjo. Shoup is an avid listener of country music, which is on the rise in the East Lansing area.

Julie Dawes/The State News

march 4–march 10: get out. get down.

happenings
get out and do something.
Go online for a list of upcoming events.

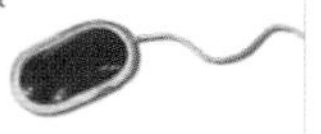

www.statenews.com

tada!
jot down your inner emo.
Make your very own fabulous, fabric-covered angst receptacle — adorned with buttons.
page 6B

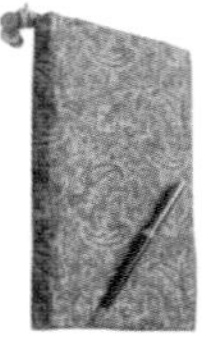

film
screen king
'Rings' star moves on to new project with Friday's release of 'Hidalgo.'
page 4B

Elysia A. Smith MS&U editor • **phone** (517)355-8252 • **fax** (517)353-2599 • **e-mail** msandu@statenews.com

FIGURE 8.1 The arts and entertainment section of a student newspaper should be an indispensable guide to what is happening on and near the campus. *The State News*, Michigan State University.

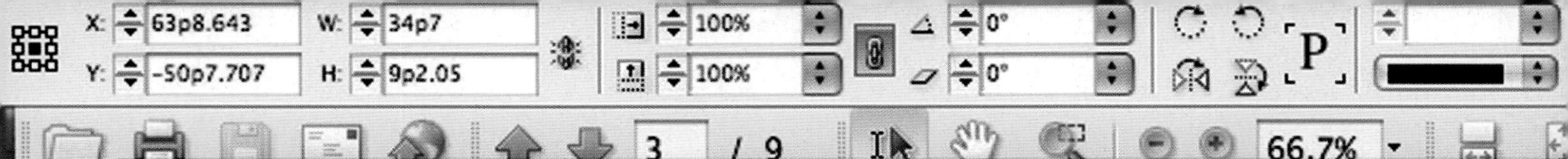

CHAPTER 8 ARTS AND ENTERTAINMENT WRITING

It's Friday afternoon and a bunch of friends are sitting in a dorm room planning for the weekend. What's playing at the multiplex? Is that student production of "Midsummer Night's Dream" worth seeing? What band is performing at the student union tonight?

If your arts and entertainment section is any good, the savvy students will depend on your paper to find out what's hot and what's not.

College students are among the biggest consumers of pop culture. While everyone else is raising kids, going to work and getting up early in the morning, students are out late, soaking up the local culture. So arts and entertainment coverage should be a major component of any student newspaper.

While you want to be an authoritative source of information, don't make the mistake of trying to imitate the daily newspaper – or even the funky alternative weekly – in town. Instead, set your own course.

"Student newspapers should offer up-close reporting on college life and culture," advises Peter S. Scholtes, a music writer, who got his start at the *Minnesota Daily*

The Student Newspaper Survival Guide, Second Edition. Rachele Kanigel.

CHAPTER CONTENTS

(mndaily.com) at the University of Minnesota. "Most of the time, student papers focus on the same things other papers focus on when it comes to arts and entertainment. Young journalists want to be like older professionals and don't realize that their greatest resource is being themselves – young and surrounded by student life."

Arts writing should be evocative and distinctive, like this piece on the band the Cramps Sean McCourt wrote for *Golden Gate [X]press* (goldengatexpress.org), the weekly newspaper at San Francisco State University:

> If the creatures, monsters, demons and derelicts that haunted many of the classic B-movie horror films of the 1950s came to life, invaded the Memphis recording studio of Sun Records, and partied with Carl Perkins, Elvis Presley, Johnny Cash and Jerry Lee Lewis, the end result of those sessions might have sounded something like the Cramps.
>
> For nearly three decades now, the Cramps have been unleashing their fiendishly twisted and mutated style of rock 'n' roll on an unsuspecting world – surviving revolving door line-up changes, disastrous record label deals, and a myriad of obstacles that would have caused any lesser group of musical monsters to drive a stake through their own hearts. But through it all, the mainstay devilish duo of Lux Interior on vocals and Poison Ivy on guitar have proved that staying sick (and true to their ideals) pays off in the long run.

Chances are, you wouldn't find that in a mainstream daily newspaper.

Entertainment coverage should be diverse. It's fine if the music reviewer is a Shania Twain fanatic, but the A&E editor should make sure the section covers more than country music. Your A&E pages should have a mix of music, dance, film, theater and visual arts and cover many different genres within each category.

Arts and entertainment sections primarily run five types of stories:

- Previews
- Reviews
- Columns
- Feature stories
- News stories.

Since we've covered features and news stories in other chapters, we'll stick here to previews, reviews and columns.

PREVIEWS

Previews, or advances, are stories that tell about upcoming performances and exhibits. These are often the most useful stories because they help readers plan what they want to see. An A&E section with strong previews becomes an essential guide to culture in your community.

Advances may be written as briefs or as longer feature stories. You can take a general approach or focus on a specific aspect of the artist or performance. For example, if a student group is staging a play on campus, you may write a story that takes readers behind the scenes of a rehearsal or one that focuses on the hopes and aspirations of the director. For a preview of an art show, you may decide to bring readers to the artist's studio or interview the curator about what the work represents. If an out-of-town band is coming to town, try to interview members a week or two before by phone to give readers a sense of what's in store.

When writing a preview, be sure to include practical information for the reader, such as dates, times and location of performances or exhibits; phone number for the venue; and, if appropriate, ticket prices. This information may be written in italics at the end of the story or, better yet, included in an information box packaged with the story and photo.

REVIEWS

Nearly every writer who has sat through an embarrassingly bad film or been transported by a glorious musical performance has fantasized about becoming a critic. What could be more fun than sharing your fervent opinions with thousands of readers dying to know what you think?

But reviewing isn't simply about dumping your opinions, says Harry Kloman, a film critic who advises *The Pitt News* (pittnews.com) at the University of Pittsburgh. "To be a real critic, and a good critic, you need to have three things: First, you need to have the ability to write well. Second, you need to have the ability to report. And third, you need to have the ability to think."

A review is a critical analysis of a performance, exhibit or other artistic work. Most reviews include five basic elements:

- A catchy opening that draws readers into the piece
- Identifying information, including the name of the work, the primary artists involved, where and when it can be seen
- A concise summary of the content of the work

Q&A Roger Ebert

Before becoming a celebrated film critic, Roger Ebert was a columnist and editor for *The Daily Illini* (dailyillini.com) at the University of Illinois. Ebert has written for the *Chicago Sun-Times* since 1967 and is well known for his TV work opposite critic-colleague Gene Siskel on *Siskel and Ebert* (they were formerly hosts of PBS's *At the Movies*). In 1975, he became the first film critic to win a Pulitzer Prize. He is the author of several books on the cinema, including *A Kiss Is Still A Kiss* (1984), and screenplays, most notably Russ Meyer's cult classic, *Beyond The Valley of the Dolls* (1970).

You were editor of *The Daily Illini*. What memories do you have of working on the college paper? How did your experiences as a student journalist influence your career?

I published and edited a weekly alternative paper as a freshman, then went over to the DI as a columnist and became news editor before I was editor. It was, and is, a real daily newspaper, independent of the university, and the best education was working with a union printing shop, which of necessity made deadlines real.

What can college papers do to make their arts and entertainment coverage interesting and relevant to their readers? What can they do to set their coverage apart from professional papers?

Find and develop colorful, quirky first-person essayists, and the taste of the majority of the students be damned.

What advice do you have for young arts and entertainment writers? What tips do you have on writing reviews?

Always write in the first person. Be closely in touch with what you really felt, even more than what you really thought. Experiment with form.

What can student reviewers do to research and become more knowledgeable about the films they review?

Simple. See lots of movies, read about them, talk about them, study them, teach them.

Any other tips, advice, words of wisdom for young journalists?

1 The muse visits during the act of composition, not before.

2 No article will ever be finished unless it is started.

3 If you procrastinate, play with deadlines and delay doing assignments, get out of the business. You're not enjoying it.

A critical assessment of the work, including its strengths and weaknesses and whether the audience would appreciate it

Background and history, such as other creative works by this artist and how this work compares with others in the genre.

"Do your homework," advises Scholtes. "Learn how to use libraries and book stores and Google and Lexis-Nexis so that you really know where a piece of art or music or film is coming from, and you aren't just using press releases."

In his book *Five Stars! How to Become a Film Critic, the World's Greatest Job* (Sutro Press, 2005), Christopher Null, editor-in-chief of Filmcritic.com, offers one simple rule to writing a good review: BE HONEST.

"That's it!" writes Null, who worked on *The Daily Texan* (dailytexanonline.com) when he was a student at the University of Texas at Austin. "Whether you are writing your first review or your 3,000th review, if you aren't honest with yourself, with the film, and with your readers, your review is useless. You can 'be nice' about your criticism or you can get really detailed with your complaints, but all of this is meaningless if you don't tell the truth and provide an analysis that comes from your heart."

That said, you may want to use tact when criticizing student artists. It's one thing to slam the latest Jim Jarmusch movie or Kanye West CD; it's another to skewer a student actor or musician who has screwed up his courage to get on stage. That doesn't mean you should give a glowing review to a dull, lifeless performance. But save the big guns for someone making the big bucks.

Whether you're writing about music, dance, theater, film or visual art, every review should have a clear message and a distinctive point of view. Don't just say the concert was weak or the movie was bad; use examples and vivid description to drive your point home. What about the dance

CHECKLIST
Entertainment review

When writing a review, ask yourself these questions:

1 Do you clearly identify the performance, CD, film, exhibit, etc. being reviewed?
2 Does the review include relevant information (perhaps in an accompanying information box) about times, dates, locations of performances or showings, prices, etc.?
3 Does the review clearly identify the genre (such as classical, hip-hop, reggae, country and western for music; comedy, drama or thriller for film; modern, ballet, flamenco for dance, etc.) and describe how this work fits in with other pieces in this genre?
4 Do you explain how the performance, film or other work being reviewed achieves its intent? Does the work make you laugh, cry, think the way you're supposed to? Why is it effective or not effective?
5 If there's a story, do you give enough of a synopsis to help the reader understand the work without giving away the whole plot?
6 Do you offer a critique of the work, detailing what was effective, what wasn't and why? Do you back up your criticism with telling examples?
7 If relevant, do you critique individual performances, explaining what worked, what didn't and why?
8 Do you include background information or history about the artists involved? Is this the first time this actor has performed at this theater? Is this band homegrown or visiting from afar?
9 Do you include audience reaction if that's relevant?
10 Do you give readers a sense of whether they would enjoy this work or performance?

performance was so exciting? Why did you want to throw a tomato at the movie screen?

THE FIRST-PERSON DILEMMA

To write in first person or not to write in first person; that is the question for every critic. And even professional reviewers can't agree on the answer. Some see first-person writing as arrogant, unprofessional or just plain lame. "The use of 'I' is a crutch for a young critic," says Kloman, the Pittsburgh critic and *Pitt News* (pittnews.com) adviser. "You should do more than just *discourage* it. You should *banish* it."

Others say first person adds personality and intimacy to a review. Pulitzer Prize-winning critic Roger Ebert of the *Chicago Sun-Times*, for example, advises reviewers, even students, to *always* use first person.

Perhaps the best advice is to write what feels natural to you. Each reviewer has to find his or her own style, a persona in print.

TIPS FROM A PRO Sean McCourt

When I was working on my student newspapers, co-workers sometimes would come up to me and ask, "How in the world did you ever get to interview (insert band name here)?!"

It doesn't take a miracle, or having some shady connection in the music business, to set up interviews with bands – even famous ones. But it does take a little effort, patience and passion on your part. Here are some tips for making it as a music writer:

1 **Take advantage of time spent on your student newspaper.** You will probably have more freedom to do what you really want to do now, when your editors and co-workers are fellow students, than when you're working at your first job. Don't put off trying to set up the interview with the band or musician you have always dreamed of meeting. It may take a while for you to establish yourself after you graduate, and if you follow rock 'n' roll, you know there is a distinct possibility that the performers you most want to interview will have broken up (or even be dead) by the time you're a pro.

2 **Make contacts.** Come up with a list of local clubs, venues and promoters, and call or email all of them. Tell them who you are and ask to get on their mailing lists and to receive their press releases. Chances are that your readers are their target customers, and they should be happy to work with you.

3 **Maintain a professional attitude.** Don't expect to immediately get in to every concert for free or expect special treatment. Professional relationships in the music business can take as long to cement as romantic ones do.

4 **Reach out to local bands and record labels.** They are more likely to get excited about coverage and can be a great source for other contacts as well – not to mention the fact that many independent bands playing in smoky dive bars are just as good as, if not better than, the ones getting all the radio airplay or MTV coverage.

5 **Spend a night out on the town.** Try to make it out to as many concerts and shows as your schedule and budget allow. You'll get a much better sense of the pulse of the local music scene and hopefully, enjoy yourself while doing it.

6 **Make it happen.** When you see that a band or musician you want to interview is coming to your town, get in touch with your contact at that particular venue and ask for the band's contact information. The act's manager or record label will arrange to set up the interview and provide you with a press kit, advance CDs, etc. Most of the time you will do the interview over the phone – that way the article can run in advance of the group's local appearance. With local bands, it is more likely that you'll be able to do the interview in person, which can give you a better feel for the people involved.

7 **Be persistent.** If you can't get an interview the first time, try again. It took me three years to get an interview with Mike Ness of Social Distortion, but it was well worth the effort.

8 **Remember to relax.** Don't get intimidated by a big interview. It can be hard at first, but if you are comfortable and at ease, your subject will most likely be as well.

9 **Do your research.** Even if you think you know all there is to know about the history of the band or musician you are going to interview, take the time to really get to know them. Listen to as much of their music as possible, read old interviews, look them up on the Internet, etc.

10 **Think your questions through, and write them down.** Don't throw together 10 random questions right before the interview. Try to think of as many different queries as possible. Try for something a little meatier than the standard "what are your influences?" or asking for drunken tour stories (although they can occasionally be entertaining).

11 **Use an audio recorder when conducting an interview.** But take written notes as well. You never know if the equipment will break, the batteries will run out, or the recorder will suddenly seem to be possessed. If you at least have some basic notes, you can usually salvage the interview –not to mention face your editor when he or she asks what happened to the great story you promised the week before.

12 **Avoid using clichés.** It can be tempting, especially if your deadline is looming, and we are all guilty of it as beginners, but try to work around them. In this business, it's all about setting yourself apart from others. If you sound just like everybody else, you won't make a name for yourself.

13 **Most of all, have fun!** That's why we're doing it, right? If you're passionate about something, it shows – especially in your writing.

SEAN McCOURT is a freelance writer who specializes in music. While attending San Francisco State University, he worked on the *Golden Gate [X]press* newspaper as a staff writer and arts and entertainment editor. During his time on *[X]press* (and at his junior college newspaper) he interviewed both local bands and world-famous musicians, including members of Nirvana, the Pixies, Social Distortion, X and the Cramps. He has written for *The San Francisco Bay Guardian*, *Sierra* magazine, *7×7* magazine, and *Rockabilly* magazine.

COLUMNS

Just like columns in your sports section, A&E columns provide unique perspectives that add personality to your paper. Some newspapers have columnists who regularly cover film, music or another artistic arena. Columnists should understand their topic well and be able to provide background and context.

Columnists should have a deep understanding of the art they cover. You needn't be a film major to cover film,

Q&A Rob Owen

As a student at Syracuse University, Rob Owen dreamed about becoming a full-time television critic. In his freshman year he started writing about TV and movies for *The Daily Orange* (dailyorange.com), the campus newspaper, and went on to become the paper's lifestyle editor. After graduating in 1993, he went to work for the *Richmond Times-Dispatch* as a feature writer and co-creator of a teen section called inSync. He got his first TV critic job at the *Times Union* in Albany, N.Y. in 1996 and in June 1998 got his dream job – full-time TV editor at the *Pittsburgh Post-Gazette*. In 1997 he published the book *Gen X TV: The Brady Bunch to Melrose Place* (Syracuse University Press, 1997), an account of the TV programs members of the Generation X age group grew up watching, the shows they watch now and the programs that depict their lives.

When did you decide you wanted to be a TV critic?
Pretty much my senior year of high school. I was the first entertainment editor of my high school's newspaper and I decided I preferred TV over film as a medium.

What intrigued you about writing about TV?
I'm very drawn to character-driven storytelling and in TV writers have 22 episodes to tell a story, which allows for a lot more nuance and realistic development than one can get in a two-hour movie.

Were you a TV junkie as a kid?
Not really. I liked TV, but we never had cable growing up and my parents did limit my TV viewing time. TV was not a babysitter for me.

What experiences at *The Daily Orange* helped shape you as a writer and a critic?
Hmmm, all of them. *The Daily Orange* was like an incubator for real-world journalism. I learned about internal politics at a newspaper and dealing with writers who can't meet a deadline. I learned to manage difficult personalities, encourage younger writers and balance work at the paper with schoolwork. They're all useful skills that translate into real post-collegiate life.

What advice do you have for students who want to cover arts and entertainment?
Just do it. By that I mean, don't be afraid to approach the student newspaper and its editors with your ideas. My first year at Syracuse University in 1989, I wrote up a preview of the fall 1989 TV season and walked it up to *The Daily Orange*, figuring they'd never run it.

Little did I know campus papers are constantly starved for copy. They ran that story and every other movie/TV review I wrote during the next four years.

Specifically, it's great to cultivate a network of sources, whatever beat you take on. If it's the movie beat, try to get passes to press screenings of movies before they open. If it's the music beat, call the record companies and get on their mailing lists. Don't expect things to come to you, you have to go after what you want.

How can student journalists and critics get film, music and other entertainment industry people to take them seriously?
By acting professionally and by not being a flake. If you ask for an interview and they grant it, send them a clip. If you ask for a CD to review and you review it, send them a clip. Do not request a pass to a movie just because you want to see the movie.

Learn to work with the publicity folks. That doesn't mean you do what they tell you or take every pitch they send your way, but building rapport and relationships will definitely help you get taken more seriously.

How can college papers provide a fresh angle on entertainment coverage when there's so much coverage in professional newspapers?
College newspapers are at ground level of youth culture, which is what seeps into the pop culture, so college papers can be at the forefront of covering what bubbles up from youth culture, particularly when it comes to music.

What kind of research is involved in entertainment criticism? What can student critics do to be more authoritative and knowledgeable in their criticism?
Read, read, read. Read as much criticism as you can. Not to copy it, but to get examples of different styles of critical voice. It also does not hurt to have a broad liberal arts base, particularly when it comes to movie/TV criticism

(wish I had more of that). Take courses in the subject area that's your beat and become an expert in that area. Talk to the critic on your beat at the local paper to get his/her advice.

Any other words of wisdom for entertainment or lifestyle writers and editors?

Be organized! Your life will be much easier if you plan ahead. That said, also be prepared to rip up a page to make it more timely. That will happen in the real world.

FIGURE 8.2 A good arts and entertainment section should be an essential guide for students who want to explore the cultural life of their campus and community. *34th Street*, the online and print A&E section of *The Daily Pennsylvanian*, offers readers a variety of options, from movies and music to restaurants and bars. *The Daily Pennsylvanian*, University of Pennsylvania.

but you had better know your Spike Lee from your Spike Jonze.

TO DO

1 Invite a professional critic to give a lecture on reviewing to your A&E writers or to your entire staff.

2 Invite professors from your theater, film, music, television, dance or art departments to participate in a panel discussion or a series of workshops for your staff on arts coverage.

3 Contact the visual and performing arts groups and classes on campus to find out when they are having exhibits and performances.

4 Assign a reporter and photographer to follow one production from beginning to end. Ask if you can sit in on tryouts, rehearsals, set and costume design sessions. The reporter and photographer's collaboration could become a series, a long feature or multimedia piece on the making of the production.

TO READ

Corrigan, Timothy. *A Short Guide to Writing About Film, 5th ed.* Upper Saddle River, N.J.: Longman, 2003.

McCoy, W.U. *Performing and Visual Arts: Writing and Reviewing.* New York, N.Y.: University Press of America, 1992.

Null, Christopher. *Five Stars! How to Become a Film Critic, the World's Greatest Job.* San Francisco, Calif.: Sutro Press, 2005.

Titchener, Campbell B. *Reviewing the Arts, 3rd ed.* Mahwah, N.J.: Lawrence Erlbaum Associations, Inc., 2005.

TO CLICK

American Theatre Critics Association

The American Theatre Critics Association, Inc., the only national association of professional theatre critics, is open to people who review theatre professionally for print, electronic or digital media.

www.americantheatrecritics.org

Broadcast Film Critics Association

A group of critics who broadcast on television, on radio, or on the Internet, sponsors scholarships for students interested in becoming film critics.

www.bfca.org

Screen Actors Guild

SAG represents nearly 120,000 actors in film, television, industrials, commercials and music videos. Members of the press can get names of talent agents for most actors.

www.sag.org

COMING UP
Columnist Aaron Lalic discusses what the university can do to compete with other campuses for new students.

OPINION

ABOUT OPINION
Brock Rutter, editor
opinion-editor.shorthorn@uta.edu
Opinion is published Wednesday and Friday

Friday, September 14, 2001 — THE SHORTHORN — Page 3

EDITORIAL/OUR VIEW

Cutting Class

The UT System should have canceled classes Tuesday so the community could recover

EDITORIAL ROUND-UP
The issue: The UT System should have given students Tuesday off.
We suggest: UT System officials exercise more consideration in the future.

The UT System did its students and employees a disservice by not cancelling classes Tuesday in the wake of the day's disaster. The decision was unproductive, unprecedented and disrespectful to students and employees who were fearful for loved ones' lives.

Whatever UT System administrators hoped to accomplish not canceling classes was surely not accomplished. Many students simply were too shocked or too transfixed by the news to come to class at all. Others who did go to class, did so with the burden of the day's news weighing heavily on them, diminishing their ability to pay attention. Still others went to class to find that the day's lecture had been turned into a discussion of the horrible events — something better done in the company of friends and loved ones. Whether or not any progress was made in any specific classes, almost without exception, the material covered will have to be re-covered because of absences.

Tragedies of this magnitude are fortunately few and far between. Perhaps the only two tragedies on par with this in any living person's memory are President John F. Kennedy's assassination and the Japanese attack on Pearl Harbor in 1941. Tuesday's tragedy, involving more deaths than either of the two — and civilian deaths at that — is arguably the worst of the three. In the previous cases, nearly everything in the United States shut down.

New York is a big city — some say a business capital of the world. As a consequence, many at UTA and through the UT System have friends, family and loved ones there. For some, the first reaction to Tuesday's news was to telephone or e-mail acquaintances living there to be sure they were safe. That is more important than class. Anecdotal stories from students who were berated for being late or missing class because they were trying to contact loved ones are particularly disturbing.

Let us hope we will not live to see another such tragedy. However, if we are unfortunate enough that that should happen, let us hope the UT System will have learned a message in human nature and good taste and give us all, students and employees, the day off.

GUEST COLUMN

A New Patriotism

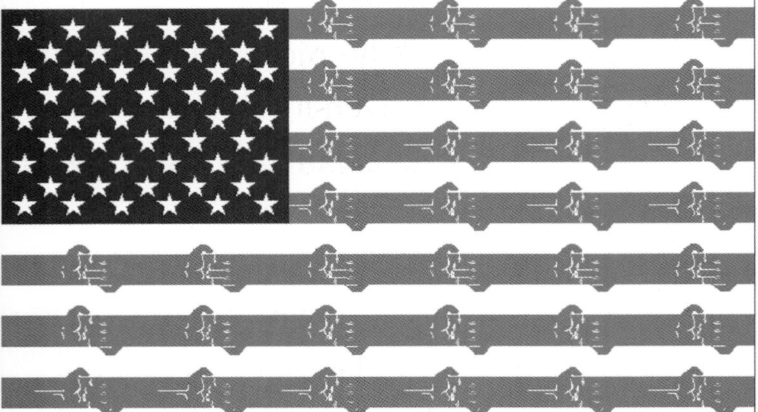

The Shorthorn: Jeff Shaw

Terrorist attacks spur a forgotten sense of American pride

Joel Fish is a journalism senior. He can be reached at opinion-editor.shorthorn@uta.edu

Buried under the piles of rubble and depressing emotion in the aftermath of the worst terrorist attack ever on American soil is a glimmer of something wonderful.

Let me demonstrate what I mean:

Several months ago a friend of mine reacted to an American flag draped on the wall of my new apartment. He laughed, asking irreverently if I was "patriotic or something?"

My answer, obvious as it seemed to me, was a confused and fervent "Yes." He chuckled and shook his head.

Tuesday evening, as I watched the White House press conference addressing the horrors in New York City and Washington, D.C., my friend phoned me to talk about the incident. His tone couldn't have been more different than it had been just several months before. Like most Americans, he felt violated and fearful. But most of all, he felt patriotic.

America has indeed gained something wonderful from this disaster. People are singing the national anthem and, miraculously, they really mean the words they sing. I can't help but wonder if I've ever experienced that before.

With media speculation teeming about who is to blame, and Osama bin Laden on the chopping block, Americans want to know who should be hunted down and punished. Their shared anger, honed like a razor, has brought them back to an "us versus them" usually reserved only for wartime.

Let's not admonish this attitude. There are bad guys and good guys, and I won't insult readers by categorizing those responsible for the attack. It's been a long time since America has faced such a personal threat, and Americans can't forget that the horrors of past wars still exist.

In closing, allow me to shock you with this statement: The terrorists involved in this attack have inadvertently given all surviving Americans a gift worth more than all of the gold and jewels in the world.

A long-needed new patriotism has materialized, just in time for the new century.

The Sleeping Giant

Terrorist attacks can't threaten America's existence.

While Tuesday's terrorist attacks on Washington, D.C., and New York were terrifying indeed, in the long run they will not serve the interests of those who carried them out. America, while shocked, is not in mortal danger but only has been awakened.

Wars of terror and attrition can sometimes be successful for a smaller party if it has limited goals, which a more powerful party can satisfy without making concessions that will threaten its very existence. In such cases, the strength of the smaller party is its superior resolve and determination, with which it gradually wears down the will of the stronger power.

Take the examples of the French in Algeria or Vietnam and the Soviet Union in Afghanistan. In all three cases, one party in the conflict was faced with what it saw as a fight for its existence, whereas the stronger party was fighting merely to maintain a superior position of wealth and influence. France's existence never was threatened by the loss of any of its colonies, nor was the Soviet Union threatened by a change of government in Afghanistan. In all three cases, the human and material cost of keeping people down eventually trumped limited advantages gained through occupation.

Brock Rutter is a history senior. He can be reached at opinion-editor.shorthorn@uta.edu

But such strategies do not work when a nation's existence is threatened. Look at Israel today or Britain during the Blitz of World War II. Nearly since its inception, Israel has been the subject of almost continuous terrorist attacks. Israel has proven time and again that its army can defeat any military combination its neighbors can field, yet still terrorist groups seek to wear down the state's will to exist. Similarly, the Germans in World War II calculated (probably erroneously) that they did not have the might to assault Britain head-on in the months after Dunkirk. Instead of attacking military targets, they sought to erode the public's will to fight by bombing British cities.

The campaign against Britain did not work, and Israel still exists despite 50 years of attrition attacks. When a nation's very existence is at stake, there is simply no point at which its people will throw up their hands and say, "It's not worth it." And in such a case, the greater power will win.

On the contrary, when terror is brought to civilians, the population is galvanized. Doves and pacifists are silenced, and the nation under attack finds a new unity. Resolve is mixed with indignity that an enemy would have the audacity to slaughter noncombatants, and the nation under attack finds a focus previously lacking.

Such is the nature of the campaign against the United States. Regardless of who is to blame, the world is awash in the rhetoric of those who call for its destruction, and any moral high ground the attackers claim to have is lost with the lives of innocents. There is no limited concession America is being asked to make that would satisfy the anti-American activists of the world.

In all likelihood, even if Americans gave up their Middle East interests or any other limited goal, extremists still would hate them.

These countries despise America's capitalism, individuality, disciplined political scene, wealth and freedoms that allegedly breed immorality. In short, some groups hate everything America holds dear and, as such, threaten Americans' right to exist. Without a feasible exit, America, or any nation, will fight to the death.

THE SHORTHORN
Since 1919

EDITOR-IN-CHIEF
Jason Hoskins

E-MAIL
editor.shorthorn@uta.edu

The Shorthorn is the official student newspaper of the University of Texas at Arlington and is published four times weekly during fall and spring semesters, and twice weekly during the summer sessions. Unsigned editorials are the opinion of THE SHORTHORN EDITORIAL BOARD and do not necessarily reflect the opinions of individual student writers or editors, Shorthorn advisers or university administration. LETTERS should be limited to 300 words. They may be edited for space, spelling, grammar and malicious or libelous statements. Letters must be the original work of the writer and must be signed. For identification purposes, letters also must include the writer's full name, address and telephone number, although the address and telephone number will not be published. Students should include their classification, major and their student ID number, which is for identification purposes. The student ID number will not be published. Signed columns and letters to the editor reflect the opinion of the writer and serve as an open forum for the expression of facts or opinions of interest to The Shorthorn's readers.

FIGURE 9.1 Opinion pages provide newspaper staff members and readers alike a place to vent. *The Shorthorn*, University of Texas at Arlington.

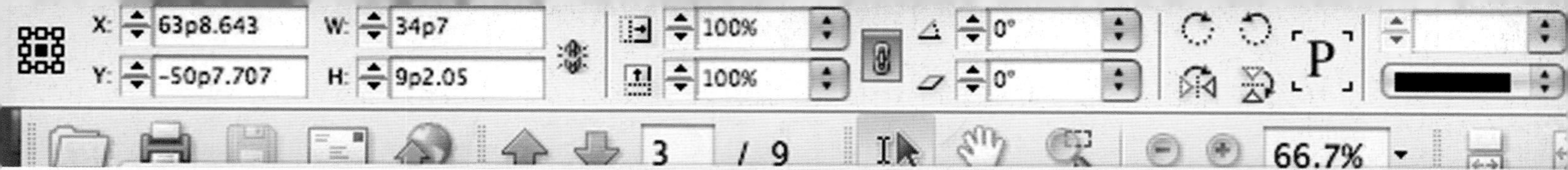

CHAPTER 9 OPINION PAGES

When *The Baylor Lariat* (baylor.edu/lariat) at Baylor University wrote an editorial in support of gay marriage, the piece didn't exactly play well on the campus of the largest Baptist university in the world. Within days of publishing the editorial, the Waco, Texas college paper was lambasted by faculty and administrators on the school's student publications board, as well as the university president, who said espousing a view "so out of touch with traditional Christian teachings is not only unwelcome, it comes dangerously close to violating university policy."

If you think opinion pages have to be stodgy and dull, think again.

The editorials, cartoons and columns that grace opinion pages can be among the most popular and well-read features of a student newspaper. A good opinion section is a virtual town square for your college community, a place where students, faculty, staff and community members can debate the issues of the day. But this is also the place where student newspapers are most likely to stir up trouble. Because they are so, well, opinionated, opinion pages can be lightning rods for controversy.

Clearly the line between what is provocative and what is simply offensive is narrow – and sometimes ill-defined. What passes for edgy on one campus may be

The Student Newspaper Survival Guide, Second Edition. Rachele Kanigel.

CHAPTER CONTENTS

considered insulting on another. In this chapter we'll look at how to create a stimulating, provocative opinion section – and how to deal with the flak that sometimes goes along with that.

THE OPINION SECTION

The classic opinion section comes in two parts – the editorial page and the op-ed (opposite-editorial), or commentary, page. In professional newspapers, the opinion page and op-ed pages are generally on facing pages, often the last two facing pages in the main news or local news section. With less space, college newspapers often combine editorial and op-ed sections into a single page.

The editorial page (Figure 9.2) usually includes:

A masthead. Names of the publisher and the principal editors

Editorials. Opinion pieces that comment on the news and reflect the views of the paper's editorial board

Editorial cartoons. Humorous sketches that comment on news and politics

Letters to the editor. Responses from readers.

Let's take a closer look at each of these elements.

The masthead

At professional papers, the masthead usually names the publisher and top editors, such as the executive editor, managing editor and editorial page editor, and the editorial board. Many student papers, especially those with a small staff, include the names of all editors or even all staffers in their mastheads. Some papers include email addresses for each staff member to increase accessibility.

Editorials

Professional papers generally have dedicated editorial writers whose job is to do research, form opinions and write cogent editorials on the issues of the day. These people are often senior staffers who came up through the ranks as reporters or editors. Typically they meet as a group on a regular basis to decide what issues they want to weigh in on and what stance the newspaper will take. "At its most basic, the editorial board is a debating club of sorts," Al Lanier, an editorial writer for the *Chicago Tribune*, wrote in a column explaining the process to readers. "We meet three times a week to talk about world events, large and small."

Student newspapers usually have an opinion editor and many have columnists, but few have dedicated editorial writers. Depending on the publication, editorials may be written by the editor-in-chief or individual editors or reporters. Typically, these are unsigned. It's important to keep in mind that unsigned editorials represent the institutional voice of the paper and the opinions expressed should speak for the editorial board, not just the individual writer.

Editorial cartoons

Want to get readers to your opinion section? Find a great cartoonist.

Like professional papers, student newspapers use editorial cartoons to comment on the news in a graphic and often humorous way (Figure 9.3).

While editorial cartoons can bring fans to your paper, they can also win you some foes. But that's not necessarily a bad thing, says Dan Carino, whose cartoons for *The Daily Aztec* (thedailyaztec.com) at San Diego State University were syndicated through KRT Campus and U-Wire for several years. Carino has won numerous national awards, including the prestigious John Locher Memorial Award from the Association of American Editorial Cartoonists.

He's also stirred up a heap of trouble.

On one occasion, students seized thousands of copies of *The Daily Aztec*, demanding apologies from the paper for publishing two racially charged cartoons. One depicted then-Iraqi President Saddam Hussein and Palestinian leader Yasser Arafat as camels with President Bush in the middle, thinking, "Definitely time for a regime change." The other cartoon showed an overweight man labeled "China" speaking in broken English in reaction to the North Korea nuclear weapons program.

In another incident, students and faculty at Indiana University in Bloomington demanded the resignation of the *Indiana Daily Student* (idsnews.com) editorial staff for running a syndicated Carino cartoon concerning affirmative action.

Despite the flak, Carino, who graduated from San Diego State University in 2003, says he appreciates the liberty he had as a student. "I believe that there's more freedom in student newspapers and that's something that an aspiring cartoonist should use to his/her advantage," he says. "The nature of political cartoons is to take issues and push them to the extreme, hoping to draw readers into a debate."

Letters to the editor

Printing letters to the editor is one of the best ways a newspaper can show it's listening to its readers. Your paper should clearly state its letters policy on the editorial page, giving guidelines on length and acceptable language and explaining your right to edit.

Many college newspaper editors complain they don't get enough letters to the editor. If readers aren't coming to you,

The Editorial Page

Masthead
A list of the editorial board members, usually the editor-in-chief, editorial page editor and other representatives of the newspaper staff appointed by the top editors.

Editorial
An opinion piece that comments on the news and reflects the views of the paper's editorial board.

Editorial policy
An explanation of whose views are expressed in editorials and columns and restrictions on opinion section content.

VIEWPOINT

Page 7 — Wednesday, April 6, 2005

DAILY BRUIN

Serving the UCLA community since 1919

Editorial Board

UC should overcome private bids to keep lab

Cochran's life crusade for justice admirable

Americanism welcomed abroad

David Keyes

Pope's political force important to legacy

LETTER TO THE EDITOR

Jewish, Muslim circumcisions more humane

EDITORIAL CARTOON
by Alex Hoffman

THE BOTTOM LINE — DOSE OF STATISTICS: 18,000 — QUOTE TO NOTE: "The new authorities are unable to guarantee security. ... Once the constitutional order is restored ... and calm returns to the country, I shall return to my home." Kyrgyzstan President Askar Akayev — SEND YOUR THOUGHTS: UCLA researchers found that nearly half of the sixth graders in L.A. public schools are bullied at least once a week. Were you bullied as a kid? Why are kids so mean? — Do you have an opinion? — E-MAIL: — MAIL:

Column
A personal opinion piece by a staff columnist, staff writer or other contributor. Some newspapers label columns as "staff column" and "guest column."

Column logo
A label for a column that includes the writer's name and head shot. Also known as column sig.

Columnist bio
A brief biographical note about the columnist that may include the writer's major, year in school and position on the newspaper staff or, job title if it's a faculty or staff person. It may also include the writer's email address.

Letters to the editor
Letters from readers.

Editorial cartoon
A humorous sketch that comments on news or politics.

Contact box
Information on how readers can contact the newspaper opinion section, including mailing and email addresses.

Contribution policy
An explanation of how readers can contribute columns or letters to the opinion section.

FIGURE 9.2 The Editorial Page. The *Daily Bruin*, University of California, Los Angeles. Graphic by Eugenia Chien.

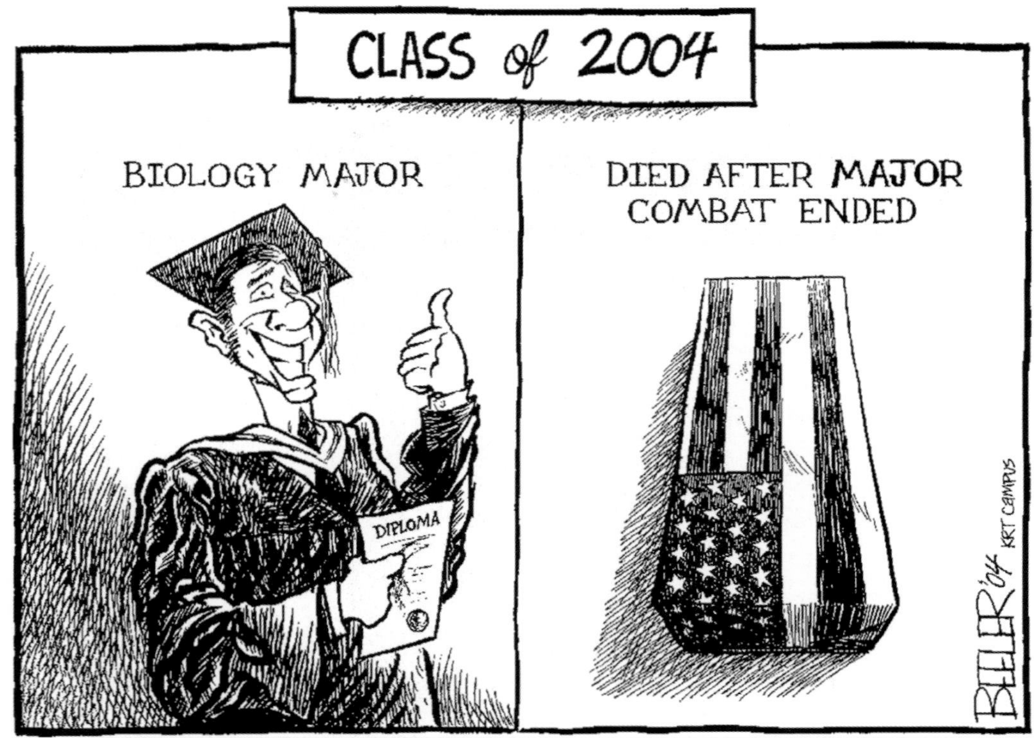

FIGURE 9.3 Editorial cartoons present opinions in a graphic, often humorous way. Reprinted with permission from Nate Beeler.

consider reaching out to them. "You have to go out and sell the idea of writing a letter to the editor to people who don't normally write letters," advises Denny Wilkins, who teaches opinion writing at St. Bonaventure University in New York.

A former editorial page editor for *The Recorder* in Greenfield, Mass., Wilkins recommends opinion page editors actively seek out letters by telling everyone they meet – faculty, staff, students – about the letters section and the role it serves. "You should put up posters and fliers; market the page as a place where students can write to tell you what they think about what you think. Go on the campus radio station or TV station and say, 'We want letters to the editor.'"

Wilkins also suggests putting a prompt line on your editorial page each week asking readers to respond in 75 words or less to questions like: What do you think of the new sculpture in front of the student union? Does the school spend too much money on athletics? How is the new registration system working?

Another sure way to get more letters, Wilkins says, is to provide "provocative, evocative content that people will respond to. Write editorials that piss people off."

The op-ed page

The op-ed page is a spot for columnists and community members to share their views. Unlike editorials, which reflect the views of the editorial board, pieces that appear on the op-ed page represent the opinions of individual authors.

To make your op-ed page inclusive and lively, solicit contributions from around the campus. If there's a controversial issue on campus – a labor contract dispute, a new smoking ban, a scandal in the administration – solicit opinions from faculty, staff and students who have a stake in the matter. Be sure to seek divergent views. Read campus blogs to find students who have strong opinions and who express them well.

Some student newspapers try to get a variety of opinions when a topic galvanizes the campus or the country. When a Rutgers freshman and several other gay teens committed suicide after being bullied or humiliated, the *Indiana Daily Student* invited its regular columnists to comment on the issues raised by the rash of suicides (Figure 9.4). They put together a poignant and compelling group of columns. "My personal intention was to raise awareness about the negative treatment of the GLBT community in our nation's schools and the very serious and very real impact that has on peoples' lives," says Zach Ammerman, who was co-editor of the opinion page at the time. "This was something that I have experienced first hand."

The editorial page

Masthead. A list of the editorial board members, usually the editor-in-chief, editorial page editor and other representatives of the newspaper staff appointed by the top editors.

Editorial. An opinion piece that comments on the news and reflects the views of the paper's editorial board.

Editorial policy. An explanation of whose views are expressed in editorials and columns and restrictions on opinion section content.

Column. A personal opinion piece by a staff columnist, staff writer or other contributor. Some newspapers label columns as "staff column" and "guest column."

INDIANA DAILY STUDENT | TUESDAY, OCTOBER 5, 2010

OPINION

EDITORS
Zach Ammerman zammerma@indiana.edu
Stephen Hammoor schammoo@indiana.edu

PHOTO ILLUSTRATION BY DREW ANDERSON AND SARAH THACKER | IDS

"We have the ability to talk directly to them right now.
We don't have to wait for permission to let them know that it gets better."

-**Dan Savage** on his "It Gets Better" outreach project for struggling LGBTQ youth. Join it now at www.youtube.com/itgetsbetterproject

FRANCISCO TIRADO
is a sophomore majoring in comparative literature.

There is no specific cure for bullying.

There is no prescription for bigotry, and there is no pill for intolerance. There is no all-encompassing first aid kit to console those who suffer quietly. However, something that we can offer, in short, is our voice.

In response to the recent suicides of teenagers who were harassed and bullied in their schools due to sexual orientation, outpourings from people have risen to the occasion to make sure that the devastation of these deaths are not unheard.

A billboard was put up to create awareness in Greensburg, Ind. The parents of Seth Walsh are working for an anti-bullying campaign in Tehachapi, Calif. Dan Savage has initiated a YouTube channel in which hundreds are uploading videos just to offer comfort to those who struggle, boldly saying, "it gets better."

It is fair to say that in response to a crisis, only a small portion of people will have the mentality to take such public action. To ask everyone to make a poster or start an organization would simply be irrational, but there is a tendency for people to tell themselves that someone else will fix it. But the time for excuses has long passed.

SEE **TIRADO,** PAGE 11

ZACH AMMERMAN
is a junior majoring in French.

The story I'm about to tell you is a personal one, but it is, tragically, not even close to being an uncommon one.

Five gay teenagers have killed themselves in the past three weeks alone, including a 15-year-old student in Greensburg, Ind., and a 19-year-old just last Friday.

This is a national problem of epidemic proportions.

My parents found out I was gay in a suicide note. Needless to say, this was devastating to them and to me. After years of serious bullying in high school for being gay — despite the fact that I wasn't even sure if I was gay yet dand wasn't even close to coming out of the closet yet — I had developed pretty serious self-esteem and depression issues that I still struggle with to this day as a result of harsh bullying.

These recent suicides point to a larger problem I experienced firsthand: We have a very serious gay bullying problem in this country.

I was bullied in high school for being gay. Other students would play a game where they would shove their friends into me in the hallway as a joke, as if even brushing by me in the hallway was repugnant and disgusting.

On another occasion, a student

SEE **AMMERMAN,** PAGE 11

DREW ANDERSON
is a senior majoring in journalism.

Teenagers find themselves in an ever-evolving identity crisis and adding sexuality throws fuel into the fire. While adults categorize this as teenage angst, the recent Andrew Shirvell scandal in Michigan reveals the online homophobia existing in the corporate world.

Chris Armstrong currently serves as president of University of Michigan's student body and is the first openly gay person to serve in the school's history. Since being sworn in in March, he has been the target of Michigan's Assistant Attorney General, Andrew Shirvell's obsession.

Shirvell's strategy to "expose Armstrong's radical homosexual agenda" became clear during recent weeks and has received national coverage. He started a blog, Chris Armstrong Watch, detailing the day-to-day actions of the student leader. Shirvell went even further by harassing Armstrong's friends and family members, videotaping him and describing his leadership as "Nazi-like."

The absurdity is endless and yet, Shirvell still has his job. Michigan's Attorney General, Mike Cox, has publicly criticized Shirvell's actions to the local press, saying he was "clearly a bully" and his actions were "unbecoming." But according to Cox, the obsession was not

SEE **ANDERSON,** PAGE 11

JUSTIN KINGSOLVER
is a junior majoring in political science and international studies with a LAMP certificate.

While much progress has been made in the fight for equality for homosexuals, the struggle is far from over.

We, as college students, seldom think of ourselves as bigoted people, but for many of us (myself included), entrenched stereotypes can shape unfair opinions of people because of their sexual orientation.

These often lead to tragic results, as was seen in the heartrending case of 15-year-old Indiana high school student Billy Lucas, who recently committed suicide after being taunted about his sexuality by bullies at school.

As a straight member of the IU Greek community, this has become abundantly clear to me during my experience here. The terms "fag," "homo" and "gay" are thrown around so carelessly and in such a derogatory manner that those students who struggle with their sexual identities retreat further into the closet for fear of social retribution for coming out.

Enter "IU Greek Project 10." This organization seeks to support closeted gay, bisexual and lesbian members of the Greek community as they struggle with their true identity.

The introductory e-mail, sent to all members of the IU Greek system, states

SEE **KINGSOLVER,** PAGE 11

FIGURE 9.4 Opinion editors should seek a wide range of opinion from students, faculty and staff on campus. When a Rutgers freshman and several other gay teens committed suicide after being bullied or humiliated, the *Indiana Daily Student* invited its regular columnists to comment on the issues the suicides raised. They put together a poignant and compelling group of columns. *Indiana Daily Student*, Indiana University.

Column logo. A label for a column that includes the writer's name and headshot. Also known as "column sig."

Columnist bio. A brief biographical note about the columnist that may include the writer's major, year in school and position on the newspaper staff or job title if it's a faculty or staff person. It may also include the writer's email address.

Letters to the editor. Letters from readers.

Editorial cartoon. A humorous sketch that comments on news or politics.

Contact box. Information on how readers can contact the newspaper opinion section, including mailing and email addresses.

Contribution policy. An explanation of how readers can contribute columns or letters to the opinion section.

THE EDITORIAL PROCESS

Editorials are designed to do more than simply report. Their role is to explain, persuade, warn, criticize, entertain, praise or lead. Some editorials may call for action on a local issue, such as the resignation of an embattled campus official or the overturning of an unpopular policy. Others, like *The Baylor Lariat's* piece on gay marriage, take a stance on an issue of national or international importance.

Many student newspapers have an editorial board that discusses the editorials for each issue. The editorial board may be made up of all the editors of the paper or some subgroup of editors. At the *Iowa State Daily* (iowastatedaily.com) at Iowa State University, for example, the editorial board comprises the opinion editor, the editor, the managing editor and two or three others chosen by the opinion editor through an application process.

"They meet, bring topics to discuss, discuss them, vote on the editorial stance, assign someone in the majority to write the editorial," says Mark Witherspoon, adviser to the paper. "Then that person goes and researches further, but also uses the debate to frame the editorial argument."

While most professional papers have one person, usually the publisher or the editorial page editor, guide the direction of the editorial page, many student editorial boards decide positions by taking a vote of the board. This can be difficult, particularly on divisive issues, and you may want to leave final decisions to the opinion editor or editor-in-chief. Whatever your approach, make sure you have written guidelines in place on how decisions will be made. Such a policy can help prevent conflicts later on.

FINDING EDITORIAL SUBJECTS

Typically the lead editorial for each edition focuses on an issue that's been covered in the news pages of your paper. If your school's governing board recently approved a hefty tuition increase or the college president has just resigned or a fraternity was recently disciplined for hazing, your editorial board will most likely want to comment on it.

But what do you write on those slow news days? Jill "J.R." Labbe, editorial director for the *Fort Worth Star-Telegram*, says the best way to find ideas is to look at and listen to the campus around you. "The place you get editorial ideas is the same exact place you get story ideas," she says. "You should be writing about what people care about. Listen to what people are talking about in the cafeteria or in the laundromat or in the bar after class."

Robert Bohler, director of student publications at Texas Christian University where he advises *The Daily Skiff* (tcudailyskiff.com), recommends students focus on local news. "Nearly anybody can offer up a solution, informed or otherwise, on the strife in East Timor or some other exotic locale, but there are a lot of writers who can do it better than can most college students. What those other writers can't cover or offer opinions on is what's happening locally. If the college newspaper thinks enough of local issues to write stories about them, then those issues have enough impact to warrant thoughtful commentary. It's the next logical step in the citizen's thought process."

WRITING AN EDITORIAL

Writing an opinion piece, be it an editorial or a column, doesn't mean you can simply spout off on the topic of your choice. Opinion writing requires solid reporting. "Most college opinion pages are heavy on the opinion but light on the facts and sources that add any credibility to them," says the *Fort Worth Star-Telegram*'s Labbe.

"You must do your homework. It's easy to have an opinion; it takes hard work to have a reasoned opinion. A plausible argument depends on evidence that is accurate, pertinent to the main assertion and sufficient to support. And there's only one way to gather evidence. You must be a good reporter before you can be a good opinion writer."

Before you sit down to write an editorial, gather your facts. First, read whatever news articles you can find on your subject from your newspaper and others. Next, seek out reports, studies, lawsuits and other documents that will inform your decision. Then pick up the phone and do some original reporting. "I don't know any editorial writers who don't do their own reporting," says Harry Austin, editorial page editor for the *Chattanooga Times Free Press*.

Once you've collected the facts, it's time to write. Editorials usually follow this general format:

Introduction

Reaction or stance

Discussion and details

Conclusion.

Bear in mind that unlike news stories, editorials are supposed to state an opinion. A good editorial synthesizes the news for your readers, puts the issue in context and tells them what to think about it.

CHECKLIST
The editorial

When writing or editing an editorial, ask yourself:

1 Does the editorial have one primary message?
2 Does it sufficiently support the argument it's trying to make?
3 Are the facts accurate?
4 Does the editorial give the reader adequate background and context?
5 Does the editorial make a clear statement about what could or should happen next?

But be wary of letting your fervor or rage for your topic carry you away. "Don't mistake hyperbole for persuasion," Labbe says. "Yes, editorials and columns should be strongly worded, but if you are trying to persuade someone to at minimum consider your viewpoint, you can't make that happen if you take their heads off with a blowtorch."

Wilkins offers this simple advice on writing opinion pieces:

1 Make one point.
2 Support it.
3 Shut up.

A good editorial, he says, is written with equal parts of passion and logic. "You have to be pissed about something to get the passion you need to drive you through," he says. "But at some point you have to let your outrage and passion slide into the construction of a credible argument to support your point."

TIPS FROM A PRO Jill "J.R." Labbe

The letters to the editor feature in your newspaper gives your readers one of the few chances they have to speak their minds in public. Letters also help create interest in your editorial pages and, theoretically anyway, should increase readership.

That said, handling letters to the editor can be one of the bigger pains in the butt that an editorial page editor – or, in most of your cases, the editor-in-chief – has to deal with. If you're doing it right, that is. Because if all you are doing with the letters you receive is slapping on a headline and sticking them in the paper, you are asking for trouble.

You take responsibility for what you publish, and that includes the letters. If they are factually incorrect, or if they contain potentially libelous statements, you're putting yourself and your newspaper in a position to be sued.

That is why a written letters to the editor policy is not just suggested; it should be mandatory. You need to set the ground rules for how letters will be handled, and you need to stick to them. Outline for your readers a suggested length, and tell potential letter writers that you reserve the right to edit their submissions for taste, grammar, libel, length, etc.

Editing letters takes time and a delicate touch. Sometimes, however, no matter how delicate that touch, no matter how hard you tried to maintain a writer's voice and salient point while cutting out the superfluous, you will be accused of violating a writer's First Amendment right to free speech by editing the letter or, even worse, by not running it at all.

Such calls provide you with the wonderful opportunity to gently deliver a constitutional lesson. Only the government can violate someone's free speech right. Last time I checked, I don't work for the government. The letter writer may call it censorship; I call it editing.

If that isn't good enough for your upset contributor, you can even cite a court case. In *Miami Herald* vs. Tornillo, the Supreme Court ruled there is no legal right of access to a paper's letters to the editor column.

All that said, know that some readers will react – some of them vigorously – if you shorten, alter or refuse to print their letters.

Verify, verify, verify. Require name and address and a telephone number at which the letter can be verified. You don't want to get burned by someone writing a letter and then signing someone else's name. Trust me, it happens. I know from experience.

It is the policy at my newspaper not to accept anonymous letters. Some newspapers publish a letter and withhold the author's name upon request. This is dicey territory. Our feeling at the *Star-Telegram* is that credibility comes with signing one's name. It allows the reader to judge for himself or herself the veracity of what the writer is saying.

All of our reporters and columnists have to sign their work; we rarely allow an anonymous source to be quoted in news reports. We think readers have a right to know who's expressing an opinion in the letters feature.

It can also trigger interesting responses. At my former paper we ran a letter to the editor singing the praises of a certain elected politician. It wasn't until we got a response that we found out that the original letter writer was the politician's mother. Had we known, we probably wouldn't have run that first letter – it's only news when your mother says you're a turd, not when she says you're marvelous.

A common complaint among college newspaper editors is that you don't get letters. So, what can you do to spark interest?

1 The most obvious thing is to put something in the rest of the paper that's worth commenting about. I have to tell you, I've seen some pretty dull front pages from college newspapers. Dry stories, boring art. Come on, people. You're in college! You should be shaking things up!

2 Make it easy for your readers to respond to stories they see in your paper. Add a letters link at the end of every online story. Add an email address at the end of printed stories and columns where readers can email responses.

3 Include a box with one of your editorials that says, "Now it's your turn to weigh in on this topic. Send us your letters." Include the mail address and how to respond online.

JILL "J.R." Labbe is the editorial director for the *Fort Worth Star-Telegram*. When hired in 1992, she became the first female editorial writer in the newspaper's history. Labbe is a former president of the National Conference of Editorial Writers.

THE OMBUDSMAN

If you've got a provocative opinion section, chances are you'll hear from your readers. And they're not all going to be sending flowers and words of praise. One way to deal with the inevitable criticism is to hire a news ombudsman, or reader's advocate.

Beginning in the late 1960s, a number of professional newspapers created positions for news ombudsmen – sometimes called reader representatives or public editors – to monitor their coverage for fairness and accuracy and to respond to readers' complaints. (Ombudsman is a Swedish word meaning "representative of the people.") Today, more than a dozen newspapers in the United States and Canada have such positions, including *The Washington Post*, *The Toronto Star*, the *Miami Herald* and the *Los Angeles Times*. *The New York Times* hired its first public editor in 2003 after reporter Jayson Blair was fired for plagiarizing and fabricating stories.

The Organization of Newspaper Ombudsmen, formed in 1980, defines a news ombudsman as someone who "receives and investigates complaints from newspaper readers or listeners or viewers of radio and television stations about accuracy, fairness, balance and good taste in news coverage. He or she recommends appropriate remedies or responses to correct or clarify news reports."

The organization offers these reasons for having an ombudsman:

To improve the quality of news reporting by monitoring accuracy, fairness and balance

To help his or her news provider to become more accessible and accountable to readers or audience members and, thus, to become more credible

To increase the awareness of its news professionals about the public's concerns

To save time for publishers and senior editors, or broadcasters and news directors, by channeling complaints and other inquiries to one responsible individual

To resolve some complaints that might otherwise be sent to attorneys and become costly lawsuits.

When he was public editor for *The Oregonian* in Portland, Ore., Michael Arrieta-Walden said he saw his role "as fostering the conversation between the newspaper and the readers. I encourage that conversation by serving as a contact for the public, and get that feedback to the appropriate staff. I also evaluate and comment on that feedback as well as the performance of the newspaper, with the interests of readers in mind."

Arrieta-Walden says student newspapers could benefit from having a news ombudsman. "I think the position strengthens the newspaper and its journalism. I also think that, given a college campus, the discussions and debate about the journalism would be especially lively and interesting."

The Daily Illini (dailyillini.com) at the University of Illinois at Urbana-Champaign; *The Washington Square News* (nyunews.com) at New York University; *The Fulcrum* (thefulcrum.ca) at the University of Ottawa; *The Diamondback* (diamondbackonline.com) at the University of Maryland, College Park; *The Cavalier Daily* (cavalierdaily.com) at the University of Virginia; *The Daily Northwestern* (dailynorthwestern.com) at Northwestern University; and *The Pride* (csusmpride.com) at California State University, San Marcos, are among the college papers that have had an ombudsman in recent years.

TECHNICIAN focused TUESDAY, JANUARY 13, 2009 • PAGE 5

CONFLICT IN GAZA CONTINUES

DEEP HISTORY BEHIND STRUGGLE, FAMILY RELATIONS AFFECT STUDENT OPINIONS ON ISSUE

STORY BY DEREK MEDLIN | ILLUSTRATION BY SUSANNAH BRINKLEY

The latest conflict between Israel and Palestine, which intensified Dec. 27, 2008 when Israel began an air assault on Gaza, has now cost almost 900 Palestinians and 15 Israelis their lives.

The newest round of fighting has been another example of the decades old conflict between the two groups.

When Israel became a nation in 1948, Palestinian people in the region between the Jordan River and the Mediterranean Sea were effectively left homeless, creating a volatile situation that has once again flared up.

Since then, multiple periods of fighting have done very little to solve the problem of Palestinian statehood.

Land issues, religious differences and even a discussion about how to handle Jerusalem, the holy city for Christianity, Islam and Judaism, have come together to create a truly unique situation that has proven time and again to appear somewhat unsolvable.

Bob Moog, an associate professor in political science, said the roots of the conflict have come from a land dispute between the two sides.

"At the core of the conflict is an issue of land and Palestinian nationalism," he said. "It's not really a religious issue at its core. The founding of the state of Israel left the Palestinians without a land of their own."

Moog said both sides of the equation know what must be done to solve the problem but also said those same people have known potential solutions for years.

"For the last 15 to 20 years, most of the world has agreed that there would be a two-state solution," he said. "There are issues obviously as to exactly how this two-state plan would work out, but basically both sides agree."

This two-state plan, according to Moog, would make the Gaza strip and the West Bank territory an official Palestinian state.

"The vast majority of people involved agree that there is going to have to be a two-state solution," he said.

The fighting that began in late December has once again highlighted the long running dispute between Israel and Palestine, and has students on both sides speaking out.

Ben Mazur, a senior in religious

> "The vast majority of people involved agree that there is going to have to be a two-state solution."
> Bob Moog, associate professor of political science

GAZA continued page 4

FIGHTING FOR REPARATIONS

Israel is more than a war zone

How heartbreaking to wake up yet another day knowing that another promising cease-fire has been eradicated. It is painful to see it in the news so much, to have lived with this feeling of not knowing if my "homeland" would still be here tomorrow, and to see that yet again, my hopes for peace have been shattered.

Broken cease-fires and the conflicts between Israel and its neighbors are nothing

Blaire Davidowitz, sophomore, communication

DAVIDOWTIZ continued page 4

{OUR VIEW} Educate yourself about the Gaza strip

The conflict between Israel and Palestine in the Gaza strip affects millions around the world, and this includes people at this university.

Though it may seem like we, as students, can't do anything to help the situation, one of the best things we can do is to stay educated. If you feel strongly about one side of the issue, then become

EDITORIAL continued page 4

Israel is responsible for genocide

I am a Palestinian-American. It gives me great pride to call myself Palestinian and be from a nation that will never give up and will never surrender.

I am proud to be an American, but I am dismayed at our government sending at least $3 billion of our tax dollars to Israel each year. I am ashamed and appalled at the stance taken by our government to excuse the actions of the Israelis as self-defense, but to con-

Julie Abdelrahman, junior, textile and apparel management

JULIE continued page 4

Hamas is to blame for Israeli deaths

What would you do?

Imagine a situation in which you and your family are forced to dodge bombs over a period of eight years.

Imagine living in fear knowing that when the alarm sounds you have 30 seconds to reach safety.

This is the case for the citizens of southern Israeli cities. For the past eight years, Hamas, a terrorist organization based in the Gaza Strip, have been shooting mis-

Ori Tuvia, senior, engineering

TUVIA continued page 4

U.S. should only be a mediator

There's no doubt that both Israel and the Palestinians are guilty of committing some pretty terrible acts. A quick glance at the news is all it takes to see that. Under international law, however, the actions of Israel are far less excusable.

Gaza and the West Bank are occupied territories, and under international law, its occupants have the right to resist Israel's military occupation. I don't

Travis Seymour, junior, international studies

SEYMOUR continued page 4

Stop targeting Palestinian civilians

Today is the 18th day of the illegal and savage Israeli military campaign on the innocent civilian population of Gaza.

According to the few reporters who have somehow managed to get around the Israeli block of international news coverage on the atrocities being committed in Gaza, a staggering 45 to 50 percent of the injured, and 25 to 30 percent of those killed, are women and

Mariem Masmoudi, junior, political science

MASMOUDI continued page 4

FIGURE 9.5 An opinion section needn't be gray and boring. Graphics and color can enliven the text, making it more appealing to readers. *Technician*, North Carolina State University.

INDIANA DAILY STUDENT | TUESDAY, FEBRUARY 22, 2011

OPINION 7

WTF IS GOING ON IN THE STATEHOUSE?

CONNOR CAUDILL

Get the government off of my baby

PAIGE HENRY

Get the government out of our health care

DANIELLE FLEISCHMAN

Get the government out of my relationship

BRENDAN IGLEHART

Get the government to kick out immigrants

JARROD LOWERY

FIGURE 9.6 An opinion page needn't stick to the traditional format. Some newspapers devote a page to multiple viewpoints on a single issue. *The Indiana Daily Student*, University of Indiana.

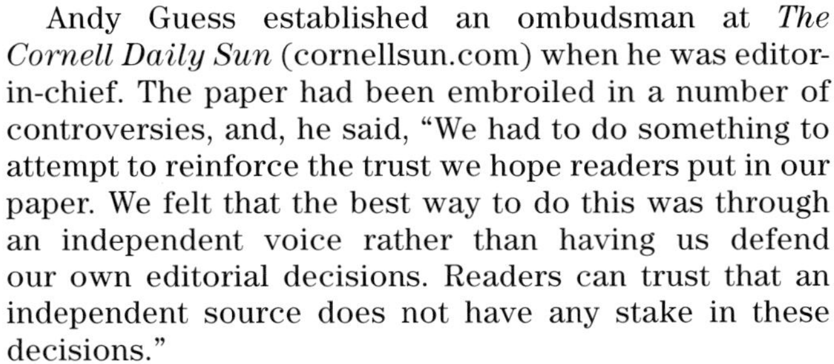

Andy Guess established an ombudsman at *The Cornell Daily Sun* (cornellsun.com) when he was editor-in-chief. The paper had been embroiled in a number of controversies, and, he said, "We had to do something to attempt to reinforce the trust we hope readers put in our paper. We felt that the best way to do this was through an independent voice rather than having us defend our own editorial decisions. Readers can trust that an independent source does not have any stake in these decisions."

Under Guess' tenure, *Daily Sun* ombudsman Jason Perlmutter wrote a biweekly column in the opinion section called "The Public Editor." In it, he freely commented on the paper, criticizing stories he thought were boring and offering suggestions for enlivening the coverage.

Newspapers generally take one of two routes to select an ombudsman. Either they choose a reporter or editor who has been on the paper, remove him from the editorial staff and hire him solely as ombudsman, or they select someone with knowledge or interest in journalism who is not involved at all with the paper. In any case, the ombudsman should not be part of the regular editorial staff.

Guess has one final word of caution: "Before you decide to add an ombudsman, realize that there will be inevitable clashes and resentment from the editors and staff. And make sure the ombudsman knows that too!"

Q&A Nate Beeler

NATE BEELER has been drawing editorial cartoons since he was a sophomore in high school. During his college years at American University, his cartoons ran every week in the student newspaper, *The Eagle*. He graduated with a degree in journalism in December 2002. As a student, Beeler received the Charles M. Schulz Award for best college cartoonist from the Scripps-Howard Foundation and the John Locher Award for best college editorial cartoonist from the Association of American Editorial Cartoonists. He also won first place in the national Society of Professional Journalists' Mark of Excellence Awards. He was the first cartoonist ever to win these three major awards in the same year.

Beeler's cartoons are syndicated by Knight Ridder/Tribune Information Services to nearly 300 campus publications nationwide. His cartoons have appeared in *The Arizona Republic*, *The Providence Journal*, *USA Today* and *The Northern Virginia Journal*. In 2005, he was hired as a cartoonist for *The Washington Examiner*.

What do you see as the role of opinion pages in a student newspaper?

I think the role of the opinion section in a student newspaper is the same as for professional newspapers: to promote debate on issues affecting the community and be a venue where differing perspectives can be offered. They certainly shouldn't be a pulpit for specific people or institutions, but every reasonable person should, in theory, be able to have their side of the debate aired. Op-ed pages, while running biased, unbalanced content, should strive to be fair and balanced as the sum of their parts. However, I don't have that big a problem with the newspaper taking an ideological stance on the op-ed pages if its community has another newspaper with a different ideology. The more perspectives on issues the merrier.

When did you start drawing cartoons? Which professional cartoonists have inspired you?

I started drawing editorial cartoons my sophomore year in high school in Columbus, Ohio. I was initially very influenced by Jeff MacNelly, Mike Luckovich and Jim Borgman, but after a year or so I was introduced to Pat Oliphant's work, and he has since been my biggest influence. In middle school I drew comic books, so comic artists have played a huge role in what I think makes for dynamic, dramatic art. Of course, comic strips also played a big role, and Bill Watterson, Bill Amend, Berke Breathed, Charles Schulz and Winsor McKay have been the big ones for me.

Where do you get ideas for editorial cartoons?

I get my ideas living out the day: talking to people, reading newspapers, watching TV, surfing the Internet. The other night I was struggling to think up a cartoon when a confluence of ideas fused together to form a seed of one. I was sitting on the couch watching TV after just having read a couple of newspaper front pages online when it happened. A segment on the Masters golf tournament came on. There was an image of Phil Mickelson putting on the green with a sand trap behind him, and I thought to myself, "Sand wedge." From there, I thought, "Wedge issue." Combine them together: "Sand wedge issue." In golf, that brings to mind someone having trouble getting out of a sand trap. In terms of "wedge issue," Iraq immediately popped into mind. So, I drew George Bush shoulder-deep in a sand trap (labeled "Iraq") whacking away at a ball but only digging a deeper hole for himself. To add a further layer to the cartoon, I had him facing the wrong way with the hole marker behind him in the distance, and two other guys are waiting by it and saying, "George! The hole's over here!" I tried to be clever with it, but the most important thing, to me, is that it says what I think and makes a valid editorial statement about a newsworthy situation.

What do you do when you don't have an idea?

When I don't have an idea, I keep trying. There's always a new idea out there floating in the ether, and you just have to work hard to catch one.

What makes a successful cartoon?

I think a successful cartoon is one that makes readers want to talk about the topic. If it makes them grin or laugh, that's a bonus. Humor is a device that can be used to help get your point across. It's not the end; it's the means. An editorial cartoon must have a point, because if it didn't, it should be on the comics pages. My most successful cartoons have done this, I hope. One way you can tell they're successful is if people want to share them with their friends or family by cutting them out or talking about them. Even having people write letters to the editor about a cartoon shows that it was successful.

What do you see as the role of an editorial cartoonist on a student paper? Is it any different in the professional world?
The role of an editorial cartoonist on a student paper is the same as one on a professional one: Draw something that says how you feel about an issue that's important to you and your neighbors in the campus, city, state, nation or world community. Help lead the public debate.

What advice do you have for up-and-coming editorial cartoonists?
Aspiring editorial cartoonists need to remember first and foremost that they are journalists. Their cartoons can skewer people, but they need to be fair and balanced in their research for the cartoons. Reading different newspapers and books is a must. Also, the power of cartooning is derived from its visual nature. Therefore, cartoonists should strive to draw dynamic-looking cartoons. A good idea can be ruined by a poorly drawn cartoon, just as a bad idea can turn an artistic masterpiece into junk.

TO DO

1 Analyze the editorials that have run in the past few issues of your paper. Are they well researched? Do they help readers understand the issues explored? How could they be better?

2 If your newspaper needs a strong cartoonist, start hunting for one. Put up fliers around campus, especially around the art or graphic design departments. Sponsor a competition for the best editorial cartoon and offer the winner or winners a regular spot on your editorial page. If you can't find a cartoonist, consider buying cartoons from a syndication service such as MCT Campus.

3 To beef up your opinion section, solicit submissions from leaders of campus groups, faculty members, administrators and other prominent people on campus. When you have a major issue brewing, invite the players to submit commentaries.

4 Consider hiring an ombudsman. Invite former staffers and outsiders to apply. Have each write a sample column or two.

TO READ

Casey, Maura and Michael Zuzel. *Beyond Argument: A Handbook for Editorial Writers*. Harrisburg, Pa.: National Conference of Editorial Writers, 2001.

Fink, Conrad C. *Writing Opinion for Impact*. Ames, Iowa: Blackwell Publishing, 2004.

Rystrom, Kenneth. *The Why, Who and How of the Editorial Page*. State College, Penn.: Strata Publishing, Inc., 2004.

William, David Sloan and Laird B. Anderson. *Pulitzer Prize Editorials: America's Best Editorial Writing, 1917–1993, 3rd ed.* Ames, Iowa: Blackwell Publishing, 2003.

TO CLICK

Association of American Editorial Cartoonists
The organization's website features cartoons from members, including some student members, from around the country, as well as a Q&A with Mike Keefe, editorial cartoonist for *The Denver Post* on how to become a cartoonist. The organization sponsors an annual contest for student cartoonists from the United States, Canada and Mexico. The winner receives a plaque and an expenses-paid trip to the AAEC annual convention. The organization offers discount membership for students.
http://editorialcartoonists.com

Many professional newspapers run explanatory notes about their opinion pages on their websites. Among them:

The Chicago Tribune Guide to the Editorial Page
http://www.chicagotribune.com/news/opinion/chi-001231 editorialpage,0,7278167.htmlstory

National Conference of Editorial Writers
The NCEW website has information about editorial writing. The organization sponsors an annual national convention and offers discount membership for students.
www.ncew.org

Organization of News Ombudsmen
The ONO website has a blog and links to ombudsman columns.
www.newsombudsmen.org

SUPER BOWL: 36.6 PERCENT OF VIEWERS TUNE IN FOR ADS PG. 5

THURSDAY, FEB. 3, 2011

DN

THE DAILY NEWS
BSUDAILYNEWS.COM

Freshman nursing major Lauren Bauerbach slides past her friends on a dining tray outside Woodworth Complex on Wednesday. **DN PHOTO** JESS LANNING

SNOW DAYS

Students react to Ball State's decision not to cancel class Wednesday

SARAH BOSWELL EDITOR-IN-CHIEF
editor@bsudailynews.com

This was one of those storms - conditions still good enough to hold classes, but bad enough to send students sliding across campus.

Senior Michal Knappenberger had to defrost her car for 40 minutes before driving to campus Wednesday morning. She had even more trouble after parking her car.

"I slid down the stairs at the commuter lot like a slide," she said. "I knew I wasn't going to be able to walk down them."

The storm that spanned 2,000 miles across the nation resulted in more than 86,800 power outages around Indiana on Wednesday. Today's forecast called for a 40 percent chance of snow showers overnight, wind chill values as low as -2 degrees and gusts as high as 20 mph, according to the National Weather Service.

A special weather statement from the NWS warns that untreated surfaces may continue to be slick and icy for several days. Temperatures will remain below freezing through at least Friday.

At Ball State, classes after 3:30 p.m. Tuesday and before 11 a.m. Wednesday were canceled. Grounds crews worked 16-hour shifts Wednesday, and students took extra caution, holing up in their residence hall rooms, charging electronics and traveling slowly outside when it was necessary.

Other students took advantage having some of their classes closed and brought sleds or borrowed food trays

See **SNOW**, page 8

《 I didn't fall, but I slid down the stairs at the commuter lot like a slide. I knew I wasn't going to be able to walk down them. 》

MICHAL KNAPPENBERGER, senior

DN|BRIEF

How sure were you that classes would be canceled Wednesday?

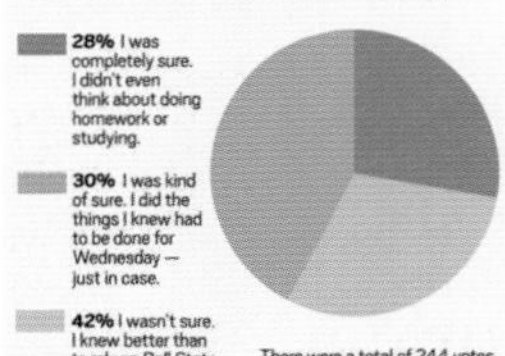

28% I was completely sure. I didn't even think about doing homework or studying.

30% I was kind of sure. I did the things I knew had to be done for Wednesday — just in case.

42% I wasn't sure. I knew better than to rely on Ball State to bail me out.

There were a total of 244 votes
DN GRAPHIC

ONLINE

To see a Q&A with the creator of the "Snowpocalypse" Facebook group go to **bsudailynews.com**

INSIDE

To see an opinion column about how students with disabilities are dealing with the weather, and how students are heading to the bars to stay out of the cold **see page 3.**

INSIDE

To see a graphic about the difference between rain, snow and sleet **see page 8.**

Icy roads lead to injuries

Health Center handles students with winter-related ailments

JACLYN GOLDSBOROUGH
ASST. NEWS EDITOR
jmgoldsborou@bsu.edu

Sid Ullrich's two morning classes were canceled when the university delayed opening until 11 a.m. on Wednesday.

But it was just as hazardous for him in the afternoon - when he slipped and broke his arm walking to a 3 p.m. class. He wishes that one had been canceled, too.

"I was basically told if I didn't show up to class my option was to fail the class for the semester and stay at Ball State another year, or go to class because it wasn't canceled," the junior theatre production major said. "So I had to put my body on the line and I paid for it. I was very upset with that."

On Facebook, students created a group called "2011 Snowpocalypse Petition for Sensibility at Ball State University."

The page criticized the school's ice-clearing efforts along with the decision to hold classes.

"Ball State University fails to care for their students," a note on the page said. "Roads have not been treated, ice has accumulated up to an inch in areas, and safety is at the least of concern for Ball State. ... To all students who felt they were at risk going to class today, join the group and share your opinions."

Ullrich wasn't the only person to take a spill. Lori Cox, a 911 supervisor for Delaware County, said she took two emergency phone calls about other students who fell on campus.

《 I was basically told if I didn't show up to class my option was to fail the class for the semester and stay at Ball State another year, or go to class because it wasn't canceled. 》

SID ULLRICH, junior production major

See **ACCIDENTS**, page 8

Commuters cope to road conditions

Ball State's decision to start class affects students, faculty

JACK MEYER CHIEF REPORTER
jmeyer3@bsu.edu

Students who commuted to school by car had to face hazardous roads in addition to hazardous campus sidewalks.

Some, including junior accounting major Emily Patz, said they had no choice.

"When the classes aren't canceled, you get penalized for not coming," she said.

Her classes are concentrated into just two days per week.

"So when I miss one, it's like missing half a week," she said. "When they aren't canceled and I can't come, there's a huge impact."

Amy Etchison, a junior elementary education major who has a 25-minute commute to class, said she stayed in Muncie on Tuesday night so that she could be sure to make it to her classes Wednesday.

"[Commuting] is a lot harder than people realize," Etchison said. "I usually play it by ear. I've got later classes so my friends usually let me know how things are. If it's icy, I usually don't go because it's not worth it."

Etchison said she doesn't think university administrators take commuters into account as much as they should.

Tony Proudfoot, associate vice president for marketing and communications, said class schedules are usually not interrupted as long as crews can get the main sidewalks cleared.

WINTER ACTIVITIES

Students find fun ways to beat the winter ice storm

HEATHER WATTS STAFF REPORTER
hlwatts@bsu.edu

After suffering through a winter storm which covered the campus with snow and ice, Ball State students have a few options: stay inside cuddled under a blanket or get out of their rooms and partake in winter activities.

Ball State students prove that even if they aren't kids, they can still have fun in the winter.

"Over winter break, my hometown received 20 inches of snow," Angelina Zulas, sophomore social work major, said. "The snow was so tall that my brother and I stood outside then fell backwards and let the snow embrace us. It was impossible to make a snow angel because you would fall so deep."

ICE SKATING

One activity students can participate in is ice skating. However, there are no ice skating rinks in Muncie.

"To fight Muncie's lack of ice rinks, I'll just use the streets," Zulas said.

Last year, Ball State's Late Nite had an ice rink set up in LaFollette field, which gave students a little piece of winter fun. The closest ice skating rink is 55 minutes away at The Forum in Fishers, a twin rink that also has an arcade. An alternative to ice skating is roller skating or blading.

Gibson Roller Skating Arena in Muncie used to have ice skating when it opened in 1940, but now the arena is home to other fun indoor attractions such as a mini-golf course and an arcade, in addition to the skating rink.

Gibson owner Ann Sheridan said she sees a good amount of Ball State students come in to skate and play.

DN GRAPHIC

SLEDDING

Sledding is another activity many people do at least once in their lives.

An unusual way to sled is on flat ground in trash bags or to use food trays from the dining facilities around campus. While students were trying to hike through icy and snowy sidewalks Tuesday, one group of Indiana Academy students were sliding down them in the Quad.

Lauren Snyder, Indiana academy junior, said Tuesday was the first time she had ever been trash bag sledding.

The group had strong trash bags, which they ripped holes in for either their legs or head and then crawled inside. They ran and threw themselves on the ground, attempting to slide as far as they could, or they had someone push them.

"It's pretty fun," she said. "I've heard people talking about it and really wanted to try it myself."

A good hill for sledding near Muncie is by Prairie Creek Reservoir in Perry, Ind.

It is a 25 minute drive, but worth it, said Patricia Hunter, sophomore psychology major. She said she went there with her family when she was younger and had a blast. Hunter is from Muncie and said there were a lot of hills in the countryside where she grew up as well. Other places to sled include McCullough Park and the hills around the White River.

See **ACTIVITIES**, page 4

MUNCIE, INDIANA — THE BALL STATE DAILY NEWS — VOL. 90, ISSUE 78

REMINDER: SPRING IS COMING SOON! THE GROUNDHOG SAID SO!

CONTACT US
News desk: 285-8255
Sports desk: 285-8245
Features desk: 285-8247
Editor: 285-8249
Classified: 285-8247
Fax: 285-8248

DOWNLOAD US
Get today's news, sports and weather delivered straight to your iPod.
Visit bsudailynews.com/podcast.

TWEET US
Receive news updates on your phone for free by following **@bsudailynews** on twitter.com.

FORECAST
TODAY High: 15, Low: -1 mostly sunny
TOMORROW High: 23, Low: 17 mostly sunny

FIGURE 10.1 As news breaks, it's the job of editors to plan coverage, from stories and photos to graphics, multimedia packages and social media posts. When a major snow and ice storm struck the Muncie, Ind., region in the winter of 2011, editors at *The Ball State Daily News* at Ball State University planned a comprehensive package.
The Ball State Daily News, Ball State University.

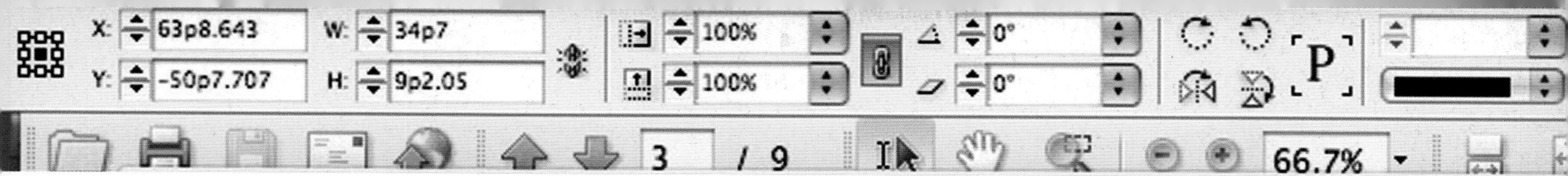

CHAPTER 10
EDITING

An editor – be it a section editor, managing editor, or editor-in-chief – does far more than simply edit words.

A good editor needs skills in diplomacy and leadership, in organization and managing people, in boosting battered egos and smoothing ruffled feathers. You've got to be able to inspire your staff to produce prize-worthy stories while making sure the pages you're responsible for get to the printer on time. One minute you're planning photos, graphics and text for a big package and the next you're on the phone with an irate reader.

And you've got to be open to new ideas. Journalism is quickly evolving; the nimble, flexible editor who embraces innovation is the one most likely to succeed.

The Student Newspaper Survival Guide, Second Edition. Rachele Kanigel.

CHAPTER CONTENTS

STAFF ORGANIZATION

In the professional world, learning this wide array of skills often happens gradually. Typically, a reporter interested in editing starts by helping out with an occasional night or weekend shift on the desk. With that experience she may be promoted to assistant desk editor, then city editor and then managing editor. This move up the ladder usually takes years.

But at a campus newspaper, a reporter may find herself in an editing position – even a top management job – after only a few months or a year on the staff.

"At a student newspaper, you go from being a peer and a colleague and a friend to a being a boss," says Ralph Braseth, manager of student media at Loyola University Chicago. "It's a difficult transition. You can lose friends, you can lose respect. It's a dangerous job to take, especially if you're not prepared for it."

Being responsible for other people and their work can be an overwhelming experience. In this chapter we'll discuss what it takes to be a good editor and provide tips and strategies for developing these skills.

EDITOR SELECTION

How does one get to be an editor at a student newspaper? Most student publications have a relatively rigorous procedure for selecting the top editor, usually called an editor-in-chief, executive editor, managing editor or, simply, editor. Generally candidates have to go through a formal process that may include writing a letter of application or an action plan, interviewing with a selection committee and making a presentation to the staff.

Typically, the top editor is selected by a newspaper adviser, a publication board or an ad hoc committee made up of advisers, current editors, faculty members and sometimes professional journalists. Whoever makes the decision should look for these qualities in a top-ranking editor:

- Maturity
- Ability to deal with pressure
- Good organizational skills
- Strong leadership skills
- News judgment
- Creativity
- Excellent people skills
- Ability to multitask, to deal with many issues at once.

Once the top editor or editors are chosen, they are usually charged with hiring the rest of the staff, including section editors, art directors, photo editors, online editors and sometimes reporters and photographers (Figure 10.2). Some editors inherit a staff from the previous school term; others have to recruit a whole new team.

Whatever the tradition is at your newspaper, the incoming editor should make the hiring process as professional as possible. Don't choose your three best friends to lead the news, sports and opinion sections, unless they are without a doubt the best qualified for the positions. When stories need to be assigned, copy needs to be edited, pages need to be proofed and tough decisions need to be made, you want to have people who can do the job.

To make the hiring process fair, create a professional looking application and have everyone who is interested in a leadership role fill one out. (An example of an editor application is at the end of this chapter.) Interview each applicant, asking about previous work experience, skills, strengths and weaknesses. You may even want to ask for references – professors, student newspaper advisers and employers who can speak to their character and ability to handle responsibility.

Staff Organization

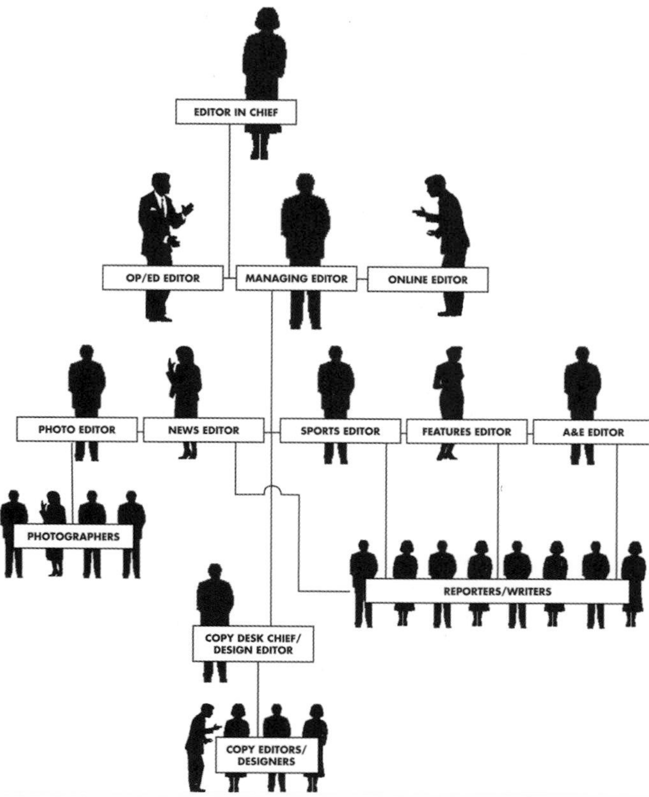

FIGURE 10.2 Most student newspapers have a hierarchical structure similar to those found in professional newsrooms. However, decision-making at student newspapers may be more collaborative than at professional newspapers. Graphic by Bradley Wilson.

DEVELOPING A LEADERSHIP STYLE

As soon as you accept an editing position – whether you're an editor-in-chief overseeing an entire newspaper, a section editor commanding a small group of reporters or a photo editor in charge of a photography staff – it's time to start thinking about your leadership style.

Do you want to be an authoritarian leader, who confidently tells people what to do, or a more democratic chief, who asks for others' opinions before making a decision? Or do you see yourself as a leader who gives others autonomy to make their own decisions? Most people have a natural tendency toward one style or another, but good leaders use a mix of all three approaches, depending on the situation.

To be a good leader, you have to be able to read people and figure out what they need. If, for example, a reporter is feeling mortified about misspelling the name of the university president in a story, he probably doesn't need to be chewed out. You should, however, remind him of the importance of getting names right and of double-checking the spelling of all names.

Sometimes, however, you have to be stern. If few people are meeting deadlines, you may need to institute penalties. Some editors pull bylines or refuse to run stories if copy comes in late. You need to decide when to use the carrot and when to use the stick.

Keep in mind that praise can be a motivating force. If you're constantly pointing out errors and telling people they've done a lousy job, you're not going to get good work out of them. People work harder and better when they feel appreciated.

"One of the single most important things you can do as a leader is to recognize the accomplishments of other people," says Braseth. "If you're not thanking folks, you're not leading. You have to do it every single day."

Recognition can come in the form of a pat on the back or paper certificates passed out in front of the whole staff. When she was managing editor of the weekly *Golden Gate [X]press* (goldengatexpress.org) newspaper at San Francisco State University, Misha Rosiak handed out homemade cookies and chocolate bars to deserving staffers at semiweekly staff meetings. When someone's done excellent work or gone beyond the call of duty, slip a note in their box or send a congratulatory email. Such words of encouragement keep people committed and motivated.

EDITING COPY

Most newspaper stories are reviewed and edited by multiple people – a section editor, two or three copy editors and often the managing editor and/or editor-in-chief. At professional newspapers, section editors primarily edit for content (structure, logic, holes in the story) and copy editors usually focus on mechanics (spelling, grammar, punctuation, math, adherence to the newspaper's style guidelines).

At student newspapers, the line between what section editors and copy editors do is often a bit blurry; everybody is doing their best to make the story better.

In their excellent book, *Coaching Writers: Editors and Reporters Working Together Across Media Platforms, 2nd ed.* (Bedford/St. Martin's, 2003), Roy Peter Clark and Don Fry of the Poynter Institute suggest the best approach to editing is to *coach writers* rather than to *fix copy*. That means talking about stories throughout the reporting, organizing and writing process rather than simply whacking away at stories after they come in. This may sound time-consuming, but many editors find that brief but frequent conversations with writers can often save time in the long run.

"One mistake I know I made was fixing errors in articles rather than editing them," says Erika B. Neldner, who was editor-in-chief of *The Sentinel* (ksusentinel.com), the weekly paper at Kennesaw State University. "It always came down to crunch time, and I never had enough free time to sit down with each writer. If I had, I would have saved hours fixing the same errors every Tuesday morning."

Your newspaper should have its own style guide, even if (like most student newspapers) you rely on the *Associated Press Stylebook* for most things. A style guide specific to your publication might include:

Proper names of campus buildings and departments

Names of campus officials

TIPS FROM A PRO Steve Buttry

As you work with a reporter on a story, you have two jobs: to help the reporter produce the best possible version of this story and to help the reporter produce better stories in the future.

Inexperienced editors who are good at editing copy sometimes think this job requires them to rewrite the story, using their superior touch with the copy. But rewriting by the editor doesn't help the reporter write a better story next time. You produce the best story now and better stories in the future by working effectively with the reporter throughout the storytelling process.

Below are some tips for helping reporters improve their stories.

Before the reporter turns in a story

Talk early and often. From the idea stage through revision, talk with the reporter about the challenges the story presents and how she is addressing them.

Discuss story ideas with the reporter. Many story weaknesses rest with the fundamental idea. The direction you provide at this stage can save work later in the process. Ask why we're doing this story now. That forces the reporter to address two questions: Why are we doing this story at all and why now?

Focus on the reader. Ask reader-oriented questions early and often, to keep a strong focus on serving the reader. Why will the reader care? Who is likely to read this story? How might the reader act on this story? What information can we give the reader to help her act on this story?

Ask what the story is about. At various stages of a reporter's work on a story, ask what the story is about. Sometimes the answer will change from the idea stage through the rewriting and asking that question repeatedly will help the reporter keep the evolving story clearly focused. Sometimes the answer will remain the same and asking the question will help the reporter stay focused.

Discuss social media. If people might be discussing this topic or event on Twitter, make sure the reporter is searching for appropriate keywords and hashtags to connect with sources and/or aggregate tweets. Encourage the reporter to check whether some person or organization has a Facebook page where the issue is being discussed. Searches of YouTube and Flickr might turn up videos or photos that could accompany the story (as well as good sources to interview). The Foursquare "Mayor" of a restaurant or entertainment venue might be a good source to interview if that location is in the news. If a story unfolds heavily in social media, Storify may be a helpful tool for curating social content, either for the main story or in a sidebar.

Discuss records. Ask what records the reporter will examine. Start with general questions that push the reporter to consider where she might find records to help with this story. If she doesn't identify some records you think might help, follow with more specific questions that steer her toward specific records. Know the federal, state and local open-records laws and push reporters to gain access.

Discuss data. Discuss where the reporter might find data to help with the story. Discuss access issues such as open-records laws, cost and which officials might be most likely to provide the records promptly. Discuss whether the story should include an interactive database where readers can search for the facts most relevant to them. Discuss whether the reporter has the skills to analyze the data and develop an interactive database. The student may need some help from a colleague or a professor, or the story may be an opportunity for the student to develop database skills.

Discuss liveblogging opportunities. If a reporter is covering an event or a breaking news story, he should tell the story as it unfolds. Discuss the best way to liveblog the story: a chronological account using CoverItLive (with opportunities to field questions and comments from the community and to aggregate tweets from the community and other reporters), a reverse chronological blog with the updates always at the top (the reporter might rewrite later for a print edition) or live tweeting (perhaps compiling them into a single story file using CoverItLive or Storify). For more about using social media tools like these see Chapter 19.

Discuss audio and video. Should the story have an accompanying video or should video be the primary vehicle for the story? Will the story present some opportunities for audio clips to run either alone or as the soundtrack for a slideshow?

Discuss interactivity. How can the reporter involve the reader in the story? Would a quiz help tell the story? Or should the reporter ask readers to vote on a particular question (or multiple questions) in a poll? Should you crowdsource some of the reporting, asking (on your website, Facebook page and/or Twitter) students or the broader public what they know about an issue or what they saw at an event.

Debrief. After an interview, ask the reporter how it went. What did she learn? What surprised her? What moved her? What did she hope to learn that the source would not tell? Who else might have that information? Encourage the reporter to start writing, even if much reporting remains.

Ask about the lede. The reporter probably is thinking about the lede without prompting from you, but talking may be helpful if the reporter is struggling with the lead.

Suggest sidebars and graphics. Ask the reporter what facts you can tell better in graphics than in prose. Ask what points should be told in sidebars, rather than bogging down the main story. Can a photo make a point better than prose? Should a YouTube video or a widget pulling in related tweets accompany the story?

Discuss maps. If the story unfolds in multiple locations, a map might illustrate the story. Or a map might become the primary storytelling vehicle. Perhaps the story will be a brief introduction, followed by a Google map, with each bubble opening to tell the story for that location.

Suggest an outline. If a reporter appears disorganized, suggest that he write an outline. If the reporter resists or has not outlined effectively in the past, talk through an outline. You might write down the outline yourself as the two of you identify main points.

Suggest writing without notes. Notes can distract a reporter. The story should be in the reporter's head. Suggest that she review the notes, then set them aside and write without pausing to find facts and quotes. When she's finished, she must return to the notebooks and get the facts and quotes right.

Encourage rewriting. Perhaps the best way to see dramatic improvement in a reporter's work is to encourage a reporter who turns in first drafts to spend some time rewriting. Don't approach this as remedial work, but as professional development. Even great stories benefit from revision. Set a deadline for finishing the first draft, then another deadline for finishing the rewrite. Talk about specific things to look for in rewriting: strong verbs, sentence length, redundancy, etc.

After you get the first draft

Promote alternatives. Encourage the reporter to try a different lede. Even if you both like the first lede, have the reporter try a different approach. Coaching should not concentrate only on making bad work good, but on making good work and even great work better.

Ask the reporter to read aloud. If a lede is long or a story is laden with long sentences or does not flow well, ask the reporter to read it aloud, to you or to herself. Often that will help the reporter identify the fat sentences and weak passages. Also ask the reporter to read aloud the passages you love. That will underscore how well those passages work.

Suggest areas to condense. Avoid cutting stories yourself. Instead, suggest that a particular passage could be condensed, that a particular sentence seems too long.

Don't rewrite the lede. Tell the reporter what's wrong with the lede. Suggest possible alternative approaches. Demand a shorter, brighter or clearer lede. But make the reporter rewrite the lede.

Don't insist on your approach. If you do rewrite the lede, or suggest a different approach, don't insist that the story has to use your lede, or your approach. Explain why the original version didn't work and explain the thinking behind your revision. Then challenge the reporter to write something better than either.

Explain editing changes. Whether you changed because of style, grammar, clarity, brevity or some other reason, explain why you changed a story. Those changes will help the reporter turn in a better story next time. Learning is a primary function of the student newspaper and explanation hastens learning.

STEVE BUTTRY is director of community engagement for TBD, a digital local news operation that covers the Washington, D.C. area for Allbritton Communications. He spent more than 30 years in the newspaper business and was named Editor of the Year by *Editor & Publisher* magazine in 2010 when he was at the *Cedar Rapids (Iowa) Gazette*. While a student at Texas Christian University, Buttry spent four years on the staff of *The Daily Skiff* (tcudailyskiff.com), including two semesters as editor. He was a leader of the *No Train, No Gain* website, where the first version of this appeared.

Coaching writers

The best editors see themselves more as coaches than as bosses, or even editors. They talk with reporters throughout the reporting and writing process, asking questions and listening.

Here are some questions you can pose to help a writer craft a story:

What's the story about?

What's your lede?

What's your nut graph?

What's new?

Why are we writing this story now?

Why should readers care?

What's your headline?

What's the most interesting thing you learned in your reporting?

What's your best quote?

Who are the most interesting characters in your story?

What does the reader need to know?

How would you explain this story to a friend?

What would make a good ending?

Student organizations

College or university boards, commissions, organizations

Course titles

Campus nicknames for teams, mascots, places, streets, buildings, etc.

Exceptions to AP style, which might include academic departments and degrees, team names, etc.

For a cheat sheet on AP style, see Appendix I Associated Press style cheat sheet at the end of the book.

EDITORIAL BUDGETS

Editors generally plan each issue by creating an editorial budget, a list of every story assigned. Formatting varies, but the editorial budget generally includes this information for each story:

A slug, a one-word title for the story

Its length, usually in words or column inches

The byline, the writer's name

A one- or two-sentence description of the story

Notations about photos (this may include whether a photo has been assigned or shot, the name of the photographer)

Notations about graphics (whether a map, chart, graph or other graphic element has been assigned or completed).

It should look something like this:

> **DOWNTOWN**–600 words, Chin–The College of Business has announced it will open a new downtown campus next year to better serve working students. **Photo** of new building shot by Green. **Graphic**: Locator map assigned.

Writers typically send a budget line to their section editor and the section editors send their section budgets to the managing editor or editor-in-chief. Some newspapers use a story planning form (Figure 10.3) to help plan stories, photos and graphics. The top editor then makes up an editorial

PACKAGING OPTIONS FOR PRINT:
(check all that apply)

Visuals
❑ Photos (new)
❑ Photos (file)
❑ Illustration
❑ Map
❑ Chart
❑ Diagram
❑ Table
❑ Timeline
❑ Other:

Text pullouts
❑ Bio box
❑ List
❑ Excerpt
❑ For more info ...
❑ Glossary
❑ Key players
❑ Key stats/facts
❑ Q&A
❑ Multiple quotes
❑ What's next
❑ If you go
❑ Other:

Furniture
❑ Column logo
❑ Series logo
❑ page topper
❑ About this story

PROMO ELEMENTS
❑ On the Web
❑ Coming next
❑ Inside
❑ Twitter
❑ Other:

ELEMENTS FOR ONLINE:
❑ Video
❑ Slide show
❑ Poll
❑ Database
❑ Interactive map
❑ Other:

SECTION:	PUBLISH DAY/DATE:	PLANNING EDITOR:

Story Planner

Working title:

What's the news and why should readers care?

If you can't answer this in one or two simple sentences, narrow your focus

Reporter(s):	Photographer(s):	Designer(s):

❑ **Single story** ❑ **Mutli-story package** ❑ **Series**

QUESTIONS READERS WILL HAVE:

HEADLINE IDEAS (5 words or less):

KEY SOURCES	PHOTO / ART IDEAS	PAGE LAYOUT IDEAS

FIGURE 10.3 *Northern Star*, the daily newspaper at Northern Illinois University, uses this form to plan stories, including graphics, photos, information boxes and multimedia elements. *Northern Star*, Northern Illinois University.

CHECKLIST
Editing a story

Editing a story can be a daunting task. There are so many things to look for. Editors should read stories at least three times:

- Once for content, including accuracy, organization, sense and meaning
- Once for mechanics – style, spelling and grammar
- Once for legal and ethical issues, such as libel, fairness and cultural sensitivity.

After you're finished editing, it's a good idea to read the story over one last time to make sure you haven't introduced any errors.

In editing a story ask yourself these questions:

Content

1 Does the lede capture the essence of the story? Is it short and punchy, usually no more than 25 or 30 words? Does it entice the reader to read more?

2 Does the story flow smoothly and logically? Is it architecturally sound?

3 Are there any holes in the story – an important perspective that's not represented, an obvious question that isn't answered?

4 Are all the assertions in the story backed up by facts? Are all quotations and facts attributed to an appropriate source?

5 Has the writer provided the appropriate background information to put the story in context? Will readers who are just reading about this issue for the first time be able to understand what's going on?

6 Does the timeline of events make sense?

7 Are the basic facts correct? Make sure names, dates, times, phone numbers, titles, criminal charges, addresses, Web and email addresses are accurate.

Mechanics

8 Are there errors of grammar, syntax, spelling or style?

9 Does the story follow Associated Press (and/or your newspaper's) style guidelines?

10 Does the math add up? Do the numbers all make sense?

11 Is there any unnecessary redundancy or repetition?

Law, ethics and taste

12 Is the story fair and balanced? Does it present all sides?

13 Are there any potentially libelous statements?

14 Is the story written in good taste?

15 Does the story include any profane language? If so, does it conform to your paper's standards? (For example, some newspapers only run swear words if they are in a quote from a source.) Is it journalistically justifiable?

16 Are there any references some people might find offensive?

budget for that entire issue of the paper. Editors usually discuss the budget – or at least the lead stories for each section – at a news meeting or budget meeting.

Editors at daily papers generally meet every morning to go over the editorial budget. These meetings should include the top editors; section editors; and the lead photo, graphics, online and design editors. At some papers, a smaller group of editors meets again later in the day to choose stories for the front page. At a weekly paper, editors typically meet once or twice during the week to plan each issue.

MEETINGS

At their best, editors meetings are a quick and efficient way to communicate and collaborate. At their worst, they drag on for hours, boring everyone involved. Here are some guidelines to ensure your meetings are meaningful, productive and blissfully brief.

Make sure someone is in charge. The top editor of the paper should run most editors meetings. If that person is unavailable, the next person down the line should take charge.

Create an agenda. The leader of the meeting should have an agenda for each meeting. This might include going over the editorial budget for the paper, discussing front page possibilities, making decisions about packaging stories and doing a brief critique.

Invite key players. Newspaper planning meetings should include top editors; section editors; and the lead photo, graphics, online and design editors. If someone can't attend, another representative of that department should be there.

Start promptly. The top editor should set a reasonable hour for the meeting and make it clear the meeting will start on time. If meetings don't start promptly, people tend to arrive late for the next meeting.

Rein it in. The meeting leader should keep everyone on track, curbing digressions. If an important issue arises that isn't on the agenda, set another time to discuss that topic.

End promptly. Set an end time for each meeting and stick to it.

PLANNING SPECIAL PROJECTS

Once your staff is in the routine of covering your campus on a daily, weekly or monthly basis, it's time to start thinking about special projects – packages that may include multiple stories, photos, graphics and multimedia elements on a single issue. Projects can bring attention to your news organization, help you win awards and give your staff an added sense of purpose. But keep in mind they can be a lot of work, requiring extensive planning and decisive leadership by one or more editors.

The first step to embarking on a team project is to come up with a good idea – one that's topical, interesting to your readers, and worth exploring in depth. Some projects follow up on a topic in the news, such as the departure of an important college official, the opening of a new campus or a change in campus policy. Others explore a trend or issue, such as suicide, gay marriage or enforcement of drinking laws. Newspapers sometimes plan a project to mark an important anniversary. The staff of the *Daily Kent Stater* (kentwired.com) at Kent State University in Ohio, for example, plans special coverage for the first week in May every year to mark the anniversary of the May 4, 1970 shootings of four students by National Guard officers. The newspaper produced a major project for the 40th anniversary, which included a separate Web page with videos, slideshows and live coverage (Figure 10.4).

While projects may require weeks or months of planning, a savvy staff can put together a news package – a mini project – in a matter of hours. When a major winter storm struck the Muncie, Ind., area in 2011, editors at *The* Ball State *Daily News* (bsudailynews.com) at Ball State University recognized the opportunity for a package of stories and photos (Figure 10.1). It included a news story on the storm and how it affected the campus, reports on storm-related injuries and commute conditions, a feature on winter activities, a poll on whether students thought classes would be canceled, a graphic explaining the difference between rain, snow and sleet and a compelling photo of students frolicking in the snow. The package, which took up the whole front page and jumped inside, was assigned, reported, shot and assembled over the course of a few hours.

When planning a special project, it's important to consider all the elements – stories, photos, graphics, multimedia and design – from the very beginning. Too often editors putting a project together have to scramble for photos or graphics at the last minute because no one has considered the visual elements. Once you've made a commitment to a project, call a meeting of all the key players – the reporters, editors, graphic artists, multimedia producers, photographers and designers – who will be involved. An editor should lead the discussion, asking these questions.

FIGURE 10.4 *The Daily Kent Stater* produced a major project on the 40th anniversary of the May 4, 1970 shootings that included videos, a slideshow with historic photos, remembrances and live coverage of the commemoration ceremony. *The Daily Kent Stater*, Kent State University.

- What's the main focus of the project?
- How can the story be told in text – what stories, sidebars and information boxes will be included?
- How can the story be told in photos – what can photographers shoot? Does the story warrant a slideshow, photo page or gallery?
- How can the story be told in graphics – what maps, infographics, illustrations and other graphic elements would enhance the story?
- How can the story be told with multimedia – what videos, slideshows, interactive maps and graphics and other tools would help the online presentation?

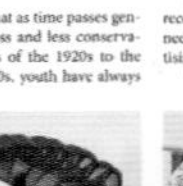

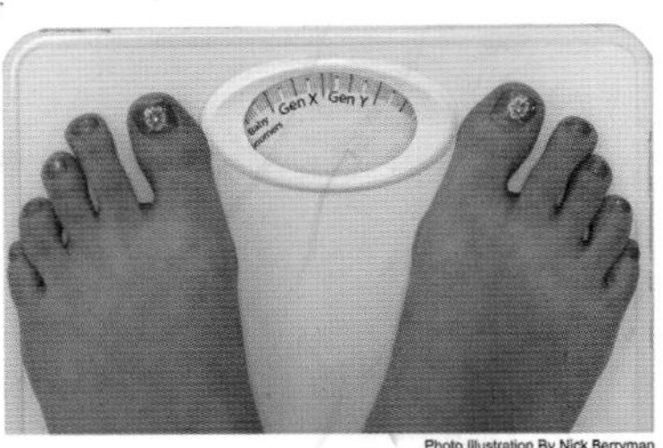

FIGURE 10.5 In the fall of 2010, Nick Dean, then editor-in-chief of *The Baylor Lariat*, assigned his staff to produce a 20-page special section, Redefining Gen Y. Dean assigned stories, photos and videos covering different angles on the topic. "This special issue of *The Lariat* is an attempt to altruistically redefine Generation Y," he wrote in an editor's note introducing the project. "While working on this special issue, I have seen my staff (full of Millennials) demonstrate the highest regard for work ethic." View the section and related videos at http://www.baylor.edu/lariat/index.php?id=77900.

- How can the staff use social media to help report and promote the story?
- Should the project include commentary – an editorial or opinion columns from your staff or others on campus?
- How should the package look? As the staff comes up with ideas for photos, stories, graphics and sidebars, the designer can sketch out a layout that integrates the different story elements. Editors should also think early on about creating a title and/or logo for the project that ties the package together.

Once the planning group has outlined the basics of the project, an editor should draft an editorial budget that includes a line for each element and assign a reporter, photographer or artist and deadline to each. Be sure to set realistic deadlines; give staffers enough time to do the necessary work but don't set target dates so far in advance that everyone is going to forget about them.

The editor leading the project should plan subsequent meetings so that the staffers involved have a chance to check in and discuss challenges and new information. Stories may fall through; new ideas may arise. Photographers may not be able to get the access or the shots editors were expecting. Editors must be flexible enough to change direction if the material they were expecting doesn't come together.

Once editors know what they have they should discuss how much space – online and in print – they want to devote to the project. Should it be given a full page, a double truck, a four-page insert? Should it run on one day or be presented as a series over multiple days? Editors may want to talk with the business staff about securing extra pages or reserving open pages for the project.

Visual presentation of the project is as important as the content. Once you have the various elements, be sure to package them together in a way that's easy for readers to navigate. Have the designer use borders, boxes, fonts and other design devices to group related elements together and let readers know this is special. An index that lists the various stories may help readers find their way in a project with many elements. You may want to present and archive all the materials on a dedicated Web page on your news organization's website. That way, readers will be able to access the project for months or even years to come.

DEALING WITH CONTROVERSY

Every college paper will sometime stir up controversy. It may be an offensive cartoon, an article that makes the school look bad or a column that goes a little too far. Sometimes you see the hate mail coming. Other times the angry letters and phone calls seem to come out of nowhere. Whatever the situation, the editors have to deal with the flak.

"You have to be prepared to handle a lot of angry phone calls and a lot of hostile office visitors," says Mandy Phillips, who was editor-in-chief of *The Standard* (the-standard.org) at Southwest Missouri State University. "I know when I first stepped into the editor's position and got my first few angry students and professors sort of 'in my face,' I probably backed off too much and too soon. I learned pretty quickly there's a fine line between being passive and being stubborn, and you've got to learn to walk it."

The key to handling controversy is to listen to all sides and keep your cool. If a source or reader has a complaint with the paper, or a staff member has a problem with a fellow staffer, make sure each person feels he is heard. Listen to the complaint and don't act rashly. Take time to formulate a response.

When you or the paper has made an error, admit it, run a correction or clarification, apologize to the injured party and move on. You have another issue to get out.

STUDENT MEDIA BOARDS

While most campus newspapers are run by student editors, many have a student media board, publications board or advisory board to provide consistency, advice and support. Such boards are typically composed of anywhere from five to 15 members (usually some mix of faculty, staff, university administrators, professional journalists and representatives of student government and/or the student body as a whole). The editor of the student newspaper and the college media adviser sometimes sit on such boards, as well; if they do, they may or may not have voting privileges. Media boards may meet as often as once a month or as infrequently as once a year.

Student media boards generally don't oversee the daily operations of the college media organizations they advise; that's the job of the student and/or professional staff. "Our Publication Board exists to provide financial guidance and oversight, and to approve the budget," says Jim Killam, adviser to the *Northern Star* (northernstar.info) at Northern Illinois University. "It does not touch editorial content or policy, nor day-to-day operations. It interviews editor-in-chief candidates each semester and gives a recommendation to the Management Board, which is made up of student managers at the paper.

"We view this as an ideal arrangement that protects both the students and administration from conflicts of interest," Killam adds. "The board's constitution was set up by our university council, so whenever there's a question about who ultimately controls the paper's budget, there's a quick answer. That's been a useful thing to have."

A media board can act as a shield that protects the paper from administrators, student government officials or others who may not like the newspaper's content. "The student media board can provide a good buffer to attempted punishments of the newspaper," says Kelly Wolff, general manager of Educational Media Company at Virginia Tech, Inc., which publishes the *Collegiate Times*.

A media board may oversee multiple student media organizations, such as radio stations, television stations, newspapers, literary journals, magazines, yearbooks and websites.

Responsibilities of media boards vary but may include:

Updating and determining the mission and policies for each student media organization

Selecting each media outlet's senior leaders

Determining an annual budget for the student media organizations

Taking disciplinary action against college media employees who violate policies or don't fulfill their duties

Setting compensation for student media leaders or the entire staff

Acting as a sounding board when there are disputes within the college media organization

Reviewing and ruling on complaints against the media organization

Providing fiscal and operational guidance to student media organizations.

Editors should feel comfortable consulting the media board when they run into problems or challenges.

At most schools, the student media board does not oversee or influence the content of the publication. At the University of Arizona, for example, the advisory board governing statement has a passage on Freedom of the Press:

> The student press at the University of Arizona is free of censorship and advance approval of content. Student editors, managers and news directors must be free to develop their own editorial policies, content, programming and news coverage. An independent and active press – print, online and broadcast – is a basic right in a free and democratic society and is valuable in promoting the development of students as socially responsible persons.
>
> Freedom of expression is guaranteed by the First Amendment to the Constitution of the United States and by the Constitution of the State of Arizona. Accordingly, it is the responsibility of the Board to ensure a free student press and to resist interference with this principle. Students alone are responsible for the content, character and design of their publications, and students alone are responsible for their broadcast programming, consistent with FCC regulations.
>
> However, it is the Board's expectation that editorial and programming decisions be consistent with the accepted principles of journalistic/broadcasting ethics and procedure and that the student media strive for accuracy, fairness and service to their readers/listeners. The Board expects student editors, managers and news directors to seek professional advice and legal assistance when confronted with editorial and operational questions.

EVALUATING STAFF

Part of your job as an editor is to review the performance of your staff. Every paper should have a process for doing this that includes written evaluations (see evaluation forms for editors, reporters, photo editors, photographers and designers at the end of this chapter) and private conferences.

Evaluating another person's work can be difficult, particularly when the person is a fellow student. Let's face it, most people don't like giving criticism and most people don't like getting it.

But a solid evaluation process can help both of you grow as journalists.

Here are some tips for conducting performance evaluations:

Set the time and place. Don't just grab the staffer on the fly. Make an appointment in advance and choose a place where you won't be disturbed.

Plan what you're going to say. Don't just talk off the cuff. When giving criticism, you need to be prepared.

Put the staff member at ease. Don't launch right into the review. Evaluations are stressful; recognize that and help the person relax.

Review the process. Explain that this is a discussion, not a lecture.

Start with a self-evaluation. Get the staff member's assessment of his performance. (You may ask the staff member to fill out a self-evaluation form before the meeting.)

Sandwich criticism between compliments. Start and end each category of performance by telling the person what they've done well. In the middle, focus on what they need to work on.

Focus on the future. Don't dwell too much on what a person has done poorly in the past. Discuss what needs to be done to move the person to the next level.

Get specific. Prepare examples of what the staffer is doing well or needs to work on. Show the person grammatical errors they make again and again or ledes that are particularly good.

Look for trends. Don't focus *too* much on individual incidents. Point out trends – that the photographer has a great eye for feature photos, that the writer needs to dig deeper or look for more compelling quotes.

Write it down. Your review process should include a written evaluation. If your newspaper doesn't already have evaluation forms for key posts, use the ones at the end of this chapter or write a narrative evaluation.

Come up with an action plan. Together, come up with specific steps the staff member can take to improve.

Ask for feedback. Discuss how you can be a more helpful and effective supervisor.

End on a high note. Thank the staff member for coming in and for contributing to the paper.

Headline writing cheat sheet

Looking for a short word for earthquake? Need a catchy synonym for organization? Try these:

Accident: collision, crash, wreck

Accuse: charge, cite

Acquire: get

Advocate: urge, push, spur

Agreement: accord, compact, deal, pledge, pact

Alteration: revise, fix, change

Appointment: post, job

Apprehend: arrest, capture, catch, nab, seize, snag

Arrange: plan, set, shape

Arrest: seize, hold, net

Assemble: meet, gather, rally

Attempt: try

Beginning: opening, start

Business: company, firm, plant, shop, store

Celebrate: fete, mark, perform, stage

Celebration: bash, event, fete, party, do

Commander: chief, guide, leader, ruler

Company: firm, house, concern

Compete: vie

Competition: race, contest

Contract: deal, pact

Damage: harm, hurt, impair, injure, wreck

Decision: decree, order, rule, writ

Decline, decrease: dip, fall, plunge, slip

Defeat: fall, loss

Destroy: raze

Earthquake: jolt, quake, shock, temblor, tremor
Encourage: aid, help, spark, boost, push
Examine: scan, study
Expose: bare, reveal
Fire: blaze
Former: ex
Increase: add, hike, rise, up
Investigate: examine, probe, study
Leader: chief, expert, guide, head, ruler
Limit: curb, restrain, soften, temper
Meeting: confab, session
Murder: kill, slay
Organization: board, body, band, club, firm, group, unit
Organize: form, join, link, merge
Overcome: beat, win
Plan: deal, plot, scheme
Postpone: delay, defer, put off, shelve
Position: job, post
Prevent: ban, bar, curb, stop
Promise: agree, pledge, vow
Resign: quit, leave, give up
Revise: alter, change, modify, shift, switch, vary
Solicit: seek
Schedule: arrange, plan, set
Steal: loot, rob, take
Storm: gale, squall
Zealous: ardent, avid, fervent

WRITING HEADLINES

Some people are born headline writers; they practically come out of the womb spouting clever, catchy phrases that capture the essence of a story. Unfortunately, those people usually go into advertising.

That leaves us mere mortals to write newspaper headlines.

At professional newspapers, headline writing is generally the job of copy editors. At student newspapers, reporters and editors at various levels may share the task.

Here are some tips to get you started:

Read the story first. Yes, the whole thing. Often you'll get an idea for the headline or deck deep into the story.

Play with words. Choose a few key words and then play around. Look for synonyms, puns, twists of phrase, rhymes, alliterations that work well.

Avoid groaner puns. There's a fine line between what's clever and what's corny. If you think you've got something but you're not sure, try it out on some other people in the newsroom. You'll know soon enough when you've got a hit.

Use present tense. That keeps the news fresh.

Use active voice. Have the subject of the headline doing something rather than having something done to it.

Write a skeleton sentence. Then try to shorten that sentence to five to seven words, then make it shorter yet.

Leave out unnecessary words. Don't use articles like *the, a, an*. Use a comma instead of *and*.

Don't cannibalize the story. Avoid headlines that scoop the reporter on a great opening or a surprise ending.

Cont'd on page 127

SINGLE LINE

Campus alcohol use increases

DOUBLE LINE

Cell phones outlawed in classrooms;
text messaging common way to cheat

HAMMER

TEEN CRIME
Judicial Commission hears 'absurd' stories

UNDERLINE

You win some, you lose some
Football team loses championship in last quarter

OVERLINE

For Rebecca Heslin, dreams become reality
Imagination runs wild

WICKET

"Intramurals give me a chance
to play in sports I normally couldn't"
Jocks of all kinds

TRIPOD

DRUM CORPS WINS Local musicians take championship in DCI national competition

FIGURE 10.6 Headlines can be written in a variety of styles. Graphic by Bradley Wilson.

Sample copy flow schedule for a weekly newspaper

In the age of Web-first publishing, most stories tied to an event – a speech, a crime, a game, a rally – should be posted to your website immediately, within minutes or hours of the event. But features and in-depth pieces may be produced at a more leisurely pace. Here's a copy flow schedule for non-breaking stories at a weekly newspaper.

Day 1. Writer pitches story to assigning editor in a proposed budget line or story-planning sheet that includes a brief description of the story, approximate length, photo and graphic possibilities and contact information for photographers. After a discussion and some fine-tuning the assigning editor OKs the story.

OR Editor assigns a story to the writer. Writer sends budget line to editor.

Editor sends graphics assignment form to the graphics editor and/or photo assignment form to the photo editor.

Day 2. Graphics editor assigns graphics to graphic artist. Photo editor assigns photo to photographer. Writer reports story, checking in with photographer and graphic artist on their related assignments.

Day 3. Editor coaches reporter through the story, asking questions, troubleshooting problems and helping the reporter organize the story.

Day 4. Reporter turns in first draft of story to assigning editor.

Day 5. Assigning editor edits story (editor-in-chief and/or managing editor may review story here, too).

Day 6. Assigning editor and reporter discuss suggested revisions. Reporter revises story.

Day 7. Reporter hands in second draft to editor. Graphic artist turns in graphic to graphics editor. Photographer turns in photos to photo editor; together they select the best photos. Photographer writes captions.

At budget meeting, editors discuss placement of stories and assignments for next week. Assigning editor edits second draft of story and turns it in to copyediting file. Copy editor edits story and writes headline, calls reporter or assigning editor with questions. (Managing editor may review story here.)

Day 8. Page designer puts story, photo and graphics on the page. After all pages are finished, paper is sent to the printer.

Day 9. Newspaper comes out and is distributed around campus. Staff meets in the afternoon to critique the paper.

TIPS FROM A PRO Becky Sher

The top job at a student newspaper isn't easy. But it's a lot of fun, and an amazing opportunity to grow as a journalist, and as a leader. A few things to keep in mind as you get used to your new role:

1. **Be fearless.** Who cares if other people think a project will never work? If you think it will, give it a try. The same goes for newsroom policies. Just because the last editor didn't do it that way doesn't mean it won't work for you. Student journalism is your chance to try things that seem a little crazy or unconventional.
2. **Act like a "real" journalist.** If you want to be taken seriously by readers and sources, then take your job seriously. Act ethically and responsibly in everything you do. Whether you're reporting on the university president's alleged financial improprieties or the outdoors club's latest fund-raiser, treat the story like it's important to you.
3. **Know your limits.** You are a real journalist, but you're also a student. And you need to be a good student; that takes time and energy. Be realistic about what you can and can't commit to.

4 **Learn from your mistakes.** It sounds pretty basic, but it's more important than you think. There are very few times in your post-graduation life when you will have the chance to make mistakes without dramatic consequences. That's not to say mistakes are never a big deal at a college newspaper – they are. But for the most part, the kind of mistakes you'll make as a college editor won't cost you your job or your lifelong reputation. So take the heat while it lasts and then concentrate on the next issue. And don't do it again.

5 **Critique.** It's important to look at your work critically, and it's always nice to have an editor from another section of the paper look at your section with a critical eye. If you're the big boss, let your staff know that constructive criticism is welcome.

6 **Ask for guidance.** There are plenty of people out there who know a lot more than you do. Find them, and ask for their feedback. Look for professional journalists who are willing to critique your paper, give a seminar on a specific topic or offer help by phone when a reporter, editor or designer is struggling.

7 **Do what you say you're going to do.** You can't expect anyone else to be committed to the job unless you're setting a good example. If you say you'll do a final read on a story by 3 p.m., do it. If you say a meeting starts at 6 p.m., that's when it starts.

8 **Be fair, but flexible.** It's a management myth that you should treat everyone on your staff exactly the same. If a good reporter has mononucleosis, she needs to be cut some slack. Special circumstances don't mean lower expectations; they just demand a different approach.

9 **Make your expectations clear.** True, many of your staffers aren't getting much in return other than the satisfaction of a job well done, but that doesn't mean you can't expect good work. Don't be wishy-washy. Your staff should know that if a deadline is 7 p.m., that doesn't mean 7:15 or 7:45. Don't seethe under the surface when you read a bad lede, but never say anything to anyone. Your staff is talented, but they can't read your mind!

10 **Make it fun.** Yes, this is a job, and yes, you should take it seriously, but this is also college. Have some fun. But also make sure your staff knows that there are times to be serious, like when the 11 p.m. press deadline is approaching. Encourage fun outside the office as well – sign up for intramural sports, have parties, go to dinner. You'll make a lot of great memories that will get you through long nights in the office.

11 **Treat your job like a job, not just an extracurricular activity.** Even if you're not getting a paycheck, or your newspaper only comes out once a month, this is still your job. Set office hours when staffers know they can find you in the office. Answer emails, voice mails and letters in a professional fashion. If you're meeting with a source, dress up a little (at least take off your flip-flops).

12 **Cultivate a good relationship with the business staff.** The setup is different at every newspaper, but regardless of the way yours works, it almost always behooves top editors to be friendly with the business and production staffs. You need them to do your job – sometimes even more than they need you.

BECKY SHER teaches journalism at George Washington University's School of Media and Public Affairs. Previously she worked for Knight Ridder/Tribune in Washington, D.C. in a number of editing positions. Sher worked for *The GW Hatchet* (gwhatchet.com), the independent student newspaper at George Washington University, from 1995 to 1999, where she was a staff writer, assistant news editor and news editor before being elected editor-in-chief her senior year.

Sample job descriptions

Editor-in-chief

1 Sets overall editorial direction for the publication.
2 Oversees hiring of all editorial staff.
3 Conducts all editorial and staff meetings.
4 Represents the paper to the public, including the school administration and campus community.
5 Oversees layout, design and production of newspaper.
6 Consults with adviser and student publication board (if the paper has them).
7 Works with adviser, business manager or student publication board to formulate a budget for the paper.
8 Maintains communication with business and/or advertising manager.

9 Sets, explains and enforces deadlines and policies for the editorial staff.
10 Sets and maintains office hours to be available to the staff and community.
11 Oversees training of new staff.
12 Ensures the timely publication of the newspaper.
13 Leads editorial board, which decides subject and stance of editorials.
14 May write staff editorials.
15 Reviews all controversial material for potential ethical and legal concerns.
16 Acts as liaison to printer.

Managing editor

1 Assists the editor-in-chief and acts as second in command.
2 Reviews stories after they've been edited by section editors and makes additional comments and changes.
3 Makes all final decisions when editor-in-chief is not available.
4 Attends budget meetings.
5 Works with editor-in-chief, art director, section editors and designers to manage production of the paper.

News editor

1 Oversees assignment of all news stories.
2 Oversees production of news pages.
3 Peruses press releases, public service announcements and other newspapers for story ideas.
4 Approves hiring of all news reporters.
5 Supervises, coaches and evaluates news reporters.
6 Reviews and edits all news stories.
7 Reviews all news headlines and captions.
8 Enforces deadlines among news reporters.
9 Attends regular budget meetings.
10 Coordinates all graphics and photos for news pages.
11 Conducts regular news staff meetings and brainstorming sessions.

Online editor/webmaster

1 Oversees production and maintenance of newspaper's website.
2 Makes sure all stories and images are posted in a timely fashion.
3 May supervise and evaluate team of online editors and/or producers.
4 Devises ways to enhance Web content with links, interactive features, slide shows and other special elements.
5 Ensures that important breaking news stories are updated between editions.
6 Attends budget meetings.
7 Responds to email related to the newspaper's website.
8 Assures adherence to all copyright law and corrects mistakes on the site.

Lifestyle editor

1 Oversees assignment of all lifestyle stories.
2 Oversees production of lifestyle section.
3 Peruses press releases and other newspapers for lifestyle story ideas.
4 Approves hiring of all lifestyle staff.
5 Supervises, coaches and evaluates lifestyle staff.
6 Reviews and edits all lifestyle section stories.
7 Reviews all lifestyle section headlines and captions.
8 Enforces deadlines among lifestyle reporters.
9 Attends regular budget meetings.
10 Coordinates all graphics and photos for the lifestyle section.
11 Conducts regular lifestyle staff meetings and brainstorming sessions.

Arts and entertainment editor

1 Oversees assignment of all A&E stories.
2 Oversees production of A&E section.
3 Peruses press releases and other newspapers for A&E story ideas.
4 Approves hiring of all A&E staff.
5 Supervises, coaches and evaluates A&E staff.
6 Reviews and edits all A&E section stories.
7 Reviews all A&E section headlines and captions.
8 Enforces deadlines among A&E writers.
9 Attends regular budget meetings.
10 Coordinates all graphics and photos for the A&E section.
11 Conducts regular A&E staff meetings and brainstorming sessions.
12 Keeps track of arts events and maintains contact with arts and entertainment officials and producers in the community.

Opinion editor

1. Oversees assignment and collection of material for opinion pages, including editorial cartoons, letters to the editor, editorials and columns.
2. Oversees, with the editor-in-chief and editorial board, writing of editorials.
3. May write unsigned editorials or bylined opinion columns.
4. Handles contributions from freelancers and community members.
5. Oversees production of opinion section.
6. Writes or reviews headlines and captions for opinion section.

Sports editor

1. Oversees assignment of all sports stories.
2. Oversees production of sports section.
3. Approves hiring of all sports staff.
4. Supervises, coaches and evaluates sports staff.
5. Reviews and edits all sports stories.
6. Reviews all sports section headlines and captions.
7. Enforces deadlines among sports reporters.
8. Attends regular budget meetings.
9. Coordinates all graphics and photos for the sports section.
10. Conducts regular sports staff meetings and brainstorming sessions.
11. Keeps track of sporting events and maintains communication with athletics officials.

Photo editor

1. Works with other editors to coordinate photography for the paper.
2. Supervises, coaches and evaluates all staff photographers and freelancers.
3. Distributes assignments to photographers and tracks the progress of all photo assignments.
4. Helps photographers edit their work.
5. Advises designers and other editors on selection, cropping and placement of photos.
6. Conducts regular photo staff meetings.
7. Makes sure all photos are properly identified.
8. Attends budget meetings.
9. Maintains or oversees the maintenance of photo files.
10. Keeps track of all photographic equipment owned by the newspaper and makes sure equipment is in good condition.
11. Tracks stock and orders photo supplies, as needed.
12. Advises editor-in-chief or others responsible on photography equipment purchases.

Art director

1. Sets overall design of the newspaper, including the use and placement of fonts, photos and graphic elements.
2. Supervises and evaluates designers, graphics editor, graphic artists.
3. Reviews and updates design style guide for the newspaper.
4. Oversees layout of the newspaper, making sure the pages conform to the design style guide and are finished on time.
5. Attends budget meetings.
6. Assigns information graphics and graphic elements, such as charts, logos and maps; creates graphics if other staff aren't available.
7. May coordinate with printer.

Copy chief

1. Oversees all copyediting and fact checking.
2. Supervises, trains and evaluates all copy editors.
3. Meets with copy editors on a regular basis to discuss common errors and copy flow problems.
4. Reviews headlines and captions.
5. Reviews and updates newspaper's stylebook.
6. Meets regularly with editor-in-chief and other editors to discuss copy flow problems and changes to the copy system.
7. Produces style and grammar memos to the staff, highlighting common problems and changes.

Don't put information in the headline that isn't in the story. This isn't the place or time to add more information.

Avoid unfamiliar acronyms and abbreviations. In fact, use abbreviations sparingly and only when you're sure most readers will know what they mean.

Challenge your headline. Is it too obvious? Could it have a second, unintended meaning?

Avoid bad line splits. Don't divide: two-word nouns, adjectives/nouns, verbs/adverbs, prepositions/nouns, etc. And don't leave prepositions hanging.

Run a spell check. Typos are doubly embarrassing in large type.

Consider the tone of the story. Don't put a light, clever headline on a serious story. Likewise, don't get overly serious on a fun story.

Be specific. Vague headlines, even catchy ones, don't make readers want to read a story. Decks – lower headlines that run below the main headline – can help here. If you've got a snappy but imprecise headline, use a deck to explain it.

Consider photos and graphics. A headline, photo, graphic and story are one package. Make sure the headline doesn't contradict or undermine the photo or graphic.

Check other elements on the page. Make sure you're not repeating key words or creating an unintended meaning by placing your head next to a photo from another story.

Punch up your verbs. Strive for fresh, strong, specific verbs.

Be conversational. Avoid "headlinese," words like "solon" and "confab" that only headline writers use.

Be accurate. A mistake in a headline can be as serious – or even more so – than an error in a story.

See Figure 10.6 for samples of headline styles and the Headline writing cheat sheet for useful synonyms.

TO DO

1 Arrange for a group of your editors to sit in on an editors meeting at a newspaper in your area.

2 Before taking on a new editing job, call a professional editor in your position and ask if you can spend a day shadowing her. If that's not possible, set up a brief interview to ask about her job and get advice.

3 If you don't already have one, organize a training session for editors before the new term begins. Invite professional journalists, student newspaper advisers, journalism professors and others to lead sessions on managing people, leadership skills, project planning, time management and other skills editors need to succeed.

4 Organize occasional training sessions for editors throughout the school year to address particular problems that arise. If, for example, reporters are consistently missing deadlines, have editors meet to discuss strategies to combat the problem. If conflict management becomes a problem, organize a role-playing session to practice these skills.

5 If you supervise writers, set aside time for coaching, using tips listed in this chapter.

TO READ

Bowles, Dorothy A. and Diane L. Borden. *Creative Editing, 6th ed.* Belmont, Calif.: Wadsworth/Thomson Learning, 2010.

Fellow, Anthony R. and Thomas N. Clanin. *Copy Editors Handbook for Newspapers, 2nd ed.* Englewood, Colo.: Morton Publishing Company, 2003.

Fry, Don and Roy Peter Clark. *Coaching Writers: Editors and Reporters Working Together Across Media Platforms, 2nd ed.* New York, N.Y.: Bedford/St. Martin's, 2003.

Hill, Linda A. *Becoming a Manager: How New Managers Master the Challenges of Leadership. 2nd ed.* Cambridge, Mass.: Harvard Business School Press, 2003.

Rooney, Edmund J. and Oliver Witte. *Copy Editing for Professionals.* Champaign, Ill.: Stipes Publishing, 2000.

Ryan, Leland "Buck" and Michael J. O'Donnell. *Editor's Toolbox: The Reference Guide for Beginners and Professionals.* Ames, Iowa: Blackwell Publishing, 2000.

TO CLICK

American Copy Editors Society
www.copydesk.org

American Society of Newspaper Editors
www.asne.org

Associated Press Managing Editors
www.apme.com

"Coaching Writers: The Human Side of Editing" videotape
This 30-minute videotape teaches the fundamentals of coaching writers. It's available for a nominal fee at the Poynter Institute website.
http://about.poynter.org/about-us/store/bzqcxq

Confusing Words: A database of more than 3,000 words that are troublesome to readers and writers.
www.confusingwords.com/

Institute for Midcareer Copy Editors: Resource Page for Copy Editors
http://www.ibiblio.org/copyed/resources.html#fact

Newsroom Leadership
www.newsroomleadership.com

The Slot: A Spot for Copy Editors
www.theslot.com

Editor Application

Name ______________________________

Phone number ______________________________

Other phone number ______________________________

Email address ______________________________

1. What staff position or positions are you interested in? (rank your top choices in order from 1 to 5)

Editor-in-chief	Special projects editor
Managing editor	Online editor
News editor	Copy chief
Lifestyle editor	Copy editor
A&E editor	Photo editor
Sports editor	Art director
Opinion editor	Graphics editor

2. List all relevant coursework:

3. List other relevant experience, including internships, jobs, leadership positions, etc.:

4. Why do you want this position(s)?

5. If named to the position of your choice, what changes and improvements would you try to make?

6. What ideas do you have for special projects or packages your section and/or the paper could tackle?

7. What strengths will you bring to the position? What skills do you still need to develop to succeed?

8. What do you think are the paper's greatest strengths? How could the paper improve?

Adapted from an application created by *The Observer*, Central Washington University.

APPENDIX 10.B PERFORMANCE EVALUATION FORMS

Editor Performance Evaluation

Editor: ______________________________

Evaluator (Name and Position): ______________________________

Please rate the editor's contributions in each category according to the following system:

4	Exceeds expectations
3	Meets expectations
2	Needs some improvement
1	Needs significant improvement

Coaching reporters through stories	1	2	3	4
Editing copy	1	2	3	4
Leadership skills	1	2	3	4
Ability to give constructive criticism	1	2	3	4
Ability to handle stressful situations or conflict	1	2	3	4
Organizational skills	1	2	3	4
Communication	1	2	3	4

Other comments

Reporter Performance Evaluation

Reporter: ____________________

Evaluator (Name and Position): ____________________

Please rate the reporter's contributions in each category according to the following system:

4	Exceeds expectations
3	Meets expectations
2	Needs some improvement
1	Needs significant improvement

Meeting deadlines	1	2	3	4
Quality of research and reporting	1	2	3	4
Quality of copy (spelling, grammar, punctuation, AP style)	1	2	3	4
Quality of writing (ledes, nut graphs, story organization, sentence structure)	1	2	3	4
Ability to accept feedback	1	2	3	4
Beat coverage/story ideas	1	2	3	4
Communication with editors	1	2	3	4

Other comments

Photo Editor Performance Evaluation

Photographer: ____________________

Evaluator (Name and Position): ____________________

Please rate the photo editor's contributions in each category according to the following system:

4	Exceeds expectations
3	Meets expectations
2	Needs some improvement
1	Needs significant improvement

Coaching photographers	1	2	3	4
Editing images	1	2	3	4
Organizational skills	1	2	3	4
Ability to give constructive criticism	1	2	3	4
Assignment of photos	1	2	3	4
Teamwork/willingness to work with others	1	2	3	4
Communication	1	2	3	4

Other comments

Photographer Performance Evaluation

Photographer: ______________________________

Evaluator (Name and Position): ______________________________

Please rate the photographer's contributions in each category according to the following system:

4 Exceeds expectations

3 Meets expectations

2 Needs some improvement

1 Needs significant improvement

Meeting deadlines	1	2	3	4
Editing images	1	2	3	4
Quality of images	1	2	3	4
Creativity in handling assignments	1	2	3	4
Technical skills (lighting, use of flash, focus, etc.)	1	2	3	4
Teamwork/willingness to work with others	1	2	3	4
Communication	1	2	3	4

Other comments

Designer Performance Evaluation

Photographer: ________________________________

Evaluator (Name and Position): ________________________________

Please rate the photographer's contributions in each category according to the following system:

4 Exceeds expectations

3 Meets expectations

2 Needs some improvement

1 Needs significant improvement

Meeting deadlines	1	2	3	4
Proficiency with design software	1	2	3	4
Understanding of and adherence to basic design principles	1	2	3	4
Creativity in handling assignments	1	2	3	4
Ability to follow editors' directions	1	2	3	4
Teamwork/willingness to work with others	1	2	3	4
Communication	1	2	3	4

Other comments

APPENDIX 10.C PRODUCTION CHECKLIST

Before sending the newspaper to the printer, editors should proof each page for accuracy, punctuation, style, spelling, design consistency and grammar. All staffers who read a page should initial their approval.

Design

	Section Editor	Copy Editor	Photo Editor	Art Director	Managing Editor	Editor-in-Chief
Are the pictures/headlines/graphics/ stories packaged logically?						
Is the date correct?						
Are volume/issue numbers correct?						
Are the fonts and spacings consistent?						
Are folios (newspaper name/date/ page number) correct?						
Are section headings/standing heads correct?						

Stories

	Section Editor	Copy Editor	Art Director	Managing Editor	Editor-in-Chief
Are days/dates correct?					
Are headlines/teasers accurate and spelled correctly					
Are bylines (name, title and email address, if included) correct?					
Are all names in the articles spelled correctly and consistently?					
Are jump pages correct? Does the jump pick up where the story left off?					

Art

	Section Editor	Copy Editor	Photo/Graphics Editor	Art Director	Managing Editor	Editor-in-Chief
Are pictures/graphics placed with correct stories?						
Are captions correct and written in present tense?						
Do numbers in graphics add up?						
Are photo/graphics credits correct?						

Serving the students and the University community since 1893

The Daily Tar Heel

VOLUME 118, ISSUE 16 | www.dailytarheel.com | TUESDAY, MARCH 23, 2010

university | page 3

SERVE ONE AT ME

Senior Calvin Young learned how to play pingpong in high school by watching and imitating YouTube videos. Now he works his skills against table tennis veteran 81-year-old Walter Shur.

arts | page 3

MOVE, DANCE

The Pilobolus Dance Theater's performance Monday pushed the limits of athleticism and flexibility.

state | page 4

I'M JUST A BILL

The Senate is expected to take up legislation today that would reform financial aid and change amounts of Pell Grants.

CORRECTIONS

Due to an editing error, Monday's front-page brief, "On the road again," incorrectly stated when the men's basketball team beat Mississippi State. They played Saturday.

Due to an editing error, Monday's front-page story, "Colleges closer to policy change," misquoted William Gheen, president of Americans for Legal Immigration PAC. He said, "This is part of a broader national agenda to incorporate illegal immigrants into American society."

The Daily Tar Heel apologizes for the errors.

CLARIFICATION

Monday's front-page story, "Health care bill headed to Obama's desk," was unclear about the next steps for the health care bills.

President Barack Obama can sign the bill passed by the Senate on Sunday, but the reconciliation bill still must be passed by the Senate before going to him.

every moment counts

Give extra encouragement to a friend.

The "Every Moment Counts" project is a monthlong campus initiative to honor former Student Body President Eve Carson's generosity and compassion through random acts of kindness.

Today's weather

A shower in the morning ain't bad H 63, L 44

Wednesday's weather

Sun rises at 7:14 a.m. and stays out H 76, L 47

index

UNC BUDGETED $490,072 TO FIND THESE THREE:

HOLDEN THORP

Position: Chancellor
Years of search: 2007-08
Firm: R. William Funk and Associates
Amount paid for search: $213,581
Candidates: Individuals unknown, but six finalists included Thorp, two black males and two white females

KAREN GIL

Position: Dean of College of Arts and Sciences
Years of search: 2008-09
Firm: Witt/Kiefer Executive Search Firm
Amount paid for search: $131,791
Candidates: Joel Martin of the University of Massachusetts at Amherst, Gil of UNC, Paul Armstrong of Brown University and Katherine Newman of Princeton University

BRUCE CARNEY

Position: Executive vice chancellor and provost
Years of search: 2009-10
Firm: R. William Funk and Associates
Amount allocated for search: $144,700
Candidates: Philip Hanlon of the University of Michigan, Anthony Monaco of the University of Oxford, Jeffrey Vitter of Texas A&M University and Scott Zeger of Johns Hopkins University

Searches draw from narrow pools, limiting UNC's options

BY ELIZA KERN
ASSISTANT UNIVERSITY EDITOR

When it came time to hire a new provost, UNC did everything by the book.

But when another search begins, administrators might need to find a new approach to solve the hiring equation.

For this year's search, UNC followed a well-worn path:

SEE HIRING, PAGE 11

UNC cleans up offensive errors in final games

Tar Heels seek NIT semifinal berth

BY POWELL LATIMER
SENIOR WRITER

After Larry Drew II's game-winning layup fell through the basket Saturday, there was a conspicuous absence from the postgame stat sheet.

North Carolina was missing its usual allotment of turnovers.

With only 11 giveaways on the day, the Tar Heels didn't let their offense stall. Mississippi State didn't bury the Tar Heels with a killer run as so many teams have this season.

In fact, UNC has quietly cleaned up its act in its last three games.

For the season, UNC is averaging 15.1 turnovers per game — 273rd in the NCAA. But in its last three games, one a loss in the ACC Tournament and the others two NIT wins, the Tar Heels are averaging 10.7 turnovers per game.

"We ... have played better in the last three weeks. I wish we hadn't waited such a long time."

ROY WILLIAMS, HEAD COACH

SEE NIT, PAGE 11

Former trustee investigated

Perdue turns over contributions

BY C. RYAN BARBER
ASSISTANT UNIVERSITY EDITOR

Gov. Bev Perdue's campaign surrendered $48,000 in donations Friday after a report revealed suspicious contributions from nine donors linked to former UNC Board of Trustees member Rusty Carter.

Rusty Carter

Carter, 60, a two-term trustee and owner of the Wilmington packaging company Atlantic Corporation, is suspected of having reimbursed employees and relatives for contributions they made to Perdue's 2008 gubernatorial campaign.

Gary Bartlett, executive director of the State Board of Elections, said Carter is being investigated for possibly violating an N.C. campaign law that prohibits donations made "anonymously or in the name of another," or by corporations.

The same law states that individuals are permitted to contribute a maximum of $4,000 per campaign cycle to political candidates.

Bartlett said he does not believe Atlantic Corp. made illegal contributions to Perdue's campaign.

"Companies cannot make direct campaign contributions, and in this case it does not look like a corporate donation but bonuses that were given to individuals," he said. "And the individuals made the contributions to the candidates."

In a letter delivered to Bartlett on Friday, the governor's campaign treasurer, Oscar Harris, expressed doubts as to the legality of the donations and surrendered the contributions to the state board with a $48,000 check.

"We are concerned that some or all of the contributors involved may have been reimbursed by their employer," Harris wrote in the hand-delivered letter.

The nine donors listed on the report made a total of 12 campaign donations, each worth $4,000.

Three of those donors contributed during two election cycles, making a contribution to the general campaign and another to Perdue's bid in one of the two primaries.

In a statement, Carter's legal counsel, Michael Murchison, said the former UNC trustee was aware of the decision to forfeit the donations, has contacted relevant authorities and intends on complying with any inquiry into the matter.

"The company and its senior management looks forward to working with those authorities to bring the matter to an appropriate resolution," he said, in the statement.

Carter, who served on the UNC board from 2000-08, was unavailable for comment.

Perdue appointed Carter's wife, Susan Carter, to UNC-

SEE CARTER, PAGE 11

FIGURE 11.1 *The Daily Tar Heel* has been doing investigative projects since it formed an investigative team in 2003. In 2010, the newspaper revealed that the University of North Carolina at Chapel Hill had spent a total of nearly $500,000 in search firm fees and travel expenses to recruit three top administrators. *The Daily Tar Heel*, University of North Carolina at Chapel Hill.

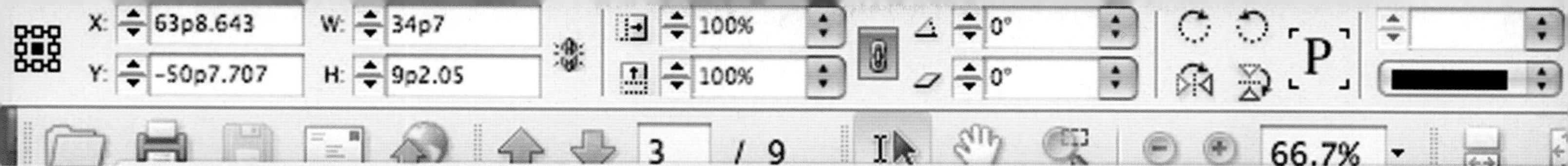

CHAPTER 11
INVESTIGATIVE REPORTING

Soon after taking on the position of investigations editor at *The Daily Tar Heel* (dailytarheel.com) at the University of North Carolina at Chapel Hill, John Frank posted a mission statement near the entrance to the newsroom:

> As the forefathers of *The Daily Tar Heel* Investigative Team, we hereby set these goals that we will uphold in our daily reporting:
>
> Be the paramount guardians in maintaining the watchdog mission of *The Daily Tar Heel*
>
> Ask the questions others are afraid to ask and dig deeper than others are willing to go for the truth
>
> Be the catalyst that sparks dialogue about underrepresented issues in the campus community
>
> Maintain the journalistic mission to 'Comfort the afflicted and afflict the comfortable'
>
> Through professionalism and diligence, improve the paper's respectability in the campus community

The Student Newspaper Survival Guide, Second Edition. Rachele Kanigel.

CHAPTER CONTENTS

Impact the way policies and laws in the campus community are created.

The Daily Tar Heel had never had an investigative team before. But after taking a computer-assisted reporting class and attending an Investigative Reporters and Editors conference, Frank, along with Editor-in-chief Elyse Ashburn, decided the paper should take its watchdog role more seriously.

In that first year, Frank and his five-person investigative team completed numerous investigative reports. Among them:

- A story on how UNC Radiology Department employees had misused more than $300,000 in university funds
- An analysis of the university chancellor's weekly calendars that offered a glimpse into the inner workings of the university
- A four-month investigation into the university's summer reading book selection committee, a secretive group that had chosen several controversial books
- An investigation into a lawsuit that could have cost the university $11 million in parking ticket revenues
- A six-part series on the university's efforts to increase the university's enrollment cap for out-of-state students.

The payoff was tangible. The following spring, the paper won the top award for student journalists from Investigative Reporters and Editors for the "Raising the Cap" series. "We had never even entered a story before," says Frank, who later became a reporter for *The News & Observer* in Raleigh, N.C. "We won on our first try."

Setting up an investigative team didn't just enrich the newspaper experience for the reporters involved, Frank says. It inspired the whole newsroom. "We had that investigative mindset going down to the freshmen reporters. They would see what we were working on and they would want to do it themselves."

The Daily Tar Heel's successes in setting up an investigative team are inspiring, but you don't have to be a big daily to do investigative reporting. The *Hampton Script*, a biweekly paper serving the 6,000-student campus of Hampton University in Hampton, Va., won accolades for its investigative report on health violations at the campus cafeteria. *The Collegian* (collegianwired.blogspot.com) of Los Angeles City College revealed that out-of-state basketball players had falsified residence information so they could play on the team and pay in-state fees. And Brian Krans, a reporter for *The Winonan* (winona.edu/winonan), a weekly at Winona State University in Minnesota, won awards for a 10-week investigation of underage drinking and the bars in town that most frequently served minors.

"You needn't have a big staff to do investigative reporting," says Frank. "Two or three reporters committed to doing professional journalism at a student level can get a lot done."

WHAT IS INVESTIGATIVE REPORTING?

Investigative reporting sounds so sexy, so Woodward and Bernstein, so Pulitzer Prize. But what exactly is it? Investigative Reporters and Editors, Inc., the leading organization of investigative journalists, defines it as "the reporting, through one's own initiative and work product, of matters of importance to readers, viewers or listeners. In many cases, the subjects of the reporting wish the matters under scrutiny to remain undisclosed."

That's it?

"People have this misguided notion that investigative journalism is this voodoo thing only select people can do," says Matt Waite, a Pulitzer Prize-winning reporter for the *St. Petersburg Times* who has been doing investigative journalism since he was a reporter for the *Daily Nebraskan* (dailynebraskan.com) at the University of Nebraska. "It's pulling documents, reviewing routine matters and keeping an eye out for trends for when something different happens. It's watchdog journalism."

Brant Houston, former executive director of IRE and a professor of journalism at the University of Illinois at Urbana-Champaign, advises students who want to do investigative journalism to start by asking a simple question: "What's not working?"

Why is the university parking garage already full at 9 a.m.? Why has tuition gone up? Why does a physically fit athlete have a handicapped-parking placard for his car? Why is the roof on the new building leaking?

WHEN LAWS DON'T WORK

Brian Krans got the idea for his first big investigative project shortly after his 21st birthday when he found himself running into younger friends in the local bars. Clearly, thought Krans, then a junior at Winona State College in Winona, Minn., the laws that set the drinking age at 21 were not working.

"It started as kind of a joke, really," says Krans. When his advanced reporting professor assigned students to survey students for a Top 10 list, Krans blurted out, "How about the top 10 bars that minors go to?"

The professor liked the idea, and over the next two months Krans surveyed more than 300 students about which bars were the easiest to get into. He accompanied underage high school and college students as they entered bars with fake IDs and even used a counterfeit identification card to get himself into a club.

Here's how his story in *The Winonan*, the weekly college newspaper, began:

> Andre 'Dre' Klonecki, a senior at Winona Senior High School, wanted to go to the bars with friends from Winona State.
>
> He did – using a fake ID.
>
> The only shared trait between Klonecki and the ID, the top corner cut off and expired in 1999, was the red tint in Klonecki's strawberry blond hair.
>
> Klonecki – a tall 18-year-old man – used the ID of a man 3 inches shorter, 6 years older and 25 pounds lighter.
>
> Given a quick glance, the ID might have resembled Klonecki, and that is all it took.
>
> On Jan. 18, manager Tony Haglund was checking IDs at the front door of Bulls-Eye Beer Hall, a popular college bar.
>
> Haglund inadequately checked Klonecki's fake ID at the front door and let him in with little hesitation.
>
> At Bulls-Eye, Klonecki was served by 3 different bartenders and despite having 15 drinks, no one asked for ID again.

When the story came out in the newspaper, much of the community was incensed. Both students and the town's bar owners challenged his reporting. One pub threatened to sue. Someone made up posters with Krans' photo saying businesses had the right to refuse service to anyone and distributed them to bars around town. The newspaper even received a death threat against Krans.

But some appreciated Krans' truthtelling. After reading the story, a Winona City Council member recommended underage drinking violations be considered when a bar's liquor license came up for renewal. The Minnesota Newspaper Association awarded Krans first prize for investigative reporting.

And Krans learned something about himself: he loved investigative reporting. "I became addicted to this stuff," says Krans, who went on to become a professional journalist who writes for newspapers and magazines.

PUBLIC RECORDS

To hear reporters like Krans tell it, investigative reporting is lots of fun. And it can be. But there's also a lot of drudgery involved. For every hot tip, there are 10 bum steers.

"It's painstaking work," says Krans. "It takes a lot of time. You've got to dig and then when you think you have your story you have to wait a little while and dig some more. There's usually more there."

Often that digging involves public records, documents that can shed light on an issue. "You've got to get into a document state of mind," advises Houston. "Every time you talk to someone and they say something is a certain way, you should ask: 'Is there a memo on this? Is there a report on this? Is there an audit on this?' Everything someone says can either be supported or contradicted by documents."

Among the documents students can look for:

- Health department records on cafeterias and restaurants on campus
- Lawsuits filed against the university
- University or department budgets
- University salary data
- Accreditation reports
- On-campus crime reports
- Criminal records on faculty members, administrators, athletes, staff
- Emails sent to your university president or athletics officials
- Research contracts.

At a public university, just about any expense can be traced through public records – often with interesting results.

The Daily Tar Heel published a major investigative story after inquiring about paper use at its campus labs, which at the time allowed unlimited free printing for students, faculty and staff. Using records obtained from the school's information and technology service, the newspaper found that students had printed an average of 2.4 million pages per month that year and that printing had been on the rise since instructors had started assigning more online readings. Many readers were shocked not only by the amount of paper used, but also by what it was costing in student fees. In response, the university adopted a new policy limiting the number of pages students could print for free and it began to charge students who went over their allotment.

The Daily Tar Heel also took a close look at the high costs of administrative searches. In 2010, the newspaper revealed that the university had spent a total of nearly $500,000 in search firm fees and travel expenses to recruit three top administrators (Figure 11.1). All three were already working at the university.

While universities are rich hunting grounds for investigative stories, Houston concedes that they can also

Investigative and enterprise story ideas

Crime

- Get crime statistics from your university police department for the last five years. Take note of trends – which crimes are up, which crimes are down.
- Ask for arrest records from your campus police or the city or county law enforcement agency that covers your campus. Look for familiar names, trends, evidence of raids. Were a slew of students arrested for marijuana possession in the dorm last month? Was the dean of students arrested for driving under the influence?
- Run key school officials – the chancellor, president, provost, deans, controversial professors – through a criminal records check.
- Do the same for high-profile students, such as members of the football team or student governing board or leaders of other student groups.
- Get information from the agency that handles parking on campus. Ask for lists of people who get handicapped placards, people who have their parking tickets waived, people issued faculty (or other premium) parking passes. Make sure these people are legitimate. (One year the *Daily Bruin* revealed that 19 able-bodied football players at UCLA had been cited for illegal use of disabled parking placards).

Budget

- Get your college or university budgets for the past five years. Note which departments are getting more or less funding. Take note of the biggest changes.
- Compare budgets for different departments. Divide by the number of students in each department to find out how much the university is spending on different groups of students.

Athletics

- Find out how much your school is spending on team recruiting.
- Check the graduation rates for each NCAA team on campus. Compare those numbers to the graduation rates for the campus as a whole.
- Look at funding for athletic scholarships. You might compare it to financial aid for academic achievements.
- Find out what kind of perks your athletes get. Schools have been known to lavish gifts on their top players, particularly if they win an important game.

Health and safety

- Check the health inspection reports on the cafeterias and other food service establishments on campus or favorite off-campus eateries.
- Find out which popular bars near campus have been cited for serving underage drinkers.
- If you've got a medical school on campus, check the licensing records of all M.D. faculty members with the state medical board.
- Use sex offender registries to find out about offenders who live on or near your campus.
- Check fire inspection reports on dorms, fraternity and sorority houses and other buildings.

Academics

- Look up the grade records on controversial or popular classes. You won't be able to get grades for individual students but you should be able to get records without names. If Human Sexuality 101 is reputed to be an easy A, report on the grade distribution. Compare different sections of the same course or different professors.
- Find out which departments are undergoing accreditation reviews. Study the accreditation reports to find the department's strengths and weaknesses.
- Request salary data for all faculty members. Find the highest paid professors and compare how professors in different departments are paid.
- Peruse the latest accreditation report for your school. Some colleges and universities routinely keep copies of these reports, which can run to hundreds of pages, in the library. If you can't find it there, try the university registrar's office.

be hard places to probe. "It's difficult to get information out of universities. They have a certain arrogance about the information they have. They don't believe they have to share it."

But they do, particularly if the school is public. State colleges and university documents are all subject to open records laws. Want to know how much your biology professor makes? It's a public record. Curious about how much the student health center spends on condoms? It's a public record. Wondering how many students have flunked out of school? You guessed it; it's a public record (although the names of the students are confidential.) Open record laws vary state by state. But they share certain exemptions. Personnel files, student records and health records are usually exempt.

INVESTIGATING PRIVATE SCHOOLS

Private colleges and universities are not subject to the same open records laws that make public schools such gold mines for investigative reporters. But you can still get plenty of documents. Colleges and universities that participate in federal financial aid programs, for example, must be accredited by a nationally recognized accreditation agency and those reports are public records.

Whenever a private school contracts with a public agency (for garbage pickup or police services, for example), that contract is public. And like other tax-exempt organizations, most private universities are required to file Return of Organization Exempt From Income Tax annual information forms, better known as IRS Form 990s. These forms can provide valuable windows into a private university – and also into the private foundations set up by public schools.

According to the Student Press Law Center, The IRS Form 990 and the supporting schedules that go with it disclose

- the amount of money the organization has taken in each year (including grants), with a breakdown indicating the general sources and amounts of that money
- a comprehensive listing of where the money was spent, how much was spent and for what
- a detailed balance sheet indicating both the assets and liabilities of the organization at the end of each fiscal year
- information on the sale or purchase of the organization's investments (such as stock portfolios, bonds, trusts and endowment funds) and how they have fared each year
- the identities and salaries of the top organization employees, consultants and professional service providers making more than $50,000 a year
- any legal fees paid by the organization.

Under federal law, tax-exempt organizations, such as private schools, college foundations, charities and nonprofit corporations, are required to provide the form upon request. Copies of a tax-exempt organization's Form 990 and supporting documents can be obtained through the Internal Revenue Service, inspected on the institution's premises or acquired online, according to the SPLC. Federal law requires that the organization make both its application for recognition of tax-exempt status and its annual information returns (Form 990 and supporting documents) for at least the last three years available to the public upon request either in person or by mail.

The SPLC offers these directions for obtaining the documents:

To make an in-person request, contact the organization's business office during regular business hours. Ask to inspect the form or ask to be directed to the office where the form is kept. The organization must allow you to inspect the form and take notes. Unless the form can be easily obtained on the Internet, copies must be provided on request, although a reasonable photocopying fee may apply. Except in unusual circumstances, the law requires that you be allowed to inspect and obtain a copy of an organization's Form 990 on the same day you make your request. If you encounter reluctance, you should submit a written request, citing the law (including the penalties for noncompliance, discussed below) and stating that you will go to the IRS if denied access. You may also wish to send a copy of your request to the organization's attorney.

If your request is solely by mail (or email) the organization has 30 days to mail you a copy of the form.

COMPUTER-ASSISTED REPORTING

Got some data? Crunch it! With simple spreadsheet programs like Microsoft Excel and online tools like Google Docs, reporters can now sort through vast amounts of data and spot trends or interesting facts that may lead to juicy stories.

Much university data is kept in digital form and you can request that officials provide the records in an electronic format. The federal Freedom of Information Act and open records laws in many states mandate that a public agency must provide the records in any format in which they are capable, according to the Student Press Law Center.

Among the data you might seek are budget and salary information; grades by course, department or professor; admission rates; campus demographics; and graduation and retention rates for your school or for particular groups, such as college athletes. Ask for data from multiple years so you can analyze changes over time.

The Lumberjack (thejackonline.org), the student newspaper at Humboldt State University in California, used Excel, a spreadsheet program, to analyze travel records after the university pledged to spend $75,000 in travel on Delta Airlines in a community effort to draw the airline to the nearby Eureka airport. The original idea was the university would encourage employees to fly Delta when they needed to travel and would use the account over 18 months. But as the deadline to use the travel money approached, more than $51,000 remained in the account. The university sent

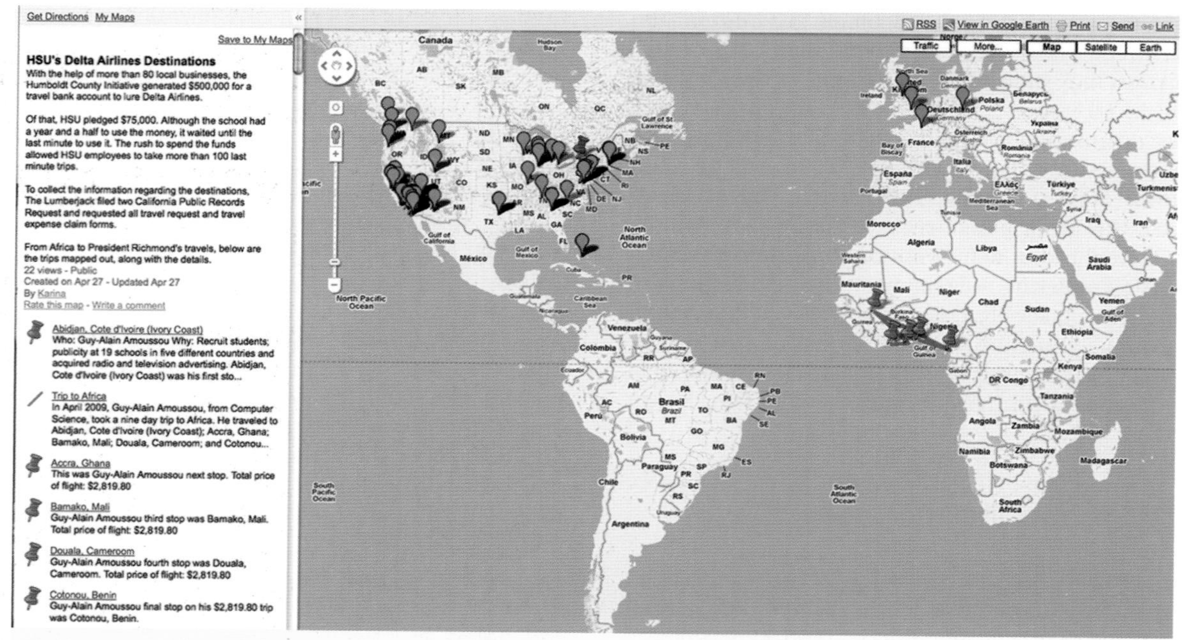

FIGURE 11.2 With computer-assisted reporting techniques and data visualization tools investigative reporters can analyze data. *The Lumberjack* at Humboldt State University in California created an interactive map to show that faculty, staff and students booked more than $50,000 in travel over the course of a month, including some trips of dubious necessity to far-flung places like Cote d'Ivoire, Ghana, France, Germany and Cameroon. *The Lumberjack*, Humboldt State University.

How to request a document

1. Figure out what documents you need.
2. Get a copy of your state's open records laws (often available from your state press or newspaper publishers association) and keep it handy.
3. Consult with an editor, adviser or the Student Press Law Center to figure out if the document you need is exempt from Freedom of Information laws.
4. Find out which office and which person is responsible for keeping the record you need – the "custodian" of the record.
5. Talk to the custodian of the record and verbally request the document. When possible, ask for the document in person. Be polite and friendly. Make a point of telling any officials you speak to that you intend to make a formal request.
6. If you are denied access, note the name of the person who is denying access and ask him or her to cite the law that enables the withholding of the record. If you are certain of your legal right to access the document, you might point to the law and ask the custodian to refute it. Take notes.
7. If you are looking for a document held by a state or local government agency (e.g., city or campus police, state board of health, etc.), use the SPLC's fully automated, fill-in-the-blanks State Open Records Law Request Letter Generator (www.splc.org/foiletter.asp) to draft an official written request for the document. If you need a federal document, go to a similar letter generator created by the Reporters Committee for Freedom of the Press (www.rcfp.org/foi_letter/generate.php).
8. States and the federal government each have a set number of days (varying between three and 20 working days) from the time the written request is received to either supply the requested document or offer a valid legal reason for withholding the document.
9. During the countdown, continue to call or visit the custodian of the record and issue reminders of the upcoming deadline.
10. If at the end of waiting period, you still have not received the records or you have received an insufficient response, contact a media law expert or the SPLC.

Adapted from a guide written by Amy Emmert, media adviser to UCLA Student Media.

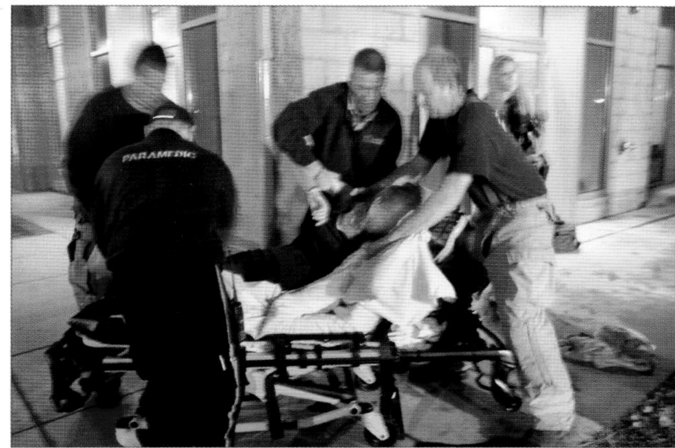

CHRISTY AUMER/THE DAILY IOWAN

A woman is lifted onto a stretcher by two paramedics and two firefighters on the evening of Oct. 25. The woman was later taken to UI Hospital and Clinics for medical care.

STORY BY DANNY VALENTINE • PHOTOS BY CHRISTY AUMER

YOUNG men and women in Iowa City aren't just going out and getting drunk anymore. Compared with five years ago, a greater number of them are going out and risking blackouts, injury, and even death, a *Daily Iowan* investigation shows. They are often hysterical and obliterated, bloodied and vomit-soaked. And more of them require the services of Johnson County ambulance paramedics. METRO, 4A

MORE ON THE PROJECT

- Read the Editorial Board's approach to effectively confront binge drinking. 6A
- Log on to **dailyiowan.com** to see photos and video from eight ride-a-longs.
- Watch Daily Iowan TV (campus channel 4, cable channel 17) at 9:30 p.m. today for an exclusive report.
- Go behind the scenes with reporters at noon today on The Lab @ KRUI: www.kruiradio.org/listen

Hawk Nation eyes Miami

Fans ready to fly south to Florida for bowl berth.

By CHRIS CURTLAND

Local travel agents began feverishly booking fans' trips to Miami on Sunday night as the news broke that the Hawkeyes will play in the Orange Bowl on Jan. 5, 2010.

Unclear if Iowa would play in the Orange Bowl or Fiesta Bowl until early Sunday evening students, alumni, and other Hawkeye football enthusiasts scrambled to snag the best deals.

Packages are selling for upwards of $2,000.

Until the Hawkeyes officially started seeing orange around 7 p.m., Winebrenner Red Carpet Travel in Iowa City had already booked some 700 Hawkeye fans on a Fiesta Bowl package.

SEE BOWL, 3A

Family, friends honor Ponseti

Celebration brings together Ponseti family, patients, and supporters.

By SAM LANE

While riding in a taxi cab with wife Helena Ponseti and son Bill on a vacation to Spain, Ignacio Ponseti noticed the driver had an interesting name.

Ponseti, perhaps the UI's most well-known medical professional, explained to the driver he had treated a patient with a similar name during the Spanish Civil War.

"Oh," the driver remarked. "You must be Dr. Ponseti."

Ponseti had helped the taxi driver's father after he had been injured during combat.

This was just one of the memories shared on Sunday as hundreds gathered at the Coralville Marriott Hotel and Conference Center to celebrate the doctor who continues to gain worldwide recognition. Ponseti died on Oct. 18 at age 95.

Many attendees came from Iowa, where Ponseti practiced medicine for over 60 years, while others came from half a world away.

"This showed great support for a wonderful man," said Bill Ponseti, the doctor's son. "Few people have the chance to affect something that heavily."

Ponseti, a UI professor emeritus, was known for his groundbreaking treatment of a congenital disease called clubfoot. With this disease, newborns' feet are turned inwards and, if gone untreated, may cause the child to walk with the sides of her or his feet.

"The Ponseti Method," a non-surgical treatment which the doctor developed in the 1940s, involves a careful stretching and casting of the foot in order to make it normal.

Sunday's event featured speeches from a number of Ponseti's peers, friends, and family.

Ponseti

ROB JOHNSON/THE DAILY IOWAN

Ralph and Marcia Compton speak with Helena Percas-Ponseti at the memorial service for her husband, Ignacio Ponseti, on Sunday at the Coralville Marriott Hotel and Convention Center. Marcia was cured of her scoliosis by Ponseti when she was 12. Ponseti, known worldwide for his non-surgical method of curing clubfoot, died on Oct. 18.

SEE PONSETI, 3A

DAILY IOWAN TV

To watch Daily Iowan TV, go online at **dailyiowan.com** or tune into UITV. The 15-minute newscast is on Sunday through Thursday at 9:30 and 10:30 p.m., with reruns at 12:30 and 1:30 a.m. and 7:45 and 8:45 a.m. the following day.

INDEX

Arts 7A · Opinions 4A · Classifieds 9B · Photo recap 5B · Crossword 8B · Sports 1B

WEATHER

28 · 21

DAILYIOWAN.COM

The Hawkeye football team is BCS-bound. Check out our web edition to see Daily Iowan sports reporters discuss Iowa's bowl bid.

FIGURE 11.3 When Danny Valentine, a reporter for *The Daily Iowan*, started to examine a rise in ambulance calls to downtown Ames, he found that alcohol abuse was the prime culprit and that toxic drinking, mostly by students, was straining the city's emergency services system. His investigative report, documenting how binge drinking, drunk driving and blacking out by students had all risen dramatically, won several national honors. *The Daily Iowan*, University of Iowa.

out a desperate email urging employees to book flights on Delta. *The Lumberjack* found that faculty, staff and students booked more than $50,000 in travel over the course of a month, including some trips of dubious necessity to far-flung places like Cote d'Ivoire, Ghana, France, Germany and Cameroon.

Using data collected from Freedom of Information Act requests, the reporters created a database and map (Figure 11.2) to show how far Humboldt State University employees flew with the public funds. As it turned out, Delta pulled out of the Eureka airport; the university's expensive effort to keep the airline at the local airport failed.

Here are a few tips for writing data-driven stories.

- **Find stats on the Web.** Visit the websites of your university and public agencies you cover to learn what reports and statistics are available online.
- **Get budgets.** Obtain the budgets and spending records of your university and other agencies in electronic form so you can use a spreadsheet to look for changes and irregularities.
- **Look for trends.** What do the numbers tell you? Does your university have more people of color than it used to? Are there more arrests for drinking-related offenses? Does it take longer for students to graduate than in past years? How much have tuition and fees gone up in recent years? Follow patterns over time.
- **Explain the trend.** Ask sources to analyze possible causes for the statistical trends you identify. When a reporter for *The Daily Iowan* (dailyiowan.com) started to examine a rise in ambulance calls to downtown Ames, he found that alcohol abuse was the prime culprit and that toxic drinking, mostly by students, was straining the city's emergency services system.
- **Use numbers sparingly.** Try to limit yourself to three numbers in a paragraph. Other data can go into charts and graphs.
- **Substitute words for numbers.** Instead of writing 25 percent, use "one-quarter." If you are writing about increases, say the numbers "more than doubled" or "dropped by a third."
- **Find the people behind the numbers.** Once you've got your numbers, look for people to illustrate your findings. If you find graduation rates are down, find students who have dropped out and ask them why they did. If your school is admitting more international and out-of-state students because they pay higher fees, interview students who have been affected by the change.
- **Understand basic math and statistics.** Numbers scare a lot of reporters. Review basic math skills, particularly percentages and averages (see Chapter 4). If you feel uncomfortable working with numbers, find someone – a newsroom colleague, an adviser, a professor, a professional journalist – who can help you.
- **Use examples.** It's hard to understand large numbers. Use comparisons to help people

TIPS FROM A PRO John Frank

Covering higher education is the best of all reporting worlds. It's a lot more than the chancellors and trustees and faculty council. There are elements from nearly every other beat – from local government and business to cops and politics.

One of the best parts about covering higher education is the wealth of information available.

These are just a few of my favorite sources of information.

- **The weekly calendars.** For the chancellor (and/or president). Also maybe the top two lieutenants. It allows you stay on top of what's happening at the institution and it's important to look at who is getting precious face time with top leaders. If nothing else, it gives you an idea of the leaders' top priorities.
- **Audits.** Get these at the college, university system and state level. I find the best ones at the university level. Auditors have a schedule for the year of what departments are going to be examined. Get the schedule, but also regularly ask for a list of the "special request" audits under way. These are typically the juicy ones because a tip or some indication of wrongdoing has prompted the review. And then call regularly to see if they've been completed.
- **Salary database.** This is probably a no-brainer. But the stories it can produce are limitless. It also adds valuable context to plenty of other stories by just plugging in average salaries for a top administrator or assistant professor.
- **Correspondence.** The best are the emails, but just request general correspondence in order to receive memos and mailed letters.
- **IRS Form 990s.** Form 990s are the Annual Information Return, which most tax-exempt charities and social welfare organizations must file with the IRS. The best place to get them is from Guidestar (guidestar.com) but the nonprofit must also keep a copy for public inspection. It is one of the best sources for information about private universities – salary disclosures are a main reason for that. Don't forget the athletic booster clubs, investment offices and other scholarships that are run by foundations.
- **Contracts.** There is a contract for nearly everything, from chancellors and athletic directors to corporations and dining hall operators. Also licensing contracts with athletic apparel companies and other advertisers are important to have on hand.
- **Fundraising brochures.** These give you a glimpse at the people who are playing a larger role at the university than most know. They can also be great sources.
- **Google News Alerts.** You can do this through Lexis and Factiva, too, but getting an email anytime your school is mentioned helps tremendously when other schools are trying to steal away your university's personnel.

JOHN FRANK was the investigations editor at *The Daily Tar Heel*, an independent student newspaper covering the University of North Carolina, Chapel Hill, from May 2003 to May 2004. He has received numerous honors for his investigative work, including top awards from Investigative Reporters and Editors, Society of Professional Journalists and the Hearst Foundation. He was a political reporter for the *St. Petersburg Times* and went on to work for *The News & Observer* in Raleigh, N.C.

This is adapted from a presentation Frank did at IRE's Annual Conference in June 2004 in Atlanta.

conceptualize. In *The Daily Tar Heel* article on campus printing, the reporter compared the number of pages printed to a familiar campus landmark, the 172-foot tall campus bell tower. In just one month that year the campus printed 5,259,757 pages – enough sheets to form a stack taller than 10 bell towers, the newspaper reported.

FOLLOWING UP ON TIPS AND HUNCHES

Investigative stories can arise from any number of sources – a phone call from a frustrated administrator, an email from a fired employee, an offhand comment by a professor in class.

Robert Faturechi of the *Daily Bruin* (dailybruin.com) at UCLA broke a major investigative story on preferential admission practices by the university's prestigious orthodontics residency program after receiving an email tip.

"Most of the time when you get emails like that there's nothing to them," says Faturechi, who went on to become a reporter for the *Los Angeles Times*. "I gave the guy a call and he sounded fairly legitimate so I drove out to his house. He had some documents to support what he was saying."

In an investigation that took more than four months, Faturechi, then the newspaper's enterprise editor, found that the residency program had violated University of California policy and standards governing public schools by giving special admissions consideration to relatives of major donors.

"In this unprecedented practice within the School of Dentistry, applicants related to donors giving six-figure gifts were automatically advanced over other students despite their lower test scores and grades," the story said. The *Daily Bruin* found evidence, including email messages and internal documents, showing that the orthodontics program had systematically advanced applicants related to major donors over more qualified students.

The *Daily Bruin* website linked to the relevant documents, including the audit and a letter of resignation from a faculty member who quit in protest of the university's inaction on the allegations of admissions impropriety. It also included graphs depicting the university's increasing reliance on private donations.

The story was picked up by several major media outlets, including the *Los Angeles Times*, *The Chronicle of Higher Education*, and even *The Drudge Report*.

Faturechi says it was a difficult story to report because many of the key sources declined to be interviewed or were hesitant to talk. "I had to be persistent," he says. Others, however, were outraged and willing to share their views. "Some of the folks I talked to take great pride in the program and they were frustrated with what they had seen happen. They wanted to clean things up."

KNOWING THE LAW

Waite, who won an IRE award while a reporter for the *Daily Nebraskan* (thenebraskan.com) at the University of Nebraska, says one key to good investigative journalism is knowing the law. "Know it in and out, up and down, left and right," he says. "Know it better than your administrators."

TIPSHEET
A dozen ways to avoid being burned by a hot story

Student Press Law Center

As more student media move from being merely a showcase for football players and prom queens to being serious news organizations, not afraid to address controversial or sensitive subjects, they face many of the hazards that have long confronted their commercial counterparts: threats of libel lawsuits, invasion of privacy claims, charges of bias, etc. While such problems are daunting, they need not be crippling. With the exercise of proper caution, the risks of covering a hot, or sensitive, story can be significantly reduced. Toward that end, the Student Press Law Center offers our suggestions for how you can avoid getting burned when the story you are covering is a hot one.

1 **Activate your common sense.** While the nitty-gritty details of libel or privacy law can be confusing, the main ideas are fairly straightforward, generally conforming to common sense. For example, libel law in a nutshell: 1. Don't publish things that aren't true or that you don't have the evidence to reasonably support and 2. Don't be a sloppy reporter. Privacy law: don't publish or gather information that is nobody else's business. Common sense also dictates that if you don't understand something or if a story simply doesn't make sense ask enough questions of enough people until it does. If you are confused, rest assured that your readers will be as well.

2 **Remember your role as a journalist.** Your job is to accurately relate the facts of a story to your readers. Go into a story with an open mind and not just looking for information that supports any preconceived version of the story that you might have. Your job is to find and report the facts as they exist. Do not be content with anything less. Good reporting is hard work. Be prepared to invest the time and energy necessary to get the story right. No excuses. If you're not willing or can't do so, leave the story for someone else.

3 **Take good notes.** The "Golden Oldie" of libel lawyer advice. Record facts and interviews scrupulously, including who said what and when. If you know you are a weak note taker, invest in an audio recorder.

4 **Documents, documents, documents.** Get it in writing. If your source tells you during an interview that she acquired her information from an internal memo, ask for a copy of the memo. And then read it to make sure that what your source told you jibes with what's in the memo. Also, whenever possible, cite a public record as your source for information. In most cases, doing so will protect you from liability even if it later turns out the information contained in the public record was wrong.

5 **Don't overstate the facts.** You are a reporter not a salesman. Get rid of the "bigger is better" mentality. Your football coach who can't account for $1,000 of the team's budget does not need to be labeled "corrupt" or the "ring-leader of the largest financial scandal in school history." "Two sources" is not "many sources" or "a number or sources" – it is "two sources." And it is perfectly okay for a problem to just be a "problem" and not a "crisis." You get the idea. Finally, you should generally avoid the temptation to interpret the facts or reach a conclusion or an opinion for your readers. In covering a sensitive story, it is safer to let the facts speak for themselves.

6 **Don't overstate the credibility of a source.** Either to yourself or to your readers. When interviewing a source, ask yourself if you think he's telling the truth. Does he have a reputation as a liar? Does he have any reason to harm the subject? If you are relying on statistical data or some other published report, establish that source's reliability. If, for example, the manner in which the statistics were compiled has been reasonably questioned, say so in your story. Remember that one exceptionally credible source is worth far more than a dozen semi-credible sources. Finally, anonymous sources should be used sparingly. And at least you should know the identity of your confidential source.

7 **Be fair.** Always give the subject of your story an opportunity to present his or her side. Not only does this give a story an essential element of fairness, it also provides you with an opportunity to catch – or at least confirm – parts of a story that may be subject to debate or question.

8 **Eliminate the non-essential.** Sensitive stories are not the place to show off your literary talents. Leave the flowery prose and melodrama for the features page. Write carefully and purposefully. Edit out sources or subjects that do not contribute to the "core" of a story. They are potential plaintiffs. Delete unnecessary (even though interesting) allegations. Tell what you know and how you know it. No more. No less.

9 **Seek the input of others.** Prior to publication, ask others to look at your story and offer their criticisms or suggestions. After you've worked endless hours on a story, "fresh eyes" are essential for catching gaps, inconsistencies, confusing phraseology, mistaken attributions and all of the other small traps that are forever hidden to one who has already read the copy 20 times. This is also the time to contact your adviser, an attorney, the Student Press Law Center or someone else well-versed in media law if you have specific questions about the legality of a story. An ounce of prevention sure beats sitting in court.

10 **Prior to publication, step back and look at the "Big Picture."** Forget the little details upon which you have focused so long and hard. Read the story through one last time. Taken as a whole, are there any obvious questions you failed to ask or glaring sources you didn't contact (for example, a person in a room who witnessed a key – and disputed – meeting)? Look at your story from different points of view. Do you believe each of your subjects and sources would feel they were treated fairly (even if they didn't like the story itself)? What about headlines and subheads – are they fair and accurate? Are the graphics, photos and accompanying captions correct and not misleading? The bottom line: make sure the story makes sense to you and fairly presents the facts as you know them.

11 **After publication, respond to complaints courteously and fairly.** Studies have shown that a person who perceives that he or she has been treated rudely or arrogantly by a media organization is far more likely to sue than one who believes that they have been shown the proper respect. Select one person –preferably a "people person" – to whom all complaints should be referred. While that person should not admit fault or provide information about specific newsgathering practices, he or she should listen carefully to the caller's complaints, promise to investigate the matter – and then do so. Where a correction or retraction is appropriate, publish it in a timely fashion.

12 **Finally, if you need help – legal or otherwise – don't be afraid to ask for it.** As a student, you're not supposed to know it all. And ask for that help sooner rather than later. It's much easier to put out a brush fire than a forest fire.

In fact, he recommends carrying a copy of your state's open records law in your back pocket – literally. (Some state press associations have pocket-sized guides to open records and open meeting laws. If yours doesn't, find the law and put it into a handy format). "That way, when a school administrator says, 'I'm not going to give you that document,' you can say, 'The law says this.' "

CULTIVATING HUMAN SOURCES

While many investigative stories begin with documents, like all stories, they need human sources to really come alive. Once you've discovered that your school is spending thousands of dollars to recruit a few high school jocks to the football team or that the chief of the radiology department at the university hospital just had his license revoked, you need to flesh out the story with interviews.

And, as you might imagine, getting people to talk may not be easy. Try to enlist sources to your cause, explaining why readers are entitled to know what's going on.

Waite recommends a combination of politeness and persistence. He remembers spending hours outside a key source's office waiting for the man to come out. When the source finally emerged, he refused to be interviewed. Waite thanked him politely and kept calling. "A week later I got the interview."

Q&A Matt Waite

Even before he had unpacked the boxes in his dorm room in his freshman year at the University of Nebraska, Matt Waite showed up at the *Daily Nebraskan* looking for a job. An editor assigned him to write a story about the city police's new electronic parking ticket writer. It was a routine story, but Waite was thrilled to be working as a reporter. Over the next four and a half years, Waite wrote dozens of stories for the paper, including a series of dispatches from Bosnia. (He got the university's College of Journalism and Mass Communications to finance his trip.) In his senior year he won a citation from Investigative Reporters and Editors for "Rethinking Malone," a computer-assisted reporting project that used census data, crime records and mortgage information to analyze a much-maligned neighborhood near the university. After graduating in 1997, Waite landed a night cops reporting gig at the *Arkansas Democrat-Gazette*. In 2000, he became a general assignment reporter for the *St. Petersburg Times* and in 2009 he won a Pulitzer Prize for developing PolitiFact.com, a website on which *St. Petersburg Times* reporters fact-check statements by politicians.

How can a student newspaper develop a watchdog or investigative spirit?

It really helps to take a group of editors, get them out of the newsroom and sit them down to have a fundamental discussion. What are we going to cover? What do we want to emphasize? What kind of newspaper do we want to be?

The thing that builds that watchdog attitude is success. If you can teach reporters at your paper to get into a document frame of mind, to look at internal audits, to ask for documents the university isn't used to having people ask for, to assess what kind of a job they are doing, then those stories end up in the paper.

Those stories get noticed by people, other papers, other editors. And you know what? That kind of success gets addictive.

What are some documents student reporters should look for?

Lawsuits are a perfect example. Go to the courthouse to look for professors suing the administration, harassment suits, breach of contract actions. It's boring and there will be weeks when you don't find a thing. But it's worth making sure. When I started going down to the courthouse the stories started dropping out of the sky.

Get the budget. It's the very lifeblood of the entire campus. Money makes the world go round. Every department has a budget and they spend money.

Look for audits. All kinds of stuff on a university campus is audited. Research grants are ruthlessly audited, extension services are audited. If you look at them you may find some people are wasting money.

What tips do you have for getting government and university officials to release documents?

Saying please and thank you and being polite works wonders. I have avoided having to write dozens and dozens of open records request letters and gotten out of countless fights over records by saying "please" and "thank you."

Get to know people on your beat. Look at what's on the walls, what they have pictures of. When I was a police reporter, I got so much out of the cops by finding out what their favorite football teams were and remembering them. I'd walk in and say, "Hey, the Longhorns won this weekend." That had an impact. You start to present yourself as a decent person.

What advice do you have for reporters dealing with reluctant sources?

Be polite. If you ask somebody for a comment and they say, "No," say, "I'm sorry. Thanks a lot." It's much easier for someone to turn you away if you're rude and act stupid. If you're polite to a fault, it's only a matter of time until they start feeling bad about it and talk to you.

How can student papers start doing computer-assisted projects?

You have to build a lot of shacks before you can build the Taj Mahal. Start small with campus crime numbers or by comparing budget figures over the last five years. Use that to learn about the budgeting process or crime and how to do percent change comparisons or summing and sorting and ranking in Excel. Treat these stories asskill-building exercises. Each time you'll learn something new.

One fairly easy story to do is to compare your campus to other schools. Get a list of peer institutions and compare tuition, graduation rates, campus crime statistics, graduation requirements. All these things are interesting to your readership.

TO DO

1 If you don't already have one, create an investigative team with some of your newspaper's most experienced reporters. Pick one or two manageable projects to start with. Invite a professional investigative reporter to act as mentor for the team.

2 Send a delegation to an investigative reporting conference or training workshop. (Investigative Reporters and Editors, Inc. and the National Institute for Computer-Assisted Reporting each hold an annual national convention and many regional workshops throughout the year.) Have participants share what they learned in a workshop for the staff.

3 Organize a brainstorming session for editors or for the whole staff focused on investigative reporting. Have people throw out ideas around the theme "What's Not Working?"

4 Organize an investigative reporting workshop for your staff or regional or state college press association. The IRE website has information on how to do this. You might be able to collaborate with professional newspapers or other student papers in your area.

5 Invite an investigative reporter from a local news organization to give a lecture or workshop for your staff.

6 Find an interesting database (faculty salaries, campus crime statistics, parking ticket fine information) and assign a team to crunch the numbers in Excel or another spreadsheet program. Have them look for possible story ideas.

7 Get a copy of your school's most recent budget and one from five years ago and assign a team of reporters to delve into it in search of story ideas.

TO READ

Burstiner, Marcy. *Investigative Reporting: From Premise to Publication.* Scottsdale, Ariz.: Holcomb Hathaway, 2009.

Houston, Brant. *Computer-Assisted Reporting: A Practical Guide, 3rd ed.* New York, N.Y.: Bedford/St. Martin's, 1999.

Houston, Brant, Len Bruzzese and Steve Weinberg. *The Investigative Reporter's Handbook, 5th ed.* New York, N.Y.: Bedford/St. Martin's, 2009.

Sankey, Michael L. *Public Records Online: The National Guide to Private & Government Online Sources of Public Records, 5th ed.* Tempe, Ariz.: Facts on Demand Press, 2004.

TO CLICK

Campus Coverage Project

The Campus Coverage Project offers investigative reporting training to college and university students with the goal of helping student journalists serve as better watchdogs on campus.

The website includes resources, updates on upcoming training and links highlighting some of the great watchdog work being done by student journalists around the country.

http://campuscoverage.org

Center for Investigative Reporting

The center is the nation's oldest nonprofit investigative news organization and produces multimedia investigative projects. The center sponsors internships.

http://centerforinvestigativereporting.org

Federal Open Government Guide

Published by The Reporters Committee for Freedom of the Press, this online guide explains how to use the Federal Freedom of Information Act.

http://www.rcfp.org/foiact/index.html

A Guide to Computer-Assisted Reporting

Pat Stith, Poynter Institute Online Veteran investigative reporter Pat Stith, who won a Pulitzer Prize for *The News & Observer* in 1996, shares tips on computer-assisted reporting.

http://www.poynter.org/content/content_view.asp?id=83144

Investigative Reporters and Editors, Inc.

The leading organization of investigative journalists sponsors conferences and training for professionals and students. Members have online access to more than 3,000 reporter tipsheets and investigative stories produced by leading journalists from around the world. Students get a membership discount.

www.ire.org

Making the Grade: Access to College Accreditation Reports

The Student Press Law Center offers this guide to getting information on colleges that participate in federal student loan programs.

http://splc.org/knowyourrights/legalresearch.asp?id=17

National Freedom of Information Coalition

The FOI Center is a reference and research library in the Donald W. Reynolds Journalism Institute at the Missouri School of Journalism on the campus of the University of Missouri. It specializes in open government research and education and promoting the public's right to government accountability.

www.nfoic.org/foi-center

National Institute for Computer-Assisted Reporting

National Institute for Computer-Assisted Reporting is a program of Investigative Reporters and Editors, Inc. and the Missouri School of Journalism.

www.nicar.org

The Scoop

Derek Willis' blog on investigative and computer-assisted reporting offers handy tips.

http://blog.thescoop.org

The Search Systems Free Public Records Directory

An online directory of free public record databases on the Internet.

www.searchsystems.net

Student Media Guide to the Clery Act

The Student Press Law Center answers frequently asked questions about the federal campus crime reporting law.

http://splc.org/legalresearch.asp?id=19

12 Wednesday, Sept. 15, 2010

Focus

xpress.sfsu.edu - GOLDEN GATE [X]PRESS

DESTROYED: A fireman digs through rubble in the 2700 block of Concord Way in San Bruno Calif., on Friday, Sept. 10. A fire ripped through the suburban neighborhood Thursday night leaving more than 100 homes affected by the blaze.

ALEX WASHBURN — [X]PRESS

San Bruno fire ravages area

Neighborhood devastated by a massive inferno.

ERIC SORACCO — [X]PRESS

INFERNO: Firefighters from Truck 94 of Daly City try to put out one of the smaller fires during the San Bruno fire on Sept. 9.

BRITTNEY BARSOTTI — SPECIAL TO [X]PRESS

EMOTION: Susan Bullis (center) breaks down after finding out that her house has been destroyed in the fire on Sept 9.

APOLOGY: PG&E President Chris Johns apologizes for a gas explosion that caused the San Bruno fire at a news conference in the Bayhill Shopping Center on Friday Sept. 10 in San Bruno, Calif.

ERIC SORACCO — [X]PRESS

ALEX WASHBURN — [X]PRESS

RUBBLE: A group of firemen dig through remains of houses on the 2700 block of Concord Way in San Bruno Calif., on Friday, Sept. 10. The fire damaged many homes and left some completely destroyed.

FIGURE 12.1 Sometimes photos can tell a story better than words. In September 2010 photographers Brittney Barsotti, Eric Soracco and Alex Washburn of *Golden Gate [X]press* went out to the scene of a gas main explosion and fire that consumed a neighborhood in San Bruno, just south of San Francisco. *Golden Gate [X]press*, San Francisco State University. Reprinted with permission.

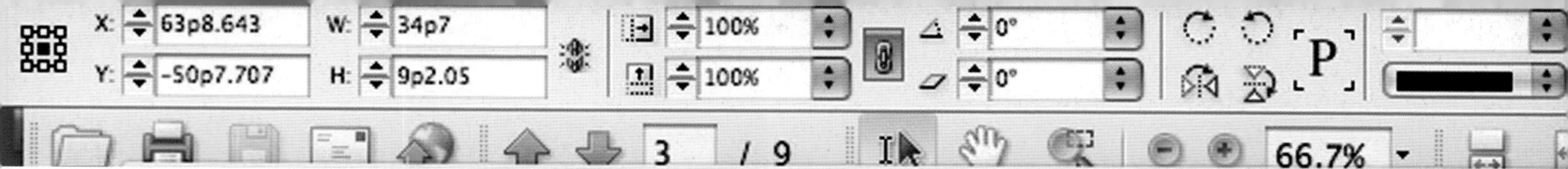

CHAPTER 12 PHOTOJOURNALISM

It was the second round of the NCAA men's basketball tournament and the University of North Carolina Tar Heels were locked in a tight battle with the University of Texas Longhorns. *The Daily Tar Heel* (dailytarheel.com) photographer Brian Cassella had gotten plenty of good action shots during the game. But when the Tar Heels lost 78–75, Cassella knew he'd need a reaction photo to truly capture the mood of the season-ending game.

After snapping a few shots of the disappointed players leaving the court, Cassella went to the locker room. "The atmosphere was overwhelmingly morose," says Cassella, who went on to become a staff photographer for the *Chicago Tribune*. "It was difficult to raise my camera. (It was like) shooting a funeral."

Cassella noticed one player sitting on a bench with a jersey over his head and he shot a few frames. Then another player went to comfort the visibly upset team manager sitting a few feet away. "The moment lined up perfectly right in front of me, and I was able to squeeze off just one frame (before other people got in the way). One minute later the coaches kicked us out, but I had a photo that was part of our front-page package the next day."

The Student Newspaper Survival Guide, Second Edition. Rachele Kanigel.

CHAPTER CONTENTS

Photojournalism is about seizing moments, about showing readers what writers try to – and sometimes can't – describe. Cassella's photo (Figure 12.2), with its slumped shoulders and bowed heads, captures the Tar Heels' utter sense of defeat as no text story could.

Photojournalists need sensitivity and intuition to find these moments, as well as the technical skills to arrest them and make stirring images. They also need access. Unlike reporters, they can't get the story over the phone. Photographers must be enterprising and assertive enough to get to the action when it's happening.

In this chapter we'll discuss what it takes to make great newspaper photos.

WHAT IS PHOTOJOURNALISM?

Photojournalism is telling stories through photos. Photos don't just break up gray text; they add value to a newspaper

FIGURE 12.2 This shot taken in the locker room after the University of North Carolina Tar Heels lost a key NCAA basketball game captures the team's utter sense of defeat. Brian Cassella, *The Daily Tar Heel*, University of North Carolina, Chapel Hill. Reprinted with permission.

by providing additional information and insights. They can be poignant or entertaining, silly or serious. They take readers to places they can't go and show them things they can't normally see.

And they bring readers to your newspaper. Numerous studies have shown readers are more likely to read a story if it's accompanied by a photo. In a landmark 1991 study, researchers from the Poynter Institute used Eye-Trac technology (a device that tracks eye movements) to monitor how readers read newspapers. They found:

Photos are usually the first thing readers see on a page, even before headlines.

Readers process photographs 75 percent of the time (as compared to 56 percent of the time for headlines and 25 percent of the time for text).

The larger the photo, the more likely readers will scan it. Pictures that run three columns across or wider are read 92 percent of the time (Figure 12.3).

Photos lure people to pick up the paper and read it, so it's in everyone's interest to make sure your paper is chock full of good photos.

One trick to making good photos is to take a lot of shots. In the past, when professional photojournalists mostly used film, they'd often shoot three or four 36-exposure rolls on a routine assignment. Now, with digital, it's not unusual for a photographer to shoot hundreds of photos to get one or two great images for a story.

One difference between shooting as a photojournalist and shooting for fun is that now you're trying to document reality. That means you don't set up photos. Unless you're shooting a portrait or creating a photo illustration, you want to capture life as it unfolds, not as you want it to look. A photojournalist doesn't tell his subject to "say cheese." Most photojournalism shots are candid. In addition, a work of photojournalism mustn't just be well composed and in focus. It has to tell a story.

California State University, Northridge

DAILY SUNDIAL

sundial.csun.edu | Monday, September 15, 2008 | Since 1957

CSUN student among dead in Metrolink crash

ABEL MACIAS / CONTRIBUTING PHOTOGRAPHER

Commuter train headed to Moorpark station collides head-on with freight train, killing 25 and injuring 135

ADOLFO FLORES
STAFF REPORTER

Like many undergraduates, Aida Magdaleno wasn't sure what she wanted to do with the rest of her life until last week when she decided to be a social worker after taking some sociology classes.

"Last weekend she told me that's what she wanted to do, she wanted to help people," her sister Gabriella Magdaleno said. "Her passion was in helping other people."

The sophomore CSUN student donated clothes, blood and money when she could. In fact she recently donated most of her clothes and was planning to go shopping this weekend, but never had the chance.

She was one of the 25 people who lost their lives on a train accident this past Friday, after a Metrolink engineer failed to stop at a red light causing the passenger train to collide head-on with a freight train leaving 135 people injured as well.

Gabriella was waiting for her sister at the Moorpark station when the accident occurred and in the hours following the accident, hoped that her sister would come out alive. The following morning her worst fears were confirmed when she was notified that her sister had passed away.

"It's just so sad, so sad," Gabriella said in tears moments before attending a mass dedicated to her late sister and the others who lost their lives on Metrolink #111.

The blue-eyed ambitious A-student never stopped dreaming or setting higher goals for herself, her sister said.

"Aida really did want to make the world a better place in anyway she could," Gabriella said.

Her brother Juan Magdaleno, who was on the phone with Aida minutes before the crash agreed and knew that one day she would give back to the community just as much as it had given her.

"She appreciated this country because it gave her the opportunity to study and get an education," he said.

Both sisters were attending CSUN this semester, Aida as an undergraduate and Gabriella as a graduate student. Gabriella plans on becoming a school counselor now more than ever.

See AIDA, page 4

PHOTO COURTESY OF MYSPACE.COM

19-year-old sociology major Aida Magdaleno was on her way home to Moorpark on the Metrolink train when it crashed into a Pacific Union train.

"Aida would always offer us food, she would always look for ways to help those around her," said her roommate, Michelle Do.

INDEX

ONLINE EDITION

Watch exclusive footage taken minutes after the crash at dailysundial.com

INSIDE

- CSUN administrator on train retells the events of the crash
- Photos of the collision site

Volume 51 • Issue 12 ©2008 Daily Sundial • A financially independent student newspaper

FIGURE 12.3 Studies show nearly all newspaper readers will look at a photo that runs across the entire width of a page. The *Daily Sundial*, California State University, Northridge.

Though digital photography offers myriad opportunities for manipulating images, **resist the temptation**! Photojournalists take varying positions on digital manipulation but most agree photographers shooting news should limit themselves to basic photo techniques traditionally used in the darkroom – cropping, taking out dust spots, adjusting contrast, dodging and burning (lightening and darkening areas of the photograph). Be aware that altering photos beyond these simple changes – especially in ways that fundamentally alter the meaning of the image – may be unethical and can even cause legal problems.

SHOOTING PERSPECTIVES

For virtually any assignment, you want to get a variety of shots, including a long shot, a medium shot and a close-up. Each type of photo offers a different perspective on an event.

The long shot

A long shot, sometimes called a full shot or a wide shot, is one that sets the scene, giving the reader an overall impression of the event and where it takes place. If there's a demonstration on campus, the long shot might show the quad where the protest is happening. If you're covering a fraternity house fire, you might take a picture from across the street showing the firefighters hosing the building. If you're covering a football game, you'll want an overall shot of the entire stadium.

Long shots demand height. When taking the long shot, try to find a way to lift yourself above the crowd. That may mean standing on a chair, scrambling on top of a car (better make it your own) or taking a picture from a balcony across the street. Photojournalists have been known to climb trees, rent ladders, even hire helicopters all in the quest for a good long shot.

The medium shot

The medium shot is one that tells the story in a single image. Like a news lede, it should capture all the major elements in one tight package.

A medium shot at a fire might show tearful survivors in the foreground with firefighters battling the blaze in the background. At a basketball game, it might show a player making a basket with the crowd watching in awe. At a demonstration it might focus on a heated argument between a protester and a police officer.

Ideally, the medium shot should capture action. That means photographers have to be on their toes, ever watchful for movement. A photojournalist must learn to anticipate action, waiting for the swimmer to dive off the diving board or the campus police officer to slap the handcuffs on the demonstrator. Medium shots are best caught with a wide-angle lens, such as a 24mm or a 28mm, but a 50mm will suffice.

The close-up

The close-up shot captures drama and emotion. It puts the reader right in the event, showing the grimace on the athlete's face (Figure 12.4) or the blissful glow on the singer's. Close-ups are often used as part of a photo story or as a secondary shot grouped with a medium or long shot.

A close-up needn't focus on a person's face. It might be a hand taking a brush to a mural or a plume of smoke coming from a beaker in a scientific lab.

A telephoto lens enables a photographer to be less conspicuous when shooting a close shot. But don't rely on a long lens if you don't have to. Get as close as you can to the action.

High and low angles

One of the challenges of photojournalism is to offer readers a unique perspective on a subject. That often means shooting from an unusual angle – down from a tall building or up from the ground. Good photojournalists shoot from a variety of viewpoints for each assignment. They move their bodies, climbing up on furniture for a high shot, scrunching down on the floor for a low shot, standing in back of a speaker to capture reaction from the crowd.

When shooting an assignment, try to get the subject from as many angles as you can.

FIGURE 12.4 A close-up shot can capture facial expressions, giving the reader insights into the subject. Sean Gallagher, *Columbia Missourian*, University of Missouri. Reprinted with permission.

FIGURE 12.5 A photographer needs to anticipate action and be quick on the draw. At this rally, photographer Jordin Thomas Althaus was able to catch the peak point of the confrontation between protesters and police. Jordin Thomas Althaus, *Golden Gate [X]press*, San Francisco State University. Reprinted with permission.

FIGURE 12.6 Photographer Derek Montgomery knew the Halloween revelry on Madison, Wisconsin's State Street often turned violent so he stuck around to capture the news as it broke. "I knew the best images would come from these two people who decided to stay and confront the police," he says. "Using a wide angle lens I was able to get most of the street scene before being blasted myself with a pepper spray cannon. It was an irritating experience, but I'm happy with the results." Derek Montgomery, *The Badger Herald*, University of Wisconsin, Madison. Reprinted with permission.

BREAKING NEWS

It may be a raucous rally on the quad or a motorcycle accident near the entrance to the campus, professors picketing against budget cuts or a dorm being evacuated during a flood. News happens, even on a seemingly sleepy college campus. The role of the photojournalist is to document that news when it's happening (Figures 12.5, 12.6, 12.7, 12.8 and 12.9).

Student photographers often don't have the resources of professional newspaper photographers – police scanners crackling in their cars, high-powered lenses and other fancy equipment – but they can cover breaking news.

In fact, student photojournalists have certain advantages over pros because they're part of the community they cover. A professional photographer may be responsible for covering a city, a county, a whole state. A student newspaper photographer can focus on a single campus.

The key is to be prepared at all times. That means carrying a camera (or two or three) wherever you go and being on the lookout for photo stories at all hours. You should also have a GPS device with you at all times, so that you can find a location easily if an editor calls with a breaking assignment. A good photojournalist is always on duty.

Do you hear people chanting political slogans outside your dorm window? Grab your camera and shoot the protest. Do you see police handcuffing someone across the street? Pull out your long lens and take a few shots. That just may be the suspect in the recent string of robberies on campus.

When shooting breaking news, try to take a single picture that encompasses all the elements of the story. Look for an angle that shows the injured student as well as the damaged motorcycle in one photo.

Record a visual moment that reflects the most intense part of the event – the angry faces of the demonstrators or the tearful faces at an accident scene. These moments – often the

FIGURE 12.7 Photographer Cera Renault was able to capture an argument between a Bush opponent and Bush supporter at a get-out-the-vote rally the day before the 2004 presidential election. Cera Renault, *Golden Gate [X]press*, San Francisco State University. Reprinted with permission.

FIGURE 12.8 Photographer Tom Whisenand was with Stephanie Seiler (center), the mother of a University of Wisconsin, Madison student who was missing for four days, when she learned her daughter had been found alive and well. He was able to show her relief at the news. Tom Whisenand, *Minnesota Daily*, University of Minnesota, Twin Cities. Reprinted with permission.

FIGURE 12.9 Photographers generally don't use a fisheye lens to shoot news, but occasionally one can be effective. Erik Jepsen wanted to capture both the size and intensity of the March 4, 2010 rally at the University of California, San Diego, one of more than 100 demonstrations organized that day in a national "Day of Action" for education.The fisheye lens allowed him to shoot wide but get extremely close to the action. Erik Jepsen, *The Guardian*, University of California, San Diego. Reprinted with permission.

key ingredient to a powerful photo – happen without warning. A good photographer is constantly watching for them.

SPEECHES AND MEETINGS

Whether it's the president of the school giving the annual state of the university speech or a political activist speaking at an anti-war rally, speeches are a big part of campus coverage. They're also a challenge for college photographers. How do you get an interesting shot of a person standing on a stage? How do you capture a reaction when the speaker is up there and the crowd is back here? How do you make this photo look different from the speech in the same hall last week or last month?

Scott Strazzante, a staff photographer for the *Chicago Tribune*, advises photojournalists to try to gain access to the speaker before and after the talk. "Arriving at a speech early and staying late is the best way to avoid having to depend on the traditional podium shot," says Strazzante, who was a photographer for *College Days* (riponcollegedays.com) when he was a student at Ripon College in Ripon, Wis.

When shooting the actual speech, he says, "try to mix up your approach. Shoot extremely tight on the speaker's face or shoot loose, giving the photo context. Shoot from the crowd using the audience as a framing device. If possible, photograph the speech from outside a doorway or window."

If speech photos can be dull, meeting photos can be even duller. Who wants to see a bunch of people sitting around a conference table talking?

When it comes to covering meetings, photographers may want to skip the actual meeting altogether. A more effective approach is to cover the issue being discussed.

Say, for example, the faculty senate votes to restrict smoking on your campus. Don't shoot the senators discussing the issue; shoot the smokers on the quad. Get shots of smokers lighting up outside buildings, standing in the rain, gathering in doorways. If the student government board is discussing whether to fund the new Filipino student group on campus, shoot participants doing something – making decorations for the Filipino Cultural Night, eating lumpia and roast pig at a celebratory dinner.

SHOOTING SPORTS

Like the athletes they cover, sports photographers must be nimble, energetic and fast. They have to be able to capture fast-moving action one second and the emotional reaction to a decisive play the next (Figures 12.10, 12.11 and 12.12).

FIGURE 12.10 In sports photography, the challenge is to arrest the action and capture emotion. Sean Gallagher, *Columbia Missourian*, University of Missouri. Reprinted with permission.

FIGURE 12.11 Sports photographers must capture reaction as well as action. Brian Cassella, *The Daily Tar Heel*, University of North Carolina, Chapel Hill. Reprinted with permission.

Knowing the sport you cover is essential. That way you can foresee where the ball is going to end up and what's likely to happen next. "For sports photography you have to anticipate," says Joe Jaszewski, a staff photographer for *The Idaho Statesman* in Boise. "Once you've observed, it's too late."

It's also useful to know the players, says Jaszewski, who was a photographer, photo editor and reporter during his three and a half years working for *The California Aggie* (theaggie.org) at the University of California, Davis. "It helps to have one photographer who shoots all the football games or all the basketball games and knows this player likes to shoot off his left foot or this football player likes to catch passes over the middle," he says.

You need the appropriate lens for shooting sports. To cover football you should have a 300 mm or longer; for basketball a much shorter lens will do. Shooting a burst of pictures with a motor drive helps nail the peak-action play.

Shooting inside a poorly lit gymnasium can be a hassle. Sometimes you can go in before the game and set up strobes

FIGURE 12.12 Photographer Derek Montgomery had shot enough University of Wisconsin basketball games to know Bo Ryan, the expressive head coach, was a man to watch. In this situation, Wisconsin's Devin Harris was getting into foul trouble and Ryan was reacting to a call against him late in the game. Derek Montgomery, *The Badger Herald*, University of Wisconsin. Reprinted with permission.

high above the court and trigger them from your camera. By lighting the gym you will improve the quality of your images.

Just like sportswriters, sports photographers need to go beyond covering the game and hang out at practices, in the locker room, at post-game celebrations. The more the players know you, the more they'll be willing to let you into their world.

FEATURE PHOTOS

Some of the best newspaper photographs don't come from an assignment sheet or even run with a story. They're standalone, or feature, photos. Feature pictures document the life of the community you're covering and provide a visual break for readers.

To find feature photos, look around you. Look at the couple kissing under that stone arch, the soccer players who gather for a late afternoon pick-up game, the tired student who has fallen asleep over her book in the library carrel. Once again, the photographer is looking to capture a moment.

But that moment needn't be completely spontaneous or unexpected. A good photographer can plan for feature photos. "Instead of just wandering around looking for people doing things, read your paper, the activities bulletin board or posted notes for things going on at your school," Strazzante advises.

Find an area of the campus that you can go back to over and over so that you can anticipate what is going to happen and when you'll have the best light. Late afternoons on the quad may give you long shadows and intimate moments, for example. If you hang around the drama department, you'll know when students are going to try out for the play, when set designers will be painting the sets, when actors will be rehearsing in costume.

Shannon Guthrie, a staff photographer for the *State Journal-Register* in Springfield, Ill., advises feature-hunters to keep a close eye on the weather. "If the wind is blowing really badly or it's raining or snowing, get out there," says Guthrie, who won numerous awards while working for the *College Heights Herald* (wkuherald.com) at Western Kentucky University. Umbrellas, snowdrifts, ice crystals on trees all make for interesting photos.

CANDIDS

Often the best way to photograph a story is to focus on a single person at the center of the tale or issue. Candid shots of subjects working, studying, and interacting with other people can offer readers windows into their world.

To start, talk with the subjects. Ask about their roles in the story and how their work or hobby has brought them into the headlines. "Often as young photojournalists we bury ourselves so deep in our cameras we forget to ask questions," says Brian Wagner, a staff photographer for *The Daily Herald* in Provo, Utah. "The more you talk to a subject, the more important and relevant the photos are. You communicate what you're trying to do and they communicate who they are."

Wagner, who worked for *The Daily Beacon* (utdailybeacon.com) at the University of Tennessee, Knoxville and the *College Heights Herald* at Western Kentucky University, mentions a story he shot about a senior volunteer who visits elderly people. During an hour-long chat, the man mentioned he got his inspiration from a higher source. He told how he kneels down alone each night before going to bed. Wagner asked if he could photograph that and the man agreed. So Wagner came back in the evening and photographed the man kneeling at his bedside.

"If I hadn't spent an hour talking with him, he probably wouldn't have told me that and he certainly wouldn't have let me take a picture of him praying," Wagner says. "As young journalists we tend to think that the picture is the only thing that matters. These days, I find that I'm talking to people more than I'm shooting."

Wagner says talking with subjects also helped him overcome his fear of intruding.

"When I was a college photographer, I was more leery of imposing on people than of coming back to the newsroom empty handed. I had to overcome the mindset that sticking a camera in someone's face is a nuisance. Eventually, I became more confident and realized it isn't such a bother. I realized I wasn't just taking from the situation, I was giving. I was showing people that they were important in my eyes, important enough to show other people."

PORTRAITS

Once you have some good candids, try some posed shots. Look for props – an astronomer's telescope, an athlete's basketball – that will help tell the story. Or look for an interesting background or setting. If you're shooting a swimmer, for example, it makes sense to shoot in a pool; if you're shooting a geography professor, a geography lab with maps all around will help tell the story.

Lighting is a key part of shooting portraits. When shooting indoors, turn off overhead lamps and look for natural light. Position your source next to a window. Side lighting is more dramatic and telling. Putting the camera on a tripod will allow you to use a slow shutter speed. The subject easily can hold still for a half-second exposure.

Even when shooting a posed portrait, try to capture a "real" moment – an expression, a hand gesture, a movement that says something about the person. If you're shooting more than one person, watch for a look or a natural gesture of affection between them. You want to catch a revealing moment.

PHOTO ILLUSTRATIONS

Digital photography has given photographers a multitude of tools for manipulating images. Now even an amateur can use multiple photos to create new images, putting the university president's face on the body of a bodybuilder or allowing people who have never met to shake hands.

If you do decide to go with a photo illustration, make sure it's clear to the reader that this is an illustration and not a representation of something real. "If a reader can look at the image and have any questions about whether it's real, you shouldn't use it," says Jim Merithew, a picture editor for *Wired* magazine who worked on *The News Record* (www.newsrecord.org) when he was a student at the University of Cincinnati.

When creating a photo illustration, be careful not to violate copyright protections. Don't scan or steal someone else's images from the Web. You may only use images you have shot or ones that you have express permission to use. Taking other people's work to enhance your photo illustration is illegal, regardless of how much you change the original.

In his book, *Photojournalism: The Professionals' Approach, 6th ed.* (Focal Press, 2008), photojournalism professor Kenneth Kobré offers practical and ethical guidelines for using photo illustrations.

- **Eliminate the docudrama.** Never set up a photograph to mimic reality, even if it is labeled a photo illustration.
- **Create only abstractions with photo illustration.** Studio techniques, for example, can help to make situations abstract – the use of a seamless or abstract backdrop, photo montage, or exaggerated lighting. Contrast in size and content, juxtaposition of headline and photo – all can give the reader visual clues that what appears on the page is obviously not the real thing.
- **Always clearly label photo illustrations as such, regardless of how obvious you may think they are.**
- **Never play photo illustrations on news pages.** Restrict them to feature pages or to section fronts. Display them so that they are obviously distinct from news or feature pictures.
- **If you haven't the time to do a photo illustration right, don't do it.** Find another solution.

PHOTO STORIES

Photo stories are stories told in pictures. They may be pegged to an event, like move-in day at the dorms or homecoming weekend, or be tied to a theme. After a University of California, Davis student died of an alcohol overdose the night he turned 21, Jaszewski, the former *California Aggie* photographer, set out to document how other students spent their 21st birthdays. "I'd spend the evening with them and document what happened," he says. "There was some pretty reckless behavior."

Often, photojournalists look for a story line with a beginning, middle and end, such as preparations for a big race or performance or the creation of a class project. Follow a nursing student learning to give an injection or an art student creating a sculpture from beginning to end. Such stories offer a natural narrative arc.

Photo stories may have an accompanying text story or simply a collection of captions that explain the photos.

When planning a photo story, look for a variety of types of photo that illustrate the challenges your subjects encounter and how they overcome them. Show the fear on the nursing student's face as she encounters her first patient, the grimace as she holds the syringe to the arm, the relief after she's completed the injection.

A photo story should offer a variety of shots that may include:

An establishing shot, or overall photo, that shows where the action is taking place

A medium shot that focuses on one activity or aspect of the story

A close-up of a person's face

A detail shot that shows one element of the story, such as a person's hands doing something

A portrait of a key person

An action shot that captures people doing something

A shot that captures emotion.

PHOTO ASSIGNMENTS

How does a photographer find out where to go, what to shoot, what the story is about? Most newspapers have a set photo assignment process.

At some papers, reporters or editors fill out old-fashioned paper photo assignment forms that photo editors distribute to photographers. But more and more, newspapers rely on Web-based or email forms that can be filled out and sent electronically.

At a minimum, photo assignment forms should include:

Slug (one word name) of the story

A description of what the story is about

Time, date and location of event

Contact name and phone number

Name and contact information for the reporter

Section the story is planned for

A space for additional information.

Once the photo editor assigns a photographer to the story, the photographer and reporter should talk about the story. Sometimes photographers and reporters go out to cover stories together. This kind of teamwork is effective for certain types of assignments – breaking news events, for example, or in-depth stories where the reporter and photographer should focus on the same subjects.

For other stories, however, it may work better for the photographer and reporter to meet with the subject separately. Reporters and photojournalists are looking for different things, after all. Reporters generally want their subjects to sit and talk, while photographers want them to move and do what they normally do. Separate photo and interviewing sessions allow both journalists to get what they need without either interfering with the other's work.

WHERE CAN YOU SHOOT?

Whether you're photographing a professor lecturing in a classroom or students drinking in a campus pub, it's important that you understand where you are allowed to shoot and where you're likely to face restrictions (Table 12.1).

Photographers can shoot photographs in most public places. You can take pictures on any public street, on a public beach, in a public airport, bus station or train station.

You can also shoot in many areas at a public college or university – in the quad, in the student union, in the hallway of an academic building – without permission. However, you may be restricted from shooting in certain places or at certain times. If a class is in session, for example, you must get the professor's consent before taking pictures. If you want to shoot a concert in the student union, you'll have to get permission from organizers of the event. And photographers usually need to get an OK from residents

Where and when a photojournalist can shoot	Anytime	If no one objects	With restrictions	Only with permission
Public area				
Street	X			
Sidewalk	X			
Airport			X	
Beach	X			
Park	X			
Zoo	X			
Train station	X			
Bus station	X			
In public school				
Preschool			X	
Grade school			X	
High school			X	
University campus	X			
Class in session				X
In public area				
Police headquarters			X	
Government buildings			X	
Courtroom				X
Prisons				X
Military bases				X
Legislative chambers				X
In medical facilities				
Hospital				X
Rehab center				X
Emergency van			X	
Mental health center				X
Doctor's office				X

Table 12.1
Where and when a photojournalist can shoot.

Reproduced with permission from *Photojournalism: The Professionals' Approach, 6th ed.*, by Kenneth Kobré, 2008.

Table 12.1 Where and when a photojournalist can shoot. (cont'd)

	Anytime	If no one objects	With restrictions	Only with permission
Clinic				X
Private but open to the public				
Movie theater lobby		X		
Business office		X		
Hotel lobby		X		
Restaurant		X		
Casino				X
Museum			X	
Shopping mall				X
Store in mall				X
Private areas visible to the public				
Window of home	X			
Porch	X			
Lawn	X			
In private				
Home		X		
Porch		X		
Lawn		X		
Apartment		X		
Hotel room		X		
Car		X		

and/or housing officials before they can take photos in dorm rooms, on-campus apartments and other residential areas.

Private colleges and universities – and most other private businesses – are allowed to limit access. Photographers generally need permission to shoot anywhere on a private campus.

PHOTOS ON THE WEB

With its virtually unlimited space, the Web is an ideal venue to showcase the work of your newspaper's photographers. Do you have lots of great photos from a campus event or game? Create a photo gallery. Do you have a story that's best told with a set of sequential images? Post an online slideshow.

A number of student newspapers have regular places on their websites to show off photographers' work. *The College Heights Herald* at the Western Kentucky University has a photo tab on its navigation bar that leads to photo galleries. The *Cornell Daily Sun* (cornellsun.com) at Cornell University puts together a "Week in Pictures" slideshow each week.

As discussed in Chapter 18, the Web also offers multimedia capabilities. An audio clip with ambient sound and dialogue can add a whole new dimension to a photo story.

Golden Gate [X]press, the student newspaper at San Francisco State University, has used multimedia storytelling to great effect on its website. Photographers and online producers frequently work together to create multimedia stories, not just for in-depth projects but for breaking news, such as protest rallies and other campus events. Typically, a photographer shoots the photos while a producer records interviews and ambient sound. They stay in close touch during the reporting process, so that they get sound and pictures that work well together. After capturing their assets, the two often sit down together to edit their work and discuss how best to tell the story. Sometimes photographers shoot the photos, record sound and edit the piece themselves.

PHOTO EDITING

Like word editors, photo editors play many roles, from managing the photo staff and ensuring all assignments are shot to making decisions about which photographs will run and how they will be cropped.

The photo editor often acts as a liaison between the top editors and the photographers and must have excellent communication skills and judgment.

In choosing images, photo editors look for several qualities:

News value: Does the photograph have journalistic value? Does it illustrate the "who, what, where, when, why or how" of a story?

Information: Does the photo provide information beyond what's in the story it accompanies? For example, does a portrait give readers a fuller sense

CHECKLIST
Photo editing

In editing photos, ask yourself these questions:

1 Will photos enhance or advance this story?
2 Which photos best complement the story?
3 Has the photographer chosen the most graphic, most compelling images from the shoot?
4 Do the photos support or conflict with information in the story? Do they add information?
5 Do the photos have news value?
6 Are they graphically appealing? Emotionally appealing?
7 Will the photos draw the reader's eye?
8 Should the photos be cropped? How?
9 Are the photos composed well?
10 Do the brightness or contrast need adjusting?
11 Would anyone find the photos offensive? If so, do they need special explanation? Should other people be brought in to discuss the photos?
12 Does one photo say enough or are multiple images needed to tell the story? If multiple images are used, how can they tell different parts of the story?
13 What is the best size for the photos?
14 How do these photos and this story relate to others on the page?
15 Does this photo warrant placement as the dominant art on the page?
16 Is the caption complete?

TIPS FROM A PRO Kenneth Kobré

"The first step in becoming a professional photojournalist is to shoot twice as much as you now shoot," says Kenneth Kobré, professor at San Francisco State University, whose book *Photojournalism: The Professionals' Approach* (Focal Press, 2008), now in its sixth edition, has been used by more than 200,000 students and is a standard text at more than 125 universities around the United States. "One difference between an amateur and a professional is the professional shoots and throws away a lot more images than the novice."

Kobré offers these 10 suggestions for transforming ordinary snapshots into memorable, award-winning front-page images:

1 **Get closer.** This was the advice of Robert Capa, legendary war photographer and founder of Magnum photo agency, who said, "If your pictures aren't good enough, you're not close enough." Often the key to giving a photo pizzazz is to move in and capture the details of your subject, leaving out extraneous things in the background. Don't be afraid to invade a person's personal space. If you are shooting the college president, put your camera within a few inches of his face for an up-close-and-personal portrait that might reveal his "true" nature.

2 **Have patience.** When you're photographing students or professors, let them get used to you before you start shooting pictures. When they forget the camera is there, you can take more natural candid shots.

3 **Frame the photo.** With a photograph, like a painting, the edges of the image are just as important as the central action. Suppose you are taking pictures of a merit scholar on the college green. Before snapping the shutter, ask yourself if you need to include the blank sky above the student's head or the boring building on either side of the scholar. If the sky and building don't help to tell the story of your brainiac, move your camera closer to eliminate the extraneous elements, leaving only the parts of the scene that are really important to your image.

4 **Avoid the "jumbled effect."** This occurs when surrounding shapes and colors compete for attention with the subject of the photo. If you are taking pictures of a juggler on the quad, for example, you may see other people in the viewfinder eating, studying, taking naps. These extraneous students add nothing to the picture of the juggler. Try setting a wide aperture and selecting a telephoto lens. Then get as close as you can to the juggler; that will help throw the other players out of focus.

5 **Cut the on-camera flash.** When you use the strobe light on the camera, the resulting pictures often look unnaturally lit. If you're using film, try an 800 ISO film for shooting the indoor college graduation ceremony. With a digital camera, select 800 ISO or even 1200 ISO for indoor low-light shooting without an on-camera strobe.

6 **Avoid the noontime sun.** Middle-of-the-day light, from about 10 a.m. to 2 p.m., comes straight down from the sky, leaving your subject's eyes in shadow and giving them the look of a raccoon. Scenic landscape pictures lose detail under this harsh light. Instead, try capturing your subjects in the rich tones and long shadows at sunrise and sunset. If you must shoot an outdoor portrait of the winning football coach during the day, move your coach into a shaded area out of direct sunlight.

7 **Shoot at night.** Nighttime offers interesting shadows and light for taking unique shots. At night, without flash, shoot by the rays of a street lamp or the light from an unshaded window. In low light, you can use a tripod to allow longer exposure and avoid camera movement. Explore what is happening inside the buildings on your campus, from late-night dorm parties to all-night study sessions.

8 **Take candids.** For more interesting shots, don't insist on having students and faculty pose in front of your camera. Instead, capture them in the middle of an activity so the photo says something about their personalities or interests. Rather than set the chemistry professor in front of her blackboard, follow her around for a few hours and see what she does. Snap pictures when she flails her arms in an attempt to explain a difficult concept to a student or colleague.

9 **For portraits, include a telling prop.** When you do choose to take an arranged portrait, find an object that will tell the reader something about the person. If you're shooting a professor who specializes in nuclear physics, pose the person in front of the school's cyclotron.

10 **Make your subject comfortable.** If you want the new library director to pose with a volume of Shakespeare, have her find a comfortable, natural position. Here's when a little leaning on the stacks or slouching against a chair is permitted. Avoid having her stand or sit straight up; these tense postures make the subject look uncomfortable and don't say anything revealing about the person.

For more information on writing cutlines, see the checklist in this chapter.

The Ten Commandments for photographers and reporters working together **Elinor J. Brecher**

For the reporter:

1 **Thou shalt not wait until the last minute to assign photographs or video requests.** Reporters should be thinking about photos as soon as a story is assigned and should begin talking with the photo department then about picture possibilities.

2 **Thou shalt not tell the story subject what the photographer will shoot.** There is nothing worse than showing up at an assignment and having

the subject say, "The reporter said you would photograph me doing…"

3 **Thou shalt give as much information as possible on the assignment form, including street address, contact name and number, and email, and a summary of what the story is about.** Due to assignment load, photographers cannot always check with reporters or editors before going to assignments. Often, the form is all they have to go on. The more information they have, the better job they can do.

4 **Thou shalt respect a photographer's professionalism.** Reporters should let photographers shoot assignments as they see fit. Suggestions are welcomed, but the final call on whether something will work should be the photographer's.

5 **Thou shalt not schedule interview photographs if there is something more active to shoot.** Interview photographs are generally predictable and visually uninteresting.

6 **Thou shalt not introduce the photographer as "my photographer."** You're part of a team and the photographer has a name.

7 **Thou shalt get to know photographers and videographers learn the basics of what they do.** Stop by and visit the photo department.

8 **Thou shalt give photographers/videographers feedback.** If you like or dislike a photograph or video, let the shooter know. Constructive criticism and communication can only help everyone do their jobs better and foster better understanding between reporters and photographers.

9 **Thou shalt stay out of the picture.** When on assignment with a photographer, be conscious of what he or she is shooting and make every effort to stay out of the line of fire.

10 **Thou shalt bear with photographers/videographers while they deal with equipment problems, and help out if you can.** Lights, cameras, and other gear are necessary to get the job done. Lend a hand if a photographer asks. You may learn something.

For the photographer:

1 **Thou shalt not depend only on the photo request information.** The assignment form is only a starting place. Photographers should talk with reporters and get as much information as possible about the story before going to the assignment.

2 **Thou shalt not barge into interviews, cameras and flashes blazing.** Be sensitive to the reporter's needs and understand that interviews can be easily thrown off-kilter with an ill-timed interruption.

3 **Thou shalt share information with the reporter.** Photographer should pass on to the reporter information, quotes and any tidbits that he or she may pick up when reporter is not around.

4 **Thou shalt act like a journalist.** Be aware of the world around you. Understand your community and what is going on and making news in it.

5 **Thou shalt use common sense and know the law.** Photographers tend to be gung-ho risk-takers, which is all well and good. However, common sense and restraint should prevail as shooters are not much good if they are in police custody or the emergency room.

6 **Thou shalt not set up photos.** Staged photographs are as misleading and unacceptable as fabricated quotes. The exception: a portrait.

7 **Thou shalt have thine technical act together.** Fooling around with lights and equipment endlessly can ruin an interview.

8 **Thou shalt respect reporters' professionalism.** Photographers/videographers should listen to reporters' suggestions and consider them carefully since many reporters have good visual sense and care about how the final package looks.

ELINOR J. BRECHER has been a reporter for *The Miami Herald* since 1989. She was a Nieman Fellow at Harvard University in 1988 while reporting for *The Courier-Journal* in Louisville. She is the author of *Schindler's Legacy: True Stories of the List Survivors* (Dutton, 1994). While attending the University of Arizona, Tucson, in the mid-1970s, Brecher was a reporter and city editor for the *Arizona Daily Wildcat* (wildcat.arizona.edu), and reporter and news editor of *The Tombstone Epitaph*. She graduated from the UA in 1977 with a degree in journalism and was inducted into the department's Hall of Fame.

of what a person looks like? Does a fire photo show readers the scope of the damage?

Emotion: Does the photo capture emotion – laughter, pain, love, anger?

Action: Does the photo capture movement, action, something happening?

Intimacy: Does the photo offer a glimpse into the subject's private world?

PRE-SHOOT RESEARCH

Photojournalists are not just photographers, they are reporters. You need to know the who, what, where, when, why and how behind every story you cover and every shot you take. Photographers should always carry a notebook and pen and get names, titles and other basic information about every subject they shoot.

Just like reporters, photographers should do advance research (if there's time) before they go out on a shoot. Unless you're covering a breaking story you should take at least a few minutes to find out what you're shooting. If you're going to cover a Diwali festival, for example, you should do some research on the Hindu holiday; study up on the customs and learn what you're likely to see. If you're covering move-in day at the dorms, you should find out which dorms have mostly freshmen (who are more likely to have emotional goodbye scenes with parents) and what time they open. This kind of background research will come in handy when you're actually out on the shoot.

Whenever possible, reporters and photographers should talk as soon as an assignment is made. They should share what they know about the topic and the direction they are each planning to go in. That way, the photos and story are more likely to mesh.

WRITING CUTLINES

Good cutlines, or photo captions, do more than simply explain a photo; they lure readers into the story. Cutlines accomplish four important things:

1 Explain the action

2 Name the principal people in the photo

3 Explain how the photo relates to the story

4 Note the important or telling details in the photo.

Photojournalists are journalists and should report every story they shoot. That means getting names and other relevant information (age, academic major, title, city of residence, etc.) from the sources they shoot.

Because a photograph captures a specific moment in time, the first sentence of a cutline is typically written in present tense. Additional sentences may be written in present tense or past tense, depending on the publication's style.

A standard cutline is usually written like this:

(Noun) (verb) (direct object) during (proper event name) at (proper noun location) in (city) on (day of the week) and/or (month) (date), (year). The second sentence should amplify the information in the first sentence, offering more details about the story.

Example: Paramedics carry a burn victim to a waiting ambulance while firefighters fight the blaze at the Sigma Phi Epsilon House on Central Avenue in Brownsville. Five students were hospitalized as a result of the fire, which destroyed the two-story building.

CHECKLIST
Writing cutlines

1 Does the caption answer the relevant who, what, where, when and why questions?

2 Is it written in present tense?

3 Is it written in active voice?

4 Does the cutline thoroughly identify all prominent people?

5 Does it identify subjects from left to right?

6 Are the names spelled correctly?

7 Does it include titles, ages, hometowns, academic majors or other identifying information appropriate to the story?

8 If it includes quotations, are they accurate and properly attributed?

9 Are all mysterious objects or circumstances clearly explained?

10 Does it tell when the scene happened?

11 Does it tell where it was taken?

12 Does the cutline go beyond the obvious, expanding on what is visible in the photo? If the basketball player is holding a basketball and wearing a uniform you don't need to say that he is a basketball player in the caption – let the picture tell the story. Add what is not evident in the photo, such as how many points he scored during the season.

COPYRIGHT AND SELLING PHOTOS

We'll discuss copyright in more depth in Chapter 13 but it seems relevant here to discuss who owns the copyright of photos produced for student news organizations.

Generally, the creator of a work owns the copyright, according to the Student Press Law Center. However, under the "work for hire" exception, an employer, such as a newspaper, owns the copyright of work created by employees working in the scope of their employment. On the other hand, if a photographer is classified as an "independent contractor," the photographer, not the employer owns the copyright.

Sounds tricky? It is, particularly when a third party wants to buy a photo.

In the case of a student publication it's sometimes difficult to determine whether staffers are employees or independent contractors. Student reporters and photographers often work for little or no money, particularly if a campus newspaper is produced as part of a class or student activity. That's why it's good to for student publications to have a copyright policy (see a sample in Chapter 13) that each staff person reads and signs before submitting work.

Many student news organizations now sell photographs created for the publication on their websites. Some contract with commercial photo reprint companies like Detroit Softworks, which sells photos and merchandise like mugs, playing cards, refrigerator magnets and T-shirts with the photo on them through a service called Fotobroker. Revenue is divided between the publication (or the photographer) and the company.

TO DO

1. Invite a photographer or photo editor from a professional newspaper to critique your paper.
2. Arrange for your photo staff to spend a day at the local paper, sitting in on budget, Page One and photo selection meetings.
3. Re-evaluate your photo assignment system. Does it work well? How could it be improved? If it's not working well, assign a team of photographers, photo editors, word editors and reporters to come up with a new system.
4. Plan a workshop for photographers, reporters and editors to discuss communication problems. Use Elinor J. Brecher's Ten Commandments for Photographers and Reporters Working Together as a way to open the discussion. Try role-playing or other techniques to open the lines of communication.
5. Pair up photographers and reporters and assign them to work together on a story. Make sure the story has strong possibilities for text and photos.
6. Set up a coaching program for your photo staff. Invite photographers from local newspapers to act as mentors who will meet regularly with your staff photographers to discuss their work.
7. Plan a training multimedia training session for photographers to learn skills in audio recording and shooting video.

TO READ

Giles, Matthew, ed. *Facing the World: Great Moments in Photojournalism.* New York, N.Y.: H.N. Abrams, 2001.

Horton, Brian. *Associated Press Guide to Photojournalism, 2nd ed.* New York, N.Y.: McGraw Hill, 2000.

Kobré, Kenneth. *Photojournalism: The Professionals' Approach, 6th ed.* Woburn, Mass.: Focal Press, 2008.

London, Barbara, John Upton, Jim Stone, Kenneth Kobré, and Betsy Brill. *Photography, 8th ed.* Upper Saddle River, N.J.: Prentice Hall, 2004.

National Press Photographers Association. *The Best of Photojournalism.* Durham, N.C.: National Press Photographers Association, Annual.

Parrish, Fred *S. Photojournalism, An Introduction.* Belmont, Calif.: Wadsworth/Thomson Leaning, 2001.

Zavoina, Susan and John Davidson. *Digital Photojournalism.* Alleyn & Bacon, 2001.

TO CLICK

American Society of Media Photographers

ASMP offers online tutorials, educational seminars, a blog, scholarships and a mentoring program for young photographers.

www.asmp.org

American Society of Picture Professionals

ASPP sponsors a mentoring program for college students.

www.aspp.com

College Photographer of the Year

The College Photographer of the Year Competition was founded by Cliff and Vi Edom in 1945. The University of Missouri administers the contest with support from its co-sponsor, Nikon Inc. The website displays past winners and tips on photography.

www.cpoy.org

Detroit Softworks

The company sells reprints and other merchandise created from a publication's photographs or pages through a secure ecommerce website. Detroit Softworks also provides hosted content management systems and Web-based ad management for news organizations.

http://detroitsoftworks.com

The Digital Journalist

The Digital Journalist has been on hiatus after it lost funding from its key sponsor Canon USA on 2009 but its archives are still full of helpful information, reviews and articles about digital photography and videojournalism.

http://digitaljournalist.org

Eddie Adams Workshop

The Eddie Adams Workshop (named for the famed photographer who died of Lou Gehrig's disease in 2004) is an intense four-day gathering of top photography professionals, along with 100 students. The photography workshop is tuition-free, and the 100 student participants are chosen based on the merit of their portfolios.

www.eddieadamsworkshop.com

National Press Photographers Association

NPPA, one of the leading organizations of photojournalists, sponsors educational programs, mentoring, scholarships, portfolio reviews and contests for students.

www.nppa.org

NPPA Code of Ethics

The NPPA Code of Ethics is used by most professional photojournalists as guidelines for appropriate ethical behavior.

http://www.nppa.org/professional_development/business_practices/ethics.html

Sports Shooter

Sports Shooter is an online community and resource for professionals, students and hobbyists interested in sports photography and photojournalism.

www.sportsshooter.com

GOLDEN GATE

[X]

[X]PRESS

Muni Fare Hike On Horizon

SEE **NEWS**_PAGE 2

NEXA on the Chopping Block

SEE **NEWS**_PAGE 3

Ring in the Lunar New Year

SEE **A&E**_PAGE 12

[February 17, 2005] [www.xpress.sfsu.edu] [Issue 3 Vol. LXXVIIII]

WAS THIS STUDENT SILENCED?

SPECIAL REPORT PAGE 2

Photojournalist Says Arrest Violated His First Amendment Rights

KELLY ADAMS/STAFF PHOTOGRAPHER

FIGURE 13.1 Shortly after San Francisco State University photojournalism student Omar Vega took photographs of other students allegedly burglarizing a car, university officials had him evicted from the dorm. He was also charged by the district attorney's office with burglarizing and tampering with a vehicle, even though he claimed he was acting as a photojournalist, not a participant. The charges were ultimately dropped as part of a plea agreement, but the case launched a national debate about the rights of student photojournalists to document activity by students. *Golden Gate [X]press*, San Francisco State University.

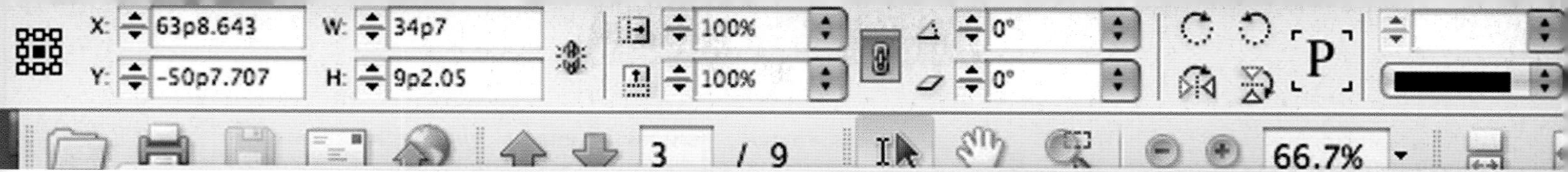

CHAPTER 13
LEGAL ISSUES

In Tennessee, stacks of a state university student newspaper were stolen the day the paper printed a story about a star basketball player's arrest for drug possession. In California, a photojournalism student was evicted from his dorm and threatened with expulsion after photographing a group of students burglarizing a car. In New York, a community college student governing board locked the newspaper staffers out of their office for a week during a funding dispute.

On paper, student journalists have virtually the same legal rights and responsibilities as professional journalists. But in reality, they face a host of added challenges.

Some administrators try to exercise prior restraint against student newspapers to keep controversial material from appearing. Official sources sometimes try to bar student journalists' access to public meetings and public records. Even fellow students – student governing boards, fraternity members and others – occasionally attempt to squelch expression by cutting funding, firing editors and stealing newspapers when they don't like what's being written.

The best way to prevent or combat these problems is to know your rights – and to know where to turn when these rights have been abridged. In this chapter we'll explore some of the major legal issues facing student journalists.

The Student Newspaper Survival Guide, Second Edition. Rachele Kanigel.

CHAPTER CONTENTS

CENSORSHIP AT PUBLIC SCHOOLS

Every year, the Student Press Law Center in Arlington, Va., the leading legal resource for student journalists, fields dozens of complaints from students who believe their free-press rights have been censored.

Former SPLC Executive Director Mark Goodman says censorship can take many forms, including:

Demanding prior approval of content by an adviser, publication board, administrator or others

Confiscating newspapers

Restricting distribution of papers

Cutting funding on the basis of content

Disciplining editors or advisers for the content of the paper.

The First Amendment protects journalists from government censorship and more than 60 state and federal court decisions have concluded that freedom of the press applies to student publications at public colleges and universities.

As the SPLC writes in its Legal Brief on Student Press Freedom at Public Colleges:

> School officials cannot:
>
> 1. Censor or confiscate a publication, withdraw or reduce its funding, withhold student activities fees, prohibit lawful advertising, fire an editor or adviser, "stack" a student media board, discipline staff members or take any other action that is motivated by an attempt to control, manipulate or punish past or future content. …
> 2. Demand the right to review publications before distribution. …
>
> Student government officials are subject to the same First Amendment restraints as school administrators. For example, they cannot punish a paper's staff or adviser or withdraw a publication's funds for content-based reasons.
>
> However, school officials can:
>
> Regulate non-content-based aspects of a publication. For example, school officials can review the financial records of student media organizations and prohibit staff hiring policies when they discriminate on the basis of race.

In Canada, the Charter of Rights and Freedoms works much like the American First Amendment in protecting the rights of journalists, both professionals and students. Despite these protections, however, attempts at censorship continue in both countries.

CENSORSHIP AT PRIVATE SCHOOLS

Student journalists at private colleges and universities in the United States do not enjoy the same free speech protections as those at public schools. The First Amendment only limits censorship by government officials or others, such as student governing board officials, who act on their behalf.

However, some private schools voluntarily give student journalists rights to free expression through written school policies, which may be published in a student handbook, code of conduct or other document. Your newspaper should know if your school has a free expression policy. Courts have suggested that schools that adopt such policies are contractually bound to abide by them.

Some states, most notably California, have statutes that protect free expression at private schools. The California law reads, in part, "It is the intent of the Legislature that a student shall have the same right to exercise his or her right to free speech on campus as he or she enjoys when off campus."

For more information about the rights of private school journalists, see the Student Press Law Center's Legal Guide for the Private School Press, available at the center's website listed at the end of this chapter.

CENSORSHIP PREVENTION

Student journalists can try to prevent censorship by building relationships with the campus community before problems arise. Effective strategies include:

Meeting regularly with top school officials and leaders of student groups

- Publishing periodic columns, articles or editor's notes explaining the editorial decision-making process. This step is particularly important with the publication of controversial material.
- Hosting a panel discussion, open house or other public event where you can educate the campus about press freedom in general and specifically about your editorial policies.
- Reaching out to student groups that feel least served by the publication and soliciting their concerns, thoughts and story ideas.

You can often keep censorship at bay just by opening communication lines.

FIGHTING CENSORSHIP

If you do encounter any sort of censorship, contact the Student Press Law Center immediately. The center provides free information, advice and legal assistance to students and the educators who work with them.

In Canada, the Canadian University Press, a cooperative of more than 60 student publications, offers legal advice and assistance to member newspapers; about three-quarters of the student newspapers in the country belong to the cooperative. "In terms of censorship, student papers here have a lot of the same problems as those in the States," says Sean Patrick Sullivan, a former CUP president and former editor of *The Brunswickan* at the University of New Brunswick.

If a Canadian University Press member paper reports a censorship problem, CUP officials typically make phone calls or write letters in support, Sullivan says. "A lot of times in those situations, lobbying works. If it doesn't, we get a lawyer involved."

The professional media in both the United States and Canada can also be important allies in the battle against censorship. Journalists are usually quick to jump on a censorship story and the public scrutiny media coverage can bring may intimidate censors. Professional news organizations may provide other kinds of assistance, such as legal advice and letters of support.

NEWSPAPER THEFT

Maybe some fraternity brothers don't like your coverage of a rowdy party. Or perhaps your college president is embarrassed by the racy sex column that came out the day of an open house for prospective students. So they quietly remove stacks of newspaper from around campus, tossing them in a trash Dumpster or out-of-the-way recycling bin.

Every year thousands of student newspapers disappear under suspicious circumstances. But if a paper is free, is this theft? Campus police departments often don't see it that way, but the Student Press Law Center says stealing newspapers, even free ones, is a crime (see Figure 13.2).

"Just because a newspaper doesn't have a sales price doesn't mean it doesn't have value," says Goodman, who left the SPLC to become the Knight Chair of Scholastic Journalism at Kent State University. "That value can be measured in different ways – in the cost of printing, in the advertising revenue the copies of the publication represent."

In several states, including Florida, Kentucky and Texas, individuals have been successfully prosecuted for stealing "free" student newspapers. In 2005, Binghamton University adopted a policy banning newspaper theft after two student publications were reported stolen.

Stealing newspapers can be seen as an act of censorship. By taking newspapers out of circulation, thieves are

TIPS FROM A PRO James M. Wagstaffe

James M. Wagstaffe, a San Francisco attorney who specializes in media law, offers this simple advice for journalists who want to avoid legal trouble:

1. Be a skeptic.
2. Get it right.
3. Get permission.
4. Write sensitive subjects sensitively.
5. Do not promise confidentiality lightly.
6. Watch for an unexpected plaintiff. (If you write a story about a teen drug addict, for example, you may inadvertently defame the teen's parent.)
7. Be wary of sources you yourself don't trust.
8. Obtain public record or documentary support.
9. Make sure your headlines and teasers are factually accurate.
10. Treat demands for correction seriously.

JAMES M. WAGSTAFFE is partner and co-founder of Kerr & Wagstaffe, LLP, a San Francisco law firm that specializes in First Amendment and media law. He successfully defended *The New Yorker* magazine in the libel trial Masson v. *New Yorker*. He teaches constitutional law and civil procedure at Hastings College of the Law and media law at San Francisco State University.

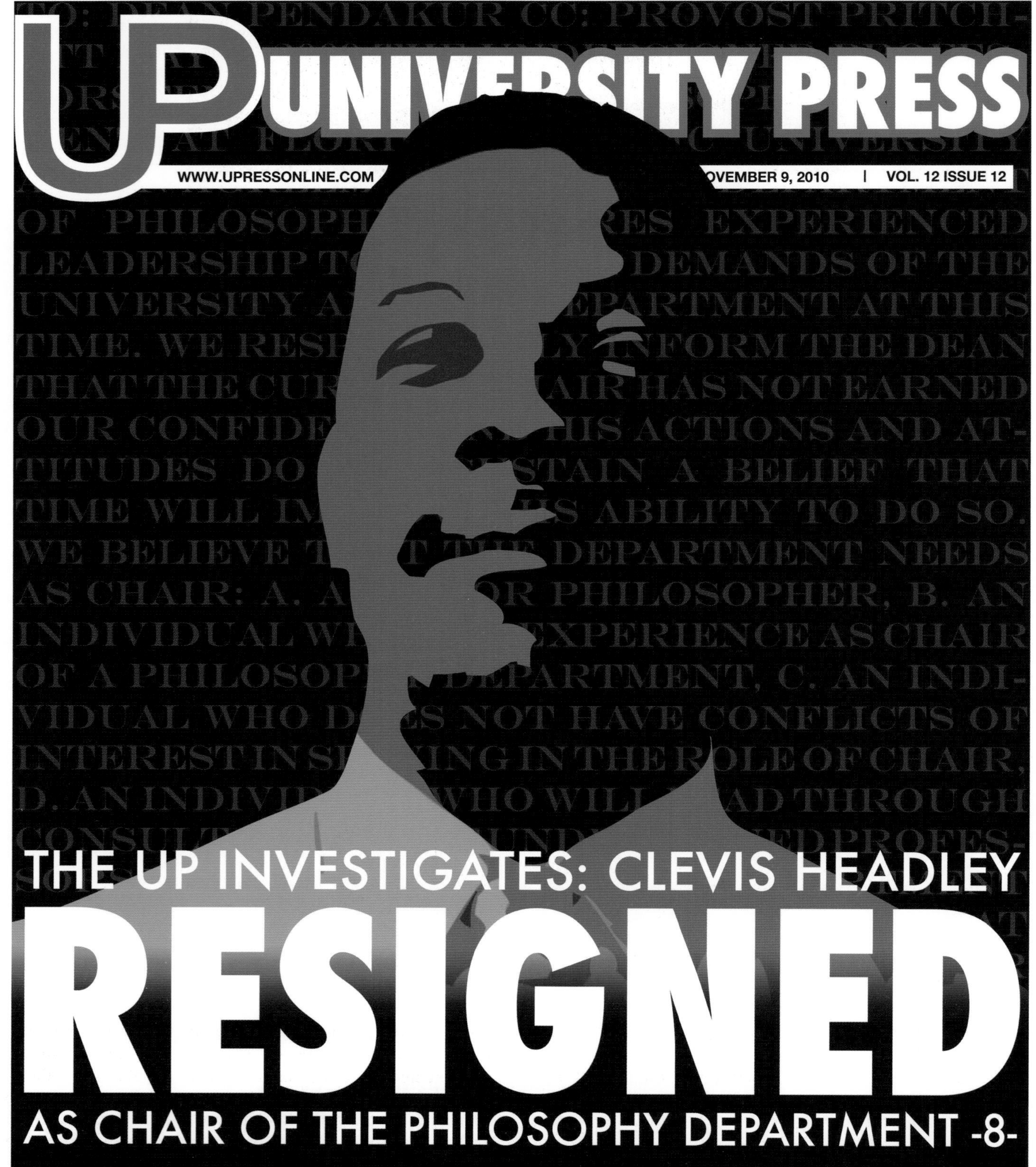

UP UNIVERSITY PRESS

WWW.UPRESSONLINE.COM | …VEMBER 9, 2010 | VOL. 12 ISSUE 12

THE UP INVESTIGATES: CLEVIS HEADLEY

RESIGNED

AS CHAIR OF THE PHILOSOPHY DEPARTMENT -8-

First issue is free; each additional copy is 50 cents and available in the UP newsroom.

FIGURE 13.2 Even if a newspaper is distributed for free, stealing it is a crime. When the *University Press* at Florida Atlantic University ran an investigative cover story on the resignation of the chair of the school's philosophy department, someone tossed 2,000 copies of the paper into recycling bins around campus. University police took the case seriously. After reviewing security camera videotapes, police nabbed a suspect, a philosophy major, who was arrested on charges of grand theft, trespassing and resisting arrest. *University Press*, Florida Atlantic University.

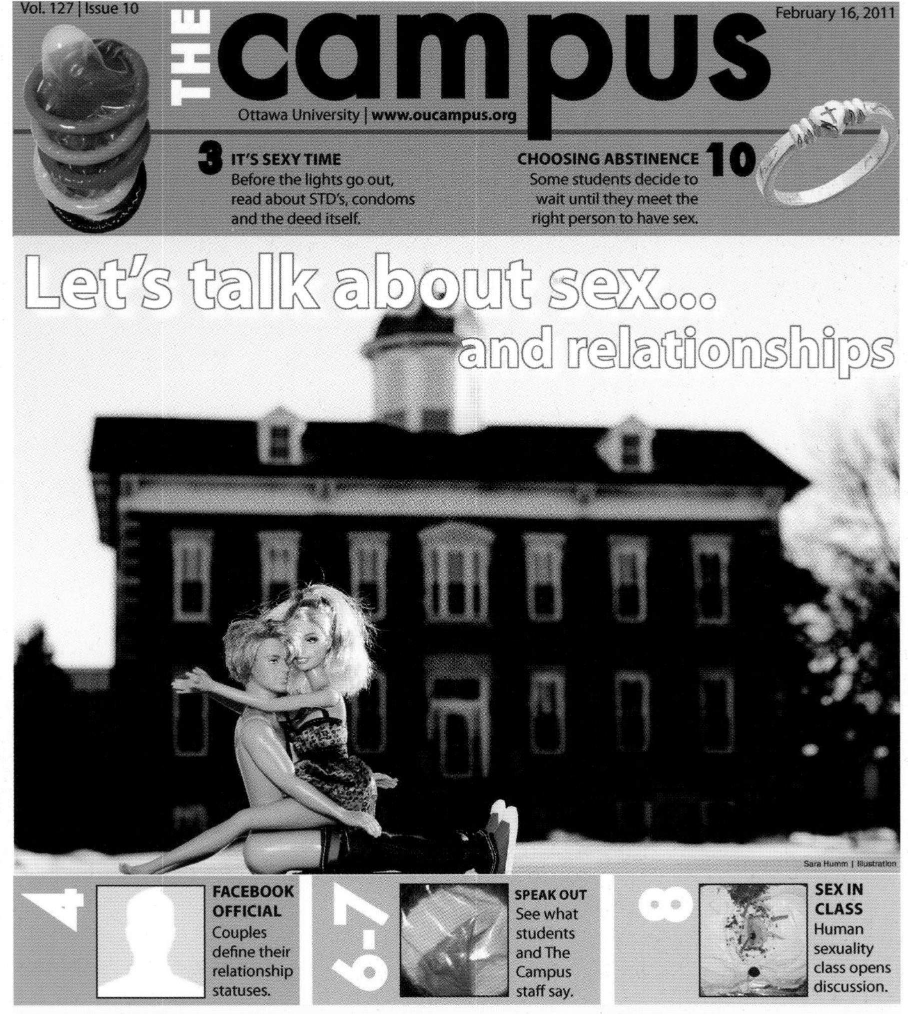
Vol. 127 | Issue 10

February 16, 2011

THE campus

Ottawa University | www.oucampus.org

3 IT'S SEXY TIME
Before the lights go out, read about STD's, condoms and the deed itself.

CHOOSING ABSTINENCE 10
Some students decide to wait until they meet the right person to have sex.

Let's talk about sex... and relationships

Sara Humm | Illustration

4 FACEBOOK OFFICIAL
Couples define their relationship statuses.

6-7 SPEAK OUT
See what students and The Campus staff say.

8 SEX IN CLASS
Human sexuality class opens discussion.

FIGURE 13.3 Hundreds of copies of *The Campus*, the student newspaper at Ottawa University in Ottawa, Kansas, were stolen from the private Christian university in February 2011 when the paper published a special issue devoted to sex and relationships. The cover featured a photo of partially clad Barbie and Ken dolls in a provocative position in front of a university building. "There was a lot of controversy on Ottawa University's campus because many thought this issue did not openly embrace a 'Christ-centered community,'" said Danielle Jurski, who was editor-in-chief at the time. "Because we are also a liberal arts institution, staff members responded by stating that we have rights to artistic and academic freedom." The issue went on to win first place in special section and illustration categories in the Kansas Associated Collegiate Press competition. *The Campus*, Ottawa University. Page design by Danielle Jurski, photo by Sara Humm.

preventing the dissemination of information, opinion or images (see Figure 13.3).

If you've been the victim of newspaper theft, don't just let it go. Follow the Student Press Law Center's Newspaper Theft Checklist.

LIBEL

One of the greatest fears of every journalist – professional or student – is being sued for libel.

Libel is anything written or printed that defames a person; defamation that is spoken is considered slander. Stories, editorials, headlines, photos, captions, graphics, cartoons, display advertisements, classified ads, letters to the editor, even comments posted on your website can potentially contain libelous statements. Even if the statement didn't originate with your staff, if your newspaper or website publishes it, you can be held liable.

To successfully sue for libel, a person must prove the following:

Defamation. The statement must damage the person's reputation. Any statement that says something negative about a person, group or business, causing them shame, disgrace or ridicule or injuring the person's livelihood, is potentially libelous.

CHECKLIST
Newspaper theft

The Student Press Law Center offers these tips on preventing and handling theft of newspapers.

Before a theft

- **Include a price tag.** In lieu of a price, include language such as the following on your flag: "Single copies free." In your masthead and rate card include additional information indicating that single copies are free to members of the school community. Also indicate that multiple copies may be available for purchase at an established price by contacting the newspaper's business office. The following language is an example: "Because of high production costs, members of the State University community are permitted one copy per issue. Where available, additional copies may be purchased with prior approval for 50 cents each by contacting the *Student Times* business office. Newspaper theft is a crime. Those who violate the single copy rule may be subject to civil and criminal prosecution and/or subject to university discipline." Of course, determining the actual price is up to you. It's not necessary that you always collect the money. You remain free to give copies away when you feel it is appropriate.
- **Establish ties.** Meet now with campus and law enforcement officials. Explain your concerns regarding newspaper theft and the danger it poses to your publication. Try to obtain their assurance that they will take newspaper theft incidents seriously. Be available to answer any questions they might have and to provide additional information.
- **Be alert.** In some cases, thieves have actually warned a newspaper staff that they intend to confiscate the publication when it is distributed. Tell staff that they need to report such warnings to editors immediately. Carefully record the source, nature and time of the warning. If you learn of a theft in progress or have reason to believe that such action is imminent, notify law enforcement authorities. Then, position your staff at likely theft locations to take photographs of those involved. Safety dictates that staff do not interfere with the thieves but simply record the criminal activity as it occurs.

After a theft

- **Get a number.** Attempt to determine how many copies of the paper were stolen.
- **Get a dollar figure.** "Free" distribution newspapers are not free. In dealing with law enforcement officials and prosecutors, it can be very important to provide a reasonable estimate of the monetary harm your publication has suffered as a result of the theft. To come up with a price tag, the following costs should be determined: 1. printing costs, 2. delivery costs, 3. production costs (e.g., wire/photo service charges, graphic art fees, telephone and postage expenses, office supplies, photo supplies, etc.), 4. special printing/production fees associated with a "rush" job should you decide to reprint the paper, 5. salary for publication staff, 6.revenue that may need to be refunded to advertisers, etc. Do your best to be accurate and reasonable in your estimates, but also don't hold back. For example, if an advertiser paid $2,000 to run an ad and only 50 percent of the newspapers were actually circulated, advertiser goodwill, if not the law, suggests that you may owe the advertiser a refund of $1,000. That is a legitimate, quantifiable loss and should be included in your tally. Prepare an itemized list to submit to law enforcement officials, news media and school officials.
- **Notify campus and/or local law enforcement agencies.** File a formal police report and request a copy. Also notify the local prosecutor's office as they will eventually be the agency responsible for determining whether a prosecutable crime has occurred. Be careful to note who you talk to and what is said. Inform officials that newspaper thieves around the country have been successfully prosecuted. If you determine the thieves are government officials (public college administrators, campus police, etc.), additional legal claims may also be available. For information about past prosecutions that you can share with "reluctant" law enforcement officials, contact the Student Press Law Center.
- **Launch an investigation.** Unless your efforts would impede police efforts, attempt to identify and interview witnesses to the theft. Send a campus email or use other campus communication resources to ask for information that may lead to the thieves' apprehension. In a few cases, professional journalism groups or interested alumni have offered modest rewards for valid "tips." Carefully document all witness statements.

- **Notify school officials.** Contact the college president and/or other high-ranking university officials in writing and request that they issue a strong public statement condemning the thefts that encourages law enforcement officials in their investigation, promises to appropriately discipline the thieves if caught and generally reaffirms the school's commitment to free speech on campus. Their refusal or agreement to do so is news.
- **Set up a "Dumpster patrol."** Search all university trash collection sites or other likely "dumping" locations. If copies are found, call for a photographer and the police to record the scene before removing them.
- **Alert local and state news media.** Prepare a short press release for distribution. As with a news story, report only what you know and how you know it. Be careful about publishing unconfirmed reports about the identity or motivation of the thieves. Include information about how many copies were printed, the number of copies stolen, the cost to the publication, the response (or lack of response) of law enforcement and school officials. You may also want to include contact information for the Student Press Law Center to assist reporters who may want to obtain a national perspective of the serious problem of newspaper theft.
- **Inform your readers.** Publish your own story – and perhaps an editorial – about the theft in the next issue of your publication.
- **Let us know.** If you haven't done so already, please report the theft to the Student Press Law Center. The SPLC is the nation's leading authority on newspaper theft and the only group to consistently track such incidents. It is very important that we know about yours. Law enforcement and campus officials have sometimes refused to act, viewing a theft as an isolated "prank." Help us remind them that there is nothing isolated or prankish about newspaper theft, that yours is part of a serious and threatening trend. Additionally, the SPLC can provide you with additional information and legal help in successfully prosecuting the theft of your publication.

Punishing newspaper thieves

- **Criminal prosecution.** Possible charges include: larceny, petty theft, criminal mischief or destruction of property. Though not necessary to prosecute a theft, Maryland and Colorado have a specific state law making the taking of a free distribution newspaper a crime. Ultimately the decision to pursue criminal charges is up to the local prosecutor.
- **Campus disciplinary action.** Even if there is insufficient evidence or grounds for criminal prosecution, newspaper thieves can be punished by campus officials for their misbehavior. While pursuing such punishment is also up to those issuing the discipline, student media can keep pressure on campus officials to take appropriate action and then follow up on the outcome.
- **Civil lawsuit for damages.** This type of claim is solely in your hands and can be a way to recover financial losses suffered by the newspaper. Depending on the amount of loss (frequently a maximum of $2,500), student media may be able to pursue this claim on their own in small claims court for minimum cost and without the expense of an attorney. You will need to have carefully documented evidence of your losses. If small claims court is not an option, you will probably need to hire an attorney. The SPLC can discuss this option with you in more detail.

Reprinted with permission of the Student Press Law Center.

Identification. The statement must clearly identify a person, either by name or by some other designation that will make at least some readers understand the statement is about the victim. In addition, if the story involves someone with a common name (like John Jones), it is important to give other identifying information, such as an address or middle initial, to make it clear that the story is about a specific John Jones and no others in the community.

Publication. The statement must be published or broadcast, meaning it was read or heard by people other than the author and the subject of the story.

Falsity. The statement must be false.

Injury. The person must prove that the defamatory statement has led to "actual injury," meaning injury to his or her reputation, humiliation, mental anguish or financial loss.

Fault. The plaintiff must prove some degree of fault; the degree depends on whether the person is a private or public figure. Private individuals only have to prove negligence on the part of a reporter (such as failing to check public records). The U.S. Supreme Court has said public figures, including public officials, must prove "actual malice" in publishing the defamation. That means the reporter:

a Knew facts that would disprove the story but published it anyway

b Did not check information that might have disproved a story

c Used obviously unreliable sources

d Made up a story.

The best defense against libel is truth. If a defamatory statement is true and you can prove it, it's not libelous. The other defenses for libel are:

Consent. If a person consents to the media using a defamatory statement about him, he can't later sue if the statement injures his reputation.

Privilege. A newspaper is not liable when it publishes fair and accurate accounts of official public proceedings and reports, even if the information turns out to be false. To qualify for this privilege

The information must come from an official record or proceeding, such as a court hearing, official public meeting or public document.

The media report must be "fair and accurate," meaning it is balanced and presented in context.

The source of the statement should be clearly noted in the media report.

Opinion. Statements of pure opinion cannot be libelous. But that doesn't mean phrases like "in my opinion," labeling a piece as a "review" or "commentary," or publishing something on an opinion page will automatically protect you from a libel charge. According to the Student Press Law Center's Legal Brief on Libel Law, "The test is whether the expression is capable of being proven true or false. Pure opinions, by their very nature, cannot be proven true or false."

Red Flags: Reporter beware
Student Press Law Center

The following is a list of particularly sensitive categories and topics that, if published inaccurately, will almost always satisfy the "Harm to Reputation" requirement for libel. These topics should be given special attention:

1 **Statements that accuse or suggest that a person has been involved in serious sexual misconduct or is sexually promiscuous.** A special problem: identifying an unmarried woman as pregnant.

2 **Statements that associate a person with a "loathsome" or socially stigmatizing disease.** For example: leprosy, some mental illnesses and any sexually transmitted disease such as herpes or AIDS.

3 **Statements that accuse another of committing a crime, of being arrested, jailed or otherwise involved in criminal activity.** For example, depending on the context or inferences made, it might be defamatory to falsely report that a person was "questioned by police." And be careful: even if you do not flatly accuse a person of, for example, committing the crime of perjury (lying while under oath), you might still invoke a red flag by reporting that a person had answered "yes" to a question on the witness stand yesterday but had responded "no" to the same question over a year ago.

4 **Negative statements that affect a person's ability to engage in his livelihood, business, trade, profession or office.** For example, a story that accused a teacher of being erratic, disorganized, absent from the classroom for extended periods and otherwise unable to teach was held to be libelous. As libel attorney and author Neil Rosini has pointed out, this is an especially broad category and lawsuits can come from unexpected sources. For example, a story that reported that a section of a new hospital was "plagued with air conditioning problems relating to the design of the system" was found to have injured the professional reputation of the building's architect even though the architect was never named. And a high school football coach successfully argued that his professional reputation was damaged when a newspaper falsely reported that he cursed and belittled his players from the sidelines, yelling such statements as "Come on, get your head out of your &!(!!(. Play the game." The coach claimed he said, "Get your head up."

5 **Statements that attack a person's honesty or integrity.** For example: calling a person a "liar" or a "thief" or stating that a person has a "selective memory."

6 **Negative statements about grades or academic ability.** A special problem: stories about "special education" or remedial learning programs.

7 **Statements that allege racial, ethnic or religious bigotry.**

8 **Statements that accuse a person of associating with criminals, "shady characters," or publicly disfavored groups.**

9 **Statements that question a person's creditworthiness, financial stability, or economic status.**

10 **Any negative statement about a lawyer.** As one writer has noted, "lawyers, in a class by themselves, are the most prolific libel plaintiffs in America. …" Because lawyers do sue and do know their way to the courthouse, all references to them should be flagged and verified.

Reprinted with permission from *Law of the Student Press*, published by the Student Press Law Center (1994).

Satire and Cartoons. A statement made in a publication that is clearly a parody or spoof cannot be libelous. This defense also covers cartoons.

If someone threatens to sue you and/or your newspaper for libel, treat the threat seriously. Investigate the person's claims and if you've found you've made an error, run a retraction or correction as soon as possible. While a retraction or correction will not absolutely protect you from a libel suit, people are far less likely to sue if you correct the mistake. Many states have retraction laws that limit the damages a plaintiff can win if a publication corrects the mistake within a specified time. If a potentially libelous error is published on your newspaper's website, be sure to correct it there, too.

PRIVACY

Everyone has a legal right to privacy, to be left alone. Unlike the freedom of the press, which is guaranteed in the First Amendment, the right to privacy has developed over time in a series of court cases.

There are four kinds of invasion of privacy:

1 **Public disclosure of private or embarrassing facts**. This may include information that is:

A. Sufficiently private: known only to a small circle of family or friends, B. sufficiently intimate: personal habits, details or history that the person doesn't ordinarily reveal, C. highly offensive: the information would humiliate or seriously offend the average person if it were revealed about him/her.

2 **False light**. The portrayal of a person – in words or pictures – in an inaccurate and unflattering way. False light is similar to libel but the plaintiff need not prove injury or damage to reputation, only that the statement was highly offensive.

3 **Intrusion into a person's solitude**. This can occur when a reporter gathers information about a person in a place where that person has a reasonable right to expect privacy, such as a home. Generally, reporters are allowed to enter privately owned public places such as a private school campus or a restaurant. However, private business owners can ask a journalist to leave if they feel someone's privacy is being violated. The three most common types of intrusion are:

Trespass–going onto private property without the owner's consent

Secret surveillance–using hidden cameras or bugging equipment to surreptitiously record information

Misrepresentation–using a disguise to gain access.

4 **Misappropriation of name or likeness**. You may not use a person's name, photograph, likeness, voice or endorsement in an advertisement.

The best defense against all four forms of invasion of privacy is consent. When getting consent, explain to the subject what you're going to use and how you plan to use it. If possible, get it in writing, making sure you seek permission from a person with a legal right to give it.

OBSCENITY

Obscenity is generally more of an issue of taste than law. Most potentially offensive content, such as profane language or ideas, is not obscene; obscenity refers exclusively to sexually explicit material.

The standard test for obscenity involves three elements described by the Supreme Court in the 1973 case of Miller v. California:

Whether a reasonable person, applying contemporary community standards, would find the work, taken as a whole, appeals to a prurient interest

Whether the work depicts or describes in a patently offensive way sexual conduct specifically defined as obscene by the applicable state law, and

CHECKLIST
Legal issues

When writing or editing a story, ask yourself the following questions:

1 Could any statements damage someone's reputation? If so, do you have public records or other credible information to back up the claim?
2 Do you trust the reporter's sources? If you have doubts, confirm suspect information with other sources.
3 Have you inadvertently identified any person who the writer meant to be unidentifiable?
4 Has the reporter or photographer invaded anyone's privacy?
5 Do you have permission to use photos or graphics taken from the Internet or other publications?
6 When writing about crime, are all potentially defamatory statements based on police records, court testimony or other credible sources? Be careful of unofficial statements made by police, attorneys or court officials outside of a court proceeding; these are not privileged.
7 When printing sexually explicit material, can you justify the content journalistically?

Whether the work, taken as a whole, lacks serious literary, artistic, political or scientific value.

Student newspapers have successfully printed nude photographs, sexually explicit descriptions and profane cartoons, without being charged with obscenity. "If the material is not more graphic than what appears in *Playboy* or *Penthouse*, it will not be considered legally obscene," says Goodman.

Sexually explicit material is far more likely to generate an attempt at censorship than an obscenity charge, Goodman says, but in most cases the courts, including the U.S. Supreme Court, have ruled in favor of free expression.

ACCESS TO INFORMATION

As explained in Chapter 11, student journalists have the same access as professionals (indeed, the same access as anyone) to public meetings and public records. However, some sources don't know this or intentionally try to keep information from students, thinking they won't know their rights.

Students frequently report being denied access to campus police records despite a federal law designed to make information about campus crime public, according to the Student Press Law Center. Under the federal Clery Act, any college or university that receives federal funding (that includes most private schools) must provide three different types of records:

An annual statistical report of campus crime

A daily campus crime log

"Timely reports" regarding crimes that present an ongoing threat to the campus community.

Schools that fail to release this information can be investigated by the Department of Education and fined for noncompliance.

It's essential that student journalists know what records and meetings are public. To understand the open records and open meetings laws that affect you, contact your state or provincial newspaper publishers association or the Student Press Law Center.

You can also go to the Reporters Committee for Freedom of the Press's website, which includes "Tapping Officials' Secrets," an online version of its 1,300-page report on every state's open records and open meetings laws. The website address is listed at the end of this chapter.

COPYRIGHT LAW

For college journalists, understanding copyright law is important both as it applies to the work they create and how they use other people's work. Copyright protects the creator of an original work (music, articles, photos, graphics, etc.) from unauthorized use of the work.

Copyright is a kind of property right. In its Legal Brief on Copyright Law, the Student Press Law Center explains:

> A person owns a copyright in much the same way he owns a car. Just as it is against the law to use or borrow someone else's car without the owner's permission, it is generally against the law to use someone's copyrighted work without first obtaining her consent. Additionally, just as no one but the automobile owner can legally sell, give away or change the appearance of a car, no one but the copyright owner, with a few exceptions, may legally transfer or alter a copyrighted work.

To be able to copyright something, it must be original and it must be "fixed in any tangible medium of expression," such as a newspaper or magazine, a book, a video, a CD-ROM disk, etc. You cannot copyright a slogan, word, phrase or title. As a result, you can use a familiar advertising slogan like "Got Milk?" for a headline.

Copyright ownership is a rather fuzzy issue for student newspapers. In the professional world, the creator of a work owns the copyright, but an employer may own the copyright of works created by employees while working in the scope of their employment. Professional publications generally own the copyrights for staff-produced material and often contract for those rights when they hire a freelance writer, photographer, cartoonist, etc.

At student papers, it's often not clear who owns the copyright to published material. What happens if a

Q&A Student Press Law Center on copyright and fair use

Can we copy and publish material that we find through an online search engine like Google Images?

The fact that material is available and easily copied on a website does not lessen its copyright protection.

The best practice is always to get consent (and if you can't, consider creating your own alternative). You may be able to make a "fair use" of a limited amount of someone else's material, but it's always best to avoid copying material from a professional news service like The Associated Press that offers such material for sale (unless you so greatly alter the material that you transform it into a new work).

Does it protect you against a copyright claim if you properly credit the artwork you are copying?

Not at all. Copyright is concerned with consent, not credit. Properly attributing a photo or a cartoon is ethically correct, but it is not a legal defense if the creator believes that your reuse of the work infringes his copyright.

Can we use the logo of a business – like Pepsi or Facebook or Google – without getting permission?

Yes, in connection with a news or feature story about the company or the industry, like a story about the popularity of Facebook. But you cannot use it without permission for purely marketing purposes, such as putting the Facebook logo on your yearbook cover in hopes of selling more books.

Isn't it safe to reuse only 30 seconds of a song, or only 10 percent of an article?

You'll hear various rules of thumb, but the Copyright Act itself contains no numerical or percentage "safe harbors." Material can safely be reused – a "fair use" – if the amount taken is limited to only what is necessary and is used in a new and different way (such as a clip from a film to illustrate a movie review) that does not detract from the economic value of the original.

Where can you find photos, videos and documents online that are fair game to be used without permission?

Start with federal government (.gov) sites like the White House, FEMA, NASA and others. Content created by federal employees in the course of their work is unprotected by copyright and can be freely reused. Also look for materials carrying the Creative Commons (CC) license, a voluntary alternative to copyright. Typically, such materials can be used in a nonprofit publication as long as proper attribution is given.

Who owns the copyright in work done by student journalists?

Unless the work is done for a salary ("work for hire") or under a contract or an employee handbook that specifies ownership, the normal rule is that the creator owns the work. And that is true even if school equipment is used.

Reprinted with permission from the Student Press Law Center.

photographer wants to sell photos or a writer wants to sell a story first published in the student newspaper?

If the photographer or writer is on staff, receives a salary and gets direction from a supervisor, it's presumed the copyright belongs to the publication, Goodman explains. If the person contributes to the newspaper on an occasional basis, makes their own assignments and is paid by the piece (or not at all), the individual generally owns the copyright.

"The problem is most situations fall somewhere in the middle," says Goodman. "The best thing is to have a written agreement that staff members and contributors can sign." See the Staff Copyright Policy at the end of this chapter.

While the Internet now makes it easy to copy and use work produced by others, just swiping material from the Web generally violates copyright law. "The fact that something is easily found or copied in no way indicates it is "public domain." explains Frank LoMonte, executive director of the Student Press Law Center. "The public domain is a very, very limited concept that consists of material that A. has aged out of copyright protection, B. never was copyright protected (e.g., works by federal government employees in the course of employment, such as official White House photographs) and C. has been voluntarily placed into the public domain by an express waiver of copyright."

That means student journalists can't just copy a photo from a Facebook page, Flickr or another website and use it in their publications. You need to get permission from the copyright owner. If you see a photo or other material that you'd like to use, send a message to the owner, requesting permission to reprint it.

TO DO

1 If your newspaper doesn't already have a relationship with a media law attorney, find someone who will be

on call for legal emergencies. Your state press association, state newspaper publishers' association or local newspaper may provide legal services or be able to help you find an attorney. The Student Press Law Center, listed in the "To Click" section of this chapter, will also answer media law questions.

2 Invite your media lawyer, a local media law expert or a law professor on campus to give a workshop to your staff on what student journalists need to know about the law.

3 Sponsor a First Amendment event for your campus community. It's a good way to educate readers and sources (including your school's administrators), as well as your own staff about press freedom. For ideas on First Amendment programs, see the Freedom Forum website listed in the "To Click" section of this chapter.

4 Try to build relationships with officials and groups that might feel poorly served by your newspaper. Invite leaders to meet with your editors or ask if you can visit their offices. Ask about their concerns and what they'd like to see in the paper.

TO READ

Fishman, Stephen. *The Copyright Handbook: How to Protect and Use Written Works, 7th ed.* Berkeley, Calif.: Nolo Press, 2003.

Fishman, Stephen. *The Public Domain: How to Find and Use Copyright-Free Writings, Music, Art and More.* Berkeley, Calif.: Nolo Press, 2004.

Newspaper Association of America Foundation. Press Freedom in Practice. A Manual for Student Media Advisers on Responding to Censorship. Available for free download on the SPLC's website at http://www.splc.org/knowyourrights/legalresearch.asp?id=72

Student Press Law Center. *Law of the Student Press, 2nd ed.* Arlington, Va.: Student Press Law Center, 1994.

TO CLICK

Canadian University Press

Canadian University Press is a national, nonprofit cooperative owned and operated by more than 80 Canadian student newspapers. CUP retains a lawyer to provide emergency legal advice for libel threats against member papers.

www.cup.ca

Copyright Crash Course

This interactive website produced by the University of Texas offers clear explanation of copyright basics.

http://copyright.lib.utexas.edu

Freedom Forum

The Freedom Forum, based in Washington, D.C., is a nonpartisan foundation that champions the First Amendment as a cornerstone of democracy.

The Freedom Forum is the main funder of the operations of the Newseum in Washington, D.C., the First Amendment Center and the Diversity Institute. It sponsors conferences and educational programs about press freedom.

www.freedomforum.org

How to File a FOIA Request

The First Amendment Center offers an extensive guide to the Freedom of Information Act and how to file requests for information.

http://www.firstamendmentcenter.org//press/information/topic.aspx?topic=how_to_FOIA&SearchString=student.

National Coalition Against Censorship

NCAC aims to educate and mobilize the community against acts of censorship. The coalition offers educational resources and advocacy support to individuals and organizations responding to incidents of censorship.

www.ncac.org

Open Records Legal Request Generator

The SPLC has a fully automated, fill-in-the-blanks state open records law request letter generator on its website. The online service asks the person seeking records to answer a series of questions, including which records they want to request, in which state the records are located and to whom the request will be sent, and then creates an appropriate letter.

http://splc.org/legalassistance/foiletter.asp

Reporters Committee for Freedom of the Press

This nonprofit organization provides free legal assistance to journalists. Its website offers many publications useful to journalists, including guides to electronic records, police records, open records and meeting laws, etc.

www.rcfp.org

Student Press Law Center

The Student Press Law Center is the only legal assistance agency in the United States devoted exclusively to educating high school and college journalists about the rights and responsibilities embodied in the First Amendment and supporting the student news media in their struggle to cover important issues free from censorship. The center provides free legal advice and information as well as low-cost educational materials for student journalists on a wide variety of legal topics. In addition, the SPLC operates a formal Attorney Referral Network of approximately 150 lawyers across the country who are available to provide free legal representation to local students when necessary.

http://splc.org

U.S. Copyright Office

The website of the U.S. Copyright Office lays out the basics of copyright law, explains how to register a copyright and answers other questions journalists and other content creators may have about copyright.

www.copyright.gov

APPENDIX 13.A STAFF COPYRIGHT POLICY

All content produced by (NAME OF PUBLICATION) staff members is copyrighted by (NAME OF PUBLICATION).

As a condition of being a member of the (NAME OF PUBLICATION) staff or applying to join the staff, you must agree that (NAME OF PUBLICATION) has exclusive and unlimited copyright ownership of any content you submit for publication or other uses by (NAME OF PUBLICATION), including material that is not published or not otherwise used.

Content includes words, photographs, graphics, illustrations, cartoons, designs, "spec" ads and any other creative work that may be subject to copyright.

(NAME OF PUBLICATION) staff members include all students in the Business Division and the News Division: reporters, columnists, photographers, artists, account executives, representatives, specialists, editors, managers and any other positions that may be created.

This policy means if you submit anything for publication by (NAME OF PUBLICATION), you may not give someone else permission to publish that material. Further, (NAME OF PUBLICATION) may sell reprints or copyright permissions. (All revenue received by (NAME OF PUBLICATION) is used exclusively to fund (NAME OF PUBLICATION) operations and programs.)

For photographers: If you submit a photograph for publication, you must also agree that (NAME OF PUBLICATION) owns the image, even if you used your own image. (NAME OF PUBLICATION) will reimburse you for the cost taking the photograph, if you submit a valid request.

NAME OF PUBLICATION grants you the following permissions: Unlimited use of your own work (a) for your own personal portfolio, (b) for exhibitions, (c) as entries for awards contests and scholarship programs, and (d) for internship applications and job searches.

AGREEMENT

As a condition of my participation in a (NAME OF PUBLICATION) educational program or as a (NAME OF PUBLICATION) staff member, I hereby agree that (NAME OF PUBLICATION) has exclusive and unlimited copyright ownership of anything subject to copyright that I create or prepare and submit to (NAME OF PUBLICATION) for any use in any medium, including items not published or otherwise used. Further, I hereby agree to the terms of the (NAME OF PUBLICATION) Staff Copyright Policy.

Signature ________________________________ Date __________

Printed name ____

Adapted with permission from a license agreement used by Collegian, Inc., publisher of *The Daily Collegian* at Pennsylvania State University.

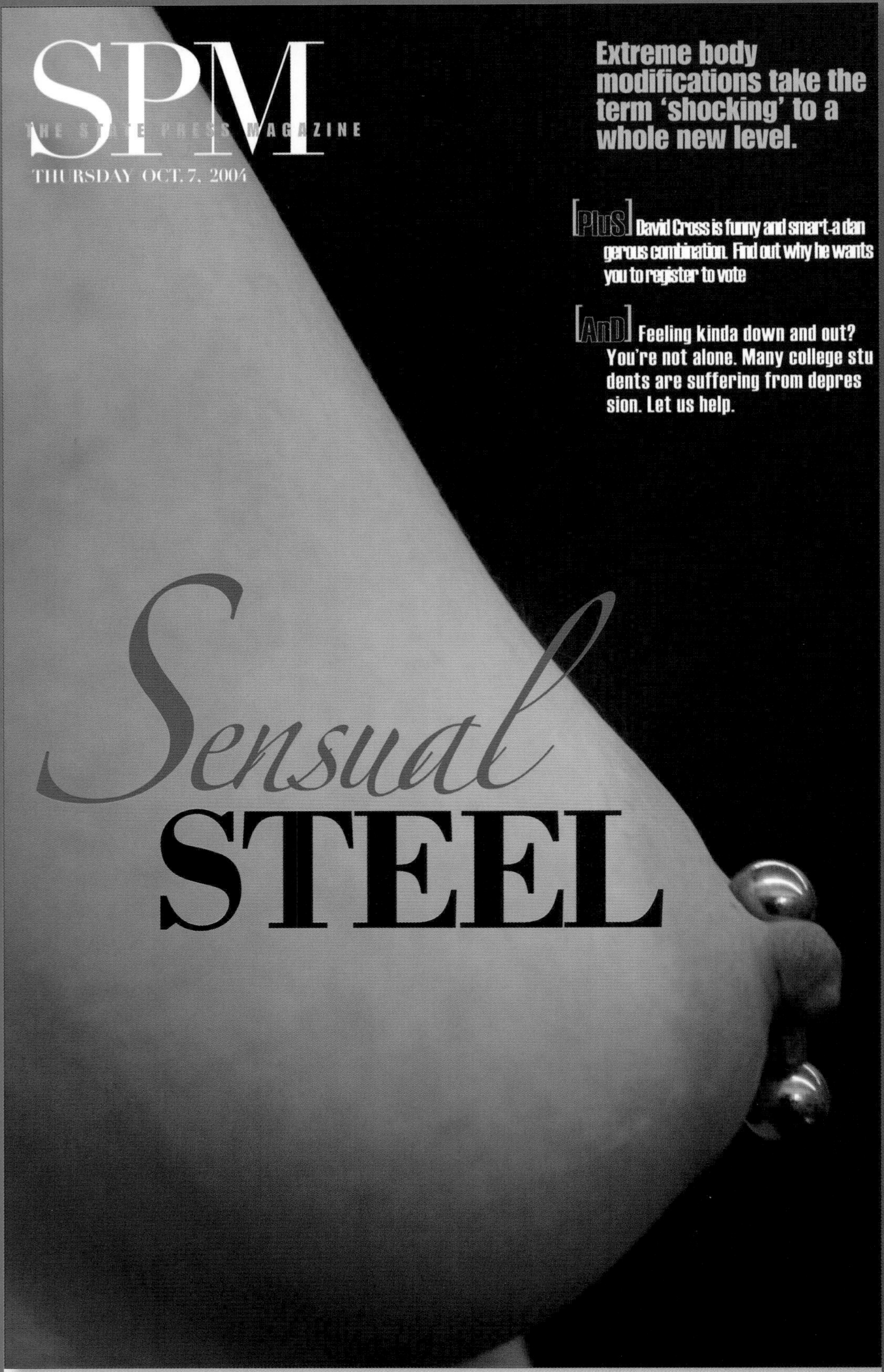

FIGURE 14.1 Would you run this photo? *State Press Magazine*, the weekly magazine affiliated with *The State Press* newspaper at Arizona State University, published this image on the cover of the magazine to illustrate a story on extreme body piercing. University officials responded with a threat to cut the newspaper's funding if the paper continued to run such controversial material. But the newspaper's editors refused to apologize. Instead, they established formal guidelines for making news decisions, working with administrators and explaining their actions to others. The newspaper won a Payne Award for Ethics in Journalism for its responsible handling of the controversy. Photo by Andrew Benson, *State Press Magazine*, Arizona State University.

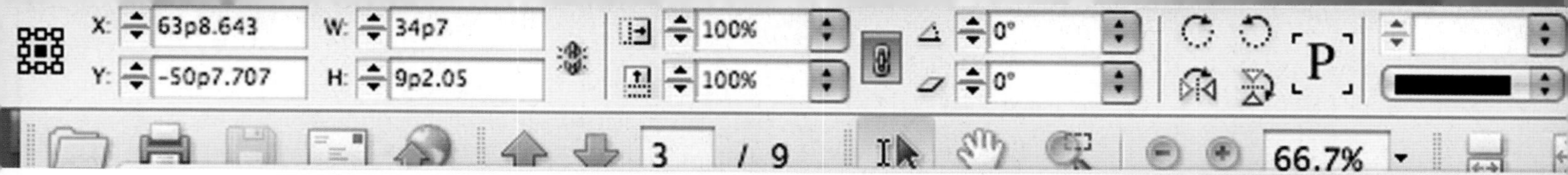

CHAPTER 14
ETHICAL ISSUES

Student journalists face all the ethical challenges professional journalists face – and more. Just like the pros, you have to deal with the moral dilemmas associated with reluctant sources, conflicts of interest and potentially offensive words and images.

You also have the complications of being a student at the very college or university you're covering. What are the ramifications of writing negative things about administrators who can discipline you or professors who can dock your grade or the health professionals who treat your sore throat in the campus health center?

In this chapter we'll look at some of the ethical problems unique to student journalists and offer some suggestions and guidelines for walking this landmine-strewn path.

The Student Newspaper Survival Guide, Second Edition. Rachele Kanigel.

CHAPTER CONTENTS

DEVELOPING A CODE OF ETHICS

Sooner or later your newspaper will face an ethical dilemma. Perhaps the police reporter will want to use an anonymous source in a story about drugs in the dorms. Or a photographer will start freelancing for the local newspaper. Or the arts and entertainment editor will take home a stack of review CDs sent to the newspaper.

Are you prepared?

The key to addressing such dilemmas is to have a comprehensive code of ethics, a set of guidelines that helps newspaper staffers make ethical decisions.

Many student newspapers incorporate their code of ethics into the employee manual distributed to each new staff member. Some, including *The Daily Illini* (dailyillini.com) at the University of Illinois, *The Gazette* (westerngazette.ca) at the University of Western Ontario, the *Daily Trojan* (dailytrojan.com) at the University of Southern California and the *Campus Times* (laverne.edu/campus-times) at the University of La Verne, post their code prominently on the newspaper's website. This allows the entire community – including advertisers, sources and readers – to understand how the newspaper operates.

Some college papers adopt the code of the Society of Professional Journalists (included in this chapter). The SPJ code is comprehensive, but it does not specifically address issues unique to student newspapers, such as whether staffers can sell work to competing professional newspapers or whether students can write about professors from whom they have taken classes. For this reason, many papers develop their own codes or adapt the Associated Collegiate Press Model Code of Ethics for Collegiate Journalists. (For information about getting a copy, see the resources list at the end of this chapter.)

A student newspaper code of ethics typically addresses the following areas:

Conflicts of interest–including membership in campus organizations, work for competing media, and freebies (free tickets, travel opportunities, gifts and review products)

Plagiarism and fabrication

Confidentiality of sources

Photo ethics–including photo illustrations and digital alteration (for more information see Chapter 12)

Obscenity and profanity

Advertising–(for more information see Chapter 20).

In recent years, journalists drafting a code of ethics have also dealt with issues related to social media, such as how student reporters present themselves on Facebook and Twitter. (See a sample social media policy in Chapter 19).

CONFLICTS OF INTEREST

Professional papers often have strict guidelines to avoid conflicts of interest. Newsroom employees are typically restricted from writing for competing media, accepting gifts or meals from sources, and engaging in political and social activities that could be seen as compromising their coverage.

But at a college newspaper, conflicts can be harder to avoid. For one thing, most student journalists are part of the college community. They typically rent, buy food, take classes and get health services from the college or university. Many of the people they write about may be acquaintances, classmates, dorm mates, friends of friends. That makes it pretty hard to cover the campus objectively.

In addition, college is a time to explore a variety of interests and many students want to take part in student government, clubs and other political and social activities. Career-minded young journalists often want to intern or freelance for local media organizations while they are in school.

Student papers take different stances on these potential conflicts. For example, a newspaper serving a large college campus may ban student journalists from taking any role in student government. But on a smaller campus – where newspapers may have difficulty recruiting "untainted" staffers – some newspapers allow staff members to serve on student government as long as they don't write about issues that come before the board.

Competition clauses also vary among student newspapers. Some student papers don't allow staffers to write for competing professional media. Others encourage students to get professional experience but draw the line at "double-dipping" – writing the same story for the campus and community newspapers.

There's no single right answer to these questions; each paper is entitled to its own approach. But your newspaper's leadership should anticipate these conflicts and have policies in place before such situations arise.

PLAGIARISM AND FABRICATION

Plagiarism and fabrication have become major issues in journalism in recent years, both in the professional world and at the student level. The revelations about plagiarized and fabricated work by Jayson Blair, who was a reporter and editor at *The Diamondback* (diamondbackonline.com) at the University of Maryland, College Park, before going to work for *The New York Times*, and Stephen Glass, who served as executive editor of *The Daily Pennsylvanian* (dailypennsylvanian.com) at the University of Pennsylvania the year before he started writing for *The New Republic*, have brought increased attention to these journalistic crimes.

In 2007, a columnist at the *Brown Daily Herald* (browndailyherald.com) was fired after editors discovered that six of his columns included plagiarized material. In 2006, a film critic for the *University News* (unews.com) at the University of Missouri at Kansas City resigned from the paper after being accused of plagiarizing parts of 38 movie reviews published over the course of a year. Even cartoonists can be prone to plagiarism. In 2006, *The Harvard Crimson* (thecrimson.com) fired a staff cartoonist for copying a cartoon by Pulitzer Prize-winning cartoonist Walt Handelsman.

Your newspaper should have a written policy on how to handle plagiarism, fabrication and other journalistic sins. These are serious offenses; at some student newspapers even a first offense may be cause for termination.

While it may seem obvious that copying other people's work and making things up is verboten, it pays to discuss such issues as each new staff comes on board. It's not sufficient to simply say, "Don't do it." Advisers or editors should explain exactly what plagiarism and fabrication are and how to avoid those temptations. In addition, they should outline the consequences if a staff member is found to copy or make up material for a story. Some student newspapers have staff members sign an oath saying they understand the newspaper's policy and pledging they will not plagiarize or fabricate.

One strategy for plagiarism prevention is to have reporters submit with each story a source list that includes phone numbers and email addresses for all people interviewed, website addresses for online sources, and citations for all books and articles used for research.

Editors who suspect a staff member has plagiarized or fabricated should investigate the situation immediately and report it to the top editor and the adviser, if there is one.

A number of websites listed at the end of this chapter offer guidance in preventing and detecting plagiarism.

OBSCENITY AND PROFANITY

Many student newspapers relish the freedom of being able to set four-letter words in type. Others see using obscene language as unprofessional. Whatever your stance, you need to have a policy.

The Whetstone (whetstone.wesley.edu), the student-run newspaper at Wesley College in Dover, Del., for example, includes this obscenity clause in its code of ethics:

> There is never a good reason to print vulgar language just to get a reaction. The staff should be sure that the words are a justifiable part of the story.

The Banner News (bannernewsonline.com) at Des Moines Area Community College is even more specific in its position on obscenity:

> *The Banner News* makes every attempt to exclude profanity from its articles, columns, and editorials. In order for an obscenity to be printed, it must give added insight into the character of the speaker. The full word is not printed. The first letters are printed and the rest of the word is replaced by dashes (-). Words such as *hell, damn, bitch* are not considered obscene. The section editor, managing editor, and editor-in-chief must be consulted before an obscenity is printed.

Newspapers should also have a policy – and a process – for dealing with sexually explicit material. The *State Press Magazine* (statepress.com/magazine) at Arizona State University learned this the hard way in 2004 when it published a story about extreme body piercing. "The problem was how to illustrate the story without watering it down and without totally grossing people out," says Megan Irwin, who was editor of the magazine at the time.

Irwin and other editors reviewed a batch of photos, dismissing some as too graphic, before choosing a simple close-up of a breast with a pierced nipple (Figure 14.1) for the magazine's cover. "We understood that some people would be offended but we felt it was still in good taste and made sense within the context of the story," Irwin said.

After one of the university's largest donors complained, the president demanded an apology and threatened to withdraw the newspaper's funding if it continued to publish similarly explicit material. But the newspaper's editors refused to apologize. Instead, they established formal guidelines for making decisions, working with administrators and explaining their decisions to others. The newspaper won a Payne Award for Ethics in Journalism for its actions.

"I always knew I would stand up for the First Amendment," Irwin said. "It was just kind of funny standing up for First Amendment rights over a nipple."

TIPS FROM A PRO **Harry Kloman**

When you decide to become a journalist, you have to give up certain things. One of them is your freedom of speech.

Well, maybe that's a little bit extreme. But only a little bit. In a profession where people count on you to present information fairly and accurately, and where you publish your name for all to see, thus making yourself a public figure, journalists have a certain obligation to conduct their private lives along some guidelines that can restrict their freedom.

Here are some general rules your paper should consider to reduce the risk of creating real or apparent conflicts of interest:

1 When reporters join the staff of your paper in any capacity, even just to write one or two stories, they must disclose to the newspaper any campus, city or hometown organization to which they belong so editors can avoid conflicts of interest. In fact, you may want to include an entry for such information on application forms. Editors should also explain the importance of this to new reporters and urge them to make full disclosure.

2 Reporters should not interview relatives, friends or roommates for a story, nor should they interview a professor if they currently have that instructor. As a corollary to this, editors should avoid assigning a story on, say, the history department to a student who majors or minors in history. Such an assignment might cause a reporter to hesitate to ask challenging questions, or the reporter might intentionally not ask certain questions to avoid making the department look bad.

3 Reporters should avoid socializing with people – students, university professionals or citizens of the community – on the beat they cover. There's certainly nothing wrong with attending a large, casual social event or having lunch with a source. (Reporters must make sure, of course, that they pay for their own meals.) But attending a party at the source's home is discouraged because it threatens to build a personal relationship that will make it more difficult for reporters to treat all sources fairly when doing a story.

4 News reporters should limit their political activities to the voting booth. They should not take part in political campaigns, speak out publicly on political issues, and/or take part in any activity or event that in some way might be considered "political" – for example, marching for or against abortion rights, gay rights, women's rights and so forth. If someone on staff decides to run for an elective political office on campus, he should resign before declaring candidacy. If he loses the election, he may choose to return to work for the newspaper.

5 Culture and arts reporters should not take part in the kind of activity on which they report. For example, a student who performs as a local musician should not review local bands. A student who performs in local theater should not review local plays. Permitting this puts the newspaper at risk of being charged with bias.

6 Sports reporting often involves a high level of fandom on the part of the reporter. Nonetheless, readers count on sports reporting to tell the whole, on-the-record truth. So sports reporters should try especially hard to maintain a professional distance from the coaches and athletes whom they cover.

7 Editors can't know everything or be everywhere. So when reporters accept a story, they must think seriously about whether they face any conflict of interest. If reporters fear that even the slightest of conflicts might exist, they should tell the editor immediately.

8 In addition to not joining organizations that might put them in a conflict situation, reporters should disclose any jobs they hold to see if those positions might create a conflict. Sports writers, of course, should not work or intern for any sports-related department of the university, nor should news writers work or intern for the university's office of public relations or police department.

9 Reporters and editors should never show a story to a source before publication. Doing so could lead to a discussion or argument about what the newspaper can or cannot print. Reporters can, however, read quotes and facts to a source if they feel a need to confirm them, although some newspaper attorneys advise against doing this. A reporter should never promise a source a copy of a story before publication.

10 The newspaper should try never to use its own people as sources for a story. If a staff member is involved with a group that is in the news, that person can suggest other sources of information. Do not let the staffer who is involved in the story read it before publication. Don't put your reporters in a position of conflicting loyalties.

11 Newspapers should try to avoid writing stories about themselves unless the news is unavoidably big and important. When a newspaper does write a story about itself – the appointment of new leadership, for example, or when it wins awards – it should work diligently to make the story as fair and balanced as possible.

In conclusion: When you work for a newspaper, you should think about every non-newspaper thing you do and consider how it might put you in a conflict situation. Always err on the side of caution, and always feel free to discuss your situation with an editor or adviser. The willingness to introduce these discussions and the sensitivity to conflict of interest issues distinguish top journalists from the rest of the field.

HARRY KLOMAN is the news adviser for *The Pitt News* (pittnews.com), the daily student newspaper at the University of Pittsburgh, and the journalism program coordinator for the university's English Department. This piece is adapted from "Ethics, Standards and Practices in Newspaper Journalism", an ethics manual he wrote for *The Pitt News*.

Society of Professional Journalists' Code of Ethics

The SPJ Code of Ethics is voluntarily embraced by thousands of journalists, regardless of place or platform, and is widely used in newsrooms and classrooms as a guide for ethical behavior. The code is intended not as a set of "rules" but as a resource for ethical decision-making. It is not – nor can it be under the First Amendment – legally enforceable. The present version of the code was adopted by the 1996 SPJ National Convention, after months of study and debate among the Society's members.

Preamble. Members of the Society of Professional Journalists believe that public enlightenment is the forerunner of justice and the foundation of democracy. The duty of the journalist is to further those ends by seeking truth and providing a fair and comprehensive account of events and issues. Conscientious journalists from all media and specialties strive to serve the public with thoroughness and honesty. Professional integrity is the cornerstone of a journalist's credibility. Members of the Society share a dedication to ethical behavior and adopt this code to declare the Society's principles and standards of practice.

Seek truth and report it. Journalists should be honest, fair and courageous in gathering, reporting and interpreting information.

Journalists should:

Test the accuracy of information from all sources and exercise care to avoid inadvertent error. Deliberate distortion is never permissible.

Diligently seek out subjects of news stories to give them the opportunity to respond to allegations of wrongdoing.

Identify sources whenever feasible. The public is entitled to as much information as possible on sources' reliability.

Always question sources' motives before promising anonymity. Clarify conditions attached to any promise made in exchange for information. Keep promises.

Make certain that headlines, news teases and promotional material, photos, video, audio, graphics, sound bites and quotations do not misrepresent. They should not oversimplify or highlight incidents out of context.

Never distort the content of news photos or video. Image enhancement for technical clarity is always permissible. Label montages and photo illustrations.

Avoid misleading re-enactments or staged news events. If re-enactment is necessary to tell a story, label it.

Avoid undercover or other surreptitious methods of gathering information except when traditional open methods will not yield information vital to the public. Use of such methods should be explained as part of the story.

Never plagiarize.

Tell the story of the diversity and magnitude of the human experience boldly, even when it is unpopular to do so.

Examine their own cultural values and avoid imposing those values on others.

Avoid stereotyping by race, gender, age, religion, ethnicity, geography, sexual orientation, disability, physical appearance or social status.

Support the open exchange of views, even views they find repugnant.

Give voice to the voiceless; official and unofficial sources of information can be equally valid.

Distinguish between advocacy and news reporting. Analysis and commentary should be labeled and not misrepresent fact or context.

Distinguish news from advertising and shun hybrids that blur the lines between the two.

Recognize a special obligation to ensure that the public's business is conducted in the open and that government records are open to inspection.

Minimize harm. Ethical journalists treat sources, subjects and colleagues as human beings deserving of respect.

Journalists should:

Show compassion for those who may be affected adversely by news coverage. Use special sensitivity when dealing with children and inexperienced sources or subjects.

Be sensitive when seeking or using interviews or photographs of those affected by tragedy or grief.

Recognize that gathering and reporting information may cause harm or discomfort. Pursuit of the news is not a license for arrogance.

Recognize that private people have a greater right to control information about themselves than do public officials and others who seek power, influence or attention. Only an overriding public need can justify intrusion into anyone's privacy.

Show good taste. Avoid pandering to lurid curiosity.

Be cautious about identifying juvenile suspects or victims of sex crimes.

Be judicious about naming criminal suspects before the formal filing of charges.

Balance a criminal suspect's fair trial rights with the public's right to be informed.

Act independently. Journalists should be free of obligation to any interest other than the public's right to know.

Journalists should:

Avoid conflicts of interest, real or perceived.

Remain free of associations and activities that may compromise integrity or damage credibility.

Refuse gifts, favors, fees, free travel and special treatment, and shun secondary employment, political involvement, public office and service in community organizations if they compromise journalistic integrity.

Disclose unavoidable conflicts.

Be vigilant and courageous about holding those with power accountable.

Deny favored treatment to advertisers and special interests and resist their pressure to influence news coverage.

Be wary of sources offering information for favors or money; avoid bidding for news.

Be accountable. Journalists are accountable to their readers, listeners, viewers and each other.

Journalists should:

Clarify and explain news coverage and invite dialogue with the public over journalistic conduct.

Encourage the public to voice grievances against the news media.

Admit mistakes and correct them promptly.

Expose unethical practices of journalists and the news media.

Abide by the same high standards to which they hold others.

INTERVIEWING VICTIMS OF TRAGEDY

One of the scariest things for a fledgling reporter is having to pick up the phone and call – or, even worse, having to knock on the door of – a person experiencing a tragedy. It's also one of the best lessons you can get for a career as a reporter.

No one really wants to interview the mother of a college freshman who just overdosed on drugs or the girlfriend of a young man who was shot to death outside a nightclub. But as you screw up your courage to call, remember this: You're doing a service, both to your readers and to the people touched by the tragedy.

The Dart Center for Journalism & Trauma, a network of journalists, journalism educators and health professionals dedicated to improving media coverage of trauma and violence, offers these tips for interviewing victims of tragedy and their families.

- Journalists can help victims and survivors tell their stories in ways that are constructive, and in ways that make for great journalism.
- Sometimes you can't avoid intruding upon someone in grief. If you can't postpone your contact, remember to be sensitive and respectful in your approach.
- "I'm sorry for your loss," is a good way to start the conversation.
- Don't assume a victim or family member won't want to talk; often they are eager to share their story and memories with a journalist.
- If someone doesn't want to talk to you, be respectful and polite. And don't forget to leave your business card; at some point, the person may decide to talk to a reporter, and they will likely call the one that made the best impression.
- Make sure the person understands the terms of the interview. Tell them: "This is an interview for a story I'm writing. Your quotes will appear in the newspaper along with your name." Remind them of the terms periodically.
- Pay attention to your own emotions during the interview and let your reactions inform your reporting (while remaining professional). If you find something emotionally stirring, chances are readers will, too.

COVERING SUICIDE

Deciding whether and how to cover a suicide is one of the most common and most poignant ethical dilemmas a student editor may face. And unlike with many other ethical issues, looking to the professional press isn't necessarily instructive. Most professional newspapers don't cover suicide unless:

It causes a public spectacle (a jump onto a freeway streaming with cars, for example, or after a standoff with police)

It's committed in connection with a homicide, kidnapping or other serious crime

It involves a public figure.

Student newspapers, however, frequently do cover suicides of students or faculty, particularly if they happen on campus. Why? For one thing, the suicide of a member of the campus community often has a significant impact on a large segment of the school – an entire academic department or a whole dorm may feel traumatized by the event.

For another, suicide is a major social problem among college students (it's the third leading cause of death among 15- to 24-year-olds, after accidents and homicides, according to the U.S. Department of Health and Human Services), and many newspapers use a suicidal incident as a news peg for an educational piece about the problem.

A year after a freshman at Northwestern University killed himself in his dorm room, for example, *The Daily Northwestern* (dailynorthwestern.com) ran a seven-part series on mental health. The series, "State of Mind," looked at eating disorders, obsessive-compulsive disorders and mental health care, as well as depression and suicide.

"There were all these issues that didn't find a place in our regular news coverage," says Elaine Helm, who worked on the series in the fall of 2003 and became editor-in-chief of the newspaper the following year. "We wanted to find an appropriate way to reflect on those issues and find a context for this one incident that touched so many lives." The series won several awards, including one from the National Mental Health Association.

When deciding whether to cover a suicide in your own paper, ask yourself these questions:

Was the suicide committed on campus?

Was the suicide committed in a public place, such as a park or downtown street?

Was the student or faculty member prominent on your campus?

Does the suicide appear to be part of a trend?

Will coverage of the suicide help the campus community in any way?

If the answer to one or more of these questions is yes, your newspaper may decide it's important to run a story.

Some newspapers also consider the family's wishes when deciding whether to write about a suicide. Journalists rarely contemplate the impact their stories will have on family members, but in the case of a suicide, editors may want to take into account how open the family is to talking about the circumstances of the death.

Another factor to consider is the risk of "suicide contagion" or copycat suicides. Researchers have found that suicides tend to increase when a particular incident gets a lot of media play. This copycat phenomenon is particularly evident when coverage is sensational and when media stories highlight the mode of suicide. For example, in the year after a student fell to his death at New York University, four other students there took their lives the same way.

The Dart Center for Journalism & Trauma offers these guidelines for covering suicide:

Be careful when approaching friends and relatives for comment; they might not have heard the news.

In your story, avoid speculating about the motivation for the suicide. Likewise, avoid quoting the speculation of others. Often, there is not a simple "reason" for a suicide. If you include one in your report, you may cause someone else to feel unwarranted responsibility for the suicide.

Be careful not to romanticize the suicide with lurid or gratuitous detail.

Consider running a sidebar with contact information for local suicide hotlines and other mental health resources.

Journalists can include information that can help the public view suicide more accurately by including such contextual details as trends in suicide rates, myths about suicide, warning signs, actions that individuals can take to prevent suicide by others.

CONFIDENTIAL SOURCES

A student with HIV tells a reporter she's willing to share her story, but only if she isn't named in the news report. A football player admits that he and several other players on the team are using performance-enhancing drugs but says if you identify him he could be disqualified from playing. An administrative clerk sends your newspaper a complaint filed against your college president claiming that he has sexually harassed her for years. She, too, asks to remain anonymous.

Would you grant these sources anonymity?

Anonymous, or unnamed sources, chip away at the credibility of a news organization and many editors avoid them at all costs. But some important stories – the Watergate scandal that led to the resignation of President Richard Nixon, for one – would never be told unless a reporter protected a source's identity.

When considering whether to grant a source anonymity you have to balance the importance of the information against the risk to the source. If you're getting reaction from students about the new football stadium and one source who criticizes the design asks not to be named, throw the quote out. There's no compelling reason to protect the source or use the quote.

But what if you're writing an investigative story about illegal activity or malfeasance? Then the stakes are higher. A source who divulges information could be fired from a job or charged with a crime. Stories about sensitive topics, such as AIDS, abortion, sexual abuse or mental illness could put a source at risk for ostracism.

Every student newspaper should have a written policy on confidential sources. *Technique* (nique.net) at Georgia Institute of Technology, for example, includes this policy on anonymous sources in its ethics code:

> Anonymous information is not as credible as information that is directly attributable to a source. A reporter should not promise confidentiality to a source without the permission of the editor-in-chief; additionally, a reporter should urge the source to allow an attribution.
>
> In general, the *Technique* will not print information anonymously unless the information is corroborated by at least one additional trustworthy source. Anonymous sources should only be used when the story is of compelling or vital interest, and only as a last resort.
>
> In general confidentiality will be granted only when there is a danger of physical, emotional or financial harm if the source goes on record. When names are being withheld, the editor-in-chief must always know the full name of the source, even though this information is being withheld from print and the circumstances surrounding the request for confidentiality.
>
> Because of the legal issues involved, there can be no exceptions to this rule. Reasons for granting anonymity should be outlined in the article so the paper's image and credibility are maintained.

Here are some steps for considering a source's request for confidentiality:

Evaluate the information. Is it credible? Is it vital to your story? Could you get this information from another source who would be named?

Talk to your source. Ask what the likely consequences would be if you name him. Explain your news organization's policy on unnamed sources. Try to convince him to go on the record.

Find other sources. Get someone else to confirm the information, ideally sources who will speak on the record.

Talk to your editor. Discuss the pros and cons of using an anonymous source with your news organization's top leadership.

If you decide to use an unnamed source, briefly explain in the article why you are protecting the source's identity.

DOING AN ETHICS AUDIT

How do you know if you're doing a good job of covering your campus? How can you tell if you're being fair and equitable to all segments of the community?

College newspaper ethics policy: *Northern Star*

This code supplements the Society of Professional Journalists' Code of Ethics. Together, these two documents are the expected code of conduct for all *Northern Star* and NS*Radio employees. Note: "*Northern Star*" refers to the newspaper, the online edition and NS*Radio.

Travel

The *Northern Star* does not accept free travel, accommodations or meals during coverage of events. Journalists must remain free of any perception that sources are buying favorable coverage. For sports coverage, *Star* reporters, photographers and broadcasters may travel on team buses or planes, or stay in the same hotels as a team, but the *Star* will pay for employees' transportation, food and lodging costs.

Products

The *Northern Star* often reviews new consumer products – music CDs, DVD movies, video games, computer software, books, electronic gadgets, etc. Some are sent by companies' PR offices and some are purchased locally by the *Star*. It is important that staff members adhere to a firm ethical policy regarding these materials.

In choosing which products to review or otherwise feature in the paper, use normal standards of news judgment. Do not choose based on what was received for free. That amounts to a company "buying" publicity.

Any materials given to or bought by the *Northern Star* for review become the property of the *Northern Star* and not of any individual staff member. Materials are to be stored at the *Star* office. Editors, at their discretion, may dispose of old material in an equitable way. (Adapted from *ACP Model Code of Ethics*)

Reviews and event coverage

Movies: The *Star* will pay for a ticket for the reviewer. Do not accept free admission.

Concerts: If the *Star* is covering the concert as a news event, arrange for media credentials beforehand with the concert promoters. We do not need to buy tickets for reporters or photographers. However [...] If a reporter or critic attends a concert in order to review it, then the *Star* will pay for that person's ticket. The reason: There could be public perception that organizers "bought" a positive review by giving the reporter free admission.

Sporting events: These generally are covered as news, and reporters and photographers may arrange for media credentials and free admission.

Abuse of media credentials: If a *Northern Star* employee is found to have accepted media credentials for a concert, sporting event or other public event, but then attends the event for non-*Star* purposes, the employee is subject to disciplinary action, possibly including dismissal.

Free tickets or passes may be accepted by staff members for personal use only if tickets are available on the same complimentary basis to non-journalists. (*ACP Model Code of Ethics*)

Radio promotional events

NS*Radio and the *Northern Star* sometimes will promote concerts with ticket giveaways for listeners/readers. Under no circumstances should tickets or other prizes be given to or won by *Northern Star* employees, their relatives or friends.

Gifts

Gifts should not be accepted. Any gift should be returned to the sender or sent to a charity. If the gift is of no significant value, such as a desk trinket, a small food item or a pen, the staff member may retain the gift. As a guideline, if the value is under $10, the gift may be kept. More than one gift in one year, even if under $10, from the same giver, may not be accepted. (*ACP Model Code of Ethics*)

Use of *Northern Star* equipment

Northern Star equipment – computers, software, printers, photo equipment – is the property of the state of Illinois. It may not be used for outside-NIU, for-profit activity by any individual or group. Such use violates university policy and could result in penalties to the *Northern Star*. Further, the *Star* sometimes reports on similar, questionable practices within other NIU organizations. It cannot ethically report on these situations if it is not itself beyond reproach.

Northern Star equipment may not be used to produce any publication – print, online or broadcast – which competes or potentially competes with the *Northern Star* for advertising revenue. Exceptions: Publications or services that enter into formal partnership with the *Northern Star*.

Northern Star equipment may be used on occasion to assist other NIU offices or outside, not-for-profit entities, but always on the employee's own time, with the prior knowledge and approval of the editor-in-chief, and never at times when the equipment is needed for *Northern Star* work.

Outside employment and activities

The *Star* strives to remain free of any potential conflict of interest – real or perceived.

All managers, and all persons involved in gathering, reporting and/or presenting news and commentary for the *Northern Star*, are prohibited from serving elected or appointed positions in the NIU Student Association, the NIU University Council, any DeKalb, Sycamore or DeKalb County governmental body, or any other policy-making committee of these organizations. Other employees may be members of the aforementioned organizations as long as there is no conflict of interest, as determined by the *Northern Star* Management Board. Such situations should be disclosed to a manager immediately. Employees may be members of clubs, committees or organizations which are funded by the Student Association but do not help formulate SA policy. In conflict-of-interest cases and hiring appeals, the Management Board will make final judgments.

The press serves as an independent watchdog of government. That responsibility will not be compromised.

Star employees may not cover or do other *Star* business with any organization which they belong to or work for. It is the responsibility of the employee to alert his/her manager or editor of potential conflicts of interest.

Star employees may participate in political rallies, clubs, protests or demonstrations, but this practice is discouraged. Such participation disqualifies them from ever covering such an event or group. Again, the employee is responsible to alert his/her manager of this potential conflict of interest.

Relationships

Staff members should not cover or have *Star*-business dealings with "family members or persons with whom they have a financial, adversarial or close sexual or platonic relationship. Intra-staff dating is not recommended if one person assigns or evaluates the work of the other person or if one is in a position to promote the other to a higher staff position. (*ACP Model Code of Ethics*)

Drinking while on the job

Even though a staffer may be able to drink legally, no, or only light drinking, in a social setting such as a dinner or reception is recommended to avoid any suspicion by a source or the public that the staffer's judgment, credibility or objectivity is impaired by alcohol. When covering an event where alcohol is served, staffers should not accept free drinks unless all drinks are free to everyone in attendance. Staffers should avoid the appearance that they are being "wined and dined" by any source or group. (*ACP Model Code of Ethics*)

Influence of advertisers

Editors should guard against attempts made by advertisers [...] to influence the editorial content of the print or online publication. The editorial staff reserves the right to make all decisions about any editorial coverage an advertiser may get in the publication, including advertising supplements. Readers should not perceive that an advertiser is getting favorable editorial mention simply because the advertiser has bought space in the publication. (*ACP Model Code of Ethics*)

In addition, business-side employees should, when needed, explain this policy to clients and potential clients.

Corrections

An inaccuracy is never knowingly published. If any error is found, the *Northern Star* is obligated to correct the error as soon as possible – regardless of who made the error. At editors' discretion, corrections may be made to the website immediately. Any online story which results in a correction should clearly state that it has been corrected, and how. (*ACP Model Code of Ethics*)

Plagiarism and fabrication

What is plagiarism?

- Presenting someone else's work as your own, without proper acknowledgment and/or permission.
- Using some else's opinions, word arrangement, design or sequence of ideas without proper acknowledgment and/or permission.

What is fabrication?

- Making up quotes or information from a real source.
- Attributing real quotes or information from a source other than the person who actually said it.
- Making up quotes or information from an imaginary source.
- Making up information and not citing a source at all.

Any *Northern Star* employee found to have plagiarized or fabricated content for print, online or radio is subject to immediate termination.

The ACP Model Code of Ethics, 3rd ed. by Albert DeLuca and Tom Rolnicki, Associated Collegiate Press, 1999. Excerpts used with permission. Reprinted with permission from the *Northern Star*.

Deni Elliott, professor and Eleanor Poynter Jamison Chair in Media Ethics and Press Policy at the University of South Florida, St. Petersburg, suggests newspapers do ethics audits. Such audits can help editors take a critical look at how they cover the campus.

Before embarking on an audit, collect demographic information about your campus, including racial, ethnic and gender composition of students and faculty; average age of students; numbers of part- and full-time students, etc. Much of this information will be readily available from the admissions, public information or institutional research offices – or even your university's website.

Then study several issues of the paper, asking these questions:

1 How many men and women appear as subjects in news photos or as sources in stories? What is the racial balance of people pictured in the paper? What are those people doing?

2 What words are being used to describe the people in the news?

3 What gets the greatest attention in the paper? What gets the least?

4 Who's missing from your coverage?

5 How does your coverage of the campus square with the demographic statistics you collected?

Discuss in groups how you can better cover the community you serve. Then come up with an action plan to make sure you follow up on suggestions for improving coverage.

TIPSHEET
Dealing with potentially controversial content

Nearly every newspaper has controversial content at some point – the provocative column that fills your comment box with vitriolic responses, the offensive cartoon that sparks a boycott of your paper, the revealing photograph that prompts a call from the university president.

These breaches of taste aren't necessarily a bad thing; student newspapers are supposed to push the envelope a bit. But they do present challenges for the editors and other staffers who have to take the criticism. Often this kind of content is seen as insensitive or offensive to a particular ethnic, racial or religious group and may jeopardize relationships with individuals and groups far into the future.

Here are some tips that will help you avoid publishing offensive material – or deal with the flak when you do.

1 **Diversify your staff.** A diverse staff helps a newspaper cover a multicultural community with sensitivity and a sense of responsibility. The more diverse your staff, the more you'll have "cultural experts" to advise you on a range of sensitive issues. And think beyond racial minorities. A truly diverse staff includes people of varying religions, ethnic groups, political persuasions, sexual minorities and disabilities.

2 **Train your staff.** Teach your student newspaper staff to be on the lookout for sensitive material – words and images that people might find offensive or disturbing. Be sure to include the whole staff – photographers, copy editors, designers, graphic artists, multimedia producers and reporters, as well as editors – in the training. Show examples of controversial content run by other newspapers and discuss how you would handle such challenges. Invite experts who can educate your staff about the communities you cover.

3 **Use the *News Watch* Diversity Style Guide.** (ciij.org/publications_media/20050321-133409.pdf). This guide, developed by the staff of *News Watch* at the Center for Integration and Improvement of Journalism at San Francisco State University, offers guidance on a host of terms, from "able-bodied" to "Zapatistas." It explains the Five Pillars of Islam, the meaning of "down low," and when it's acceptable to use the word "Eskimo."

4 **Reach out.** Build relationships with campus and community groups representing different ethnic, racial, religious and political groups. Learn about their cultures, traditions and beliefs. The more you understand, the less likely you are to make a cultural faux pas.

5 **Ask hard questions.** When considering content that some may find offensive – be it a news story, a cartoon, an editorial, an opinion column, a video, or a photograph – ask yourself: What does the piece say? Is it fair? Are there words or images that might hurt people? Try to look at it from different points of view. Weigh whether the benefits of the piece – the insights and information it will convey – outweigh the trouble and pain it may cause.

6 **Encourage group decision-making.** Young editors sometimes feel they should be able to make important decisions on their own. Try to create an environment where decisions are made after discussion among several people. Train editors to seek and consider multiple points of view before making judgments and taking action.

7 **Warn the reader.** When you do decide to run controversial material, explain what you're doing and why you're doing it in an editor's note. Show readers you've really thought this through.

8 **When the flak hits, listen.** Be open to criticism. Respond to angry letters and phone calls in a calm, rational and timely manner. Don't get defensive. Offer to meet in person with school officials, student leaders or others who are upset.

9 **If you've made a mistake, take responsibility.** If you've got something to apologize for, apologize quickly and publicly. Don't let wounds fester. Give your apology at least as much play as the error or offensive content.

10 **Consider disciplinary action carefully.** If an individual acted with negligence or malice, you might want to suspend or fire that person. But also remember that student publications are supposed to be learning experiences. If people involved made an honest mistake and take responsibility for their actions, they may deserve a second chance.

11 **Stand by sound decisions.** If after careful thought you believe you did the right thing, even in light of criticism, explain your actions to your readers and your community. Be responsive to community concerns, but stick to your guns.

12 **Heal wounds.** If your publication offended a particular community, try to make amends. Reach out to that group and make it clear you want to improve your coverage. Appoint a diplomatic staff member as a liaison to that group.

13 **Learn from your mistakes.** While it can dangerously strain relationships between a publication and its readers, running controversial content nearly always provides important lessons. Figure out what this experience is teaching you and use it to educate current and future staff members. Re-evaluate policies and systems that allowed this error or offensive content to go through.

REFLECTIONS ON AN ETHICAL DILEMMA **Joel Elliott**

In May 2003, Joel Elliott, editor of *The Talon* (my.tfc.edu/talon) at Toccoa Falls College in Toccoa, Ga., published a story in the student paper revealing that the evangelical college's president, Donald O. Young, did not hold the master's degree that was listed on his résumé. Many on the campus criticized Elliott for his actions, saying it wasn't Christian of him to reveal the unpleasant facts. A few weeks later, Young resigned from his job.

In the end, it took a five-minute call to Fuller Seminary to determine that my college president had not earned a master's degree as he claimed. It had taken me several months of examining financial statements, working contacts and poking through the college's hallowed archives to find it.

The president's skeleton had initially peeked from the closet when one professor hinted vaguely of a scandal he planned to disclose upon his own retirement. He wouldn't specify so I had to dig for it.

I first caught wind of the story while shooting the breeze with a fellow reporter at *The Toccoa Record*, where I worked to pay my school bills. He said it was rumored the college had run into difficulty trying to renew accreditation because the president was underqualified.

The rumor was a little misleading, but I eventually dug out the kernel of truth.

I didn't have much time to contemplate whether to publish the story, as we had only one issue of *The Talon* left before students went home for the summer. The situation didn't look good. President Donald O. Young had threatened to shut down *The Talon* earlier in the semester, so I could only guess what he'd do in retaliation for this. My mother asked me not to do it, for fear Young would expel me with only one semester before graduation. I'd already been kicked out of one college, so it was a real concern. However, I felt I'd made my decision and commitment to reporting the news the previous year, when I'd taken the position as editor. Fear for personal loss couldn't be a consideration.

As for *The Talon,* I knew it would cease to exist as a truthful news-reporting organization the instant I spiked the story. I felt that gambling on the consequences of telling the whole truth was a better bet than going for the seemingly safe certainty of destroying our integrity.

Folks at the school seemed to think that the school's Christianity should throw a warm fuzzy into my editorial decision-making process. Quite the opposite. I feel Jesus and the prophets never depended on the suppression of truth for the promotion of their agendas. I saw no reason why a newspaper should, either.

The day the story ran, Donald Young compared its impact to an earthquake. He announced the catastrophe during chapel that morning and evoked a more emotional response than the time he announced the bombing of the Twin Towers. Students and faculty members cried, wailed and prayed for God to deliver them from evil as they surged to the front to embrace and lay hands on Young, while I scribbled notes for a follow-up story. Soon, I was alone in my seat with nearly every Toccoa Falls College student and professor at the stage, facing back toward me.

One student gave Young a hug and borrowed his microphone to shout up at the few who dared remain in their seats.

"Satan's trying to destroy this school and this man of God," he said. "You're either for us or against us."

"This school" was also my school, and I was sickened by the hypocrisy. Even a dean, who, the previous day, had offered to help blackmail the man into resigning in exchange for me killing the story, stood behind Young with head dutifully bowed. The dean would later denounce me to a *New York Times* reporter as having chosen the way of the newspaperman over the way of the Christian. However, his false dichotomy served only to solidify my knowledge that I had made the right decision. If journalism is worth doing, it's worth doing right. I believe it's worth doing.

JOEL ELLIOTT graduated from Toccoa Falls College in 2003 with a degree in journalism. He won numerous awards for reporting the story on Donald O. Young, including the Payne Award for Ethics in Journalism from the University of Oregon School of Journalism and Communication, the Weltner Hero Award from the Georgia First Amendment Foundation and a citation from the Georgia General Assembly. He writes for *The Caravan*, a narrative journalism magazine run by Delhi Press, and has freelanced for *The New York Times* and *The Christian Science Monitor*.

10 ethical dilemmas for student journalists

The following ethical dilemmas may be used for discussion at an editors' training or staff orientation.

1 A reporter is doing a story on students who sell prescription drugs like Ritalin as a study tool. She's been having trouble finding sources for her story and she comes to you, the editor, asking if she can use her roommate as an unnamed source. She is willing to give you her roommate's name as long as it's kept confidential.

What would you do? What is your newspaper's policy on unnamed sources? Do you have a policy on reporters interviewing friends, relatives and acquaintances?

2 A student photographer gets a great shot of three freshmen drinking beer at a party for a story on underage drinking. The students are easily identifiable in the photo. The photographer said he identified himself as a photographer for the paper and that the students knew they were being photographed. They said they didn't care if the photo was in the paper and they gave the photographer their names. The story is slated to run on the front page and you need art. It's an hour before deadline and this is the only decent shot you've got.

Do you run the photo? Do you publish the students' names?

3 The director of your advertising department heard that you're planning a story on bars for celebrating St. Patrick's Day. She suggests that you write about O'Callahan's, a local Irish bar that she's been trying to get to advertise in the paper. She notes that advertising revenue has been down this year and the paper will have fewer pages if she doesn't sell more ads. She also notes that the bar offers drink specials for the holiday. Your reporter has already written the story, which features half a dozen bars but doesn't include O'Callahan's. You have time and space to add in a brief paragraph about the bar and you want to stay on good terms with the advertising director.

What do you do?

4 A local animal park is holding a special day for local media and invites your paper to send two staffers to enjoy a media day at the park. As part of the day, the staffers will get free admission and lunch and be able to attend special information sessions about the park's new additions. A reporter has lined up an interview with a tiger trainer (an alumnus of your school) during the event. The animal park does not require students to publicize the event, but does ask to receive a copy of any clips that result from the event.

What do you do? Does your newspaper have a policy about "freebies"? How do you handle free books, CDs, movie tickets, products, etc. sent to your office?

5 A female student is killed off campus and her boyfriend is arrested and charged with murder. A reporter is trying to get a photograph of the victim from family and friends but so far you haven't been able to get one. A photographer takes a photograph into her apartment through an open window that's accessible to the public. The photo shows police working at the crime scene.

Do you run the photo – in print, online or both? Does your paper have different standards for what it runs in print and on the Web? Should it? How do you decide what's tasteful?

6 You learn that a new student at your university set himself on fire at an off-campus gas station and was pronounced dead at the scene. You call the gas station and the manager tells you that the young man bought 53 cents worth of gasoline and drenched himself with it before lighting himself on fire. Police confirm the death was a suicide.

Do you report the student's death? Do you say it was a suicide? What details of the death do you include in the story? Under what circumstances would your newspaper cover suicide by a student or faculty member? What if the family asked you not to report on it?

7 The president of your public university is concerned that your paper doesn't cover the governing board for the system, which meets several hundred miles away. He offers to give the newspaper money for transportation and lodging so you can send a reporter to cover the meetings. Your newspaper is strapped and can't afford to send a reporter to the meetings.

Do you accept the travel funds from the president? If so, do you do anything special in your coverage that notes where the travel funding came from?

8 A bunch of students stage a protest rally on your campus that turns into a melee. A police officer uses a Taser to stun one of the protesters and a member of your staff catches the incident on video. You publish an edited version of the video on your news website. A few days later the police department asks your news organization to submit the raw video as evidence for the investigation into the Tasing.

Do you comply with the police request?

9 You're a reporter working on a story about the homeless and you go out to the streets looking for people to interview. You find a great source who gives you a lot of information. He says he hasn't eaten in two days and asks you to buy him lunch.

What do you do?

10 A graduate of your school calls to say he is applying for jobs and the first thing that comes up on a Google search of his name is an article your paper published three years ago about him being arrested on a charge of public drunkenness. The charge was dropped but the paper never followed up. He asks that you take the article off your website.

What do you do? Does your newspaper have a policy about deleting content from the website?

TO DO

1 Assign a team to review your code of ethics. Is it as complete as it could be? Are there important issues it doesn't address? Once your code is revised, consider different ways of distributing it, including posting it on your website, making it part of your staff manual and publishing it in your newspaper.

2 Invite an ethics expert on campus (perhaps a journalism or communications professor) or a journalist from a professional paper to speak to your staff about media ethics.

3 Devote a training session to discussing ethics. You might assign staffers to small groups to discuss real or theoretical ethical dilemmas such as those presented in this chapter or at Journalism Ethics Cases Online (see the website listed in the "To Click" section).

4 Assign a team of people to conduct an ethics audit of your paper. Present the results of the audit to your entire staff and break people into small groups to discuss how to improve your coverage.

5 Break your staff into small groups and assign each group to pretend to be a certain kind of student – a person who uses a wheelchair, an African-American, a lesbian, a student who lives at home with his parents, a Muslim student, a 40-year-old student who is returning to school after 20 years in the working world. Have each group brainstorm story ideas that might appeal to that type of person. Then have each group share their ideas with the whole staff and put together a list of story ideas for the paper.

6 Rent a movie with a media ethics dilemma, such as *The Paper*, *Absence of Malice*, or *The Insider* and show it to your staff. Then discuss the movie as a group.

TO READ

Black, Jay, Steele, Bob and Barney, Ralph. *Doing Ethics in Journalism: A Handbook with Case Studies.* Greencastle, Ind.: The Sigma Delta Chi Foundation and The Society of Professional Journalists, 1993.

Cote, William and Simpson, Roger. *Covering Violence – A Guide to Ethical Reporting About Victims and Trauma.* New York: Columbia University, 2000.

Patterson, Philip and Wilkins, Lee C.. *Media Ethics: Issues and Cases, 7th ed.* New York: McGraw-Hill Humanities/ Social Sciences/ Languages, 2010.

TO CLICK

American Society of Newspaper Editors' Codes of Ethics

The society has links to ethics codes from dozens of American newspapers.

http://asne.org/key_initiatives/ethics/ethics_codes.aspx

Dart Center for Journalism & Trauma

The center's website offers a wide range of materials on the ethics of covering traumatic events, from earthquakes and fires to suicide and murder.

www.dartcenter.org

Ethics AdviceLine for Journalists

Sponsored by the Chicago Headline Club Chapter of the Society of Professional Journalists and Loyola University Chicago Center for Ethics and Social Justice, the Ethics AdviceLine is a free service for professional journalists in need of guidance on reaching ethical decisions while covering the news. The line also answers questions from student journalists as long as they are working for a publication (including student publications), not just writing a paper for a class. All conversations between callers and respondents begin as confidential although callers will be asked if information can be shared with the AdviceLine team or with others for educational purposes.

Call Toll Free 866-DILEMMA
www.ethicsadvicelineforjournalists.org

Journalism Ethics Cases Online

This collection of cases put together by the Indiana University School of Journalism would work well for an ethics-training seminar. The cases raise a variety of ethical problems faced by journalists, including such issues as privacy, conflict of interest, reporter-source relationships, and the role of journalists in their communities.

http://journalism.indiana.edu/resources/ethics

Onward State

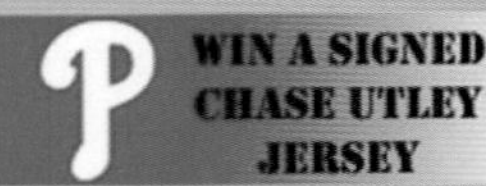

GO TO
WWW.THEPSBC.COM
TO BUY A TICKET

NEWS | SPORTS | ARTS | COMMUNITY | TOPICS | ARCHIVES | SEARCH

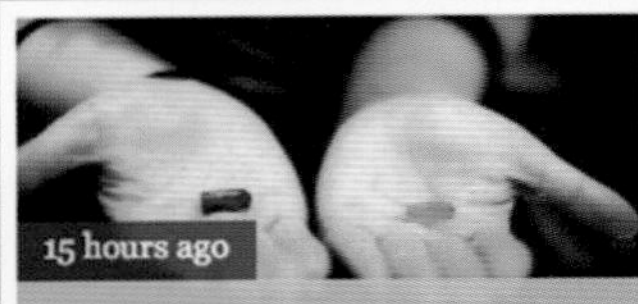

15 hours ago

State College PD Collects Unused Pills

17 hours ago

Controversial Call Leads to Loss for Men's Soccer

8 hours ago

Biden Takes Over The HUB

THON

SPA

UPUA

CCSG

IFC

Joe Paterno

Liz Goreham

Established in 2008, Onward State is an online news organization serving the Penn State community.

Stay Connected

Onward State Penn State YAF posted a video of its protest at today's rally featuring Vice President Joe Biden.

Penn State YAF Protests Joe Biden

www.youtube.com

Members of Penn State University's chapter of Young Americans for Freedom explains why

2,914 people like Onward State

Bobbie-Jo | Mike | Patrick

Facebook social plugin

Community

Submit

If You Could Start a Company or Initiative at PSU, What Would It Be?

Jon Co-founder (Innoblue)

What business, student organization, or civic initiative would you launch if you had access to the resources to make it happen?

Comments 2 — Read Full Post

Question of the Day: Non-Alcoholic Fun

Alex Federman Community Manager (Onward State)

Despite Penn State's nationally ranked party scene, there are plenty

Biden Takes Over The HUB

An update 8 hours ago in News about HUB by Tom

Vice President Joe Biden attended a rally today at the HUB-Robeson Center to address the Penn State community regarding the upcoming legislative elections in November.

Speaking to a crowd of over a thousand students, professors, and townspeople in the HUB, the vice president spoke on behalf of President Obama about the issues that Americans will face when they go to the polls in two months.

Facebook 1 — Twitter 0 — Comments 0 — Read Full Post

[Pics] HUB Preparation for Joe Biden Rally

An update 15 hours ago in News by Davis Shaver

Joe Biden will be speaking in the HUB this

FIGURE 15.1 Davis Shaver, a freshman at Pennsylvania State University, created *Onward State* in 2008 with two classmates who shared his vision to start a hyperlocal, social media-driven news website that would have "the snark of Gawker, the aggregation of *The Huffington Post*, the political coverage of Politico." *Onward State*, Penn State University.

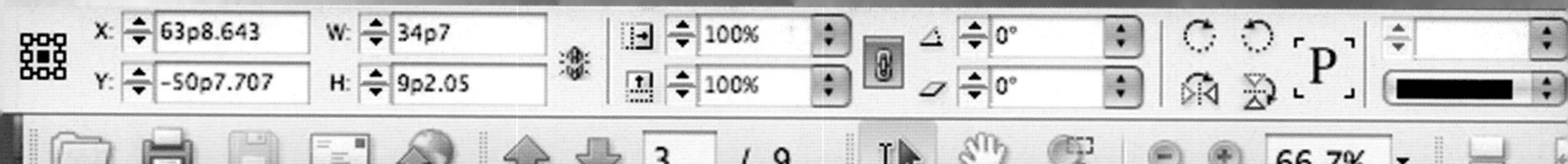

CHAPTER 15
STARTING A NEW NEWSPAPER

As a freshman at Penn State University, Davis Shaver wasn't satisfied with the campus newspaper. Though *The Daily Collegian* (collegian.psu.edu) had won countless awards and maintained an active website, Shaver felt the century-old news organization was too print-focused and didn't take full advantage of the Web's potential. So within weeks of arriving on campus he set out to create a new media venture, a hyper-local, Web-only, social media-driven news blog.

"I had been partly inspired by blogs launched at New England schools such as *MiddBlog* (midd-blog.com) at Middlebury and *Wesleying* (wesleying.org) at Wesleyan," Shaver says. "These sites provided event listings and secondary content (links to other people's content). I wanted to take that model and enhance it, creating basically a hyper-local for the student community." His vision was to create a website that would have "the snark of Gawker, the aggregation of *The Huffington Post*, the political coverage of Politico."

Shaver found two classmates – Evan Kalikow and Eli Glazier – who shared his dream and together they began to create the technical backend of the site and to recruit additional contributors. On Nov. 17, 2008 they launched *OnwardState.com* (onwardstate.com), named for a phrase taken from the Penn State football fight song.

The Student Newspaper Survival Guide, Second Edition. Rachele Kanigel.

CHAPTER CONTENTS

Onward State

COVERAGE OF ALL PENN STATE ATHLETICS AND A DAILY NEWSCAST
NEWS. SPORTS. TALK. COMRADIO.

NEWS SPORTS ARTS COMMUNITY TOPICS ARCHIVES SEARCH

about a year ago Davis Shaver News Comments 222

Penn State Student Missing

Penn State freshman Joseph Dado ~~is currently missing~~ *has been found dead. Our deepest sympathies are with the family and friends. Details to follow soon.*

He was last seen at a FIJI party on Sunday, September 19th at 3:00 AM. He is supposed to have begun walking back to East Halls, but no one has seen or heard from him since he left Fiji (Phi Gamma Delta). At the time, he was wearing jeans, a yellow shirt, and a blue hooded sweatshirt.

If you have any information about Joseph, please contact Natalie Dado at 724-858-9809 or Penn State Police at 814-863-1111. Anonymous tips can be directed to Centre County Crime Stoppers at 877-992-7463.

Update 10:00 pm: A small candlelight vigil is being held on Pollock Road immediately outside the cordoned off area. Auxiliary Police are still stationed around the perimeter of the police tape while high-intensity flood lights are seen on the other side of the wall where the investigation is being carried out.

Update 7:51 pm: Joseph Dado appears to have fallen 15 feet and sustained severe trauma to his head. Repairmen found his body when responding to a service call. [source] The Collegian also has a story up.

Update 7:05 pm: Dado found dead in stairwell by Steidle and Deike. Foul play not suspected, however alcohol was involved.

Update 7:01 pm: There is no ambulance at the scene. Police bringing in generators and lighting equipment now.

Update 6:50 pm: The area between Steidle and Deike is quartered off by police. It looks to be an area containing dumpsters and other maintenance apparatus. In total it looks like 5 police cars with more en route. Gavin Keirans and IFC president Luke Pierce are on the scene.

Update 6:10 pm: Penn State posted a note on Facebook saying that,

Police have found no record of activity on Dado's student ID card, bank debit card and cell phone since before he

Established in 2008, Onward State is an online news organization serving the Penn State community.

Stay Connected

follow us on twitter

Onward State on Facebook

Like

2,914 people like Onward State

Jen Craig Brian Jerry Andrew Natalie

Facebook social plugin

Calendar

September 2010

Powered By PSUevents.com

FIGURE 15.2 When Penn State University freshman Joseph Dado went missing after a frat party, *Onward State* posted frequent updates and made extensive use of social media tools to report the story. The student was later found dead at the bottom of a stairwell, where he had apparently fallen. *Onward State*, Penn State University.

Unlike more traditional college media outlets that primarily run staff-generated content, *Onward State* embraced new media guru Jeff Jarvis's mantra: "Cover what you do best. Link to the rest." For example, the blog's first post was a brief on an unconfirmed rumor that remix artist Girl Talk would be performing at Penn State the following month. The site followed up with links to a *New York Times* review of a recent Girl Talk concert, a *Harvard Crimson* Q&A with the performer and a report on Girl Talk's Wesleyan University show on the *Wesleying* blog. *Onward State* next reported on a student arts group's efforts to bring Girl Talk to campus and finally updated the post to confirm the performance.

While *The Collegian* rarely mentioned its upstart rival, *Onward State* devoted a corner of its home page to *Collegian* headlines and frequently linked to the newspaper's stories.

Born at the dawn of the social media age, *Onward State* from the get-go relied heavily on social media tools for generating story ideas, scoping out rumors, finding sources, promoting content and conversing with readers. "As a staff we use a lot of online tools to stay connected since we don't have a brick and mortar office," says Shaver, who started the online news outlet out of his dorm room and met weekly with his staff in the dormitory basement. "A lot of our work happens over Google Wave (a now-discontinued Google tool for collaboration), Google Chat, even Facebook."

Onward State staffers were also quick to embrace mobile technology. A contributor wandering around in downtown College Park might snap a cell phone picture of a sign announcing that a popular watering hole had closed and post it immediately to the site.

But *Onward State* didn't just report on light matters. When a freshman went missing after a frat party one night, the blog covered the story with minute-by-minute updates. "That was the same year we were named the No. 1 party school in the country (by the *Princeton Review*) so it was a hot story," Shaver says.

Onward State posted a description of the missing student and told readers how they could volunteer to help out. The blog linked to its rival's stories as well as a Facebook page set up to help with the search. "Our posts became the things people were sharing on Facebook and Twitter," Shaver says. "That positioned us as the best aggregator on the story. We covered it really well." When the student was found dead the following day, *Onward State* was the first to report the news. More than 200 comments on the coverage – first prayers for the missing man and suggestions for where he might be found and, later, condolences for the family – were posted to the blog.

Onward State quickly became the darling of the blogosphere. *The Huffington Post*, the media blogs *Mashable* and *College Media Matters* and *The Chronicle of Higher Education* all wrote about the online news outlet and its old media-new media rivalry with the venerable *Collegian*.

Just two months after *Onward State's* launch, *The Paper Trail, U.S. News and Report's* college blog, nominated it for Best Alternative Media Outlet in its Best of College Newspapers competition, inviting readers to vote for their favorite. Thanks in part to an aggressive get-out-the-vote campaign by staffers on online forums, Facebook and Twitter, *Onward State* won. Beginner's luck? Perhaps. But when the blog won the same award the following year, *The Paper Trail* wrote: "Face it, *Onward State* is to alternative student media outlets what Ohio State football is to the Big Ten."

NEWSPAPER COMPETITION

Like most North American cities, the majority of college campuses are one-newspaper communities. But in recent years alternative publications like *Onward State* have sprouted like mushrooms, turning many schools into true marketplaces of ideas. Such rivalries have led to experimentation and a healthy spirit of competition.

The University of Wisconsin, Madison, has one of the longest running newspaper wars in the nation. On any weekday the 40,000 students there can pick up two dailies – *The Daily Cardinal* (dailycardinal.com), founded in 1892, and the *Badger Herald* (badgerherald.com), founded in 1969 as a more conservative voice. (It's since swung to the center.) The two newspapers celebrate this spirit of competition with an annual *Cardinal–Badger Herald* football game in the fall and a softball game in the spring. According to tradition, the losing newspaper must run a report of the game by one of its rival's reporters.

Competition also thrives at Vanderbilt University in Nashville. In 2001, a coalition of liberal and minority groups launched *The Vanderbilt Orbis* (vanderbiltorbis.com) to compete with *The Vanderbilt Hustler* (vandymedia.org), the official student newspaper for more than 100 years. Soon after, another band of students announced plans to start *The Vanderbilt Torch* (vutorch.com), a conservative/libertarian paper. "The belief was that *The Hustler* wasn't doing a very good job covering some aspects of the campus," says Chris Carroll, director of student media.

A decade later, all three news publications (as well as a political magazine, a literary review, a humor magazine and a weekly arts supplement) were still around; in fact, the *Hustler* increased from twice-a-week to three-times-a-week publication in 2004. *The Nation* named *The Vanderbilt Orbis* one of "Ten Papers We Like" in an article about alternative campus newspapers.

Carroll once had doubts about whether Vanderbilt, a campus of only 6,000 undergraduates and about 10,000 students total, could support so many publications. In fact, the *Hustler* is the only one that brings in substantial advertising revenue. "To have so many publications, you're stretching to get the best writers, the best photographers. There's an overload of media, an overload of message."

However, he notes, the newer publications have encouraged many more students to get involved in campus media than ever before. "Our chancellor makes a big deal about how many publications we have, how many outlets for expression, which he sees as a demonstration of the vitality of the campus."

ALTERNATIVE MEDIA OUTLETS

Since most colleges and universities have a campus paper, the majority of the new publications that have sprung up in recent years are alternative papers – ones that provide an alternate perspective to the mainstream campus newspaper. John K. Wilson, former coordinator of the Independent Press Association's Campus Journalism Project, divides alternative publications into six categories:

Conservative: Publications that provide right-of-center perspectives.

Progressive: Newspapers created to discuss progressive or liberal ideas.

Humor: Non-partisan newspapers that offer satire. "Harvard's *National Lampoon* was a forerunner," Wilson says. "Today *The Onion* inspires many imitators."

Religious: Newspapers that offer a religious slant are rare but growing in number with a recent Supreme Court decision decreeing that religious newspapers are entitled to student fee funding.

Alternative weeklies: Campus papers patterned after urban alternative weeklies.

Identity: Newspapers based on identity politics, such as African-American, gay and lesbian and feminist newspapers.

"Alternative newspapers work best by filling an ignored niche," says Wilson, who in 1995 co-founded the University of Chicago *Free Press*, an alternative monthly, and in 2001 founded the *Indy* (isuindynews.com), an alternative weekly at Illinois State University. "The mainstream campus newspaper has all of the advantages of being established, and no alternative newspaper can really hope to beat it at overall campus news coverage. Therefore, alternative newspapers specialize in things that mainstream papers do poorly." Alternative papers tend to run longer pieces, including investigative, magazine-style and opinion articles.

In recent years, Web-centric blogs and online magazines have emerged to challenge traditional college newspapers with edgy, sometimes irreverent writing and unconventional reporting techniques. "Everyone knows that you can 'get away' with more on the Web," Alana Taylor, then a New York University journalism student, wrote in a post for *PBS MediaShift* about *NYU Local* (nyulocal.com), an upstart blog that covers her campus. "Most college newspapers have advisors and editors working over the writers' shoulders, making sure they don't write anything too brash that will upset the dean of the school. But on the Web, writers are posting straight from laptops in their dorm rooms or from iPhones as they stroll down the street."

NYU Local was launched with funding from the Reynolds Foundation Program in Social Entrepreneurship and under the supervision of NYU faculty, but its hip, brash writing and tell-it-like-it-is style made it clear that students were running the show. On its "about" page, *NYU Local* says, "Our goal is to deliver all the discussion-worthy happenings in the school and city we call home. The site is conversational, the setup straightforward and the information useful. Read us often to learn about what's happening in your neighborhood, the most recent J-Sex fumbles and the worst Lil Wayne videos."

"The idea was it would be like a collaborative effort where everyone was writing the news and people were having conversations," says Charlie Eisenhood, one of the original writers who went on to become the publication's third editor-in-chief. "We had more of a crowd-sourced model rather than a journalist-to-reader model."

Eisenhood says *NYU Local* and its chief competitor, the well-established *Washington Square News* (nyunews.com), both grew from the rivalry. "We've both adapted. We tend to do a little more on-the-ground reporting now and they tend to do a little more quick coverage. From the beginning we got pigeon-holed as the Gawker-style, snarky alternative but were not seen so much as a respected news source. I'm trying to take the site to a higher level. Just because we're a blog doesn't mean the work we do has to be sloppy or too fast or not researched enough."

STARTING A NEW PUBLICATION

So what does it take to launch a new college newspaper? Ideas, people, production facilities and money.

First off, you need a vision. Think carefully about what kind of publication you want to create. Does your college or university need a mainstream, general-interest publication that covers the whole campus or a forum for alternative voices? Do you want to start a newspaper that caters to a particular group – such as Asian Americans, night students, summer students – or one that has a specific political bent? Or do you want to break with tradition and experiment with a news blog?

Next, you need to recruit a staff that believes in your vision. Announce an organizational meeting. Print fliers and post them all over campus. Make recruiting visits to journalism, English, political science, creative writing, photography and graphic design classes, as well as clubs where you're likely to find people interested in writing, photography and design. Recruit on Facebook and Twitter.

Once you have a core group, it's time to come up with a name. Student newspapers often play on the school's mascot, landmarks or nicknames such as *The Pitt News* (The University of Pittsburgh), *The Spartan Daily* (San Jose State University), *The Foghorn* (University of San Francisco), *The Daily Tar Heel* (University of North Carolina), and *The Northern Light* (University of Alaska-Anchorage). Some unusual college newspaper names include: *The Good 5-Cent Cigar* (University of Rhode Island), the *Tulane Hullabaloo*, *Le Provocateur* (Assumption College) and *The Mass Media* (University of Massachusetts, Boston).

WRITING A MISSION STATEMENT

The next step is to write a mission statement for your newspaper. The mission statement should reflect the goals and aspirations of your staff. What does your publication stand for? Who do you want to serve? What values do you want to uphold?

In discussing your mission statement be sure to give everyone on the staff a say in what the paper should be; a newspaper is a team effort, not just one person's soapbox. Early on, decide how you want to make group decisions – by consensus or by majority rule – and stick with your process.

As you make decisions, start writing down rules and policies that can be used in a constitution and/or staff handbook. Some newspapers have one of each; others have a single document that serves both functions.

Sample mission statements

The Unfiltered Lens (ccri.edu/unfilteredlens), Community College of Rhode Island

The overall mission of *The Unfiltered Lens* is to inform and improve the quality of student life at the Community College of Rhode Island. We strive to accomplish this standard by reporting and writing the truth in an ethical and responsible fashion that enlightens the entire college community, while providing information in an unvarnished manner that seeks thoughtful responses, dialogue and, of course, action. We fully understand serving students is our clear objective and recognize the impact and, more importantly, the importance of this endeavor. We realize we do not make news but cover events that stimulate our community, improve college life and strengthen our democracy.

Reprinted with permission

The Flip Side (flipsidepress.org), University of Wisconsin-Eau Claire

The Flip Side is a publication dedicated to providing an alternative media outlet and forum on the UW-Eau Claire campus by welcoming the writings, views, and involvement of all students and community members. By reporting on news, perspectives, and opinions on all issues, we seek to develop and maintain our freedom of speech.

Reprinted with permission.

DRAFTING A CONSTITUTION

A constitution is a formal document that outlines the rules that govern a student newspaper; you may be required to draft a constitution in order to get funding or recognition as a club or activity from your student government.

A typical constitution articulates its policies in a format like this:

Article I – Name of the organization

Article II – Membership

Explain who can join your staff, such as whether they must be students or whether they have to take a prerequisite course. You might want to include a non-discrimination clause explaining that the organization does not discriminate against anyone on the basis of gender, race/ethnicity, sexual orientation, political affiliation, religion or disability status.

Article III – Officers

Outline the titles and responsibilities of your paper's officers/editors.

Article IV – Editor selection

Explain how you select your editor-in-chief (and, if applicable, other top editors).

Article V – Removal of staffers.

Explain the terms under which a staffer can be removed from a position.

Article VI – Ratification and amendments

Explain the terms for ratifying and amending the constitution.

CREATING A STAFF MANUAL

Generally less formal but more detailed than a constitution, a staff manual is a guidebook that will help staffers do their jobs. At a minimum it should include:

A mission statement

Job descriptions

Code of ethics

Stylebook

Policies on deadlines, meetings, copy submission and other issues related to the functioning of the organization.

You may also want to include important campus phone numbers, maps, department listings and other documents to help new staff members.

DRAFTING A BUSINESS PLAN

Early on in the process you need to figure out your expenses and how you're going to pay for them. The biggest cost at most professional papers is salaries, but new student papers typically pay staffers little or nothing. Many student papers compensate staffers by giving them independent study or course credit. If you're interested in doing this, contact a journalism, English or writing program faculty member about how to arrange credit for the work you're doing. Other fledgling papers compensate staffers with small stipends.

At student newspapers that don't pay their staffers, the largest expenses are generally printing costs. The cost of paper and printing can vary widely; it pays to shop around. It may also pay to beg. Some community newspapers may be willing to print your paper at little or no cost as a community service.

With an online publication, production costs are minimal. You can start a website with little or no capital using free content management systems like WordPress. (Read more about websites in Chapter 17.)

Many student newspapers rely on some or all of their funding from student activity fees, often doled out by student government. Since your paper is serving the student body, this can be a legitimate use of student fees. However, there's a danger to using these funds. If student governing board members don't like what you run, they may decide to stop funding your paper (see Chapter 13 on legal issues for a discussion of this kind of censorship.) In the best situations, student government bodies understand the basic principles of press freedom. But student newspapers critical of student government or administrators have been the victims of reprisals.

Grants are another possible source of income. A number of ideological groups, including the liberal Center for American Progress and the conservative Collegiate Network, provide grants to help establish new student newspapers. Friends and family members or local corporations may also help out. Once again, however, these sources of funding may have strings attached. If your Aunt Thelma agrees to contribute $2,000 toward your effort on the condition you make the dean's list, you may want to want to think twice about the offer.

Probably the easiest way to support a student newspaper is to do what professional papers do – sell ads. Once you've put together a prototype or a first issue you can approach campus organizations and local businesses about buying ads. (For more about developing a media kit and selling ads, see Chapter 20.)

PRODUCTION

Not that long ago, producing a student newspaper was a complex process that required expensive equipment. But new advances in printing technology and Web publishing make starting a newspaper easier than ever. All you really need to get started is a single personal computer (though the more computers your staff has access to the better) loaded with some kind of design or publishing program. If you don't have Adobe InDesign or Quark Xpress, you may be able to get access to them at a school computer.

While money can be an obstacle, don't let it keep you from publishing. *The Flip Side* (flipsidepress.org) at the University of Wisconsin-Eau Claire started on stapled sheets of copy paper with almost no money. "We printed it on campus printers," says Jeremy Gragert, who started the paper in the fall of 2003. "A bunch of us spread out to different printers on campus. It took about three or four hours to print it. Then we got together stacks of the papers and formed an assembly line to the put the papers in order and staple them."

The *DoG Street Journal* (dogstreetjournal.com) at the College of William and Mary delayed the burden of printing costs by publishing first on the Web (see Figure 15.3) and adding a print edition later (see Figures 15.4 and 15.5).

And increasingly many publications start – and remain – Web-only. With the Internet's immediacy and social media capabilities, many students editors see no need for a print publication.

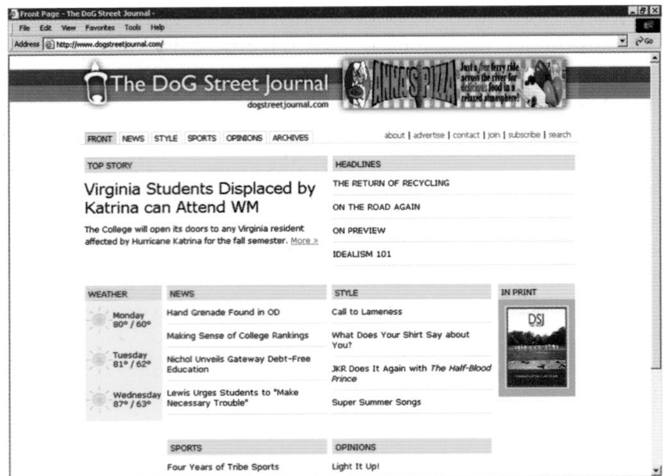

FIGURE 15.3 *The DoG Street Journal* at the College of William and Mary started as an online publication. *The DoG Street Journal*, College of William and Mary.

CREATING A NEWSROOM

One of the most challenging parts of starting a new campus newspaper is finding – and being able to afford – a newsroom. Sometimes you can secure an unused classroom or office space on campus for little or no cost, but on-campus space is a finite commodity. If you can't find a free or affordable space, you may need to start by sharing an office with another campus organization or running the newspaper out of someone's dorm room or apartment.

The Otter Realm (otterrealm.net), the newspaper at California State University, Monterey Bay, operated for years out of a tiny office space on the far edge of the campus. The cubicle had room for just three computers, castoffs that were donated, along with the office space, by the university. The newspaper shared a fax machine with several other campus organizations housed in the building. Students did much of the production work in a campus computer lab. It was far from an ideal situation, but the newspaper got out, first every month and later every two weeks. (*The Otter Realm* finally got a newsroom in 2005.)

If you don't have a space large enough to accommodate your whole staff, hold staff meetings in an empty classroom, library discussion room or quiet public gathering spot. *Onward State* started in Davis Shaver's dorm room and as the staff grew larger it met in the basement of his residence hall. "I'm not opposed to having a physical space," he said nearly two years after the blog launched. "It's something we're looking into."

Once you are able to find office space, make up a budget of what you'll need to outfit it. Look for grants to help you buy equipment and supplies. You may be able to get castoff computers, software and other equipment from the university. In addition, make a plea to local professional newspapers, which may be willing to give you old equipment. When the *San Francisco Chronicle* photo department switched from Nikon to Canon

VOLUME 1, NUMBER 7 dogstreetjournal.com

AND WHO ARE THEY?

The DSJ took some time to mill around with the Board of Visitors during their most recent meeting over Charter Day weekend.

>>>see pages 6 & 7

WEDNESDAY, FEBRUARY 11, 2004

CAMPUS news

'LOVE YOUR BODY WEEK' SET FOR 23-27 FEBRUARY

The CARES team on campus has begun planning for their annual "Love Your Body Week" festivities, this year to be held 23 – 27 February.

Events already set for the week include a Body Fair featuring tips and hints on how to pamper your body and mind through massage, Pilates, meditation, yoga, manicures, the showing of "Barbie Nation," (a documentary on the rise and influence of the Barbie doll), residence hall programs to promote healthy habits for your mind and body throughout campus, joining President Sullivan on one of his morning walks (with free Daily Grind beverages to follow!), and an Eating Disorders Panel composed of students who have both suffered from eating disorders and had first hand experience helping others with them.

"We really want to raise awareness about body image and eating disorders on campus," said Michelle Alexander, Health Educator on campus.

TRIBE sports

TRIBE FOOTBALL ANNOUNCES RECRUITING CLASS

Tribe football head coach Jimmye Laycock announced the signing of 10 letters of intent from high school players who will join the team in the fall including one transfer from Kent State.

"We are pleased with the group of student-athletes that we've identified and brought into the program," Tribe head coach Jimmye Laycock said. "It is a versatile class, in terms of positions, and our staff has worked very hard in bringing in a fine quality group of young men."

Eight of the ten players are from out-of-state.

THE DSJ contact us

757.221.7851

letters@dogstreetjournal.com

ATTN: THE DSJ
The Campus Center
One Jamestown Road
Williamsburg, VA 23185

College Celebrates 311th Birthday

MEGHAN McCARTHY staff reporter
email: mkmcca@wm.edu

Celebrating the 311th anniversary of the Royal Charter, members of the William and Mary community gathered in Phi Beta Kappa Memorial Hall on 7 February for the annual Charter Day exercises. The ceremony included readings from the Royal Charter and Royal Proclamation, as well as remarks from John H. Chichester of the Virginia Senate and President of the College Timothy J. Sullivan.

Attended by students and alumni alike, Charter Day is an example of the appreciation the College of William and Mary instills in its members, past and present.

"Charter Day is an important part of the William and Mary tradition. It's birthday time! I came to support the College, because William and Mary gives so much to us" said Owen Gentry, Class of 2007.

Alumni Dave Peckens and Mary Tine-Peckens of the Class of 1956 agreed.

"We come every year!" said Tine-Peckens. "I like to come back because it's always a good ceremony with very interesting speakers," added her husband Dave.

Designed to appreciate the rich past of the College while admiring present achievements, this year's Charter Day festivities also included many remarks on the future of William and Mary.

"Virginia has lived for the moment too long. We have let serious discussions about tomorrow be waylaid by today's distractions. We cannot continue to follow that path and produce a Virginia that is not 'worthy of its past.' Our current debate is about how we are going to define and fund our future" said Chichester.

Chichester also addressed the question that seemed impossible to ignore: the state of

>>>see CHARTER, page 3

State Senator John Chichester-R, addresses attendees of this year's Charter Day exercises at Phi Beta Kappa Hall. Photo by Tim Aiken.

CONTROLLING THE PENNIES

JAMES EVANS staff reporter
email: jeevan@wm.edu

Nancy Pulley sits opposite a panel of nine of her fellow students as they question her. Something about her story doesn't add up, and the Committee is intent on catching her mistake.

No, this isn't an Honor Council hearing. To some students it's worse than that. It's the Executive Appropriations Committee (EAC).

The EAC's job over the past several weeks has been to take over half a million dollars that will be paid by students next semester in their Student Activities Fee, and decide how much of it each club and organization on campus will get. They received applications from about 75 groups and held hearings like the one described above for 48 of them.

Despite the questioning of her budget request, Pulley, who represents the Graduate Education Association, was glad to have the opportunity to make her case on behalf of her organization. She had seven minutes to present and take questions before Ankit Patel from the Hindu Students' Organization was shown in and the whole thing started over again.

The EAC is a wing of the Student Assembly, which controls all student activity fee distribution. Supervising the EAC was Stephen Mutnick, Secretary of Finance for the SA.

"I thoroughly enjoyed working with the EAC this year," said Mutnick. "I think that we have been able to produce a strong, working budget for the President and Senate."

After the EAC finished its work, the budget moved on to SA President Brian Cannon who heard appeals from organizations and may make some changes to the budget.

When Cannon finishes with the budget he will introduce it to the SA Senate in his Spring Semester "State of the Student Assembly" address. This is expected to take place next Wednesday. The Senate will deliberate over the budget and make any final changes needed to pass it through the Senate.

"The EAC was great," said Cannon. He praised the new system over last year's budget group called the "Finance Committee." "The students really took control of the process," he said.

"The new process will strengthen the ability [of] the Student Assembly to create a fair and equitable budget for the students," said Mutnick.

Both Cannon and Mutnick described the EAC as a bottom-up process, while the President and Senate's changes are top-down – meaning the EAC works with all organizations to reach their goals while the President and Senate look at the whole budget and ensure it is fulfilling the collective goals of the College community.

"I think this ensures the maximum amount of fairness to the organizations at the College," said Mutnick. He thanked both the members of the EAC and members of the College's Office of Student Activities for their work on the budget.

Graduate student and EAC member Aftab Hossain also thought highly of the new process, saying the EAC had its disagreements but always reached a compromise.

"I think we managed to work together pretty well," said Hossain.

According to Hossain, hearings with the EAC were optional. This is a change from last year's system, and he suggested there might be more appeals due to the lost chance to communicate with some groups.

"As the custodians of this budget it could be difficult for us to discern what these groups were going to do with this money," said Hossain. Overall, however, he was happy with the EAC's work.

After the Senate receives the budget it will have several weeks to pass it. A committee will most likely review it before the entire Senate debates it.

"I know that Brian worked hard on it, and if he has every dollar where it is needed, he will have no trouble passing his budget," said Sophomore Senator Matt Wigginton.

HOW IT WORKS...

1) The College's Office of Student Activities notifies organizations of the upcoming budget process and organizations get a Budget Request Package.

2) Organizations attend pre-budget seminars and submit their budget requests.

3) Organizations may choose to have a hearing with the EAC to argue for the amount they have requested. The EAC takes this information and proposes a budget.

4) After the EAC's budget is announced, organizations may appeal the EAC's allocations to the SA President.

5) The President submits the budget to the SA Senate, who may also make changes.

6) Upon passage in the Senate the budget waits for distribution at the beginning of the next school year, unless the Board of Visitors changes the student activities fee.

THE BREAKDOWN...

Current Organizations - 28%
Student Government - 19%
New Organizations - 3%
One Time Purchases - 1%
Special Activities - 32%
Miscellaneous - 17%

FIGURE 15.4 While maintaining the website, *The DoG Street Journal* staff began to put out a biweekly print newspaper. *The DoG Street Journal*, College of William and Mary.

cameras, it donated tens of thousands of dollars worth of photo equipment to the San Francisco State Journalism Department and its laboratory newspaper, *Golden Gate [X]press* (goldengatexpress.org). The cameras and lenses might no longer have been state-of-the-art, but they were certainly more sophisticated than individual staffers or the student newspaper could afford to buy.

Every newsroom should have a communication center. Use inexpensive organizers to create mailboxes for each staff member. Many newsrooms also use whiteboards or blackboards to leave phone messages. Boards can also be used for editorial budgeting to keep track of stories.

Think about adding furnishings and equipment that will make the newsroom comfortable for your staff. Get a small refrigerator, a microwave oven and a table and chairs and encourage staff members to eat their lunch in the newsroom. (But if you do, make sure people are responsible about throwing out their garbage; leftovers will quickly attract rodents and insects.) A sofa, even a bedraggled one, can make a room cozy and provide an oft-needed space for power naps during marathon production sessions.

You should also have a television and radio to keep up with breaking news. Consider buying a police scanner, which will help you monitor police and fire calls on your campus and in your community.

Many student newspapers invest in photo and recording equipment – cameras, lenses, tripods, video cameras and audio recorders – that staffers can check out as needed. If you do, it probably pays to get insurance in case of loss, breakage or theft.

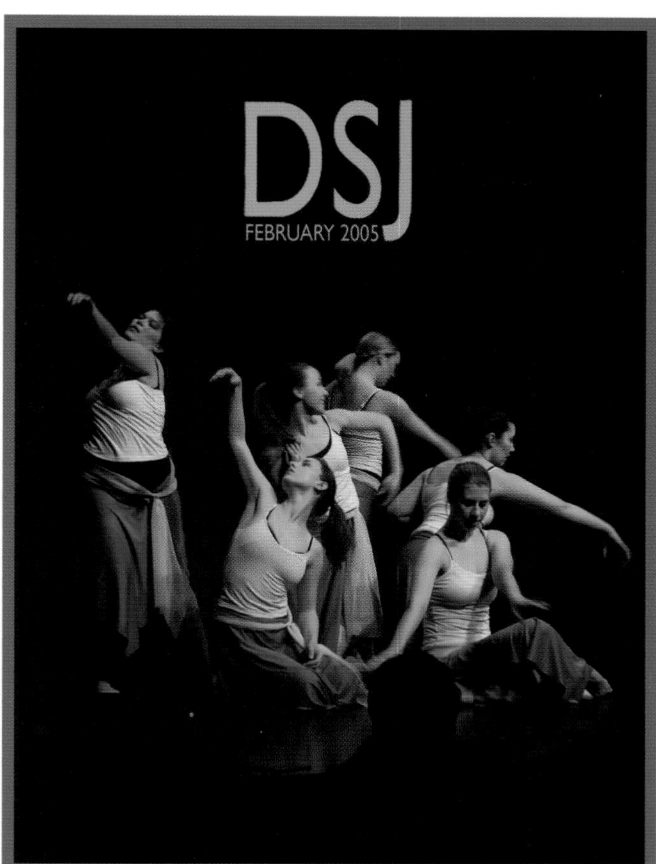

FIGURE 15.5 *The DoG Street Journal* later switched to a monthly news magazine print format. *The DoG Street Journal*, College of William and Mary.

PUBLICITY

When you're ready to publish the first issue, get the word out. Put up fliers and banners announcing the new publication. If your school has a campus radio or TV station, ask them to publicize the new publication. (In fact, you could establish a trade arrangement by which you run ads or a regular guide to their programs and they run public service announcements about your paper.) Staffers advertised the launch of *The DoG Street Journal* at the College of William and Mary, which started as an online newspaper, by donning T-shirts with the paper's launch date.

Social networking sites are a great way to publicize your publication, whether it's print or online. Even before you produce your first issue or post your first material, you can start to build a buzz on Facebook and Twitter. (For more on social media read Chapter 19).

Q&A George Srour

In 2003 George Srour and Dan FitzHenry, two sophomores at the College of William and Mary in Williamsburg, Va. launched *The DoG Street Journal*, an online publication, to compete with *The Flat Hat* (flathatnews.com), the campus weekly. The following semester, the *DSJ* staff began publishing a print edition of the newspaper. In the publication's first two years, more than 100 students contributed to the effort. Srour describes the joys and challenges of starting a new college paper:

Why did you want to start a new campus newspaper?

Originally *The DoG Street Journal* was a joke. A friend of mine and I took an International Relations course together and every week, we'd toss around the idea of starting a new paper because we weren't really happy with the options that existed. Midway through the semester, that joke turned into a real desire to try and build a publication. As freshmen, we figured we had little to lose so we began meeting and started to spell out what we wanted to accomplish and how best to do so.

How did get you the publication together?

We went to friends of ours and just shared with them what we wanted to do. To our more witty friends, we asked if they'd be willing to write a column. To those who loved photography, we asked them to join the photo staff. To those who'd shared stories at some point with us about high school journalism, we asked them to climb aboard too.

What has been very rewarding is to see how many of those people, nearly all, who came out to the first interest meeting we ever had are still actively involved and encouraging others to join in and take a position at the paper.

How did you come up with the name?

The name is derived from Duke of Gloucester Street, the main throughway of Colonial Williamsburg that ends at the tip of the college's campus. Everyone on campus refers to it as "DoG Street," so we thought we'd take it a bit further and have a little fun with a name that everyone on campus could relate to.

How is *The DoG Street Journal* different from *The Flat Hat*?

The main difference is that we're an online daily newspaper, which is what we really wanted to accomplish when we first started. *The Flat Hat* offers a thorough weekly publication, but we felt that the demand and talent were there to come out more often in a format more in tune with what students favor.

Another major element that has set *The DSJ* apart from other publications is that the staff has grasped what I believe is an important aspect of journalism – that of using our media outlet as not only a way to cover the less fortunate around us, but to also do something about it. Be it raising money to replace trees lost to Hurricane Isabel or collecting contributions for the construction of a school in Uganda, our staff tries to unite the community in efforts to benefit those we've written about. I think this has helped define *The DSJ* and those who work for the publication.

***The Dog Street Journal* started as an online newspaper. Why did you start that way? When did you add the print edition?**

Money. After we took some time to look at the costs involved in a print publication, we realized that it would be far easier to start online, and if that met some success, to go ahead and venture into the print edition. When we got started, we didn't have a dime to our name, a computer for ourselves, let alone a place we could meet. Going online made more sense to start.

The print edition came in after our first semester of online publication. Originally it was produced twice a month with plans to increase our frequency. We had to modify our plans because of the resources available to us – an office that can fit three people at one time and just two computers. Coming out more often, and even twice a month, was simply too much of a strain.

That said, our current print edition, a monthly magazine, has been a big hit. We've seen an increased number of advertisers per issue, and more importantly, the readership rates are far higher than they were for the initial publication. I think that's a combination of being around for more than two years now and being able to discern our exact niche in the print world.

How did you publicize the online newspaper?

We had about 25 people when we got started and we had shirts made through an advertiser with our name and our release date and we sent our entire staff out with fliers to post around campus. It was great fun periodically checking the statistics for Web visits because they started on a steep incline, which we still see to this day when school is in session. Once people knew there was a source for news that was as current and up-to-date as *The DSJ*, many people started logging in and checking out the site.

What were some of the greatest challenges you faced in starting *The DoG Street Journal*?

Our venture was a lofty one. We met administrators, students and even close friends who doubted how successful *The DSJ* could be in the face of a publication that's been around campus for nearly 100 years. Over time, however, I think the very same people who voiced some apprehension would agree that *The DSJ* has become a part of the publications scene at the college and is well read. We had to show that we were after something different than any other publication and that we had a solid number of people who wanted to get involved and keep things going.

What kind of reaction did you get?

I have a stash of emails we printed out during our first week online – friends from all over, alumni, random visitors and many others wrote to say how much they enjoyed reading about college and Williamsburg news online. That said, we also got a handful of suggestions that we looked at and were able to make improvements to the site as a result.

How did you finance the publication? What have your greatest costs been?

Initially, everything was financed through ad sales. We had months where we skimped and made it on $20 and $30 to cover the hosting costs, but once we were able to prove ourselves, more ads came in and helped finance purchasing a computer, furnishing an office and other such things. Our greatest costs are really printing costs, which are offset by ad sales. We also receive a subsidy from the college and we're hoping that in two to three years' time, the paper will be fully independent and not reliant on such funds.

What advice do you have for other students who want to launch a new campus newspaper?

Take some time to construct a vision. One of the best things that happened to us was that we took almost a year before our first day online to hash out what exactly we wanted to do, who would be able to help us get there and the most efficient means for starting a publication. Even in the face of doubts, we found old advisers, local people and friends who believe in the vision we constructed and by building *The DSJ* around their words of wisdom and insights, we were able to put together a publication that far exceeded any expectations we ever had.

With print publications don't just drop stacks of your first issue around campus and expect people to pick the paper up. Have staffers pass them out in classes, cafeterias, dorms, the student union and the library. Come up with a catchy slogan and announce it over a megaphone.

Reach out to professors as well as students. Brian Vander Kamp, co-founder and editor-in-chief *of The Flip Side* at the University of Wisconsin-Eau Claire, says, "The first issue we had a handful of professors come over to our table and ask for twenty or thirty copies to take to their classes. One batch I delivered myself and overheard the professor announcing some assignment based on *The Flip Side* for the next class period. Right there, I was able to go back to my room and cross one of my journalism fantasies off my list. It was so great."

TO DO

1. When starting a new newspaper, study what publications already serve your campus, including professional newspapers, faculty newsletters, university magazines and publications put out by your public affairs office. Ask yourself: What's missing? What's not being covered? What could we do better?
2. Study mission statements. To get ideas, browse other student newspapers on the Web. Then assign a group of staffers to write a mission statement for your new newspaper.
3. Create a launch campaign for your publication. Get ideas from marketing professors or marketing students on campus. You might even get a marketing class to take your newspaper on as a project.
4. Create a social media campaign for launching and stimulating interest in your new publication.

TO READ

Ridgley, Stanley K. (editor), *Start the Presses! A Handbook for Student Journalists*. Wilmington, Delaware: Intercollegiate Studies Institute Books, 2000.

TO CLICK

Campus Progress

Campus Progress, the youth division of the Center for American Progress, provides funding, training and editorial guidance to a diverse network of print, online, and broadcast media on college campuses across the country.
http://campusprogress.org

The Collegiate Network

A branch of the Intercollegiate Studies Institute, the Collegiate Network supports conservative college newspapers. The network sponsors training workshops and seminars, paid internships and fellowships and grants for starting new publications.
www.collegiatenetwork.org

NOVEMBER 19, 2009 THURSDAY WWW.KYKERNEL.COM

KENTUCKY KERNEL

CELEBRATING 38 YEARS OF INDEPENDENCE

PHOTO ILLUSTRATION BY ADAM WOLFFBRANDT | STAFF

First issue free. Subsequent issues 25 cents.

Newsroom: 257-1915; Advertising: 257-2872

FIGURE 16.1 Good design uses text, images, headlines and graphics to communicate information effectively, but sometimes a single image will do the trick. When the University of Kentucky implemented a campus-wide ban on smoking the *Kentucky Kernel* devoted the entire front page to a picture of a crushed cigarette butt. *Kentucky Kernel*, University of Kentucky.

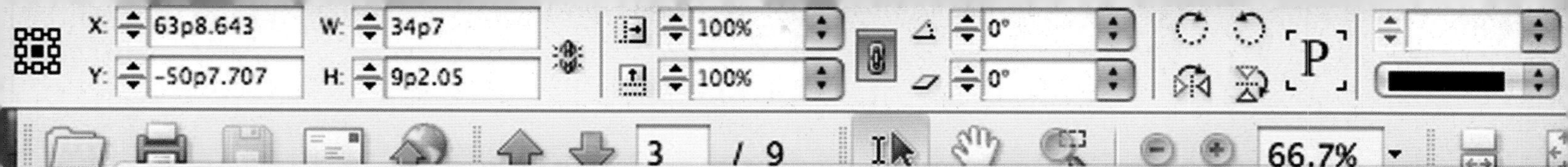

CHAPTER 16 DESIGN AND GRAPHICS

Your staff has produced some great stories and eye-catching photos for this issue. But where are you going to put them on the page? How will you entice readers into each story? In fact, how are you going to get people to pick up the paper at all? The answers to all these questions lie in design.

Newspaper design is about getting people who don't want to read, to read. It's about making text so effortless, so captivating, so compelling, that they can't help themselves.

Newspaper design is governed by a set of basic principles based on studies of how people read type. Once you understand these rules, you can follow them, bend them and even occasionally break them.

The Student Newspaper Survival Guide, Second Edition. Rachele Kanigel.

CHAPTER CONTENTS

CHECKLIST Designing for content

Each time a story is conceived, ask yourself the following questions:

1 What kind of photos would help tell this story – a news photo, a portrait, a detail shot, a scene setter?

2 If no photos are obvious, would a photo illustration be appropriate?

3 Would a map help tell the story?

4 Would a chart help? If so, which kind of chart (pie, line, graph, etc.) would be most effective?

5 Would an information box help? If so, what information should it contain?

6 Would a timeline help readers follow the story? Would a process graphic (one that illustrates how something works) help?

DESIGN IS CONTENT

The first rule of newspaper design is that design should be dictated by content.

Design isn't about making the paper pretty; it's about making it easier to read and easier to navigate. Good design guides the reader through the paper, showing what's important, where to find things, how to make sense of information.

"Design is journalism," says Amy Emmert, a former page designer for the *Orange County Register* who went on to advise the *Daily Bruin* (dailybruin.com) at the University of California, Los Angeles. "Visual choices should be about information, not decoration."

LAYOUT AND DESIGN

Every publication has a "look." That look is consistent day after day, week after week. *The New York Times* is recognizable among all other newspapers on the newsstand. So are *USA Today* and *The Wall Street Journal*. What gives these papers such distinctive appearances is that they follow the same design for every issue. When they want to change the design after a number of years, they go through a redesign process.

For each issue, page designers place the stories, photos and graphics onto pages; this process is known as layout (Figure 16.2). The designers may change the size of the headline or where the photos are placed from issue to issue, but all their decisions follow the basic design of the paper. Typefaces used for headlines and text, the size of margins and the location of certain regular features should all remain consistent, maintaining the basic design scheme of the publication.

PRINCIPLES OF DESIGN

What are the elements of good design?

Balance. Every element on a page has a visual "weight." In general, large objects are "heavier" than small ones, color elements are heavier than black and white. If you put all the pictures at the top of the page, for example, it will look top-heavy. If all the images are on one side of the page, it will look lopsided. A well-designed page is balanced horizontally and vertically.

Consistency. Consistent design helps build trust and loyalty among readers. They know where to find what they're looking for and what certain things mean. To maintain consistency, use the same margins, fonts and color scheme throughout the paper (Figure 16.3).

Elements of a Front Page

Monday, March 8, 2003

INDIANA DAILY STUDENT

OPHELIA REVIVED
Creator of National Ophelia Project speaks at Saturday conference

OUT ON A LOSS
Wisconsin repeated its dominance of IU during Saturday's defeat.

D'OH!
Simpsons producer gives IU students behind-the-scenes look at series

WEATHER
45
34

Volume 137 • Issue 11

www.idsnews.com

16 pages • Free

Court to hear appeal late Tuesday

■ Decision might end up tied because 1 justice studying abroad

By Mallory Simon

RHA ELECTIONS

Final RHA election results

A tough goodbye

Voters choose to 'Connect' in RHA

■ Ticket sweeps Amplify after Eigenmann re-vote

By Michael Zennie

■ 2 seniors lead scoring, bid farewell to Hoosier fans in last home game of careers

By Natalie A. Trout

Amplify wins 3 of 6 elections complaints

■ Loophole allows disqualified VP-elect's reappointment

By Michael Zennie

"The problem with RHA elections is that there is no universal policy."

Target holds grand opening at College Mall location

■ New larger store features groceries, Pizza Hut, Starbucks

By Melanie Knapp

ids

Flag
The name of the newspaper, usually set in a distinctive type. Also known as **nameplate**.

Headline
The title of the story set in large type above or next to the text.

Display head
A fancy headline that uses special fonts or graphic treatment to highlight a story.

Cutline
A line of text describing or explaining a photograph or illustration. Also known as **caption.**

Cutout
A photo in which part of the background has been cut out. Also called a **silhouette.**

Logo
A graphic symbol used to label stories in a series or about a certain topic.

Refer
A reference to a related story in another part of the paper or on the Web.

Deck
A smaller headline, usually under the main headline, that gives more information about the story.

Photo credit
The photographer's name.

Teasers
Text and images used to promote stories inside the paper. Also known as **promos** or **skyboxes.**

Standing head
A label used for recurrent features or stories on a certain topic.

Infographic
A chart, map or graphic that conveys information in a graphic way.

Byline
The writer's name, sometimes followed by title. Some newspapers print the writer's email address under the byline.

Jump line
A line directing the reader to the page the story continues on.

Pull quote
A quotation from the story pulled out and set in large type for emphasis. Also known as **liftout quote** or **breakout.**

Sidebar
A short, related story that is packaged with the main story.

Index
A table of contents for the newspaper.

FIGURE 16.2 Elements of a page. *Indiana Daily Student*, Indiana University. Graphic by Eugenia Chien.

Contrast. While you want to maintain consistency, you don't want to be boring. You can make a page visually interesting by varying shapes, colors and sizes. The key is to provide just enough contrast that a page is interesting without looking cluttered or confusing.

Visual hierarchy. A well-designed page tells the reader what's most important by putting key elements in the most visible positions. Stories with the greatest news value should be at the top of the page and have the largest headlines. As the reader reads down the page, the

Just as a logo gives a product, company or service an identity, the identity of a newspaper begins with its nameplate. It continues into standing heads at the top of each section and even into column heads such as "Letters to the Editor" and "News Briefs." This consistency ensures that readers will know what publication they are reading without even seeing the nameplate. Such consistency also helps establish brand loyalty.

Daily News (Ball State University, Muncie, Ind.; Justin Hesser, editor; Vince Filak, adviser)

The Shorthorn (University of Texas at Arlington; Amber Tafoya, editor; Lloyd Goodman, adviser)

Technician (North Carolina State University, Raleigh, N.C.; Rebecca Heslin, editor; Bradley Wilson, adviser)

FIGURE 16.3 Design consistency. Graphic by Bradley Wilson. (Images from *The Ball State Daily News* (Ball State University, Muncie, Ind.; Justin Hesser, editor; Vince Filak, adviser); *The Shorthorn* (University of Texas at Arlington; Amber Tafoya, editor; Lloyd Goodman, adviser); *Technician* (North Carolina State University, Raleigh, N.C.; Rebecca Heslin, editor; Bradley Wilson, adviser).

headlines should become smaller, indicating that the stories are less important.

Simplicity. Simplicity in page design means fewer elements and more white space. Pages should be functional and uncluttered.

TYPOGRAPHY

Ever since Johannes Gutenberg started printing Bibles in the 15th century, people have been playing with type. They've scrunched it, stretched it, curled it and twirled it, all with the hope of making the 26 letters of the alphabet more interesting or fun to read.

But as a newspaper person you have to remember that the primary function of type is to make reading easy. Type should be clear and legible. It may look cool to use funky typefaces or run words up one side of the page or run pink text on a black background, but if people can't read the text, you've failed.

Type has its own language. Here's a typography vocabulary that will help you talk about type (Figure 16.4):

- **Typeface, or font**–a set of characters (letters, numbers and punctuation marks) in one size, style and weight (such as lightface, heavy, extra bold).
- **Font family**–a group of related fonts with a variety of weights (lightface, regular, boldface) and styles (roman, italic, condensed).
- **Serif type**–a font with tiny strokes, or serifs, at the tips of each letter. Most body text is set in serif type.

TIPSHEET
Good page design

1 **Select a dominant visual element for each page.** The lead art should be at least twice as big as any other visual element on the page.

2 **Divide the page into rectangles.** Each story, including art, should fit into a rectangle.

3 **Shoot for a 2:1 text-to-art ratio.** That means each page should be about one-third art.

4 **Think in terms of packaging.** Group related stories together.

5 **Try to have a visual element for each story.** If you don't have a photo or infographic for a story, use an infobox or pull quotes to break up text and create another point of entry.

6 **Avoid jumps as much as possible.** When you do jump, run at least 4 inches of the story before the jump line and at least 6 inches after jumping. Don't jump a story more than once.

7 **Use graphics to explain complicated information.** Even if you don't have a gifted graphic artist on staff, you can use maps and simple charts to convey information visually.

Sans serif type–a font without serifs. Sans serif type is slightly harder to read than serif type, so newspapers generally use sans serif fonts for larger type, such as headlines, reverse type (white type on a black or colored background) or small blocks of type, like photo captions.

Type size–all type is measured two ways. The face of each letter is measured vertically in points, with 72 points to the inch. The width of a line of type is measured horizontally in picas, with 6 picas equal to 1 inch. So a headline set in 72-point type across an 18-pica column would be one inch high and 3 inches wide.

Leading–the space between the lines of type. Body text is generally set with 2 points of leading.

Body type–small type, usually 12 points or smaller, used for text.

Display type–large type, usually 14 points and larger, used for display information, such as headlines.

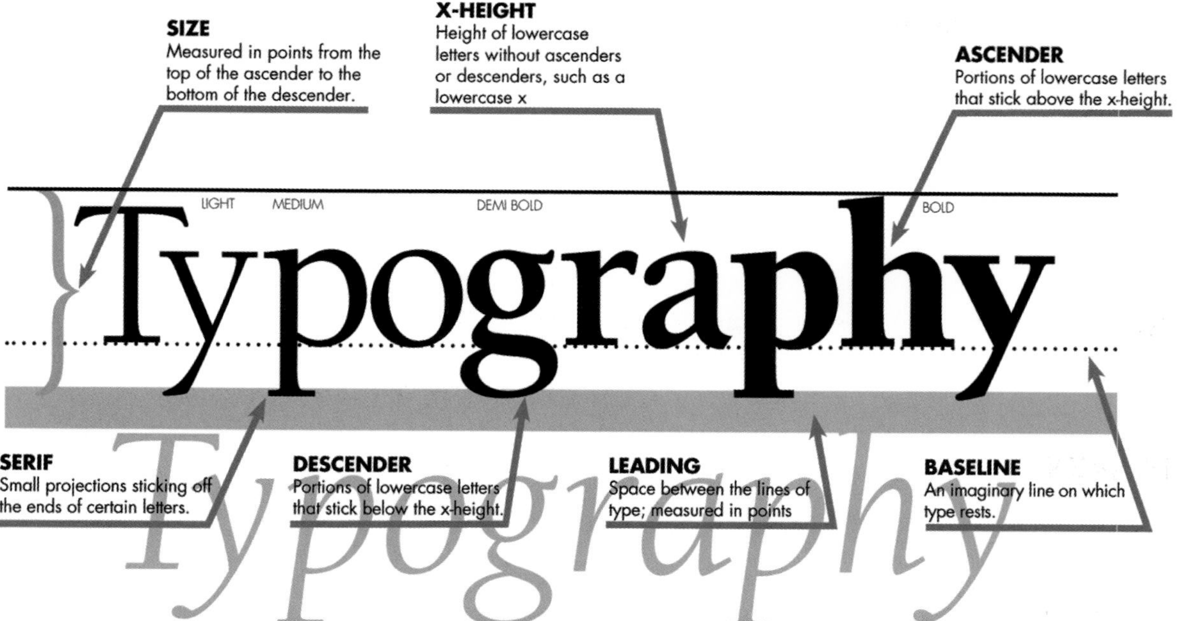

FIGURE 16.4 Type vocabulary. Typography, the study of type, is a field with its own unique vocabulary. Understanding this vocabulary makes it easier to communicate expectations to designers. Graphic by Bradley Wilson.

Agate type–the smallest point size type (usually 5 or 6 points) that can be read, often used for sports scores and stock quotes.

Alignment–the way type starts and ends on a line. Left aligned means the type starts on the left margin and ends in an uneven arrangement on the right. Centered type is set to the middle of the line. Justified type lines up on both the left and right edges. Computers can force justify a line of type by adding spaces between words or letters.

THE BUILDING BLOCKS OF A PAGE

Every newspaper page is made up of four basic building blocks:

Headlines–the oversized type that labels each story

Body text–the stories themselves

Images–graphics or photos that complement the stories

White space–the space around the text, headlines and images.

Let's examine each of these building blocks in more detail.

Headlines

As we discussed in Chapter 10, headlines are designed to grab the readers' attention and give them a sense of what the story is about. They also help organize the page and anchor each story.

Headlines are written in larger type than the stories themselves. The general rule is the more important the story, the larger the headline. And since the most important stories generally run at the top of the page, headlines usually get smaller as you move down the page.

Small headlines range from 12 to 24 points, midsize headlines from 24 to 48 points and large headlines are above 48 points.

Many papers also include a deck under the headline. This smaller headline generally has more words than a main headline and can offer a more complete explanation of the story.

Body text

Body text in newspapers is generally 9 or 10 points and set in columns.

Text is hard to read if it's set in columns narrower than 10 picas or wider than 18 picas; most newspapers set columns at 12 to 15 picas across.

Long columns of type also tire the reader. The best depth for text is between 2 and 10 inches per leg of type.

Images

Newspapers use art – photos, graphics and illustrations – to break up columns of type and help tell stories in a visual way. Photographs provide emotional depth; graphics explain complicated concepts. These visual elements also serve as a nice contrast for the eye to long columns of gray type.

Each page should have one dominant piece of art – a single large photo or graphic. The dominant art should be at least twice as large as any other piece of art on the page.

White space

What's left? White space. These empty areas give readers a break. But white space isn't just space that's left over after all the other elements are put on a page. It should be planned like any other element on a page. White space should be treated like a visual element in itself.

White space is best used in the corners or outer areas of a page. Large areas of white space in the middle of a page can get "trapped" and distract readers from other elements – like body text, photos and headlines.

Like other elements of a page, white space should be consistent throughout your paper. Gutters, the vertical spaces between columns, should be the same size, usually about 1 pica, unless you're using a special design treatment.

MODULAR DESIGN

If you look at a newspaper from 50 or 100 years ago, you'll see a clutter of stories and photos. You'll have a hard time figuring out what's most important or where you should look first.

The 1970s and '80s ushered in a new style of newspaper design, one marked by simplicity and organization. One of the most important results of this revolution was the development of modular layouts.

In modular design (Figure 16.5), each element – photo, headline, cutline, body copy – is treated as a rectangular building block. These blocks are then packaged together to form larger rectangles.

Modular design makes a paper easier to read and navigate. It helps readers know which photos, stories, sidebars and infoboxes go together and where to find the next column of type.

MULTIPLE POINTS OF ENTRY

To attract readers to a story, newspapers increasingly rely on multiple points of entry – different doors readers can use to enter a story. Some readers, for example, might enter a story through a headline; others might be attracted by a photo, while someone else might start by looking at a graphic (Figure 16.6).

Designers have a number of tools to help create multiple points of entry. Among them:

Information boxes, or infoboxes, summarize information such as key points of a story, details of an upcoming event, actions at a meeting, biographical details about a key person in a story.

In each of these modular units, the headline covers the entire module, captions touch the photos; the upper left corner of the story touches the headline; copy blocks form L shapes, U shapes or rectangular blocks; and white space is to the outside. With consistent internal spacing (1 pica), the reader will perceive each of these units as a package of related elements. And in no case does the reader have to jump over any elements.

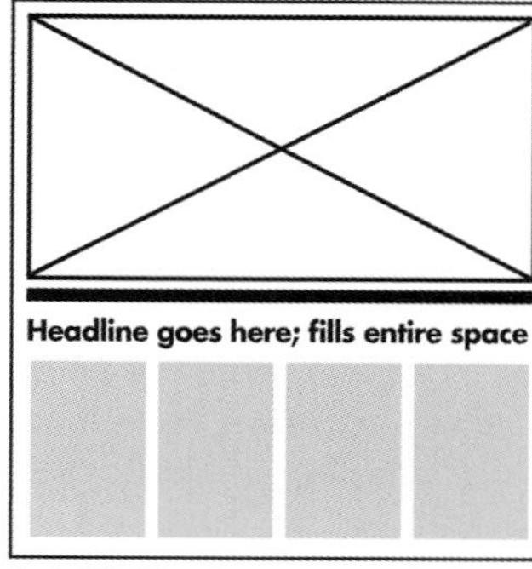

Vertical Module • photo (on top), caption, headline, story

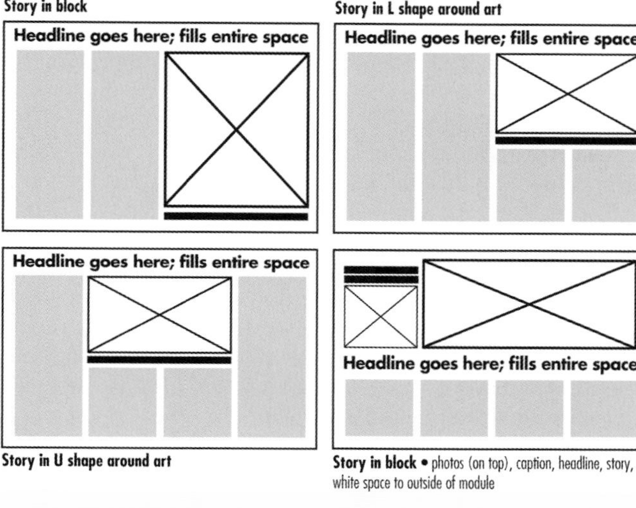

FIGURE 16.5 Modular Design. Graphic by Bradley Wilson.

CYAN MAGENTA YELLOW BLACK

Friday, March 25, 2005

INDIANA DAILY STUDENT

TURKISH DELIGHT Ballantine Hall to play host to 2 weekends of Turkish film

RE-CYCLING The 55th Little 500 season officially begins Saturday with qualifications

MR. AND MISS ASIA Candidates strut their stuff this weekend at Buskirk-Chumley Theater

WEATHER 52 38

Volume 138 • Issue 16 www.idsnews.com 16 pages • Free

Fife named new IPFW head coach

■ Former player, current assistant will be youngest in Division I basketball at age 25

By John Rodgers

'Game' over for local promoters

■ Canceled rap concert coinciding with Little 500 sparks skepticism

By Rick Newkirk and Adam VanOsdol

DECLARING A RIGHT-TO-DIE

Indiana citizens can fill out an Indiana Living Will Declaration and must check one of the three options below:

Matters of life and death

■ A living will may enable loved ones to make medical decisions for incapacitated patients

By David A. Nesko

■ Schiavo's parents all but run out of options for dying daughter after Supreme Court rejection

By Jill Barton

Students descend on campus to celebrate Masti 2005

■ Annual event to promote awareness of southern Asia's culture

By Daria Kamalipour

CORRECTION

FIGURE 16.6 Information boxes, graphics, decks, photos and teasers give readers multiple points of entry to stories on this page. *Indiana Daily Student*, Indiana University.

Refers guide readers to a related story or stories on a different page or on the Web.

Information graphics, such as pie charts, bar graphs and maps, help explain the story in a visual way.

Pull quotes, also known as pullout quotes and liftout quotes, are quotations from the story that are set in larger type to attract readers to the story.

THE DESIGNER'S TOOLBOX

Your design kit should also include tools to make pages easier to read and visually attractive. Among them:

Subheads are bolder than regular type and are used to break up long stories. In general, they're set every eight to 10 inches, usually where there's a shift in topic.

Rules are lines that are used to isolate or organize elements on a page. Rules can be used to create boxes, separate stories or indicate which elements go together, such as which story goes with which photo.

Screens are background tints, either in gray or a color, that can be used to add contrast to a page. They're particularly effective for highlighting sidebars and infoboxes, but they should be used sparingly. Screens should be light – no more than 10 percent or 20 percent – and you may want to use slightly larger or bold text to compensate for reduced legibility.

BROADSHEETS AND TABLOIDS

Newspapers come in two formats: broadsheets and tabloids. Broadsheets are full-size papers, usually about 22 inches long and 12 to 13 inches wide. Tabloids are roughly half that, 11 inches wide by 13 to 15 inches deep. Broadsheets generally run five or six columns across; tabloids generally have four or five.

In a 1999 study of more than 250 American college newspapers, researchers Lillian Lodge Kopenhaver and

Ronald E. Spielberger found that nearly two-thirds of college and university newspapers were tabloids. In Canada, the vast majority of college newspapers are tabs.

Tabloids tend to be easier to design, because they offer fewer options and generally include fewer stories on a page. Because of their smaller size they're handier for students to read on a bus or at a desk. They're also thicker; a 16-page tabloid becomes an 8-page broadsheet, which might strike some readers as thin.

Broadsheets offer the advantage of greater flexibility and some think they look more like professional dailies. In addition, broadsheet newspapers can generally charge more for a full-page advertisement because the format is larger and that can help bring in more revenue.

Some newspapers offer a mix of formats. *The Exponent* (purdueexponent.org), the newspaper at Purdue University in Indiana, for example, publishes a broadsheet five days a week during the school year and a tabloid three days a week during the summer months.

THE ROLE OF DESIGNERS

At many college newspapers (and even some professional papers), the work of the designer doesn't begin until after the stories are written and the photos are shot. This is a mistake. Designers need to be part of the planning process from the beginning. Design shouldn't be the last consideration at a newspaper; it should be among the first.

Amy Emmert, the *Daily Bruin* adviser, challenges student newspapers to ask themselves these questions.

- Do designers and/or design editors have a voice in planning coverage?
- Do they attend budget meetings?
- Do they read stories and regularly contribute their own ideas about story quality, placement, photography, etc.?
- Do your designers consider themselves to be journalists?

If the answer to any of these questions is no, you're underutilizing some of your greatest resources.

Emmert says designers must think of themselves as journalists – and everyone else in the newsroom should too.

STYLE GUIDES

Designing a single newspaper page from scratch can take hours – or even days. Each page involves an infinite number of decisions, from the size and font of the headlines to the placement of the stories to the size of the rule under the flag.

That's why newspaper designers generally work from a style guide. Ron Reason, a Chicago-based designer, educator and consultant, says any newsroom larger than two people should have at least a basic design stylebook. "It will reduce questions of style relating to your design and production for newcomers and old-timers alike and reduce inconsistencies in the paper. A stylebook will also allow your staff to focus on more important issues, like writing better headlines, selecting and cropping better photos, and originating better ideas for illustrations and graphics."

MODELS

Nearly every designer interviewed for this book had the same advice for student designers: Learn from other publications. When you find a newspaper you like, try

TIPSHEET
Creating a design style guide

Every newsroom should have a design style guide – a manual that sets in place the rules and policies of how the newspaper is produced. This may be packaged with an editorial stylebook or exist as a separate document.

A design style guide typically has the following elements:

An index. This makes it easy to find things.

A statement of philosophy. What is the design of the paper trying to do?

A font palette. Most newspapers have one font for text, one or two others for headlines. You may choose one other typeface for special touches, such as logos and section flags. Some newspapers also select a separate font for special text, such as sidebars, graphics, jump lines and cutlines.

A graphics policy. This should explain how graphics get done at your paper and lay down the rules for type fonts and sizes for infographics and other graphical elements. This section should include a copy of your graphics request form, the document you use to assign infographics.

A photo section. This should include policies on cropping, cutlines, running text over photos and other issues related to photography. This section may include your photo ethics policy and a photo request form.

Numbers confuse and scare away readers. But a simple graph can show a trend in a way that number embedded in a story can't.

- A bar chart shows the relationship between items with differences conveyed by the height, color and/or shade of the bar. They can also display trends such as the increase in enrollment.
- A pie chart divides a "whole" into "parts" such as the university into colleges. Even without the numbers present, a reader can determine what is the largest piece of the pie.
- A line graph is a quick way to display a trend usually with time on the horizontal axis.
- A chart displays the data and leaves it up to the reader to identify the trends.
- Identify the source of all data.

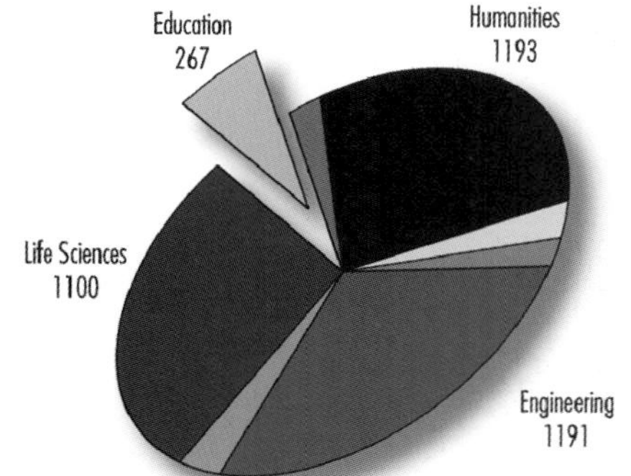

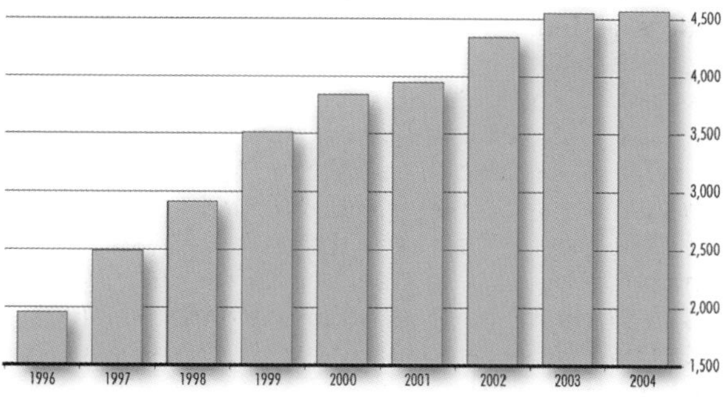

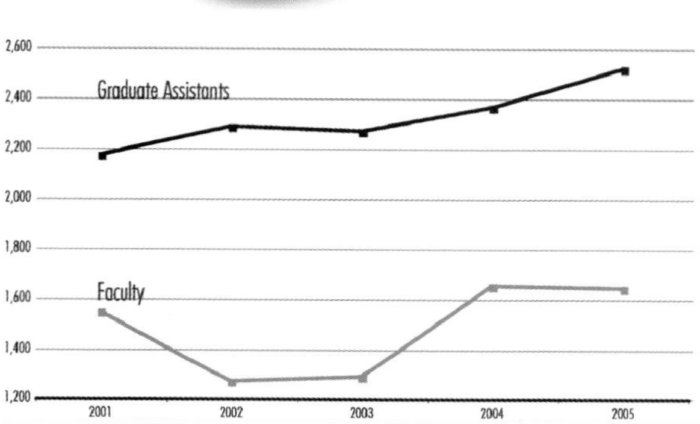

STUDENT STATISTICS	2005	2004	2003	2002	2001
1. Total Headcount Enrollment	30,149	29,957	29,854	29,637	29,286
2. Total Undergraduate Enrollment	22,879	22,754	22,971	22,780	22,418
3. Total Graduate Enrollment	7,270	7,203	6,883	6,857	6,868
4. Female Percent of Enrollment	43.5	43.2	43.3	42.8	42.7
5. In-State Percent of Enrollment	86.4	86.8	87.1	87.0	86.3
6. Black Percent of Enrollment	9.1	9.7	9.8	9.7	9.7
7. Number of Entering Freshmen	4,253	3,847	3,851	3,628	3,831
8. New Freshman Average SAT	1186	1192	1195	1193	1175

FIGURE 16.7 Graphs and charts. Graphic by Bradley Wilson.

writing a style sheet for that newspaper. Then, modify the style sheet for your particular publication. You can add, subtract or modify elements that you think will give your paper a distinctive look that reflects something about your campus. And while everyone should look at mainstream daily newspapers, don't stop there.

Tim Harrower, a newspaper design consultant and author of *The Newspaper Designer's Handbook* (McGraw-Hill, 2007) (a must-buy for newspaper designers), says too many college newspapers "have the same bland personality as the big dull daily down the street. You have to update your design vocabulary so that you're as modern looking as the publications you yourself read."

Alternative weeklies, magazines and foreign newspapers can be excellent sources for design ideas, Harrower says.

DRAWING A DUMMY

While most newspaper pages are put together on computers using page layout programs such as Quark XPress or Adobe InDesign, designers usually start on paper with a dummy, or sketch. Dummy sheets are grids that represent newspaper columns. They are generally smaller than the actual paper but proportional.

Dummying saves time and helps you see your mistakes before they get into print. By drawing a sketch you can figure out in advance what kind of headline you'll need, how photos should be sized and cropped and whether you need more information for an information box. A dummy can save you hours of computer time. While moving an element on a computer can mean major rearrangement and take lots of time, a dummy can be changed with the stroke of an eraser.

INFOGRAPHICS

Increasingly, newspapers use graphics to visually explain information; these are called information graphics, or infographics for short. Pie charts, maps, bar charts and diagrams are all examples of infographics (Figure 16.7).

Infographics help readers process complex or hard-to-understand information, such as statistics, geography and dollar amounts. A locator map, for example, can show where a fire happened and put the event into context. A pie chart can quickly show readers what proportion of their tuition goes toward faculty salaries, facilities and other expenses. An explanatory graphic (Figure 16.8) can show a process or explain how something works.

Certain types of information are best conveyed with particular sorts of infographics.

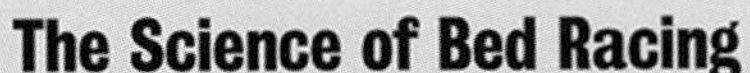

The Science of Bed Racing

It's time for the annual Bed Races and with a wealth of physics and engineering knowledge on campus, racers may benefit from a few tips for maximum speed.

According to Robert Bruntz, lab manager and physics research scientist, there are three main areas of concern for racers who want to achieve lightning speed: mass, friction and force.

Bruntz also said that pushing in a line as straight as possible will help to maintain forward momentum.

"They don't have any aerodynamic issues because they won't be going fast enough for it to matter," said Lena Gerry, mechanical and aerospace engineering freshman and Formula SAE team member.

— *Justin Sharp*

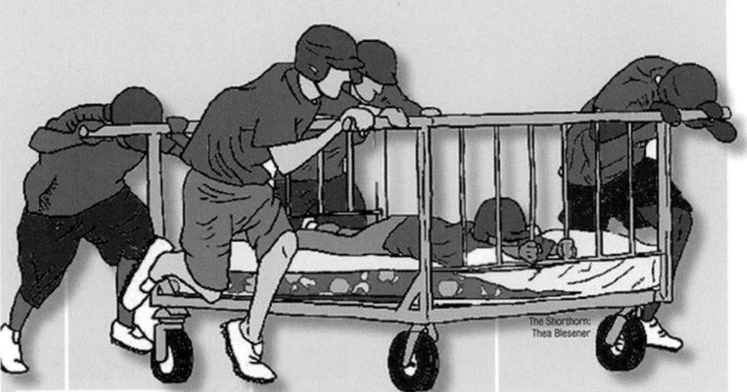

Pushing: Keep handlebars parallel to shoulders. Lena Gerry, mechanical and aerospace engineering freshman and Formula SAE team member, said having the bars at a pusher's shoulder height prevents energy from being lost in upward or downward force.

Friction: Wear shoes with deep treads for maximum purchase on the surface of the field. Physics doctorate student Elizabeth Mitchell said good shoes will allow more force to move the bed.

Mass of the bed and rider: You want to put the smallest person on the bed because greater mass requires greater energy to move it, said Robert Bruntz, lab manager and physics research scientist. Find the strongest, fittest people to use as pushers. The amount of force applied to the bed in acceleration and maintenance of speed will likely be the deciding factor, he said.

FIGURE 16.8 Explanatory graphics explain how something is done. *The Shorthorn* created this graphic to explain the science of bed racing for the annual campus bed race. *The Shorthorn*, University of Texas at Arlington. Text by Justin Sharp, graphic by Thea Blesener. Reprinted with permission.

CHECKLIST
Page layout

1. Is the file name of the page correct (according to the conventions of your newspaper)?
2. Are the date and page numbers correct in the folio?
3. Do continued stories jump to the correct page?
4. Does the text of jumped stories flow correctly (no words repeated or missing)?
5. Do you have one dominant piece of art? Is it at least twice as large as other photos or graphics?
6. Do the numbers in infographics and breakout boxes make sense?
7. Does the page correspond to the story budget? Are you missing any stories, photos, graphics, infoboxes or other elements?
8. Do all stories have bylines? Are names and titles correct?
9. Do all photos have cutlines and credit lines?
10. Are the headlines correct? Do any of the headlines repeat major words?
11. Do the refers direct readers to the correct page?
12. Are the photos cropped correctly? Does the image fill the frame?
13. Do all elements – headlines, body text, cutlines, bylines and photo credit lines – adhere to your design style guide?

CASE STUDY Anatomy of a newspaper redesign

In 2003, the staff of *The Harvard Crimson* (thecrimson.com) decided to add color to the newspaper, which – despite its name – had been black and white for 130 years. The staff commissioned Ron Reason of Garcia Media, the design firm that helped bring color to *The Wall Street Journal,* to redesign the entire newspaper. (See Figure 16.9 for the *before* version and Figure 16.10 for the *after* version.)

In addition to creating nearly 100 prototype pages for the consideration of the editors, Reason presented a number of formal and informal training sessions to bring the staff up-to-date on modern editing, planning and visualizing techniques.

"Ron left *The Crimson* with more than just a new style – he spread the Gospel of Visual Thinking," Michael Conti, one of the paper's design chairs, wrote in a column for the newspaper on the redesign. "From the early stages of a story, reporters, photographers and designers have started working together to display our content in a fashion that is both exciting and easily accessible to our readers. The results have been absolutely astounding.

FIGURE 16.9 Before undergoing a redesign in 2003, *The Harvard Crimson* relied primarily on headlines, text and photos to tell its stories. *The Harvard Crimson*, Harvard University.

FIGURE 16.10 The redesigned *Harvard Crimson* uses infographics, story labels for recurring topics and front-page teasers to lure readers into stories and guide them to information. *The Harvard Crimson*, Harvard University.

'Visual thinking' has become the catchphrase of *The Harvard Crimson*."

The redesign brought together a nice mix of the old and new, Conti says.

"In terms of its design, *The Crimson* has always been relatively conservative. With our redesign, we were looking to maintain some degree of conservatism, while introducing some important modern design elements."

A big priority was making the content more accessible to readers. The old *Crimson* relied simply on headlines, pictures and text to tell its stories. With the redesign, the paper added new elements, such as infographics, story labels for recurring topics and front-page teasers and an index to guide readers to inside stories and sections.

"We wanted to give our readers more entry points to our content, so that when they scanned the pages important information would jump out at them and pull them into the stories," Conti says.

Reaction to the redesign was overwhelmingly positive. In fact, the paper won two design awards from Associated Collegiate Press in 2004.

Conti offers this advice to other student papers undertaking a redesign: "Take your redesign very seriously and give a lot of thought to every change you make. The smallest details, from colors to fonts, can make or break a page design. Most importantly, think about your changes from the perspective of your readers; the goal of any redesign should be to make content more attractive and accessible to the reader."

Q&A Emmet Smith

As a designer at *The Ball State Daily News* (bsudailynews.com) at Ball State University in Muncie, Ind., Emmet Smith won design awards from the Society for News Design, Indiana Collegiate Press Association and the Columbia Scholastic Press Association. In 2002 he was named the College Designer of the Year by the University of Missouri's student chapter of the Society for News Design. Smith, who also served as editor-in-chief of *The Ball State Daily News*, graduated with a bachelor's degree in journalism in 2003. After interning at *The Virginian-Pilot* and the *Detroit Free Press*, he got a job as a designer at *The Plain Dealer* in Cleveland, Ohio, where he later became the deputy design director.

What do you see as the role of design at a college newspaper? Is it any different from the professional world?

The question I always struggled with as a student was 'What is the role of a campus paper?' Is it the same as a professional paper, that is, to deliver the news best suited to the readership in the form best suited to the readership? Or is it to give student journalists practice writing, reporting, editing and designing as they will in the 'real world'? Those are two different audiences we're talking about – the 18- to 24-year-old college audience and your average newspaper editor.

In my mind, college journalists should be crafting their papers for their readers, not their future employers. With that attitude, it's evident that shorter stories, use of infographics, breakouts, alternate story forms and all of the things that design can lead the way on are integral to the fabric of what a college newspaper should be.

How can students with little design experience put out attractive, visually compelling newspapers? What can designers do to encourage people on campus to pick up their paper?

That's easy. Hire someone to set up a solid, clean base design for you and follow their rules. There are a ton of people that can do this affordably; you don't need Mario Garcia. Look at good design; the Society for News Design annuals are a great place to start. Edit well, write smart headlines. Someone (who?) once said that a great headline

Christmas Past

The history and evolution of the holidays

Big, bad snowmen and the island of misfit toys; our fascination with claymation

Six

From Saint Nick to shopping malls; how Santa Claus has changed over the years

Eight

FIGURE 16.11 Emmet Smith designed the cover of this holiday supplement for *The Ball State Daily News*. Design by Emmet Smith, *The Ball State Daily News*, Ball State University.

set in Cooper Black looks a million times better than even a mediocre one set in a beautiful face. Use photography well. Great pictures can make or break a page. And above all, keep it simple. Make everything earn its way onto the page.

What are some of the challenges you faced as a student designer?
Resources and time are the two great scarcities in college journalism. Your paper has no money and not nearly enough staff. What do you do? Work all the time, which is rough because there are classes, not to mention the rest of life. Plus, the entire staff is learning. They're going to come up short and make mistakes, even when all of the things necessary for success are there.

What were some of your greatest accomplishments as a student designer?
Our greatest accomplishments were the days when you couldn't tell that we were a college paper, or better yet, that you could because we took a risk that no professional paper would and pulled it off.

What do you wish you had known about design when you were in college?
That there are a million approaches and the only right one is the one that works for your readers. Not everyone can or should be *The Washington Post, San Jose Mercury News, The Hartford Courant, The Virginian-Pilot*, etc. Stop emulating and start looking for the things that work for you.

What other advice do you have for student designers?
Look at professional newspapers as much as possible, talk to as many people as possible. Develop relationships with professionals who could become mentors and advocates. Try things, be crazy. You've gotta go there to come back. And besides, it all ends up in the trash the next day.

- **Line charts**, or fever charts, show how quantities change over time. These are useful in showing a trend, such as falling numbers of foreign students or rising tuition rates.
- **Bar charts** use horizontal rectangles to represent amounts, while column charts use vertical rectangles to represent figures. These are best used to compare two or more items, such as student fees for last year compared to student fees for this year.
- **Pie charts** allow readers to compare the parts that make up a whole, such as the percentages of students from different ethnic groups on your campus.
- **Timelines** are great for showing a chronology, such as the major events in the tenure of a university president or the life of a school.
- **Diagrams** illustrate how things work or explain a process.
- **Maps** show readers where events have taken place and may offer context.

TO DO

1. Invite a professional newspaper designer to critique your paper. Ask for specific suggestions on how to make the paper more visually effective. The Society for News Design has a database of speakers that allows you to search by state and topic (typography, ad design, redesign, etc.). See the website listed below.
2. If you don't already have one, create a design style guide for your newspaper following the steps listed in this chapter.
3. Send a delegation from your staff to visit the design department of your local or regional newspaper.

Steps to designing a page

STEP 1. Assemble and measure the elements of your page. That includes text, headlines, photos, cutlines, information boxes and graphics. Decide which elements are related and how to group them.

STEP 2. Rank your stories. Generally, the editors will decide the lead story, and sometimes the secondary story for each page. If there are other stories for the page, rank them, considering their importance and reader appeal.

STEP 3. Select the dominant art. It may be a photo or an infographic, but you must have one dominant image for each page. "You need something to draw your reader in," says Matt Garton, a designer at the *Cleveland Plain Dealer* who got his start at the *Oregon Daily Emerald* as a student at the University of Oregon. "You are establishing a hierarchy on your page. Lead art tells them where to start."

STEP 4. Place the dominant image on the upper half of the page. It may be in the middle or to one side. The dominant photo will usually run at least three columns if it is a vertical shot and four columns if it is a horizontal shot.

STEP 5. Select and place your secondary visual element. Be sure to vary the sizes and shapes of your photos and graphics. If your dominant photo is a large horizontal photo, try to use at least one vertical shot on the page. The dominant image should be at least twice the size of any other visual element on the page.

STEP 6. Place your lead story. The lead story may or may not correspond to the lead art. Lead stories are generally placed across the top of the page or down the right-hand column, but some papers run them down the left side. Give your lead story the largest headline. Package the story, headline and accompanying elements (photos, graphics, cutlines, info boxes) into a rectangle.

STEP 7. Build more rectangles out of the other stories and photos. Remember that your most important stories should go on the top half of the page and have the largest headlines. Don't forget to leave room for cutlines, jump lines, photo credits and other necessities.

Ask if you can sit in on a planning meeting. And don't just send designers. Invite at least one reporter, photographer and editor so they can see how the design process works, too.

4 Arrange a one- or two-day design workshop for your staff. Invite designers to lead sessions and allow time for group discussions about how you want your paper to look.

5 Create a design library for your newspaper. It should include a wide range of newspapers and magazines as well as books on design, and design annuals from the Society of News Design and the Best of Collegiate Design series.

6 Send a delegation of students to attend a design seminar sponsored by the Society for News Design, the Poynter Institute, the Society of Publication Designers or your state newspaper association. Most groups list training opportunities on their websites.

TO READ

Ames, Steven E. *Elements of Newspaper Design.* New York, N.Y.: Praeger, 1989.

Berry, John D. *Contemporary Newspaper Design: Shaping the News in the Digital Age: Typography and Image on Modern Newsprint.* West New York, N.J.: Mark Batty Publisher, 2004.

Bohle, Robert H. *Publication Design for Editors.* Englewood Cliffs, N.J.: Prentice-Hall, 1990.

Conover, Charles. *Designing for Print: An In-Depth Guide to Planning, Creating, and Producing Successful Design Projects.* New York, N.Y.: Wiley, 2003.

Garcia, Mario R. *Contemporary Newspaper Design: A Structural Approach, 2nd ed.* Englewood Cliffs, N.J.: Prentice-Hall, 1987.

Graham, Lisa. *Basics of Design: Layout and Typography for Beginners.* New York, N.Y.: Thomson Delmar Learning, 2001.

Harrower, Tim. *The Newspaper Designer's Handbook, 6th ed.* New York, N.Y.: McGraw-Hill College, 2007.

Moen, Daryl. *Newspaper Layout and Design: A Team Approach, 4th ed.* Ames, Iowa: Iowa State University Press, 2000.

The Society for News Design. *The Best of Newspaper Design.* Gloucester, Mass.: Rockport Publishers, Inc. (annual)

White, Jan V. *Editing by Design: For Designers, Art Directors, and Editors: The Classic Guide to Winning Readers, 3rd ed.* New York, N.Y.: Allworth Press, 2003.

Williams, Robin. *The Non-Designer's Design Book: Design and Typographic Principles for the Visual Novice, 3rd ed.*, edited by Nancy Davis. Berkeley, Calif.: Peachpit Press, 2008.

TO CLICK

College Front Page

Although this site is no longer being updated, it still has some good examples and interesting columns about college newspaper design.

www.collegefrontpage.com

Design with Reason

News design consultant Ron Reason writes an interesting blog about news design and visual thinking.

www.ronreason.com

The Edmund C Arnold Chapter of the Society for News Design at Michigan State University

MSU/SND, the student affiliate at Michigan State University in East Lansing, sponsors the Michigan State University Design Contest for College Students.

http://msusnd.org

The Society for News Design

The leading membership association for news designers has a great website and sponsors training workshops and competitions. The SND Foundation sponsors scholarships for students and grants that help students attend the annual national workshop and exhibition.

www.snd.org

The Society of Publication Designers

The website of this membership organization for publication designers includes a job board, several blogs about publication design and a special section for students.

www.spd.org

Student Society for News Design

The University of Missouri-Columbia Chapter of this national organization sponsors an annual College News Design Contest.

http://ssnd.wordpress.com

Today's Front Pages

This online gallery of front pages from more than 800 newspapers worldwide is a great resource for designers looking for inspiration.

http://www.newseum.org/todaysfrontpages

lsureveille.com

THE DAILY REVEILLE

Search the Archives

Search

FRONT PAGE | NEWS | SPORTS | ENTERTAINMENT | OPINION | RADIO | CLASSIFIEDS

Live streaming: Mayor-President Holden to address the media at 5:30 p.m.

Click here to watch live coverage

Top Story

BR stores closing ahead of Gustav

As Hurricane Gustav barrels toward a Monday morning landfall on the Louisiana coast, campus area stores are running low and supplies and beginning to close their doors.

- Gustav aims at those Katrina hit
- New Orleans preps for storm
- Oil rigs evacuating Gulf

Latest Campus Headl

- Volunteers work at PMAC
- Football team to remain on campus
- Greek community prepping for Gustav
- Students mapping out plans to stay busy in dorms
- LSU sports teams scattered across continent
- Campus elevators to close
- Chancellor offers safety tips to students

Hurricane Gustav Tracking Center

- **Click here for** a tracking map of Gustav.
- **Click here for** computer models of Gustav.
- **Click here for** LSU's Emergency Operations Center.
- **Click here for** emergency numbers.
- **Click here for** updated closures on campus.

Most Commented | Most Popular

Gustav explodes to Cat 4 strength -- 1:10 p.m. 3 comments

Campus elavators to close 1 comment

Snapshots: Campus hairdos 2 comments

Planning begins for work on Lee Drive 3 comments

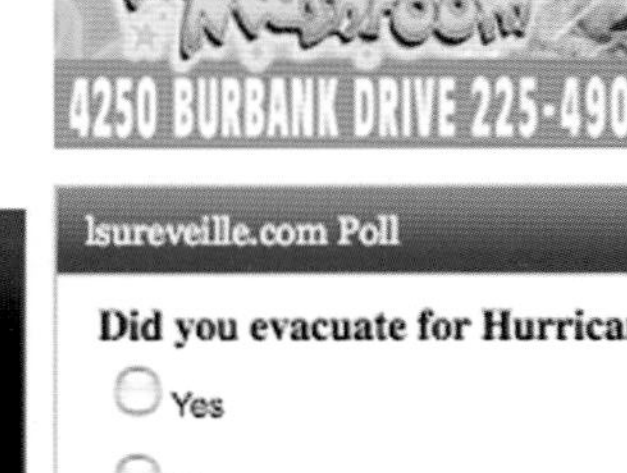

FIGURE 17.1 When a big story breaks, editors sometimes choose to simplify their websites. When Hurricane Gustav slammed into the Gulf of Mexico in 2008, editors at *The Daily Reveille* changed the layout on the website to better present the news as it evolved. They added a bright red bar across the top of the homepage to report breaking news, a "Hurricane Gustav Tracking Center" with links to external weather and government sites relevant to the storm, and a news blog where the *Reveille* staff could post updates. *The Daily Reveille*, Louisiana State University at Baton Rouge.

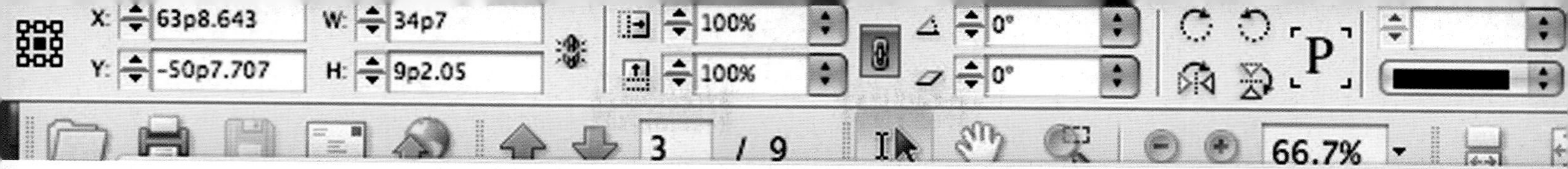

CHAPTER 17
WEBSITES

It was the week before Labor Day 2008, exactly three years after Hurricane Katrina had devastated the Gulf Coast. The staff of *The Daily Reveille* at Louisiana State University in Baton Rouge was preparing its anniversary coverage of the 2005 disaster.

But there was a bigger story brewing; another major storm was heading toward the region. Hurricane Gustav had already ravaged parts of Haiti and the Dominican Republic, leaving a path of death and destruction. Now it was on its way toward the hurricane-weary communities around the Gulf of Mexico. The staff of *The Daily Reveille* produced its Friday paper, the final print edition of the week, with the front-page headline "Planning for Gustav … but never forgetting Katrina."

The next print edition wasn't due to come out until Monday but Editor Kyle Whitfield wasn't concerned; the staff would use the newspaper's website (lsureveille.com) as the primary vehicle for reporting the news. "The idea was to execute a plan of coverage that would be Web-first, information-first, with a 24-hour news cycle as its core value," Whitfield says.

A native of New Orleans who had lived through Hurricane Katrina, Whitfield was ready to cover a disaster. In keeping with *Daily Reveille* tradition, he had already designated an "E-team"– an emergency team of top reporters, photographers, editors

The Student Newspaper Survival Guide, Second Edition. Rachele Kanigel.

CHAPTER CONTENTS

and videographers who had committed to cover any major breaking news that occurred. As soon as the weather service reported that Gustav was on its way, Whitfield mobilized the team by sending out alerts to all members and calling a series of planning meetings.

As the university braced for the coming storm, Whitfield and his E-team prepared to hunker down in the newspaper's office in the basement of Hodges Hall. They brought food, sleeping bags, blankets and clothes, knowing they might be stuck there for several days. They stockpiled equipment, too – cameras, video cameras, cell phones, batteries and chargers.

The Daily Reveille editors decided to change the layout on the website to better present the news as it evolved (Figure 17.1). They added a bright red bar across the top of the homepage to report breaking news, a "Hurricane Gustav Tracking Center" with links to external sites (such as weather and government sites) relevant to the storm, and a news blog where the *Reveille* staff could post updates. The night before the hurricane was expected to make landfall the staff set up a video camera and computer on the fourth floor of their building so they could stream live video of the storm via Mogulus (later renamed Livestream).

On Monday, as the hurricane whirled around them, the staff posted 17 updates and 17 blog posts; dozens more followed in the following days. One of the website's most popular features was an interactive map where readers could click on particular areas of the campus and view pictures or read reports of closures, flooding or damage. "That became a sort of hub for all the information as far as damage," Whitfield says.

"Our mission was to serve the community by giving them information right away and making it as accessible as we could," says Whitfield, who went on to get a job as an online producer for the *Dallas Morning News*. "To be able to serve people the way we did, it confirmed for me why I was in this business."

The Web offers a host of opportunities for covering news. Unfortunately, even now many college news organizations fail to take full advantage of the medium. Some student newspapers still simply "shovel" stories and photos from the print paper without updates or enhancements. This chapter will teach you some of the basic principles of online journalism and help you make your website an indispensable resource for your campus community.

NEWSPAPER OR NEWS ORGANIZATION?

Do you work for a college newspaper that has a website or do you work for a college media organization that produces a 24/7 news website, a newspaper and perhaps other media products (such as a magazine, TV broadcasts, radio programming, etc.)?

If you're living in the 21st century, you should be working for the latter.

No matter how small your school is or how tiny your staff may be, you should think of your print publication as part of an integrated news operation that's ready to cover news about your campus community at every hour of the day and night.

How do you know if you work for a news media operation?

- You publish content to your website first, not waiting for the daily, weekly or monthly deadlines of your print publication.
- You post new content to your website every day – or pretty close to that.
- You cover news – including sports, arts and cultural events – as it breaks.
- You use multiple media – audio, video, text, graphics, photos – to tell stories.
- You use social media, now a vital arm of journalism, to find, report and distribute the news.

With the Web there's no excuse to wait for your print publication or limit yourself to what works best in print.

Some journalists worry about cannibalizing their print publication by posting to the Web first; they think people won't pick up their print product if it includes information

CHECKLIST
Breaking news shift

Whether you have a breaking news desk, a team of general assignment reporters or a rotation where all staffers cover a news shift, your news organization should report news as it breaks on or near your campus. Here is a checklist to help your staff find news as – or even before – it happens.

- Call university police and community police and fire agencies to check if they are working any crimes or other incidents on or near your campus.
- Check university calendar listings for planned events your staff might have missed or forgotten to cover.
- Check websites of local media – television, radio, newspaper and online – to see what they're reporting this hour.
- Check Twitter feeds of university and city officials, local media and other key sources.
- Do a Google news search on your school and other relevant keywords.
- Monitor traffic reports on the radio and online for serious accidents or other incidents that could be disrupting traffic near your campus.
- Call major transit authorities to ask about major delays on bus or rail service.
- Check weather reports for big storms, heat waves or other unusual weather coming your way.
- Call your university public information office.

that's already been published online. But they have to understand three fundamental truths:

1 **Audiences for print and online are different.** While your print newspaper strictly circulates on campus and in your community, your website goes to the world where alumni, parents of students, prospective students and random Googlers will find it.

2 **Print and online products are different.** Print publications offer after-the-fact news accounts of the day, week or month in text and images. Online publications report news as it happens in text, video, audio, microblog posts, photos, interactive graphics and other media. They can be updated at a moment's notice.

3 **Consumers now expect to read about news as it happens.** Your readers don't want to wait for your next print publication to find out what the college president said at the press conference or who won the last basketball game. They want to know as the news unfolds.

We're not just talking here about "breaking news," the hurricanes and shootings and other major news events that force publications into Web-first publishing mode. We're talking about game stories, crime reports, theater reviews, news accounts of routine speeches and events.

The good news is it doesn't take a major overhaul to move to a Web-first publishing model. You can do it today.

Take that game story you're holding onto for next week's newspaper. Publish it to your website now. Why not? People want to find out what happened. Tell the music critic reviewing tonight's concert to file the piece right after the event and then make sure the editor edits and publishes it immediately. Better yet, have the reviewer tweet her first reactions and tell readers to look for the review on the website.

This is not to say student journalists should disregard their paper newspapers. Print is not dead and most student publications still get the lion's share of their advertising revenue and their most loyal readers from their print edition. The lesson here is that online and print must work together, each serving their distinct audiences as best they can.

The more you start to think of yourself as a round-the-clock news source, the more your readers will see you that way and come to look to your website as the go-to destination for news about your community.

How do you cover news around the clock when your reporters, photographers and editors have classes, jobs and other things to do?

At the *Daily Sundial* (sundial.csun.edu) at California State University, Northridge, all staffers – editors, photographers, reporters, copy editors – are required to work a two-hour news shift every week or two. During the shift, staffers are expected to monitor local professional news outlets – radio, television, print and online – and check in with local police and fire officials to find out what's happening. If a story breaks, they're expected to report the news by Twitter and in short news updates. News that warrants further coverage is followed up in longer, more in-depth pieces for the website and print newspaper.

"If you see an ambulance on campus, it may not be worth a 500-word story but it might be worth a two- or three-paragraph brief," says Melissa Lalum, publisher of the *Daily Sundial* and former managing editor of the *Los Angeles Daily News*.

"We're getting away from what I call the 'newsdump' at the end of the day," Lalum adds. "The editors are examining our online traffic and staggering content throughout the day."

TIPSHEET
Breaking news online
Chris Snider

Readers are busy people, and believe it or not they're not always on your website. It's important to reach out to readers to let them know when big news is happening. That might mean reaching them by text message, email or Facebook.

It's also important to understand all of the tools you can use during breaking news situations. That might mean setting up a live chat, creating a poll or creating an RSS feed so that readers can easily subscribe to updates on the story.

Perhaps you need your readers' help to tell the story. That might mean setting up a hashtag that they will use on Twitter or asking them to send in photos through your site or via email.

And if the news is big enough, you might even need to go to a DEFCON version of your homepage to let people know at a glance that something big is happening.

The hard part, of course, is remembering all the tools and options you have in breaking news situations while you're scrambling just to report the news. To help, here's a checklist of tools to use and ways to share information when big news breaks.

Promote the news

- Post to Twitter (and have staffers post to their Twitter accounts).
- Post to Facebook.
- Send breaking news text alert.
- Send breaking news email alert.
- Create a widget so others can add news to their site.
- Buy keywords on Google/Yahoo/Facebook.
- Send to Drudge, Reddit, Digg, Fark.
- Send info to bloggers/sites who cover that topic.
- Post info in forums related to that topic.
- Put together a plan for promoting your unique online content in print.

Tools to use on your site

- Use an alternative homepage design.
- Create a poll.
- Start a breaking news blog.
- Should any of your staff bloggers promote on their blog?
- Are there community members who can blog about this topic?
- Link to blogs outside your site.
- Start a discussion forum.
- Ask readers to submit photos.
- Create a live chat.
- Create a hashtag for Twitter/Flickr/etc.
- Ask readers for YouTube videos.
- Ask readers what questions they have/what info they know.
- Add a Google locator map.
- Create a Google map that allows readers to add content.
- Create a searchable database.
- Q&A with reporter or editor or source.
- Ask Twitter followers for feedback or help.
- Add links to more coverage elsewhere on the Web.
- Create a site that captures social media conversation on the topic.
- Aggregate content from other sites onto your site.
- Create an RSS feed for continuing content.
- Allow readers to subscribe to that RSS via email.
- Post large photos online (in a blog or story).
- Offer print pages for sale.
- Highlight the best comments from readers.

CHRIS SNIDER is an instructor in the journalism department at Drake University in Des Moines. He was formerly assistant managing editor for digital at the *Des Moines Register*, where he created his breaking news checklist. Find him online at ChrisSniderDesign.com.

THE ONLINE MEDIUM

To better understand online journalism, let's look at some of the important ways in which the Web differs from print.

Immediacy. Stories and photos can be posted minutes after news breaks and be updated any number of times as a story changes.

Space. There's virtually no limit to what you can run.

Multimedia. In addition to text, photos and graphics, the Web offers the ability to transmit audio and video and to create interactive databases, maps and graphics, allowing you to tell stories in new and creative ways.

Interactivity. Polls, quizzes, reader feedback, user-generated content and discussion forums can all enhance news coverage, engage readers and help the newspaper gauge interest in particular issues.

Linking. By connecting readers to other parts of your site and to other sites you can add context and depth to your stories.

So how does all this apply to your online newspaper and your stretched-to-the-max staff? Let's go over each of these elements in more depth.

Immediacy

There's nothing like having a big story break just after deadline and being forced to wait for the next issue to deliver the news. If you work for a daily, it means holding the story till the next day – and possibly getting scooped by your professional competition. If your newspaper publishes weekly, or even less frequently, it means your story is old news even before it sees print.

The Internet, the ultimate breaking news vehicle, has revolutionized the news cycle for countless publications – from the small college weekly to *The New York Times*. But taking advantage of this 24/7 medium requires some planning. Large professional newspapers have staff assigned to night and weekend shifts. The majority of college newspapers don't. In addition, most students are juggling classes, homework, jobs and social activities with their newspaper commitments – and the newspaper doesn't always come out as the No. 1 priority.

This means that editors must plan for breaking news and develop a breaking news culture in their newsrooms. Reporters and photographers need to know to check in when there's a crisis; editors must know how to get in touch with staffers at a moment's notice. If the staff is large enough, you may want to assign people to night or weekend shifts or at least have certain people on call. Forward-thinking editors may want to set up an E-team like the one at *The Daily Reveille*, where selected staffers sign contracts saying they'll report for duty in the event of a disaster.

You also need to make sure that editors can publish Web stories and photos quickly and easily. Most student newspapers now have content management systems that allow reporters and photographers to file copy, videos and photos and editors to publish content on the Web without requiring them to be in the newspaper office. If you don't already have such a system, consider creating one or find ways to handle breaking news by email and phone.

Space

As we've discussed, the Web offers virtually unlimited space – a true luxury in times of shrinking newspaper budgets and rising paper and printing costs. But this doesn't mean that you should publish photos and stories that aren't good enough to appear in your print paper. Web reports should meet the same standards for accuracy and readability that you have for your print edition.

Think, too, about creative ways to use this extra space. If, for example, you can't print all the letters to the editor that you receive in your paper, print them all online. (Make sure you put a note on your print letters page referring readers to the online letters section.)

If you have a great collection of photos from an important campus event, create a digital slideshow or photo gallery. During the football season, the *Collegiate Times* (collegiatetimes.com) at Virginia Polytechnic Institute and State University publishes a gallery of each week's game photos. Editors say it's one of the most popular features on the site.

You can also use the website to publish documents related to your story. The online editor of *The Otter Realm* (otterrealm.net) at California State University, Monterey Bay did just that when a group of students "kidnapped" the university president's plastic lawn flamingo. The newspaper got hold of the email "ransom" note and published it on the newspaper's website, along with the tongue-in-cheek story (Figure 17.2). More serious documents – letters, police reports, audit reports – that back up news stories can also be scanned and published this way, adding credibility and depth to your stories.

The *University Daily Kansan* (kansan.com) at the University of Kansas, for example, has a documents section on its website where the staff can post court papers, important press releases, updated bus schedules, newsworthy letters and other documents of interest to readers. Each document has a place for comments so that readers can discuss them. *The Red and Black* (redandblack.com) at the University of Georgia includes documents with its daily "Crime Notebook" whenever possible. The newspaper posts arrest warrants, police reports, complaints, email correspondence and any other documents related to crimes that reporters can collect.

The *Northern Star* (northernstar.info) at Northern Illinois University was one of the first student newspaper sites to take full advantage of this unlimited space. By including everything under the sun, from campus, national and international news, to bus schedules, local restaurant menus and movie listings, to MP3 files from local bands and video clips from Huskies football games, the site has made itself an indispensable resource for the entire campus community.

Jeremy Norman, the paper's online editor from 1999 to 2003, explains the philosophy behind flooding the audience with material: "Sure, students can find residence hall menus on our university website, but where? Sure, they can find information regarding utility hook-ups for apartments, but there's no central location. Sure they can find a calendar of events for our community, but how many sites should one have to go to find local band dates, CD releases, late-night talk shows and university events? With us, it's just one." Norman took over as online editor in his freshman year. At the time, the newspaper's website, which simply posted campus news from the *Northern Star's* five weekday editions, attracted about 400 hits a day, mostly from alumni.

He revamped the site completely, looking for models not in other college newspaper websites but in CNN.com,

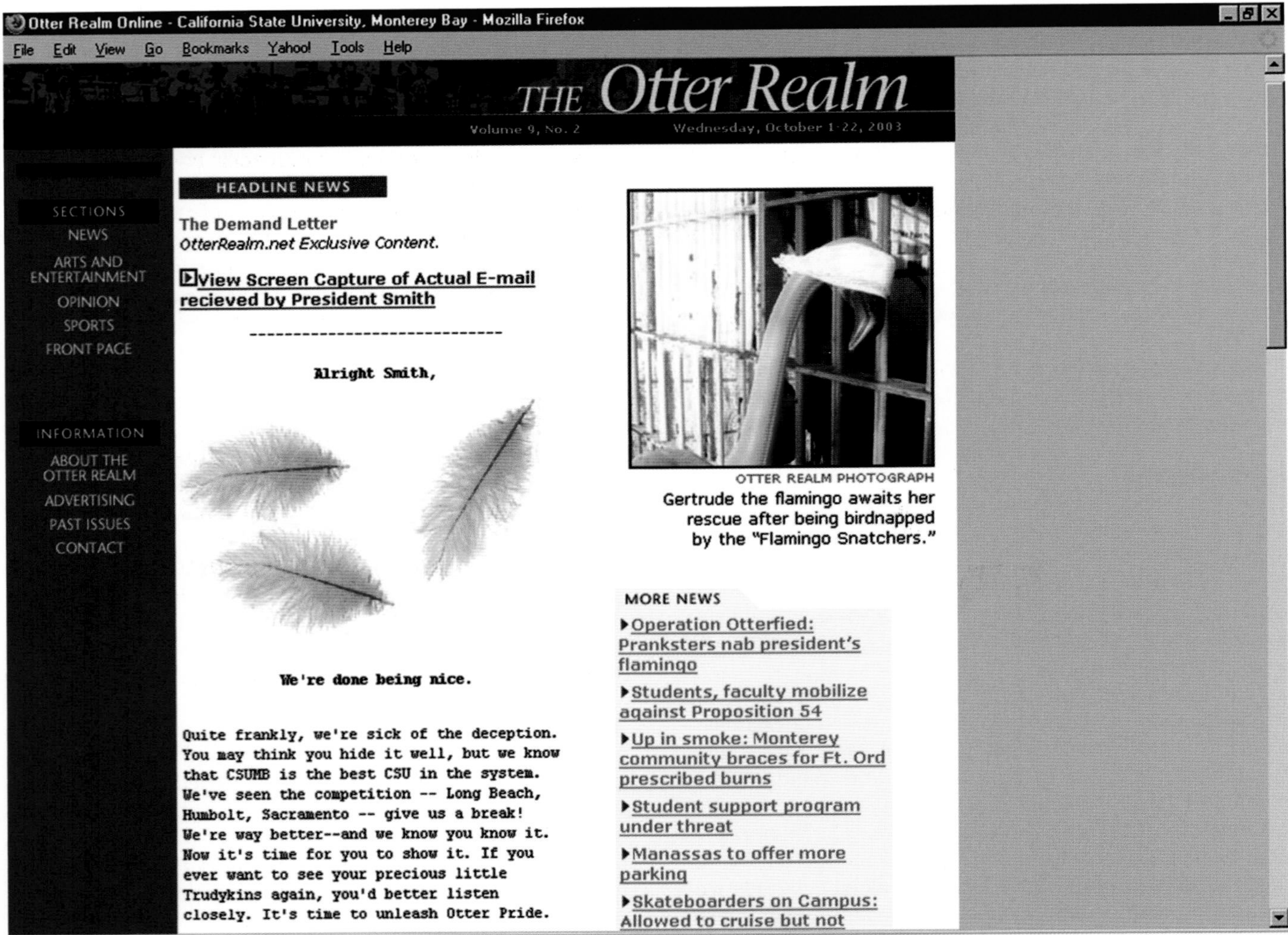
Otter Realm Online - California State University, Monterey Bay - Mozilla Firefox

File Edit View Go Bookmarks Yahoo! Tools Help

THE Otter Realm

Volume 9, No. 2 Wednesday, October 1-22, 2003

SECTIONS
NEWS
ARTS AND ENTERTAINMENT
OPINION
SPORTS
FRONT PAGE

INFORMATION
ABOUT THE OTTER REALM
ADVERTISING
PAST ISSUES
CONTACT

HEADLINE NEWS

The Demand Letter
OtterRealm.net Exclusive Content.

View Screen Capture of Actual E-mail recieved by President Smith

----

Alright Smith,

We're done being nice.

Quite frankly, we're sick of the deception. You may think you hide it well, but we know that CSUMB is the best CSU in the system. We've seen the competition -- Long Beach, Humbolt, Sacramento -- give us a break! We're way better--and we know you know it. Now it's time for you to show it. If you ever want to see your precious little Trudykins again, you'd better listen closely. It's time to unleash Otter Pride.

OTTER REALM PHOTOGRAPH
Gertrude the flamingo awaits her rescue after being birdnapped by the "Flamingo Snatchers."

MORE NEWS
- Operation Otterfied: Pranksters nab president's flamingo
- Students, faculty mobilize against Proposition 54
- Up in smoke: Monterey community braces for Ft. Ord prescribed burns
- Student support program under threat
- Manassas to offer more parking
- Skateboarders on Campus: Allowed to cruise but not

FIGURE 17.2 News organizations can use the Web to publish documents, such as police reports, court documents and "ransom" notes. *The Otter Realm*, California State University, Monterey Bay.

WashingtonPost.com and NYTimes.com. By 2004, the site, with its eclectic mix of news, information and entertainment, was attracting more than 80,000 unique visitors a day and garnering national awards from Associated Collegiate Press, *Editor & Publisher*, College Media Advisers and the Student Society for News Design.

Norman's advice to others who want to enhance their website: "Don't be afraid to go crazy. Chase those stories that happen in your community and abroad, then add what you can to make them more important than a standard article template. You can add important stats, photo galleries, interactive surveys and local resources to a multitude of stories each day. You will become the source for all news and entertainment in your community."

MULTIMEDIA

Photos, video, audio, text. Multimedia means telling stories using several media at once. It may be an interactive graphic, a slideshow with an audio track or a video clip that runs on the Web. Not that long ago, many student newspapers saved multimedia tools for big stories or special projects, but more and more reporters are using video cameras and audio recorders to capture the sights and sounds of everyday life and more routine news stories.

Most student news websites now have a multimedia section that showcases videos, audio slideshows, podcasts and interactive graphics. And some student reporters are getting in the habit of taking a video camera – or even a cell phone capable of recording video – wherever they go so they're always ready to report a multimedia story.

(We'll discuss multimedia in greater depth in Chapter 18.)

INTERACTIVITY

The Web's interactive capabilities are part of what makes it such a fun and engaging medium, particularly for today's tech-savvy generation of college students. Many college newspaper editors understand this and have given polls, bulletin boards and other interactive features space on their sites. *The Daily Tar Heel* (dailytarheel.com) at the University of North Carolina actually has an "Interact" tab on its website – along with more traditional categories like News, Sports and Opinion – that helps readers access games, polls and Twitter and Facebook pages.

Soliciting content from your readers is another way to make your site interactive. When Hurricane Gustav struck, *The Daily Reveille* invited readers to submit photos; the best ones were published on the newspaper's website. "We were a little disappointed because we only got 10 or 15 photos," said Whitfield. "But when you think that no one had power and even cell phones weren't working, that's pretty good."

Such interactive features aren't just fun for your readers. They give your staff a sense of what your community cares about. If you've got a story that draws dozens of comments or a poll that elicits more responses than usual, you know that's an issue you need to follow up on.

LINKING

Adding links is the easiest and most obvious way to turn a conventional newspaper story into an online story. By linking to other Web pages, you can enhance the story, providing more information and giving the reader a fuller, deeper understanding of the issues, people and events you write about. That, in turn, makes your site more useful and valuable. (For tips, see Linking Do's and Don'ts in this chapter.)

Linking also provides a way to give your readers information they want or need without taxing your staff's resources. Many student newspaper sites link to local weather reports, government agencies and other sites with information of interest. At Orange Coast College in Costa Mesa, Calif., for example, the homepage of *The Coast Report* (coastreportonline.com) offers a link to a website that monitors surf conditions – a popular feature for a school that's practically right on the beach.

MOBILE JOURNALISM

You're at a major intersection near the entrance to your campus and you see that a car has collided with a motorcycle. An ambulance is on the scene. What do you do?

If you don't have a conventional camera, whip out your cell phone and snap a picture. Send it back to the newsroom with a text message reporting the basic details of the accident. Within seconds you can have a brief news report up on your news website. If the accident is causing a traffic jam you may want to send out a news alert via Twitter or short message service (SMS).

Linking Do's and Don'ts

While links can take just a few minutes to post and they enhance stories, you need to think carefully about what you're linking to and whether the links truly add value to the story. Before doing your Google search, think about what search terms you want to use and what kind of site you want to connect your readers to. Here are some tips on adding links:

DO add links that provide additional information about an event, exhibit, show, etc. Virtually every arts and entertainment story can benefit from links. On sports stories, think about linking to athletics department homepages, particularly if they have game schedules and other useful information. However, check the site out first; if it doesn't have helpful or interesting information, don't bother making the link.

DO add links to sites that will give readers information about related events. If, for example, your story is about an exhibit for Black History Month and your school has a Web page listing other commemorative events, link to it.

DO link to sites that offer multimedia elements that you may not have legal access to, such as music clips for a band you are writing about or video clips of a film you're reviewing.

DON'T link to the website of every business, program and person you write about. Check out the site to see if it has information that will enhance your story. Avoid linking to commercial sites for products or businesses unless the reader can truly gain added information. There's no reason to link to Amazon.com if you're writing about a book or Toysrus.com if you're writing about a new board game.

DO link to sites you mention in your story. If you're writing about a dating website or a teacher review site, put the links in your story. Sure, your readers can do a Web search to find these sites but it's so much easier if you provide the link.

DO link to related stories and photos on your own site, particularly if this is part of an ongoing issue such as faculty contract negotiations or student government elections. By connecting your coverage to previous reports you can add background and context.

DON'T link to your competitor's stories.

DO link to published studies or journal articles about research you're writing about. If, for example, you're reporting on a professor who has just published in a scientific journal, link to the study if it's online.

DON'T, however, link to the press release about the study. Press releases are secondary sources. Stick to primary sources for links.

TIPSHEET
Writing breaking news

Student journalists assigned to write breaking news for the Web often take too long, thinking they need to have all the details before they can post. That's a mistake. Paul Conley, a consultant to publishers who frequently speaks to student journalists, notes that reporting breaking news on the Web is all about speed and updates.

He recommends journalists follow the formula used by Bloomberg News, where business reporters start by posting a simple headline, usually within seconds of the news happening. After that, a reporter should write a two-paragraph story, and post it within minutes. Next comes a four-paragraph story, which will generally follow this format:

Paragraph 1: Theme–what happened and why

Paragraph 2: Authority–a quote

Paragraph 3: Details–more information

Paragraph 4: Why it matters, what's at stake.

"This is the fastest and easiest way to move to 24/7 publishing," Conley says. "It's possible to impose this system tomorrow on your website."

Breaking news should be edited quickly, he adds, even with the editor looking over the shoulder of the reporter as she's writing. "It's not quite publish first, edit later, but almost," Conley says. "Since it's the Web, it's not permanent."

When writing breaking news for the Web, think about what readers need to know. If campus officials have decided to close the campus during an emergency, for example, that's a vital piece of information that needs to get out as soon as possible. If the football coach resigns, report that fact and save the reasons for later. You can send out news alerts on Twitter, Facebook and mobile phones and pledge to release details as they come in. In this way you're telling readers your news organization is the go-to site for important information.

That's mobile journalism.

Mobile technology puts the basic tools of multimedia journalism into every journalist's – really every person's – pocket.

The trick is knowing when and how to use these tools.

While some journalists carry a backpack of equipment – a digital camera, a video camera, an audio recorder, mics and tripods – with them at all times, others rely on their cell phones to help them capture the news.

But to be a true mobile journalist, you don't just need the right equipment, you need the right mindset. You have to think: *There's news here. I'm a reporter. I need to cover this. Now!*

Mobile journalism means not waiting to get the complete story, the verification from police, the quote from the official source. You need to go with what you have. That doesn't mean spreading groundless rumors, but if you see fire crews in front of a building with smoke coming out of it or you witness police arresting a man outside the Humanities Building, you can report that and get additional facts and details later.

Steve Buttry, director of community engagement for TBD, a local news operation covering the Washington, D.C., area, says news organizations need to take a "mobile-first" approach at every level. "Reporters, editors and visual journalists need to think first about how to package and deliver news for mobile devices," he wrote in a 2009 post for his blog, *The Buttry Diary*. "Information technology staffs need to work first on development of mobile applications for popular devices. … Designers need to present content that is clear and easy to read on the small screen (even if this means spending less staff resources on the design of print or Web products)."

As Buttry notes, mobile technology isn't just changing the way journalists collect information, it's changing the way they distribute it. You no longer can assume that readers are looking at your site on a wide computer screen; they may be checking you out on their cell phones or iPods. That means you need to optimize your site for mobile devices, simplifying your pages so they are easy to read on a 1- or 2-inch screen.

If your news organization doesn't already have a mobile strategy, it may be time to craft one. Think about who your readers are and what will be useful to them. Keep in mind that mobile readers tend to be more local than online readers. In that way, they're more like your print readers. But they also tend to be younger and more technologically savvy – more students, less faculty and staff.

Think about what your audience wants. "Mobile users like local information, video, breaking news and weather," Regina McCombs, who teaches multimedia at the Poynter Institute, writes in a column for Poynter.org. "Mobile users are socializing, multitasking, and passing time. And they're conscious of data rates and battery life, so they want it fast."

Among the topics of interest to college mobile readers: on-campus activities, sports, building or campus closures, traffic conditions, disruptions in public transportation, crime, giveaways.

SEARCH ENGINE OPTIMIZATION

It may sound like geekspeak but search engine optimization, or SEO, is a fundamental tool of online publishing and one that all student journalists should be familiar with. "Today's (and tomorrow's) journalists need to learn search engine optimization techniques as much as, if not more than, their predecessors who worked in the print industry needed to

CHECKLIST
The newspaper website

In setting up or evaluating your newspaper's website, ask yourself:

1. Does it have a clear and easy navigation system? Can readers get around easily?
2. Does it have contact information for the newsroom, including street address and phone number, and email addresses and phone numbers for top editors?
3. Does it include information for advertisers, such as a rate card or contact information for the advertising department?
4. Does it have a search function?
5. Does it have an easy-to-access archive?
6. Does it offer readers ways to interact, such as response forms, polls, forums, chat rooms?
7. Does it make good use of photos, such as slideshows and photo galleries?
8. Does it take advantage of multimedia storytelling techniques?
9. Do you routinely use the site to break news?
10. Can you update the site easily?

learn AP (style)," Robert Niles, a digital journalist and Web designer, wrote in the *Online Journalism Review*.

SEO is essentially about helping search engines find your content so they can drive readers to it. "Even as Facebook and social media provide an increasing share of referrals to online news sites, search engines still provide the initial point of entry for millions of new visitors to websites each day," Niles writes. "If there are techniques that allow you to jump to the front of the line, to attract more of those potential readers, you need to be using them."

Search engines help users find what they are looking for by analyzing words on Web pages, particularly words that are highlighted in some way – in headlines, in subheads, in bold face or italics, in a link or in a bulleted or numbered list – and in tags encoded in the Web page's HTML, or coding language.

When a person searches for particular words, the search engine tries to find the best matches from the pages it has analyzed and then comes up with a list of links, organizing them from the best match to the worst. People usually click on the first links that show up on the search page so you want your Web pages near the top of the list.

The first step to effective SEO is to let search engines know that you exist. Search "submit site" on Google, Yahoo and other search engines and you'll get some quick forms to fill out.

Next, start thinking about keywords, the words people use when they are doing a search. Look at your website traffic report. What keywords generate the most traffic? A little common sense will also help you come up with keywords. If someone is a fan of your men's basketball team and wants to look for information about the team, they'll search for your school, your team, basketball, maybe the name of the coach or a particular player.

When choosing keywords, though, you have to be aware that common keywords bring up millions of sites. When you do a Google search on baseball, more than 300 million sites come up. When you narrow it down to SFSU baseball, Google finds 26,000 sites. But *Golden Gate [X] press*, the student newspaper at San Francisco State University, doesn't come up until the second page of results. By considering search engine optimization, the newspaper could improve its results.

Journalists naturally include keywords when writing about a topic, but there are ways to employ them more strategically. By writing and editing with search engine optimization in mind, you can increase the number of visitors to your stories.

SEO isn't strictly the domain of your resident geeks, your webmaster and online editors. All journalists, particularly copy editors, should be aware of the basic concepts and incorporate them when they write headlines, stories and photo captions. At *The Oklahoma Daily* (oudaily.com) at University of Oklahoma, copy editors routinely write different headlines for print and online, keeping SEO in mind.

"Although we write tight for print, I also have our copy editors write a longer Web-only headline using complete proper nouns (names, location, etc.), since those are the words people are typing in their Google searches," says Chris Lusk, who was online editor in 2010–2011. "When we run articles and columns about our football team, I tell the writers and editors that the first graph needs to have the phrase 'OU football' as soon as possible, instead of referring to the sport as 'Sooner football.' Why? Because analytics show that 'OU football' is a more popular search than 'Sooner football.' So, I put these key phrases in our headlines, story teases, leads, meta data fields, etc."

Some tips for making your website more search engine-friendly:

Use full names and proper nouns in headlines.

BEFORE: College names new president
AFTER: George Johnson named president of Kent College

Don't have a separate archive for older content. Keep all content on your main site.

Be specific in headlines. Name the city, state, agency, etc. you are writing about.

BEFORE: State adopts new budget
AFTER: California adopts new budget

Add or optimize tags. Search engines look for title tags, headline tags, keyword tags.

Use keywords as links.

BEFORE: For more information about the Associated Students, click here.
AFTER: For more information, go to the Associated Students website.

Avoid abbreviated names and initials on first reference and in headlines.

BEFORE: TU named biggest party school in the state
AFTER: Truman University named biggest party school in Utah

Avoid puns and vague references. Write clear, direct, literal headlines.

BEFORE: Knocked out
AFTER: University Health Center focuses on treatment of concussions

Spread content out. When you put content on YouTube, Google Maps, Flickr and other sites it comes back to you.

Add or optimize tags to your images. Make sure all images on your site have relevant titles. You can get a lot of hits through Google image searches.

WRITING FOR THE WEB

Reading text online is different from reading printed text and journalists need to consider this in writing and editing for the Web. Reading on a computer screen takes longer. Numerous studies have shown that people tend to scan Web pages rather than read every word.

Eye-tracking research, which follows a reader's eye movement, reveals that eyes often sweep across a page from left to right when people read online and that they tend to focus most on the top left corner of a Web page. They primarily pay attention to headlines and subheads, boldfaced terms and images and often stop reading when faced with long blocks of uninterrupted text.

To keep readers' attention, writers and editors need to present text in a different way online than they would in print. Text needs to be easier to scan. And because readers may come from beyond your campus community, you should write for a global audience.

The savviest editors actually reformat stories from their print newspapers for the Web.

Choose from a range of features to make your website more readable.

- **Write short.** Use short sentences and short paragraphs.
- **Use bulleted and numbered lists.** When you have multiple points to make, create a list like this one that puts the most important information in boldface.
- **Position your content where people are most likely to see it.** Put the most important content in the upper-left area of the screen.
- **Frontload your content.** Put the most important words at the beginning of sentences, headlines, subheads and lists.
- **Write clear headlines and subheads.** Use direct, literal language rather than puns or turns of phrase.
- **Don't assume readers know where you are.** Avoid writing "the state" or "our country."
- **Avoid or explain local references.** Readers may not understand in-jokes or nicknames.

BLOGS

Web logs, better known as blogs, can add personality and vitality to a student news website. Staff writers and editors can use blogs to report up-to-the-minute and/or personal observations on campus events and issues. But as professional newspapers have found, the most engaging blogs often come from outside contributors rather than staffers.

To add blogs to your website, launch a contest inviting readers to submit a sample blog. You may set categories – sports, Greek life, dating/relationships, first-year students, particular dorms or academic departments – or ask for general musings on college life. Another strategy is to invite specific students – the head of a campus group, a player on one of your teams, a student studying abroad for a year – to share their reflections with your readers.

Staff writers and editors can also blog. Reporters often find a beat-related blog gives them a space to share vignettes and observations that aren't quite right for a full-fledged news story. It's also a way to build a relationship with readers.

An editor's blog is a good way for editors to share information about the newspaper – to announce staff changes, to introduce a redesign or a new feature, to discuss errors and problems. Editors at *The Daily Evergreen* (dailyevergreen.com) at Washington State University have announced staff changes and awards and explained an April Fool's Day prank. *The Daily Californian* at the University of California, Berkeley, has used *The Editor's Blog* (blog.dailycal.org/editors) to seek reader input for a redesign, share comments from readers and explain why the paper was cutting its Wednesday edition.

One of the most talked-about features on *The Harvard Crimson's* website is its *FlyBy* blog (thecrimson.com/section/flyby) (Figure 17.3) which the newspaper describes as a "more-than-daily source for Harvard news, gossip, and oddities." The blog has run everything from a guide to French kissing to a post on a new kind of candy being sold in campus vending machines to a July 4 video asking students to sing

FIGURE 17.3 *The Harvard Crimson's Flyby* blog offers a breezy, amusing counterpoint to the usually serious newspaper. *The Harvard Crimson*, Harvard University.

"The Star-Spangled Banner." The blog has some recurring features like "The Golden Dozen," in which people around campus are asked the same 12 questions, and "Bargain Hunting," guides to the easiest courses, the coolest course titles and courses that still have openings late in the semester. It's a great example of the more casual, conversational and off-the-wall approach a blog can take.

As many professional newspapers have found, blogs should be edited. There's no point in showcasing writing with misspelled words and sentences that don't make sense. But

10 tips for successful blogging **Daniel Reimold**

Student readers can recognize in an instant when a newspaper's blog is an afterthought. To impress instead of bore, your blog needs to be central to your paper's editorial and online plans. The best blogs possess what I call the IOU – interactivity, originality and an understanding of the Web's full potential. To harness this potential, here are a few things your newspaper's blog should be:

1 **Be consistent.** Like fish and visitors, blogs without fresh content stink after three days. Update your blog often, at regular intervals, so it becomes part of readers' Web browsing routine.

2 **Be complementary.** Do not simply parrot your print edition or hype your homepage content. Your blog should have a voice, an attitude and an identity at least somewhat separate from everything else in the newspaper. It should have its own name, tagline, editor and staff of dedicated writers. It should provide its own distinct news and notes.

3 **Be brief.** Keep most posts under 600 words. Break up longer pieces into multiple posts. Blog readers are scanners. They are searching for a quick sip of information, not a huge gulp.

4 **Be bold.** Your blog's writing style can veer from sheer objectivity. You can be more informal and talk to readers directly. You can occasionally even get in people's faces with the news, if you choose.

5 **Be beautiful.** Your blog must be interesting to read *and* nice to look at. Design an alluring header. Hand-code from scratch or adapt a template to create a blog free of clutter and, most important, full of readable text. In addition, integrate bullet points, numbered lists, subheads and multimedia elements such as photo slideshows, podcasts, tweets and video reports to break up streams of text.

6 **Be Google-friendly.** Over time, a quality blog can generate major online traffic for a newspaper, especially from random Googlers. The key to driving traffic to your blog: Practice search engine optimization techniques. Link frequently to outside websites, the more popular the better. Fashion post headlines so that the first few words relate directly to an anticipated Google search. Also, check trending Twitter topics and have bloggers sound off on the current events that people will be searching for.

7 **Be collaborative.** A quality blog has both readers and commenters. Your newspaper blog should serve as a sounding board for the student body. Start discussions. Ask questions. Run instant polls. Invite student readers to write guest posts. Think dialogue, not monologue.

8 **Be newsy.** A blog is basically obsolete if not utilized for breaking news. As the residence hall fire burns, the police sirens outside the frat house blare, the fans on game day scream, and the tuition hike protest marches on, your newspaper's blog should be setting the scene and reporting in the moment. Embrace live-blogging tools, such as CoveritLive, and integrate tweets into the mix of posts. Instill in your writers the following breaking news blogging philosophy: observe, interview, interact, follow up, triple-check, and share with the world, as soon as possible.

9 **Be prepared.** Develop and distribute a workflow sheet so that every aspect of your blog's editorial cycle is clear – from posting drafts to clicking "publish." Keep a story ideas log on a shared online space so all staffers can stay in the loop on upcoming content. Also, decide how the newspaper will handle the most common blogging ethical dilemmas, including anonymous commenting and sources' requests to erase information after its posting.

10 **Be what you want to be.** Blogs are meant to be experimental. They are expected to reinvent, repeatedly. They should attempt creative reporting techniques. Never be afraid to shake things up.

Four super student news blogs to check out:

Harvard Crimson's FlyBy (thecrimson.com/section/flyby) "Harvard Life. To go."

IvyGate (ivygateblog.com) "The Ivy League blog"

NYU Local (nyulocal.com) "A 24-hour website about the school we call home"

Wesleying (wesleying.org) "Real students, real student life at Wesleyan University"

DANIEL REIMOLD, Ph.D. is a college journalism scholar who has written and presented about the student press throughout the United States and in Southeast Asia. He is an assistant professor of journalism at the University of Tampa, where he also advises the student newspaper, *The Minaret* (theminaretonline.com). He maintains *College Media Matters* (collegemediamatters.com), a daily blog focused on student journalism 2.0 that is affiliated with the Associated Collegiate Press. His book on modern college media, *Sex and the University: Celebrity, Controversy, and a Student Journalism Revolution*, was published in 2010 by Rutgers University Press.

edit lightly. Even as you correct obvious errors and check for potentially libelous statements, be careful to keep the writer's voice. After all, that's the whole point of running a blog.

POLLS

Some newspapers, such as the *Indiana Daily Student* (idsnews.com) at Indiana University and *The Eastern Echo* (easternecho.com) at Eastern Michigan University, post daily or weekly polls, asking such questions as "Were you able to get all the classes you registered for?" or "Do you think grade inflation is a problem here?"

Other polls link directly to breaking news. When *The Daily Reveille* was covering Hurricane Gustav, the editors came up with poll questions related to the storm: Do you think Saturday's football game should be canceled? Did you evacuate for Hurricane Gustav?

Polls aren't just for fun; they can give your newspaper a sense of what your readers care about. Editors should monitor poll results, looking for trends. Which poll got the most responses this month? What times of the day or week do the bulk of the responses come in? On the day *The Chronicle* (dukechronicle.com) reported that the university's longtime basketball coach Mike Krzyzewski had been offered an $8 million contract to coach the Los Angeles Lakers, the paper ran the poll question: "Will Coach K leave Duke for the Lakers?" Within hours nearly 1,000 votes had been cast – and this in the middle of the summer on the eve of a holiday weekend. Clearly, this was an issue readers cared about.

But be careful not to use these informal polls as scientific data. Online polls are notoriously unreliable. It's too easy for people to stuff the virtual ballot box, and those who respond generally don't represent a cross-section of the readership. On top of that, the small number of responses most student newspaper polls elicit is generally not statistically significant. So have fun engaging your readers with polls, but don't take the results too seriously.

PUBLISHING OPTIONS

Student newspapers can publish independently or use the services of digital publishing companies. College Media Network has emerged as the leader in the field. With the company's software you can post text, photographs, videos, podcasts and graphics; supervise forums; conduct polls; and post advertisements.

College Media Network's content management system is appealing to some college newspapers because its simple templates allow students to create professional-looking websites without a lot of technical know-how. The company offers technical support and a selection of templates. And because you're part of a national network, you may actually get more advertising revenue.

However, many student editors and webmasters complain that the software limits what they can do. Even though the templates can be customized, the sites don't have the fresh, individual look of a tailor-made site.

In recent years, many student newspapers have moved to open-source content management systems

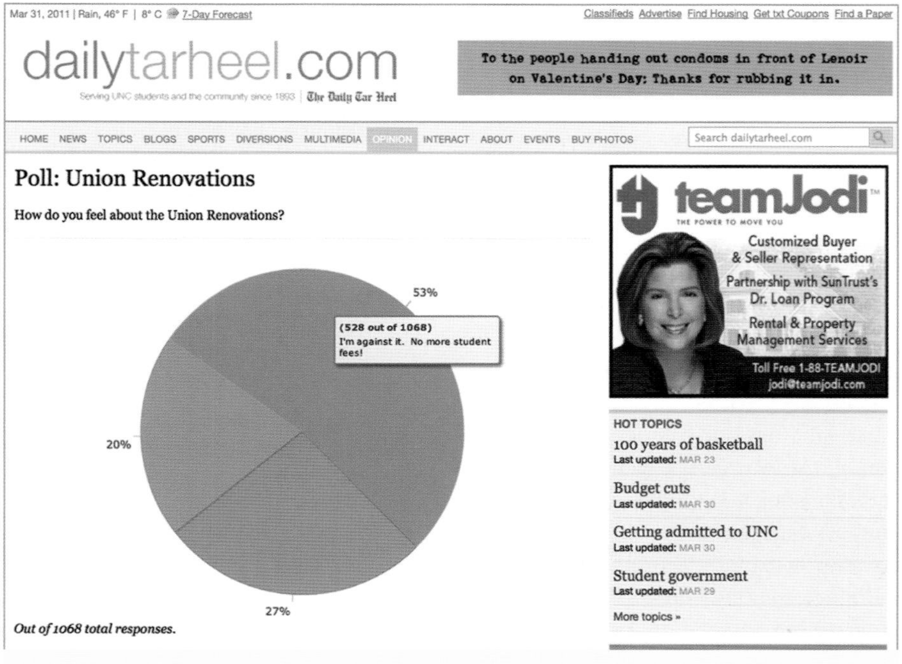

FIGURE 17.4 Polls give readers an opportunity to interact with your news organization – and give your staff a sense of what readers care about. A successful poll can draw 1,000 or more votes like this one by *The Daily Tar Heel* on renovations to the student union. *The Daily Tar Heel*, University of North Carolina.

TIPS FROM A PRO Jake Ortman

A newspaper's website shouldn't simply be an online repository for material that's already appeared in print. It should be a dynamic online publication with original content, breaking news, blogs and other cool stuff. Here are some tips for making your newspaper's website all that it can be:

1 **Put someone in charge.** Have a dedicated online person on staff – be it somebody with computer or news experience – or, better yet, both. While many publishing systems allow easy uploading of story content, you want that person around if something goes wrong or if you want to do something more advanced. This person will also act as a liaison for the online edition – attending editor meetings, putting pressure on editors and reporters to consider online possibilities and suggesting additional content for the website.

2 **Color, color, color.** In the print world, you can only publish color if **A** you can afford it, or **B** you have an advertiser pay for it. On the Web, color doesn't add to the cost and it really brightens up the site. If the print edition only runs black and white, the online edition should always have color.

3 **Class up your classifieds.** Classifieds should be online and searchable, and people should be able to submit classifieds via your website. You can mark up your classified ad rates for this privilege and make a few bucks.

4 **Promote your staff.** Put their pics online with their beats or titles and email addresses (use professional-looking, non-personal addresses, like JoeBlow@yournewspapername.com). Add some personal biographical details and plug your staffers' accomplishments, such as awards they've won, big stories they covered, etc. This kind of information also helps them land internships and jobs.

5 **Break news online.** If an important story is breaking before the next issue goes to print (and this is especially the case with non-dailies), get it online. Now. Faster. Even if a story isn't fully written, get a blip on your website about it. If your site is set up right, you can get a story online anywhere with an Internet connection. I've posted stories from hotel lobbies, my parent's house, the library, even a gas station on a mountain pass. Get it up, and make a spectacle out of the local media who get thrown off guard. Scooping the pros will give the staff a jolt and will keep readers checking the site and the next morning's paper for more information.

6 **Get personal.** You're in college. You know who your readers are. You share in-jokes and frames of reference. Bring that personal connection to your website. Be it a daily note from the editor(s), a random quote, a funny picture, whatever, give your site a personality.

7 **Experiment.** Another perk about being in college and not on some major corporation's dime is that you have a lot more leeway. Take advantage of it. Experiment – don't be afraid to screw up. This applies to the print edition as well. Figure out what works and what doesn't and what you can and can't do now, and bring that enthusiasm to the real world.

8 **Interact.** Give folks reasons to come back to your site. Local weather, polls, surveys, events, forums, whatever – the news can't be the only thing that brings people to your online edition. Give people an option to express their voice, and they will – either via a simple letter to the editor feedback form, or via comments on individual articles. This is especially important if you don't update your site's content on a daily basis. You have to keep people interested.

9 **Run next-day teases.** Along the same lines as the breaking news, put up next-day teases the day before – a "here's what's coming in tomorrow's issue" type of thing. These don't need to be detailed, just little blips to entice people to pick up a paper or come back to your website the next day.

10 **Get an RSS/syndication feed.** If you use some sort of content management system for your website, this will be a trivial thing to produce, but it's very important. Why? Traffic and exposure. If you set up an RSS feed (which can stand for Really Simple Syndication, Rich Site Summary or RDF Site Summary, depending on who you ask), your headlines (and even story summaries, if you like) can be subscribed to and syndicated all over the Web in feed readers and portal sites. That way, every time you post a story, all these sites and feed readers will be updated with your new headline. Folks can even subscribe via email to many RSS feeds. When breaking news hits, this is a great way to get people to come to your site.

11 **Get social.** While the jury's still out as to whether doing things like posting your newsroom meeting

notes on Twitter is worth the effort, Twitter and Facebook are both vital to keep the campus community following your news. Set up a fan page on Facebook, and get your headlines and breaking news teases on both Twitter and Facebook. You can use your site's RSS feed (see above) to automate much of this and have it dump headlines to your Facebook and Twitter feeds automatically.

12 **Post online exclusives.** This is a no-brainer. Put content online that readers can't find in the print edition. Be it an exclusive column, more letters to the editor, more photos, a longer story, full details on a student senate vote, or whatever, it's not too hard to get at least one online exclusive per issue. Tease your exclusives in the print edition with a nifty little icon.

13 **Search engine submission.** Submit your site to as many search engines and directories as you can think of. If you can't find yourself on a "(insert college name) news" search on Google, you have some work to do.

14 **Advertise.** Put your paper's URL on everything – Fax cover sheets, T-shirts, letterhead, business cards, the front page of the paper (in type larger than 12-point font), receipts, tear sheets, office doors, distribution boxes ("Are we out of papers? Find the news online at www.campusnewspaper.com"), etc.… Anything that leaves the office should have it on there.

15 **Market your site.** Do promotions to get people to visit your site. Advertise an online contest in your print edition with some sort of student-friendly prize (pizza, beer, money and sex will get their attention 99 times out of 100). Give out bumper stickers with your Web address on them. Form a partnership with the local student-run TV or radio station; have them plug the site in exchange for a free newspaper or Web ad.

16 **Get your link everywhere.** Your campus has a ton of student organizations, university offices, alumni groups, and fan groups that have websites. Get your Web address on them. This will not only bring you more traffic via those links, but it's one of the most important factors in increasing your search engine rankings. Be sure you give people an easy way to link to your site.

17 **Name that site.** Get an easy-to-remember URL. I've seen too many URLs for college newspapers that look like the *Emerald*'s old one did: http://darkwing.uoregon.edu/~ode. How are people supposed to remember that? Talk to your folks on campus and see if they will host a domain for you, or give you a more friendly URL (like http://ode.uoregon.edu). Most domain registrars will point domains to an existing URL for free or very low cost. If you have a slash or some other non-alphabetic character in your URL that isn't a dot, it needs to be fixed.

JAKE ORTMAN was the online editor and technology columnist for the *Oregon Daily Emerald* (dailyemerald.com) at the University of Oregon in Eugene from 1997 to 2000. During his tenure, the website won awards from the Associated Collegiate Press, College Media Advisers, Society of Professional Journalists and the Oregon Newspaper Publishers Association. He is the geek, SEO guru and marketing guy at Discover Sunriver Vacation Rentals and writes a popular blog at utterlyboring.com.

such as WordPress, Joomla and Drupal. Two other options specifically designed for newspapers are SchoolNewspapersOnline.com, which is popular with high school newspapers and small college publications, and TownNews.com, which is used by more than 1,500 news outlets, including several college news organizations.

If you are thinking about a move to a new content management system, carefully consider the needs of your particular news organization. Are you looking for something simple and easy? Do you have a strong technical support staff? Make sure you choose a system you can maintain and update even as your online editors come and go. In making your decision you may want to consult other student and professional newspapers about their experiences with different options.

ARCHIVING CONTENT

The Web provides an instant archive for your content, making it easy for people to search for stories and photos and giving your publication a historical record of your coverage.

But this easy archive can also present problems. What do you do if a former student asks you to remove a story about an embarrassing comment she made five years ago? What if a crime brief reports that someone was charged with marijuana possession and then the charge was reduced or dropped? What if a former staffer calls to say a poorly written story composed in her youth is damaging her chances of finding a job?

Every year student newspapers receive requests from people asking that stories be removed from their websites or that corrections be made to articles written months or years earlier.

To deal with such requests it's useful to have a written policy. Here's an example from *The Daily Tar Heel* at the University of North Carolina at Chapel Hill:

Manipulation of archives

The *Daily Tar Heel* and its website, DailyTarHeel.com, strive to report the truth as accurately as possible on news events of the day. Online archives are a part of the institutional memory of the newspaper and a historical record of our community. As such, we will not remove nor attempt to hide from commercial search engines any material in our online archives – news stories, story comments, editorials, opinion columns, photographs or graphic illustrations. If an error in our archived content is brought to our attention and documented to our satisfaction, we will append the original article with an editor's note acknowledging the change made to the original archive. That decision is solely at the discretion of the current student editorial management.

To make a complaint that archived content is inaccurate, contact the editor-in-chief in writing by letter or email with the following information:

Name, telephone number and email address,

The URL address of the content in question, and

The specific content that is inaccurate and an explanation of how the information is inaccurate.

In the case of content published more than one year ago, the complainant must provide reasonable proof to the editor-in-chief that the content in question is no longer accurate. For example, a copy of expungement papers should be provided in case any criminal charges are dropped. If published more than a year ago, contested quotes are highly unlikely to be amended without written or audio documentation.

If the contested content was published less than a year ago, normal internal procedures for checking the material's accuracy will apply, and you may be asked to provide written documentation. Updates or corrections may be added if the material is factually inaccurate, but nothing will be removed. In the event of a correction, a note detailing the date and time of the change will be included.

The request will be reviewed and checked by the editor and if the editor determines it to be valid, an update or correction will be posted.

REPRINTED WITH PERMISSION FROM *THE DAILY TAR HEEL*

Having a policy like this – and posting it to your website – will make your position clear and save hours of discussion for future generations of editors.

TO DO

1. Look at other student newspaper websites (see list at the end of this chapter) to get ideas about design, navigation, use of photos, interactive features and story placement. When you find a site you like, send an email to the online editor or webmaster and ask for ideas about your site.
2. Invite an online editor from your local newspaper to critique your website in front of the staff. Ask for constructive criticism about how you can improve the site.
3. Assemble a focus group of students from your campus and ask them to discuss what they like and what they don't like about your website. Reward them with cookies or pizza.
4. Review how your staff is presented on your website. Do you include short bios and photos? Are staffers labeled by position or beat? Can readers send email directly to the sports editor, for example, or the reporter who covers student government? Make sure your staff is accessible.
5. Create special projects for your website that take advantage of multimedia, interactivity, linking, immediacy and other online attributes discussed in this chapter.
6. Set up a publicity team to promote your website. Sponsor a contest or giveaway. Make up amusing bumper stickers, pencils, keyrings or other inexpensive trinkets with your site's URL and hand them out at campus events.
7. Enroll in one of the online training workshops or webinars co-sponsored by the Online News Association and the Poynter Institute. Most are free or low-cost.
8. Check out winners of the latest Online News Association contest (journalists.org). For each winning entry, jot down a few ideas that you could apply to your newspaper website.
9. If you don't already have a mobile strategy for your news organization, appoint a team to develop one. Consider your audience and what they want. Think about how to design your site for mobile users and about special mobile features you can offer. Train your staff to think in a mobile-first mindset.

TO READ

Briggs, Mark, *Journalism Next: A Practical Guide to Digital Reporting and Publishing*, Washington, D.C.: CQ Press, 2010.

Luckie, Mark S. *The Digital Journalist's Handbook*, CreateSpace, 2010.

McAdams, Mindy. *Flash Journalism: How to Create Multimedia News Packages*. Burlington, Mass.: Focal Press, 2005.

Williams, Robin and Tollett, John. *The NonDesigner's Web Book, An easy guide to creating, designing, and posting your own website, 3rd ed.* Berkeley, Calif.: Peachpit Press, 2008.

TO CLICK

Knight Digital Media Center

The Knight Digital Media Center offers workshops for mid-career journalists to enhance their expertise and multimedia skills. The center's website offers free tutorials for a range of multimedia skills, including data visualization, video, audio, Flash and Web development.

http://multimedia.journalism.berkeley.edu

Media Bloggers Association

The Media Bloggers Association is a nonpartisan nonprofit organization dedicated to promoting, protecting and educating its members; supporting the development of "blogging" or "citizen journalism" as a distinct form of media; and helping to extend the power of the press, with all the rights and responsibilities that entails, to every citizen.

www.mediabloggers.org

Online News Association

Founded in 1999, ONA is the leading organization of professional digital journalists. Discounted membership is available to high school, undergraduate and graduate students with an interest in online journalism. The organization's website features winners of ONA's annual contest (which honors student work in several categories), discussion groups and information about training.

http://journalists.org

School Newspapers Online

School Newspapers Online helps student newspapers – mostly high school but a few college publications – create or enhance their presence on the Internet.

www.schoolnewspapersonline.com

Town News

This site provides easy-to-use content management systems and revenue-generating tools to community and student newspapers.

www.townnews.com

Check out these award-winning campus newspaper websites:

Arizona Daily Wildcat, University of Arizona
http://wildcat.arizona.edu

The Auburn Plainsman, Auburn University
www.theplainsman.com

Collegiate Times, Virginia Tech
www.collegiatetimes.com

The Daily Collegian, Penn State University
www.collegian.psu.edu

Daily Illini, University of Illinois
www.dailyillini.com

DENNews.com, Eastern Illinois University
http://www.dennews.com

Golden Gate [X]press, San Francisco State University
www.goldengatexpress.org

The Harvard Crimson, Harvard University
www.thecrimson.com

Indiana Daily Student, Indiana University
www.idsnews.com

Northern Star, Northern Illinois University
http://northernstar.info

The Red and Black, University of Georgia
www.redandblack.com

The Sentinel, North Idaho College
www.nic.edu/sentinel

The Shorthorn, University of Texas-Arlington
www.theshorthorn.com

The Sun Online, Southwestern College
http://southwesterncollegesun.com

The Temple News, Temple University
www.temple-news.com

University Daily Kansan, University of Kansas at Lawrence
www.kansan.com

You can find links to other college newspaper websites at Newslink (http://newslink.org/statcamp.html), which lists campus newspapers by state.

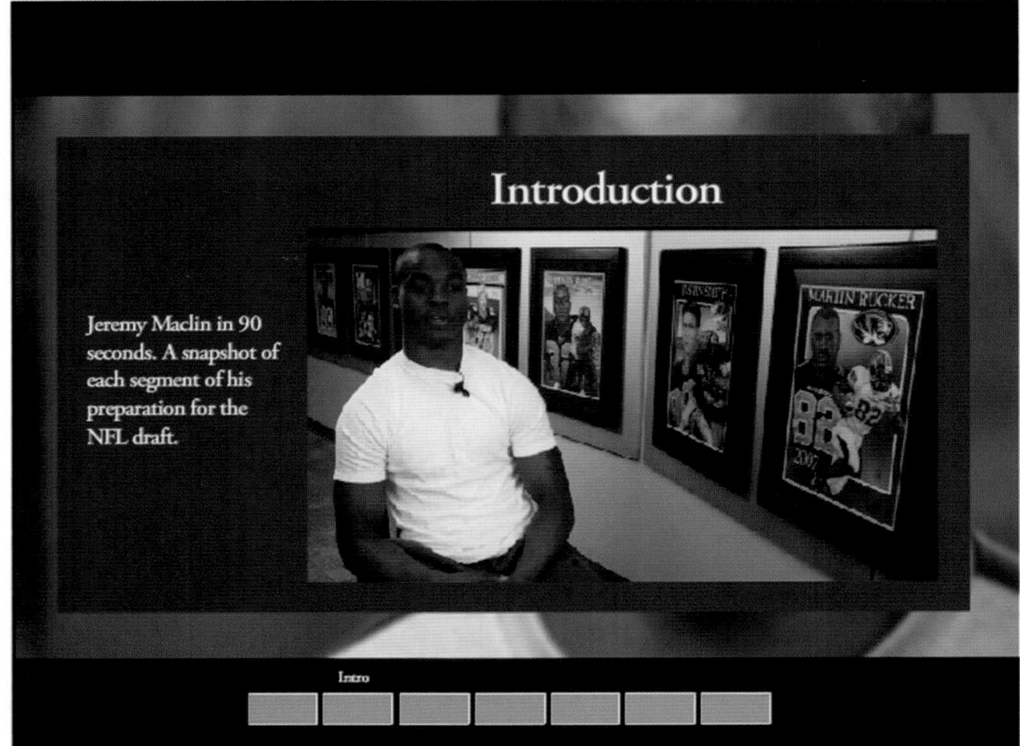

FIGURE 18.1 When University of Missouri Tigers wide receiver Jeremy Maclin appeared headed for the pros in the winter of his sophomore year, it seemed the perfect opportunity for a big multimedia project. Brian Singler, a multimedia producer, and writer Robert Mays III spent three months following Maclin around and produced a project that brought together text, interactive graphics, video and still photos. *The Missourian*, University of Missouri.

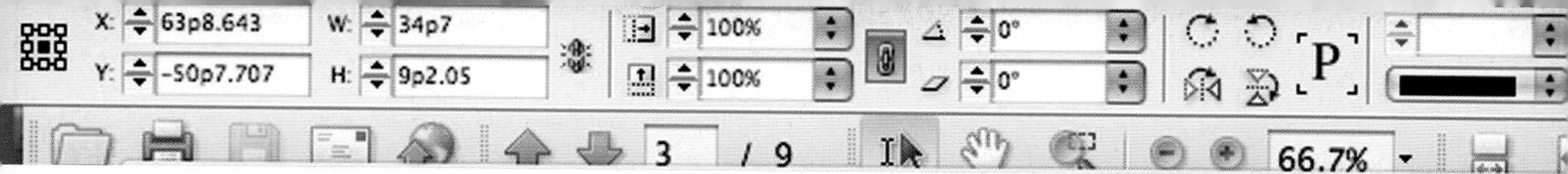

CHAPTER 18
MULTIMEDIA STORYTELLING

Your basketball team wins the NCAA championship for the first time in 26 years and the whole school goes wild. A group of militant students commandeers the Business Building on campus to protest fee hikes and budget cuts. A candlelight procession for a missing student snakes its way through campus as participants sing the young woman's favorite songs.

You could tell these stories with photos and text but multimedia storytelling offers even more compelling ways to capture the sights and sounds, the emotion and action of such news stories. Don't simply describe the jubilation at the victory game or the solemnity of the vigil; let your readers hear and see these events as they unfold.

As prices for equipment fall and new tools make creating, editing and posting audio and video to the Web easier than ever, even the smallest student newspaper can now be a full-scale multimedia news operation. In this chapter we'll talk about how to make every journalist on your staff a multimedia reporter and how to make the most of your multimedia projects.

The Student Newspaper Survival Guide, Second Edition. Rachele Kanigel.

CHAPTER CONTENTS

WHAT IS MULTIMEDIA JOURNALISM?

Multimedia journalism is the converging, or bringing together, of multiple media – audio, video, text, animation, photos and graphics – into an integrated product. It may mean marrying sound and still photos into an audio slideshow or pulling together video, text and graphics into a comprehensive package. Though multimedia storytelling may use new techniques and tools, the basic fundamentals of good storytelling – strong characters, plot, a narrative arc, a climax, a conclusion – remain.

Some things to think about when considering multimedia:

Multimedia can be nonlinear. Rather than a structured single narrative that people read or watch from beginning to end, multimedia may offer multiple ways into a story, allowing readers to decide how they want to navigate through the material.

Multimedia is multisensory. It stimulates the eyes, the ears, the fingertips, but most of all, it excites the mind. It offers both creators and readers a chance to explore information in new ways.

Multimedia is constantly evolving. What was fresh and new yesterday may be considered tired or passé tomorrow. Good multimedia makes use of new technologies, new storytelling forms and new delivery devices as they become available.

"New multimedia tools, now reproducing themselves exponentially, provide reporters and editors with sometimes awe-inspiring ways to tell our stories," Marc Cooper, an associate professor at the University of Southern California and director of Annenberg Digital News, wrote in an article for the *Online Journalism Review* (ojr.org). "Learning to master these tools and when to choose them, however, can be as important as which tool a surgeon requests for a certain procedure in the compressed atmosphere of an OR."

CHOOSING THE RIGHT MEDIUM

As Cooper suggests, part of the art to multimedia storytelling is selecting the right medium for each story or part of a story. It's a mistake to send a videographer out on every assignment or to make a slideshow just because you have a lot of photographs.

The Web offers journalists choice. In the past, television reporters had to tell stories that had strong visuals, radio reporters were limited to stories they could tell well with sound alone and print reporters could describe but they were restricted in how much they could show – usually only what could be captured in a photo or two. Online journalists – and aren't we all online journalists now? – have the opportunity to choose the best way or ways to tell a story.

To determine how to best use the multimedia tools in your toolkit, you need to first think critically about what each medium offers – and also what it takes to produce. Let's consider the attributes and limitations of each type of media.

- **Text** is good for explaining concepts, for providing background and context. If the administration announces plans to renovate the library or the academic senate changes the English composition requirement for incoming freshmen, text may be the best way to explain the news to readers.
- **Video** captures action – a parade, a sporting event, a talent show. It can also be useful for showing emotion – the tears at a beloved professor's surprise retirement party, a passionate outburst at a protest rally.
- **Audio** is useful for stories with a strong sound component – when the marching band plays at the homecoming game or the new president gives his first public speech, your readers want to hear it.
- **Graphics** come in handy when you've got a lot of numbers or a complex process to explain. An infographic is the most effective way to demonstrate how tuition has risen over time or to show the proportion of your school's budget that goes to athletics. Maps are useful when there's a geographic element to your story, showing where a crime was committed, for example, or the path a marathon is going to take.
- **Photos** are best for capturing a particular moment in time. When you've got a collection of images that together tell a story, a slideshow or audio slideshow may be the best vehicle to use.

Once you've decided that a certain medium would be useful for telling a particular story, you also have to consider

Which medium should you use?

Slideshows	Video
Time: Quick to create & edit **Resources:** One person; easy to learn **Shelf life:** Can be short or long **Interactivity:** Somewhat, readers can go through photos at their own pace	**Time:** Consuming (plan, shoot, edit) **Resources:** Extensive training; videography skills and equipment needed **Shelf life:** Short or long **Interactivity:** Very limited, readers generally simply watch from beginning to end
Interactive graphics	**Podcasts**
Time: Very time consuming **Resources:** Considerable staff time; can require text, photos, video, graphics **Shelf life:** Should be long **Interactivity:** Extremely interactive	**Time:** Relatively quick to create & edit **Resources:** One person; easy to learn **Shelf life:** Can be short or long **Interactivity:** Limited interactivity but consumers have the option to listen on the Web or download to an mp3 player
Audio slideshows	**Interactive maps**
Time: Somewhat time consuming **Resources:** A moderate amount of staff time because they involve capturing and editing images and sound **Shelf life:** Short or long **Interactivity:** Limited interactivity	**Time:** Quick to create and edit **Resources:** One person, easy to learn with Google Maps and other mapping software **Shelf life:** Can be short or long **Interactivity:** Very interactive

FIGURE 18.2 How do you decide which medium to use to tell your story? Michael Roberts, project director for NewsTrain, recommends journalists consider four factors – time, resources, shelf life and interactivity – when determining which medium is most appropriate for telling a particular story. This chart was adapted from one Roberts helped develop when he was a deputy managing editor at *The Arizona Republic*.

whether your publication has the time, staff, equipment and other resources to devote to that story. Michael Roberts, project director for NewsTrain, a training organization sponsored by Associated Press Managing Editors, suggests journalists consider four factors when selecting a medium for telling each story (Figure 18.2):

Time–How much time to prepare for publication

Resources–People, hours and equipment required

Shelf life–The amount of time it will still be valuable to users

Interactivity–Opportunities for users to control what they see and hear.

"Each medium has its own limitations and advantages," Roberts says. Over the course of developing their convergent newsroom, the editors at *The Arizona Republic*, where Roberts was a deputy managing editor, carefully analyze audience and use of resources for different types of stories.

TIPSHEET Multimedia reporting

- **Choose the medium that best tells the story.** If you've got action, use video. If a story has a strong sound component, like music, include audio. Use graphics to simplify numbers or explain complex information.
- **Make it interactive.** Give readers something to do – a clickable map, places to comment, polls that allow them to share their opinions or experiences.
- **Keep videos short.** Make them one to two minutes, three at the most. People don't have patience to watch long videos on the Web.
- **Don't be afraid to get close.** Whether you're gathering sound, video or still shots, you need to get the detail shots and sounds that are telling. "If you are shooting a painter, for example, put your lens six inches away from the brush and your microphone so close you can hear the bristles bending," says Brian Singler, a multimedia journalist who blogs about the field at BrianSingler.com.
- **Write a script.** "It can be as simple as making a Word document with two columns," says Singler, "one that has all audio (soundbites, nat sound, voiceover) on one side and all the video on the other. This allows you to match the video and audio, see your story as a whole, find the weak spots and present it to an editor. It also saves time in the long run because your story is laid out for you before you edit, and you don't waste time endlessly swapping around shots and trying to figure things out as you go."
- **Work to get high-quality audio.** If users can't understand what's being said they'll lose interest quickly.
- **Think about the sequence of images.** Plan the string of images in videos and slideshows carefully. Images should not be selected at random. They should fit together to create a story arc.
- **Show, don't tell.** You've heard that old adage about text stories and it holds true for multimedia, too. "Think about what it means," Singler says. "If you're doing a story about an athlete who's motivated by his deceased father's memory, don't show me practice video and tell me about it. Take me into the dorm room, let me see the pictures on the wall, the tears running down the face, the special technique the Dad taught. Go the extra mile to make stories personal."

- **Provide links to relevant resources.** Arm readers with sources they can go to for follow-up or more information. But make sure all sources you link to are credible.
- **Be judicious when manipulating images and sounds.** Don't re-enact events, add sound to a story or manipulate images in any way that can mislead viewers or misrepresent subjects.

CHECKLIST Multimedia equipment

A well-equipped multimedia newsroom should have a collection of equipment including:

Video cameras (whether they are expensive full-size cameras or cheap pocket-style cameras, make sure they have jacks for external microphones)

Digital cameras

A variety of lenses for your cameras

Tripods (ideally ones with a fluid head that allows for smooth panning when shooting video)

Good-quality microphones (lavalier and shotgun, wireless if you can afford them)

Appropriate cables and power cords

Extra DV tapes or SD cards

Extra batteries for all devices, including still and video cameras and microphones

Camera bags for carrying equipment

Computers loaded with photo and video editing software.

Newsroom equipment should be kept in a locked room or cabinet and your newspaper should have a checkout policy, as well as staff to monitor when equipment is removed and returned.

Many student news organizations rely on their staffers to have their own equipment; most student journalists have at least some of their own gear. Multimedia journalists should learn to carry some kind of digital recording device wherever they go. Even a cell phone with a camera or an iPod that records video can come in handy when news breaks.

"We decided to quit covering breaking news with video," Robert says, noting that video took too long to produce and usually held little interest for readers after a day or two. "We decided to use it for stuff with more of a shelf life."

However, video can be useful for certain types of breaking events, particularly if you can livestream it or post lightly edited video quickly. If, for example, a prominent person speaks at your campus or the basketball coach holds a press conference to announce his retirement, you might want to stream the event or post it immediately after.

In addition, your news organization may have a different experience with breaking news video than *The Arizona Republic*. College students are so accustomed to watching video on the Web that you may find breaking stories do well on your site. The key is to watch what your audience likes and doesn't like. Take a hard look at your website traffic. Are your sports podcasts tanking? Are readers flocking to your weekly slideshows of football games? Pay attention to what does well and adjust your coverage accordingly.

SOUND

Audio can be used to enhance other media, such as still photos or text, or for standalone reports like podcasts or radio shows. Podcasts, digital audio files posted to the Web, can be an important tool for providing content on mobile devices, particularly now that smart phones and iPods have become ubiquitous on college campuses.

When capturing sound, think about the three different types of sound.

- **Interviews** with sources – experts, witnesses, people reacting to a story – will provide the backbone of most audio stories.
- **Natural sound,** also known as "nat sound" or ambient sound, are the sounds around your subject – the click of shoes on the floor, the shutting of a door, street traffic, crowd noises, music playing in a nightclub.
- **Voiceover,** or narration, provides context so listeners can better understand the story.

Edited audio stories, like those broadcast on radio, typically capture all three types of sound.

Among the ways your news organization can use audio:

News bulletins. A number of student papers feature podcasts that recap the top stories of the day or week. These may be produced by your college radio station or by your newspaper staff.

Themed podcasts. Many student news organizations run regular podcasts on sports, entertainment or other topics. Often these are in the form of roundtable discussions or interview shows. *The Arbiter* (arbiteronline.com) at Boise State University, for example, has had two weekly sports podcasts – "Sports Talk," where two or three sportswriters talk about the latest news in campus sports, and "Boys in Blue," an interview show about sports. In addition, it has produced "Lights On," a weekly podcast about sex and relationships. Each podcast has had its own Facebook page and Twitter account.

Event coverage. Take an audio recorder to a lecture, conference, rally or other news event. If the audio is evocative or interesting you could run a brief sound clip along with your text story, join it with photographs of the event to make an audio slideshow or create a standalone podcast about the event.

Q&As. This format works well for interviewing student government candidates, campus officials, noted visitors to campus and other newsmakers. Reporters for *The Daily Eastern News* (dennews.com) at Eastern Illinois University have interviewed college sports figures, musicians, the departing university president and even a recovering methamphetamine addict. *The Arbiter* at Boise State did a moving two-part interview with Vietnam veteran Tom Titus about the life and death of his son, Brandon Titus, the sixth soldier from Idaho killed in Iraq.

Media roundtables or interviews with reporters. The *Oregon Daily Emerald* (dailyemerald.com) at the University of Oregon has produced a series of interesting "In the Newsroom" podcasts featuring interviews with staff reporters and special guests about stories in the news. These not only give the back-story on issues of the day, but also give the news organization transparency; readers get a window into how the news operation works. Editors at *The Daily Californian* (dailycal.org) at the University of California, Berkeley have produced audio interviews with staff reporters about major issues they've covered and linked those podcasts to the related news stories.

Audio feature stories. Reporters can also produce National Public Radio-style audio feature stories that incorporate ambient sound, interviews and narration. When a reporter for *Golden Gate [X]press* (goldengatexpress.org) learned that a blind student had installed chimes around the San Francisco State University campus to help other blind students orient themselves, she invited the artist to give an audio tour of the installations. The listener got to experience the sound of the chimes as the blind artist did and also hear him explain the project. Audio was the perfect medium for this story.

When recording audio, remember that sound quality is paramount. Do interviews in a quiet room and use the best microphones you have. The *Daily Sundial* (sundial.csun.edu) at California State University, Northridge has set up four podcasting stations in its newsroom – one in a dedicated multimedia room and three more in a former editor's office that's been turned into a podcasting room. Each station has a soundboard, a telephone, microphones, headphones and a computer loaded with audio editing software. "Students can record phone interviews, do voiceovers, bring in audio files and piece together a full podcast," says Melissa Lalum, publisher of the newspaper. "It's a really nice option to have."

In planning your sound offerings – podcasts, radio shows, audio clips paired with other media – pay attention to who is listening. While some student news organizations have succeeded in developing strong and loyal audiences for their podcasts, others have given up on podcasting for lack of listeners. "The key to a podcast is consistency," says Brad Arendt, director of student media at Boise State University. "I tell my students if you don't do a podcast (or can't) on a regular basis, then don't do it."

TIPSHEET
Audio reporting

Whether it's for a standalone podcast, an audio slideshow or some other purpose, make sure to capture clean audio that's free of distracting noise. Find a quiet place to conduct the interview even if you plan to capture ambient sound – the shouts of protesters, the chants of the cheerleaders at halftime – to add in later. You want to make sure voices can be heard. Some other tips for audio recording:

Invest in high-quality microphones. When it comes to mics you generally get what you pay for. A few audio recorders come with good built-in mics, but most need an external microphone to capture broadcast-quality sound.

Do your research. A recorded interview needs to be more tightly focused than an interview for print. Do some background research and have a list of questions handy. Make sure that you can accurately pronounce the interviewees' names.

Always wear headphones when recording. You may feel self-conscious wearing those big things on your ears, but listening through headphones is the only way to truly hear what you're recording. "A lot of reporters are a little skittish about wearing big headphones in an interview situation, but for me there's a Murphy's Law," *New York Times* multimedia reporter Amy O'Leary told journalists at the 2009 Nieman Conference on Narrative Journalism. "If you're not wearing headphones anything can go wrong and you won't know. It's like trying to take a picture without a viewfinder."

Check your mic placement. Generally you want the microphone to be about a fist's length from the subject's mouth, set just under the chin. If the microphone is too close or positioned directly across from the source's mouth, the sound may be distorted. If the mic is too far from the source, the sound may be too distant.

Check your sound levels. Before you begin recording, sample different volumes and microphone distances to help you find the best levels. Mic up close. Mic further away. Listen to how it sounds. A sound check involves more than simply saying, "Testing, testing, 1, 2, 3." Listen for sound quality, volume levels and distracting noises like humming computers or refrigerators. Some radio reporters even ask if they can turn off machines while they conduct an interview.

Hold the microphone or recorder yourself; never give it to your source. There is a psychological reason for this as well as a technical one. You want to be in control of the interview. In addition, it takes practice to hold a mic still; don't leave that up to your subject. Even a slight move of the hand or a tap on the microphone can ruin your sound. Be careful not to move your fingers, hand or arm while you are recording.

Mic yourself. Even if you plan to edit your questions out, mic yourself when you pose a question. You might need it to provide context.

Have sources speak their names as you record. That way you'll have a record of the proper pronunciation.

Deconstruct the scene. Try to isolate individual sounds like a dog barking, a door creaking open, a seagull squawking. You may want to mix these into the audio.

Shut up and listen. Don't say "hmm" or "uh-huh" or other listening noises. Nod, smile and use eye contact to let your source know you are listening.

Phrase your questions strategically. In most circumstances you will edit your questions out so construct them in a way that encourages your source to speak in full sentences. You can explain this to your subject at the beginning of the interview. Be careful not to ask questions that will elicit a yes or no answer. But be specific; you don't want your source to go on and on. You want a nice, tight response.

Watch out for background music. Even soft music in the background can make it difficult to edit an interview. Record the music playing and then step away from the music or turn it off for the interviews.

Practice, practice, practice. Recorded interviews are a bit stilted when you're starting out. It takes a while to feel comfortable with the equipment and to get your technique down. Practice on a friend a few times before recording for broadcast.

Collect ambient sound. If you're doing more than a simple Q&A, collect sounds from the environment. A story on a ceramics class, for example, might include the whirring of the pottery wheel, the sounds of people slapping and kneading the clay, the chatter before class as students admire each other's work.

Pay attention to your voice. Use inflection to add emotion to your comments and questions. This will prompt your source to be more animated and it will make for more interesting conversation if you don't edit out your questions.

Record a minute or two of room tone. You can use this to cover the sound gaps under the narration or between audio clips.

Re-record the key points. Mindy McAdams, a professor of journalism at the University of Florida, offers this strategy for recording audio interviews on her blog, *Teaching Online Journalism* (mindymcadams.com/toujou): "When you've finished, stop the recorder. Put on your headphones. Start a new recording, and explain to your subject that you need to put some audio online." Then repeat two or three of the most important questions, the ones that yielded the most interesting or relevant answers the first time around. "There are two benefits," McAdams explains. "1. The subject's answers are often more compact and organized the second time. 2. Your job of editing is easier, because the short (second) audio file will take less time to cut."

Add some professional touches. Use music, intros and outros to give your podcast some style. Introduce your report and guest at the beginning and sign off at the end by saying your name and the name of the podcast and or your news organization.

EDITING AUDIO

While your student news organization may have expensive audio editing software like Apple's Soundtrack Pro or Avid's Pro Tools, there are also a lot of cheap or free options available. GarageBand, which is installed in most Apple computers, and Audacity, which can be downloaded for free, are good alternatives and do most of what you'll need to create professional-quality audio reports.

One of the best ways to become a skilled audio editor is to listen to a lot of good audio. If you're not already a radio news junkie, flip on your local public radio station or check out podcasts of shows like "Morning Edition," "All Things Considered," "Fresh Air," "To the Best of Our Knowledge," "This American Life" and "Radio Lab." Listen carefully to how each piece is constructed, noting what's included and what's left out. Pay attention to the use of natural sound, supplementary music and narration. Some radio shows publish transcripts and it can be helpful to look at these before writing your own script.

For an edited podcast or radio show, audio editors usually follow these steps:

1. Transcribe all interviews – or at least the parts of the interview you're likely to use.
2. Choose the actualities, or "sound bites" you plan to use, usually 10- to 20-second clips of an interview, and highlight these on your transcript.
3. Write your script, including the actualities you plan to use and narration that will tie the sound bites together into a story.
4. Choose natural sound clips or music you will use to help tell the story or set the mood.
5. Record your narration.
6. Edit the actuality, narration, natural sound clips and music together.

For training in particular audio editing software, such as GarageBand or Audacity, see the tutorials listed at the end of this chapter.

SLIDESHOWS AND AUDIO SLIDESHOWS

A photographer comes back to the newsroom with 75 photos of the new student orientation week. Do you put them all into a slideshow or gallery? No! Just because you've got the space online doesn't mean you should put up every photo you've got. Choose photos carefully.

In planning a slideshow, with or without a soundtrack:

Look for variety – different subjects, different angles, different moods make for a more interesting slideshow.

Shoot in sequences. Think like a videographer; take wide shots, medium shots and lots of close ups. Consider how you can weave them into logical sequences

Find a narrative arc. Look for a clear story line with a beginning, middle and end.

Be ruthless in choosing images. Just because you have five great shots of the mascot at your football game doesn't mean you should use all of them. Choose the best one or create a sequence that simulates action.

Select your opening shot carefully. The first photo of the slideshow should establish the scene. Look for a shot that tells viewers where they are or one that introduces the main subject.

End on a mood. Choose a final shot that gives viewers a sense of closure or completion.

Many photographers find an audio soundtrack can enhance a slideshow. Soundslides, an inexpensive program for creating audio slideshows developed by photojournalist Joe Weiss, has made making audio slideshows easy. Audio slideshows can also be made in Final Cut Express, Final Cut Pro and other video editing software.

If your slideshow will include a soundtrack, keep these additional tips in mind.

- **Match audio and images.** If your slideshow about tailgate parties shows images of hamburgers cooking on the grill, let your viewer hear the sizzle.
- **Use lower thirds titles.** Don't have sources introduce themselves. Use titles to give name, position, major or other identifying facts.
- **Use natural sound clips to help set the mood.** Include protest chants at a demonstration or the mooing of a cow on the vet school farm.
- **Find an evocative opening sound.** "It's best to open your show with a bit of natural sound rather than with a subject talking," Colin Mulvany, a multimedia producer at *The Spokesman-Review* in Spokane, Washington, wrote in a post for his blog, *Mastering Multimedia* (masteringmultimedia.wordpress.com). "The ramp up into your story is important. If you don't pull the viewer in fast they will bolt. Natural sound eases the viewer into your story without jolting them with dialogue."
- **Pace your show deliberately.** Make sure the images move slowly enough that viewers can really take in the photos but not so slow that they get bored.

WEB-BASED VIDEO

Web-based video has exploded in the past few years as equipment costs have plummeted and as Internet connections have gotten faster. Even a financially challenged student newspaper can afford a pocket video camera or two and many students already have video capability on their cell phones and MP3 players. The key to video is figuring out how and when to use it.

There are several different kinds of video stories and it's important to understand the differences between them so you can choose the right video approach for each story.

Raw video footage–good for breaking news; gives news consumers a sense of what's happening as the story unfolds (good for natural disasters, riots, demonstrations, spirit activities); may run with a text story that provides context.

Live webcast–ongoing coverage of a planned news event, such as a public meeting or an important speech. For example, when the president of the University of Kentucky held a news conference to announce his retirement, the *Kentucky Kernel* (kykernel.com) streamed a live video of the event.

Quick news video–lightly edited video that can be completed and posted within minutes or hours of an event (good for community events, such as festivals, parades, holiday celebrations); can run with a text story that provides context.

Polished feature video–a more thoroughly reported and edited video, usually on a person, place or issue rather than an event; may stand alone or run with a text story.

User-submitted video–video of an event submitted by a user that can supplement news coverage.

Broadcast-style video reports–video reports of the day's or the week's news. *The Crimson White* (cw.ua.edu) at the University of Alabama, for example, does a weekly video "Week in Review" broadcast.

Man on the street–many student publications do regular person-on-the-street interviews on a topical issue. Some papers transcribe these interviews for the print edition.

Web videos should be short – generally no more than three or four minutes – and 90 seconds may be plenty. Don't feel you have to tell the whole story in video. You may use text, graphics or other media to add to the story, explaining complex concepts or offering background and context.

FIGURE 18.3 *The Daily Tar Heel* has a regular video feature called "Close Ups" offering intimate profiles of people on campus. *The Daily Tar Heel*, University of North Carolina, Chapel Hill.

TELLING STORIES WITH VIDEO

A video story should be tightly focused. Don't try to tell the entire story of budget cuts on your campus in one video. Leave the big issues to text or tell them in a multimedia package. Video is better for a narrow story, a small slice of life or a portrait of a person that represents an issue.

An edited video piece is made up of A-roll – interviews – and B-roll, supplementary footage that illustrates some aspect of the story, either what the subject is talking about or what he's doing when he's not being interviewed. Once you've introduced the speaker, keep talking heads to a minimum. A video on your football coach, for example, might include B-roll of the coach instructing players at a practice, training an athlete, joking with team members in the locker room and throwing up his hands on the sidelines at a game. Each B-roll scene should complement what the coach is saying in the interview.

Find a narrative arc for your video – a clear and logical way of telling the story that has a beginning, middle and end. It may be chronological, following your college president through a day, for example, or showing a process, such as blowing a glass figurine or mounting a theatrical performance, from beginning to end. Or you may present a narrative arc that sets up a conflict and then finds some kind or resolution.

The best videos have well delineated characters. Even if your story focuses on an issue or trend, it will be stronger if it has a distinctive protagonist. If you're focusing on the long hours worked by residents at your university hospital, find one and follow her through an entire shift. If your story is about tuition increases, focus on one student who has to work extra hours at her waitressing job and show her at work while she talks about the extra burden.

The Daily Tar Heel (dailytarheel.com) has run a feature called "Close Ups," video profiles of students. The videos, all shot in black and white, offer intimate portraits of the subjects. One focused on a freshman's first night as a radio DJ (Figure 18.3) another on an ROTC cadet. One of the most powerful portrayed a fraternity president who was elected after his predecessor, one of his best friends, was shot and killed by police.

When capturing video, make sure to shoot a lot more than simply your interview. Collect footage of the medical resident examining patients, conferring with colleagues, catching a catnap, writing a prescription. Shoot in sequences. Show the young doctor knocking on a patient's hospital room door, opening the door, walking in, greeting the patient. Get a variety of shots – wide shots, medium shots and lots and lots of close-ups. Focus in on her hand as she writes a prescription or when she holds the stethoscope

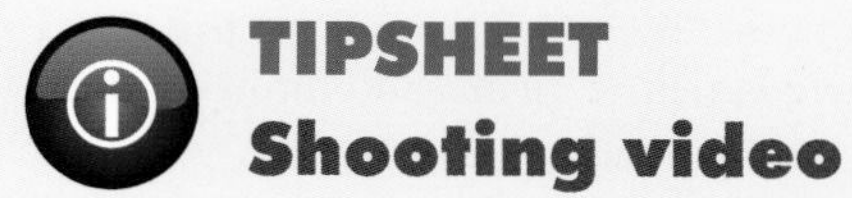

TIPSHEET
Shooting video

1 **Think before shooting.** Plan your shots even before you go out and shoot. Make a list of the shots you know you'll need. Write the story in your head and think about what shots you can get to illustrate the major points.

2 **Monitor your audio.** As with audio reporting, always wear headphones.

3 **Use a tripod.** It's hard to hold a video camera still. Whenever possible, use a tripod to steady your shot. If a tripod isn't available, plant your feet firmly on the ground and hold the camera with both hands, pressing your elbows against your sides.

4 **Limit your dependency on the built-in mic.** Whenever possible, use an external microphone to capture sound. Video depends on high-quality sound and most on-board mics aren't up to the job.

5 **Shoot selectively.** Remember that you're going to have to review everything you shoot. Stop the camera between shots or in dead moments when nothing is really happening. The less you shoot, the less you'll have to edit out.

6 **Shut up.** As with audio recording, don't make listening noises.

7 **Look for a good establishing shot.** Keep an eye out for a sign, the outside of a business or another shot that will help establish a sense of place.

8 **Include people.** When shooting a scene – a park or outside a building, for example – try to get people in it. A shot of a building, for example, will be more interesting if you can capture people walking in or out rather than simply a shot of the building with no action.

9 **Hold your shots.** Keep your camera on the subject for at least 10 to 15 seconds before moving to another shot.

10 **Limit panning and zooming.** When you first get behind a camera it's fun to zoom in and out and pan across a scene. Resist the urge. Overuse of panning and zooming makes your video look shaky and unprofessional. When you do pan or zoom, use slow, smooth motions to limit shake.

11 **Frame your shots carefully.** Remember the rule of thirds. Divide your screen into three equal strips vertically and horizontally, like a tic-tac-toe pattern. When framing a person, you want their eyes on the top line and the center of their head on the left or the right line. Fill the frame with your subject and everything else you want to include – the bookshelf behind the professor in the interview, for example, or the flag behind the politician in her office. But be careful of plants, sticks or other things in the background that could look like they're growing out of the person's head.

12 **Make eye contact with your interview subject.** In interviews, use the LCD monitor on the camera to watch the interview while you look over the camera and at the subject. This will make your subject feel more comfortable.

13 **Leave headroom and nose room.** Position your subject a little to the left or right of center and leave a little room in front of the nose and above the head. A three-quarter view of the face is ideal.

14 **Get in close.** The best videos have a lot of close shots – people's hands doing things, expressions on faces. Don't be afraid to get up close and personal.

15 **Watch the light.** Don't shoot your subject in front of a window or with the sun behind him, unless you want the person to appear in silhouette (a technique sometimes used for anonymous sources). The best light source comes from behind the camera.

16 **Vary your shots.** Get a mix of wide shots (a whole room, for example, or an outdoor scene), medium shots (such as a person doing something), close-ups (a person's face) and extreme close-ups (a smile, a hand).

17 **Vary your angles and perspectives.** Shoot from up above, down below; look for interesting perspectives, such as through a bicycle wheel in a bike shop. If you're shooting a dance class, focus on people's feet as well as their faces and bodies. Try for unique and creative angles that will make your video more interesting.

18 **Shoot in sequences.** Get shots of each step in a process – a person reaching for a door handle, opening a door, walking through the doorway, etc.

19 **Shoot action and reaction.** If you're shooting two people conversing, focus on the speaker and then focus on the other person reacting to the speaker. With every action, try to find a reaction.

20 **Anticipate action.** If you're shooting a game, position your camera where you think the ball is going to go.

to a little boy's chest. Show her face as she sleeps on the doctors' lounge couch.

Some videographers combine still photos with video footage to catch particular moments in time.

Remember that just as with a text story you need to seek multiple points of view on every story. If you're profiling a basketball coach, interview players, fans, the university president, the coach's wife. Though in-person video interviews often take more time to set up than phone or email interviews for a text story, that doesn't excuse one-source stories. A good video must be thoroughly reported.

MULTIMEDIA PROJECTS

Multimedia storytelling lends itself to big projects and collaboration because you can tell different parts of a story in different ways. In the 2008–09 academic year the student media organizations at Colorado State University – *The Rocky Mountain Collegian* newspaper (collegian.com), KCSU radio, CTV television and *College Avenue* magazine (collegeavenuemag.com) – collaborated monthly on a series of multimedia projects. Topics included AIDS, living with disability, Black History Month, faith and marijuana. Staffers prepared podcasts, videos, text stories and slideshows and packaged the projects for television, radio, newspaper, magazine and the Web.

"It went really well," says Jenny Fischer, creative services manager for student media at Colorado State and adviser to the magazine. "We had a lot of buy-in from the staff." The collaborative projects helped bring different factions of the college media operation together. Leaders of the four media met weekly while they were working on projects, brainstorming ideas and sharing information. "It was important to make sure all areas were represented and to keep the lines of communication open," Fischer says.

The following year the student media organizations collaborated on just one big project, Project Earth on the 40th anniversary of Earth Day.

Fischer says collaborative projects are a good way to foster strong relationships between different media on campus. They also give student news organizations a chance to do more ambitious projects than they could take on alone because they can combine resources.

But of course you don't need multiple media organizations or a cast of dozens to take on a big project. Sometimes just two or three people can produce an impressive project.

When University of Missouri Tigers wide receiver Jeremy Maclin appeared headed for the pros in the winter of his sophomore year, Brian Singler, a master's student at the journalism school there and multimedia editor for the *Columbia Missourian* (columbianmissourian.com), saw an opportunity for a major project. "Maclin was easily among the top skills players to ever come out of Missouri, with a legitimate shot at being an NFL superstar," Singler says.

"Not many of those have come out of Missouri over the decades. I recognized that following his path to the NFL would likely be the best story I would be able to cover at MU, one that may not come around again for years."

Around the time that Singler started working on the video, Robert Mays III, a magazine writing student, also became intrigued by the Maclin story and decided to write a profile of the athlete. "We quickly realized this story was a chance to showcase how print and multimedia work together," Singler says.

"I could tell the story of 'now,' the diet, training, the family, the thought process. That was what I could show. Robert could tell you about the high school and PeeWee days and other aspects of the story without a strong visual component."

Over the course of three months, Singler documented every part of Maclin's life from his workouts and practice sessions on the field to his diet and room at home with his foster parents (see Figure 18.1).

"The thinking behind the video was to capture the three-month portion of Maclin's life before the NFL draft," Singler wrote on his blog.

"The training videos alone took upwards of 15 visits to the Mizzou Athletics Training Complex to catch each phase of his routine. Throughout the project, I had to be able to drop everything and go where Maclin was going to be, which was early in the morning, late at night, on weekends and at many different locations around Columbia and the state."

Singler advises videojournalists to approach multimedia stories like any other reporter.

"Too often an editor just says 'ooh, that would make great video' and sends a reporter out without thinking about the *story* itself. Video stories need narrative, thought, sources from all sides, structure and a compelling open and close, among a host of other things. Does that sound like a newspaper article? It should because I think of great multimedia like an awesome print story that has come to life through images, graphics, video text and interactivity. Way, way too often (I think because good multimedia can have a high technical ceiling) there's no story development or at best, a bunch of pretty shots strung together with audio filler. That's not great storytelling, but surprisingly, a vast majority of multimedia and video, especially at the newspaper level, follows this same tired formula."

OTHER MULTIMEDIA TOOLS

The Web offers journalists a number of other tools that are not available in print, including interactive maps, searchable databases and animated graphics that can be used to enhance stories or as standalone features. And there are constantly new tools being developed that help journalists tell stories and present information in new ways.

Databases

One of the most popular Web-based features in journalism today is the searchable database, and a number of student newspapers have started displaying these on their websites. In fact, some, like the *Collegiate Times* (collegiatetimes.com) at Virginia Tech (Figure 18.4) and *The Daily Illini* (dailyillini.com) at the University of Illinois have devoted special sections on their websites to databases.

Databases are a big hit with consumers. According to a survey published in 2010 by the Pew Research Center's Internet & American Life Project, "40 percent of adult Internet users have gone online for raw data about government spending and activities."

COLLEGIATETIMES THE EXTRA POINT

VIEW TODAY'S PAPER

Advertising | Photo Reprints
Donate | Event Calendar | Financial

NEWS SPORTS FEATURES OPINIONS SPOTLIGHT DATABASES BLOGS CLASSIFIEDS

Search

Databases

PUBLIC UNIVERSITY SALARIES | GRADES | CRIME

Virginia Tech Public Salaries

VirginiaTech

Available Years:
All - 2007 - 2008 - 2009 - 2010

Faculty Name: Department:

School: Virginia Tech Years: All Search

Currently viewing 150 of 27,653 records matching your query.
Please refine your search using the fields above.

Name	Department	Salary	Year
Charles Steger	President - Admin.	$457,040	2008
Charles W. Steger	President - Admin.	$457,040	2009
Charles W. Steger	President - Admin.	$457,040	2010
Charles Steger	President - Admin.	$439,461	2007
Cynda A. Johnson	Provost - Administration	$414,000	2009
Robert E. Foster	Athletic Department	$404,460	2010
James C. Weaver	Athletic Department	$380,596	2010
Robert E. Foster	Athletic Department	$378,000	2009
James C. Weaver	Athletic Department	$362,472	2009
Robert Foster	Athletic Department	$350,000	2008
James Weaver	Athletic Department	$345,211	2008
Mark McNamee	Provost - Administration	$327,937	2008

facebook
The Collegiate Times
Like 1,055

MOST VIEWED

- Updated: Virginia Tech student who fell from balcony identified
- Updated: Two Virginia Tech cadets in intensive care after Saturday accident
- Burrito connoisseurs camp out for Chipotle grand opening
- Lewis execution underscores immorality of death penalty

MOST COMMENTED

- Updated: Virginia Tech student who fell from balcony identified
- Boucher not adequate representation for district

FIGURE 18.4 The *Collegiate Times* annually publishes a searchable database of salaries of all employees at Virginia Tech, as well as salary databases from other schools. *Collegiate Times*, Virginia Tech University.

The hands-down most common data student newspapers publish is salary information, which is available by law at all public universities. (Student journalists at private schools are at a disadvantage here; few schools make this information available if the law does not require them to.) While this information is a matter of public record, some school officials may be resistant to hand it over. *The Daily Illini* at the University of Illinois, for example, had to file a Freedom of Information Act request to get the university to release salary data. Once the information was obtained, the newspaper published a database searchable by employee's name, department, title, campus or salary range. The newspaper's report on the data included a list of top earners, those making more than $300,000. The database allows readers to learn how much the Fighting Illini football team pays its coach and see who makes more, an adjunct history professor or the janitor who cleans her office.

"As soon as we decided to print a salary guide, we realized that the power of an online database may be even stronger than a print product because of its ability to be searchable and reach so many more people," says Melissa Silverberg, who was managing editor at the time and later went on to become editor-in-chief.

"Needless to say, the online database is one of the biggest things we've ever done. From launch to today it has had nearly 750,000 page views. Nothing we have ever done even comes close to that. On the day it launched it had about 168,000 page views."

Response to the publication of the database was heated; the newspaper received dozens of comments, some focusing on the content of the database but many remarking on the paper's decision to publish it. Some people applauded *The Daily Illini* for revealing the information, giving the community a window into how the state university system spent its money. Others said it was irresponsible for the paper to publish salaries, even though the data came from public records. "Do your friends, neighbors and fellow co-workers know how much you make?" wrote one reader. "Would you want them to? Are you really that naive to think that A. co-workers won't look at this information B. hold it against you. Employees in my department couldn't wait to discuss what others make."

"The phone was ringing the whole day and we even had a few people come in and confront us about the salary guide," Silverberg says.

"Many people believed we were wrong to publish their private data when actually since this is a public university their salaries have always been public and available for anyone to research in the university library. All we did was make it more accessible."

On its website, the newspaper provided this explanation of why it was publishing the data:

> Employee salaries are one of the largest items on the University's budget. With the recent mandatory furloughs and changes in the administration, there has never been a more important time for continuing the transparency the University has started. In addition, this list allows the public to see how their tax and tuition dollars are being spent.

The Daily Illini followed up on the publication of the database with a two-part series looking at salary inequalities based on race and gender.

"I think publishing databases is important for any publication because it allows the users to really massage the information, analyze it themselves and use our coverage to better understand what it means to them," Silverberg says.

FIGURE 18.5 *The Ball State Daily News* uses an interactive graphic to show the flight path of an airplane that crashed near Ball State University. *The Ball State Daily News*, Ball State University.

"I think this is particularly important because of the audience we are reporting to. Younger generations know how to get information online because of growing up with computers in front of us, and now in our pockets basically, so as a student newspaper it's important that we are the ones providing them with that information."

At Virginia Tech, the *Collegiate Times* maintains a vast database on its website that includes not only all faculty and staff at the Blacksburg, Virginia school but also data from peer institutions in more than a dozen states. So you can compare the salary of the Hokies' football coach with the coach for the rival Cavaliers at the University of Virginia. Job-hunting professors can use the information to check out how different universities pay.

"The *Collegiate Times* continually updates the database," says Peter Velz, who was editor-in-chief of the paper for the 2010–2011 academic year. "We email a letter to the university's public relations or FOIA compliance office, and we typically receive the data in an Excel file," Velz wrote in an email interview.

"The response to the database is often mixed. About once a week I receive an email or phone call from an irate professor or staff member who wants his name removed from the database. I have to explain that the information is a matter of public record, but more often than not the person understands the situation."

The *Collegiate Times* also developed a grades database that allows readers to search average grades by course, professor and department over the course of several semesters. "This information is collected by Virginia Tech for research purposes, and we post it online so people can research what classes they're signing up for," Velz said.

Andrew Dunn, who describes himself as a "huge data nerd," decided to make databases a top priority when he became editor-in-chief of *The Daily Tar Heel* in 2009. He created a data page for the newspaper's website. "Honestly, none of the things we have on our data page were original ideas, but I looked at what I liked from news organizations around the country and found a way to get the data," says Dunn, who went on to become a reporter for the *Wilmington Star News*.

The Daily Tar Heel started with a salary database and bought a license for Caspio, an online database-publishing tool that allows users to create interactive databases without the need for programming. "The Caspio program makes it extremely easy for student newspapers to publish databases online at relatively little cost," says Dunn. (Caspio offers discounts to nonprofits and educational organizations.) "It's worth it. While a story can sum up trends found in data, readers enjoy being able to delve into the data itself, finding the little nuggets of information most interesting or relevant to them."

Once *The Daily Tar Heel* staff became comfortable creating online databases, reporters began to see how they could use them to help tell stories. A reporter on the newspaper's investigative team who was looking into the distribution of free Tar Heels football tickets to elected officials decided to publish a database of his findings. Readers can search it by an elected official's name, office or even particular football opponent to find out how many tickets were given out.

Dunn says the searchable databases continue to be a big draw to *The Daily Tar Heel* site, even months after they are first published.

"We found that databases were an extremely popular feature for our readers, and were projects that took relatively little time on our part, but were popular for a long time. When we talk about shelf life, this had the greatest of just about anything on our site."

It may be tempting for student journalists to simply publish databases and let readers explore on their own. But don't stop there. Often this kind of data warrants further explanation and context. Like *The Daily Illini*, use data as a starting point; then ask probing questions. How many of the top-paid faculty members at a school are in the athletics department? Why is the university spending more on athletics than on the English department? Why does the women's tennis coach make less than the men's? Once you've got the data, you can tease it out into stories, graphics and lists.

Data visualization

Online databases like the ones described above make data more interesting, but even in an interactive form pure data can be boring. When you've got data, particularly numbers, it's better to say it in pictures. Data visualization – the graphical representation of information – helps readers see what data means. "Visualizations allow us to understand and process enormous amounts of information quickly because it is all represented in a single image or animation," says Mindy McAdams, Knight Chair, journalism technologies and the democratic process at the University of Florida.

Traditional types of data visualization include maps, bar charts, line graphs and pie charts. But new Web-based tools have taken data visualization to a new level, offering online journalists new ways to tell data stories.

New types of data visualization used by online journalists include:

Word clouds

Interactive maps

Animated graphics

Interactive timelines.

10 simple tools for creating interactive graphics and databases

Not that long ago news organizations needed an experienced Web developer and a gifted graphic artist to produce snappy online graphics. But new tools, many of them free, make it easy for almost any journalist to create maps and charts that will help your readers visualize data. Among them:

1. **Many Eyes**–Part of IBM's Collaborative User Experience Visual Communication Lab, this site allows users to upload data and produce graphic representations and then share them with others. **http://manyeyes.alphaworks.ibm.com**
2. **Open Heat Map**–This tool lets you tell stories through heat maps in literally seconds with either an Excel spreadsheet or a Google Docs spreadsheet. You can use the maps to illustrate patterns, highlight intensity levels, showcase regional differences and much more. **www.openheatmap.com**
3. **MapAList**–At this site you can generate a geocoded map from a list of addresses. **http://mapalist.com**
4. **Google Chart Generator**–This tool allows you to generate simple charts using Google Chart API and then add them to any Web page. **http://code.google.com/apis/chart**
5. **Dipity**–Dipity allows you to create embeddable timelines for your website. You can upload photos and links to videos. Use this the next time you report on an anniversary or a story with a number of key events that took place over time. Timelines are great for tracing a person's career, such as a college president or a basketball coach, or for looking back at a series of events like a rash of crimes. **http://dipity.com**
6. **Tableau**–This site offers a set of tools for building interactive graphics based on spreadsheet data. Graphics built with Tableau Public can then be embedded into blogs and websites. **http://tableaupublic.com**
7. **Google Maps**–Probably the most commonly used mapping program, Google Maps offers a simple and fast way to generate easily embeddable interactive maps. Use maps for plotting crimes, multiple venues at a music or film festival or other stories that involve multiple locations. **http://maps.google.com**
8. **Caspio**–For a relatively modest fee you can quickly create online databases and Web forms without writing a single line of code. **www.caspio.com**
9. **Google Fusion Tables**–Set up much like Google Docs in that you can share them with others, Fusion Tables allows you to upload data and use it to create maps, timelines and charts. **www.google.com/fusiontables**
10. **Wordle**–With this toy you can create "word clouds" from text that you provide. The clouds give greater prominence to words that appear more frequently in the text. Try this the next time a celebrity gives a commencement address or your football coach speaks at a press conference. **http://wordle.net**

The Ball State Daily News (bsudailynews.com) created an interactive graphic to show the erratic flight path of a single-engine plane that missed the airport where it was supposed to land and crashed in 2009 near the Ball State University campus (see Figure 18.5). The graphic, which features an audio soundtrack and photos of the crash site, includes information about the airplane, air traffic control procedures and other details that would be clunky to explain in straight text.

Sophisticated data visualizations like the ones produced by *The New York Times* are usually created by experienced Web developers and graphic artists. But there are a bunch of free tools available now, no programming required.

Nathan Lau, a doctoral student in statistics who spent a summer as an intern for *The New York Times* graphics department, says the best examples of data visualization tell a great story. "Maybe the story was to convince us of something, compel us to action, enlighten us with new information, or force us to question our own preconceptions," he wrote on his blog, *Flowing Data* (flowingdata.com). "Whatever it is, truly great data visualization reaches us at a very human level and that is why we remember them."

FIGURE 18.6 Interactive maps have become the modern crime blotter. On the *Arizona Daily Wildcat's* website (wildcat.arizona.edu), viewers can click on a map and read about crimes. *Arizona Daily Wildcat*, University of Arizona.

Multimedia skills training opportunities

Do you want to be a multimedia journalist but your school doesn't have the classes you need?

Here are some online resources for picking up a range of multimedia skills:

BBC Academy–The folks at the BBC offer face-to-face courses and online training in audio, video and multimedia storytelling.
www.bbctraining.com

BBC News School Report–Don't worry that this site is designed for school kids; it offers some great tips on producing audio reports, everything from using a microphone and writing for radio to editing and presentation.
http://news.bbc.co.uk/2/hi/school_report/5275764.stm

J-Learning–J-Learning describes itself as a "how-to site for community journalism." It offers free articles and tutorials on a host of multimedia skills including Web design, blogging, photography, audio, video and databases.
www.j-learning.org

Knight Digital Media Center–A partnership between USC Annenberg and UC Berkeley Graduate School of Journalism funded by the Knight Foundation, the center runs workshops for professional journalists and journalism educators. Its website offers free and easy-to-understand tutorials on video, audio, photography, Web design, Flash, multimedia storytelling and mashups.
www.knightdigitalmediacenter.org

lynda.com–Whether you're into digital photography, Web design and development, motion graphics, or just need to brush up on Excel, you can learn all the software skills you need to gain a competitive edge with these online tutorials. Cost: $25 monthly/$250 annual membership.
http://lynda.com

News University–This online branch of the Poynter Institute offers free and low-cost, Web-based self-directed courses, group seminars and Webinars covering a range of multimedia techniques, as well as other journalism skills.
www.newsu.org

Teaching Online Journalism/Mindy McAdams–Mindy McAdams' Teaching Online Journalism blog offer lots of free advice and tutorials on multimedia skills. Her Reporter's Guide to Multimedia Proficiency, a collection of many of her blog posts, is available as a downloadable PDF at http://mindymcadams.com/tojou/2009/now-printable-reporters-guide-to-multimedia-proficiency/.
http://mindymcadams.com/tojou

Interactive maps

Has there been a rash of thefts on your campus? Map them. Are there a dozen bars near your school offering special events for the Super Bowl? Map them. Did a recent storm down tree limbs and power lines around campus? Map them.

Interactive maps, sometimes called map mashups because they mash together content from different sources, are an engaging way of sharing information that has a geographic element. Unlike static maps found in print, these maps are dynamic; users can click on a spot and find out more information, see a photograph or even view a video. And with free programs like ZeeMaps, Google My Maps, MapAList and MapBuilder, they're easy to make and embed on your website.

Probably the most popular use of interactive mapping in the college press is crime data. The interactive crime map has replaced the traditional police blotter at many college newspapers, including *The Daily Collegian* at Penn State University, *The Red and Black* (redandblack.com) at the University of Georgia, the *Arizona Daily Wildcat* (wildcat.arizona.edu) at the University of Arizona (see Figure 18.6) and *The Nevada Sagebrush* (nevadasagebrush.com) at the University of Nevada, Reno.

But don't stop at standalone maps; interactive maps can provide geographic context to feature stories and breaking news. When *The Daily Pennsylvanian* (dailypennsylvanian.com) did a story on dining venues open late at night during finals week, the website ran an interactive map showing the location and hours of the restaurants. When *Golden Gate [X]press* at San Francisco State University reported on seismically unsafe buildings on California campuses, the staff produced an interactive map showing just which buildings were at high risk of collapsing during an earthquake.

Maps can enhance breaking news stories, too. If a natural disaster strikes your community, you can map the damage – as *The Daily Reveille* (lsureveille.com) did with Hurricane Gustav – showing closed roads, ruined buildings or power outages. If a shooting occurs on your campus you can use a map to track the gunman's path.

You can even involve your readers in the mapping process. When gas prices shot up in 2007, *The Independent Florida Alligator* at the University of Florida, Gainesville (alligator.org) built a map showing prices at gas stations around town. A box on the website allowed users to report prices they had found.

TO DO

1. Look critically at the way your news organization has used multimedia. Are your multimedia stories compelling? Are you using each medium to its best advantage?
2. Plan an ambitious multimedia project that brings together different factions of your staff or different media organizations from your university. Appoint a leader to oversee the project and to make sure all voices are heard.
3. Look for funding to buy new equipment. Many state and regional journalism organizations, such as state newspaper publishers associations or a Society of Professional Journalists chapter, offer grants for student news organizations. Your school may also have funding for equipment.
4. Organize a multimedia workshop for students and professionals in your city or region. Many professionals would facilitate a training session for little or no money if you provide the space and possibly the equipment.
5. Have a brainstorming session for your staff geared toward multimedia storytelling. Think about new ways you can use interactive databases, maps, video and audio to tell the stories of your community.

TO READ

Briggs, Mark, *Journalism Next: A Practical Guide to Digital Reporting and Publishing*, Washington, DC: CQ Press, 2010.

Luckie, Mark S. *The Digital Journalist's Handbook*, CreateSpace, 2010.

McAdams, Mindy. *Flash Journalism: How to Create Multimedia News Packages*. Burlington, Mass.: Focal Press, 2005.

TO CLICK

Association of Independents in Radio (AIR)
The website of this global social and professional network of 750 producers offers training materials and advice on interviewing, choosing equipment, capturing ambient sound and other topics.
www.airmedia.org

Interactive Narratives
Sponsored by the Online News Association, Interactive Narratives is designed to capture the best of online visual storytelling as practiced by online and print journalists from around the world.
www.interactivenarratives.org

The Kobré Guide to the Web's best videojournalism
Kenneth Kobré, a professor of photojournalism at San Francisco State University, leads viewers on a tour of the best videojournalism around. Come here for inspiration.
www.kobreguide.com

Mastering Multimedia
Multimedia journalist Colin Mulvany shares tips and techniques about multimedia storytelling in this blog.
http://masteringmultimedia.wordpress.com

Multimedia Shooter
This blog started by Richard Koci Hernandez is chock full of tutorials, advice and inspiration from a team of multimedia journalists.
www.multimediashooter.com

thebattalion

• wednesday, march 24, 2010 • serving texas a&m since 1893 • first paper free – additional copies $1 • © 2010 student media

Grammar not affected by Web sites, texting

Katy Ralston
The Battalion

Facebook, Twitter, texting, Second Life, e-mail — the list goes on. In the past few years, technology has saturated the life of the college student. These new mediums have opened the door to shorthand typing, abbreviations, emoticons and instant message lingo, causing some people to fear the decline of the formal English language. The question of whether it is making a difference in student's formal writing is debatable.

Texas A&M University Writing Center Executive Director Valeria Balester says it does not have an effect.

While there are still mistakes in student's grammar usage, Balester said she has not seen an increase or decline in the amount of errors in the 20 years she has taught writing.

"Any teachers who are assuming [errors] are increasing don't have any evidence for that. It's just anecdotal," Balester said.

Freshman architecture major Corinne Nelson said she doesn't think social networking plays a role in student's grammar abilities either.

"If someone has good grammar it's not going to make it worse," Nelson said.

See **Grammar** on page 4

Game plan

Students can waste days fake farming or collecting Farkle chips on Facebook. Avoid these games or try to log off the site before it becomes an addiction and sucks all the studying from your life.

voices | 7

Workplaces should avoid stalking employees online

Gloria Gadsden, a sociology professor at East Stroudsburg University in Pennsylvania was suspended for comments made on her Facebook page.

Ian McPhail

As social networking sites grow in popularity, more businesses are disciplining employees because of online content. Instead of overreacting to off-color remarks made outside of work, employers need to stop invading employees' personal lives.

Sites like Facebook and MySpace are well-known even to those technologically illiterate. Content placed online, especially on networking sites, has become accessible to almost anyone. Gadsden believed her Facebook status would remain private, and despite having no student listed as a friend, a pupil

See **Facebook** on page 7

this day in world history

March 24, 1874

Harry Houdini (1874-1926) was born (as Erik Weisz) in Budapest, Hungary. He came to the U.S. with his family as an infant and lived in New York City. He began as a Coney Island magician, then became a world famous escape artist, known for escaping from chains, handcuffs, straightjackets, locked boxes and milk cans filled with water. He died from a burst appendix and was buried in Queens, N.Y.

'Dwell time' for military to change

Samantha Johnson
The Battalion

Lt. Gen. David Huntoon Jr., the director of Army Staff, spoke to a group of junior and senior Corps of Cadets under contract with the military about changes to time length between deployments.

"I want to thank you for raising your hand and volunteering to serve your country in a time of war," Huntoon said. "You have lots of options, but you decided to put on this uniform when we need you."

One issue that Huntoon addressed is referred to as "dwell time," the amount of time that soldiers spend home in between deployments. The rate is one year deployed, followed by one year at home.

"We know that if we want to sustain an all-volunteer military, we have to improve that," he said.

Huntoon said the goal was by early 2011 soldiers can begin to have two years at home for every year they are deployed, but the time spent at home will not be all rest.

"There will be a deep breath where you

See **Army** on page 4

Sam Smith — THE BATTALION

Lt. Gen. David Huntoon Jr., the director of Army Staff, speaks to a group of junior and senior Corps of Cadets under contract with the military about their future.

Student loans to shift hands

Robert Carpenter
The Battalion

Beginning this summer, Texas A&M students seeking student loans will be doing business with the federal government.

The change comes as the University transitions from the Federal Family Education Loan Program to the Federal Direct Loan Program. Formerly, students received student loans through private banks, however, these loans were insured against default by the federal government.

Under the new program, students seeking loans will skip the middleman and receive loans directly from the U.S. Department of Education.

Joe Pettibon, assistant provost of student financial aid, said the University could have made the transition as early as 1993, but rejected the opportunity because private banks typically offered better options to students.

This changed, he said, when the credit crunch began driving banks

See **Student loans** on page 4

Fast facts

- 17,500 Texas A&M students have student loans
- Approximately half of A&M undergraduates will have student loans upon graduation
- The Congressional Budget Office anticipates $61 billion in federal savings over the next 10 years
- 4.4 million direct student loans in the U.S.

Pg 1-03.24.10.indd 1 3/23/10 10:37 PM

FIGURE 19.1 Social networking has revolutionized the news media, transforming the relationship between journalists and their sources and raising new ethical quandaries. *The Battalion*, Texas A&M University. Illustration by Evan Andrews.

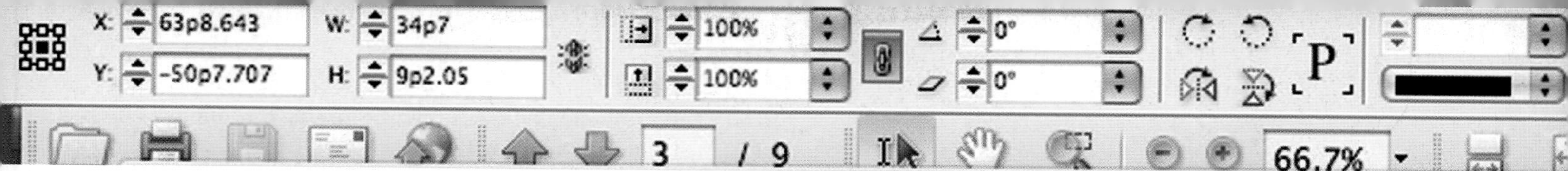

CHAPTER 19
SOCIAL MEDIA

In 2010 the University of Nevada was in the midst of the worst budget crisis it had ever encountered. When the Board of Regents met in June, students, faculty and staff from Las Vegas, as well as other schools in the eight-campus system, knew that the cuts were going to be severe. But no one knew just where the axe would fall.

Only a tiny fraction of the thousands who would be affected were able to attend the two-day meeting in Reno. But readers of *The Rebel Yell* (unlvrebelyell.com), the student newspaper at the University of Nevada, Las Vegas, didn't need to be in the room to know what was going on. Haley Etchison, then news editor of the paper, reported live from the meeting using CoveritLive. "I covered every single thing that happened," says Etchison, "I was typing frantically for 20 hours over two days."

CoveritLive is a live blogging tool that allows users to report on meetings, speeches, games and other events in real time. Reporters can post text, links, photos and videos, and viewers can follow along and even comment on the coverage as it unfolds. Etchison posted a minute-by-minute report on the meeting, including quotes from faculty begging that their programs be spared and comments from regents as they discussed the tough decisions they would have to make. When the board was about to

The Student Newspaper Survival Guide, Second Edition. Rachele Kanigel.

CHAPTER CONTENTS

move on to a new issue, she'd sometimes add a poll to see how readers felt about it. She was able to add links to articles and documents on the Web. And she recorded each vote as it happened.

"We provided the most comprehensive coverage of any media outlet there," Etchison says. "The local professional press covered maybe 5 percent of the amount of information I was able to cover. And because I had really good notes, my print coverage was more comprehensive, too."

Social media tools like CoveritLive, Facebook, Twitter, Flickr and others that continue to emerge, are revolutionizing the way journalists find, report and distribute news. "Social media is the biggest advance in the Internet for journalists since the debut of the public Web," says Sree Sreenivasan, dean of student affairs at Columbia University's Graduate School of Journalism and a noted expert in new media.

Consider this:

Social media has transformed the relationship between journalists and sources. Sources who may have once kept their distance are now "friending" and tweeting the very reporters whose phone calls they wouldn't return.

Social media has changed the relationship between journalists and readers. Journalists needn't wonder anymore what their readers want to read; they can ask them by sending out queries and monitoring discussions on social networking sites.

Social media has blurred the line between journalists and non-journalists. Many college and professional news organizations now routinely use photos, videos and other content from citizens in their coverage.

WHAT IS SOCIAL MEDIA?

Everyone's talking about social media these days, but what does the term really mean? In 2010, the social media blog *Mashable.com* posed this question and asked people to respond in up to 140 characters, the length of a Twitter post. Among the responses:

> Social media is a phenomenon which creates a personalized network for sharing digital content among all people in the cyberspace.
>
> ROHAN AURORA, BIOMEDICAL ENGINEERING STUDENT, INDIA

> It's a conversation in an instant with anyone, anywhere, anytime that gives control back to the individual and consumer in unprecedented ways.
>
> CHARLES UBAGHS, WRITER, LONDON

> Relationshipping on steroids.
>
> PAT GRAHAM-BLOCK, ENTREPRENEUR, MARYLAND

Clearly, social media means different things to different people. For news consumers it means they can go beyond simply listening, watching and reading to actually interacting with the information they consume – and with the journalists who produce the news. For journalists, it means they can connect with readers in a more instantaneous, more intimate and more meaningful way than ever before.

Charlie Eisenhood got a taste of that kind of instantaneous connection when he liveblogged a student takeover of a campus cafeteria at New York University for the news blog *NYU Local* (nyulocal.com) (Figure 19.2) For nearly 30 hours, Eisenhood posted minute-by-minute video, photo and text updates of the demonstration from inside the building where members of the left-leaning group Take Back NYU had barricaded themselves. Eisenhood used Twitter to post brief updates and Ustream to post live video. He incorporated comments from readers in his posts and demonstrators responded to his coverage as he was reporting the news. It was social media journalism at its best.

"I didn't really plan out what I was going to do, I just documented what was happening all around me," says Eisenhood, who went on to become editor-in-chief of *NYU Local*. "I knew people would want to see pictures and look at videos so I uploaded them as quickly as possible."

Eisenhood's coverage was unlike anything a traditional news organization would write. It was raw and real, laced with editorial commentary and, he admits, a few errors. "It was this crazy story happening. Sometimes with hard news you need to just report the facts. But in this case having the (tools) of social media and the editorial freedom of blogging made it a much more interesting story."

NYULOCAL

Home About Masthead Join Advertise City Entertainment National On Campus

FEATURED, ON CAMPUS, ON-CAMPUS DEVELOPING - by Charlie Eisenhood on Wednesday, February 18, 2009 21:15 - 134 Comments - 1,750 views

Exclusive: NYU Students Barricade Doors, Occupy Kimmel

TBNYU

9:18 PM – I'm sitting on the 3rd floor of Kimmel watching as a ton of students roll in for Take Back NYU's 2nd New School sit-in round 2?

I will be here all night live-blogging and posting photos and video of the happenings.

Got any tips/news for me? Send me an email at charlie@wnyu.org. Blog after the jump.

9:23 PM – Security guards took a walk through; there seemed to be no incident.

9:33 PM – I was wrong! Dance party started!

9:44 PM – A security guard told me he doesn't know *what's* going on. He's "just keeping us safe."

Lily Q also rolled through

FIGURE 19.2 *NYU Local* took social media to the max in its coverage of a student group's takeover of a cafeteria at New York University. Reporter Charlie Eisenwood embedded himself with the protesters and liveblogged the takeover for nearly 30 hours. *NYU Local*, New York University.

USING SOCIAL MEDIA FOR JOURNALISM

Social media is vital to journalism today and to journalists who know how to use it. In a 2010 survey of professional journalists by Middleberg Communications and the Society for New Communications Research, 70 percent of journalists said they used social networks to assist in reporting, up from 41 percent the previous year. While journalists across all age groups said they were using social media tools in their everyday work the greatest usage was among "millennial generation" journalists, those in the 18-to-29-year-old age group. In the Middleberg survey, 92 percent of journalists strongly or somewhat agreed that social media enhances journalism, but 100 percent of adults under 30 agreed with this statement.

Columbia University's Sreenivasan says social media can help journalists:

- find new story ideas, trends and sources
- connect with readers and viewers in new ways
- bring eyeballs, traffic and attention to their work
- create, craft and enhance their personal brand.

"Smart journalists understand that social media is for listening, not just broadcasting or sharing what's on your mind," Sreenivasan says.

But social media is still evolving, and it's not always clear how best to use it. You don't want to bombard readers with so many tweets and wall posts that they stop following you. You don't want to be so informal that you alienate your readers.

Lilah Raptopoulos, who was editor-in-chief of *The College Voice* (thecollegevoice.org) at Connecticut College, notes that while student journalists are comfortable with social media they don't necessarily know how to use it for journalism. "As students we're all media fluent," she says. "But as student journalists we need to think about how to use recreational tools in an effective way, in essence how to do business on our playground."

TYPES OF SOCIAL MEDIA TOOLS

Though new applications and services pop up every week, social media can be divided into five main categories: social networking, bookmarking, blogging/microblogging, content sharing and location-based mobile apps.

Social networking sites like Facebook, LinkedIn and Myspace are like Swiss Army knives for journalists. They provide ways to recruit staffers, find sources, connect with readers, promote stories, solicit content and check facts. Every student publication should have a presence on Facebook that is updated regularly. Don't just post headlines and beg readers to pick up your newspaper; be creative. The *Minnesota Daily* (mndaily.com) at the University of Minnesota, for example, offers movie passes and other freebies on its Facebook page, as well as headlines. *The College Voice* uses Facebook for fact checking and finding photos. "If we need to verify a student's class year or dorm of residence (or various other facts), Facebook can be a quick help," says Raptopoulos. "If the night before a deadline we need a photo for a story, we can find one on Facebook and then call or email the photographer for their permission and a hi-res version."

Curation tools like Storify allow journalists to pull social media content, such as tweets, photos, blog posts and videos, from a variety of sources and create them into a single story. *Golden Gate [X]press* (goldengatexpress.org), the student newspaper at San Francisco State University, used Storify when the app was still in beta testing in 2011 to cover a national day of protest against cuts to public education. Coverage included tweets and photos from demonstration organizers, participants, faculty and students, as well as reporters in the field. Together these news tidbits offered a fuller, more complete picture than a single journalist (or even a group of staff reporters and photographers) could create.

Social bookmarking tools like Delicious and Digg are designed to organize, store, manage and search information on the Internet. Reporters can use them to keep track of online research materials, such as articles, reports and websites, creating their own personal libraries of information. This is particularly useful at student publications where staffers switch beats frequently; a reporter can now leave a trail of resources for the next student covering his beat. Many news organizations put bookmarking plug-ins for Reddit, StumbleUpon, Delicious, Digg and other bookmarking tools on their websites so readers can easily share content with their friends.

Content sharing sites like YouTube and Flickr provide storage space as well as access to videos and photos produced by community members. Many student newspapers have a channel on YouTube to display staff-produced videos. Editors can search for campus photos and videos on these sharing sites when they need visuals to go with their stories. (If you do this, be sure to get permission from the creator before publishing a photo or video on your website.)

Blogging/microblogging tools like Twitter have quickly become an important tool for communicating with readers and promoting content. But again, don't simply publish headlines and link to stories. Make it a conversation. Ask questions. Retweet what your readers say. Liveblogging tools like CoveritLive and Livestream can be great for reporting breaking news as it happens or for having conversations with readers. The *Kentucky Kernel* (kykernal.com) at the University of Kentucky, for example, has used CoveritLive for everything from reporting on big games to webcasting the university president's announcement that he was retiring.

Location-based services like Foursquare and Gowalla started out as a sport for geeks. But journalists have begun to use them to report the news. For example, you can quickly find a source at the scene of an event or alert people to news at a particular location. *The Chronicle* (dukechronicle.com) at Duke University has used Foursquare to create an interactive guide to landmarks on and near campus. Users can then add their comments, reminding people of $1 concessions on Thursday nights at the Durham Bulls ballpark, for example, or recommending the crab burritos at a local Mexican restaurant. At *The Daily Collegian* (collegian.psu.edu) at Penn State University, film critics have used Foursquare to promote their reviews. "When reviewers are out covering a movie, they'll check in at the movie theater and then tell people to check Friday's paper for their review," says Elizabeth Murphy, who was editor-in-chief. "It's showing our readers we're out there getting the story, we're out there talking to people."

FINDING STORY IDEAS

Social media sites can be treasure troves for story ideas. By monitoring what's being written about your school or about particular relevant issues you can spot stories quickly. *The Spartan Daily* (spartandaily.com) at San Jose State University, for example, has a search set up on HootSuite, a social media dashboard that allows you to track key words, for anyone who mentions the university on Twitter. "That has proved invaluable in a handful of cases," says Suzanne Yada, former online editor for the newspaper. "We can be alerted to news stories posted by the mainstream media the moment they appear, and we can take action."

Yada also picked up leads for stories that no one else has. For example, one San Jose State Twitterer mentioned a blind classmate in an orchestra class.

"I messaged her and got more details: Apparently the Braille technician on campus had moved on to another job, and the blind student wasn't able to have the sheet music printed in Braille, so the orchestra had to be limited to pieces that were already available in Braille. It was an interesting story I don't think I would have found any other way."

REPORTING WITH SOCIAL MEDIA

Reporters are increasingly using social networking tools to identify and develop sources and learn what readers want to know. When Emily Stephenson at *The Daily Tar Heel* (dailytarheel.com) was working on a series about health care reform, she used Twitter and Facebook to ask readers what they wanted to know and to solicit opinions on the legislation. She incorporated these comments into her story.

When Raptopoulos of *The College Voice* got a message from her college president saying that a student named Elizabeth Durante had died in a car crash, her first instinct was to look Durante up on Facebook. There she found, not only Durante's friends, photos and status updates, but a list of 25 things about her, written just a month before she died. She learned that Durante, a pre-med psychology major, was passionate about medicine and that she loved bad movies. Number 5 was especially chilling: "*The concept of Death – specifically, the eternal, infinite, endlessness of it – scares the hell out of me,*" Durante wrote. "*Always has.*"

"The most intriguing thing about Facebook is that it doesn't just tell you about a person – it tells you how they choose to portray themselves to their social sphere," Raptopoulos says

"I think the way someone defines him or herself on Facebook, within the site's predetermined layout, says just as much about the person as the content itself. These were pictures Liz uploaded, articles she recommended, interests she wanted people to know about her. They were her words, sprinkled with her eager vernacular and personality."

From the Facebook page and other sources, Raptopoulos was able to find friends and relatives of Durante to interview.

"Once I had all the puzzle pieces and was preparing to mold it into a story, I kept coming back to her list of 25 things, because they so strongly reflected the qualities people described about her. They were also 25 things Liz felt were important to know about her. I could put her voice into the article with no opportunity to meet to her myself. It fit."

Raptopoulos crafted a poignant piece based on Durante's list that offered a window into the dead woman's soul.

After a gunman opened fire on the campus of Northern Illinois University, shooting 24 people, Facebook became an important reporting tool for the staff of the *Northern Star* (northernstar.info) the daily campus newspaper. "We were able to trace what happened from the posts on students' Facebook," says John Puterbaugh, who was editor-in-chief of the paper at the time of the February 2008 shootings. "From wall posts – condolence messages and things like that – we were sometimes able to figure out who had died even before the police released the names." (Out of respect to the victim's families, the *Northern Star* didn't report the names until police released them.) The newspaper also used the social networking site to contact hard-to-reach sources.

"After phone calls weren't successful, we'd sometimes send out Facebook messages to friends and family members of victims saying, 'We're here if you want to talk.' It was a different kind of approach and some people really responded to that. They're there on Facebook in their private, intimate moments and sometimes that works better than calling them up on the phone."

ENGAGING READERS

Stephanie Romanski, Web editor and social media coordinator at the *Grand Island Independent* in Nebraska, has one word of advice for student publications trying to make the most of social media: Engage.

"Don't just spit out headlines and links," she says.

"Have a real person man the Twitter account and inject their personality into it. Don't be afraid to tweet a link to some cute otter video or funny meme once in a while. Respond to followers who mention you or ask you a question. Of course, the main purpose is to drive traffic to the website, but when you do post an update or new story, try to do it manually and give a little tease to the story to make followers want to click."

"Though Twitter posts and Facebook news updates are brief, they should be carefully crafted. Make them conversational," advises Yada, former online editor of *The Spartan Daily*. "We made sure we asked questions of readers, at least one every day, about the issues of the day. We tried some different things with that. For example, if two columnists wrote opposing views on one subject, we asked the Facebook fans to 'like' the article they agreed with the most."

The Daily Tar Heel also tries to make the news a conversation. When a pair of basketball-playing twins decided to transfer from University of North Carolina, the newspaper's Facebook page asked what readers thought – and the comments pored in. When there's a big game, the newspaper invites readers to contribute photos and predict the score.

Some examples of engaging tweets and Facebook page updates:

North by Northwestern (Northwestern University): University library is closed, cops on the scene, but there is no danger to the student body. Check NBN for the story.

The Daily Collegian (Penn State University): Penn State is drawing closer to naming a quarterback for 2010. Who's your pick?

Onward State (Penn State University): It's the first day of classes! Are there any that you're excited for? Or conversely, not ready for at all?

The Torch (St. John's University): Has anyone had any frustrating experiences with the Financial Aid office this summer? If so, let us know!

The Daily Tar Heel (University of North Carolina): Do you remember the Rathskeller? We'd love to hear about your memories. Email (editor's personal email address) or DM (direct message) us your phone #.

Student news organizations can also use social networking sites to build relationships with other student organizations and with professional journalists. "We have a LinkedIn account and a *College Voice* alumni LinkedIn group, which we use to reconnect with alumni that used to be involved in the Voice," Raptopoulos says. "This network of support has been fantastic. It's a group of unofficial advisers for the editors, of interesting people willing to come in and speak at our various events, and it's great for fundraising."

CROWDSOURCING AND USER-GENERATED CONTENT

One way to connect with readers is to seek their content – quotes, news updates, photos, videos, etc. This process is often called "crowdsourcing." When a major ice storm struck the University of Oklahoma campus in Norman in January 2010, *The Oklahoma Daily* (oudaily.com) asked readers to send in photos. The newspaper was deluged with reader photos of icicle-encrusted trees, bike racks and statues and

FIGURE 19.3 Seeking content from readers helps build a relationship between a news organization and its audience. When a major ice storm struck the University of Oklahoma campus in Norman in January 2010, *The Oklahoma Daily* asked readers to send in snapshots. The newspaper was deluged with reader photos; the best were posted to a gallery on the website. *The Oklahoma Daily*, University of Oklahoma.

students playing in the snow. The newspaper posted a slideshow of the best photos, which became a popular feature.

Crowdsourcing is particularly useful for breaking news events when you're trying to gather multiple points of view quickly.

Robert Hernandez, an assistant professor at the University of Southern California Annenberg School for Communication & Journalism who worked as an online journalist for seattletimes.com and SFGate.com, offers these steps for crowdsourcing on his blog, *WebJournalist* (twitter.com/webjournalist):

Step 1. The moment you know you are going to an assignment/event/location, announce it. Tell people you are covering the event and ask who is attending. The sooner, the better … and do it multiple times … without looking like a crazy spammer.

Step 2. When you arrive to the scene, tweet that you are there … again, ask who is there, too. The point is to find sources! Also, get people to join your reporting … ask for tips, suggestions and possible questions.

Step 3. Give updates from the scene … not only text, but send out images and videos when applicable. Again, do a call out for tips, suggestions and questions. You are giving people direct access and getting them an opportunity to get involved.

Step 4. When you are done, tell people when they can expect to see or read your completed, "official" piece. And, if you got responses, thank people for their help.

Step 5. After piece runs, ask for feedback, comments, thoughts and tips. Engage with your community before, during and after these acts of journalism … be genuine and social in social media!

Additional tips from Hernandez:

Make sure you use hashtags throughout the process! Either use the established one or create a logical one the community would use.

You may or may not get responses, but doing this doesn't cost you ANYTHING. Remember, it takes less than a minute per tweet!

If you get responses, don't feel forced to use them, but be grateful you have people engaged enough that they want to HELP you. Make sure you respond and thank them.

Everyone knows that "If your mom says she loves you, check it out." That old journalism saying applies to tweets, as well as your mom. Just because someone tweets that they are there or gives you a juicy tidbit of info, it does not mean that it is fact. Check it out! What do we call this … reporting! Do some of that. If you get lazy, you get burned. More importantly, credibility is hard to build, but easy to lose.

SOCIAL MEDIA EDITORS

Many news organizations are developing new positions with titles like community editor, engagement editor and social media manager to oversee increasingly complex social media efforts. *The Daily Tar Heel* at the University

Wanted!

Social media manager

So you want to hire a social media manager or engagement editor for your news organization? Here's what a job description might look like:

- **Social media fanatic**–must spend ridiculous amounts of time on Twitter and Facebook, especially in the wee hours of the morning.
- **Innovative**–must have wacky ideas about how to use social media to promote the student paper, develop sources, find story ideas.
- **Good training skills**–able to teach staff members how to use social media tools to their best advantage.
- **Multitasker**–must be able to type a tweet while talking on a cell phone, browsing the Web on an iPad and studying for their French final.
- **Geeky**–should know their way around HTML, RSS and PHP.
- **Inquisitive**–must be curious about people and be able to come up with stimulating questions that will provoke discussion online and off.
- **Creative**–can come up with new ways to present a bunch of photos readers send in from yet another homecoming game or breast cancer walkathon.
- **Friendly**–can meet with people in the flesh as well as online.
- **Passionate**–must have an evangelical approach to social media.
- **Good manager**–able to spot raw talent and recruit photographers, videographers, writers and artists from the campus community and form them into a network of correspondents (some of whom might ultimately join the staff).

FIGURE 19.4 The *Minnesota Daily* makes it easy for readers to "connect with the *Daily*." The home page prominently features links to pages that allow readers to submit a story idea, send a press release, write a letter to the editor, pose a question to the newspaper's advice columnist and submit an event listing. *Minnesota Daily*, University of Minnesota.

TIPS FROM A PRO Using social media effectively
Josh Shannon

It's no secret that Facebook and other social media tools are a big part of most college students' lives. We use them to keep in touch with friends, plan events and "stalk" classmates. So why shouldn't we, as college journalists, use social media as yet another platform for reporting news?

The answer is that we should. In fact, I would argue a strong social media presence is crucial for a college newspaper. Our generation uses social media more than any other demographic does, so it only makes sense to use it to better reach our audience.

At *The Review* (udreview.com) at the University of Delaware, we created a Facebook fan page toward the end of the 2008–09 school year and joined Twitter the following summer. We started it more as a side project – an experiment to see if social media would serve our purposes. Almost immediately, the results were astounding: We soon found that more than 15 percent of our Web traffic was coming from social media (12 percent from Facebook and 3 percent from Twitter.)

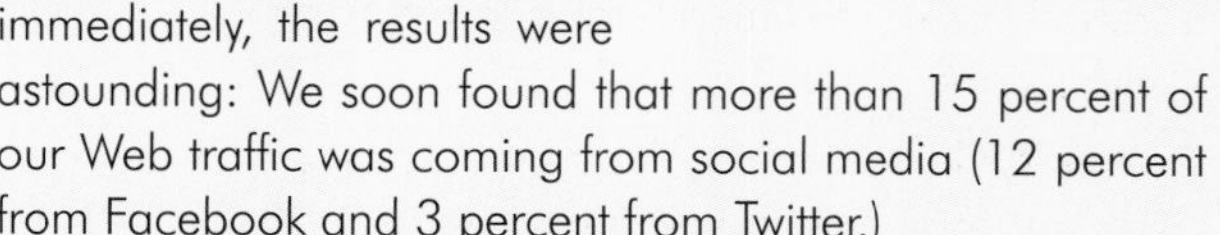

What's even more exciting is that once we began to foster a social media community, readers started to post our content themselves, either by retweeting or posting links to our stories on their own Facebook profiles. Not only does that bring in more readers, it means people are reading our content and finding it useful enough to pass on – an instantaneous way to see which articles are resonating with readers.

When thinking about using social media, it's important not to alter the way you write or choose news; your idea of newsworthiness and ethics should not change. But it is important to think about which stories you choose to link to through social media.

A few tips for using social media effectively:

Pick stories that will resonate in the social media community. Don't make the mistake of tweeting links to all your articles; pick a few that will have the most impact. And don't just choose the articles you put on your front page. Select stories you think people will click on to read and then pass on to others. Crime stories almost always do well on social media, as do articles about unpopular laws and policies. Feature stories, no matter how well written, rarely do well online.

Look for stories that have a chance to go viral. Post links to the stories that have that "I'll-be-darned" factor – something unusual, weird or funny – that people will be likely to pass on to their friends. A good example is a story we ran about a student who was walking home from a party and managed to get trapped in a shuttered auto plant near campus. It went viral through social media, eventually got picked up by CollegeHumor.com, and got more than 35,000 hits on our website.

Don't go overboard. Nobody likes the person who tweets 20 links at one time or posts numerous Facebook updates in one day. Doing that is the quickest way to lose followers. If you are more selective about your tweets, people will pay more attention to them.

Use Twitter to break news. Post a quick summary of what happened and then direct readers to your website for more in-depth coverage. If you have a smart phone, tweet a picture from the scene of the news. The same technique can be used for sports coverage: tweet periodic score updates, then direct readers to your website for the game story.

Use social media to find sources. If you're looking for people to interview about a particular issue – for example, students who planned a spring break trip close to home because of the economy – post that on Facebook and Twitter. You might be amazed at the response you'll get. More than once, I've gotten a crucial source on deadline thanks to social media.

Develop niche social media accounts. For example, create a separate Twitter account where the sports desk can post game scores. That way, you can provide followers with more detailed sports news without boring the non-sports fans who follow your general account. Reporters, especially entertainment writers and columnists, can also use social media for their work. For example, one of our columnists seeks input from readers about upcoming columns via Twitter.

Be responsible with social media. Remember that the same rules and ethics apply to anything you publish, whether it's a 700-word article or a 140-character tweet. You can use more casual language, but careless spelling and grammar will still undermine your credibility. Also, remind your staff to be mindful of posting information on social media that could damage their credibility or objectivity. For example, news reporters should refrain from tweeting their personal opinions on news topics or filling in the "political views" section on Facebook. And, though letting readers see you as a real person is a good thing, the dean you're scheduled to interview tomorrow might not be too impressed with the pictures of your drunken homecoming party.

JOSH SHANNON was the editor-in-chief of *The Review* (udreview.com), the independent weekly student newspaper at the University of Delaware, from 2009–2011. He also managed the paper's website and led *The Review*'s transition into multimedia production and daily Web updates.

of North Carolina created a new position of community editor in 2009–2010 to increase communication between the paper and the university community (both on campus and in the town of Chapel Hill). "My efforts primarily focused on Twitter and Facebook, promoting stories, asking questions and responding to readers," said Emily Stephenson, the paper's first community editor. "Student newspapers have to be present and active where students go for news, and that means using social media as much as possible."

TIPSHEET
Twitter for journalists

Twitter, a microblogging tool that allows users to send out brief messages (called "tweets") of up to 140 characters, is a great tool for promoting content, engaging readers and building community. But poorly phrased tweets, offensive content or too many automated posts can alienate readers. Here are some pointers for making the most of your news organization's Twitter presence.

1 **Set up a profile.** Establish a profile that includes your news organization's name, basic information, a Web address and an image, such as your logo. Select a user name, probably a variation of your news organization's name or a commonly recognized nickname (such as @IDSnews for the Indiana Daily Student's news account).

2 **Follow, don't just lead.** Follow as many people and organizations linked to your school and your town as you can find – school officials, professors, teams, clubs, nearby businesses, alumni, staff and individual students. (To follow a person or organization, simply click a button on their profile that allows you to subscribe to their Twitter feed.) The more people you follow the more you'll know what's going on in your community – and the better you'll be able to develop an audience. For sources check out the Twitter directory of college students, faculty and alumni organized by school at *CampusTweet.com*.

3 **Make it a conversation.** Don't just push out links to your content; ask readers what they think about the new football coach or the controversial cartoon in your paper this week.

***The Hustler,* Vanderbilt University:** First-year students: what did you think of orientation? Reply to @hustlernews and let us know!

4 **Proofread your posts.** There's no excuse for misspellings and grammatical errors. You've only got 140 characters; make sure each one is correct.

5 **Report news.** Twitter is a powerful vehicle for reporting breaking news. Even if you don't have the complete story you can quickly alert readers to urgent news as it unfolds and then point them to your website for more information.

***The Battalion,* Texas A&M:** Code Maroon: Tornado warning – tornado activity near College Station moving toward campus. Seek shelter immediately.

***Talon Marks*, Cerritos College:** There is a natural gas leak in the Physical Science Building students are being evacuated.

6 **Shorten your URLs.** Every character counts in a Twitter post. Use free Web-based services like bitly (http://bit.ly), ow.ly (http://ow.ly) or is.gd (http://is.gd) to compress Web page addresses.

7 **Cover sports live.** Use Twitter to post scores and other developments at big games.

***Mustang Daily,* Cal Poly San Luis Obispo:** Doug Shumway connects with Dominique Johnson on a 25-yard TD pass to put the Mustangs up 35-20.

8 **Retweet.** Send out interesting comments or news alerts from other news organizations or twitterers that would interest your readers. Simply click on the "retweet" button that shows up when you slide your mouse over the bottom-right corner of each tweet.

***The New Hampshire*, University of New Hampshire**: Living off campus this year? This @fostersdailydem article about new ordinance changes in Durham is a must read.

9 **Make your tweets useful.** Your Twitter feed should be a go-to place not just for news alerts but for resources your readers will be interested in. Is there a new sushi bar in town? Tweet it! Is today the first day to register for fall parking permits? It may not be worth a news story, but it warrants a tweet.

***Talon Marks,* Cerritos College:** A student wearing a green sweater, a cap and two backpacks claiming to be a teacher on campus is asking for money. Students should be aware.

10 **Alert readers to your coverage.** If you're sending a reporter to an out-of-state game or planning to liveblog the Board of Regents meeting, let your readers know.

***The Daily Orange,* Syracuse University:** Can't catch the game? Read live updates on Twitter RIGHT NOW.

11 **Ask for news tips.** Remind your readers you want to hear from them.

***The Tower* at Catholic University of America:** Got news for us? email news@cuatower.com or tweet us.

12 **Promote campus events.** Let your readers know what's going on as it happens.

***Daily Sundial,* California State University Northridge:** Temporary tattoos, laser tag, fortune tellers, caricature portraits ... it's all going on right now at matador nights!

13 **Use hashtags.** Set up a hashtag – a # sign followed by a keyword ("#SFSU" or "#Big10") for your school and for major stories to make it easy for readers to follow you and the issues you're covering.

***The State Press*, Arizona State University:** Tired of expensive textbooks? #ASU launched a book printing service at the #Tempe campus.

14 **Consider setting up multiple Twitter accounts.** You may want to establish separate Twitter feeds for certain sections, such as sports, A&E and news, or for certain people, like the editor-in-chief, a columnist or a beat writer. But don't set up too many; you don't want to fractionalize your audience. If you've got multiple Twitter feeds, you may want to put a Twitter directory on your website to make it easier for readers to find the Twitter account they want.

15 **Keep private information private.** Your news organization's Twitter feed is not the place to post your reaction to last night's date. If you want to tweet about your personal life, do it on your own Twitter account.

16 **Tweet interesting facts.** Got a tidbit that's not worth a full story? Report it in a tweet.

***The Daily Athenaeum,* West Virginia University:** A record crowd of 41,382 people attended tonight's game at Joan C. Edwards Stadium. Stadium capacity is 38,016.

***The Daily Illini,* University of Illinois:** Out of power right now? According to Ameren's outage data, 4,646 Champaign customers are suffering power outages this evening.

17 **Respond to your audience.** Let readers know you're listening to them. If readers tweet to your news organization, make sure someone responds. To answer a message, click on the "reply" button that shows up when you move your mouse over the bottom-right corner of each tweet.

18 **Recruit.** Let your readers know when you're looking for a cartoonist or taking on new writers.

***The Breeze,* James Madison University:** Breeze open house tonight at 7 p.m. Come learn more info and get involved!

19 **Avoid headlinese.** Don't capitalize all the words, as you might for a headline, or write in the sometimes-stilted language of headline writers. Use a more informal tone.

20 **Solve mysteries.** If people are wondering why there are three police cars outside the Humanities Building or why the cafeteria is closing early tonight, let them know.

***The Daily Californian,* University of California, Berkeley:** Helicopters above campus just now are filming a BBC documentary on earthquake faults, according to campus public affairs.

21 **Correct errors immediately.** If you make a mistake or if something you reported turns out not to be true, put out the correction on Twitter as soon as you can.

***The Famuan,* Florida A&M University:** Tear gas, NOT gunshots fired in response to series of fights in front of student services center.

22 **Don't punch out all your tweets in one blast.** Unless you're covering a breaking story you should tweet throughout the day.

23 **Use Twitter judiciously.** Don't tweet every story you publish or post every thought that enters your brain. Consider whether your readers would care.

One of *The Daily Tar Heel's* most successful endeavors was a weekly feature in the print paper that highlighted tweets, Facebook comments and photos from readers. "We used local trending topics and tweets directed at @dailytarheel, comments on our Facebook fan page, and photos emailed in by readers," says Stephenson. "We called it 'That's What You Said,' and we got great feedback from students on that."

The Daily Tar Heel created a special tab on its website called "Interact," which includes links to games, polls, Twitter and Facebook.

Stephenson's successor, Sara Gregory, expanded *The Daily Tar Heel's* community outreach efforts by organizing a series of in-person meet-ups for the community at the newspaper's office. "Online is great, but face-to-face talks can't be beat," she wrote in a column to readers. She also stationed herself at a local coffee house once a week, making herself available for informal chats with readers.

Whether you have a social media editor on your staff or not, you need to make it crystal clear to readers how they can connect with you. Too many college newspapers want reader interaction but don't make it easier for readers to contact them.

The *Minnesota Daily* at the University of Minnesota does. It has a "Connect with the *Daily*" box prominently displayed on its home page. At the top are icon links to the newspaper's Facebook page, RSS feed and Twitter accounts for news, sports and A&E. Under that are invitations for readers to connect, with links to submission forms for story ideas, letters to the editor, event listings, press releases, the "Overheard on Campus" feature and questions for the site's popular "Dr. Date" advice column. (see Figure 19.4)

ETHICAL ISSUES

While social media tools offer new opportunities for student news organizations, they also present new questions and ethical dilemmas.

How do you decide who posts on your newspaper's Facebook account? Should staffers create different Twitter accounts for their personal use and their newspaper work? Can the editor of a college paper share her political beliefs or views on campus issues on her personal Facebook page? Is it a conflict of interest for reporters to quote their Facebook "friends" in a news article? How should sources found on Twitter or Facebook be verified?

To help staffers sort through these questions, many newsrooms – professional and student – are adopting social media policies. *The New York Times*, *The Washington Post*, The Associated Press and countless other professional news organizations have drafted such guidelines. (For one example see *The Oklahoma Daily's* Social Media and Blogging Guidelines.)

But some say strict rules governing journalists' social media behavior are old-fashioned. Social media strategist J.D. Lasica says such policies sometimes go too far, violating the spirit of social media. "It's as if the top editors in the country got together and decided to roll back the clock to 1995, with no appreciation of the enormous forces that have reshaped media in the year 2009," he wrote that year on Socialmedia.biz.

"The notion that journalists don't have personal lives or opinions, that they shouldn't reveal political preferences or engage in civic causes regardless of their beat, that they should be shielded from direct interaction with the public for fear of disclosing a compromising point of view – this is sheer lunacy."

If your news organization chooses to adopt social media guidelines, think carefully about the wording and the

Social media guidelines

Thinking about drafting a set of social media guidelines for your newsroom? *The Oklahoma Daily* at the University of Oklahoma adopted these guidelines, based on policies drafted by Radio Television Digital News Association and *The Daily Tar Heel* at the University of North Carolina, Chapel Hill. Reprinted with permission.

The Oklahoma Daily Social Media and Blogging Guidelines 2010

The following is a set of *guidelines* for *The Oklahoma Daily* staff members. In addition to the following, staff members are strongly encouraged to avoid referring to *The Oklahoma Daily*, OUDaily.com or Student Media on their Facebook, Twitter or other social networking account without first discussing it with their immediate supervisor.

Image and reputation

Personal and professional lives merge online. Newsroom employees should recognize that their words become direct extensions of their news organizations. When you work for a journalism organization, you represent that organization on and off the clock.

- Avoid posting content that might embarrass you or undermine your journalistic credibility. Inspect your "friends" list regularly to look for conflicts with those who become newsmakers.
- Be prepared to publicly explain why you show up as a "friend" on the website of a politician, source or other newsmaker.
- Know that when you join an online group, the public may perceive that you support that group. Be prepared to justify your membership.
- Pay attention to how the public might interpret Facebook information that describes your relationship status and political views.
- Tell your supervisor if you plan to tweet as a *Daily* staff member. Likewise, tell your immediate supervisor if you plan to live tweet an event.
- Never insult or disparage readers of your social media or websites (any more than you would readers of *The Daily*).
- It is always a bad idea to criticize a colleague's work, whether it's a colleague from *The Daily*, Gaylord (the journalism school at the University of Oklahoma) or another media outlet.

- Respond to people who contact you via social media. If you aren't the appropriate person to answer their questions, refer them to whoever is.

Truth and fairness

Social media comments and postings should meet the same standards of fairness, accuracy and attribution that you apply to your journalism.

- Information gleaned online should be confirmed before reporting.
- If you cannot independently confirm critical information, reveal your sources – tell the public what you know, how you know it and what you cannot confirm.
- Twitter's character limits and immediacy are no excuse for inaccuracy and unfairness.
- Correct and clarify mistakes in social media postings – whether factual mistakes or errors of omission.
- When using content from blogs or social media, consider:

  Whether the source has legal right to the material posted

  Whether the video or photo has not been manipulated

  Whether the poster had a "reasonable expectation" of privacy

  Whether the story is of great significance

  Whether there is any other way to get the information

  Whether you are willing to disclose your methods and reasoning

  What your journalistic motivations are.

Accountability and transparency

You are responsible for everything you say on a newsroom or personal website.

- Don't post anonymously or use an avatar or username that cloaks your real identity.
- If using your account for *The Daily* reporting, identify yourself as a *Daily* reporter in your profile.
- Be especially careful when writing, Tweeting or blogging about a topic you or your newsroom covers.
- Don't use social media to promote business or personal interests without disclosing that relationship to the public.

If staff members neglect or outright refuse to follow the policy, especially after discussing the policy with the editor-in-chief, it could be grounds for termination.

ramifications. A good social media policy acknowledges that journalism is changing and finds the appropriate balance between traditional values and modern technology.

TO DO

1 If you don't already have a social media strategy, assign a committee to draft one. Think about how your news organization can use social media to build community, report stories, seek reader-generated content, promote your print and online products and improve relationships with readers and sources. Examine your current use of Facebook, Twitter and other social media tools; are you using them effectively?

2 Consider hiring a social media editor or community manager to oversee your social media efforts.

3 Next time there's a big event on campus – a protest rally or a flood or a big sports event, invite readers to submit photos, videos or anecdotes. Then put the best ones in your newspaper or on your website. It not only will give you some fresh content, it will build readership as students and their friends come to see if their contribution was chosen (this also may be a way for you to identify promising new staffers for your newspaper).

4 If your news organization doesn't already have social media guidelines, draft a policy. Consider some of the problems you've already encountered as well as situations that are likely to arise. Consult social media policies of other news organizations, including *The Oklahoma Daily.*

TO READ

Briggs, Mark, Journalism. *Journalism Next: A Practical Guide to Digital Reporting and Publishing,* Washington, D.C.: CQ Press, 2010.

Luckie, Mark S. *The Digital Journalist's Handbook,* CreateSpace, 2010.

TO CLICK

CampusTweet

CampusTweet is a directory where college students can find other students, alumni, and faculty from their campus who are on Twitter. Student journalists can use it to find out who is tweeting on their campus and what's being said.

http://campustweet.com

CoveritLive
CoveritLive.com is a Web-based live blogging tool that allows you to broadcast video, text and photos to your readers as an event is happening. It can be used to cover meetings, concerts, games and other events.
www.coveritlive.com

Delicious
Formerly known as del.icio.us, this social bookmarking Web service allows users to organize, store, manage and search information on the Internet. Reporters can use it to keep track of online research materials, such as articles, reports and websites, creating their own personal libraries of information and leaving a research trail for the reporters who come after them.
www.delicious.com

Digg
This social news website allows people to share content by sharing links and stories and then vote on content shared by others. Digg is a great place to look for story ideas as well as share your content.
http://digg.com

Facebook
The granddaddy of social networking sites offers myriad opportunities for finding story ideas, connecting with sources and promoting your content.
http://facebook.com

Flickr
This photo management application allows people to post and share photographs. News organizations can create a photo pool or group where readers can submit photos about a certain event or topic.
www.flickr.com

Help a Reporter Out
HARO is an online service set up for journalists to quickly gather feedback from the public. Journalists write in to say what topic they are researching and what kind of information they need and it's sent out to a network of tens of thousands of potential sources. The service is open to student journalists as long as they are writing for a publication.
www.helpareporter.com/reporters

Innovation in College Media
This blog, now sponsored by College Media Advisers, tracks what college media organizations are doing with new media.
www.collegemediainnovation.org/blog

LinkedIn
This business-oriented social networking tool is a must for students interested in entering the professional world of journalism – or any other field for that matter. It connects you to your trusted contacts and helps you exchange knowledge, ideas and opportunities with a broader network of professionals.
http://linkedin.com

Mashable
This blog is a must-read for journalists interested in social media.
http://mashable.com

Reddit
This social news website allows users to post links to content on the Internet. Other users then vote the links up or down, causing them to become more or less prominent on the reddit home page. It's a great way to make your content go viral.
www.reddit.com

Storify
This Web application allows people to collect material that others post on social media sites – photos, tweets, video, etc. – and create rich, complex stories that present multiple perspectives on an event or issue.
http://storify.com

StumbleUpon
This discovery engine (a type of search engine) finds and recommends Web content to its users. It allows users to discover and rate Web pages, photos and videos that are personalized to their tastes and interests.
www.stumbleupon.com

Tumblr
This livestream blogging platform allows users to post text, images, video, links, quotes and audio to their tumblelog, a short-form blog. Journalists can use it to engage readers and reach new audiences.
www.tumblr.com

Twitter
This leading microblogging site allows people to share 140-character posts or tweets.
http://twitter.com

YouTube
You know this site as a place to watch videos for hours on end, but media organizations can use YouTube to source material, connect with viewers and reach new audiences.
www.youtube.com

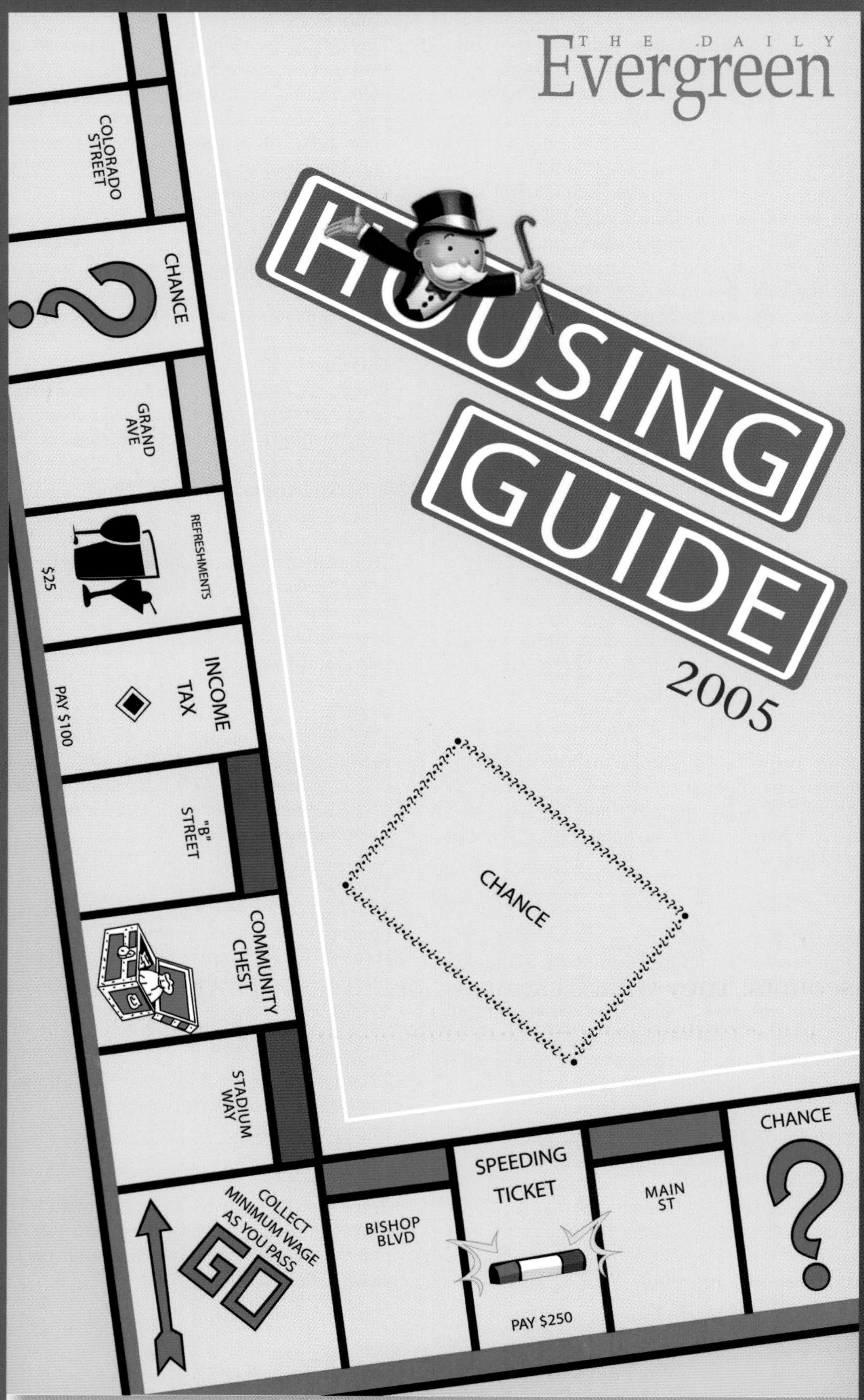

FIGURE 20.1 Special issues and special sections, such as housing guides, sports preview sections, back-to-school handbooks and graduation editions, are attractive to advertisers and readers alike. *The Daily Evergreen*, Washington State University.

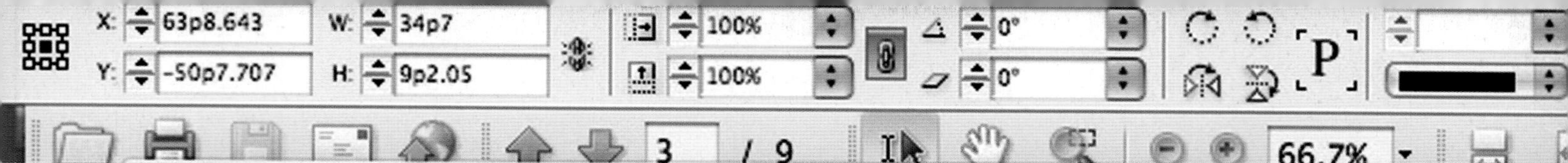

CHAPTER 20
ADVERTISING AND MARKETING

For most college newspapers, advertising is vital. While a few papers exist solely on student government or journalism department funding, most are reliant, at least in part, on a steady flow of advertising dollars. Without advertisers, many college papers would cease to exist.

But advertising isn't just a necessary evil. It also provides a community service. Your readers want to know where to get a good deal on housewares for their new apartments or what bands are playing at the local bars or which pizza places offer student discounts. They want to know where to find apartments and jobs and tickets to the upcoming Eminem concert. Running ads is another way to serve your readers and help students become part of the community where they live, work and go to school.

The Student Newspaper Survival Guide, Second Edition. Rachele Kanigel.

CHAPTER CONTENTS

RECRUITING YOUR SALES STAFF

Some student newspaper advertising departments have only professional, non-student employees; others employ only students. The majority have a mix, usually a professional business manager and/or advertising director and a student sales staff.

Whatever staffing model you use, recruiting and hiring good employees is key.

To recruit student staff, run ads in your newspaper and on the campus radio station; post fliers around campus; and announce job opportunities in business, marketing, communications, advertising and graphic design classes. Make it clear that advertising sales positions offer flexible hours, excellent pay and valuable work experience that can prepare students for professional careers.

Screen applicants carefully. You don't want someone who will spend a few weeks making contacts and then quit. Advertising sales can be a lucrative job, but it takes persistence, motivation, creativity and hard work. A flaky salesperson who drops the ball can lose hundreds, even thousands of dollars in revenue for your paper.

The Purdue Exponent (purdueexponent.org), the daily newspaper serving Purdue University in Indiana, puts new student advertising sales representatives through a rigorous interview and an eight-hour unpaid training program before hiring them. At the end of the training, students must show they can put together an effective sales presentation. "That tells us if they have the perseverance and drive it takes to sell ads," says former Advertising Director Christy Harrison.

TRAINING YOUR STAFF

Once you have a sales force in place, you need to train it. Normally the business and/or advertising manager oversees training.

Whether you're training a single new sales rep one-on-one or conducting a workshop for a dozen or more, training should include:

Basics of professional behavior–appropriate dress, phone etiquette and the importance of meeting deadlines.

How your department works–who's in charge of what, what forms need to be filled out when, deadlines, record keeping.

The rate card–how to figure out the cost of an ad, how to calculate discounts, whether color is available and what it costs.

How to submit ads–procedures for layout, design and copywriting.

Advertising policies–what sort of ads your newspaper does and doesn't accept, what to do with a potentially controversial ad.

Collection and credit policies–who handles collections, the procedures for establishing credit for an account.

Ad copy and layout basics–how to put an ad together, including headlines, illustrations, body copy, logo and contact information.

Understanding your market–demographic information on your campus, media usage and shopping patterns among your readership.

Your advertising products–print ads, online ads, special sections, coupons, etc.

The competition–how your newspaper compares to other media in the area and what advantages you offer in reaching the college student market.

Selling techniques–developing a sales presentation, how to respond to objections, building customer relations.

Social media–how to use Facebook, Twitter and other social media tools to attract and serve advertisers.

Getting to know your client

Before you can sell an ad, you need to get to know your clients, their businesses and their needs.

Some questions to ask:

1. When did the business open? How did you start in this line of work?
2. What do you enjoy most about your work?
3. Who is involved in making decisions about advertising?
4. How do you try to promote your business?
5. Where do you currently advertise? Why did you choose those media?
6. Who are your customers?
7. Are you trying to reach the college market?
8. What percentage of your customers are male? What percentage are female?
9. What is the age breakdown of your customers? Income level?
10. How far do your customers travel to do business with you?
11. Are you satisfied with your customers? If not, what changes would you like to see?
12. What are your top five products?
13. Do you foresee any major inventory changes over the next year?
14. What's your best month for gross sales? Which is generally your worst month?
15. Which media are working best for you? Which are not working well?
16. Who are your major competitors?
17. What are your competitive advantages?
18. Do you have a slogan or motto for your business?
19. What are your feelings toward our newspaper?
20. What else should I know to understand you and your business better?

If you don't have the resources or personnel to train employees, see if a professional news organization will help out. Local newspapers will often let a student sit in on a sales meeting or training session or shadow a sales representative. You can also contact your state or provincial newspaper publishers association in search of a mentor.

College Newspaper Business and Advertising Managers, Inc. is probably the best training resource for student newspaper advertising departments. This membership organization, known as CNBAM, sponsors a national training conference each spring and offers a 150-page training guide to new members. The organization's Listserv and website (listed at the end of this chapter) offer support and networking opportunities to student and professional advertising employees.

Some state college media organizations also offer training. The California College Media Association, for example, offers an annual workshop for ad sales reps at the beginning of the school year. Advertising sales professionals give students pointers on such topics as prospecting for advertisers, closing a sale, social media and helping advertisers communicate their message.

MOTIVATING YOUR STAFF

Most sales representatives are paid on commission – usually somewhere between 6 percent and 20 percent of the revenue they bring in. Some news organizations also pay a small base salary.

To motivate your sales reps and keep them selling, you've got to provide incentives. Most newspapers set goals for each sales rep and many offer higher commissions or bonuses to those who make or exceed their monthly sales goals. Some papers also pay bonuses for landing a lucrative contract or a major advertiser.

At the *Mustang Daily* (mustangdaily.net) at Cal Poly, San Luis Obispo, General Manager Paul Bittick promises all-expenses-paid trips to the national CNBAM convention to reps who meet their sales goals. One year, he notes, the newspaper "spent $10,000 to take 11 students to New Orleans. But these people sold nearly $200,000 in ads so it was worth it."

TYPES OF NEWSPAPER ADVERTISING

To sell ads you have to understand what you're selling.

- **Display ads**–bordered or boxed ads that run in the newspaper or on the website.
- **Classified ads**–ads sold by the word under classified headings such as "help wanted" and "apartments."
- **Classified display ads**–bordered display ads positioned in the classified section.
- **Pre-printed inserts**–advertisements that have been prepared and delivered to the printer to be inserted in the middle of the newspaper.

TIPS FROM A PRO Kami Hammerschmith

You walk into a business, ready to sell an ad, and the owner or manager shuts you down. Kami Hammerschmith, a former president of College Newspaper Advertising and Business Managers, Inc., offers these responses to common objections.

I won't advertise because I didn't get any response from my last ad. Advertise items that people want when they want them and in a price range they are willing to pay. Lack of results is not necessarily the medium. Look at the ad. Is it attractive? Easy to read? Is your store identification clear, your price right? Do you feature a benefit?

Other advertisers say they are satisfied with their advertising, so maybe we should take a look at your ad(s) and see how we can improve them.

I don't advertise because I don't have the money to advertise. As a merchant you must invest money to make money. One of the best investments you can make is advertising in the newspaper, because it creates sales. The secret of good advertising is frequency, not size. Let's work on developing a consistent campaign.

I won't advertise because it isn't the right time of year. Advertising is designed to build business, and it works best when repeated regularly. You have items on your shelves to sell, so you should still want/need customers to come in your door.

I don't need to advertise because I have enough business. Advertising is an investment in your future. An advertiser may have too much business today, but what

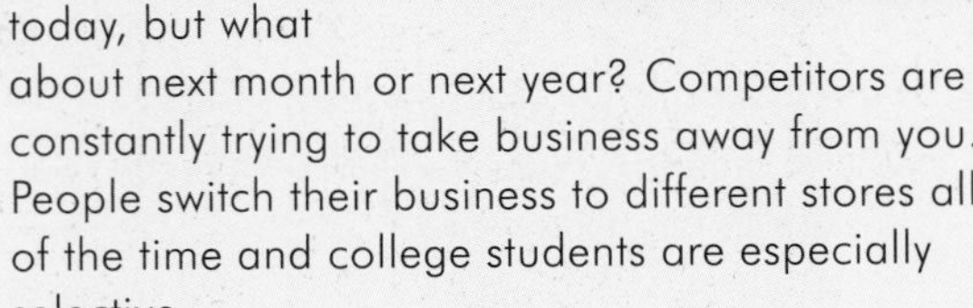

about next month or next year? Competitors are constantly trying to take business away from you. People switch their business to different stores all of the time and college students are especially selective.

Also, there are 20,000 students at the university, plus 4,000 faculty/staff, and new potential customers are moving into the area all the time. Each year there are more than 3,000 new students at the university and the faculty and staff are changing all the time.

KAMI HAMMERSCHMITH is the assistant director of student media for advertising and marketing at Oregon State University and past president of College Newspaper Business and Advertising Managers, Inc., 2007–2009.

ADVERTISING POLICIES

If your newspaper accepts advertising, you should have an advertising policy in place. It may be as simple as a one-sentence statement – "We reserve the right to accept or reject any advertisement" – or a detailed notice explaining what sort of ads are acceptable and which are not. Many student newspapers, for example, don't accept advertisements for tobacco and alcohol products; some Catholic school newspapers won't advertise birth control or abortion services.

Keep in mind the First Amendment **doesn't** mean you have to print everything that comes your way; it simply means the government can't censor the press. You may reject any ad that your editors or advertising department finds offensive, discriminatory or inappropriate.

When a controversial ad is submitted to a college newspaper, the decision on whether to publish it must be made quickly, so you should have a procedure in place. Some student newspapers leave that decision to the advertising manager; others see it as an editorial decision to be made by the top editor or the editorial board. A few leave it up to a publisher or publisher's representative, such as an adviser.

Whoever decides, it is helpful to have standards in place for what is acceptable. Among the reasons for rejecting an ad are:

- It's potentially libelous
- It will offend some readers
- It's false, misleading or inaccurate
- It violates community standards or university policies
- It discriminates against a certain group of people
- It contributes to a significant health or societal problem, such as smoking or alcohol abuse.

If you don't already have a policy and procedures for dealing with controversial ads, form a committee to draw up guidelines. Nearly every newspaper has to deal with some kind of advertising challenge at some point; you might as well be prepared.

Local/National

Ad Sizes (In inches)

1/2 Vertical
5.00 x 20.00

Full Page
10.00 x 20.00

Business Card
3.3 x 2.5

1/8 Vertical
5.00 x 5.00

1/4 Vertical
5.00 x 10.00

Full Page
10.00 x 20.00

1/16 Page
5.00 x 2.50

1/8 Horizontal
10.00 x 2.50

1/4 Horizontal
10.00 x 5.00

1/2 Horizontal
10.00 x 10.00

Contract & Rate Policies

All sizes listed are in inches wide by inches tall. Rates and charges are listed at net amount due. The Arbiter reserves the right to reject any advertising copy at any time. Rejection does not nullify the advertiser's annual contract space requirement obligations. All ads are subject to approval prior to insertion by the Editor-In-Chief. If an advertiser fails to meet the requirements of the signed contract, the advertiser's contract rate will be adjusted to either the rate earned (based on space actually purchased) or the Local Rate, and the advertiser will be billed accordingly. Advertisers are responsible for 25% of the full cost of space reserved if an ad is cancelled after deadline or has not been received by the publication deadline. Composition, artwork and photography produced by The Arbiter becomes property of The Arbiter and may not be used or reproduced in any other publication or medium or in any other form without prior written consent of the Director. The Arbiter also assumes no financial responsibility for typographical errors, omissions, failure of an ad to be published or other errors beyond our control.

Payment & Billing

Invoices are sent out at the end of each week, and statements will be mailed monthly. Terms are net 30 days. For all new advertisers, payment is required prior to publication. For multiple run contracts, 25% of the total contract price must be paid until credit is established. All political advertising must be prepaid. Visa, MasterCard and Discover are gladly accepted. If an account becomes delinquent after 30 days, the account will accrue a finance charge of 1.5% per month (18% APR) or a minimum of $15 and may be turned over to a collection agency.

Deadlines

Signed contracts are due six calendar days prior to publication. Proofed ads, or ads submitted by customer, are due three calendar days prior to publication.

The Arbiter
Boise State University
1910 University Drive
Boise, ID 83725-1335

Phone	208.426.6300	**Advertising**	208.426.6302
Fax	888.388.7554	**Bookkeeping**	208.426.6306
E-mail	ads@stumedia.boisestate.edu	**Business Manager**	208.426.6303
Web	arbiteronline.com	**Marketing Director**	208.426.6304

FIGURE 20.2 A basic rate card should include deadlines, advertising policies, a publication schedule, rates, readership demographics, specifications on submitting ads and contact information for your advertising department. *The Arbiter*, Boise State University. Reprinted with permission.

ADVERTISING RATES

Advertising rates at student newspapers vary widely, depending upon many factors, including the size of the school and the readership, frequency of publication and the economics of the community. If you're setting new rates, don't feel you have to reinvent the wheel. Study rate cards of the professional daily and weekly newspapers serving your community. Then look for student newspapers that are comparable to yours in circulation, frequency of publication, student population and type of community (rural, college town, small city, big city). To find rates, look for rate cards, which are usually available on a newspaper's website, or call other advertising departments.

Rates are generally calculated in column inches. Ads are measured by the width in columns and the depth in inches. For example, a 3×5 ad is 3 columns wide and 5 inches tall for a total of 15 column inches. If the rate is $10 per column inch, the ad would cost $150.

Ads can also be sold by the page and its fractions – a full-page ad, half-page, quarter-page, one-eighth page, etc. Newspapers often offer discounts as incentives for advertisers buying full- or half-page ads.

Some newspapers like *The Daily Skiff* (tcudailyskiff.com) at Texas Christian University and *The Red and Black* (redandblack.com) at the University of Georgia, sell puzzle sponsorships to advertisers. Businesses can buy an ad above or below a crossword or sudoku puzzle with a line saying the puzzle is sponsored by the business.

Most student newspapers have a two- or three-tier system with one rate for national advertisers and reduced rates for local businesses and university-affiliated or nonprofit advertisers. That's because national ads usually come from agencies that take a commission. If your rate is $100 for a quarter-page ad and the firm takes a 15 percent commission, your paper will only receive $85 for the ad.

The tiered system takes this into account. If the national rate is $10 per column inch, the rate for local advertisers may be $9 and the rate for university groups and nonprofit charitable organizations may be $8. That way your paper doesn't lose anything to the national ad reps and gives a break to campus advertisers.

Local (cost/run)

	1x	6x	15x	30x	Add Color Per Run
Business Card	$41.00	$38.00	$34.00	$29.00	+ $10.00
1/16 Page	$61.50	$57.00	$51.00	$43.50	+ $15.00
1/8 Page	$123.00	$114.00	$102.00	$87.00	+ $20.00
1/4 Page	$246.00	$219.00	$183.00	$153.00	+ $30.00
1/2 Page	$492.00	$390.00	$330.00	$270.00	+ $45.00
3/4 Page	$738.00	$585.00	$495.00	$405.00	+ $60.00
Full Page	$984.00	$780.00	$660.00	$540.00	+ $75.00

National (cost/run)

	1x	6x	15x	30x	Add Color Per Run
Business Card	$52.50	$51.25	$48.75	$45.00	+ $10.00
1/16 Page	$78.75	$76.88	$73.13	$67.50	+ $15.00
1/8 Page	$157.50	$153.75	$146.25	$135.00	+ $20.00
1/4 Page	$315.00	$307.50	$292.50	$270.00	+ $30.00
1/2 Page	$630.00	$615.00	$585.00	$540.00	+ $45.00
3/4 Page	$945.00	$922.50	$877.50	$810.00	+ $60.00
Full Page	$1,260.00	$1,230.00	$1,170.00	$1,080.00	+ $75.00

Classified Display

	1x	6x	15x	30x
1.25" x 2.00"	$16.40	$14.20	$12.20	$10.20
1.25" x 3.00"	$24.60	$21.30	$18.30	$15.30
2.50" x 3.00"	$49.20	$42.60	$36.60	$30.60
5.00" x 2.00"	$65.60	$56.80	$48.80	$40.80

Inserts

	Single Page	2-4 Pages	5-8 Pages	8+ Pages
Price Per 1.000*	$45.00	$55.00	$65.00	$85.00

Insert Policies

The Business Manager must approve all inserts in advance. The Arbiter reserves the right to refuse any pre-printed insert at any time. Rates quoted are for standard-sized inserts printed on paper that can be inserted mechanically. For coupon books, tabloid or large inserts, call first for pricing and insertion requirements. Inserts simulating editorial style must carry the identification "this is a pre-paid advertisement" on each page of the insert.

Position Requests

Except for Classified Display Ads, position may be requested. Position guarantees are available for a minimum of 15% of the total ad cost (including color) or a minimum of $30, whichever is greater. Without payment of a premium, The Arbiter will make every effort to honor position requests, but cannot guarantee position. Position guarantees are on a first-come, first-serve basis.

Arbiter Locations

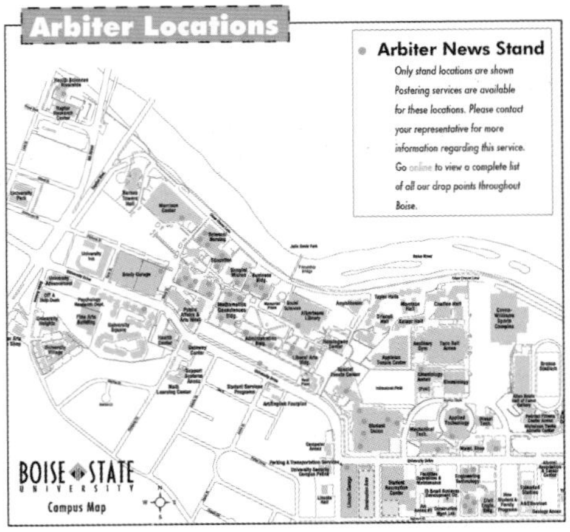

Arbiter News Stand

Only stand locations are shown Postering services are available for these locations. Please contact your representative for more information regarding this service. Go online to view a complete list of all our drop points throughout Boise.

BOISE STATE UNIVERSITY
Campus Map

Statistics

Fall 2009 Enrollment

Fall 2009 head count	18,936
Summer 2009 head count	7,483

Student Population

Freshman	4,706	25%
Sophomore	3,559	19%
Junior	3,308	17%
Senior	4,284	23%
2nd undergrad degree	839	4%
Academic graduate	2,240	12%

Student Demographics

Age Group		
18 or younger	1,824	10%
19-20 years	3,391	18%
21-24 years	5,245	28%
25-35 years	5,430	29%
36-50 years	2,367	12%
51+ years	679	3%
Gender		
Female	10,281	54%
Male	8,533	45%
Enrollment Status		
Full Time	12,875	68%
Part Time	6,061	32%

10/11 Issue Dates

August

S	M	T	W	TH	F	S
1	2	3	4	5	6	7
8	9	10	11	12	13	14
15	16	17	**18**	19	20	21
22	**23**	24	25	**26**	27	28
29	**30**	31				

September

S	M	T	W	TH	F	S
			1	**2**	3	4
5	6	**7**	8	**9**	10	11
12	**13**	14	15	**16**	17	18
19	**20**	21	22	**23**	24	25
26	**27**	28	29	**30**		

October

S	M	T	W	TH	F	S
					1	2
3	**4**	5	6	**7**	8	9
10	**11**	12	13	**14**	15	16
17	**18**	19	20	**21**	22	23
24	**25**	26	27	**28**	29	30
31						

November

S	M	T	W	TH	F	S
	1	2	3	**4**	5	6
7	**8**	9	10	**11**	12	13
14	**15**	16	17	**18**	19	20
21	22	23	24	25	26	27
28	**29**	30				

December

S	M	T	W	TH	F	S
			1	**2**	3	4
5	**6**	7	8	**9**	10	11
12	**13**	14	15	16	17	18
19	20	21	22	23	24	25
26	27	28	29	30	31	

January

S	M	T	W	TH	F	S
						1
2	3	4	5	6	7	8
9	10	11	12	13	14	15
16	17	**18**	19	**20**	21	22
23	**24**	25	26	**27**	28	29
30	**31**					

February

S	M	T	W	TH	F	S
		1	2	**3**	4	5
6	**7**	8	9	**10**	11	12
13	**14**	15	16	**17**	18	19
20	21	**22**	23	**24**	25	26
27	**28**					

March

S	M	T	W	TH	F	S
		1	2	**3**	4	5
6	**7**	8	9	**10**	11	12
13	**14**	15	16	**17**	18	19
20	**21**	22	23	**24**	25	26
27	28	29	30	31		

April

S	M	T	W	TH	F	S
					1	2
3	**4**	5	6	**7**	8	9
10	**11**	12	13	**14**	15	16
17	**18**	19	20	**21**	22	23
24	**25**	26	27	**28**	29	30

May

S	M	T	W	TH	F	S
1	**2**	3	4	**5**	6	7
8	**9**	10	11	12	13	14
15	16	17	18	19	20	21
22	23	24	25	26	27	28
29	30	31				

June

S	M	T	W	TH	F	S
			1	2	3	4
5	6	7	8	9	10	11
12	13	14	15	16	17	18
19	20	21	22	23	24	25
26	27	28	29	30		

July

S	M	T	W	TH	F	S
					1	2
3	4	5	6	7	8	9
10	11	12	**13**	14	15	16
17	18	19	20	21	22	23
24	25	26	27	28	29	30
31						

FIGURE 20.2 (cont'd)

Newspapers generally offer discounts for frequency. You should offer a lower rate to advertisers who run an ad multiple times or who sign a contract to advertise a certain number of inches during the academic year.

MEDIA KITS

Every newspaper that accepts advertising should have a media kit, a package of materials that gives potential advertisers all the information they need to buy an ad. A good media kit helps sell the publication and its readership to the advertiser and works as a reference source that your sales reps can use when making presentations. A media kit also acts as a "silent salesperson," answering questions when your sales reps aren't available.

Media kits can range from a couple of photocopied sheets to a glossy, professionally designed, full-color brochure. Small publications may think they don't need a sophisticated media kit. But keep in mind that the more professional-looking your kit is, the easier it will be to sell ads. You may be students, but you have a valuable product – a newspaper read by hundreds or thousands of people.

A media kit should include, at a minimum:

- A detailed rate card that explains ad rates for different sizes and types of ads, discounts for frequency, and deadlines (Figure 20.2)
- A publication calendar that lists publication dates for the entire year, as well as special sections
- Advertising policies that spell out what kind of ads you do not accept and your policies on cancellations, errors, etc.

You may also want to include:

- Demographic information for your campus community, including enrollment figures; spending patterns; numbers of students who live on campus, with parents, at fraternity or sorority houses, etc.
- Statistics from readership surveys
- Photos of your campus
- A list of awards your newspaper has won
- A map or list of distribution sites
- Other key information about your school or your newspaper that would sell it to potential advertisers.

WELCOME TO OUR ONLINE MEDIA KIT

The GW Hatchet's 2010-2011 Media Kit has gone green here at whatGWreads.com. You can learn more about The Hatchet, view our rates and check our technical specifications. And while you can download PDF documents of our print media kit, contracts and rate sheets, we will strongly encourage you to **place your ad and manage your contracts online** come the fall.

SIGN UP FOR OUR NEWSLETTER

Local and GW advertisers: sign up for our advertiser mailing list and receive monthly newsletters from our business staff.

Your e-mail address: [ ] Continue

WHY THE HATCHET?

REACH

The GW Hatchet has been the primary news source of the GW Community for over 100 years. Distributing to over 80 locations on campus and in Foggy Bottom, there is no better way to reach the community.

STRENGTH

While newspapers may be suffering from competition, college newspapers remain strong. Students turn to The Hatchet as a trusted source of information. Our strength is in our readers.

POWER

There is no more powerful medium than print advertising. Newspaper ads can't be blocked. You can't fast-forward past them. There is no station to change. Newspaper ads are an excellent way to reach the market. Take your business to the next level with the power of the printed word.

LEARN MORE

FIGURE 20.3 Online media kits are environmentally friendly and cheaper than slick, full-color paper media kits. From a single Web page *The GW Hatchet* makes it easy for potential advertisers to place an ad, learn about rates and special issues, and sign up for a monthly newsletter specifically for local and campus advertisers. *The GW Hatchet*, George Washington University.

Some news organizations save money on slick, full-color print media kits by directing advertisers to electronic versions on their websites. From a single colorful Web page *The GW Hatchet* (gwhatchet.com) at George Washington University makes it easy for potential advertisers to place an ad, learn about rates and special issues and sign up for a monthly newsletter specifically for local and campus advertisers. (Figure 20.3)

DESIGNING ADS

Many student newspapers offer advertising design and photography services, either for free or for an extra fee. Such newspapers generally have student designers who can translate an advertiser's concept into an effective advertisement.

Sales reps should also understand the basics of advertising copy and layout. Every ad should have:

- A catchy headline that draws the reader's attention
- A graphic element, such as a photograph, an illustration or a graph
- Body copy that explains the product or service being advertised
- Logo and contact information, including the name, street address, phone number, Web address and business hours.

Advertising sales reps and designers should study ads in other newspapers to get a sense of what makes them effective. Some ad reps even design (or have a designer design) an ad "on spec" (before the client agrees to advertise) to give an advertiser a sense of what it could look like.

COUPONS AND SPECIAL DEALS

Coupons are a win–win for student newspapers. Students love getting a bargain and advertisers appreciate having tangible proof that their ads are actually bringing readers to their businesses. Some newspapers have a special place for coupons. *The Red and Black* at the University of Georgia, for example, has a weekly "Coupon Corner" on Page 3 of the newspaper every Tuesday where regular readers know to look for special deals.

Newspaper coupons are no longer restricted to the boxed ads with the dotted lines that you clip out of a print newspaper. Online and mobile technologies have spawned a variety of digital coupon options. Some online newspapers, like *The Daily Texan* (dailytexanonline.com) at the University of Texas at Austin, produce on online page of coupons every week that readers can print out. The newspaper will even email the page to readers who subscribe to a coupon service. Other student publications send digital coupons directly to readers' cell phones.

Several newspapers, including *The Daily* (dailyuw.com) at the University of Washington and the *Iowa State Daily* (iowastatedaily.com) offer Groupon-style "daily deals" that they promote on Twitter and Facebook.

The Daily Californian (dailycal.org) at the University of California, Berkeley has a "press pass" that staffers hand out on campus and during community events. The plastic card, which is good for a full academic year, entitles users to a variety of discounts and weekly specials at restaurants, clothing stores, hair salons, bookstores and copy shops around Berkeley. "We've been doing it for a number of years," says Dante Gallan, who was advertising manager of the newspaper. "People really like it."

10 STEPS TO SELLING NEWSPAPER ADVERTISING

Selling is an art, but there's a science to it, too. Most sales reps can't just walk into a business and sell an ad. To make a successful sale, follow these 10 steps:

Step 1. Prepare before you call. Do some preliminary research on your prospective client. Has this business advertised or been approached by your paper before? Have you seen the company's ads elsewhere? What do you know about the client? What do you need to know? Rehearse what you want to say and jot down some questions.

Step 2. Find the decision maker. In most businesses, one person is responsible for making advertising decisions. It may be a store owner or manager or a media buyer at corporate headquarters. Find out who that person is and introduce yourself and your newspaper. Present your media kit and discuss the benefits of advertising with your paper.

Step 3. Collect information. Before starting your sales pitch you want to find out as much as you can about the business from the client. What are the client's most popular products and brands? When are the best and worst times for sales? What challenges does the client face? What does the client need?

Step 4. Form a proposal. Find a solution to the client's problem. If sales are weak in the late summer, suggest advertising in your back-to-school issue. If a restaurant isn't getting enough customers on Sunday evenings, suggest offering a student discount that night or running an ad in your restaurant guide.

Step 5. Present your proposal. Explain your idea, offering facts and examples that bolster your case. Show how your solution has helped other businesses in similar situations. Explain how this approach might work for the client.

Step 6. Evaluate the client's response. Listen carefully to concerns and questions the client raises. Try to determine if the person is open to persuasion or if you should try a new tactic.

Step 7. Respond to objections. Many potential advertisers will raise concerns or objections. The person might say it's not the right time of year for an ad or it's too expensive. Remember that an objection is better than a flat "no;" it opens the door to more conversation. Offer a polite but persuasive response. Or suggest a different approach – a smaller ad or a different sequence or timing.

Step 8. Close the deal. Once you see the client is ready to buy an ad, stop talking. Don't oversell. Look for buying signals, comments and body language that suggest the client is ready. Pull out the contract and get a signature. A little reassurance is fine but don't do a lot of unnecessary chatting.

Step 9. Wrap it up. Thank the client for advertising with your paper and confirm the agreement – the size of the ad, the start date, whatever details bear repeating. Invite the customer to call if questions arise.

Step 10. Follow up. Make sure you get a final proof to the advertiser, leaving plenty of time for corrections. When the paper comes out, hand deliver the ad – or, if time doesn't allow for that, send a tearsheet the same day. Later on, ask how the ad worked out. The better service you provide, the more the client will want to buy another ad in the future.

ASSEMBLING A SALES KIT

Before going out on sales calls, assemble a sales kit with everything you need to make those calls. Keep your sales kit in a briefcase or professional-looking satchel. It should include:

- Copies of the most recent issues of the paper
- Media kits (or rate cards)
- Binder, pen and layout paper
- Business cards
- Calculator
- Calendar
- Special section/promotion calendar
- Credit reference forms
- Contracts
- Insertion orders.

CUSTOMER SERVICE

Landing a new client is great, but keeping one is even more important. The key here is to provide top-notch customer service. That means returning emails and phone calls promptly, turning ad designs around quickly, delivering proofs when promised.

"It's about speed, but it's also about quality," says Mike Spohn, former advertising manager for the *Arizona Daily Wildcat* (wildcat.arizona.edu) at the University of Arizona. "That means looking over a proof before it is sent to catch any obvious errors before the client does, etc. A sales rep who has a client that says, 'Wow, I can't believe the level of customer service and attention I get from my rep' is going to be the account executive who is successful."

SPECIAL ISSUES AND SPECIAL SECTIONS

Some of the most effective and lucrative sales opportunities at college newspapers are special issues and special sections. Bittick at Cal Poly, San Luis Obispo says nearly one-third of his paper's advertising revenue comes from four special issues – the back-to-school, freshman welcome, open house and graduation editions.

"There isn't a school around that can't do a back-to-school issue," says Bittick. "It's a no-brainer. It's really easy to sell. And by doing that back-to-school issue, you've created a customer. They may not be in every issue, but you may get them three or four more times over the course of the school year."

Some of the common themes for special issues and special sections are:

- Freshman orientation
- Back to school
- Homecoming week, alumni weekend, founders day (or other special events that bring alumni, parents or other visitors to school)
- Valentine's Day
- Housing guide
- "Best of" guide (with results of reader polls on best pizza place, best bookstore, best coffee shop, etc.)
- Career guide or summer jobs guide
- Bridal guide
- Commencement
- Sports supplements or special sections to preview a season or a big game.

Be sure to plan special sections in advance. Set dates by the spring or summer before the academic year so you can present them in your annual media kit.

CLASSIFIED ADVERTISING

While online sites like Craigslist and eBay have cut into classified advertising at all publications, student newspapers remain an important forum for help wanted, housing, personals and other classified ads for your campus community. Most college newspapers have a classifieds section in their print editions and many now include classified ads on their websites.

At some newspapers, people can submit a classified ad online one morning and read it on the website that afternoon and in the newspaper the following day.

"Online advertising has been especially popular with landlords," says Jerry Bush, business and advertising director for the *Daily Egyptian* (dailyegyptian.com) at Southern Illinois University Carbondale. "Students who aren't on campus – they're on break or they haven't even started school yet – can see the ads from home."

Some student newspapers, including *The Daily Texan* (dailytexanoline.com) at the University of Texas at Austin, allow advertisers to add maps, images, hyperlinks and email links to their classified ads. An apartment manager, for example, can show readers where a rental unit is located, what it looks like and provide a link to the apartment complex's website. Readers can respond with a click of the email button.

ONLINE DISPLAY ADVERTISING

In recent years the Internet has changed the way many student newspapers sell advertising, giving papers a new product line to sell and a new way to communicate with potential advertisers. Most news websites have an advertising information page that may include:

- Media kits and rate cards in downloadable PDF files
- Interactive features that allow potential advertisers to contact the advertising department directly
- Information about theme issues, promotions and other special products and services
- Classified advertising forms that people can download or fill out on the Web.

To sell online advertising, you need to have detailed traffic data on your website. You should be able to tell your advertisers how many readers visit your site, how many of those readers come from your university and other details on usage patterns. Stress that your website offers access to a different, wider audience than your print product, one that may include alumni and potential students, as well as family and friends of current students.

Your website may well attract a different kind of advertiser – hotels and restaurants for parents planning to visit or alumni coming back for the big game rather than students looking for an apartment or cheap pizza.

Once you've collected usage statistics, you should have a simple, easy-to-understand advertising program. Don't offer too many options; that just confuses advertisers, some of whom may be venturing into online advertising for the first time. Come up with a few standard sizes and pricing packages.

The most common types of online advertising are:

- **Banner ads**–horizontal rectangles that usually run across the top or bottom of the page.
- **Tower ads**–vertical rectangles that run on one side of the page.
- **Tile or button ads**–smaller rectangles or square ads, usually stacked in the right or left margins.
- **Text link ads**–ads that use text hyperlinks to take readers to the advertiser's website.
- **Video ads**–ads that play before videos.
- **Email newsletter ads**–many student newspapers send out email newsletters to readers and some sell advertising on them.

Online advertising may be sold by the week, month or number of impressions (the number of times the ad is shown). Many newspapers sell ads in units of 1,000 impressions.

The Daily Tar Heel (dailytarheel.com) at the University of North Carolina at Chapel Hill was one of the first student newspapers to split up advertising for print and online. The news organization has two distinct units – the print newspaper and dailytarheel.com, a digital media operation – with separate advertising staffs.

Dailytarheel.com offers several digital advertising products, including banner ads, a local search directory, an online housing search site and the Campus Rec Report (dthcampusrecreport.nc.oursportscommunity.com) a website for club and intermural sports. In addition, the company sells mobile advertising via a mobile phone app and Blink (blinkcoupons.com) text coupons that are sent directly to customers' sell phones.

While his organization has invested a lot in online media advertising sales, Kevin Schwartz, director and general manager of *The Daily Tar Heel*, says a complex digital media program is not for every publication. Smaller news outlets may not have the traffic and frequency of updates to support online advertising. "You have to have the will to develop these products and you have to have the market," he says. Even in the sophisticated Research Triangle area of North Carolina, he says, some of his clients give him "a blank stare" when he talks about digital media. "We're actually ahead of a lot of our clients."

In addition to selling your own ads, you can generate online revenue by subscribing to an online advertising service such as Google AdSense (google.com/adsense). Such services place relevant ads on your pages and then send a monthly check based on the number of hits. Programs like this can bring in hundreds, even thousands of dollars each year, without taxing your sales staff.

DISTRIBUTION

Distribution is one of the most important business functions of a student newspaper. People need to know where and when to pick up you paper. Your job is to make it so ubiquitous that readers can't miss it.

Most student newspapers rely primarily on rack distribution. Racks or boxes should be strategically located in well-trafficked areas around campus – the student union, near bus stops, inside or outside dorms, cafeterias and classroom buildings. Papers may be distributed by a paid distribution staff or by student newspaper employees. *Golden Gate [X]press* (goldengatexpress.org), the weekly student newspaper at San Francisco State University, used to have a paid distribution person, but that position was cut a few years ago when the budget got tight. Now one of the editors oversees distribution and volunteers from the staff go around the campus twice a week filling or refilling boxes.

The Daily Tar Heel's marketing staff carefully monitors boxes, noting which empty first and where stacks remain virtually untouched. "Sometimes just picking up a box and moving it a few feet can make a difference," says Schwartz. *The Daily Tar Heel* has a map on its website showing readers the more than 200 locations where they can pick up a paper.

For most student newspapers, rack distribution isn't enough. Staff members should deliver stacks of papers to

Sample job descriptions

Advertising manager

1 Generates advertising for student newspaper.
2 Hires, trains and supervises advertising sales and design staff.
3 Develops and updates account and prospects lists.
4 Checks and proofreads all display ads.
5 Assigns ads to individual production pages.
6 Delivers camera-ready ads to the production manager or other designated person.
7 Handles customer inquiries and complaints.
8 Develops and updates advertising sales materials, including rate card and media kit.
9 Sets and updates advertising rates.
10 Plans special advertising sections and issues.

Advertising sales representative

1 Solicits advertising accounts assigned by telephone and in person.
2 Seeks out new accounts.
3 Works with designers to design ads when necessary.
4 Writes or assists the advertiser in writing ad copy.
5 Creates layouts for advertisers and submits them to the production department at the appropriate deadline.
6 Informs the advertiser of all charges.
7 Proofs all ads and notifies production staff of errors or changes.
8 Provides tearsheets to accounts.
9 Prepares all ads for production, including rough layouts, art and copy.
10 Completes all necessary forms for production and completes billing accurately and on time.
11 Keeps accurate records of clients and prospects for regular submission to the advertising director.

Classified advertising manager

1 Takes responsibility for classified advertising section, including entering ad copy, accepting orders, reserving space, making necessary copy changes, proofing, assisting with billing.
2 Notifies production manager of status of classified section for dummying purposes.
3 Maintains and/or develops online classified advertising section.
4 Solicits classified advertising accounts.

Marketing director

1 Directs marketing efforts for the student newspaper and website and other related media.
2 Serves as a liaison between student media and other campus organizations.
3 Develops a marketing plan for the year.
4 Plans special events.
5 Reviews the publication's logo and branding and suggests changes when necessary.
6 Reviews location of distribution racks and monitors which racks get the most and fewest pick-ups.
7 Works with the advertising department on advertising efforts.
8 Assists the online editor, webmaster or social media editor with social media marketing efforts, such as contests, giveaways, Facebook and Twitter presence, etc.
9 Plans special events to promote the publications.

classes and hand them out on the quad, at games, in the cafeteria, at bus stops – wherever students gather.

The Daily Tar Heel starts building reader loyalty even before students come to campus. "About 90 percent of our marketing efforts are targeted at new students," Schwartz says. The paper is mailed home to incoming freshman and handed out at freshman orientation events. During move-in week, every student is given a welcome issue. "We make sure they touch the paper four times before they take their first class."

MARKETING

There may have been a time when student news organizations simply dropped papers around campus and waited for people to pick them up. But more and more, campus publications are making concerted efforts at marketing and promotion. Many hire a designated marketing director or appoint a promotions team.

Q&A Leigh Sabey

LEIGH SABEY was an outside advertising representative for the *Rocky Mountain Collegian* (collegian.com) at Colorado State University for two and a half years and was honored as Salesperson of the Year for 2002–2003 and 2003–2004. She was the student advertising manager for the 2004–2005 academic year and was named Advertising Manager of the Year by College Newspapers Business and Advertising Managers, Inc. (CNBAM). Sabey was the student representative to the CNBAM executive board for the 2004–2005 academic year and helped coordinate the annual conference in New Orleans. After graduation, she took a job as an advertising representative for the *Northern Colorado Business Report*. She went on to create a blog, *Colorado Springs Giveaways*, that links consumers to local businesses.

What was your experience like selling advertising for the *Rocky Mountain Collegian*?
During my time selling advertising for the *Collegian*, I grew more confident in my abilities, gained direction for my education and career, and earned a ton of money. To be honest, I think that I learned more at the *Collegian* than in my four years of college! I had no idea what I was getting into when I applied for a sales job, but once I overcame my initial fears, I enjoyed every minute of it.

What was it like going out on your first sales calls?
I remember sitting in my car in front of the business going over exactly what I planned to say. I was surprised to find that of the few business owners that actually showed up for my appointments, most only had about two minutes to spend with me. I'm sure that my nervousness showed as I rushed through my presentations, forgetting necessities, such as a calculator or business cards. I somehow managed to come out with a few signed contracts, which gave me the confidence I needed to keep trying. Looking back, I laugh at the silly mistakes I made during my first few calls.

What was challenging about the job?
At times I felt overwhelmed by all of the numbers I had to memorize: rates, column inches, marketing stats, and, worst of all, deadlines! At first, I took every rejection personally. Over time I realized that a "no" is not the end of the world, and it's not completely my fault. Also, it was hard for me to schedule my time. Between classes, exams, sales appointments and looming deadlines, it was easy for priorities to slip between the cracks.

What did you enjoy about the job?
I loved the individual responsibility and freedom that I had. As a sales rep, I determined the most efficient use of my time and decided which clients to call on. I had opportunities to be creative as I developed ad campaigns and dreamed up new answers to common objections. I also enjoyed establishing relationships with business owners across town; I was always in the loop about new business openings, upcoming events and great deals.

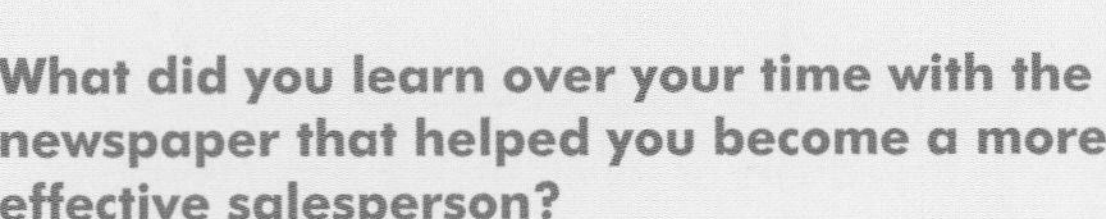

What did you learn over your time with the newspaper that helped you become a more effective salesperson?
The most valuable thing that I gained was an improvement in my communication skills. I went from stumbling through phone messages to feeling completely confident that I deserved each client's time and attention. I learned to be prepared for every single sales call. It's amazing how much more smoothly a call goes when you arrive with a typed proposal, spec ads and examples of their competitor's ads printed in your paper. I also learned customer service skills. Sometimes, it's easy for salespeople to get so excited about a signed contract that they forget to follow through with their promises. Long-term relationships are built on simple things like thank-you notes and correct ad copy.

Selling can be very frustrating. What do you suggest ad sales reps do when businesses come up with objections?
Believe it or not, you will hear the same exact objections over and over again, just with slightly different wording. Memorize responses to your most common objections. That way, you won't get stumped every time a client says that their budget is already spent or they don't believe that college students are their prime market. If you can't talk them through an objection immediately, always call back later. You will usually hear several "no's" before you finally get a "yes." I remember calling on our local bowling alley every month for about a year before I finally got anywhere. Suddenly, they changed owners and completely remodeled the building. Thanks to my

persistence, the first ad premiering their new image ran in my paper, later followed by ads in our local daily and alternative weekly publications.

How did your experiences working for the *Rocky Mountain Collegian* prepare you for the professional world?

My experiences at the college paper helped me develop a resume that was very impressive to potential employers. Words like "Salesperson of the Year" can really make one applicant stand out amongst hundreds of recent college graduates. Because of my time at the *Collegian*, I was able to secure a summer internship at a Gannett newspaper after my sophomore year. They invited me back the following summer to cover the territory of a rep on extended leave, and then offered me a great territory after I graduated. I ended up accepting a position at a business publication, which gives me the opportunity to combine my passion for sales with my interest in business. Several of my clients offered to provide references for me during my job search.

What advice do you have for student ad sales reps working for college newspapers?

1. Find a mentor, whether it's a more experienced rep, your ad manager, or even a professional ad rep at your local newspaper. Regular meetings with someone who has been through it all will give you a broader perspective.
2. Look beyond your Rolodex! I held the same territory for two years, and my major clients at the end of that time were completely different from the ones I started off with. You never know when clients will go out of business or change decision-makers, so it is important to constantly seek new advertisers. The best place to turn for new prospects is in competing publications. These businesses already understand the value of print advertising, so it should be an easy sale.
3. Maintain balance in your life. It's easy to become overwhelmed by all of your responsibilities as a student and as an ad rep, so make sure to set aside time for relaxation and fun.

Among the ways you can promote your print, online and broadcast products:

- **Maintain a visible presence on campus.** Let students know where your office is. Staff a table on the quad or in the student union at lunchtime. Hand out papers at games and other campus events.
- **Co-sponsor events with other student groups.** Offer free or discount ads to event organizers and then set up a booth and/or banners with your newspaper's name at the event.
- **Promote major stories, projects and special issues or guides before they are published.** Build some anticipation for what's coming out.
- **Send out email newsletters.** Brad Arendt, director of student media at Boise State University, says email newsletters, which include ads, drive traffic to his publication's website and generate revenue. "When we don't send it out, we notice fewer visitors," he says. "Several people use our email as a reminder of a new edition being on the stands. We are a twice-weekly publication so they don't expect a new one every day."
- **Toot your horn.** When your publication wins an award, secures a grant or breaks an important story, let people know. Write a brief story about the accomplishment and promote it on social media.
- **Reach out to new students.** Send copies of the paper to the homes of admitted freshmen and transfer students. Distribute the paper at orientation events. Create a welcome guide or orientation issue aimed at new students.
- **Evaluate your distribution system.** Monitor racks to see where people are picking up the paper and where they aren't. Make sure all boxes or racks are attractive and working properly. Clean, repair or replace boxes that aren't. Have distribution people check racks between deliveries and clean up trash that may have accumulated around them (inserts in particular can leave a big mess).
- **Survey your audience.** Find out what readers like and don't like, why they pick up the newspaper or why they don't. Respond to the feedback you receive.
- **Distribute papers off campus, too.** Even if you don't have boxes off campus you can leave stacks in coffeehouses, bars, copy shops and other popular student gathering spots.
- **Survey sources.** Ask news sources about their experiences being interviewed, whether the story was fair, balanced and correct and whether they were quoted accurately. *Golden Gate [X]press* at San Francisco State University sends out brief source response forms to faculty and staff who have been quoted in the newspaper each week. Seeking such feedback not only helps check for accuracy; it sends the message your publication cares about its reputation.
- **Put staffers to work on promotion.** Have them bring stacks of newspapers to classes, campus parties and

other events. Encourage reporters and photographers to give the newspaper to sources.

- **Meet the community.** Organize an open house or meet-the-editors event. Arrange meetings between the top editors and leaders of other campus organizations.
- **Create promotional products.** Pass out pens, mugs, T-shirts, refrigerator magnets and other swag with your logo at campus events. Have staffers wear logo T-shirts to campus events.
- **Cross-promote your products.** Advertise your print publication online and your online publication in print. Trade ads with radio and TV stations, too.
- **Sponsor contests.** Give away movie tickets, CDs and other prizes you can get for free from advertisers to people who enter your contest. The *Minnesota Daily* (mndaily.com) gives out movie tickets to Facebook fans and people who participate in a weekly scavenger hunt listed in the newspaper.
- **Use social media to promote new content.** Facebook and Twitter are great tools for driving traffic to your website and your print publication. (Read more about social media in Chapter 19.)

TO DO

1. Review and update your media kit. Make sure the statistics are up-to-date and the design and content of the kit represent your paper well.
2. Look over your advertising policies. Do you have a procedure for handling potentially controversial or offensive ads? If so, is it sufficient? If not, assign a committee to develop guidelines and policies.
3. Ask local professional newspapers if your new ad sales representatives could sit in on a sales training session or shadow a professional.
4. If your newspaper is not already a member, join College Newspaper Business and Advertising Managers, Inc. The organization's training conferences, Listserv and online resources will soon pay for the membership fee.
5. Review your training procedures. Are new ad sales representatives prepared to go out and sell? Would more workshops or training help? Look into training options from CNBAM, College Media Advisers, your state college media association or state newspaper publishers association.
6. Review your news organization's digital advertising program. Does it pay for you to try new products like digital coupons, email newsletter advertising or mobile ads?

TO READ

Blakeman, Robyn. *The Bare Bones of Advertising Print Design*. Lanham, Md.: Rowman & Littlefield Publishers, Inc. 2004.

College Newspaper Business and Advertising Managers, Inc. *Advertising Sales Resource Guide*. (Available with membership at cnbam.org).

Corbett, Michael. *The 33 Ruthless Rules of Local Advertising*. New York, N.Y.: Pinnacle Books, Inc., 1999.

Fowler, David. *Newspaper Ads That Make Sales Jump: A How-to Guide*. Cardiff-by-the-Sea, Calif.: Marketing Clarity, 1998.

Larkin, Ernest F. and Susan Schoebel Larkin. *Campus Newspaper Advertising Managers Handbook*. Minneapolis, Minn.: Associated Collegiate Press, 1994. (This book is out of print, but Associated Collegiate Press will email PDF versions to member publications upon request.)

Sullivan, Luke. *Hey, Whipple, Squeeze This: A Guide to Creating Great Ads, 3rd ed.* New York, N.Y.: John Wiley & Sons, 2008.

TO CLICK

College Newspaper Business and Advertising Managers, Inc
CNBAM is the only national organization specifically for college newspaper business and advertising employees. The organization publishes a newsletter, maintains an active email discussion list, hosts an annual convention and sponsors a national awards competition for excellence in business and advertising operations.
www.cnbam.org

College marketing firms

Alloy Media + Marketing
www.alloymarketing.com

Campus Media Group, Inc.
www.campusmediagroup.com

CampusParty®
www.campusclients.com

Collegiate Promotions
www.collegiatepromotions.com

MJS Communications
www.mjscom.com

APPENDIX 1
ASSOCIATED PRESS STYLE CHEAT SHEET

The *Associated Press Stylebook* is the most commonly used style guide for college newspapers. This "cheat sheet" is designed for quick reference. Your news organization may have its own style guide that supersedes AP style.

Abbreviations and acronyms

- Avoid "alphabet soup." Don't use abbreviations that a reader would not quickly recognize. The most common abbreviations, such as CNN, GOP and CIA, can be used on all references. Less well-known but still common ones such as OSHA and NATO can be used after you spell out the full name on first mention. In most cases, however, the stylebook suggests using a generic reference such as *the association* or *the organization* for all references after the first.
- Avoid using multiple acronyms or abbreviations in a sentence unless their meaning is clear.
- Do not use periods for most acronyms, but do use periods for two-letter acronyms: *FBI* for Federal Bureau of Investigation or *U.S.* for United States. If the acronym spells an unrelated word, use periods between letters to avoid confusion.
- Don't put unfamiliar abbreviations in parentheses after the first reference (for example, "*Online News Association (ONA)*"). Instead either repeat the full name on subsequent references or use a generic reference, such as *the association*.
- After a name, abbreviate *junior* or *senior* as *Jr.* or *Sr.* with no comma to set it off: *John Moraga Sr.*

Academic terms

Some student newspapers deviate from AP style on academic terms; check your newspaper's stylebook.

Academic degrees–AP recommends avoiding degree abbreviations after the name. Instead, use an explanatory phrase: *Walter Corrigan, who has a doctorate in psychology, will speak at the commencement ceremony.* Use an apostrophe in *bachelor's degree*, or *a master's* but there is no possessive in *Bachelor of Arts* or *Master of Science.* Use abbreviations such as B.A., M.A., LL.D. and Ph.D. only when you need to identify many individuals by degree on first reference. When used after a name, an academic abbreviation is set off by commas: *Mildred Smith, Ph.D., spoke at the meeting.*

Academic departments–Lowercase except for words that are proper nouns (*the psychology department, the department of history, the French department, the department of Spanish language and literature*) or when the department is part of the official and formal name: *San Francisco State University Department of Journalism.*

Academic titles–Capitalize and spell out formal titles such as chancellor, chairman, etc. when they precede a name. Lowercase elsewhere: *Chancellor John Smith addressed the students Tuesday. John Smith, chancellor of Cornell University, addressed the students Tuesday.*

Academic divisions–Pay attention to how departments, colleges, schools, programs and divisions are organized at your school. Generally departments are subdivisions of colleges or schools. Also be aware of the difference between deans, who generally oversee colleges or schools, and chairs, who oversee departments: *The chair of the journalism department reports to the dean of the College of Humanities.*

Courses–Capitalize the name of a specific course but don't capitalize generic courses: *Introduction to Reporting was his favorite journalism course.*

Addresses

Street, avenue and *boulevard* are abbreviated when you write the full street address; all others are spelled out. But *street, avenue* and *boulevard* are spelled out without the specific address: *The crime occurred at 790 Main St. The fraternity house on Century Boulevard was razed after the fire.*

Compass points are abbreviated in full street addresses but spelled out when just the street name is mentioned: *The carwash will take place in front of the Phi Delta Theta fraternity on Northeast 47th Street. Police foiled a robbery attempt at a liquor store at 800 N. Main St.*

When using two roads with the same designation (such as street), use lowercase street, road, etc. *The anti-war group often protests at the corner of Chestnut and Main streets.*

Adviser

Not *advisor*. However, there are advisory committees.

Alumnus, alumni, alumna, alumnae

These terms refer to people who have attended (but not necessarily graduated from) a school.

A male is an *alumnus*. A group of men are *alumnni*.

A female is an *alumna*. A group of females are *alumnae*.

Use *alumni* when referring to a group of men and women.

Board of Regents, Board of Trustees

On first reference, call it the *Board of Regents* or *Board of Trustees*. On second reference, it's *the board* or *the regents* or *the trustees*.

Capitalization

Avoid unnecessary capitalization. Use lowercase if the dictionary lists it as an acceptable form.

- Capitalize proper nouns: *James Olmos was a student at Ithaca University in New York.*
- Capitalize common nouns when they're part of the full name for a person, place or thing: *the Democratic Party, Lake Tahoe.* Lowercase when common nouns stand alone in subsequent references: *The party, the lake.* Lowercase the common noun elements of names in plural uses: *the Democratic and Republican parties. Tower and Lake streets.* Exception: plurals of formal titles *Presidents Jimmy Carter and George H.W. Bush attended the event.*
- In composition titles, the principal words in the titles of books, movies, songs, works of art, etc. are capitalized: *The New York Review of Books, To Kill a Mockingbird.*
- Lowercase the names of the seasons unless they are used in a proper name: *the Winter Olympics.*
- Lowercase the word *room* except when used with the number of the room or the name of the room: *Room 215, the Lincoln Room.*

Chairman, chairwoman

Do not use chairperson, chair or co-chair unless it is an organization's formal title for an office (academic department heads are often called chair). Capitalize as a formal title before a name: *Chairman Marc Rosen.*

Computer-related terms and styles

- byte
- CD-ROM
- database
- disk, diskette (but *compact disc*)
- dot-com
- email, e-book, e-commerce
- gigabyte
- Internet
- laptop, laptop computer
- megabyte
- online
- Web, World Wide Web, website, webcam, webcast, webmaster, Web page
- When listing Web addresses, use this format: http://www.collegenewspaper.com

Day/date/time

- Lowercase a.m. and p.m. and use periods: *The meeting will begin at 7:30 p.m.*
- Do not use :00 after an on-the-hour time. Simply use the numeral: *The game starts at 2 p.m.*
- Avoid redundancies like 7 *p.m. Thursday night.*
- Use noon or midnight for 12:00, but only use the word, not the redundant 12 noon or 12 midnight: *The party was supposed to end at midnight.*
- Spell out months when not part of a date: *The school year begins in September.* When part of a date, abbreviate these months: *Jan., Feb., Aug., Sept., Oct., Nov., Dec. Classes begin Sept. 9.* Spell out: March, April, May, June, July.
- Spell out days of the week: *The class meets every Tuesday.*
- Generally use day or date, not both. *Finals week begins on May 4* or *Finals week begins Monday.*
- Use Arabic figures to indicate decades of history. Use an apostrophe before the decade if you leave out the first two digits but don't put an apostrophe between the year

and the "s": *This economic depression is often compared to the Great Depression of the 1920s. The fraternity is planning a '70s party.*

Directions and regions

Lowercase *north, south, northwest, northern,* etc. when they indicate compass direction but capitalize when they designate regions or are part of a proper noun. Lowercase the compass point unless it's a widely known section, as in *Southern California* or *South Florida. Duke University is one of the top universities in the South. The motorcycle was traveling west on Thornton Street when it was hit by the truck. The campus is one of the biggest in Northern California, but there are larger ones in the southern part of the state.*

Greek

Always capitalized, whether you're talking about an ethnic background or the university's fraternity/sorority system: *Greek Row, the Greek system.*

Numbers

- Spell out numbers under 10; for 10 and up use numerals. Include commas for numbers in the thousands (5,000, 100,000).
- For numbers greater than 999,999, use numeral and million or billion: *7 million people; $3 trillion.*
- If a sentence begins with a number, either spell it out or rewrite the sentence, unless it is a year: *2009 was a very good year for the Tigers.*

These are exceptions (always use figures):

Ages: *She is 5 years old.* Use hyphens for ages expressed as adjectives before a noun or in place of a noun: *A 6-year-old girl, the 6-year-old.*

Days of the month: *The rally is scheduled for March 4.*

Degrees of temperature: *The temperature hit a high of 92 degrees.*

Dimensions: *The 5-foot-2-inch tennis player is powerful for her height.*

House numerals: *The president's family lives at 1600 Pennsylvania Ave.*

Percentages: *The board approved a 5 percent increase.*

Scores: *The Tigers beat the Braves 5-2.*

Speeds: *The car was traveling 45 mph.*

Sums of money: *The new library will cost $3.5 million; the pencil costs 25 cents and the notebook costs $4.95.*

Time of day: *The performance will start at 6 p.m.*

Votes: *The board voted 5 to 2.*

Years: *She was born in 1961.*

Possessives

The stylebook goes into great detail on how to handle every possible type of possessive.

- To form the possessive of a singular common noun *not* ending in "s," add an apostrophe and an "s": *The provost's speech.*
- To form the possessive of a singular common noun ending in "s," add only an apostrophe: *Mathematics' rules.*
- To form the possessive of a singular proper noun ending in "s," add an apostrophe only: *Moses' law* or *Jesus' parables.*
- To form the possessive of a plural common noun ending in "s," add an apostrophe: *The ladies' bathroom, states' rights.*
- For plural nouns not ending in 's," add "*s*": *Women's rights.*
- Understand the difference between its (possessive) and it's (contraction of it is): *It's a nice day. The snail curled into its shell.*

Punctuation

AP style uses as little punctuation as necessary. The goal is to write clearly and succinctly.

- Do not use the serial comma (the final comma before the conjunction) in a series: *She is taking chemistry, biology and English courses this semester.*
- Use a semicolon to clarify a series that includes a number of commas. Include a semicolon before the conjunction: *The university choir will perform in Tampa, Fla.; Austin, Texas; and Baton Rouge, La.*
- When punctuating quotations, always place the comma (and most other punctuation) before the closing quote: *"The surgery went well," said Jill Smith, sister of the injured player.*
- Capitalize the word after a colon only if it could stand alone as a sentence: *The chancellor announced his decision: no fee hike. The chancellor announced his decision: He will not raise fees.* Exception: In headlines, the word after a colon always is capitalized: *Provost: Smoking ban will stand*

States

- Spell out names of states when they stand alone but abbreviate when they run with the name of a city, with commas before and after the abbreviation: *Calistoga, Calif., is a great weekend getaway spot for students who attend San Francisco State University.*
- Eight states are never abbreviated: *Alaska, Hawaii, Idaho, Iowa, Maine, Ohio, Texas* and *Utah.* See the *Associated Press Stylebook* for state abbreviations.

- Be sure to use the stylebook abbreviations and *not* the U.S. Postal Service abbreviations for states *unless* you are providing a full address including ZIP code: *Send contributions to the Student Press Law Center, 1101 Wilson Blvd., Suite 1100, Arlington, VA 22209.*

Titles and jobs

- Titles are generally only capitalized when used before a name: *President Jose Lopez approved the smoking ban. Jose Lopez, president of the university, approved the smoking ban.*
- Put long titles after a name: *Sandra Smith, associate vice president for academic affairs, is scheduled to speak at the meeting.*
- Qualifying words before a title are not capitalized: *On Sunday, former university President John Mason visited the campus.*
- Do not capitalize job descriptions, even when they come before a name: *The school named janitor Marco Smith the top employee of the year.*
- Abbreviate these titles before a full name, except in quotations: *Dr., Gov., Lt. Gov., Mr., Ms., Mrs., Rep., Sen., the Rev.* When used in a quotation before a full name, spell out all except *Dr., Mr., Mrs.* and *Ms.*
- Generally avoid courtesy titles (Mr., Mrs., Ms.) except for clarity: *Mrs. Rosenbloom is 88 and Mr. Rosenbloom is 85.*

University

Uppercase when part of a proper name; lowercase when it stands alone: *Students at Harvard University launched a new social media site this week. The university will not accept new students for the spring semester.*

APPENDIX 2
CONTESTS FOR STUDENT JOURNALISTS

Associated Collegiate Press
2221 University Ave. SE, Suite 121
Minneapolis, MN 55414
(612) 625-8335
studentpress.org/acp

Contests are free but open only to ACP member publications. Contests include the Pacemaker awards for college newspapers, online publications, yearbooks and magazines. ACP also awards individuals in categories such as Story of the Year, Photo Excellence, Design of the Year, Multimedia Story of the Year and Reporter of the Year. In addition, ACP co-sponsors a cartooning contest with Universal Uclick and an advertising contest with Sierra Nevada Media Group. The deadline for the Online Pacemaker award is in February; the deadline for the yearbook Pacemaker award is in January; the deadlines for the Newspaper Pacemaker Award, Magazine Pacemaker Award and the individual awards are in June. College publications attending the ACP spring convention may also enter the Best of Show contest. The Pacemaker awards have no prize money attached; prize money for the individual awards varies.

Association of American Editorial Cartoonists
John Locher Memorial Award
3899 North Front St.
Harrisburg, PA 17110
(717) 703-3086
editorialcartoonists.com

The AAEC/John Locher Memorial Award recognizes undergraduate editorial cartoonists between the ages of 17 and 25. Contest entry is limited to student cartoonists from Canada, the United States and Mexico. Entrants must submit four copies of four of their cartoons as printed in their college or university newspaper. The winner receives an all-expenses-paid trip to the AAEC convention. The annual deadline is in March.

Black College Communication Association
bccanews.org

The Black College Communication Association conducts the annual Excellence in Journalism competition "to encourage and recognize excellence among student journalists and newspapers at historically black colleges and universities." Awards are given in more than a dozen categories, including best student newspaper, best online site, best news story, best headline writer, best editorial cartoon, etc. The contest is open to BCCA member publications. The annual deadline is in December.

College Media Advisers
Best of Collegiate Design
The University of Memphis
3711 Veterans Ave. Room 300
Memphis, TN 38152
(901) 678-2403
design@collegemedia.org
collegemedia.org

College Media Advisers' annual Best of Collegiate Design contest honors the best work produced by student media designers in more than 20 categories for college newspapers, magazines, yearbooks and online publications. Winners are showcased in an annual publication distributed to CMA members. Entry forms are available on the College Media Advisers' website; the annual deadline is in June. Entries must be submitted in an electronic version, either in JPG or PDF files. CMA also recognizes excellence in student work in the Dave L. Adams Apple Awards at its annual spring convention and acknowledges the achievements of student media advisers through various award programs and special honors and its Hall of Fame.

College Photographer of the Year
Rita Reed, director
109 Lee Hills Hall
University of Missouri-Columbia
Columbia, MO 65211
(573) 884-2188
info@cpoy.org
cpoy.org

The College Photographer of the Year awards recognize outstanding student photographers in single-picture, multiple-picture, multimedia and portfolio categories that include news, sports, features, portraits and photo stories. The winner of the first-place portfolio competition receives

The Student Newspaper Survival Guide, Second Edition. Rachele Kanigel.

a camera, an internship and $1,000. Other winners receive fellowships, or other prizes or certificates. The annual deadline is in October.

Columbia Scholastic Press Association

Columbia University Mail Code 5711
New York, NY 10027-6902
(212) 854-9400
cspa.columbia.edu

The Columbia Scholastic Press Association Crown and Gold Circle Awards recognize excellence in student media, both scholastic and collegiate. The Collegiate Crown awards honor newspapers, magazines, online publications and yearbooks. The Gold Circle Awards recognize outstanding writers, editors, designers, cartoonists and photographers. It is the largest national competition for individual achievement in college and university publications in the United States. The annual deadline for Golden Circle awards is in June; the deadline for the Crown awards is in October.

Eric Breindel Memorial Journalism Awards

1211 Avenue of the Americas, 9th floor
New York, NY 10036
(212) 843-9253
ericbreindel.org

The Eric Breindel Journalism Awards honor work that "reflects the spirit that animated the writings of Eric Breindel: Love of country and its democratic institutions as well as the act of bearing witness to the evils of totalitarianism." The competition for undergraduates offers the winner a cash prize of $10,000, as well as a paid internship of his or her choice at Fox News Channel, *The Wall Street Journal*, or the *New York Post*. In addition, residential housing in New York City can be provided for the winner for the duration of the internship position. The annual deadline is in April.

The Fund for American Studies

Robert Novak Collegiate Journalism Award
Traci Leonardo, director
Institute on Political Journalism
The Fund for American Studies
1706 New Hampshire Ave., NW
Washington, DC 20009
(202) 986-0384
tfas.org

The Robert Novak Collegiate Journalism Award "recognizes excellence in collegiate reporting in which the student's work demonstrates an understanding of the basic ideas that support a free society, including freedom of the press, freedom of speech and free-market economic principles. Judges recognize students who show initiative and original reporting, and superior writing skills, as well as an understanding of the principles of individual freedom. In addition, a quality piece will also demonstrate a skill for accuracy in reporting as well as good use of sources."

Entrants must be undergraduate students who are currently enrolled in a four-year college or university in the United States. First-place winners receive $5,000; second-place and third-place winners receive $2,500 and $1,000, respectively. The deadline is late January for work published in a print or online student publication the previous calendar year.

Hearst Journalism Awards Program

William Randolph Hearst Foundation
90 New Montgomery St., Suite 1212
San Francisco, CA 94105-4504
(415) 908-4560/ (800) 841-7048
hearstfdn.org/hearst_journalism

The Hearst Journalism Awards program includes six writing competitions, three photojournalism competitions, two multimedia competitions and three broadcast news (one in radio and two in TV) competitions, with championship finals in all divisions. Participation in the program is open to undergraduate journalism majors currently enrolled in schools accredited by the Accrediting Council on Education in Journalism and Mass Communications (ACEJMC). An exception to the journalism major rule is made for students entering the photojournalism competitions. Up to two students per university can enter each competition. The students to be entered are selected by the schools. The awards range from $1,000 to $2,600, with the schools receiving matching grants. Deadlines for entry vary from November to April each year.

Investigative Reporters and Editors

141 Neff Annex
Missouri School of Journalism
Columbia, MO 65211
(573) 882-6668
ire.org

The IRE Student Award recognizes outstanding investigative reporting by a student in a college newspaper, magazine, specialty publication or internship. The winner receives a $250 cash scholarship and a certificate for Outstanding Investigative Reporting. The deadline is in January each year.

Michigan State University Annual Design Contest for College Students

c/o Cheryl Pell
305 Communication Arts Building,
East Lansing, MI 48824-1212
snd.jrn.msu.edu

The Michigan State University Design Contest for College Students awards work done by students for a college class, a student publication, an internship or a job. Categories include newspaper sections, art and illustration, infographics and advertisements. The annual deadline is in March.

National Lesbian and Gay Journalists Association

1420 K. Street, NW, Suite 910
Washington, DC 20005
(202) 588-9888
nlgja.org

The Excellence in Student Journalism Award recognizes outstanding coverage of lesbian/gay/bisexual/transgender issues. Work must be published by a campus or student news organization. The deadline is in June.

National Society of Newspaper Columnists Education Foundation
P.O. Box 411532
San Francisco, CA 94115-6885
(415) 488-6762
columnists.com

The annual National Society of Newspaper Columnists Education Foundation Scholarship Contest awards scholarships to three outstanding student newspaper columnists who write for U.S. college or university undergraduate newspapers. The contest is open to undergraduates who write bylined general interest, editorial page or op-ed columns. Sports columns, movie reviews, magazine columnists and other specialized columns are not eligible. First prize is $1,000, second prize is $500 and third prize is $250. The annual deadline is in March.

The Newspaper Guild – Communications Workers of America
David S. Barr Award
The Newspaper Guild-CWA
501 Third Street, N.W., 6th floor
Washington, DC 20001-2797
(202) 434-7177
newsguild.org

The David S. Barr Awards competition is open to high school students and to part-time or full-time college students, including those in community colleges and in graduate programs. All entries must be of work published or broadcast that helped to right a wrong, corrected an injustice or promoted justice and fairness. Winners of the high school prize get $500 and college students win $1,500, as well as travel expenses to the annual Freedom Award Celebration in Washington, DC. Entries are due in January.

Online News Association
P.O. Box 65741
Washington, DC 20035
646-290-7900
journalists.org

Students are welcome to submit work to any category for the Online News Association's Online Journalism Awards. In addition, the contest has three student categories – Multimedia Feature Presentation, Outstanding Use of Digital Technologies on the Web and Online Video. For these categories, entrants can be full- or part-time students but cannot have been paid for producing the work entered. Work produced for pay, either for a professional media organization or through a grant or other client, should be entered in the appropriate professional category. Entrants can be graduate, undergraduate or high school students. Entrants must check a box affirming the work was done by students and explain any professional or professorial involvement. Entries are due in July.

Payne Awards for Ethics in Journalism
University of Oregon School of Journalism and Communication
1275 University of Oregon
Eugene, OR 97403-1275
(541) 346-2519
payneawrds.uoregon.edu

The Payne Awards for Ethics in Journalism honor "the journalist of integrity and character who reports with insight and clarity in the face of political or economic pressures." Students eligible for the Collegiate Media Award must be enrolled in a two- or four-year college when the nominated work is published or aired or the nominated decision and reasoning occurs. If the nomination is for published work, it must be published in a regularly distributed medium (e.g. a student or professional newspaper, magazine, broadcast or cablecast news program or an edited Internet publication). The winners of the student and professional awards each receive a $1,000 prize. The deadline is in February for material published or broadcast or decisions made the previous year.

Religion Newswriters Association
30 Neff Annex
School of Journalism
University of Missouri
Columbia, MO 652-11-2600
(573) 882-9257
rna.org

The Chandler Student Religion Reporter of the Year honors excellence in writing on religion. Emphasis is placed on "reporting skill and a grasp of religion issues that is fair, balanced and in accordance with journalistic standards." Named for Russell Chandler, former religion writer for the *Los Angeles Times*, this student contest is made possible through the Chandler Legacy Fund. First-place winners are awarded $600 plus a travel stipend to the RNA annual conference. Second-place winners are given $300 and a citation and third-place winners are given $150 and a citation. The annual deadline is in May.

The Robert F. Kennedy Center for Justice and Human Rights College Journalism Award
1367 Connecticut Avenue, NW
Suite 200
Washington, DC 20036
(202) 463-7575
rfkcenter.org

The Robert F. Kennedy College Journalism Award recognizes print and broadcast stories focusing on issues that reflect Robert F. Kennedy's concerns, including human rights, social justice, and the power of individual action. The winner receives $500 and a bust of Robert F. Kennedy to present to their school. The deadline is in February each year.

***Rolling Stone* Annual College Journalism Competition**
1290 Avenue of the Americas, 2nd Floor
New York, NY 10104
(212) 484-1616
rollingstone.com

Rolling Stone seeks to honor outstanding college journalism in the fields of entertainment reporting, feature writing and essays and criticism. The winner receives a prize of $2,500. The annual deadline is in June.

Scripps Howard Foundation National Journalism Awards
P.O. Box 5380
Cincinnati, OH 45201

(513) 977-3035
(800) 888-3000
scripps.com/foundation

The Roy W. Howard National Collegiate Reporting Competition awards nine aspiring journalists a 14-day guided study tour to Japan and South Korea, an area of special interest to Roy W. Howard. The annual deadline is in February.

The foundation's National Journalism Awards contest also includes the Charles M. Schulz Award for college cartoonists. The competition is open to undergraduate student cartoonists whose cartoons were published in print or online by a college newspaper or magazine in the United States or its territories. The deadline for entries is in January.

Society of Professional Journalists

Eugene S. Pulliam National Journalism Center
3909 N. Meridian St.
Indianapolis, IN 46208
(317) 927-8000
spj.org

The Mark of Excellence Awards offers 45 categories for print and online collegiate journalism. Entries are first judged on the regional level and then forwarded to the national competition. The deadline is in January each year.

Student Press Law Center College Press Freedom Award

Student Press Law Center
1101 Wilson Blvd., Suite 1100
Arlington, VA 22209-2275
(703) 807-1904
splc.org/aboutus/csjaward.asp

Along with the Associated Collegiate Press, the SPLC co-sponsors the College Press Freedom Award to recognize the college student or student news medium that has demonstrated outstanding support for college press freedom. The award is presented at the Associated Collegiate Press/College Media Advisers national fall convention. Winners receive a plaque recognizing their achievements. To nominate yourself or someone else, submit a written description (not to exceed 600 words) of how their situation meets the entry criteria described above, along with any relevant supporting materials or press clips and letters of support. The annual deadline for entries is August.

Student Society for News Design at the University of Missouri-Columbia – College News Design Contest

College News Design Contest
c/o Joy Mayer
313 Lee Hills Hall
Columbia, MO 65211
ssnd.wordpress.com

The College News Design Contest awards published work produced while the designer was enrolled at a two- or four-year college, whether it's for a student or professional publication or project. The contest has a variety of categories for print and for multimedia, as well as a Student Designer of the Year competition. Winners of the Student Designer of the Year award receive travel grants to the annual Society for News Design national workshop. The annual deadline is in April.

INDEX